Montserrat C

Robert Pullen graduated in law from the University of Warwick. After two years of postgraduate research, he trained as a lawyer and now works as a writer and editor specializing in employment law. He has been devoted to opera – especially to the Italian works of the first half of the nineteenth century – since first attending the main European music festivals in the mid-1970s. He lives in South London.

Stephen Taylor studied English at Oxford and trained in art history at the University of Warwick. He undertook postgraduate research in pre-Renaissance Italian art at the University of London and has worked at the Glyndebourne Festival Opera and at the Barbican Centre in London. His specialist area of interest is German opera and he is an authority on the works of Richard Strauss. He lives in North London.

'Everything you always wanted to know (and perhaps a bit more) about the legendary Spanish soprano – a sensible, readable biography . . . it is hard to see how the book could be bettered, offering as it does a full and thoughtful narrative of Caballé live and on disc.' *Kirkus Reviews*

'Surprisingly, given the subject's many years of fame, this is the first book on Caballé to appear in any language. An authorised biography, its two writers have had access to the Catalan diva's papers, family and entourage, and the singer herself in the course of their research. For all that they have avoided the dangers of the fanzine approach: this is a sympathetic but not uncritical account . . .' **George Hall,** *Opera Now*

'. . . a well-written, exciting narrative of Caballé's life and career . . . Her great worth as an artist and as extraordinary human being comes through on every page . . . This is a book that Caballé's fans will prize and, because it is scrupulously written and comes with Caballé's imprimatur, it should remain a valuable historical document.' **Stephen A. Willer,** *Opera Quarterly*

'It is a heart-warming story. If the authors sometimes appear biased in their heroine's favour in her many contretemps with opera houses and other artists, that was bound to be the case in a book that has Caballé's seal of approval, and they assess her undoubted greatness from a position of deep and dedicated knowledge of the art of singing, also displayed in a critical discography of Caballé's myriad official and unofficial recordings.' **Alan Blyth,** *BBC Music Magazine*

'She has given roughly four thousand performances so far in her career. All of this the book impressively records. It goes further, and concerns itself with the quality of this multifarious activity. If the authors' comments are almost invariably, in the loose sense, "appreciative", they are also detailed and based on intelligent observation.' **John Steane,** *Times Literary Supplement*

ROBERT PULLEN AND STEPHEN TAYLOR

Montserrat Caballé
Casta Diva

INDIGO

First published in Great Britain 1994
by Victor Gollancz

This Indigo edition published 1996
Indigo is an imprint of the Cassell Group
Wellington House, 125 Strand, London WC2R 0BB

A catalogue record for this book is
available from the British Library.

ISBN 0 575 40013 7

Printed and bound in Great Britain by
Guernsey Press Co. Ltd.
Guernsey, Channel Islands

96 97 98 99   10 9 8 7 6 5 4 3 2 1

Contents

PART VI: 'QUI LA VOCE SUA SOAVE'

Preface

This biography of Montserrat Caballé is long overdue, both in the sense of it being well past its original publication date and also in that it is the first full-length treatment in any language – including Spanish – to have been devoted to one of the most famous and best-loved performers of our time.

Caballé's place in modern operatic history is assured, thanks not least to her recordings. But although she has been acclaimed across all five continents for nearly thirty years now, it is surprising how little is known of her family background and formative years before she was catapulted into the limelight in 1965. Since then, sopranos have come and gone, yet she is still actively with us, notwithstanding illnesses that have plagued her throughout her career. At one point in the 1980s this accumulation of ailments led to a nightmarish series of cancellations, which in turn led some to conclude that her singing days were numbered. Yet these episodes need to be viewed against some 3800 performances she has given in public in the thirty-eight years since her professional début in 1956. Even if she has cancelled nearly 200 performances over the years through indisposition, this constitutes only five per cent of her 'output'.

If it is salutary to see Caballé's own career in perspective, it is positively sobering to view it in relation to those of two of her most eminent post-war colleagues who pursued, at least in part, a similar repertory: Maria Callas and Joan Sutherland. The Greek soprano's career effectively lasted from 1947 to 1965, an eighteen-year period during which, although indisputably the most famous opera singer in the world, she gave just 600 performances in total. Even in the years of peak activity – the early 1950s – Callas never once performed more than sixty times a year, and never sang a note of any non-operatic music in public. Sutherland's career extended from 1952 to 1990, a thirty-eight-year span in which she gave just over 1800 performances, venturing only very rarely into recital repertory. And beyond the similarities in all three sopranos' repertoires, there lay the differences, with Callas rarely singing anything from the German school in which Caballé was grounded, and Sutherland eschewing not only that but most of the heavier Verdi and *verismo* works as well. Montserrat's 3800 performances suddenly take on a new meaning when placed in this kind of perspective. From the purely statistical point of view, there is simply no one with whom Caballé can meaningfully be compared.

There is also the extraordinary number and range of Caballé's stage roles, far exceeding that of any of her colleagues. Even so, the tally has been estimated to be as high as 130. But this figure can only be arrived at by incorporating all her non-operatic vocal assumptions, such as nearly thirty oratorios and liturgical works, as well as concert pieces like Beethoven's Ninth Symphony and Berlioz's *La Mort de Cléopâtre*. A particular problem has arisen in France where she has been credited in print with a preposterous diversity of roles during her earliest years in Barcelona, Basel and Bremen, which no archival researches will support. She may indeed have studied such parts as Elsa, Ilia, Rusalka, Romilda (in *Xerxes*) and Susanna, as well as many others besides, as required by the system of covering, but she never sang any of them on stage. The true total of operatic roles appears to be eighty-eight, which is in itself remarkable enough without contemplating her enormous song repertory, which could well number around 800.

It is this sheer prodigality of performance, coupled with the absence of any pre-existing documentary record of Caballé's life and career, that has led to the delay in the appearance of the book, as well as influencing its shape and structure. After all, if anyone nowadays wishes to write a book about Maria Callas, their first port of call need only be any bookshop or library, where numerous volumes all recycle the known facts. Caballé's life and career, however, have had to be researched from scratch, a task complicated by the fact that she has kept neither a personal diary nor a complete record of her professional activity. Since it was intended from the outset that this authorized biography be as comprehensive as possible, the story has had to be treated chronologically for the sake of those many readers unfamiliar with the larger pattern of Caballé's activities. This approach has its dangers, of course, and another volume might well choose a more selective approach. But in Caballé's one – and we may safely assume only – authorized biography there was a responsibility, if not to set the record straight, then at least to set the whole of it before the public. In any event, as the narrative unfolds, space has been found in which to tackle certain 'themes' or specific considerations pertaining not just to Caballé's career but to the wider operatic context in which it has been conducted.

*   *   *

It goes without saying that in a book of this kind thanks are due to the people who have helped in its preparation. First and foremost, there is Montserrat herself, who has devoted an unprecedented amount of time and concentration to this project, for all that in its earlier stages she was privately unconvinced of its necessity. But as the work took shape, she happily came to think otherwise and took a highly active role which involved over forty working sessions. Roughly half of these took place in her apartment in Barcelona, with the occasional excursion to her farmstead in Ripoll or her hotel suites in Paris and London. The remainder were conducted in the apartment of her brother and life-long personal manager, Carlos, who provided a host of anecdotes and observations, as well as preventing numerous errors from creeping into print. This intensive participation of both the Caballés has, we hope, produced a story that is not simply authorized but authoritative.

Beyond these two principal players, it is doubtful whether the authors owe a debt of gratitude as great as they owe to each other. Over the seven years it has taken, ever since a fateful meeting with Caballé in Pesaro in 1987, the strengths of the one have bailed out the weaknesses of the other. Even so, there are many people – other than those whose comments are directly incorporated into the text – without whose assistance the book would not have been as it is. We therefore would like to record our thanks to the following: Claudio Abbado; Mrs H. L. Baker; Maria-Rosa Barbany of the Cultural Department of the Spanish Embassy in London; Manolo Barroso; Manuel Bertrand; Flora Bertrand; Alan Blyth; Mark Bonello; the late Edward Bridgewater; Ana Caballé; Isabel Caballé; Neil Cameron; José Carreras; L. D. Castello Cruz; John Cox; Kate Crawshaw; Dr Paul Dakin; Denny Dayviss; Carlos Diaz Du-Pond; Peter Freestone; Bruce-Michael Gelbert; Dr Albin Hänseroth; Michael Hardy; Marilyn Horne; Peter Katona; Sylvia McNair; Joaquín Martínez; Cristina Ordovás, Condessa Ruiz de Castilla; Cristina Oriols; the late Allen Sven Oxenburg; Jean Paciulli; Michel Palmer; Elizabeth Picazo; Clive Portbury; Tony Pullen; Ruggero Raimondi; Adelita Rocha; Guillermo Rosal-Bertrand; Sandra Rotondo; Josefa Subirana Villaba; Antonio Sánchez Subirana; Reuel Sherwood; Alan Sievewright; Cheryl Studer; Hermes de la Torre; Nik Walton-Jones; the staffs of the Barbican Library, the British Library, the Central Westminster Music Library and the British Newspaper Library; RCA/BMG in France and Spain; the Círculo del Liceo; *Opera* magazine; *La Vanguardia*; the Hotel Negresco in Nice; and the Ambassador and Le Meridien Hotels in Barcelona.

Lastly, we would like to thank our commissioning editor, Richard Wigmore, whose patience, though sorely tried, ultimately knew no bounds; and to pay fond tribute to Montse Caballé, Montserrat's niece and personal assistant. Over the years, she has been instrumental in sorting out itineraries and the myriad other tasks that have enabled the book to be written. She has done this with unfailing good humour and, without her help, progress would have been much more difficult.

Robert Pullen and Stephen Taylor
London, 1 July 1994

Robert Pullen wishes to append a note of personal appreciation to the following. To Mark Layton and Ron Arnold, without whose patience as my employers it would have been impossible to find either the time or money to see the book through to completion; to my long-suffering colleagues in the Legal section of IDS, and especially to fellow editors Steve Gibbons and Emelia Thorold, for whose readiness to jump into the breach – often at short notice – I am deeply grateful; to Mary Garden, whose knowledge of operatic history is as awe-inspiring as her proof-reading skills; and to Marian Bell, for her enthusiasm and encouragement in the difficult early stages of the book. Finally, there are those whose contribution has for me been as much inspirational as practical. I owe a vast debt to Tony Pullen, who gave the support that really only a brother can give. His confidence in my abilities as well as his practical advice has meant much more than these few words of thanks can express. And to Antonio Sánchez Subirana I owe an equally inexpressible debt. He played the decisive part in encouraging me to undertake this biography of his fellow Catalan. Given the demands the research and writing imposed on his time and patience, he may well have subsequently regretted this. His greatest contribution has been never to have said so. With Stephen Taylor's consent, I should like to dedicate my part in this book to these two Tonys.

Stephen Taylor, whose support and encouragement were largely self-administered, would nevertheless wish to acknowledge debts of gratitude to Margaret Church and Tadej, and simply to echo Jack's sentiment in Act III of *Lulu*: 'Das war ein Stück Arbeit.'

Preface to the Paperback Edition

In the two years since the first publication of this book in hardback, Caballé's biography has appeared in several foreign language editions. For us, the most remarkable of these was the much media-hyped simultaneous release of two versions – one in Catalan and one Castilian – where the prevailing conditions permitted the Spanish publishers to push the boat out in a fashion that is reserved these days for the book launches of the latest tales about royalty and rock stars. It was a memorable experience to find ourselves faced with a barrage of questions and flashlights at press conferences first in Madrid and then in Barcelona. Nor will we ever forget the breathless Sunday when, after a gruelling concert the night before, Montserrat materialized promptly at 10 a.m. to start a round of signings as part of Spain's annual book festival at no fewer than four Barcelonese bookshops plus the city's largest department store, all of which were under siege conditions. This is self-sacrifice on a heroic scale, given that the soprano has never stood to gain financially from a book of which originally she had not quite seen the point. It is a measure of how far she has come in terms of seeing that point and trusting our approach to it that she has thrown herself whole-heartedly into the various concert/book promotion tie-ins that other European language editions entail.

Thus far, the various editions have yielded a rich crop of reviews, virtually all of which have been gratifyingly positive. The critical discography has been particularly well received, the only recurrent criticism being to bemoan the fact that it is not complete. Originally, of course, it was, but as is indicated in the discographic preface considerations of space necessitated some stern pruning. The removal of several discussions of complete recordings did not, however, affect the integrity of the catalogue listings which appear at the end of each section and which are, to the best of the authors' knowledge, complete. Inevitably, again for reasons of space, it has not been possible to expand this paperback edition. But we have at least managed to tack on an addendum to the discography in the space available in order to bring it up to date. We have also rewritten the end of the final chapter so as to take some account of the past two years of what is obviously turning into one of the longest careers any opera singer has ever enjoyed.

If we had known in 1987, when this project started, what we know now, we might well have written a different kind of book. But in truth it would not necessarily have been any better, particularly in terms of its usefulness as a document of record. And it would probably have been even longer, so we can all be grateful for small mercies. There was a great deal of blood, sweat and tears expended in the research and writing, which perhaps naturally enough coloured our appreciation of the finished effort at the time of its first publication. But since then, its original motivation as a labour of love has crept again to the fore, not just from the authors' point of view but from Caballé's as well. It gave us enormous pleasure to learn that recently, after a recital in Tokyo, Montserrat greeted a small army of Japanese fans backstage, all bearing copies of the book (in English) which they wanted her to sign. Her eyes widened: she then impulsively grabbed a copy and held it to her heart saying: 'This is me. This is my book!' Evidently, it now is.

Robert Pullen and Stephen Taylor
London, August 1996

I

'Del Primo Pianto'

Turandot

CHAPTER ONE

To 1940: Ancestry, Birth and Childhood

Maria de Montserrat Viviana Concepción Caballé i Folch was born in Barcelona on 12 April 1933, at nine o'clock at night in the Calle d'Igual-ada, which is close to the shell of Antoni Gaudí's unfinished church of the Sagrada Familia. The baby barely survived; the labour, which was long and difficult, took place in the family home, without the advantages conferred by modern medicine. Worse, the infant was born with the umbilical cord wound tightly around her neck, her head changing colour alarmingly as she was effectively being slowly strangled. The doctor in attendance, Dr Company, was forced to perform some rapid makeshift surgery in order to free the baby. He then had the job of getting her to breathe, which met with tremendous success when she emitted a piercing yell. With a perhaps understandable excess of hindsight, Dr Company subsequently claimed that this denoted exceptional lung power, indicative of a soprano in the making: but though great Normas are in all probability born rather than bred, it is doubtful whether it would be manifest quite so early in anybody's career.

Montserrat is not strictly speaking a forename: it has only become so by association, and then only in Cataluña. It is in fact a geographical location, meaning 'cut' or 'serrated mountain' and is located some thirty kilometres north-west of Barcelona at the centre of the province. The mountain itself is an extraordinary sight, rising sheer out of the surrounding plains and visible for miles around; there has always been an unsubstantiated suggestion that Wagner drew his inspiration for the concept of Montsalvat in *Parsifal* from it. What is certain is that, simply as a geological phenomenon, it moved both Schiller and Goethe to the heights of Romantic fervour in its praise. Nowadays its fame is almost wholly due to musical association: on the one hand it boasts, in the Escolanía de Montserrat, one of the finest boys' choirs and training methods in Europe; on the other, it is both the inspiration for and (even now) the proud owner of the Llibre Vermell de Montserrat, a late-fourteenth-century compilation of pilgrimage songs considered to be one of the greatest collections of medieval music in the world.

The history of the mountain's colonization by religious orders dates back as far as the ninth century, when there is documentary evidence of there having been four hermitages, one of which was dedicated to the Blessed Virgin under her name of St Mary. The presumed presence of the saint was commemorated, some time around the year 1200, by the carved effigy which still dominates formal worship in the church. Many are surprised to discover that this sculpture portrays the Virgin as black – though this is not iconographically unprecedented – and that her familiar name to Catalans is *La Moreneta*, or 'the little dark one'. Today, whilst the effigy of the Virgin is the object of specific veneration, all Catalans regard the mountain as one of the principal focal points of their cultural identity, transcending questions of religious belief and observance to assume an almost mythic power.

A sharp distinction should be drawn between the Virgin, who is Maria, and the mountain, which is Montserrat, not least because it is quite common for Catalan girls to be called simply Montserrat, without any specific reference to the Virgin Mary. But Caballé's baptismal name is Maria de Montserrat, which shifts the emphasis away from the place and back to the person. Given Ana Folch's upbringing and religious devotion, it is hardly surprising that at the time of her greatest need, in the throes of a perilous childbirth, she should have directed her thoughts to the Blessed Virgin. So while the doctor struggled to save both her and her baby, she started praying to *La Moreneta*, if not for her own life then at least for that of her half-born child. Obviously from Ana's point of view the prayer was answered: there was no question, therefore, as to what the baby should be called. It seems fairly obvious, however, that no one – not friends, family, nor teachers – would be prepared to go on calling a child Maria de Montserrat on a daily basis. It would have had to have been shortened to either one name or the other; and since in Spanish Montserrat familiarly abbreviates to 'Montse' in everyday use, this probably decided the matter. There was also the added advantage that for foreign consumption 'Montserrat' sounds infinitely more exotic than the more or less universal 'Maria'. In any event, Caballé herself is quite clear on the subject: 'I am named after the Virgen de Montserrat. I am Maria.'

The difficulties of the birth were only part of a wider pattern of family problems and privations. Yet it had not always been so. Indeed, as one attempts to trace the lineage of both sides of Caballé's family back into the nineteenth century, an extraordinary pair of pre-histories begins to emerge.

Ana Folch i Martínez, Montserrat's mother, was born in 1911, the only daughter among the four children of Arturo Folch and Concepción Martínez.* At the time of her birth, the family was already in some degree of financial and social decline, although by contemporary standards still reasonably well-to-do. The foundations of their fortune had already been laid in the preceding mid-century when Ana's grandfather, Arturo Folch – Montserrat's great-grandfather – had been born into one of Spain's most wealthy families, with ancestors in Valencia and, in particular, the provincial town of Játiva. The Folch family were raised to the nobility by the Crown in recognition of their history of royal and state service. Arturo Folch had entered the junior ranks of diplomatic service following his years of training in the legal profession. He made spectacular progress through the diplomatic ranks, doubtless unhindered by his family's connections, becoming Ambassador at the Spanish court of Cuba and serving the Spanish Crown for a continuous period of sixteen years, covering the reigns of Alfonso XII (1875–85) and his widow, Queen Maria Cristina (1885–1902). In the second half of the nineteenth century, following the losses of Mexico and South America, Cuba was Spain's most significant surviving colonial possession. This was partly on account of its ready supply to the mother country of raw materials, including minerals, sugar and tobacco, and partly because of its status as the largest single overseas market for the export of textiles made in Cataluña, Spain's industrial heartland.

As befitted his situation, Arturo made a good marriage and proceeded

* It is standard practice in Spain for the children of any marriage to bear both their parents' surnames, in the order patronymic, then matronymic. As Montserrat herself has observed, 'In Spain, we also honour the mother.'

to father a characteristically large Victorian family. That he held his office for sixteen years against a steadily deteriorating background of social unrest and political disruption must give some indication of his calibre. But he was powerless to halt the inexorable growth of anti-colonial sentiment within Cuba, which took a violent turn in 1895 when republican forces began to promote insurrection. For three years the entire military and naval weight of what is invariably described by historians as an utterly corrupt colonial administration was thrown behind the attempt to crush this rebellion. It might even have succeeded had America not decided to intervene and, in the name of democracy (as usual, acting as a cover for its own colonial expansionist policy), offered Spain $3 billion to quit the country. This offer, however, was unacceptable, not least to the captains of the Catalan textile industry who, seeing the prospect of their one lucrative market vanishing, used their economic clout to lean on the Madrid government.

The result, in 1898, was the Spanish–American War, which ended in the most complete humiliation of any European power of the nineteenth century and Spain's abject surrender. But before this inglorious mayhem had reached its climax, Arturo Folch had been recalled. He made his way back to Madrid, where he was received by Maria Cristina, who was acting as Queen Regent until such time as her son, Alfonso, would reach the age of majority.

Most of Arturo's sons were trained in the law, just as he and his siblings had been. This meant that they formed a large group of closely related lawyers, and were able to set up a family firm in Valencia specializing in international law. We may imagine, given the prestige of Arturo's status, the kind of clientele that was attracted to his practice; indeed, the Folch family continued to enjoy royal patronage by acting as the Spanish royal family's legal advisers. But Arturo's sons could hardly be said to have enjoyed a sedentary existence since most of them at some time or another were employed as legal diplomats, negotiating on behalf of the Crown in its one remaining overseas possession – the Philippines.

Here matters had been deteriorating for much the same reasons as in Cuba. The colony had been experiencing progressive civil insurrection, countered with fierce repression by the Spanish authorities, and this, in turn, provoked massacres of colonial occupiers by armies of Filipino freedom fighters. But whereas the comparable situation in Cuba had been experienced by only one of the Folch family, Arturo, who had been withdrawn before the military reprisals began, six of his sons were present in the Philippines as representatives of the hated Spanish regime at the height of hostilities in various parts of the islands, and in the

event, were all killed. Of the elder Arturo Folch's sons, only two survived: Arturo junior and one other, who had remained in Madrid as
senior partners in the practice. 1898 therefore turned out to be a watershed, not only marking the bloody and abrupt end of Spain's history
as a colonial power, but also bringing personal tragedy into the lives of
so many families who, throughout the various levels of Spanish society,
had overseas links.

The few surviving members of the Folch family were left much
chastened, and – perhaps, like Parsifal, *durch Mitleid, wissend* (through
suffering, made wise) – turned increasingly to charitable work. But the
heartbroken elder Arturo never lived long enough to see the fruits of
this philanthropy: within mere months of the conclusion of the Spanish–
American War he was dead. With this unhappy conclusion to events,
the two brothers decided to sell off their father's law practice to those
existing partners who were not blood relatives and to split the proceeds
between them, as well as dividing the inherited moneys from the
paternal estate. Arturo junior's brother had recently married a young
woman from Argentina and, with the seeming collapse of the world
into which he had been born, decided to sell everything and emigrate
with his wife to her home country.*

Arturo junior himself, who had never married, had been financially
supporting the establishment of a collegiate orphanage in Valencia, run
by French Carmelite nuns. Many of the young orphan girls, drawn
principally from the province of Valencia, in turn became nuns; but this
was not the invariable outcome of the thorough schooling which they
received. One of them, Concepción, who was in her middle twenties,
had stayed on at the convent as an assistant to the nuns, in which capacity
she stitched and embroidered sacral vestments; but she was also a teacher
in her own right, specializing principally in French. Whether any pressures were brought to bear on her as an adult *alumna* of the orphanage is
not known, but it is certain that she fulfilled these functions without ever
taking formal vows. Arturo frequently visited the orphanage of which he
was effectively patron, and it was there that he met Concepción. Gradually, they fell in love and decided to marry. This brings the story into the
beginning of the twentieth century.

We can derive some idea of what must have been the very cloistered
nature of Concepción's previous existence from the fact that her wedding
was the first-ever occasion on which she had left the convent's premises

---

* They prospered there, and the Folch family is still prominent in Buenos Aires.
Caballé met them a few years ago and wistfully recalled: 'They don't feel Spanish
any more, but I suppose this is only normal after so long.'

as an adult. The girl's family background was not surprisingly unknown, and anyone marrying out from the orphanage with no known family name of their own would as a matter of course have been given the standard surname 'Esposito'. This, however, carried a certain element of social stigma which, especially in view of the evidently morganatic nature of the proposed marriage, the nuns were anxious to avoid. As a result, the Abbess took matters into her own hands. She prevailed upon a friend of hers to assume legal guardianship of the girl, thus enabling her to take the common enough Spanish surname of Martínez.

The wedding took place in Játiva and the newly-weds settled down to a reasonably comfortable middle-class existence. Arturo still practised law, though no longer as a senior partner in his own firm; Concepción soon had her own business to attend to, in the shape of José, the first of their four children. Alfredo and Arturo junior followed, but it was not until 1911 that their only daughter, Ana – Montserrat's mother – was born.

In many ways Ana Folch is the key figure in Montserrat's development, so it is all the more regrettable that she died no more than a few weeks before preliminary research for this biography was first undertaken. Inevitably, the story of Montserrat's maternal parentage had to rely not upon first-hand sources but upon the singer herself. It transpired, not surprisingly, that Caballé's own knowledge of the subject was limited to what she had been told by her mother piecemeal over a period of decades and that, without her consciously realizing it, some irreconcilable inconsistencies were present in these now second-hand accounts. Moreover, since Ana was the last of her generation of Folchs, there was no one who could provide clarification on certain matters.

The principal difficulty concerns the date of the Wall Street Crash, which incontrovertibly took place in 1929. It is to this event that Ana Folch always attributed the decline of her family's fortunes, which, together with the progressive impoverishment of the Depression during the early 1930s, precipitated their subsequent departure from Valencia to Barcelona. But the facts of Ana Folch's childhood, as known by her daughter, suggest an altogether different time-scale of events. From the tender age of ten or eleven, Ana had been compelled to go to work in a laundry where she was employed to do the ironing. She did this for four years, until at the age of fifteen she was obliged to stop because the constant lifting of the heavy iron platens was beginning to affect the curvature of her spine. Since Ana was born in 1911, it is clear she would have been engaged in this employment from approximately 1922 to 1926. For the youngest child of a supposedly well-to-do family to be forced to this extremity – seven years before the Wall Street Crash could have had any bearing on the family's fortunes – proves that severe financial decline must have afflicted the family at least a clear decade earlier. Why this should have happened and what particular reasons could have reduced one of the two sole heirs of what must have been in 1900 a substantial fortune to such impecunity, can now, alas, be no more than conjecture.* Perhaps Arturo invested unwisely; perhaps personal factors played a part; or perhaps the illness which would kill him shortly after the family's removal to Barcelona was already taking its toll. We simply do not know. What is certain is that within the brief space of twenty years, from the beginning of the century to the early 1920s, the once prosperous Folch family was approaching penury.

Their removal to Barcelona would therefore seem to have taken place rather earlier than Ana used to maintain, and under worse conditions than anyone had imagined, since the family are recorded as residing in the Sant Andreu quarter of the Poble Nou, an extremely poor area close by the port.† Arturo had attempted to pursue his legal career in the new city and, with the influence of friends, had secured a position in a large firm called Koch. But this was not to provide a solution to the problems, since he died of cancer within eighteen months. Montserrat tells of his widow, her grandmother, Concepción, struggling to bring up her four children by practising the only skill she knew: embroidery. But again, if the time-scale is to make sense, the four children have to be *children* rather than the young adults predicated by a chronology based upon the Wall Street Crash. All this means that the collapse of the family's fortunes would have had to have taken place no later than the mid-1920s and possibly much earlier.

In any event, it seems certain that it was the widowed Concepción who, in 1928, took her seventeen-year-old daughter, Ana, to one of the Sunday social clubs which used to be such a feature of Spanish society. At these, and with perfect propriety, the marriageable sons and daughters of respectable (and would-be respectable) citizens were put on show, closely chaperoned by their watchful parents. And it was on one of these visits that Ana Folch was introduced to a dashing and well-connected young chemistry student in the final year of his studies: Carlos Caballé.

As Montserrat herself says, 'The story of my father, Carlos, and his family is very different.' Indeed it is, as we pass from a tale of quasi-

---

* Whatever it was, it most certainly had nothing to do with the intervention of the First World War, during which Spain was technically neutral and from which, in economic terms, she benefited greatly.
† What was left of it was demolished in 1989 to make way for the Olympic Village.

aristocratic decline and fall to one of bourgeois entrepreneurial success. Already by the mid-nineteenth century, the Caballés, who hailed from the Southern Catalan town of Tarragona, were prosperous factory owners. Montserrat's great-grandfather, Pablo Caballé, owned a large brick-making company there and, boosted by the vast expansion in building programmes characteristic of the mid-nineteenth century throughout Europe, his business was highly profitable. In time-honoured tradition, he proceeded to diversify into other areas of the construction industry. With all the confidence of a self-made man and patriarch who had named the youngest of his three sons Abundio, he sent the boy to university in order to study engineering. This extraordinarily named youth turned out to be an enthusiastic and precocious student at the University of Barcelona, completing his studies effortlessly and in the process revealing an aptitude for invention. In due course he graduated, and though it was automatically expected that he would carve a niche for himself somewhere within his father's business empire, as had his brothers, he preferred the more quixotic lifestyle of an independent inventor.

However, it did not turn out to be in his – or indeed any other Caballé family member's – nature to languish unappreciated; he became the principal manufacturer of the *doble cojinete*, or double-sleeved, ball-bearing-driven cog-wheel, which revolutionized the commercial weaving process. This splendid gadget doubled the efficiency of industrial looms by permitting the shuttle to weave in both directions much more rapidly. By 1890, news of this remarkable advance had reached England, centre of the world's cotton-spinning industry, and a licensing arrangement was entered into between Abundio Caballé and the principal manufacturers based in and around Manchester. In addition, he invented and patented a machine for the processing of unfinished leather. Not surprisingly, Abundio made an absolute fortune out of these deals and with them ensured his complete independence from his father by financing the construction of his own factory on what was then the outskirts of industrial Barcelona.

The factory specialized in the manufacture of highly intricate textile machinery and parts, incorporating, of course, Abundio's own invention. This supplied the whole of Spain – particularly the northern industrial heartland of Cataluña and Navarra – the South of France and Northern Italy, and made a substantial contribution to the country's export revenues. On the strength of the personal fortune he amassed, Abundio decided to marry and raise a family. Thus Carlos Caballé, Abundio's only son, was born in 1907. He soon proved to be as fiercely independent as his own father had been, and declined to take his appointed place in the family business. As a boy at school he was principally fascinated with science, and when the time came for him to follow in his father's footsteps and enter the University of Barcelona, the subject he chose, perhaps with a nod in the direction of parental approval, was industrial chemistry. But if there had been any intention of pleasing his father by studying a subject with industrial application, it failed miserably.

Carlos stayed at the university until he was twenty-three, working in his father's factory during vacations. But relations between the two became progressively more strained: Abundio expected his son to embrace the specific interests of the family business and insisted that he master all the various textile-manufacturing, shop-floor and managerial working practices. Carlos, however, was profoundly unhappy at this enforced labour, and longed to be free to pursue his own particular interests. Matters came to a head during Carlos's last year of study when he refused to work in his father's factory any longer and instead went to work for one Señor Gaillard, a family friend, who had his own business manufacturing fertilizers and needed the particular expertise of an industrial chemist. Father and son were no longer on speaking terms, and not even Carlos's graduation the following year was sufficient to heal the rift. He remained as a full-time employee at Gaillard's from 1929 until the outbreak of the Spanish Civil War in 1936, by which time a great deal had happened and many things had changed.

Carlos had known Ana Folch for two years since their initial meeting without the friendship having become particularly serious. It was towards the end of his university career, when he was already working part-time at Gaillard's Fertilizers, that the relationship started to deepen. The unwritten rules of formal courtship which applied at the time would not permit visits to either party's family home without there being some very clear statements of intent and an indication of the probable date of marriage. In the event, this took place in Barcelona on 11 July 1932 at a time of ever-worsening economic depression and national political upheaval.

Throughout the 1920s Barcelona had acted as the powerhouse of a bloodless revolution that was changing the face of Spain. In April 1930 the Republic of Cataluña had been proclaimed by Luis Companys from the balcony of the Gothic town hall in Plaza San Jaume, at the same time as Colonel Macía declared the Republic in the Generalitat (the Catalan Parliament) opposite. King Alfonso XIII responded by abdicating, whereupon Spain became, for the second time in its history, a

Republic. The initial result of all this heady political activity was a national left-wing coalition government based in Madrid which was committed to a programme of army purges and anti-clerical legislation, including the dissolution of the Jesuit Order and the institution of divorce. But this government had entrenched opposition on both its left and right: on the one hand, the Communists and anarchists; on the other, the military, the monarchists and the Church. Its most pressing problem – the economic crisis – was effectively worldwide and beyond its control, so that the breeding ground for discontent of whatever political colour was fertile soil. Throughout 1934 strikes and demonstrations became ever more frequent: the public disorder in Asturias turned into full-scale regional civil war and was only quelled by the intervention of the combined forces of the Spanish army and the Foreign Legion, under General Francisco Franco y Bahamonde (or Franco, *tout court*).

In mid-1935, parties of the broad left sought to amalgamate and set up as the Popular Front, in direct opposition to the Falangists, a right-wing grouping modelled on Mussolini's *fascisti*. The former were especially strong in Barcelona where, at this time, over 350,000 people belonged to the anarchist groups, principally the CNT – Confederación Nacional de Trabajadores (or National Union of Workers). This new Popular Front narrowly won the national elections in February 1936 and proceeded to set about their social aims with a vengeance: thus the stage was fully set for the Civil War.

By this time, Carlos Caballé and Ana Folch had been married for nearly four years, and their daughter, Montserrat, was nearly three. What had at first seemed to be a marriage of serene promise had been severely tested by the political developments in Barcelona. The various anti-clerical measures had profoundly distressed Ana, strictly brought up as she had been by a convent-reared mother; and the army reforms had no less upset Carlos who, in 1929, had acted as a member of the royal military escort when Alfonso XIII had come to Barcelona for the Universal Exposition. The couple had set up home in the Calle d'Igualada situated just north of the Diagonal, between the Paseos de Gracia and San Juan. This was in the heart of the Gracia quarter of the city which, then as now, was a pleasant, well-to-do area. But the relative comfort of the couple's earliest years of marriage depended upon Carlos's position with the Gaillard factory and on the *rapprochement* he had effected with his father Abundio who, following the marriage, had been keen to encourage his son to maintain links with the family business, not least because it would eventually form his and his sister's patrimony.

But as the 1930s progressed, Carlos and his wife must have been wondering if there would actually be an inheritance. With effective government in Barcelona in the hands of various left-wing alliances, the position of the factory-owning classes and their scions was becoming ever more precarious. As early as 1932, during a CNT-sponsored strike in Barcelona, Abundio had been the object of an assassination attempt, although it seems unlikely that this had been engendered by any hostility within his own factory, since the 250-odd workforce there were generally better treated than many. The founding of first the Falange and then the Popular Front only served to polarize an already over-populated political battleground. From the Caballés' point of view, the situation collapsed altogether in July 1936, when the anarchists banded together all groups of the left under the umbrella of the Central Committee of the Anti-Fascist Militias, which they dominated. On 26 September, they were formally invited to merge with the Catalan Parliament and, although this was against their anarchist convictions, they accepted. Within days, a law was passed which empowered the CNT to take direct control of all privately owned factories and industrial plant.

Carlos Caballé suddenly therefore found himself performing his product-testing and development duties in an anarchist-run business; and his father, Abundio, found himself dispossessed of his own factory. Many members of the moneyed classes panicked and started to quit Cataluña. At this time, as the peseta began to plummet internationally, Lenin's old prediction that Spain would be the second country to establish a dictatorship of the proletariat began to look quite plausible. Some of the dispossessed factory owners took to staging sit-ins in their own factories, but in so doing fatally misjudged the temper of the times, since many of them were summarily shot. Abundio himself was once again the subject of an attempt on his life. He was a portly, bonhomous man who, luckily for him, wore loose-fitting clothes the better to disguise his girth, so that when he was shot at, the bullet entered the front of his jacket and passed straight through the fastening on the other side. This piece of serendipity has, of course, passed into Caballé family folklore, as has his rescue from certain imprisonment – if not, indeed, execution – by the testimony of his factory workers who were prepared to defend him as having always been an 'enlightened' employer.

But although the left-wing alliance was now firmly entrenched in Barcelona, this was not the case in the rest of the country where, following the assassination in mid-July of the head of the Parliamentary right wing, the army itself had proceeded to take the initiative and had appointed General Franco as its leader. It was only four days after the left wing had legitimately taken control of Cataluña on 26 September

1936 that General Franco, acting from his military base of Burgos in Castilla la Vieja (now León), installed himself as head of government and proclaimed himself *Generalissimo*. The legitimate seat of national government in Madrid was powerless to prevent this usurpation, and Franco's Nationalist troops started their remorseless advance across the country.

By autumn 1937, virtually the entire country was under Nationalist control, with the notable exceptions of Madrid and Cataluña. The situation in the latter was becoming nightmarish: on the one hand, there were chronic shortages of food and raw materials, and a vast pool of unemployed were nearing starvation; on the other hand, since right-wing forces were considered responsible for the plight into which left-wing Barcelona had been plunged, the usual public manifestations of privilege and authority came increasingly under attack. Thus it was that privately owned restaurants, cinemas and shops were expropriated. Of the fifty-eight churches in Barcelona, with the principal exception of the Gothic Cathedral preserved by the order of the now socialist-dominated Generalitat, more than fifty were burned. The workshops of Gaudí's unfinished Sagrada Familia were ransacked and the architect's plans destroyed. It became unsafe for anyone to wear the trappings of bourgeois respectability: a tie was a quick pass to imprisonment; a hat, an invitation to murder. Over 1200 monks, nuns and priests were killed in Barcelona alone.

In the midst of all this turmoil, Ana's overriding concern was to keep her husband and infant daughter fed, since most of Cataluña's food production was now being diverted to the ever-increasing number of Republican troops. The war from outside – as opposed to the internal strife – finally arrived on Barcelona's doorstep in January 1938 when the city was subject to the first of numerous horrifying air raid attacks carried out by Italian forces based in Majorca. On this occasion many hundreds were injured and some sixty died. On 16 March, just three weeks short of Montserrat's fifth birthday, the worst air raid left nearly 2000 wounded and over 1000 dead.

The Nationalist pressure was kept up so that by the middle of 1938 Cataluña had been more or less completely encircled. Air attacks continued and the number of starving and homeless multiplied vastly, not least because of the influx of refugees fleeing Franco's troops. In November there took place the decisive battle of the River Ebro where an enormous Republican army had been sent to prevent the Nationalists' advance. But the Catalan forces were routed, with 25,000 left dead. On 23 December 1938, despite a papal plea for a temporary cease-fire in order to observe Christmas, Franco launched his final assault on the city of Barcelona. By 15 January, Tarragona to the south had fallen; as a result all women, children and senior citizens were ordered to go and dig an enormous network of trenches around their city. But it was all to no avail. The air raids continued, during one of which an arms factory – 'Elizalde' – next to the Caballés' house in the Calle d'Igualada was destroyed, and Carlos found himself conscripted into Barcelona's defence force. By the end of the month Franco's troops had reached Llobregat – the location of the present-day international airport – and after brief skirmishing, during which Carlos was wounded in the left shoulder, the Nationalists broke through the remaining resistance.

The tanks rolled into Barcelona on 25 January 1939, only to find a city largely deserted, as it is estimated that over half a million people were in the process of fleeing northwards into the mountains. The Barcelonese are wedded to their geography: the extensive mountain range of Tibidabo, which curves behind the city, has almost symbolic significance for the people. Its name is popularly supposed to be a Latin rendition of the Devil's words to Christ during the temptation in the wilderness:'I offer this to you.' In times of crisis the citizens quite literally head for the mountains. And this is what they did in 1939, either as a temporary measure, or as the first stage of onward flight through the Pyrenees to France. But the Nationalists had already occupied Tibidabo, which therefore needed some shrewd negotiation if it was to provide safe passage.

Perhaps the majority of those fleeing were not, in fact, seriously at risk in terms of reprisals by the occupying forces, but in the panic which followed the collapse of the city's defences, they could hardly be expected to believe this. The Caballé family were among them, including the nearly six-year-old Montserrat. Just how perilous the flight into the mountains was, she only learned many years later. Her parents had put together what scraps of food they could find, and Ana had managed to contact one of her brothers, Alfredo, who joined them in the journey. As the disorganized convoys thronged up the steep sides of Tibidabo by whatever means available, it was down to the initiative of individuals as to what were the safest ways to proceed. At one point a large group, including the Caballés, were confronted by a stark choice: two tunnels loomed ahead, one a continuation of the road, the other an abandoned section of the funicular railway. A desperate dispute broke out as to which route should be followed. Alfredo Folch was quite clear about which direction to take in order to reach safety and Carlos Caballé was in complete agreement, but they were unable to persuade the whole of the group to heed their advice; a certain number therefore broke away and followed the other route. Alfredo duly led his group to safety; the others emerged into the midst of a Nationalist encampment and were shot.

Preoccupied at this time with the fundamental problem of survival, the Caballés would hardly have been given to introspection. Had they been so, they would surely have reflected bitterly upon the grim fate that had overtaken their country and the ruin that had personally overwhelmed them. As it was, they may have been cold, hungry and homeless; but at least they were together and all alive.

The subsequent return home was equally fraught with danger and uncertainty. After the first flush of Nationalist reprisals against suspected Republican sympathizers and the enforced restoration of order in the city, the vast majority of those hiding in the hills decided to make their way back to Barcelona. They found the place eerily quiet, with signs everywhere of death and destruction, not least that of Catalan cultural identity itself, the very language of which was being stripped from the city's walls. As Caballé says: 'Things were worse than ever before. There was no food, no money, no clothing, no warmth. Nothing. My family was in a desperate situation, but then so were many others.'

Her father Carlos returned to work in what was left of the Gaillard factory, but the general economic collapse in Cataluña meant that, for a while, nobody was properly paid and continuity of employment could not be guaranteed. Worse still, Carlos began to manifest the early symptoms of what was eventually diagnosed to be angina. And although in these early days of recovery after the Civil War this did not prevent him from performing his duties, it would soon become a decisive factor in the family's waning fortunes.

On the wider political scene, the legitimate government in Madrid held out against the Nationalists for a further two months after the fall of Barcelona. But it too was forced to capitulate at the end of March 1939, permitting Franco to declare a formal end to the Civil War on 1 April, evidently unaware of the significance of the date. Henceforth, the full weight of unopposed Fascist dictatorship began to be felt across the entire country, greatly helped in its practical application given that the new government had the unqualified support of the Catholic Church. It could also count on the slightly more guarded welcome of the surviving landowners and businessmen, glad to be rid of what they regarded as the scourge of the left-wing. To this end, the new administration promulgated a law by which all expropriations of property during the Civil War were to be reversed and private possessions restored to their former owners. In cases where this was to prove difficult, or only partially possible, compensation was to be paid. But, as was the case with the Caballés, in reality this amounted to little more than a political gesture by the new régime.

Carlos's father, Abundio, had died shortly after the end of the Civil War, without seeing his property restored to him. Nor, indeed, was there a great deal to restore, since the textile machinery had either been stolen or melted down for the purposes of munitions, and the fabric of the factory itself had sustained considerable damage. On his death, more or less penniless, the remnants of Abundio's property passed in theory to his two children, but not until the new law was enacted were they able to realize such assets as it represented. Carlos and his sister were only able to obtain a fraction of the factory's former worth – not surprising, given both its condition and the condition of the Spanish economy – and the compensation payable hardly made good the shortfall. By this time, of course, the World War had begun, and although Spain again remained neutral – whilst firmly allied by treaties to both Hitler and Mussolini – this could not isolate her from the economic difficulties that prevailed everywhere else. Coupled with the catastrophic losses already brought about by the Civil War, Spain's economic situation remained precarious throughout the 1940s.

These, then, were the formative years of Montserrat's childhood, unsettled and uncertain. Even so, it became possible, after all the endless social disruption of the immediately preceding years, to send Montserrat to school for the first time, and she began her formal studies at a local academia. But this was the world of ordinary education where, with the exceptions of history and geography, the young girl found little enough to stimulate her interest. What did fire her imagination was the music she frequently heard at home, either on the radio or, more particularly, when her father played his cherished shellac 78s of favourite singers. One of these was of Conchita Badía. The aria, prophetically enough, was 'Un bel dì vedremo'.

While the family was still living in the partially damaged property in Calle d'Igualada, a rare opportunity had been taken to visit the opera. As part of the busy 1939–40 season, *Madama Butterfly* was given with Mercedes Capsir in the title-role.* Montserrat recalls the occasion vividly:

---

* Mercedes Capsir, 1895–1969. One of the most famous sopranos of the inter-war years, who moved from début roles such as Gilda and Lucia into heavier repertoire, including Elsa and Tosca. Another Liceo product, with a voice perhaps best described as a full lyric with coloratura. Extraordinarily enough, she was born in the same house, eleven years later, as Maria Barrientos, who in her slightly earlier generation had been just as eminent.

My first visit to the opera was to *Madama Butterfly* at the Liceo when I was seven. It was with Mercedes Capsir. I enjoyed it immensely, but it was a great shock at the end with the death of Butterfly which I had not expected. It made a great impression on me and all night I was thinking about it and talking about the performance for days afterwards because it was something very special. It was incredible. The aria – 'Un bel dì' – I remembered from hearing on records at home and so I listened to it again and again afterwards during our last year in Calle d'Igualada and sang it for my parents as my present to them that Christmas 1940.

The bomb damage next door to the family home in Calle d'Igualada hardly made it a suitable place in which to bring up a child. Furthermore, Carlos's heart trouble was beginning to affect his capacity to work regularly, and so it was beyond both his physical and financial powers to effect repairs until such time as the matter of his paternal inheritance was resolved. In the event, after this had eventually been processed in 1940, both he and Ana decided to leave behind the now painful scene of their once-carefree family home and make a new life for themselves. With Carlos's share of the factory sale and the compensation, there was enough money to commission the building of a house in El Guinardó, just over a mile to the north-east of their old home, behind the city's largest hospital, Santa Cruz y San Pablo. Progress on the construction was continually interrupted by shortages of various raw materials and the intervention of one of Europe's worst winters, so that it was only possible for the family finally to leave Calle d'Igualada in early spring 1941. It was here in Guinardó that the Caballés experienced a sense of security and material comfort that they had not known for over five years. This in turn made possible the realization of a dream which, for some time, had been dear to Montserrat's heart: she would be sent to study music at the city's prestigious Conservatorio del Liceo.

CHAPTER TWO

1940–1955: The Conservatorio Years

What is now known as the Conservatorio del Liceo was originally founded in 1838 and soon came to rank with the finest educational establishments in Spain. Its present position above the opera house dates from the rebuilding in 1862; but it had occupied the same position and relationship in the original building of 1847. Evidently, there was always a concern that the opera house should be kept supplied with home-grown talent on a regular basis. Such was the quality of its teaching that the Conservatorio soon acquired a formidable reputation as a breeding-ground for great singers and instrumentalists, which in turn meant that it increasingly attracted those of superior ability, both as students and teachers. This astonishing institution became of vital significance to the musical life not just of Barcelona, nor even of Spain, but of the whole world. Together with the city's other principal music academy, the Conservatorio Municipal, it can list among its *alumni* Francesco Viñas, Pablo Casals, Hipolito Lazaro, Elvira de Hidalgo, Conchita Supervía, Maria Barrientos, Mercedes Capsir, Miguel Fleta, Victória de los Angeles, Alicia de Larrocha, Enriquetta Tarrés, Giacomo Aragall, Eduardo Giménez, Vicente Sardinero, Juan Pons and Dalmacio González, as well, of course, as Montserrat Caballé. It is difficult to imagine any other music academy producing a comparable galaxy of stars. Beyond the imponderables of *genius loci*, this must surely point to extraordinary standards of tuition.

We have already seen that Montserrat's first manifestation of na'ural musical talent occurred in early 1940. Once the family was comfortably settled into the new house in El Guinardó a year later, Carlos returned to work and Ana threw herself energetically into the role of proud housewife. Shortly after the move she became pregnant, and on 19 December 1941 she gave birth, this time without problems, to her second child and only son, who it was decided would be named after his father.* Thus we encounter for the first time the young Carlos Caballé, not quite nine years his sister's junior, who was destined to play such an essential part in the development and fulfilment of her career, as well as that of so many other artists.

Montserrat, meanwhile, was kept happily occupied with her musical studies. In the early stages these lessons were neither arduous nor over-frequent: one hour per week was devoted to piano, and a further hour to what is known in Europe as *solfège*, musical theory and notation. Montserrat found at the Conservatorio del Liceo all the compelling interest that for the most part had been lacking at her primary school, and began to show every sign of thriving in her new environment. Perhaps this was not solely due to the nature of the studies themselves, but also to the altogether less regimented and informal atmosphere in which her Conservatorio lessons were conducted. Whereas at school, like all the other children, she was effectively confined to a specific class within her own year, at the Liceo people from a much broader social base and age-range mingled freely, brought together more by musical affinity than by educational necessity.

During Montserrat's first year at the Liceo, however, her father's health declined sharply, obliging him to take ever-longer periods of sick leave. Gaillard's honourably paid him something, but it was insufficient to make good the sudden drop in family income. Unfortunately, the symptoms of Carlos senior's angina started to become more and more problematic: as well as his chest pains, he began to suffer from shortness of breath and general debility. On this basis alone he was not, perhaps, an employable proposition, even though he was still only in his mid-thirties. As a result, at a time when no social security safety net existed, it proved impossible for him to provide for himself, his wife, and their two children. Inevitably, but with reluctance, it was decided in late 1942 to sell the house in El Guinardó in order to finance the purchase of a grocery store over which the family would live, and which would enable them to make a self-sufficient living as small traders.

The shop was in the Calle de Calàbria, just off the Gran Via de les Corts Catalanes in the westernmost part of El Ensanche,† just a sturdy

---

* In fact, Carlos's date of birth is registered in Barcelona as having taken place on 4 February 1942. But this is incorrect, and Carlos himself attributes the anomaly to the administrative chaos still prevalent in Spanish bureaucracy after the Civil War.

† The Ensanche is a large area of central Barcelona designed by Idelfons Cerdá in the 1860s based upon Victor Haussmann's revolutionary innovations in town planning which were taking place in Paris. But Cerdá's motivation was resolutely socialist, which accounts for the absolutely unbroken – and equal – rectilinearity of the area's grid-like layout stretching from the Plaza d'España in the east to the Poble Nou in the west.

stone's thrown from the Plaza d'España. It is the first of the extraordinary coincidences that abound throughout Montserrat's life that this grocery was next door to Miguel Fleta's apartment. Fleta, the most famous Spanish tenor of his generation, whose career had reached its summit with the creation of the role of Calaf in *Turandot* at La Scala in 1926, had died shortly before the end of the Civil War. Years later, his children were to act as hosts to the young man from Aragón who was to become Montserrat's husband. Caballé's parents, both of whom were musically cultivated, would have been quite aware of the significance of their neighbours, and Montserrat recalls that the Fletas became regular customers of the shop.

The young girl was frequently obliged to help her mother in the day-to-day running of the shop when she was not deputed to look after her baby brother, who was otherwise much given to throwing oranges out into the street and demolishing the piles of carefully stacked fruit. Given the downturn in the family's fortunes, it seemed that it would be necessary for Montserrat to give up her musical studies. And so it would have proved if it had it not been for the intervention of her piano teacher, Pedro Vallribera, who was one of the Conservatorio's directors and therefore in a position to recommend that the young girl should be awarded a *beca* or scholarship. He had been deeply impressed by both her seriousness as a pupil – particularly since she was almost the youngest in her motley group – and her extraordinary determination, which seemed to him reason enough for the Conservatorio itself to act in furtherance of her education. So it was that her studies not only continued but soon took on new dimensions. After her second year, she recalls that:

I joined other classes which taught harmony, keys (including the antique modes), pitch sensitivity and how to improve your perception of it, because this is something which you can learn, not as if it was perfect pitch, I admit, but still you can get much better. The Conservatory had a large number of instruments, and in the beginning we used to listen to and play with the percussion, such as bells and triangles. Then, each month, we would be introduced to other instruments such as the oboe, the violin, the trumpet, so that we could learn their range, how they are played and how they are constructed. We were taught how to tune a violin and how this differs from how to tune a cello or a double bass. The more I studied the more I loved music and the more it became an important part of my life. I remember going to school and doing everything as quickly as I could so that I could get to the Liceo, which was for me what really mattered. I really didn't care if I got bad reports at school generally, but if I got a bad report for music it was awful; that was something I could never accept.

Carlos senior was still working, when his health permitted, at Gaillard's, which left the grocery venture wholly under his wife's management. It was therefore little short of a family catastrophe when Ana herself fell ill with lung trouble and was hospitalized in 1943. She was found to be suffering from pleurisy, and acting upon medical advice, once she had been discharged it was decided that complete rest and a change of air were necessary for her full recovery. Therefore, only one year after acquiring the shop, the family were obliged to sell it and, with the proceeds, buy a small house in the mountain pinewoods that lay beyond Tibidabo, outside Barcelona, in a place called Floresta. Inevitably, this removal to a location far from the city centre meant that Montserrat was no longer able to attend her music lessons at the Liceo. This came as a terrible blow to the ten-year-old, since by this time she was quite sure that it was through the medium of music that she was going to discover the 'something' of which she so longed to be proud. But for the time being the harsh reality of the family's circumstances precluded any further developments on this front. Indeed, it was at this time that Montserrat herself took on the role of 'little mother', increasingly charged with the responsibility of looking after her two-year-old brother. It was as a direct result of this situation – which would continue unchanged throughout Carlos junior's childhood – that the siblings became utterly inseparable. At this stage, the infant boy was, naturally enough, wholly dependent upon his older sister: but later the balance of power in the relationship would frequently tilt the other way.

In the unspoiled mountain air of Floresta, Ana's health slowly began to improve, but Carlos senior's sick-pay from Gaillard's fertilizer factory was insufficient to provide for the family. She was therefore compelled to seek employment in order to make good the shortfall. Like her mother before her, she had only one marketable commodity – the skills she had been taught as a seamstress – and opportunities for exploiting these in the sparsely populated Floresta were few and far between. Eventually it became clear that, however agreeable the air was, the family could not live on it. And so once again, with profoundest regrets, the Caballés were forced to sell up.

This time the situation was rather different. There seemed no likelihood of Carlos senior ever resuming full-time paid employment; and the need for Ana to be in a place where she could find ready work predicated a removal back to central Barcelona. Unfortunately, the sale of the house in Floresta realized less than it had originally cost to buy, so that it proved impossible for the Caballés to buy another home in the city centre. Thus, for the first time, they found themselves forced to rent their accommodation in the form of a modest apartment in the Travessera de les Corts, which runs just in front of the old FC Barcelona football stadium. This final move took place in 1945, which means that over a period of under five years, the family had moved no fewer than four times, the last three occasions each constituting an appreciable turn in the downward spiral of their social mobility. It is true that geographically they were now back not so very far from where they had started: but they had lost all their capital in the process; they had acquired a new baby in the meantime; and both parents were now suffering from poor health.

It takes no great effort of imagination to realize the profoundly unsettling effect all these vicissitudes must have had upon Montserrat during the formative years of her childhood. One inevitable result of all this enforced relocation was that she had yet to undergo any real continuity of formal schooling. Her parents were deeply conscious of this and set about finding a local school which their daughter could attend regularly. Happily, it transpired that the Academia Arpí was no more than two doors away from the Caballés' rented flat. Montserrat was sent there immediately. Many people look back on their early school days with nostalgia and affection, but not so Montserrat: for her this period was one of pain and humiliation, leaving her with scars which carried into adulthood. She was the victim of that extraordinary cruelty which is so successfully practised by children – picking remorselessly on a person's weakest point. In Montserrat's case, this was her poverty. Such was the family's decline, and the wider shortage of raw materials, that despite Ana's abilities as a seamstress, the young girl was obliged to attend school, day in, day out, always wearing the same dress.

> I wasn't at all popular; in fact I was very shy. For years I wore the same dress, as if it were the school uniform. For a young girl this is very distressing. I was always clean and tidy, but that is not enough for a girl. The young can be cruel, and some of the other children made fun of me because of my one and only dress. I found this very hurtful, but I couldn't say anything back to them because there was no answer.

Home life could be hard too. There never seemed to be quite enough to eat and Ana was increasingly preoccupied with the mechanics of keeping the family going. Caballé remembers her mother working feverishly. This was not, however, just the usual round of domestic cleaning and cooking – though it is true that Ana had a particular obsession with clean white net curtains – for by this time she had resorted to taking in other people's clothing for washing and repair. In those days of economic depression following the end of the Second World War, when linen, socks or stockings developed holes, no one would dream of throwing them away – substitutes would be hard to find and prohibitively expensive to buy. So an entire cottage industry had sprung up based on people's ability to repair these items, and even at this early age Montserrat was taught how to help her mother. Needless to say, the work was scarcely lucrative and extremely time-consuming, but it made all the difference to the Caballé family's survival.

Ana set about searching for employment in addition to these *ad hoc* arrangements for working at home and eventually managed to find a part-time job in a *merceria*.* This left even less time for her to devote to the children, who were increasingly thrown on to their own resources, inevitably in each other's company. The income generated by Ana's labours proved sufficient for it to be possible, in September 1945, for Montserrat to return to the Conservatorio in order to resume her music studies as well as continuing her normal education at the Academia Arpí. Once returned to the Liceo, the girl rapidly picked up the threads of her interrupted tuition. She met some old friends and made some new ones: indeed Montserrat still keeps in touch with one or two of them. She remembers how in the days before photocopiers the children used to band together in order to copy out full orchestral scores. In the process, they would learn how music was formally laid out and the different instruments notated, and would amuse themselves by inventing new harmonies and instrumentation. It seems quite clear from these memories that, although Montserrat's schooldays would continue periodically to be dogged by the humiliating teasing she had already experienced, these music classes in all senses provided the escape into a higher, more rewarding reality of which she had dreamed.

Finances on the home front, however, remained difficult, becoming even more so when in the latter stages of 1947 it was necessary for the five-year-old Carlos to attend school for the first time. He followed his sister into the Academia Arpí where he soon showed himself to be a highly gifted and intelligent pupil. Montserrat continued to derive her greatest satisfaction, however, not from her studies at Arpí, but from those precious hours she was able to spend at the Conservatorio. Ever since that fateful Christmas gift to her parents in 1940 – her rendition of 'Un bel dì vedremo – the young girl had eagerly seized on every

---

* There is no English equivalent to this combination of haberdasher's, perfumery and general chemist.

opportunity not only to listen to singing at home, both on records and the radio, but to break into song herself. By the late 1940s, it was quite clear to Caballé's parents that their daughter had a real, if untutored, voice, and it was equally clear to Montserrat herself that, more than anything else in the world, she wanted to be a singer.

But how was this to come about? Thus far, the cost of her three or four hours' study per week at the Conservatorio had been manageable; but the business of undertaking voice studies was an entirely different financial proposition due to the greatly increased scale of the educational programme. This would entail a change from part- to virtually full-time study, the costs of which would simply be beyond the Caballé family's means. The dilemma presented itself at the end of the Conservatorio del Liceo's 1948-9 academic year, and we may imagine the endless heart-searching that went on in the Caballé family home during the following summer. At least there was no conflict, in the sense that everybody wanted the same thing; but there seemed no financial way by which it could be achieved. Ana, however, was utterly determined: from the first time she had heard her daughter sing she had, rather like Maria Callas's mother Evangelia, been a constant source of exhortation.

In retrospect, it is hardly surprising, given the precarious, hard-driven existence she was leading, that Ana Caballé should have so eagerly seized upon her daughter's nascent talent as a commodity to be exploited. It should be remembered that Ana had known want as a child herself, but had made a marriage which she had every reason to expect would prevent its recurrence. Yet that dream had vanished over the past decade, to be replaced by a grimmer reality than anyone could have anticipated. That Ana should live to see such deprivation revisited on her own children must have been the realization of her worst nightmare. Small wonder, then, at the woman's steely determination that her daughter should succeed.

When I used to go to school, my mother would pull my hair back so tight with a ribbon that it hurt. I wanted so desperately to be proud of something, so I worked very hard to be the first in class. My voice was very high and light and I was certain I would be a singer. Never a doubt. If mama was desperate I'd say, 'Have patience, because when I am famous we won't want for anything.' And she believed me. Little Carlos believed me too.

All this belief amounted to something tangible: Ana redoubled her efforts to earn extra money through the work she undertook at home. Somehow the necessary finances were scraped together to enable Montserrat to register for the vocal classes at the Conservatorio. Thus it was that Caballé started her preliminary voice studies at the end of September 1949, euphoric at being able to do so, but deeply apprehensive about the financial implications for the family.

No sooner had Montserrat begun to settle in to her new studies than her father fell seriously ill and was diagnosed as urgently needing heart surgery. Spain in the late 1940s had no organized system of social security or free health service as such: those needing surgery simply had to find the means with which to pay for it. And so it was decided that Montserrat, in addition to her studies, would have to go to work immediately. At the very end of 1949 she started work in a handkerchief factory known as Casa Comella, situated in Calle de Petrixol – a back-alley leading northwards off the Plaza del Pi in the heart of the ancient Barrio Gótico quarter of the city. Conveniently enough, this was barely a couple of minutes' walk from the Conservatorio del Liceo on the opposite side of the Ramblas. Caballé worked in the factory during the day and attended her musical courses in the Liceo in the late afternoon. Work hours began at eight o'clock in the morning and continued until one or one-thirty, then recommenced from three until six. This routine was observed every day of the week, from Monday to Saturday inclusive.

She recalls that her job was to cut appropriate-sized pieces of cloth from larger swatches, a job for which at the beginning she had little enough aptitude since any number of cut-outs emerged lopsided and proved impossible to stitch into the correct shape. However, one soon develops the necessary skills in a sweatshop, or rapidly finds oneself without a job. So although the clouds of fine cloth particles thrown up by the cutting process made her very wheezy, Montserrat adapted to this gruelling regime, even to the extent of working overtime on Saturdays whenever possible. But the morning, noon and night regime of work and study was simply too taxing. Something had to give and, not surprisingly, following a most miserable Christmas, it was decided that Montserrat should forgo her lessons at the Conservatorio. She thus began the first year of the new decade by being forced to abandon her most cherished ambition, or at least to allow immediate contingencies to take precedence over her long-term plans.

The need for the elder Carlos to have an operation was becoming more urgent and this meant that by Easter 1950 Montserrat was not only working full-time at the Casa Comella, but also assisting her mother in the evenings darning stockings and performing general seamstress work. Ana, herself frantic with worry – partly on account of her husband's health, partly because of the enforced disruption of her daughter's training – was still working in the *merceria* as well as bringing home laundry. The result of all this effort was that enough money was saved to enable Carlos to have his operation in the early summer – successfully, as it transpired. After eight months' hard labour, Montserrat was able to give up work at the handkerchief factory. This alleviated her workload, but of course diminished the family's income. Moreover, her father was now effectively unemployable, having been hospitalized for over six months and still needing an extended period of convalescence.

It was at this juncture that Ana's brother, Alfredo, made what proved to be the decisive suggestion. He was working as night watchman in the most affluent part of the city called – aptly enough – Bona Nova, where one of the villas belonged to the family Bertrand i Mata. He suggested that Ana should write to them asking for help. This was not quite the desperate and unlikely ploy it might sound, since there was a long and honourable tradition of patronage among well-to-do Barcelonese families.

The Bertrand i Mata were an old textile-manufacturing family who, in 1935, according to the Bulletin of the Federation of Master Cotton Spinners published in Manchester, were the largest private owners in the cotton sector in the world. The head of the family, Eusebio Bertrand, had been a profoundly cultivated man, being the Honorary Life President of the Board of Directors and a part-owner of Barcelona's opera house, the Gran Teatro del Liceo. Of course, his business had suffered greatly during the Spanish Civil War, but such was the extent of his overseas investments that the greater part of his personal wealth had survived, unlike that of the Caballés, all of whose capital had been tied up in their requisitioned factory and plant. After the war, Eusebio had been instrumental in founding an association of industrialists which helped to reconstruct those factories in the textile sector that had sustained damage. It seems almost certain that the Caballé factory was one of these, though in the absence of documentation this must remain speculative. On a broader social basis, the family also privately endowed the Hospital of San Rafael for children. Eusebio himself had six – José Antonio, Mercedes, Ines, Flora, Manuel Juán and Eusebio junior – all of whom became active in public good works. He died in 1945 and his children immediately set about extending the family's reputation for philanthropy by establishing memorial trusts and sundry foundations.

Carlos Caballé senior was initially extremely reluctant to follow the suggestion that Alfredo Folch had passed on, reasoning that nobody ever did something for nothing. His somewhat jaundiced outlook was actively challenged not just by Ana, who by this time doubtless reasoned

that anything was worth trying, but by Montserrat herself. Above all
else she wanted to resume her voice studies since, as she says:

> It was very clear to me that music was my whole life and that, through
> it, I could maybe achieve a better position and earn some money so
> that the family did not continue to have to suffer, that my father
> could be properly looked after, and that my brother Carlos could
> continue with his education.

Carlos was therefore prevailed upon to compose a letter to be sent to
the Bertrand family under Montserrat's name. He had limited himself
to a simple request for some form of subsidy to enable his daughter to
continue her singing studies until such time as she secured her first
contract. The letter was sent at the beginning of July 1950 to the two
remaining unmarried Bertrand children who still lived in Eusebio's
house, José Antonio and Mercedes. A breathless wait ensued: then, on
21 July, a reply was received from José Antonio Bertrand acknowledg-
ing Montserrat's request, confirming that her music teacher, Pedro
Vallribera, had provided a glowing testimonial, and asking for an
exact breakdown of the moneys needed. The Caballés' response was
despatched the following day. On 31 July 1950, Señor Bertrand wrote
back with some specific calculations concerning the cost of hiring a
piano for Montserrat's home use and the level of fees for French lessons.
Furthermore, he would need to know what time-scale was envisaged
for his on-going patronage. The Caballés replied on 4 August, but there
then followed a long silence: by the end of the month nothing had been
heard.

In fact, it was not until 3 September that a reply was finally received,
José Antonio and his sister having been cruising the Mediterranean and
Egypt on the family yacht in the meantime. The letter outlined in detail
the Bertrands' intention of offering Montserrat a total sum of 8000
pesetas for the continuance of her musical education, and ended by
suggesting that the señorita and her mother might care to attend the
family's office in order to finalize the matter.* Following this invitation,
Ana and her daughter went to see José Antonio Bertrand for what
turned out to be a highly informal interview, during the course of which
Ana declined the offer on the grounds that if she received so substantial
a sum all at once she would undoubtedly use it to pay off the family's
most pressing debts. At this point Bertrand, amused rather than
offended by Ana's candour, asked to know rather more about the
Caballés' family situation and background. Having heard the full story,

---

* The current equivalent in sterling would be approximately £4000.

he began to think along rather grander lines about long-term and wide-ranging assistance for the whole family. From the young girl's point of view, this would mean an altogether more thoroughgoing assessment of her vocal potential, since it was one thing to 'buy off' the importunate mother at the price of two years' fees, quite another to undertake an entire five- or six-year programme of patronage and subsidy for the whole family.

To this end, an audition was arranged at which the seventeen-year-old Montserrat was invited to sing in front of half a dozen people, including José Antonio and Mercedes Bertrand. The others, selected by the Bertrands from amongst their wide circle of musician friends, included Max Lorenz, the famous Wagnerian *heldentenor* who often sang at the Liceo, (of which the Bertrands remained part-owners), Julius Katchen, the renowned American pianist who gave frequent performances in the Palau de la Musica in Barcelona and was invariably the Bertrands' house guest on these occasions, and Alicia de Larrocha. Everyone did their best to put the young hopeful at her ease, mindful of the importance, at least from her point of view, attaching to the occasion.

In front of this dauntingly high-powered gathering, then, Montserrat proceeded to sing a brief selection of arias and *canciones* which were warmly received. The musical assessors were asked by the Bertrands to provide written reports: those of Lorenz and Katchen were very positive and indeed enthusiastic, recommending that the Bertrands undertake the girl's vocal education as a matter of urgent priority. As a result, they decided to sponsor not just Montserrat but the whole of her family, and to set about tackling some of the most pressing problems. Accordingly, the Bertrands' offer to help was extensive and virtually unconditional: they would wholly take charge of bearing the costs of Montserrat's studies at the Conservatorio del Liceo; they would ensure that her younger brother Carlos was properly educated (to which end they had him transferred to a school of which they were patrons, run by the religious order Los Escolapios); and they would do whatever was within their power to help the parents, including finding a job that would not tax the father's limited energies.

This exceptionally generous act of patronage was to extend for the whole period of Montserrat's vocal studies and beyond, until such time as she secured her first permanent contract. The only condition imposed – though informally – was the verbal understanding that if and when Montserrat became a great singer, she would never neglect her native city and would sing in its Gran Teatro del Liceo every year. Some years later, shortly before José Antonio's death, she visited him and, after he had reiterated his desire that she should always retain Barcelona as the centre of her activities, she asked him why it was that he had been so generous not only to her, but to so many others. Why did he never say 'no' to anyone? His reply was that he felt himself under an obligation to help others: suppose he himself had needed help, but had been refused? The lesson was not to be lost on Caballé.

The immediate upshot of the Bertrand sponsorship was to allow Montserrat to return to the Conservatorio in time for the start of the 1950–1 academic year and to begin full-time vocal studies. It was while she was there that she encountered the three most profoundly formative influences of her musical life: Eugenia Kemmeny, Conchita Badía and Napoleone Annovazzi.

By this time Eugenia Kemmeny was a formidable woman of advanced years who in her youth had been a championship swimmer and athlete in her native Hungary. She had studied singing there, enjoyed a modest career, and had eventually graduated to singing Wagner at Bayreuth. Kemmeny's method of vocal teaching disdained such traditional concepts as 'vocal placement' – an unscientific breakdown of the human voice's perceived chest, middle and head registers in terms of their supposed physical location – in favour of an all-embracing system of muscular development and breath support unique to each individual. But the primary emphasis of Kemmeny's teaching was upon musical *feeling* and was dedicated to drawing out of each student his or her innate emotional response to what the music was trying to say. She favoured as an exercise playing sequences of simple chords on the piano and asking her students to improvise a vocal line which would harmonize not just technically but emotionally. Montserrat remembers that she was required to sing

> in accord with the different harmonies Kemmeny played. We had to feel for ourselves whether these were sad or happy or brilliant. So she made us discover how to produce a sound filled with the feeling that the harmonies inspired in us. I remember, one day I was doing an improvisation while she played a bright passage, but then suddenly I sensed she was playing in the minor, so brilliance was impossible and I began to sing with a sad sound. Kemmeny was very happy. She said, 'Well, you understood: you began so bright but ended dying away.' This way of teaching was very important to my development.

Kemmeny's insistence upon intrinsic musicianship was, and probably still is, rare enough in itself. But the technical means by which this was to be fulfilled was even more so. In the first year, the students were confined to performing nothing but scales and physical exercises designed to develop the abdominal musculature in order to stabilize the emission of breath. Kemmeny's name for all this was *respiratory gymnastics*. The object of the exercises was to build a physically perceptible wall around the diaphragm; the exercises themselves concentrated upon learning how to use and to control the musculature behind the abdomen, since it is these muscles which support the diaphragm as well as the whole of the back. Everything was geared to strengthening the abdominals so that the diaphragm itself would not have to work at all, but simply support the even exhalation of breath across the vocal cords. Or in other words, to sing properly. Kemmeny, who as both an athlete and a soprano was better placed than most to understand the mechanics of voice production, knew that the work of pushing the air out and up is all done by the abdominal muscles. Furthermore, she brought a runner's mentality into her teaching by maintaining that singing always required that the maximum expenditure of effort be reserved for the final lap. Among other endearing quirks, she kept a stop-watch and would make students hold their breath for as long as possible and then time the length of their exhalations.

> I have practised as Kemmeny taught me for decades now. Every morning I do a breathing exercise for three-quarters of an hour after having breakfast. I cannot do it before eating something because on the few occasions when I have attempted this I get very dizzy. After I have eaten I set up a stop-watch and measure how long it takes me to breathe out completely. I can usually manage one minute forty-five seconds, but my ideal is two minutes, which I can do if I'm in good form. And it is better this way because I then have more in reserve.

Many of Montserrat's classmates thought Kemmeny's acrobatics and almost year-long refusal to allow them to sing anything other than scales and improvisations were sheer perversity. Several of them complained to the Conservatorio authorities, as indeed did some of the other teachers. Some students stopped attending Kemmeny's classes altogether, believing the woman to be utterly mad. But Caballé found the whole business engrossing and was happy to go along with it because she felt that it was working for her. Eventually, when there was a dedicated band of just eleven students left, it started to become apparent that Kemmeny's methods were beginning to produce some remarkable results; at this point her classes began to seem not nearly so eccentric as people had imagined. Another factor that doubtless produced many new devotees was Kemmeny's assertion that, if followed correctly, her method of voice production would prolong any career by at least a decade. It would also prevent the development of uncontrolled

wobbling or widening of vibrato since, she maintained, those phenomena were completely unconnected with the natural vibrations of the
vocal cords but simply attributable to the progressive loosening of the
supporting musculature. As Caballé observes:

> With the kind of physical exercises she made us do – bending, stretch-
> ing, lifting – and the way she made us aware of our breathing, by
> the end of our time with her we all knew we had made it through
> the 'war'. After that none of us ever pushed our voices, and we never
> looked for a place to 'put' the voice – we had it there already. We
> had incredible breath support, and we are still singing.

This question of 'looking for a place to put the voice' refers back to
the method of voice teaching which has arguably led to the decline in
the standards of much modern-day singing. Instead of dealing with the
fundamental physical processes which enable an individual to sing, it
concentrates instead on vague quasi-mystical appeals to 'conceptualiz-
ing' or 'visualizing' the voice as an independent entity which takes up
residence in various parts of the body. On this basis, everyone can work
out where the head and chest voices are, or at least are thought to
be; but after much heart-searching, the middle voice remains elusive.
Kemmeny would have none of it. Neither does her most famous pupil:
'Voice placement is something you have to feel inside yourself. You
can't *do* it, you just *feel* it. That way what you feel inside is not just the
voice but also all the expression as well. It all fits together because it is
just the same body, the same soul, that produces the sound which
expresses what you feel.'

For Caballé, not only the question of technique but the whole matter
of musical response and feeling is so deeply embedded or, as she herself
puts it, 'internalized' in her lower musculature that the entire process
of singing – both tone and technique – is inextricably integrated. It is
almost as if the musical feeling was itself written into the muscular
response with which she summons forth the voice. This also gives her
her characteristic poise, because with this degree of 'internalization',
'nothing can disturb you because this whole process does not rely upon
external factors but comes from within'. Her fabled *pianissimi* are, for
instance, only the most obvious by-product of her physical training.
They are effectively no more than a manifestation of her musical will:
she believes that the music acquires greater shape and sensitivity, mood
and meaning by their application. The technical ability to master *pianissimo* singing came from Kemmeny, but the artistic impulse behind it
predated Montserrat's vocal studies altogether.

I was always very impressed when my father played the records of Miguel Fleta, who had this wonderful *pianissimo*, which is never a falsetto. I thought to myself, 'Why cannot a woman do that too?' It became an obsession. At home, I tried and tried, but could not make it. Then later when I was in the second year of my voice studies I asked Kemmeny, and she said, 'Of course you can do it. It is simply a matter of practising with your breath and learning how to project it. It has nothing to do with any concept of sound as such.' Through her physical methods, I learned it. The voice must never *sit* but always *float* on the breath. You cannot do this if your throat is tense. There must be no effort. So I sing *pianissimi* with absolutely no effort. You simply relax the muscles and emit small breath. I have this still, after forty years.

Sometimes Kemmeny's verbal explanations were not enough to make her points clear; then she would start manipulating the students physically, in terms of posture and musculature.* This basis of Caballé's vocal technique was more or less established after no more than two years' work with Kemmeny, lessons lasting one hour being taken nearly every day. As may be imagined, from the strenuous discipline imposed by her teacher's very strict methods, coupled with her dominant personality, the relationship between teacher and pupil was not so much warm as mutually respectful. It is very noticeable that when Montserrat talks about Kemmeny it is specifically to deal with what she taught; the enlivening personal warmth with which she speaks of her other principal teacher, Conchita Badía, betrays a significant difference in her feelings.

There may have been Spanish sopranos who were more famous than Conchita Badía – Conchita Supervía for one – but it is doubtful that any have been as important or well loved by composers themselves. Badía was born in Barcelona in 1897, and her teachers included Enrique Granados (for piano and singing), Pablo Casals (oratorio and *Lieder*) and Manuel de Falla (Spanish music in general). She made her home début at the age of sixteen, singing the première of Granados' *Canciónes amatorias*, accompanied by the composer, and subsequently collaborated with virtually all the major Spanish composers of the day, including Eduardo Toldrà, Federico Mompou, Xavier Montsalvatge and the

---

* There is nothing new about this: one has only to recall the extraordinary double-act that Callas and Schwarzkopf got up to in Biffi, the Milanese restaurant, groping at one another's ribs and abdomens, singing the while – doubtless to the astonishment of the other diners – trying to establish how certain sounds were physically produced.

Joaquins, Rodrigo and Turina. From 1938 to 1947 she lived mainly in Buenos Aires, where she worked closely with the expatriate de Falla right up to the time of his death, but also in Rio de Janeiro with Heitor Villa-Lobos. Thereafter she returned to Barcelona and eventually became a senior figure in the city's operatic life, though according to no less an authority than Wilhelm Kempff she was at least as great a pianist.

She had been a close friend of the Bertrand family even before her South American sojourn and had been a regular guest at Eusebio's renowned musical soirées, where she once found herself being accompanied by Artur Rubinstein. It is not surprising, therefore, that following her return, she was invited by Eusebio Bertrand's heirs to hear their new vocal protégée, who by this time was nearing the end of her second year of study with Kemmeny. Many years later Badía recalled this unofficial 'audition' to her own biographer, Joan Alavedra. She found herself summoned by José Antonio Bertrand to hear a girl and was asked to accompany her at the piano. She recalled that:

> The girl seemed to be about seventeen, had an agreeable face and was quite thin. When she opened her mouth she began to enchant us with that extraordinarily beautiful and individual timbre of her voice. The Bertrands were all gathered round the piano at which I was accompanying, waiting eagerly to hear my opinion. I said: 'This girl will be a remarkable singer. She deserves your help.'

In consequence, from the beginning of her third year of formal voice studies in September 1951, and in addition to her on-going training with Kemmeny at the Liceo, Montserrat became the most cherished pupil in Conchita Badía's private classes. These were devoted to the teaching of song repertory – *Lieder, mélodies, canciónes, arie antiche* – where it was not a question of Montserrat learning to produce the voice but learning instead the appropriate stylistic manner and musical background. To a large extent this involved concentrating on languages and the different expressive capabilities and nuances of French, German, Spanish and Italian as expressed through the relevant art songs of these countries. Badía also gave courses in interpretation – according to Caballé, not unlike the latter-day Schwarzkopf master classes – which paid a surprising amount of attention to difficult contemporary music, embracing not just Spanish composers but those of the second Viennese school: Schoenberg, Berg and Webern.

This extraordinarily wide-ranging musical background fed the eager enthusiasm of the young student: just as Badía increasingly came to look upon Montserrat as one of her own daughters, so did Caballé begin to think of Conchita as her musical mother. Moreover, it was Badía who taught Caballé to share her oft-expressed belief in the 'oneness' and universality of music. Montserrat remembers her always saying: 'Whatever you sing – whether it's opera, oratorio, *Lieder*, folk song, no matter – it's all music, and music is everything. And just as you have different races and you don't discriminate between them, so it must be with music.' Badía's all-embracing attitude to both music and humanity, allied to Kemmeny's technique, is ultimately the foundation on which Montserrat's own success has been built.

The Caballé family's home life at this time had improved immeasurably, thanks to the intervention of the Bertrands. Carlos senior was able to earn a little at the desk-bound sinecure which they had found for him with Barcelona's public transport system; Carlos junior was making steady progress at school, though he hated most of the lessons at the Escolapios foundation; Ana had been able to relinquish at least some of her more arduous duties; whilst Montserrat had not only, as we have seen, found true fulfilment at the Conservatorio, but was able to enjoy, together with the rest of the family, the new-fangled radiogram they had acquired courtesy of the Bertrands. This was designed to play that new invention, the LP, though Carlos senior was usually to be found polishing his beloved 78s. The piano they had been given was far less of an innovation and allowed Montserrat to practise her music at home. She had to practise her German, too, since the Bertrands had insisted that she take lessons in the language. They had also made provision for a steady expansion in the programme of her musical studies, so that by the 1953–4 academic year, Montserrat was not only still studying with Kemmeny and Badía, as well as continuing her piano lessons, but had also enrolled for classes in composition, orchestration and ballet.

At this remove we may wonder how seriously she took her dance studies, but contemporary photographs confirm her to have been as slender during her adolescence as she has always claimed, and it is worth noting that Montserrat's own daughter, Montsita, at the same age was – and remains – rapier-thin and, until recently, a keen student of ballet. The composition and orchestration classes turned out to have rather more practical application from Caballé's point of view. Some of these were taken by Napoleone Annovazzi, who was soon to prove crucial in the final stages of Montserrat's Conservatorio career and beyond. She was taught both harmony and counterpoint as part of the composition class, as well as learning how to improvise cadenzas. The practical lessons in orchestration involved her producing a full-score version of a single melodic line. As a result of all this, she developed an acute ear for instrumental balance vis-à-vis voice and orchestra. This has, on

occasion, led to some trenchant exchanges between Caballé and a conductor who thinks he knows the score better than she does.

She had plenty of opportunity for testing her aural skills when,
together with a handful of fellow students who formed the hard-core
of the various voice classes, she would rush down the stairs of the
Conservatorio after her lessons were finished and install herself in the
queue for the cheap day seats in the upper slips of the opera house (unless
that day she had struck lucky by sweet-talking the door attendants –
principal amongst whom was one Pepuchin – and had therefore been
allowed in gratis). Here the young hopefuls would sit spellbound
through performances by the likes of Mario del Monaco, Maria
Caniglia, Hans Hotter, Martha Mödl and, on one never-to-be-
forgotten occasion in 1952, the farewell of Kirsten Flagstad. But perhaps
the most powerful single memory that Montserrat retains from this
period is of the last Act of *Andrea Chénier* in which Caniglia and Mario
Filippeschi encored the whole of the final duet in response to the audience's ovation. Even so, we may doubt whether anything was quite so
significant for Caballé's future development as the début in November
1953 of Renata Tebaldi. In the space of just three years, Montserrat
heard the Italian diva in several of her greatest roles, including Violetta,
Tosca and Mimì. She vividly remembers waiting on the Ramblas for
Tebaldi to emerge from the Liceo's well-disguised stage door – then,
as now, effectively hidden at the back of a book-shop – in order to
obtain her idol's autograph.

The students argued vociferously amongst themselves as to the various merits of the singers they heard, but were all united in their determination to join their ranks as soon as possible. In fact, only Montserrat
was to enjoy international fame, but this is not to suggest that her
companions lacked talent. Indeed, of the eighteen graduates that finally
emerged from Kemmeny's classes in 1955, every single one had a professional career in music. For example, there was Francisca Callao, who
sang regularly at the Liceo, and Carmen Lluch, whom Montserrat
remembers as having a huge voice and singing a fabulous Turandot.
And then there was Mirna Lacambra, of whom rather more later.

Caballé's last year of formal studies began in September 1954, by
which time she was attending the Conservatorio morning, noon and
night. Her voice studies were due to be completed in June 1955, at
which point her final examination would take the form of an assessed
concert, together with her fellow graduates. In the meanwhile, and in
addition to the feverish activity involved in taking so many subjects,
she undertook a new vocationally oriented course, with a view to preparing her, musically at least, for a life on the boards. This was the

province of the Italian-born Napoleone Annovazzi, a composer who became a regular conductor at the Gran Teatro del Liceo in the early 1940s, also working there as music director. With the more or less vocally trained students, he advised on repertory and supervised the teaching of a number of different roles hand-picked for each of them. At this stage of their studies, many students unwittingly fall prey to inadequate or plain misguided advice, regarding both their own voice-type and the suitability of certain repertory for them. Without necessarily knowing it, however, Caballé's group were in safe hands with Annovazzi.

Some years earlier, in 1943, he had been brought in by the group of five sponsors who had banded together under José Maria Lamaña as *El Patronato* in order to finance the further studies of Victória de los Angeles. His job, as it would be at the Liceo, was to advise and train in specific repertory. This immediately brought him into conflict with de los Angeles's singing teacher, Dolores Frau, who believed that the soprano was destined for *spinto* and dramatic repertory. Annovazzi dismissed Frau's belief as dangerous nonsense and proceeded to groom the young woman as a pure lyric. The row that ensued was monumental, with Frau insisting that dramatic roles be taught; Annovazzi refused to compromise either his beliefs or his ideals, and set about teaching de los Angeles *Manon*, *Figaro* and *Bohème*. History has shown clearly enough who was right. Annovazzi was to prove equally astute in Caballé's case – not that anybody at this point thought that Montserrat had the makings of a dramatic soprano: quite the reverse. As she recalls:

In those days I could get up to the high F, which of course meant that the Queen of the Night fell within my range – just. But Annovazzi was quite clear in his assessment of my voice. He told me that I was, in reality, a full lyric soprano and that if I was stupid enough to pursue a career as a coloratura, or even spend too much time in that repertory, then without doubt I would lose my voice. In that one year he took me through four roles, two because they were right for me and two because they were not, even though I could still sing them. In this process I learned how to sing these roles effortlessly without ever having to force my voice.

The roles were Susanna (in *Le nozze di Figaro*); Mimì in *La bohème*; the title-role in Massenet's *Manon* and Marguerite in *Faust*. Additionally, she learned the principal arias of both Fiordiligi and the Queen of the Night as well as the Mad Scene from *Lucia di Lammermoor*. All Montserrat's teachers shared more or less the same viewpoint apropos her voice and actively discouraged her from delving any deeper into the coloratura repertory than she already had. Kemmeny, never at a loss for an opinion on any subject relating to her students' voices, least of all their designation, referred to Montserrat as a *lirico-pieno* (full-bodied lyric). Caballé's undoubted and, at the time, quite brilliant upward extension would, in Kemmeny's view, prove very useful for coloratura embellishment, but was under no circumstances to be thought of as the most characteristic or beautiful part of her voice. Everyone was agreed: the highest-lying role in terms of *tessitura* which Caballé should ever contemplate singing was Violetta in *La traviata*, which is moreover written up to high D♭.

The pace of life in this last year of Caballé's voice studies had become quite frenetic. The thin, intense, still rather shy twenty-one-year-old found the pressures sometimes overwhelming. On top of this, there was a not entirely problem-free domestic existence to cope with. With the passage of time – and the endurance of great hardship – Ana Caballé had become in some ways a difficult and embittered woman. As Carlos junior entered his teenage years, manifesting a precocious musical intelligence, he and his sister became ever closer. For some time already Montserrat had taken him with her to her lessons at the Liceo: many of the Conservatorio's staff, including the principal, Señor Vallribera, had developed a liking for the gifted boy, and arranged for him to have lessons. As a result, both Carlos and Montserrat now shared a consuming passion for music for itself, which tended to liberate them, in contrast to their mother's inevitably more disciplined and functional attitude. This led to some domestic friction, the upshot of which was that Montserrat had a complex and fraught relationship with her mother.

> I respected Mama, but at the same time I was afraid of her. She would not permit weaknesses. Whenever I had something difficult to discuss, or a plan, or anything that was important to me, I would never go to her first for advice. I would always speak to my brother and then to my father. Papa was more concerned with our feelings, and would listen to what we had to say and advise us accordingly. But Mama issued orders, told us what we should or should not do. So we had to find ways around her. This is the only way you can deal with someone who you know in advance will always say 'no'.

Moreover, home life was by no means luxurious. The Bertrands' sponsorship, of course, had greatly alleviated the family's situation as well as facilitating Montserrat's studies. But though it made certain things possible, it was not a magic wand capable of transforming the entire lifestyle of what was now four adult Caballés, even less so given that Carlos senior was not always capable, due to continued bad health, of contributing to the family's finances. Montserrat certainly lacked those accoutrements usually considered indispensable by teenagers: her wardrobe was severe and restricted, and she wore no makeup, primarily because she could not afford it. She had also developed a complex about the size of her nose. Nor was she eating properly – which accounts for her painful thinness.

The shyness that accompanied all this had been observed over a period of several years ever since Montserrat had first come under the tutelage of Margarita Rocha, wife of Dr Alfredo Rocha, the Bertrand family's personal physician. When the teenager had suddenly fallen ill with appendicitis, it was Dr Rocha who, at the Bertrands' bidding, had performed the operation. Montserrat was invited to convalesce at the Rochas' estate, where the doctor's wife began, subtly at first, to instruct Montserrat in the ways of the *haut monde* to which they belonged. But for all her aptitude, the girl had little enough opportunity to practise such graces in her normal everyday existence which remained tied to far more mundane considerations. It is in part due to Margarita Rocha's tactful instruction that Montserrat began to develop not just the strong character which had always been hers, but also the ability to give expression to this in public. In certain matters at least, shyness began to be replaced by self-confidence. Perhaps her residual diffidence was a manifestation of the extent to which she was torn between two social worlds, insecure about her appearance, unsure perhaps of her very identity. Only her life in music posed no problems for her.

Not surprisingly, as the date of her voice examination drew closer, Montserrat became ever more apprehensive. She slept badly and virtually stopped eating altogether (not that anyone in the Caballé family was eating particularly well in those days). Her test programme had already been settled in consultation with her teachers and was to comprise three arias: the Countess Almaviva's 'Dove sono i bei momenti' from Act II of *Le nozze di Figaro*; Amina's 'Ah, non credea mirarti' from Act II of *La sonnambula*; and Agathe's 'Und ob die Wolke' from Act I of *Der Freischütz*. Although she had the comfort and support of her family in attendance, Montserrat was profoundly nervous. The twelve-strong jury was made up entirely of voice experts largely unconnected with the Conservatorio, with the exceptions of its director, who acted as chair, and the vice-president, who was a jury member. When the time came for her to sing, Montserrat offered up a silent prayer and walked as purposefully as her nerves would allow on to the platform of the small recital hall at the very top of the Conservatorio's building.

The Mozart went well, the Bellini even better with a barnstorming rendition of its virtuoso cabaletta, 'Ah, non giunge'. And the Weber was going very nicely until, towards the end, Montserrat began to feel more and more faint. With exquisite timing she arrived at the penultimate note, was unable to sustain it and promptly collapsed.

She was carried out into a side-room where she was attended to by Dr Rocha who verified that she was genuinely unwell. Even so, one member of the jury was of the opinion that her fainting fit had been a piece of theatrical artifice, deliberately calculated to win her the sympathy vote, if nothing else. The others were unanimous in their opinion and set about trying to persuade their overly cynical colleague. In the event, for the purpose of medal placement, her contribution was declared void. Some heated debate ensued, at the end of which the still dazed Caballé was led back into the auditorium to be informed of the jury's decision. Although it has been touted as fact in every biographical sketch of Caballé that she received the Liceo's Gold Medal at this time, the simple fact is that she did not. The decision to make the award was only taken some two days later after the jury had reconvened under the chairmanship of Pedro Vallribera. But no formal presentation was ever made and the medal remained on the Conservatorio's premises during Caballé's years of foreign apprenticeship. Not surprisingly, hard on the heels of her triumphant return to Barcelona for her début at the Liceo in 1962, the academy's management was keen to make amends. When approached, however, Caballé demurred:

> Well, I was always very strong in character. I said to them: 'You may keep your medal. If I want to see it in future, I will come here.' They kept it at the Conservatorio for years. They wanted to present it to me when I was given my first *homenaje* by the theatre after I came home in 1962, but I said to them, 'No, not yet. The day will come, but not yet.'

The day finally came on 7 January 1987, when, after a spectacular gala *homenaje* (or tribute) in celebration of the twenty-fifth anniversary of her début in the house, the director of the Conservatorio formally presented Montserrat with her twenty-two-year-old medal. This time there were no dissenting voices.

❦ II ❧

'O dei Verd'Anni Miei'

Ernani

─────────────◈─────────────

CHAPTER THREE

1955–1959: To Basel and Beyond

It is common enough when reading the reminiscences of creative or performing artists to encounter long tales of woe concerning the years spent trying to establish themselves as full-time professionals. One notable example of this phenomenon is Giuseppe Verdi who, in middle and later life, complained incessantly of the long period of time he had been obliged to spend as little more than a galley slave. Some singers who have subsequently become famous look back on the period during which they sang little more than the operatic equivalent of a spear-carrier in much the same light, frequently resentful of any time spent in relative obscurity or, worse still, poverty. The rags-to-riches aspect of Montserrat Caballé's professional existence, struggling in the earliest years to establish herself as a performer, has been the object of considerable interest in the available literature, of which the most impassioned example is by the French critic André Tubeuf.[1] Here, after lengthy polemic berating public and professionals alike for their failure over so many years to recognize a surpassing talent in their midst, we encounter a sorrowful story full of the soprano's presumed anguish at the slow progress of her career. In this version of events, Caballé is portrayed less as a Norma in the making than as a moping Cinderella wondering if she will ever get to go to the ball.

The truth is entirely different. Montserrat may well have spent the better part of ten years after graduating working towards the event which was to make her an overnight success, but at no point has she ever given the least indication that she regarded her experiences in this period as other than a necessary and, indeed, invaluable training ground. She has always been quite clear that this period laid the foundations of the career which was to come, and that without it she would have been seriously unprepared. No matter what sporadic setbacks she may have encountered, she has never had any cause to look back on her 'salad days' with the least regret. Ultimately, this attitude stems from temperamental factors: her personality is little given to soulful nostalgia or self-pity. But this is not to suggest that it was roses all the way and did not entail a great deal of hard work and sacrifice, both at the beginning and, rather more unexpectedly, towards the end of these, her 'galley years'.

In the summer of 1954, one of Caballé's principal concerns was to continue her music studies at the Conservatorio del Liceo. It is true that she had just graduated from the voice classes with its highest honour but all concerned, in particular her father, thought it prudent that Montserrat should continue her studies for a further year in order to secure her *revalida*. This, at a time when the awards conferred by the Conservatorio were not – as they are now – comparable to university degrees, was necessary in order to provide a full professional qualification and teaching diploma. If all else failed, Montserrat would at least be able to teach for a living. In fact, she had not the slightest intention of failing and immediately set about the business of securing her first professional engagements as a soprano. Luckily for her, Napoleone Annovazzi had been keeping a close eye on her throughout the whole of the later stages of her voice training and no sooner was she qualified than he suggested that she should perform with the chamber orchestra which he had founded in Barcelona some years earlier, and for which he had arranged a substantial schedule of engagements during the 1954–5 season.

Montserrat's professional association with Annovazzi's orchestra began in the latter part of 1954: she remembers singing the soprano part in Beethoven's Ninth Symphony in Valencia. And then there was her professional stage début singing the role of Serpina in Pergolesi's *La serva padrona*. The venue for this brief first appearance – the work, being a comic intermezzo, lasts all of forty minutes – was the Catalan town of Reus, just a few miles inland from Tarragona. A proud Caballé hovered around waiting for the conductor to congratulate her on what she felt had been a successful début. Instead, Annovazzi stormed backstage demanding to know why the soprano had performed most of the opera facing upstage, her back to conductor and audience alike. Montserrat was obliged to admit that stage fright had got the better of her and that she had hardly dared to look out into the auditorium, hoping that this reluctance would be attributed – at least by Annovazzi – to her supreme musical self-reliance. This ploy having failed, he tried to help her deal with her common enough problem, and since the performance was repeated many times in different locations – ranging in size and significance from Figueras to Valencia – she soon came to terms with it.

In the summer of 1955, Montserrat duly secured her *revalida*, which came as a great relief to her father who had always imagined the worst calamities befalling his daughter unless she had a sound professional qualification behind her. But after a year of sporadic activity with the Opera de Camera, the soprano had no intention of teaching: she wanted to perform. At the back of several people's minds (including the Bertrands, whose judgement had been so spectacularly vindicated thus far) must have been the conventional wisdom that prophets are rarely honoured in their home land. This was particularly true of Spain in the 1950s, a country in which neither the economic infrastructure nor, more importantly, the political will was there to support any form of artistic expression, least of all operatic. These were the bleakest years of Franco's regime.* It was therefore decided that Montserrat should go to Italy in order to do the rounds of all the major opera houses with a view to securing engagements. (At that time, in stark contrast to the present day, when anyone who can lift a larynx can say where they will be singing four years hence, it was still possible then to find work as a singer on a few months' notice: even La Scala planned no more than one full season ahead.) The prospect of undertaking such a speculative venture must have seemed daunting to a young woman who had up to then never been out of her native country. Nevertheless, it was quite clear that careers were not forged by staying at home. Spain may well have been internationally famous for producing great singers, but there was scant opportunity for anybody to become one *in situ*.

At the end of 1955 when I went for the auditions, Conchita Badía warned me: 'You are so young to go into the world, so unprepared;

---

* Such philistinism, as in England, had a long pedigree: to take only one example, it was common knowledge that Conchita Supervia had laboured long in South America and spent five years in Chicago before being lionized at home.

be careful. I know you need to go; I know you have the strength, but I love you very much and I am worried for you. Please, you must promise to write to me to let me know how it all goes.'

One of the Bertrand family's innumerable musician friends was Raimundo Torres, a noted Spanish baritone who sang Scarpia to Maria Callas's Tosca. In the 1955–6 season, he had been engaged by the Teatro San Carlo in Naples to take the title role in *Boris Godunov* and sing in the local première of Henri Sauguet's *Les caprices de Marianne*. Through his influence, he had arranged for the Bertrands' protégée to audition for the theatre's impresario, di Costanzo, as well as for an important agent in Rome. With at least this much activity guaranteed in advance, Montserrat set out on her own and arrived in Naples, after a series of nightmare train journeys, on 4 December 1955. She was installed in a modest *pensione* by Torres and spent several days preparing for her forthcoming audition, as well as watching the baritone at work on the Mussorgsky. After a week, she was called to a rehearsal room in the San Carlo and, although very shy and apprehensive, gave a successful account of herself. The management seemed impressed and spoke positively about the prospects of her future employment, though nothing specific was discussed. With this somewhat inconclusive, albeit encouraging, result, Caballé departed for her Roman audition.

The agent concerned was very kind and, in Caballé's own words, treated her as if she were his own daughter.

He complimented me on my voice and its particular sound. But the shyness and nervousness I had shown, he thought would make me unsuitable for the stage. In his opinion, opera required self-assured, even exhibitionist personalities, and young people such as me who did not have them should avoid it. He said that music would always be beautiful to me no matter what I did, and that my best course of action would be to go home, marry and have children. That was the life for me.*

Exiting shell-shocked from his office just off the Foro Romano into the thick snow of an uncharacteristically bitter winter, Montserrat suddenly encountered a familiar face in the shape of Elena Doria – a Veronica Lake lookalike whom Caballé had met just days before in Naples where she had been singing in the Sauguet work alongside Torres. Doria's fiancé lived in Rome and she was visiting him in a break

---

* Montserrat and this man have long since become friends, and though she is fond of recounting the advice he gave her, she guards his anonymity tenaciously.

between performances. She stumbled across Caballé crying her eyes out in front of the Colosseum and, wanting to know what the trouble was, invited her back to her apartment for a meal. Here, she learned how badly the audition had gone and how low Montserrat's fortunes were sinking. Doria was in the process of drying out Caballé's wet shoes when she noticed how worn they were and promptly gave her a new pair, as well as offering to lend her some money. Montserrat had not planned to stay in Rome for any length of time, least of all after such a depressing rejection, but almost immediately she fell ill and was effectively confined to her meagre hotel. Elena would materialize bearing food, soothing honey and a thermos full of soup. This was a series of kindnesses that Montserrat would never forget, although in fact the two women eventually lost contact when Montserrat removed to Switzerland. Only in another decade, on a different continent, would they meet again.

After this depressing Rome experience, Caballé returned home in time for Christmas. In consultation with the Bertrands, plans were laid for a rapid return to Italy and more concentrated assault on some specific targets. But before this took place, there was an important date ahead of the young soprano when, early in 1956, she made her solo recital début in her native Barcelona at the Palau Güell, Antoni Gaudí's first major commission in the city. The programme for the recital had been decided in collaboration with Conchita Badía, to whom Caballé invariably turned for advice. In her usual fashion, it was wide-ranging in terms both of language and period. Several of the Bertrand family attended the recital and were delighted to witness their protégée so well received.

Torres had now moved on to Florence but before leaving in April had arranged for a further audition for Caballé at the San Carlo, this time on stage. It went well and, as a result, Montserrat was offered the title role in the planned revival of *Les caprices de Marianne*. At this point, however, she had not so much as set eyes on Sauget's score and so decided that before she could accept the San Carlo's offer she would need to see what it was she was committing herself to. As we have seen, her Conservatorio training had conscientiously embraced contemporary repertoire; even so, Caballé was not prepared for the surprise she received when she was given the vocal score to peruse.* She remembers being alarmed at the very high-lying *tessitura* and she decided to contact Torres in Florence and ask his advice. It was unequivocal: 'You're not

* The role of Marianne had been created in Aix in 1954 by Graziella Sciutti, which gives one some idea of the appropriate voice-type.

suited to Sauguet. I should know, I've sung it.' She therefore turned the offer down, notwithstanding the fact that this was the only concrete proposition she had received so far. In retrospect her vocal timidity seems highly uncharacteristic of a woman who, within two years, would be singing Strauss's Salome and whose repertoire would in time embrace a number of contemporary works.

Following another abortive audition in Rome, she was left with one remaining hope on this increasingly dispiriting *tournée*: an audition in Florence, again arranged by Torres. This was to be given in front of one of the most eminent and influential opera administrators in Europe, Francesco Siciliani. It was he who, at a time when the intendant in Milan had resolved to keep Maria Callas out of La Scala, arranged a now legendary series of productions for her in Florence – including *Armida* and *I vespri siciliani* – which had effectively set the seal on Callas's Italian reputation. Caballé was quite aware of Siciliani's importance and grateful that such a prestigious audition had come about through Torres's influence. She was therefore overjoyed when, having heard her sing, Siciliani offered her the principal role of Salud in Manuel de Falla's *La vida breve*, which he was proposing to mount as part of the spring 1956 Maggio Musicale. This particular festival was being planned as a celebration of the roots of modernism and was therefore to be devoted to music composed before the Great War, including works by Schoenberg, Janáček, Scriabin and Stravinsky, as well as de Falla. Caballé contacted the Bertrands to tell them the stupendous news which, of course, necessitated her remaining in Florence for three weeks or so of continuous rehearsals during which she would learn the part. They decided that she should not be left all on her own in a foreign country at such an important time, and accordingly arranged for Ana Caballé to join her daughter in Florence.

However, Siciliani's avant-garde programme had met with opposition from the outset. The Florentine authorities were horrified at such alarming modernism without so much as a single rousing patriotic chorus to sugar the pill and they were convinced that their subsidy was being misused. The *coup de grâce* to Siciliani's plans was, in the event, delivered by that unarguable arbiter of Italian public taste, the box office. With a fortnight to go and most of the artists either *en route* or already present in rehearsal, Siciliani was forced to scrap all his original plans, including *La vida breve*. In its stead, a Verdi–Wagner season was thrown together, and a Florentine public which had taken fright at the prospect of hearing the likes of Janáček could now flock to *La traviata*.

Montserrat was devastated by the turn of events. Although financially compensated – at least in terms of out-of-pocket expenses – she knew perfectly well that she had lost a golden opportunity for her first exposure on the wider international operatic scene. Siciliani, for his part, behaved honourably throughout and was determined to do something to advance the soprano's career and alleviate her disappointment. It so happened that the principal stage designer favoured by him at the Maggio Musicale was Cajo Kühnly whose relative, Ernst, ran an important singers' agency based in Stuttgart. Ernst Kühnly's particular speciality was the casting of German operas outside Germany: indeed, he performed this function for the Maggio Musicale itself. After a word in the right ear it was decided to help Caballé and her mother travel to Germany in order to audition for him. Caballé was of course apprehensive but it seemed to be the only way forward and would at least provide her with an opportunity to practise her text-book German. With the cost of the excursion borne by her Florentine expenses, she and her mother set out by train for the journey north, broken only by an audition with an agent – Signor Ansaloni – which Siciliani had arranged in Milan but which proved inconclusive.

The audition in front of Ernst Kühnly in Stuttgart at the beginning of June was very brief, serving simply to confirm the favourable impression already created by the report of Siciliani, who would recall in later years that, in his opinion, Caballé was 'the singer with the greatest technique in the world'. From his extensive contacts in other countries, Kühnly knew that Silvio Varviso, the music director of the Stadttheater Basel in Switzerland, was in urgent need of a Tosca. But Montserrat was convinced that the role was too dramatic for her, and said she needed a little time to think over the proposition. She immediately telephoned Raimundo Torres, who broke from rehearsals in Cologne and came to Stuttgart in order to coach her in the role. After three days, she informed Kühnly that she would like to test for the role, and an audition was arranged. Unfortunately, the sporadic curse that had afflicted Montserrat during her rounds of the Italian opera houses struck again in Basel. In all probability this was due to a combination of the nervousness inevitably associated with any such occasion and the fact that she was auditioning before not only the music director but the intendant, Hermann Wedekind. Whatever the reasons, however, it is certain that the high B♭ at the climax of 'Vissi d'arte' went horribly astray. Varviso attributed this to the soprano's evident inexperience and the nature of the occasion. In any event, both he and Wedekind were sufficiently impressed by the soprano's quality of voice to want to secure the possibility of her long-term association with the house, if not in the capacity of a principal, then at least that of a useful back-up. Accordingly, as Montserrat remembers, Varviso said to her:

'Well, you are not a Tosca-sized singer at present, but we like your voice. Dr Wedekind was most impressed with the way you carried on after your mishap. Do you need the money?' I guessed why he was asking, so I said 'No, I don't.' Then Varviso asked me, 'In that case, do you think you can remain here as a beginner covering performances, maybe never doing any? But you will at least have the opportunity to learn many roles, to have rehearsals, and perhaps get some stage experience.' And I thought this was wonderful because it was what I needed, and so I replied enthusiastically, 'Yes, yes, I agree.'

Of course, she had been lying when she had said that she did not need the money, but had done so in the belief that she had no alternative if she were ever to gain this toehold at the start of her career. This left Montserrat and her mother with a dilemma, however: they were now effectively committed to remaining in Basel for the foreseeable future without any means of support. Ana Caballé's first decision, therefore, after contacting her husband in Barcelona to keep him informed of events, was once more to put her seamstress skills in harness and find some paid employment in Hanro, a Swiss fabric company. Between the two of them mother and daughter managed to earn just enough money to rent an attic room on the Bachlettenstrasse, overlooking the city zoo. After no more than a couple of weeks pursuing the unexpectedly rigorous routine involved in an unpaid contract – attending rehearsals and having teaching sessions with *répétiteurs* – Caballé received a proposition from Wedekind, who was greatly impressed by her application and potential. Afraid that without at least some form of contractual remuneration the soprano might leave, he decided to offer her the possibility of singing small parts for which she would be paid a modest sum of 100 Swiss francs per performance, with an assurance of at least one performance per month. But the season was almost at an end and there would be no possibility for Montserrat to earn any living until the house reopened in September. Meanwhile, she turned up at the opera house on a daily basis to work with the principal *répétiteur*, Josef Biburger, with whom she studied not only her forthcoming roles – the First Lady in *Die Zauberflöte* and Marzelline in *Fidelio* – but also worked hard to improve her rudimentary German, which she had otherwise only picked up from lessons with the Bertrands' nanny.

The new season gave Caballé her first experience of full-length staged opera in an orderly and fully professional environment, enabling her to observe at the closest quarters what the principal roles of these operas actually entailed on stage, without (as yet) having to take on responsibility for them herself. Her operatic naïveté at this time can be judged by the enthusiasm with which she greeted another new part given to her in the form of a hand-copied vocal score extracted from Prokofiev's *Der feurige Engel* (The Fiery Angel). She noted that the part – the Third Nun – was short but compelling. Unfortunately, she had failed to realize that it was not a solo that she had been assigned but rather one part of a sextet; worse still, this was set in a convent afflicted with demonic possession.

Throughout this period Caballé and her mother were living in the Bachlettenstrasse attic, which the diva remembers as straight out of *La bohème*, ill-lit and cramped. Neither of them was eating well because often enough they could not afford to. While Montserrat went to the opera house's rehearsal rooms to study with Biburger, Ana was busy stitching, sewing and mending. It did not, however, cover the rent, and by the time the new season was underway in the latter part of September 1956, they were already some weeks in arrears.

The first fees Caballé received from singing in *Zauberflöte* were therefore wholly absorbed by the attempt to clear some of their accumulated debts. But since the soprano scheduled to sing Marzelline stayed in resolute good health throughout the run, *Fidelio* could hardly be said to have lived up to its description as a 'rescue' opera. What kept Montserrat going was the possibility that if the scheduled soprano were unable to sing, the cover would suddenly find herself thrust into the limelight. But this presupposed that the role being understudied was of undeniably principal status, and thus far Montserrat had not been at Basel sufficiently long to have graduated to such a position. So she was not the official cover for Mimì in the performances of *La bohème* which were scheduled to begin on 17 November 1956. Indeed, a whole army of covers should have been poised to take over when the Canadian soprano who had been cast in the role became ill. Instead, Montserrat found herself advancing through the lists, one by one, as the replacements all proved to be unavailable. She recalls the circumstances and their practical outcome:

The intended Mimì, Irene Salemka, was in London doing something for the BBC. I think it was *Faust*. The first cover was sick. The second had already got permission to sing somewhere else and had left Basel. So I was the only hope for them! They were very worried. But I'd been preparing myself these months and I knew *Bohème* very well because at the end of my career in the Conservatorio I'd studied

it with Annovazzi. And then, I had already been on stage for so many
different small parts in Basel that it was no longer a stranger to me.
So I sang Mimì. I am sure it was the best one I ever sang in my life
because at that time my voice was so pure, so naïve and innocent –
just right for the role.* It went so well that soon afterwards they
gave me the role of Nedda in *I Pagliacci*, which was a little heavy for
me at that time. But I felt it was a great opportunity. Now, Irene
Salemka's success in London made her ask the Opera House in Basel
to release her. The others were not so senior to me and so from
being the fourth cover I soon became the first soprano, which was
wonderful. In the same season I sang not only many Mimìs and
Neddas, but also Tosca – which was too heavy – and Martha in
Tiefland by d'Albert – which was too low! But I remember this first
full season in Basel with lots of love and happiness. From everything
I experienced I knew that it wasn't an illusion, it was the sensation
of being on stage and feeling the music the way Kemmeny had taught
me. But also beginning to be alive in the life I always wanted. A life
of music.

This meant, of course, that her position now had to be contractually
regularized. Rather than being paid on an uncertain 'per-performance'
basis, she would henceforth be treated as a principal soprano and thus
become a fully salaried employee of the opera house, with sick-pay,
pension rights and everything else. The sum was set at 500 Swiss francs
per month – not a fortune, even by the standards of the time,† but by
quite a margin the most significant remuneration Caballé had up until
then received. On the strength of this arrangement, it was decided that
the two Carloses, father and son, should immediately leave Barcelona
and rejoin Ana and Montserrat in Basel. This, of course, should have
necessitated their moving because the attic which barely accommodated
two could scarcely be expected to house four. Even so, it was not easy
to find a more spacious apartment at anything like an affordable rent,
so when the men-folk arrived shortly before Christmas 1956, they had
no choice but to move into the poky Bachlettenstrasse garret. Although
they intended to move as soon as possible thereafter, in the event, the
Caballés remained there throughout the entirety of their stay in Basel.

As they entered 1957, the Caballé family therefore found themselves
reunited under the same roof for the first time in eighteen months.
Carlos junior, who was rapidly approaching his fifteenth birthday, was

* She is well placed to judge: she has a private tape of this performance which she
treasures.
† At current rates, this would be the equivalent of about £500.

sent to continue his studies at the local *Gymnasium* (or German-style secondary school), although before attending his classes he would rise very early in order to go to the railway station where he helped unload freight trains at the princely sum of two Swiss francs an hour. Carlos senior was keen to contribute to the family's upkeep and managed, with some astute manipulation of his health record, to find employment in a furniture removals company. Montserrat, who was approaching her twenty-fourth birthday could, with justifiable satisfaction, reflect that up to now everything she had promised both to her family and to herself had come to fruition.

If Basel was not the still centre of a turning operatic universe, she was sensible enough to realize that at this stage of her career a position any closer to the centre might have exposed her to the possibility of being burned. In a sense, Montserrat was lucky in that she belonged to the last operatic generation which was allowed to grow up naturally, at its own pace, without undue pressures, able to make all the inevitable mistakes in decent obscurity. She must also have been one of the last to benefit from the kind of rigorous training and rehearsal methods which in those days obtained in opera houses throughout the German-speaking world. All these things depended upon the establishment and maintenance of a tightly organized company. With its hierarchical structure – the music director and intendant at the top and a clear line of command descending through the appointed ranks – everybody (including the singers) knew exactly where they stood, and how well they would have to perform if they wanted to stand anywhere better. The company supported; it nurtured; and in return for discipline, it provided. All aspects of opera performance involved the exercise of a professional craft, the choristers no less than the lighting technicians, and if a performer was expected to learn and develop, then he or she was given the proper time and conditions in which to do so. It was another world, one which more or less vanished for ever in the scorching slip-stream of the jet engine.

During her three years at Basel, apart from the roles already mentioned, Caballé sang Elvira in *Don Giovanni*, the title-roles in *Aïda*, and *Tosca* (her voice presumably having filled out in the meantime), Jaroslavna in *Prince Igor* and Antonia in *Les contes d'Hoffmann*. In addition, there is something almost heroic in the way she threw herself into contemporary music, particularly when one considers that the twin operatic luminaries of the day, Renata Tebaldi and Maria Callas, avoided anything remotely modern throughout their entire careers. Conversely, in November 1957 Montserrat played the soprano lead in the world première of Casmir von Pászthory's *Tilman Riemenschneider*, an opera very much in the mould of Hindemith's *Mathis der Maler* in that it treated of the creative life and loves of a great artist (in this case one of the two greatest limewood sculptors of Renaissance Europe). This première was well received, combining as it did a compelling story with reasonably accessible music. In somewhat similar vein was Montserrat's first appearance in a major role as a *Gastspielerin* – guest artist – away from her home house. This took place in Bielefeld and had been arranged by her agent, Ernst Kühnly. The role was that of Martha in d'Albert's *Tiefland*.

But the most important part which Caballé undertook during her time at Basel, and the one which has effectively remained in her repertory throughout her stage career, was the title-role in Strauss's *Salome*. Montserrat has never made any secret of the fact that Strauss is her favourite composer and her one regret is that because she became famous for singing *bel canto* heroines, hardly anyone subsequently thought to offer her the chance of singing her favourite Strauss roles: Arabella, Chrysothemis, Marschallin, Ariadne and, above all, Salome.* The Stadttheater Basel had scheduled a new production of the work at the beginning of 1958. Obviously, such an important event was not to be entrusted to one of the house sopranos, at least not for the first run of performances. The role was to be sung by the internationally renowned Swiss soprano Inge Borkh and Montserrat was her official cover, who had been promised performances of her own after Borkh's departure. But matters did not run entirely without incident.

I did all the rehearsals, nearly two months – she only came in the last week before the première. She gave the first six or seven performances and then I sang it. There was a big scandal because Madame Borkh had made a cut in the Schlussgesang which the conductor, Silvio Varviso, wanted to keep as a cut even when I took over. I made a real scene because I was so angry. I had to do seventeen performances, and after the first one, at which Varviso had refused to open the cut, *Basler Nachrichten*, the local newspaper, had a review which wondered why *I* had made the cut in the music. Well, I was furious and so at the end of the second performance I came out for the curtain call, holding the review, and said in my bad German: 'I have here a paper which says that I made a cut in Salome. I want you all to know that I have rehearsed this Salome complete but that Maestro Varviso

---

* In fact, Salome is something of an exception given that she has performed the role well over sixty times on stage in numerous different productions, the latest – and last – occurring as recently as 1989.

refused to open the cut for me.' He had already left the pit at the time. This was my first public *rebeldía* [act of defiance].

Varviso may well have left the pit, but on this showing it is a marvel that Caballé was not obliged to leave the opera house, particularly if one bears in mind that he was its music director. Inevitably, this quite literal 'curtain lecture' caused a sensation and led to further coverage in the newspapers. It is a measure of the regard that Varviso had for Caballé as a musician that she was allowed to continue, and with the cut passage duly restored. This evidently set the pattern as the first of a whole series of fiery public *denuncias* delivered to bemused audiences. In any event, she has never really understood the fuss surrounding the role and is disinclined to take Strauss's formula – a sixteen-year-old girl with the voice of an Isolde – at face value.

> Salome isn't a problem to sing. It wasn't then and it never has been. It has to have a child's sound and must be pure and innocent, yet somehow nasty – sometimes even schizophrenic. Except for the end, when maybe being an Isolde helps, the role ultimately is always a child singing.

Caballé's life at this time was largely confined to an endless round of rehearsing, covering and performing. In an average week during the season, she was on stage at least three times and very often more. Nevertheless, on the few days when she was not required to do any of these things, she would take herself off, sometimes accompanied by her brother, to other opera houses in Switzerland or occasionally Germany when there was either an opera or, more usually, a particular singer she wanted to hear. She still vividly remembers taking a train to Zurich in order to hear *Tosca* with Birgit Nilsson and Jussi Björling, and an even further-flung jaunt to hear her beloved Elisabeth Grümmer sing Donna Anna in Berlin. These 'moonlightings' were of compelling interest but not without their drawbacks: 'I used to sleep in the overnight trains coming back to Basel because I normally had an early rehearsal the following day. It was a terrible time for the body – but for the soul it was something very special.' More conveniently, she found favourites amongst the home team as well, principally Ingeborg Felderer. When Caballé had first arrived at Basel, it was Felderer who had done the most to make the new recruit feel welcome, going so far as to give her a rabbit's paw as a talisman. As Donna Anna, Felderer was simply exquisite, according to Montserrat.

In a scheduled new production of *Così fan tutte*, Felderer, who was the senior soprano, had first call on Fiordiligi, a role which Montserrat was obliged, by the pecking order of the company system, to cover. Again, Silvio Varviso was conducting all performances and supervising the rehearsals. Although the relationship between the music director and Caballé had been fully restored after their brush over *Salome*, and each had come to regard the other with warmth and respect, something of the spirit of the barricades that had prevailed during the earlier contretemps resurfaced when Caballé took over in the Mozart opera as a member of the second cast. In a rehearsal she was upbraided by Varviso for insisting upon a more flexible tempo and, therefore, by implication not knowing the score. Montserrat, with as yet imperfectly developed skills in getting her own way, showed rather less of the velvet glove than the iron fist when making her reply. The maestro was reduced to yelling: 'So it's Salome all over again. You're doing just what you want!' Montserrat instantly retorted, with a certain asperity, 'No, maestro, I'm just doing what I can.' Varviso, unmoved, said, 'If you don't do this properly, you will never make it big anywhere in opera.' With a sweet smile – and concrete dimples – she replied: 'I'm sure we will meet somewhere big in the world of opera in the future.' Indeed they did. More than a decade later, after she had been singing regularly for several years at the Metropolitan Opera House, Varviso made his début there as a guest conductor. They ran into each other backstage and fell into a whirl of nostalgic reminiscence. During this reunion, however, Caballé – who never forgets – was thinking of his jibe back in Basel. Varviso, with the innocence of a lamb to the slaughter, ventured to observe how nice it was for both of them to be at the Met together after so many years. With lightning speed and deadpan expression, she replied, 'Yes, yes, I thought you were never going to make it.'

In the early days at Basel Caballé had had the foresight to have a clause written into her contract permitting her, for a maximum period of two months within the operative dates of each season, to undertake roles elsewhere. As we have already seen, she took advantage of this opportunity during her first season to perform in *Tiefland* in Bielefeld, which had the added advantage from Basel's point of view of thoroughly preparing her for a role which she would subsequently be obliged to cover in her home house. Later, she sang Aïda as a guest artist in Hanover. But unquestionably the most important of these guest appearances took place at the beginning of the 1958–9 season, which was Caballé's last at Basel under the terms of her then current three-year contract. She was under pressure to renew for a further three years but intuitively felt that Basel, for all the excellence of its musical standards, had taught her everything of which it was capable. Kühnly's arrangement for her to make her début at the Vienna State Opera House, no less, was remarkable enough. Even more so, and indicative of the reputation she was beginning to build, was the role which he had managed to secure for her: Salome.

In all senses, this was the big time. From a modestly appointed 1000-seat provincial opera house singing everything in German, she was about to make her first appearance in a large – 2000-seat – international house that ranked as one of the two or three most important in the world. Throughout this period, the music director of the house was Herbert von Karajan who, having inherited the ensemble so lovingly nurtured by Karl Böhm, presided over the palmy days of Mozart and Strauss singing there. On any given night one might hear the likes of Lisa della Casa, Sena Jurinac, Elisabeth Schwarzkopf, Hilde Gueden, Irmgard Seefried and a host of others gracing the stage. Unfortunately, at the exact time of Montserrat's guest performance in Vienna, Karajan was on extended leave, busy supervising the dynamiting of the Mondberg in order to hew his grandiose new Grosses Festspielhaus out of the bare Salzburg rock. As a result, Caballé's performance took place in something of a void. Even so, it is clear from contemporary reports that Caballé enjoyed a real personal success – indeed, the following year she was awarded the Gold Laurel (decided by polling the audiences) for the best Strauss singing heard in the house during 1958. Given the roster of sopranos listed above, Montserrat's award as a young unknown singing Salome seems even more exceptional. Karajan's absence is perhaps regrettable, since had he and Caballé been able to collaborate at this early stage of her career, the conductor would undoubtedly have found her a more complaisant musical personality, susceptible to his moulding, than she would later prove following her international fame. On the other hand, in the light of so many other singers' experience, perhaps it is not regrettable at all.

Montserrat's last major engagement at the Basel Stadttheater in 1959 was to undertake the role of Jaroslavna, Prince Igor's long-suffering spouse in Borodin's opera. Shortly before and, indeed, during the lengthy rehearsal period she attended a number of auditions at other houses with a view to extending her career. Not that Basel had the slightest intention of overlooking her: on the contrary, they knew quite well that she had extraordinary potential. The problem was that the new intendant had very definite views about Caballé's voice and plans for its exploitation which by no means accorded with the soprano's own. It is perfectly true that, considering the repertory she had sung during her three years at Basel, there was some foundation for the intendant's views, even if some roles must have been very heavy or unsuitable for a twenty-five-year-old: Aïda, Tosca, Salome and Martha in *Tiefland* were all potentially dangerous propositions. Yet Montserrat recalls always having consciously protected her voice by ensuring that she sang these more demanding pieces strictly within the vocal resources she then had at her disposal and by exploiting the lessons she had learnt from the teaching of Eugenia Kemmeny. She remembers this being so particularly in the case of Martha in *Tiefland*, which as we have seen she sang in her very first season when only twenty-three. The role is extravagantly dramatic and relies for its effect on a stentorian chest register, yet Caballé recalls that she sang it without any of the typically Germanic heft that is standard for the role and instead managed to soften the edges, offering the Basel audience a Spanish señorita rather than a Hamburg hoyden. In cases like this she never felt she was having to force her voice.

But the incoming intendant's proposals went far beyond anything Caballé regarded as feasible. Instead of respecting her as the full lyric soprano with *spinto* potential which she then was, the opera house envisaged pushing her into *hochdramatisch* repertory by preliminary way of Senta and Leonora in *Fidelio*. Resisting these 'suggestions', she therefore began to make plans for moving on, arranging to audition before the authorities in Frankfurt (in front of Georg Solti, whose three-word rejection she still cherishes), Düsseldorf, Hanover, Munich and Bremen. In addition, she was scheduled to return to Vienna for a clutch of *Gastspiel* Neddas, in between which she found herself auditioning before the august figure of Josef Krips, who had a hand in repertory casting. The audition, together with her small but impressive track-record in the house, led to her being called into an office where she was formally offered a five-year contract which would have involved her in much the same kind of cover work that she had been doing in Basel, as well as offering her some ten to fifteen guaranteed performances in the Staatsoper itself each season. But Josef Krips also felt himself obliged to explain something to her for which she would be grateful ever after. She remembers him saying to her:

> Your voice is like a brilliant star. But the stars have to be in their proper place, otherwise you cannot see them. I think today the Staatsoper can offer you a very nice contract with good roles that will keep you here as a member of the company for five years. But you will sit here for long periods of time, just waiting, while the other, senior prima donnas and Kammersängerinnen sing most of the big roles and have all the choice of dates. I don't think you are the type of voice that should have to sit and wait. So think carefully before you sign this contract.

He inquired about the other contracts she had been offered. Munich had fallen into the same trap as Basel, and saw her principally in terms of dramatic repertory. She discussed the other propositions she had received from all the houses where she had auditioned. He considered these various offers and rapidly concluded that it was Bremen which gave her the right repertory for her type of voice. He said: 'You are a lyric soprano with a full-bodied sound. This contract from Bremen is the best for your voice. It would be a pity if you did certain things too early. Yours is a very precious instrument and you have to take good care of it.'

Caballé thanked Krips for his advice and promised to think things over before coming to a decision. In retrospect, it seems almost unbelievable that a young hopeful, just turned twenty-six, was able to walk out of an office in the Vienna State Opera House leaving a cast-iron five-year contract sitting on a desk unsigned. But then, when it comes to her voice and her career, Montserrat has always had nerves of steel. Back in Basel, she thought things over, discussing them with the other members of her family, in particular her brother Carlos. She concluded that Krips was right: she would only get bored sitting in an apartment in Vienna either waiting for somebody to cancel their own performance or for those one or two times a month when she was actually scheduled to perform. Having made her decision, she contacted Krips to thank him for his advice and told him that in all likelihood she was going to sign a contract with the opera house in Bremen. Such was the plethora of star singers at the time in Vienna that Krips can hardly have been devastated by the news. Nevertheless, whilst assuring Montserrat that he was certain she had made the correct decision, he expressed a decent regret that she was not to become a member of the Viennese company. She has always remembered his parting maxim: 'Remember, it's not a great opera house that makes a singer great; it is great singers that make an opera house great.'

Unfortunately, whilst Krips's observation is undoubtedly correct, Caballé was not to experience the truth of it in Bremen.

CHAPTER FOUR

1959–1962: Blood, Sweat and Tears

Before Caballé's full-time removal to Bremen was contractually finalized, there was one significant formality to be gone through: the ritual, in-house *Informations Gastspiel*. Ostensibly intended to enable incoming singers to familiarize themselves with the house, in practice it was an opportunity for the latter to decide whether they wanted a particular performer in front of them on a regular basis. Montserrat's brother tells a wonderful story – undoubtedly apocryphal but *se non è vero, è ben trovato* – concerning a much-hated house tenor at Augsburg who, his home audience discovered to their surprise, was scheduled to give a guest performance in Ulm. Were it to be well received, his future there would be assured. The local Augsburgers duly bought up every available ticket for the Ulm *Gastspiel* and laid on a fleet of coaches to make sure people could get to it. The tenor sang in his usual dismal fashion, but this time was met with a thunderous ovation which the Ulm authorities took as proof of his popularity, thereby ensuring his engagement, whilst the Augsburgers went home well pleased with their night's work.

Montserrat's trial by ordeal was a performance of *La bohème*, with the distinguished Hungarian tenor, Sandor Kónya, as Rodolfo. It is safe to assume in this instance that coaches had not been laid on from Basel. If they had been, the Swiss contingent might have been vastly amused, since the performance was poor and the two principals were bored and aggravated in turn with the lacklustre leadership of the conductor. During the interval following Act I, Caballé and Kónya hastily convened a council of war and decided between them that since the performance could scarcely get any worse they might just as well afford themselves a little musical mischief – and pleasure – by singing the remaining three Acts in the original Italian rather than the execrable German translation with which they had been wrestling thus far. However, they neglected to tell the conductor who, as they correctly predicted, did not understand a word of Italian and therefore suddenly found himself confronted with the necessity of accompanying very different phrasing and dynamics. Inadvertently, this had a galvanizing effect on the performance, which soon took fire and ended in a tremendous ovation from the audience for both singers. The conductor's comments were not, presumably, quite as complimentary.

Following this success, the three-year contract with Bremen was duly signed and sealed, and Caballé bowed out of Basel with what transpired to be her last-ever performance of Jaroslavna in *Prince Igor* at the very end of June 1959. The transition between the two houses was swift. In July, the entire family removed to their new apartment in Bremen, which occupied the ground floor in a house on Parkstrasse, and began settling in during the operatic summer recess. For Montserrat, however, there was no time to acclimatize: she was characteristically busy because in addition to the inaugural contract she had signed with Bremen, she was scheduled to appear at the neighbouring Göttingen Festival, devoted to performances of Handel's operas and oratorios. She was to make her début there in the rarely performed *Ariodante*, singing the role of Ginevra. The cast was very well received and, since the opera had always been envisaged as a co-production with the Bremen City Theatre, Montserrat was assured of a warm welcome when, in less than a fortnight, it opened the 1959–60 season there. It all seemed to be an auspicious start to her new career in Germany.

Bremen is a large industrial port in the north of the country, on the estuary of the river Weser. If this makes it sound as though it would at least have the advantage over land-locked Basel in reminding the Caballés of their home town, the truth is that the similarities between Barcelona and Bremen end there. Temperamentally and climatically they are worlds apart, and this would have profound repercussions for Montserrat as her contract wore on. As at Basel, she was employed as a principal house soprano, which is to say that she was a salaried employee rather than someone paid on a 'per-performance' basis. Her terms had improved marginally compared to the deal in Switzerland, but she had not reckoned with the difference in the cost of living – not to mention taxes – and was dismayed to discover that she was worse off materially than she had been before. However, in these earliest days in a very alien city, there were the artistic consolations of the new repertory that had tempted her there in the first place.

Principal among these was the role of Violetta Valéry in Verdi's *La traviata* which Montserrat had yearned to sing in Basel but never had. Now she was to be given the opportunity to do so in a brand-new production conducted by the music director, Heinz Wallberg, which would have the advantage of several weeks of preparation and rehearsal.

The première took place at the beginning of September. There is an old theatrical expression by which professionals in the industry wish one another good luck on the opening night, consisting of variations on the theme of 'break a leg!' Caballé very nearly did in both senses: Violetta had no sooner seen to the welfare of her party guests and mounted the platform on which they were seated than some of the wooden planking of which it consisted gave way. Montserrat was left trapped up to mid-calf by the woodwork and the curtain had to be lowered in order to free her. But the curtain soon rose again and the performance went on to score a considerable success:

> Montserrat Caballé . . . recovered quickly from the shock of a little accident she had right at the beginning . . . and went on to fulfil the heavy musical and theatrical demands of her dominant role in the work with surpassing understanding and cultivation of feeling. Her acting is convincing and well thought out in terms of expression, whilst her voice has the measure both of the great passionate outbursts and the moments of charming intimacy. Her coloratura functions neither as a glittering display of jewels, nor as elaborate ornamentation, but rather as a wholly sublimated form of expression within the contours of her singing.[1]

The repertory at Bremen offered Caballé the kind of development and challenge she felt she needed as a further stepping-stone towards what even then she looked forward to as her future international career. But as at Basel, this did not necessarily entail a concentration solely on mainstream works, even though she did indeed spend much of her time repeating roles she had already sung in Switzerland, such as Donna Elvira, Aïda and Tosca. And again as at Basel, there was her quota of world premières, the earliest of which was Ludwig Roselius's *Lady Godiva*, a rather unexpected operatic treatment of the English tale concerning the heroine's naked ride through the streets of Coventry. Apart from these première performances by Caballé, there were a number of new roles which she sang for the first time. In the opening season alone, she sang her first-ever Tatyana in *Eugene Onegin*, as well as her début Violettas. It is clear from these activities that Bremen was beginning to see her in terms of the heavier German lyric repertory. There is always the danger with this that the management will begin to reason to itself, 'If she can sing Tosca, Chrysothemis and Violetta, she can probably sing Senta, Fidelio and maybe even Elektra.' This, of course, is what had happened latterly at Basel, and Montserrat gradually began to realize that the fate which had determined her departure from that city, as well as her rejection of the offer from Munich, was now once again catching up with her in Bremen. She still had every intention of resisting these attempts to push her prematurely into heavier repertory, and to this end took full advantage of her contractual right to sing elsewhere during certain parts of the season. In so doing she was able to retain a degree of control over the kind of repertory she sang.

The first opportunity for her to perform away from Bremen occurred in April 1960 when she returned to the Vienna State Opera in her beloved role of Donna Elvira. Things would seem to have gone smoothly enough and the ensemble which had performed Mozart's opera so well together – including Eberhard Wächter, Teresa Stich-Randall, Erich Kunz and Lisa Otto – was approached by Ernst Kühnly with a view to doing so elsewhere. Under the baton of Michael Gielen, this starry cast, of which Montserrat was quite the least known, per-formed the work together in summer 1960 at the Teatro São Carlo in Lisbon. They were rapturously received by the Portuguese audience, but Lisbon was not – any more than were Basel or Bremen – the focus of operatic attention, and on the wider international scene this performance passed almost without notice. It would have sunk into oblivion had it not been for the fact that one performance was broadcast live on Portu-guese radio and, for archival purposes, taped. This has recently become available on compact disc and provides us with Montserrat Caballé's earliest extant public performance. Having heard it, one is better placed to understand the otherwise perverse-seeming musical authorities at Basel, Munich and Bremen in those days. This is a voice which in its fullness of tone and security of execution gives the impression of being able to sing almost anything.

Ernst Kühnly still functioned as Caballé's agent, having benignly overseen the transition from Switzerland to Germany, and remained as ever most keenly concerned to promote his artists outside Germany. To this end he secured a notable triumph in arranging for Montserrat's début at La Scala, Milan, the effective Mecca of Italian opera, which only four years earlier had refused to hear her at all. Admittedly, the role was not an overly significant one, since it was only the small part of the First Flower Maiden in *Parsifal*. But like the Nightwatchman at the end of the second Act of *Die Meistersinger von Nürnberg*, it is invariably cast from strength. The performances took place in May 1960, in sumptuous neo-realist sets by Nicòla Benois and with a fine cast which reunited Caballé with her Bremen Rodolfo, Sandor Kónya in the title-role, Rita Gorr as Kundry, Gustav Neidlinger as Amfortas and Boris Christoff, no less, as Gurnemanz. André Cluytens conducted and it seems probable that in a house better disposed towards the

German repertoire in general, and Wagner in particular, Caballé's début performance would have excited more interest.

Her next assignment back in Bremen was to sing Tatyana again in a revival of the season's earlier new production of *Eugene Onegin*, a role she was to sing so frequently over the remaining two seasons that she came to dread the opera's reappearance in the repertory. At about the same time began the first of many attempts by Bremen's principal conductor, Georg Albrecht, to inveigle Caballé into singing Elektra, presumably on the doubtful reasoning that since she had already sung Salome, she might just as well sing Strauss's other mad monster. In favour of his argument he could always point to the then current examples of Inge Borkh and Christel Goltz who did indeed sing both roles. If Montserrat had felt the need for a counter-argument other than her flat refusal, she could have pointed out that neither of these worthies was then expected to do equal justice to roles such as Violetta or Fiordiligi within a rapid turn-over repertory system. Indeed, unwillingness to be 'pigeon-holed' has remained the basis of Montserrat's musical aesthetic throughout her career. Thus, in addition to the roles already mentioned, during the three years at Bremen she also sang Leonora in *Il trovatore*, Rosalinde in *Die Fledermaus* and Mařenka in Smetana's *The Bartered Bride*.

Just as at Basel, whenever her endless round of learning, rehearsing and performing permitted, Caballé would venture further afield to hear other singers. The strongest musical memory she retains of these excursions is what she describes as her 'dream Tosca', which she heard in Stuttgart, with Renata Tebaldi and George London as Scarpia. Increasingly during her time at Bremen she began to be invited to give performances or concerts – frequently broadcast – elsewhere in Germany which included, for example, a stint in Krefeld singing Martha in *Tiefland*. In any event, the year had started spectacularly when Montserrat had been informed by the authorities of the Vienna State Opera House that she had been awarded a Gold Laurel for the second time, on this occasion in recognition of her Donna Elviras, which had been adjudged the finest Mozart singing heard in the house in 1960. Hardly had she digested this news, when it was time for her to depart once again for Lisbon, where Kühnly, following the success of the previous year's *Don Giovanni*, had organized a four-opera German season at the Teatro São Carlo.

Montserrat's share of this repertory was rather more *recherché* than hitherto, and in one respect constituted a palpable piece of undercasting: the role of Naiad in *Ariadne auf Naxos* should, by this time, have been beneath her, given that Ariadne herself was being sung by Teresa Stich-Randall, with whom Montserrat was accustomed to singing in *Don*

Giovanni on an equal footing. But she found the bait being dangled in order to secure her agreement to this irresistible: the once-in-a-lifetime opportunity to sing the title-role in Richard Strauss's rarely (and now, never) performed recension of Gluck's *Iphigénie en Tauride*. This performance was the subject of the first review consisting of more than a single adjective that Montserrat had received in the English magazine *Opera*. 'The Spanish soprano Montserrat Caballé, who is now attached to the Bremen Opera House, displayed in the title role a well-trained voice of purity and character but sounded too young and immature.'[2]

No one expects critics to have twenty–twenty hindsight, and perhaps it is slightly unfair to seize on this particular example of critical inadequacy. On the other hand, it is a reasonable expectation that critics should have ears, and since both the 1960 Donna Elvira and this 1961 Iphigénie survive as sound recordings, the irrefutable evidence of an obviously outstanding talent is there for all to hear.

Following her extended leave of absence, Caballé arrived back in Bremen to begin a period of extensive rehearsal for the 1960–1 season's great novelty: the German stage première of Dvořák's last opera, *Armida*, in which she was to sing the title-role. It is one of the ironies of Montserrat's musical life that she should have sung her first Armida in its then most contemporary musical setting, only moving backwards as her international career progressed, via Rossini, to sing Gluck's heroine in the mid-1980s. All these operas share the same narrative source – Tasso's *Gerusalemme Liberata* – and deal with the sorceress's entanglement during the Crusades with the Christian knight Rinaldo. Unfortunately, the Bremen Opera House had entrusted a revision of Dvořák's work to its resident *dramaturg*, who in association with the producer had decided to eliminate all supernatural effects from the work. Judging from surviving pictures, the sole enchantment of the production was the characteristically striking sets of Günther Schneider-Siemssen, Bremen's head of scenic design from 1955 to 1962. The conductor was Georg Albrecht, who was due to take over from Heinz Wallberg as Music Director with effect from the start of the 1961–2 season.

The performance was reviewed at length in *Opera*, two-thirds of which was spent mourning the fact that, between the *dramaturg*'s tinkerings and the conductor's cuts, the audience scarcely had the possibility of assessing Dvořák's work in a form which the composer would have recognized.* In the penultimate sentence of the review, Montserrat –

---

* Thirty years on nothing much has changed, except that this peculiarly German disease of 're-interpreting' seems to have caught on everywhere else.

the Armida – is finally mentioned. 'Her voice lacked smoothness in the quieter passages.' In the light of her subsequent vocal reputation, this criticism seems perverse, especially when one turns for verification to the recording which has recently become available. The local press, conversely, were full of praise for Caballé's performance and indeed began to give signs of an awareness that someone special was in their presence. She, however, had been profoundly unhappy with Albrecht's cuts and the wholesale demythologizing of the work. After her experiences in Vienna and Lisbon, she took less kindly than ever to the almost militaristic approach to the repertory which had increasingly become the norm in Bremen. She was rather apprehensive about the forthcoming change in musical directorship, believing that it would lead to renewed pressure to take on heavier repertory. She also felt that the standards of musical preparation were rapidly becoming unacceptable. Many revivals were flung on stage without proper rehearsal; she knew that the general standard of singing was not good; and the *esprit de corps*, so vital to the running of a company, was all but non-existent. She felt no particular affinity for most of her immediate colleagues, the women amongst whom she remembers as having only two topics of conversation: hairstyles and boyfriends. This was in stark contrast to the ethos in Basel, which took itself and its business seriously, and whose artists had shown an intelligent awareness of each other's worth.

There was also the thorny topic of Montserrat's relations with the theatre's financial director. It happened that her father had fallen ill and been diagnosed as suffering from acute appendicitis. Immediate surgery was necessary. But in those days the Caballés had no private medical insurance and Carlos senior's operation would have to be paid for. Montserrat therefore went to see the financial director in order to secure an advance against her monthly salary, clearly explaining the reason for her request. Her shock and anger knew no bounds when, after some prevarication, he declined. She picked up the inkwell on his desk and threw it down with all her force, causing the ink to splatter everywhere. And as she slammed his office door behind her, the main panel of glass smashed to smithereens, for the replacement of which she was duly charged. Eventually, the financial director gravitated up the hierarchy of Deutsche Grammophon, which in the late 1960s pursued the by then famous Caballé at exactly the same time as EMI were trying to lure her into an exclusive recording contract. The man's very presence at DG was crucial in influencing her decision to opt for EMI.

Overriding these specific problems were more general, though no less demotivating, factors. Being in the very north of Germany, Bremen is a cold city at the best of times: in winter it is often freezing for weeks on end, the light rarely other than slate-grey, and invariably dark by mid-afternoon. And their summers, like the British ones, could be nasty, brutish and short. For a family from Barcelona, where the summers give a passable impression of lasting all year long and the azure blue light extends well into evening, Bremen was a profoundly depressing experience. Small wonder, then, that Montserrat should leap so eagerly at such otherwise implausible projects as singing the third Norn in *Götterdämmerung* and the First Flower Maiden in *Parsifal* for no better reason than that the performances were taking place in Naples, at the Teatro San Carlo.

Matters reached a head in mid-October 1961 when Caballé was singing the title-role in a revival of the new production of *Madama Butterfly* that had closed the 1960–1 season. During Act I she felt increasingly unwell and fainted immediately after the end of the love duet. She was attended by the father of the conductor, Georg Albrecht, who, as an expert, was frequently consulted by singers and musicians connected with his son's house. Dr Albrecht did some preliminary tests and on the strength of these diagnosed anæmia. He insisted that she should not perform for a month. This in itself was worrying enough for Montserrat and her family; far more so was the fact that she had recently signed a contract to make her début performance at the Gran Teatro del Liceo in Barcelona, through the good offices of a Viennese agent, Vladarski, who had been busy on her behalf persuading the intendant, Juan Antonio Pàmias, to stage the Spanish première of *Arabella* for her. The first night of the production was scheduled to take place on 4 January 1962, with rehearsals throughout December. Now the entire project was suddenly in jeopardy. In the event, Caballé rested at home in Bremen for some twenty days, taking the necessary medicines and injections which Dr Albrecht prescribed. She was also placed on a special diet which involved eating raw liver and what she remembers as hundreds of apples (not surprisingly, she cannot now face the thought of either). She made good progress and as a result, on the doctor's suggestion, went rather earlier to Barcelona than was necessitated by her forthcoming début there.

Once home Montserrat met up with the Bertrands who immediately arranged an appointment for her with their family doctor, Alfredo Rocha. He conducted further tests which, as well as confirming the earlier diagnosis of anæmia, revealed a condition of hypoglycæmia (low blood sugar). Retrospectively, this was held to account for her numerous fainting fits in the past. Dr Rocha was also inclined to attribute much of her current weakness to the mild malnutrition that she had endured as a child. He was of the opinion that her immune defence system, if not compromised, was nevertheless not fully effective. At this time she was generally weak from the symptoms of anæmia and, by her own account, very thin, which raises the question of the extent to which she had ever properly remedied in Basel and Bremen the dietary deficiencies of her early years. For the hypoglycæmia, Dr Rocha prescribed glucose injections and these had an immediately beneficial effect on the young soprano, who felt a rapid improvement in her health. This, and her sojourn in Barcelona, did much to restore her spirits and led her to conclude that perhaps her depression in Bremen had physical causes which had now been resolved.

Certainly she threw herself into rehearsals for *Arabella* with a determination she had not really shown since her days at Basel. The whole cast were united in their desire to make this last, fragile fruit of the glorious Strauss/Hofmannsthal collaboration a resounding success on its Spanish première. For Montserrat, there was the additional responsibility not only of making her house début in front of her fellow Barcelonese, but also doing so in a glamorous title-role. Although Mandryka and Zdenka are both important characters, their principal function in the opera is to make the heroine look good: ultimately, any performance stands or falls by the degree of empathy which the singer of Arabella manages to establish with the audience. Thrust into the limelight, Montserrat must have wondered whether the other members of the cast and production team were sufficiently accomplished to offer much inspiration. Realizing the importance of the occasion, Caballé's parents and brother travelled from Bremen to attend the latter stages of rehearsal and all three scheduled performances. With the entire family therefore present as a support network the most important by-product was that after six years in what they regarded increasingly as the frozen north, the Caballés could once more celebrate a Christmas and New Year together in their home town. It is true that they no longer had a home base from which to operate and were therefore celebrating in an apartment rented from friends; but this scarcely detracted from the joys of warmth, light and familiar faces.

As soon as the New Year celebrations were over, it was back to work with a vengeance. But there were problems in accommodating the borrowed production to the Liceo's stage. In fact, *Arabella* was the first of a five-opera German season which Vladarski had arranged for the house, and many of the same singers, as well as the entire production team, were involved in all five works. The logistics in an opera house without on-site storage space were nightmarish: as *Arabella* neared its dress rehearsal, the technicians were wrestling with the sets for Nicolai's *Die lustigen Weiber von Windsor* as well as the *Don Giovanni* in which Montserrat was due to sing Donna Elvira immediately after the Strauss performances. As a result of all this, the conductor, Meinhard von

Zallinger, decided to postpone the eagerly awaited première for three days. Thus it was that on Sunday, 7 January 1962 Montserrat Caballé finally made her stage début in the Gran Teatro del Liceo, the opera house she had been taken to as a child, and at the top of which she had studied as an adolescent. The principal review of the first night was carried two days later by the Barcelona-based national newspaper *La Vanguardia* and was written by the eminent Catalan composer, Xavier Montsalvatge. The extended headline read: 'Dos novedades absolutas para Barcelona: *Arabella* de Richard Strauss, y la voz de Montserrat Caballé ('Two absolute firsts for Barcelona: *Arabella* by Richard Strauss and the voice of Montserrat Caballé').

With her performances of *Arabella*, which introduce her to Spain . . . the soprano has at a stroke achieved a level of prestige comparable to the most cherished of present day singers. It is admirable that Caballé has chosen for her first performances before us such an extremely difficult work which tests her to the extremity of her powers, without the compensatory possibility of applause which would have been forthcoming for *Bohème*, *Tosca* or indeed any Italian opera . . . It must surely have been chosen because Montserrat Caballé is exceptionally gifted to sing German opera. Her voice is bright, clear and of a timbre which, if not penetrating, nevertheless effortlessly overcomes the problems which Strauss's orchestra erects in the form of a 'sound barrier' between the singers and the public. This artist must have a great deal of confidence in the carrying power of her voice, which she uses with great cunning, delighting in *pianissimi* and refinements of phrasing all of which allow her to produce expressive inflections of extraordinary beauty, almost approximating to an orchestral range of colours (which probably Strauss himself would have wanted). Caballé is a great performer, not only for the quality of her voice, but also for having mastered all those aspects which are necessary in order to impose as an opera singer. Her diction is of an exquisite musicality. She moves on stage with skill, dignity and grace, without ever being inexpressive. What a pleasure it is to find that all this has been achieved by one of our artists in the first flush of her youth.[3]

Montsalvatge's review concluded with a description of the reception accorded to Caballé by the house: warm after the first Act, enthusiastic after the second, and ecstatic after the third. Montserrat, not surprisingly, retains the most vivid memory of the occasion:

You know, looking at such a big house,* everybody screaming so wildly, I thought to myself, 'How wonderful! At last they've discovered me!' I was remembering when I was seven years old at the performance there of *Madama Butterfly*, and then how many times when I was at the Conservatorio I had passed through a small door which they used to open for me so that I could see the performances. And here I was, looking out at the auditorium, thinking to myself: 'So many years waiting to be here. This is what it has all been for. I have had to work through all Europe just to arrive here. When I was a student, it was so close – from the top of the house to the bottom, just a few stairs. Yet I had to go such a long way round, so many years, so many countries just to come down that staircase. But it was all worth it. I was home at last and I was very, very happy.

Caballé's association with the Liceo was to continue unbroken for all but thirty years, during which time she faithfully appeared at her home house at least once every season, even during the extended period when they were unable to afford her fee, which she therefore waived. In the immediate short term, however, the association continued for another fortnight, embracing two further performances of *Arabella* and, on 15 January 1962, the first of three as Donna Elvira. Caballé once again found herself shoulder-to-shoulder with the Donna Anna of Teresa Stich-Randall, while Don Giovanni was now the distinguished and extraordinarily versatile French baritone Gabriel Bacquier. (Montserrat's old Conservatorio classmate, Francesca Callao, was Zerlina.) This was the first time Bacquier and Caballé had worked together, but they immediately established a close rapport and over the next few years performed frequently with one another. As for the performance itself, without repeating the eulogies inspired by Caballé's *Arabella*, the critics were none the less warmly appreciative, and it was clear that Caballé would most certainly become a house favourite with the Liceo public.

Unfortunately, however, her immediate contractual obligations compelled her to leave this adulation behind and return to Bremen. The whole family arrived back there early in February and for the first week or so Montserrat positively basked not just in the afterglow of her Liceo reception, but also in her unaccustomed feelings of good health which Dr Rocha's prescribed treatment had produced. Perhaps she had been

---

* This is no exaggeration: the seating capacity of the Gran Teatro del Liceo (before the fire that destroyed the auditorium at the end of January 1994) was almost 3000. This made it the second largest opera house in Europe after La Scala and half as large again as, for example, Covent Garden.

right after all in thinking that her previous depression in Bremen was attributable to physical factors. But she soon found otherwise when she commenced a rehearsal for yet another revival of *Eugene Onegin*, locked in the depths of a bleak German winter. As Montserrat recalls, 'I thought I was going to die singing Tatyana.' The contrast with her recent experiences was almost unbearably great. She immediately fell into a deeper depression than that which had precipitated her departure at the end of November. Nothing seemed to be working according to plan: she had become disillusioned because of the unsuitable repertory she was continuously offered, which she felt either provided her with no real sense of challenge or was simply implausible, given her voice type. And above all, she was tired of Bremen's slack and humdrum musical routine. In her own words, she felt that she had voluntarily returned to a prison, which the news that she was to be given the role of Mařenka in a new production of Smetana's *The Bartered Bride* at the end of the 1961–2 season did nothing to alleviate.

Astonishingly enough, with the memory of her Liceo triumph mere weeks old, she began quite seriously to contemplate giving up the life of a singer altogether. Almost as a numb reflex response, she again applied herself to the dreary business of entering into negotiations with other German houses, most of which failed to develop. And those that did all had it in mind to cast her in the lyric-dramatic repertoire she was keen to avoid. She had already decided that under no circumstances would she renew her contract at Bremen: the real question, which burned unanswered within her, was whether she could bring herself to renew her contract with opera itself. She temporized as best she could about most of the options – Hamburg, Munich and Frankfurt were all making vague noises – and decided to put it all at the back of her mind over the Easter period while she went off, taking advantage of her last period of contractual absence, to make her début at the 1962 Lausanne Festival.

Whilst most of her guest appearances outside Germany had been organized by Ernst Kühnly, this new excursion had been made possible by the intervention of the Lausanne-based agent, Bernard Lefort. In due course, the latter would assume several important roles in the world of opera in France, becoming in the process not only a respected stage director but also the artistic administrator in turn of the opera houses in Marseilles, Paris and Aix-en-Provence. Unlike Kühnly, whose principal interest was the casting and presentation of German works, Lefort was more closely attuned to the warm Mediterranean sound and the Italian repertory that showed it off to best advantage. It was his tastes and influence which were instrumental in extending Caballé's repertory away from the German school in which she had undergone her apprenticeship for so long.

Even so, in the immediate short term, the first task which Lefort had arranged for her fell well within her current operatic routine. The work was *Don Giovanni* in which, although Montserrat was itching to tackle the role of Donna Anna, she sang, as always, Donna Elvira. (In fact, she believes she has sung this role more than 130 times.*) Apart from getting her out of Bremen, the other advantage of this Lausanne engagement was to reunite her with Bacquier in the title-role. The rest of the cast included the veteran Benno Kusche as Leporello and Magda Laszlo as Anna, conducted by the unjustly neglected Jascha Horenstein.

Back in Bremen, rehearsing the Smetana, Montserrat's gloom and despondency reached their depths. The entire family had been worried about her for several months, but had at least been reassured by the sojourn in Barcelona and the fact that, thanks to Dr Rocha's treatment, she was steadily gaining a little weight. But the problem, as was now clear, had nothing to do with her physical condition: she was undergoing a profound psychological crisis made all the more acute by the cruel disparity she had experienced between life in Barcelona and Bremen. Morosely contemplating the offers of full-time employment she had received from the other opera houses, all of which were much of a muchness, she realized that none of them held the least appeal for her. They were all in Germany and quite simply she had had enough. She felt that she was a virtual prisoner, her real potential locked away inside her, unrealized and unacknowledged. It was as if she was losing interest in music itself.

She had prolonged discussions with her brother Carlos, who had recently married a young German woman, Brigitte Claus. (Prior to the Second World War, Brigitte's father, Rudolf Claus, had been a leading tenor at the Deutsche Staatsoper, or the Oper Unter den Linden as it was then known. His repertoire had been wide-ranging, encompassing both Tamino and Radamès at its extremes.) Throughout the whole period of the Caballé family's residence in Germany, Montserrat had increasingly come to rely upon Carlos's artistic judgement in matters relating to her career. She had virtually reached a decision to abandon music altogether and to return to Barcelona to find work exploiting her talent for languages as an interpreter, when Carlos made a shrewd

---

* Unfortunately, Caballé never kept either personal or professional diaries to cover the earlier years of her career, and it has proved impossible in many instances – of which the Donna Elviras are just one example – to be specific with regard to either number or, indeed, location of performances.

eleventh-hour proposition: for a period of one year she should entrust him with the management of her career as a singer. He would set up the necessary administration and would dedicate himself to finding the right work in the right places. With the Caballé family's instinct for a good bet, Montserrat duly accepted her brother's challenge. This was in late April 1962, and Carlos – aged twenty – decided that he would need to return to Barcelona and establish some sort of office from which he could operate, if not yet as Montserrat's formal agent then at least as her official secretary. As a result of the pact concluded with his sister, he left Bremen immediately, taking his new bride with him, who was already expecting their first child. Within a matter of weeks, Carlos had been invited by Pámias to begin working on an informal basis for the Liceo itself.

Montserrat dutifully saw out the last two months of her Bremen contract, where the season ended on 2 July 1962 with a performance of *The Bartered Bride*. Carlos had been busy on his sister's behalf in the interim and the following morning Ana, Carlos senior and Montserrat packed their bags and left Germany, heading for home.

CHAPTER FIVE

1962–1965: Finding Fulfilment

Back in Barcelona, Montserrat felt rejuvenated: an enormous weight of depression, dissatisfaction and frustration had been lifted from her shoulders. The family established themselves in an apartment rented from friends in the Avenida Carlos III and rapidly settled into the blissful and much-missed rhythms of Barcelonese life. But as Caballé's general health and spirits improved and Dr Rocha's renewed treatments took effect, her weight began to spiral steadily upwards. She herself tells how, between the return to Barcelona and her wedding two years later, she put on nearly three stones (eighteen kilos). Dr Rocha was sanguine about the consequences of this development, believing that once her hypoglacæmia was fully cured through continued glucose intake she would shed the weight she had gained. However, his prognostication about the Caballé *avoirdupois* turned out to be over-optimistic. Initially, Montserrat was not perturbed at this turn of events: although she was growing larger, this was entirely associated in her own mind with the first real period of good health she had ever experienced in her adult life. And surely Dr Rocha's predictions would sooner or later prove to be true.

In the meantime, the first fruits of Carlos's efforts had been to secure several dates – for both concerts and recitals – the most prestigious of which was probably the San Sebastián Festival where, in mid-July 1962, Caballé sang in performances of Debussy's cantata *La damoiselle élue*, Brahms's *German Requiem* and Orff's *Carmina Burana*. A real breakthrough had been achieved in securing for Montserrat the soprano role in the several European premières of Pablo Casals' *El Pessebre*. The composer/cellist, who lived in Puerto Rico in self-imposed exile from Franco's regime, became fired with enthusiasm for the young Catalan soprano. She had been brought to his attention by his brother Enrique, a musician who ran a record shop in Barcelona and who was a good friend of the Bertrands. Pablo Casals was only too pleased that a fellow Barcelonese should be instrumental in spreading the fundamentally pacifist message of his oratorio. The work had always been intended as the cellist's own personal crusade for peace and had first been heard in the Americas during the early part of 1962. Now the honour fell to Montserrat to introduce it to French and Italian audiences, though not, of course, to the Spanish since all of Casals' works were effectively proscribed in his own country. The whole of the autumn of that year was taken up with performances of *El Pessebre* under the composer's direction in Florence, Assisi and Toulouse (in the Capitole on 2 and 4 October) with Rosario Gomez, Raimundo Torres and Juan Oncina.

This tour met with great success: apart from giving Caballé herself immense musical satisfaction, it also served to plant her name, with rather more prominence than had hitherto been the case, in front of a European audience. These performances were followed during the remainder of the 1962–3 season by an extensive recital tour which embraced more than fifty different venues in northern and central Spain, including Salamanca, Valladolid, Vigo, La Coruña, León, Vitoria, Pamplona and Bilbao. Her accompanist throughout this exhausting schedule was none other than Pedro Vallribera, her former piano teacher at the Conservatorio and the man who, not so many years previously, had been instrumental in procuring the scholarship that had enabled Caballé to continue her studies. The programmes throughout remained resolutely highbrow, continuing in the tradition she had been taught by Conchita Badía and which she had encountered first-hand during her years in Switzerland and Germany. One wonders how some of these unrelieved evenings of Brahms, Schubert, Schumann, Handel, Scarlatti, Mozart and Debussy went down in provincial Spanish towns: in any event, they set a pattern to which, with little variation, all Montserrat's subsequent recitals have conformed.

In the interim, Carlos had been busy forging musical contacts with a view to furthering his sister's career, and, in particular, exploiting the possibility of her making a début recording. He had been speaking to Oriol Martorell who was the chorus-master of the Choral San Jordi (the choir which had performed in *El Pessebre*). In his further capacity as a freelance record-producer, Martorell effected an introduction between Carlos and one Señor Solís, the managing director of Vergara Records, who had heard a number of tapes which the Caballé family had in their possession from the days of Montserrat's earliest performances in Basel and Bremen. He had been sufficiently impressed to award the evidently up-and-coming young soprano her first recording contract. The first fruit of this was a record made in Barcelona on 30 November 1962 wholly devoted to orchestral songs by Eduard Toldrà, a noted local conductor and composer who had died earlier in the year. Montserrat remains proud of this, her first-ever professional studio recording, not least for the fact that all the songs were recorded in the original Catalan, a bold decision in Franco's time.

A break in this activity was provided by her first return to the Liceo since leaving Germany when in December 1962 she sang the Countess in *Le nozze di Figaro*. Singing this role was not only an affirmation to her of the esteem in which she was held, but also an active fulfilment of her promise to the Bertrands always to remain loyal to the theatre. The warmth of her reception left her in no doubt whatsoever that returning home had been the right thing to do, and the success of her continuing *Liederabend* series only served to confirm this feeling. When, in April 1963, exactly one year after the original deal had been struck, Carlos Caballé asked his sister whether she still wished to give up singing, he was told in no uncertain terms: 'You can forget all about that!' Montserrat's decision to pursue her career was just as well since both Carlos and Bernard Lefort had been extremely busy on her behalf. The contract which Carlos had negotiated with Vergara was about to be extended with the recording of songs by the Catalan composer Frederico Mompou, who in the event provided the piano accompaniment for the soprano himself.

In addition to this notable pair of début recordings arranged by Carlos – destined, alas, never to be released outside Spain and unavailable for decades – Lefort had secured a number of contracts for Montserrat to make stage appearances. One of these provided for her French début later that year in Rouen in Verdi's *Don Carlos* (all five Acts, and in the original French) to be followed by *Don Giovanni*. Thereafter, the Verdi and *Le nozze di Figaro* were to be given in Marseille in 1964, and in all four sets of performances Montserrat would be reunited with Gabriel Bacquier. Her début in the role of Pamina in *Die Zauberflöte* was arranged for the 1963 Lausanne Festival, with Mady Mesplé, Gottlob Frick and Fritz Wunderlich as colleagues.* And then there was the extensive recital tour of Central America which Carlos had organized for the early autumn, to begin shortly after Montserrat was scheduled to make her first appearance in La Coruña singing Cio-Cio-San . . .

All these arrangements had been made with Carlos acting simply in the capacity of Montserrat's 'secretary'. But, with the winning of his bet that things would radically improve within one year of leaving Bremen, and with her determination to continue, it became necessary to formalize the business nature of their relationship. She asked him to

---

* According to Montserrat, one of the performances was broadcast, and she is sure that a recording survives in the archives of Swiss radio.

prepare a contract. He did so, and (in a rather tongue-in-cheek manner) set out in it the basis of their understanding: 'I, Carlos Caballé, will undertake management of the career of my sister, Montserrat Caballé, shaping the repertory, choosing the venues, etc., on the understanding that I will be responsible for making sure that she does no bad things on stage, if she will be responsible for me and make sure I do no bad things in life.' Thus Carlos became Montserrat's worldwide general manager, disliking, as both did, the term 'agent'. In fact, following her triumphant début in New York two years later, Carlos was in a position to set up his own office on the Via Augusta, just off the Diagonal, which to this day bears the name Carlos Caballé: Artists' General Manager.

Carlos's way of organizing Montserrat's musical life came as both a revelation and a relief to her. There were, of course, risks in her being a 'jobbing' soprano since, among other things, she would have to forgo the securities and certainties she had enjoyed as a salaried employee in a German opera house. But for Caballé, her peripatetic lifestyle was in the sharpest possible contrast to the deadening routine that had so depressed her latterly, and came as a positive liberation of both the music and the spirit. All this was to prove crucial to her future development as an artist, for never again in her professional career did she submit to what she doubtless felt to be the tyranny of a permanent contract. After her fame was secured, neither record companies nor opera houses could ever manage to seduce her with the lure of what they regarded as their ultimate honour. And so, as 1963 progressed, Montserrat remembers that at last she began to find fulfilment, and her joy in music-making returned.

Halfway through that year, Caballé's career took an unexpectedly decisive step forward when, in June, Victória de los Angeles was obliged by the advanced stages of pregnancy to withdraw from her scheduled performance in the Granada Festival. Montserrat's burgeoning reputation, at least in her native Spain, made her an appropriate choice as a substitute. Since there was not much time for complicated rearrangements, the programme underwent little alteration and Montserrat found herself inheriting de los Angeles' accompanist, Miguel Zanetti.* The highly varied programme, including music by Schubert, Debussy and de Falla, scored a tremendous success with the audience and it was

---

* He was then at the outset of his career and subsequently accompanied Caballé in both recording and recital work for more than twenty-five years. He worked with nearly all the great Spanish singers, and eventually became a professor of piano studies at the Madrid Conservatorio.

decided that a permanent record of the recital should be made. Live recordings not having become fashionable at this period, Vergara took the highlights of this recital into the studio immediately thereafter, thus producing Caballé's third recording.

After *Die Zauberflöte* in Lausanne, Montserrat left for rehearsals of the solitary performance of *Madama Butterfly* at the Festival in La Coruña in August 1963. Puccini's opera had always had a fateful significance in her life hitherto: after all, it was the first opera she had ever seen and it contained the first aria she had memorized and sung. As she travelled to La Coruña, a large industrial port in Galicia on the north-westernmost tip of Spain, she must have been wondering what fate would have in store for her this time. In the event, the answer was: plenty. The tenor singing Pinkerton was Alfonso de la Morena, utterly unknown now but whom Caballé describes temptingly as sounding rather like Pavarotti. Matters had proceeded smoothly until the day before the dress rehearsal, when Morena fell ill and announced his enforced withdrawal. Panic broke out in La Coruña, since no provision had been made for a cover and the relatively isolated geographical situation of the place made getting one at such short notice unlikely. At this near-hysterical juncture Montserrat had a brainwave: she recalled the tenor she had heard only the month before when the entire Caballé family had trooped off to a performance of *La bohème* in Barcelona's Las Arenas (Bull-ring). His name was Bernabé Martí. Montserrat had first heard him in the autumn of 1962 singing the role of the Duke of Mantua in *Rigoletto* at the Teatro Calderón on the Rambla de Cataluña: such had been his success with the public that he had encored 'La donna è mobile' and had made an instant impact upon Caballé. Montserrat thinks that she was attracted to him from this very first encounter simply by the quality of his voice. As she recalls:

> After three years in Bremen singing all the standard Italian repertory in German with native tenors, I was used to voices that sounded like *bacalao* [dried salted cod]. But here I thought to myself: at last! a voice, a real voice with expression and power. THIS IS A TENOR! And then he encored 'La donna è mobile'. The second time it was even nicer, and I remember thinking how much I would like to sing with him.

That particular experience had not led to any personal encounter but the subsequent trip to the Arenas did. The Mimì at the Arenas *Bohème* was Montserrat's Conservatorio school-mate, Mirna Lacambra, and it was only natural that Caballé should go backstage after the performance in order to congratulate her. There was also the possibility of meeting the tenor she was increasingly regarding as fascinating. Mirna came up trumps and duly led Montserrat to the tenor's dressing-room. Alas, things did not go very well. 'He was so cold, so distant, so gentlemanly. Very formal and a lot of courtesy but no warmth. I was very disappointed and thought to myself, "Why can't he be more like he was on the stage, so virile and powerful?"'

Following the announcement of Morena's illness at La Coruña, Montserrat spoke to the stage director for the *Madama Butterfly*, Diego Monjo, about this new tenor who had so impressed her – at least vocally – back in Barcelona. It so happened that Monjo had worked with Bernabé before and needed no persuading as to his merits, since the tenor had made his début at the Liceo, where he had met the director, before Montserrat had made hers. Bernabé was therefore contacted, and agreed on just two days' notice to take over the role of Pinkerton. However, he had two problems: how to get to La Coruña in the shortest possible time from Barcelona, where he lived with the Fletas; and how, despite his understandable claim to know the role, to learn it overnight, given that all he actually knew was the Act II aria, 'Addio, fiorito asil' and the love duet. This state of blissful ignorance had been encouraged, at one remove, by no less than Miguel Fleta himself, who had always said, 'What else do you need to know for Pinkerton?', a piece of folklore readily picked up by Bernabé since he had lived for years in the house of the famous tenor's son, Miguel junior. And it was the latter who rapidly came up with the solution to the two problems: Bernabé would fly to Madrid, where he could buy the score and learn it on the train to La Coruña.

On arrival, Bernabé was immediately bundled into the dress rehearsal, at which point it became clear that for all his concentrated overnight study, he was very far from note-perfect. His embarrassment was made all the worse by the rather harsh treatment he received from the conductor. Montserrat tried to cheer him up as best she could by telling him what a fine voice he had, but there was no mistaking the fact that the rehearsal had been ramshackle. The performance itself was to be given the following day and the tenor spent what time was left with his head buried deeply in the score. In the opera Pinkerton is on stage from the very beginning, discussing his marriage arrangements before Cio-Cio-San makes her entrance singing from off-stage. Bernabé was therefore very much on his own as the curtain went up and Montserrat barely had time for one last piece of advice before scuttling away: 'What you know, you know; and what you don't know, it's too late. I'll do what I can when I arrive!' In fact, the duet went well musically, but so preoccupied was the tenor with remembering the role that he barely took any active part in the unfolding stage drama. Thus it was that *Madama Butterfly* Act I ended with Pinkerton forgetting to kiss his geisha bride who was busy hissing instructions at him from behind her artfully poised fan. Despite all this, the performance went down well with the good-natured public and a special ovation was reserved for the tenor who had 'saved' the opera.

Montserrat, somewhat disappointed that nothing had seemed to come of this encounter with Martí, returned to Barcelona and threw herself whole-heartedly into preparing for her forthcoming recital tour of Central and South America, which was to occupy her for most of the autumn. The tour embraced Mexico City, Chihuahua, Monterey and Puerto Rico. It was in Chihuahua, while checking into the Hotel Ritz with her brother who accompanied her throughout this tour, that she encountered a horde of ethnically dressed Red Indians coming down the street and fled into the hotel's foyer in fear of her life. Otherwise her perambulation of the Spanish-speaking musical circuit afforded Montserrat a great deal of satisfaction and her singing drew favourable reviews whenever the local press deigned to attend one of the performances.

She returned to Europe towards the end of October in order to fulfil her contract with the Théâtre des Arts in Rouen, singing her first-ever Elisabeth de Valois in *Don Carlos*. Remarkably enough for the day, these performances were sung in the original French, complete with the Fontainebleau first Act. It was in between performances of this work and rehearsals for the following *Don Giovanni* that Montserrat travelled to Paris with her mother in order to give an audition which Lefort had arranged at the Paris Opéra. This took place in one of the numerous salons backstage at the Palais Garnier where she sang 'D'amor sull'alli rosee', Leonora's aria from Act IV of *Il trovatore*. Astonishingly, she was rejected, and could take little comfort from the fact that the reason given for this rejection was that she sounded too much like Zinka Milanov. Any other opera house in the world at a similar stage in its fortunes – rock-bottom – might, one supposes, have been glad enough to have had at their disposal an entire army of such 'imitation' Milanovs; but evidently not the Palais Garnier. Thoroughly disillusioned, Caballé was trudging across the Place de l'Opéra when she walked straight into Bernabé Martí and Miguel Fleta junior who were in good spirits for Bernabé had just successfully auditioned for the forthcoming Saint Etienne Festival and had been offered the title-role in Massenet's *Werther*. Gallantly, he offered her his commiserations about her failed audition and gently reminded her that they would soon be working together again: her brother Carlos had arranged for them to repeat their pairing at La Coruña in a performance of *Madama Butterfly* to be given at the Liceo in December. She brightened somewhat at this prospect, whilst still finding his demeanour over-formal.

Back in Barcelona rehearsing for that very performance during the latter half of November, Montserrat fell into conversation on the topic with the Liceo's wigmaster, José Damaret. He volunteered the information that Bernabé had some kind of on-going involvement with a woman from Bilbao but that it was perhaps none too serious. Montserrat observed to the wigmaster that Bernabé was obviously a very timid, rather unforthcoming sort of a man: he had not even managed to kiss her at the climax of the love duet when they had first performed *Butterfly* together. She hoped things would go better this time. In the interim it would seem that the wigmaster – in the time-honoured tradition of backstage gossip and intrigue – passed on the soprano's comments, for on the opening night on 8 December 1963 Bernabé grabbed Montserrat forcibly and gave her a long and passionate kiss which she thought was never going to end. She became extremely flustered and, rather illogically, angry:

I nearly fainted, but got very offended too, shouting at him in the interval, 'How dare you take advantage of a lady like that in front of the public!' And he said, 'Of a lady, no; but of a woman who says I am timid, yes!' Oh, I wanted to kill him there and then.

Fortunately she didn't, because despite her not entirely feigned anger, in the cool light of day she was increasingly convinced that Bernabé was the man for her.

Bernabé wasn't like any of the others who would compliment me on relatively trivial things and then proceed to talk about *their* performances. The kiss came as a complete surprise. And even though I had seen him for only a few times, I knew that Bernabé was the man for my life.

Even so, there was no pursuing the matter in the short term since the performance on 8 December was the only one they gave together in *Butterfly* at the Liceo. The two met briefly ten days later just before Christmas when, to Montserrat's surprise, he invited her out for a drink. The rendezvous was to take place at the Café Milan in the Paseo de Gracia at six o'clock. Caballé remembers sitting there waiting impatiently. After twenty minutes she was convinced that he was not going to arrive and was beginning to experience the mortification of being stood-up on her first-ever date. She decided to wait another ten minutes, at the end of which Bernabé turned up breathless and apologetic. Thirty years later she can no longer recall the excuse he gave, but she remembers thinking: 'Whatever it was he said, I believed him. Someone who was so correct, so serious, would not tell a lie.' They duly had their drink and then engaged in the favourite pastime of the Barcelonese, promenading late up and down Las Ramblas. He escorted her home and extracted a promise that she would go to dinner with him the following week. A few days later they met at a restaurant called Costa Vasca. Montserrat, by this time, normally took quite grand restaurants in her stride, but even she was overawed by this special occasion when, having taken her seat, she discovered that Orson Welles was dining at the next table.

The conversation during dinner became increasingly emotional on Montserrat's part and candid on Bernabé's. Slyly, apropos of nothing in particular, he volunteered that, cherishing above all his independence, he did not think much of the idea of marriage. A pole-axed Caballé mustered sufficient self-composure to inform him that in that case it would perhaps be best if they stopped meeting each other. Bernabé affected surprise at this proposal. Weren't they having a good time together? This provoked an outright declaration from Montserrat: she was in love with him, and if he didn't think there was any future possibility of their marrying she would rather give up seeing him altogether. It was at this point that he realized not just the depth of her feeling for him, but also a significant aspect of her personality. Up to then he had assumed that such a seasoned opera singer must have been a woman of the world, her first emotional and sexual experiences behind her. The truth was, of course, entirely the opposite, which fact only now dawned upon Bernabé. All at once he appreciated just how vulnerable and insecure she was and how the whole situation was far more serious than he had imagined. Diplomatically, he sought to deflect the course of the conversation, not least because of the unexpectedly intense examination of his own feelings that Montserrat had stirred up. He suggested that they go dancing, but she demurred and the evening came to a somewhat premature and thoughtful close. Both evidently needed time to think.

On 15 January 1964 Bernabé rang Montserrat at home: he was about to depart for Paris and she was due to go to Madrid in order to perform Strauss's *Four Last Songs* and the closing scene from *Salome* with the Orquestra Nacional de España under Rafael Frühbeck de Burgos, which was broadcast by Spanish television. They wished each other good luck, and arranged to meet after she had returned from Geneva where she was due to sing the principal role in Schumann's rare *Das Paradies und*

Die Peri with the Orchestre de la Suisse Romande.* The couple met again at the very end of January, when Bernabé discussed his forthcoming engagements in France comprising Don José in Paris with the noted French soprano Géori Boué as Carmen and, later in the year, Werther in Marseilles. He believed that this exposure would lay the foundations of a substantial career and that, if his assumption were to prove correct, he would need to know where he would be able to contact her while he was away. Montserrat was herself scheduled to be in Marseilles throughout most of February 1964 rehearsing and performing Marguerite in *Faust*.

During her stay in Marseilles, Bernabé rang her twice from Paris. The first occasion was just before the opening night on the 14th in order to wish her good luck. In the event, Montserrat's luck held good, but Bernabé's sentiment really should have extended to the rest of the performers: so violently did the audience take against the tenor and bass soloists in the opening Act, that the whole of the 'Kermesse' scene up to and including Marguerite's first entrance took place against a background of rhythmic clapping from the audience, accompanied by chants of 'Remboursé! Remboursé!' ('Money back!') The second time Bernabé rang was towards the end of the run when he simply said, 'I have something very important to say to you. I cannot say what I must say over the telephone, so I am coming to Marseilles tomorrow.' Nervously Montserrat asked what it was that was so important and why he wanted to come. He snapped back, 'You always ask the same stupid questions!' and put the phone down.

The following day she sat in a fever of expectation in the hotel lobby, chaperoned – as always – by her mother. Bernabé entered, strode across to where the two women were sitting, and without addressing so much as a word to Montserrat, turned to her mother and said, 'Señora Caballé, I am a simple man; I have no diplomatic skills and am not given to any verbal ornamentation. I want to marry your daughter.' The two women sat there dumbstruck; but with a rather stern demeanour, Ana said, 'I think you had better ask my daughter.' When he repeated the proposal to Montserrat her response was momentarily guarded: 'We need to talk. Let's go somewhere.' They didn't go very far, and the talk didn't last very long. When Ana Caballé next saw her daughter she was engaged to be married.

---

* This performance took place in the old Victoria Hall on 28 January 1964 and was broadcast by Swiss radio. The critic of *Le Journal de Genève* wrote that Caballé's voice was of exceptional beauty and one of the finest to have been heard for years. Again, Montserrat believes that a tape is still extant in the radio archives.

All three left Marseilles the day after to return to Barcelona, where a great deal of heated debate ensued in the Caballé household. Carlos senior was happy enough on his daughter's account, but Ana had fundamental objections to the match, partly on the grounds of the potential disruption to the development of her daughter's career and partly because of Bernabé's avowedly humble background. Carlos junior, on the other hand, was enthusiastic and simply wanted to see whatever would make his sister happiest brought about as soon as possible. Inevitably, this led to considerable strain within the family, not helped by Montserrat's almost immediate departure to fulfil her next engagement, which was another one-off performance with Bernabé of the opera that had become the *leitmotif* of the Caballé courtship: *Madama Butterfly*. It was after this performance – including the most passionate clinch at the end of Act I thus far – that Bernabé formalized the engagement by giving Montserrat a ring.

But there was the matter of her parents to be considered, since out of the conflicting viewpoints there had emerged a very definite belief that the marriage itself should be held in abeyance until both young singers had achieved rather more in the way of fame and fortune. Ana in particular made it quite clear that this 'suggestion' should be heeded: she had no desire to see what she regarded as an unsuitable marriage so precipitately solemnized. There was also the undeniable fact that, virtually up to the time of her marriage, Montserrat had led the archetypal existence of a properly brought-up young Spanish woman. She had scarcely enjoyed any social encounters unchaperoned by her mother and her life up to then had consisted almost entirely of study and hard work. Against this background, it is perhaps not surprising that a shy, albeit romantically inclined young woman should fall in love so rapidly and on such brief acquaintance. It is equally unsurprising that, given this situation, there should have been resistance – primarily on Ana's part – to what must have seemed a late occurrence of the infatuation contingent upon first love. Montserrat herself, by this time aged thirty, had more or less given up hope of finding personal happiness. As she remembers:

> I never thought I would marry. I had always worked. I felt like an old woman inside. I was used to the idea that this was how it would always be. And then, when I met Bernabé, my life changed. Suddenly I knew who I was and what I wanted.

From her earliest days, the world of music had always provided Montserrat with both an escape from, and consolation for, the privations of her real life. But escape and consolation are, at best, only negative values: it is thus ironic but appropriate that this same world of music should have provided Montserrat with the bedrock on which her life in the real world was to come to fruition. Perhaps it is more than mere chance that the role with which she had made her début in Barcelona was that of Arabella. Certainly, in retrospect, a special significance seems to have attached to her assumption of the role, with which she identified closely. Those inclined to view Hofmannsthal's romantic tale of love at first sight as an implausible fiction would do well to consider the case of Caballé's courtship. Can there ever have been a more perfect example in reality of Arabella's credo, 'Aber der Richtige', in Act I of the opera?

> The right man for me, if he exists in this world,
> will simply, suddenly stand there in front of me.
> He will look at me, and I will look at him;
> and there will be no doubts, and no questions,
> and I will be blessedly happy and childishly obedient.[1]

In Montserrat's case, there could be no doubt that 'der Richtige' was Bernabé Martí.

Bernabé himself recalls that it was during the Barcelona *Butterfly* on 8 December 1963 that he began to realize his feelings towards Cio-Cio-San were something deeper than mere Puccinian pasteboard. At first sight, it is perhaps rather surprising that a relatively worldly man in his early thirties from a provincial background of land-workers should have been susceptible to precipitate emotions similar to Montserrat's. He had always seemed so stolid, so self-assured. In fact, his background was scarcely less deprived than hers, though without her all-pervasive family memory of lost wealth and social status.

Bernabé Martínez was born on 14 November 1928, the last of eight brothers and sisters. That he was very much an unexpected addition to the family is borne out by the astonishing facts that his mother was fifty-one years of age at the time of his birth, and that his eldest brother, Manolo, was already thirty-two, married and with children. Until the age of twenty-two, Bernabé lived in his home village of Villarroya de la Sierra, near Calatayud in the central province of Aragón. The family scratched a living from the soil, and given the extraordinary age differentials, Bernabé was effectively brought up by Manolo and his wife, Otilia. It had become increasingly obvious that the youngster had a voice, and so he was taken to see a priest in Zaragoza who taught the children who formed the chorus at the famous Basilica del Pilar. Up until this time, Bernabé's sole musical accomplishment had been to learn to play the saxophone, but after preliminary vocal studies in Zaragoza he entered the Conservatorio in Madrid and spent two years there studying *solfège* and voice with José Luis Lloret. Although he was considerably older than the vast majority of the other students, he was considered to be exceptionally promising, as a result of which he was awarded a scholarship by the town council of Zaragoza to continue his studies for a further three years at the Accademia di Santa Cecilia in Rome. Thereafter, he went to Milan for further studies where he came into contact with the conductor Alberto Erede. Bernabé's career really got underway in the very year of his belated professional début in 1958, when he sang the role of Paco in *La vida breve* at the Granada Festival with Victória de los Angeles as Salud, going on to give further performances in Brussels as part of the EXPO celebrations and at that year's Edinburgh Festival.

However, like so many other Spanish singers, not least his future wife, he was obliged to pursue his professional career elsewhere, coincidentally enough in Germany where he had some success as a *Zwischenfach* house tenor. Erede, who had been brought in to conduct the Italian repertory in the opera house in Düsseldorf, arranged for Martí to be given a two-year contract with the house. Bernabé only returned home to Spain in 1962 to make his Barcelonese début in the performance of *Rigoletto* which Montserrat and her family had fatefully attended. But their paths had almost crossed the year before when the tenor had been singing the role of Narraboth in *Salome* as part of his contract in Düsseldorf. Montserrat, of course, was still in Bremen at this time, but one night received a frantic phone call from the Düsseldorf management asking her to deputize for their principal house soprano who had fallen ill. Caballé duly made the train journey in order to sing this substitute Salome. But the very same evening, when she should have been singing alongside her future husband, Bernabé himself was summoned to Duisburg, where he was required as the Italian Singer in *Der Rosenkavalier*. Extending the coincidence, the replacement Narraboth had been a colleague of Caballé's in her Basel days and thought it odd that she had missed the original Spanish tenor in the role since he had sung all the other performances during the previous two seasons.

Considering this lost opportunity in the past and the vicissitudes of their courtship once they actually had met, it is surprising that their relationship had so rapidly blossomed. Although Montserrat's parents were urging caution in finalizing a date for the marriage, Bernabé's relatives harboured no such reservations. The people of his village were simple, direct, earthy and honest, and Caballé found the experience of meeting them salutary: 'His family really came as a surprise to me: they were all so old and, as a result, across the years I have been to so many funerals. But talking to them I realized how complicated I was. Life for them was very simple and clear-cut.'

In the interim, Carlos had taken on responsibility for the management of Bernabé's career as well, on the strict understanding between the two men that Bernabé would never be offered work simply because he was Carlos' future brother-in-law. However, there was one early exception to this rule: Carlos persuaded the president of Vergara Records to devote one of Montserrat's forthcoming scheduled recordings to a disc of operatic duets. The sessions for this recording took place at the end of May 1964 and continued into the first week of June. They took place in Milan, presumably to take advantage of in-house connections between Vergara and the Milanese publishing house of Ricordi – certainly the orchestra on the recording is labelled 'Sinfonica Ricordi', though no such ensemble existed at the time. And it was during this period that the couple began to give serious consideration to their marriage plans.

There was of course Montserrat's mother's 'suggestion' to bear in mind. But from the couple's Milanese viewpoint, perhaps fame and fortune did not seem so remote. Bernabé, whose reasoning has always been clear, and to whose judgement Montserrat usually defers, posed an unanswerable question: 'If we have to wait until we're famous and successful, we could wait for ever. In which case we might just as well wait together. Why wait separately?' In the face of such coolly logical ardour, Montserrat (not, of course, much disposed to argue anyway) agreed to name the day. They determined to marry as soon as possible, with the intention of the wedding taking place on 15 August, which in the Catholic tradition is a Marian feast day. Originally, in accordance with Spanish custom, the ceremony was to have been held in the groom's home town of Villarroya at a nearby mountain-top church. However, the logistics of transporting so many guests to such a remote location in the days before the readily available hire of fleets of cars, if not indeed helicopters, proved too difficult. Evidently determined to celebrate their nuptials up a mountain, the couple then shifted the focus of their attention to Montserrat's home territory of Cataluña. Ana, by now – in principle at least – reconciled to the inevitable, had a further suggestion: why not hold the ceremony at the monastery of Montserrat itself? Everybody thought this a splendid idea, but unfortunately no one realized that, on its founder saint's feast day, the church would be unable to solemnize any marriages since it would be entirely given over to worship. So the marriage was finally arranged for 14 August 1964. It was the most important day of Montserrat's life but, in the event, took place to a scenario which would hardly have been out of place in a Marx Brothers' film.

Anybody who has visited Barcelona at the height of summer knows that its characteristic climate is hot and humid: rain is virtually unknown. Inevitably, therefore, the wedding procession wound its way out of Barcelona for the hour-long drive to Montserrat in pouring rain, which only worsened as they began the steep ascent of the mountainside. The bridal car which followed shortly afterwards found it all too much: halfway up the mountain the engine flooded and the vehicle ground to a halt. The guests had all gone on ahead, so there was no hope of hitching a lift from any of them. In the driving rain, Montserrat and her mother sat in the car and became more and more hysterical as the time of the wedding ceremony approached. In the end, utterly desperate, they managed to flag down the only vehicle which appeared – a ramshackle and rather grimy old truck carrying livestock. Thus the bride appeared in the church late, flustered and wet. At least the couple did not have far to travel in order to begin their honeymoon, since they had arranged to spend the first five days in a hotel on the mountain. Immediately after this they departed for a further five days in Switzerland, to be spent primarily on Lake Lucerne where Montserrat was due to sing in a performance of Orff's *Carmina Burana* on 29 August as part of the local festival.

Upon returning to Barcelona, the newly-weds moved into an apartment in the Avenida Infanta Carlota. This was the first move Montserrat had undertaken since her return home from Bremen two years previously. More significantly, it was the first time she had ever lived away from her parents. Two years later, in 1966, the Martís moved a few hundred yards further down the road towards the Sants railway station, to the seventh-floor apartment in which the couple still live to this day.

Looking back over this period, Montserrat sees very clearly just what Bernabé brought into her life.

For so many years my life was difficult. It nearly killed my spirit. I lost track of what is important. I was so concerned with practical matters – study, work, travel – that I had no time to prepare for an inner life. This I found only through my husband, a man who does not know the meaning of envy or meanness. He made me human and opened my eyes to the things that really matter – to look at a star, to watch a tree grow, to understand the otherness of other people. He gave me the courage to realize I can be wrong and to accept it. Through him I found peace and equilibrium. I would not be who I am without him.

Almost immediately after the honeymoon, Montserrat began preparations for her forthcoming tour of Central and South America, which in addition to numerous recitals would this time include her operatic stage début in Mexico, singing the title-role in Massenet's *Manon*. Des Grieux at these performances was Giuseppe di Stefano, no longer at the height of his powers but still, on a good day, very much a force to be reckoned with. Additionally, there was the inescapable fact that he carried with him the residual aura of surely the century's most glamorous and best-documented operatic partnership. In fact, Montserrat never heard Maria Callas perform live on stage. Di Stefano was therefore a link not just in personal terms but as a way of re-orientating some of Montserrat's hitherto unquestioned beliefs concerning repertory. It is true that her current unusual excursion into French opera had stemmed, like her recent *Don Carlos*, from the influence of Bernard Lefort. But for a woman who had always felt that her true *fach* was the Mozart/Strauss repertory, these adventures were proving surprisingly successful.

Di Stefano's attitude towards new colleagues was customarily one of complete indifference, and there was no reason for Montserrat to presume that she would be accorded any more favourable treatment. Indeed, she remembers that not only did the famous tenor not attend any of the rehearsals, but also none of the officials of the Palacio de las Bellas Artes were in the least surprised or inclined to do anything about it. Carlos Diaz Du-Pond, who had been working at the house continuously since the palmy days of the early 1950s when Callas and di Stefano had sung there together in five operas, passed on some friendly advice to the nervous new soprano, telling her not to fret at the tenor's absence: she should not take it personally, since Pippo (di Stefano's universal nickname) never came to rehearsals. But this did little to allay Caballé's fears. She had an important stage début immediately ahead of her with, in the period before the emergence of the current trio of great tenors – Pavarotti, Domingo and Carreras – probably the most famous tenor in the world. At this rate, their first meeting would be backstage on the opening night.

Caballé decided to take matters into her own hands: she persuaded Diaz Du-Pond to give her di Stefano's private telephone number and set about ringing the tenor at home. Her appeal to him was straightforward: this was her stage début in Mexico, and her début in the role of Manon. It would be of great assistance to her and much appreciated if he would be good enough to attend the remaining rehearsals. The administrators of the opera house found the naïveté of this approach very amusing, and counselled Caballé to expect no response. They were all the more amazed the following day when an immaculate di Stefano materialized at the theatre and proceeded to rehearse as scheduled. The upshot of this visit was to instil some much-needed confidence in the soprano, since the tenor was both chivalrous and complimentary in the extreme. Furthermore, the reviews serve to confirm his response. If no one was as yet talking about Callas's successor, the time was not far off when they would be. And it has to be remembered that in late 1964 nobody could know that the Greek soprano had precisely nine operatic performances left to give before her withdrawal from the stage some nine months later. In reviewing Caballé's Mexico Manon, the critic of *Opera News* – the house magazine of the Metropolitan Opera in New York – said simply: 'The most marvellous Manon since Lucrezia Bori.'* In England *Opera* was equally enthusiastic: 'What an exciting voice! Her Massenet *Manon* is a model in every way. I hope that she will not expose herself in roles that are too heavy for her, but I can only envy any public where she appears, if she sings as she did here.'[2]

It is a pity that none of the reviewers seem to have attended her subsequent performances during the same highly concentrated season – thirteen works in less than four weeks – when she undertook her first-ever Amelia in *Un ballo in maschera*, conducted by Nicola Rescigno. Unfortunately, the major excitement that seems to have been aroused by this event was the furore surrounding di Stefano's disinclination – through ill-health, it was claimed – to sing Riccardo's Act III aria, 'Ma se me'è forza perderti'. After the operatic season concluded with performances of *Tosca*, Caballé continued with an extensive recital tour which, repeating her itinerary from 1963, took her to Venezuela, Colombia, Peru and Brazil. (It would also have taken her to Argentina, where she was scheduled to make her début in the Teatro Colón in Buenos Aires as Liù, but for the intervention of a *coup d'état* which led to the season's postponement.) A typical programme would comprise a first half of Schubert and Strauss, followed by Debussy ('Mandoline', Lia's aria from *L'Enfant prodigue*) and Granados' 'Siete canciones amator-ias'. This activity kept Caballé in South America until November 1964, at which point she returned home to Barcelona, via a *Nozze di Figaro* in Marseilles with Bacquier, in order to begin rehearsals for a production of Puccini's *Manon Lescaut* at the Liceo, in which she would be partnered

---

* Bori was herself Spanish-born and trained in Valencia. In her preferred repertory of Italian and French lyric roles she was regarded as an outstanding interpreter. Following her retirement, she became the very first woman on the Metropolitan's Board of Directors and remained a house institution even after her death in 1960. For the unknown Caballé to be compared to her in the Met's own journal was praise indeed.

by the des Grieux of her husband. There was also another recital record to be made for Vergara, this time a miscellany of opera arias with the Orquesta Sinfónica de Barcelona, conducted by a Liceo regular, Carlo Felice Cillario.

In her absence, both Carlos (as her personal manager) and Bernard Lefort (as a freelance agent) had been successfully reaping the rewards of Montserrat's steadily burgeoning reputation. She had been invited to make her début some eighteen months hence in Philadelphia singing Maddalena in *Andrea Chénier*, with Franco Corelli in the title-role; Glyndebourne had, as usual, stolen a march on everybody and arranged for her first performances in England as part of the 1965 summer festival. Most importantly of all, the Civic Opera in Dallas had offered her a series of Violettas in November 1965, which would mark her all-important North American stage début. These two American offers constituted Caballé's breakthrough into the big time: both were highly prestigious propositions and had been processed through the offices of Columbia Artists, which had been alerted to Caballé's qualities by Giuseppe di Stefano. Slowly at first, but now with gathering momentum, it was all beginning to happen.

The Liceo *Manon Lescaut*s in December 1964 were well received: one critic referred to the opera as the 'ideal vehicle for such an accomplished soprano'.[3] During and shortly after these Liceo performances, she recorded her first operatic recital for Vergara. The LP was scheduled to consist of entire scenes from *Otello* (the 'Willow Song' and 'Ave Maria') and *Un ballo in maschera* (the gallows scene), as well as arias from *Tosca* and Charpentier's *Louise*. But this left the second side short and discussions were still taking place concerning an additional item as the sessions began. Montserrat was in favour of some more *verismo*: perhaps Butterfly's Act II aria or something from *Bohème*. Maestro Cillario, however, had a completely different and very unexpected suggestion: why not tackle a *bel canto* aria instead? This struck Caballé as a quite extraordinary proposition. Of course, she had been taught the historical rudiments of that repertory as part of her Conservatorio training, and was perfectly well aware of the trail-blazing efforts of both Maria Callas and, more recently, Leyla Gencer on its behalf. She had also briefly studied the role of Lucia, but had never sung it and indeed regarded all such generic works as fundamentally unsuited to her voice. Cillario more or less bullied Montserrat into looking at the score of Donizetti's *Anna Bolena* and had a messianic line of argument to get his own way. 'In years to come you will remember what I am telling you now. Your voice is a born *bel canto* instrument.' Reluctantly, she agreed to sing the aria as a test-piece in the recording studio on 30 December 1964 with full accompaniment under Cillario's direction. The aria itself – 'Al dolce guidami', Anna's last act lament before being led off to the scaffold – was recorded in one single take at 3.30 in the morning after the orchestra and soloist had been working for hours on end. Cillario supervised one complete read-through of the eleven-minute piece, the solitary take, and an additional minute-long 'patch' to cover a small blemish in the unaccompanied cadenza. The whole process took just under thirty minutes. In the light of subsequent events, this can be regarded as the turning-point in Caballé's career.

1964 had been a year of consolidation and final preparation on the professional front. On a personal level it had seen her engagement to be married and indeed the marriage itself. She had made her first operatic recordings, both of arias and duets; she had performed with di Stefano and had a contract in the future to sing with Franco Corelli; she had accepted offers to make her stage débuts in North America and England; and, significantly, she had ended the year by making her first foray into the still relatively uncharted waters of *bel canto*. When Caballé looks back over this whole period, she realizes that it was essential for her to leave Germany in order to build her real career, and that the time between her doing so in July 1962 and the fateful day in New York less than three years later, was in many ways the richest and most rewarding time of her entire life. What is quite obvious in retrospect is not only the extent to which Montserrat's career began to take off once she had left Bremen, but also the unmistakable signs of a woman at last finding her true direction in life, personally as well as artistically. And for much of this we have good cause to be grateful to Bernabé Martí. Her marriage to him in the August was the 'bel dì' of which she had sung as a child, and now that it had at last arrived, as if in direct response, the self-confidence and personal contentment which it inspired were beginning to reap rewards in her professional life.

During her recent South American tour, mere weeks before the close of 1964, Montserrat had given a recital in the Teatro Municipal in Rio de Janeiro, then Brazil's capital. The magnificent house, a classic example of South American architectural megalomania, holds over 2200 seats. Fewer than 200 people attended the performance, which tells its own story. But the impression it made was profound, as a member of the audience that night recalls:

From the first Schubert song the small audience sensed that something special was happening, and by 'Du bist die Ruh' we were all spell-bound. As her last encore, Mme Caballé sang Joaquín Rodrigo's 'De los Álamos vengo', such a masterpiece of an interpretation (everything was there – voice, expression, line, style) that we were all released into Rio's night in a state of bliss . . . I have always since had the feeling that perhaps I witnessed the last performance of the anonymous Caballé.*

Indeed he had.

* Señor L. D. de Castello Cruz, now the Brazilian Consul-General to the Netherlands, in private correspondence to the authors.

❦ III ❧

'Ritorna Vincitor!'

Aïda

CHAPTER SIX

1965–1966: A Trip to Stardom

The American Opera Society was founded in 1951 by the twenty-four-year-old Allen Sven Oxenburg with the intention of bringing to the sophisticated New York audience performances, in concert, of rare operatic repertory. Over the twenty-year span of the Society's existence, Oxenburg provided New York with its first-ever hearings of works such as *Medea*, *Giovanna d'Arco*, *Billy Budd* and *Les Troyens*. Following Maria Callas's tempestuous and wholly factitious feud with Sir Rudolf Bing in 1958, the Greek soprano was *persona non grata* at the Metropolitan Opera House, a state of affairs which threatened to rob New Yorkers of their opportunity to hear the world's most famous opera singer. Oxenburg, with a flair for publicity and true to his avowed aim of always providing operatic novelty, arranged a concert performance of Bellini's then never-performed *Il pirata*. This took place in Carnegie Hall at the end of January 1959 in a gap that had arisen in Callas's schedules due to her dismissal from the Met. Although occurring relatively late in her performing career, and certainly well after the period when the voice had first shown marked evidence of decline, the performance caused an absolute sensation and she sang better than anyone could possibly have predicted. The AOS, already a respected institution in New York's musical life, became overnight its principal purveyor of star attractions, establishing a level of expectation amongst its audience that must have been difficult to satisfy with any regularity.

Oxenburg's talent became directed towards giving New Yorkers what it was they evidently wanted: stars. The newest to have appeared in the operatic firmament in this period was Joan Sutherland who, following a long apprenticeship at Covent Garden, had herself finally achieved 'overnight' stardom there in 1959 singing the title-role in Franco Zeffirelli's production of *Lucia di Lammermoor*. Decca had been busy and commercial records were already in circulation, which had served to whet the appetite of New York's large, vociferous and well-informed body of opera lovers. The Metropolitan was, of course, in negotiation to secure Sutherland's début; but like all creaking dinosaurs, it took an eternity for the brain to register that its tail was being bitten. Oxenburg stepped in smartly and arranged for Sutherland to sing the title-role in another forgotten Bellini opera, *Beatrice di Tenda*, in February 1962. And, following the American show-business tradition of piling Pelion on Ossa, he cast Marilyn Horne in the role of Agnese. Such was the demand that the performance was given three times to sold-out houses, two of them at the cavernous Carnegie Hall, and this event established one of the most famous of all post-war operatic partnerships. In these performances Marilyn Horne had scored no less of a personal triumph than Sutherland and, following a further joint triumph in Rossini's *Semiramide* two years later, it was thought advisable to offer the newly consecrated American star a vehicle all of her own.

This took some while to arrange. Horne was in the middle, not of a vocal crisis, but a crisis of vocal identity. She was capable of singing more or less anything that happened to appear in the treble clef, but like most natural mezzo-sopranos, hankered after the supposed extra glamour (and quite possibly fees) that attached to *prima donna* soprano status. Since she had decided that her voice was going up, her starring role for the AOS needed to be something soprano as yet unearthed in the on-going *bel canto* revival. After much discussion the work was decided upon: Donizetti's more or less forgotten *Lucrezia Borgia*, which had dropped out of the repertory twice over – once during the general collapse of *bel canto* performance in the last quarter of the nineteenth century, and again following the retirement of Ester Mazzoleni, who had single-handedly restored it in Italy during the period around the First World War. The date was finally set for 20 April 1965 in Carnegie Hall and was intended to set the seal on Horne's new vocal status:

no longer a partner to the world's great sopranos, but a rival. Weeks beforehand, the house was completely sold out and anticipation was beginning to mount steadily towards fever-pitch.

At which point Marilyn Horne cancelled. By mid-March 1965 she was entering the seventh month of a complicated pregnancy and felt disinclined to take any risks. Oxenburg was panic-stricken and uncertain of how to proceed since it was obvious that no one was likely to know a role so far removed from the standard repertory. His only hope seemed to rest with the bare handful of *bel canto* exponents who might be prepared to learn it in the time remaining. Calls for help were speedily despatched: Sutherland was one obvious candidate but she was immersed in rehearsals at Covent Garden for forthcoming *Lucia*s and *Sonnambula*s; Leyla Gencer was another possibility, but she was likewise unavailable. It is a measure of how little real progress the *bel canto* revival had made at this point that, having eliminated these two possibilities, there was virtually no one left to whom Oxenburg could turn. In situations like these agents can often prove very useful, particularly if one is familiar with them and can trust their judgement. Oxenburg outlined his problem to several of them, including Bernard Lefort. Lefort had a suggestion: he had worked for a couple of years on behalf of an unknown Spanish soprano who had recently sung a fabulous *Figaro* at the Lausanne Festival, and who he was sure could do the role justice. Her name was Montserrat Caballé . . .

Montserrat was at home in Barcelona contemplating her next scheduled role – the Marschallin in *Der Rosenkavalier* which she was due to begin rehearsing at Glyndebourne in mid-April – when at the end of March she received a telegram from Lefort. The essence of this was simple: drop everything, come to New York and sing Lucrezia Borgia. The offer was one of those once-in-a-lifetime opportunities which fuels every young hopeful's day-dreams. Even so, Montserrat proceeded cautiously, going so far as to reply that she did not think that she was well suited to this kind of material even though she was fully aware of the significance of the offer:

> I thought to myself, 'Aha! This is good, but . . .' Carlos said to me, 'No "buts". Big chances like this in your life may only come once. You're going to do it.' 'But I don't know the part and I am not at all sure I can do it.' He said to me, 'Nonsense! You are going to do this role and it is going to make your reputation.'

She contacted Carlo Felice Cillario who had conducted her recent performances of *Manon Lescaut* and was still working in Barcelona, to obtain specific musical advice about the score. His response was unequivocal: 'This is it, this is the role for you.' Caballé still had doubts, however:

I said to him, 'But how can I do this?' And he replied, 'Very easily, exactly the same way you would sing Fiordiligi.' I thought this was an extraordinary idea, but he insisted on running through the part with me at home once we had got hold of the score. So I put Fiordiligi into my Lucrezia and it was fine. Not that it sounded as if it was Mozart, because what Cillario was referring to was exactly the same vocal position of the roles, since the *tessitura* is the same for both of them. It is only the style which is different and has to be appreciated in a different way musically. We made a tape of that session and then sat down to listen to it. I was surprised because it sounded good and the part had not been nearly as hard as I imagined. So I said to him that if he would promise to study the part with me for a week then I would accept the proposal from America. He agreed, and within a few days Carlos was able to tell Lefort that I would do it.

At the end of the first week in April, having secured Glyndebourne's tight-lipped permission to arrive a few days late for rehearsals, Montserrat set out for New York on her own. Needless to say, she would have preferred to have undergone this experience with support from her nearest and dearest: but Bernabé was already contracted to sing elsewhere; and Carlos was doing his obligatory military service. She was met by a relieved but still worried Oxenburg, who promptly escorted her to a room he had booked for her in the Mayflower Hotel two blocks away from his Central Park apartment and set her to work immediately.

The situation was very funny because I was working with a *répétiteur* on Borgia, but I said to Allen, 'Well, I'm here, so please can I have one or two hours a day with the *répétiteur* for my own purposes?' And he said, 'Of course, when do you want him? My piano, my room, my music, everything is at your disposal.' Since I was saving the performance, he made everything very easy for me. The second day I was rehearsing when he came in the room. I was singing the Marschallin's Act One monologue. 'WHAT IN GOD'S NAME ARE YOU DOING!?' he screamed. I said, 'Rehearsing.' 'Yes, but what?' I replied, 'Rosenkavalier.' He said, 'Yes, yes, I know what it is. But WHY?' 'Because my next engagement is in Glyndebourne, and I want to arrive knowing the part. I've only just begun to learn it.' He exploded. 'THE MARSCHALLIN!! You cannot rehearse the Marschallin that lies so low when you are going to sing the Borgia which is so high.' I said,

'Yes I can, I know I can, otherwise I would not do it.' He looked very serious: 'I trust you will allow me to sit here and listen?' he asked. 'Yes, yes.' So I went on with my two hours of Marschallin after the rehearsal of *Lucrezia Borgia* earlier in the day. And at the end he said, 'I am astonished. You know, I never thought that you could do this.' And I told him, 'Well, you were wrong. And I never thought I could do Lucrezia Borgia. So I was wrong too.'

Just how wrong is the stuff of operatic legend.

It would be nice to report that a packed-out Carnegie Hall audience sat eagerly expectant on the evening of 20 April.* In fact, many tickets had been returned once Marilyn Horne's withdrawal had been announced; moreover, the attitude of many who had decided to attend was evidently grudging: they were used to paying high prices to hear the likes of Callas and Sutherland, and probably felt that an exotic name was not much of a substitute for the home-grown heroine. As they thumbed glumly through their programmes it would be hard to imagine that many of these seasoned New York opera lovers would have drawn much encouragement from reading that the evening's soprano had sung for many years in Basel, Bremen and Barcelona. Of course, there was always La Scala: but First Flower Maiden? Her Viennese track record may have looked a little better but seemed to be rather a long time ago. In other words, Al had lost his touch, if not his marbles. Al, however, knew different. He had persuaded some significant opera house and recording executives to attend and hear for themselves what had been overwhelming him during the rehearsals.

As the lights dimmed and Jonel Perlea began to conduct the Prologue, Montserrat sat in her dressing-room virtually immobilized with fright. So many people had said so many nice things about her voice since her arrival that she should have been assured of success; but clearly it was by no means a foregone conclusion. Everyone had agreed on one piece of advice – the need to make a really unforgettable entrance. Unfortunately, although the concert performance was being semi-staged in such a way as to afford one in theory, Lucrezia scarcely has the dramatic material to allow one in practice. The character simply wanders on after everyone else except her sleeping son, Gennaro, has left and begins to apostrophize his recumbent form in a long recitative followed by a slow, unflashy aria. Certainly not the stuff of which an immediate sensation

---

* Coincidentally, on the same day as Caballé's performance, Leontyne Price was in Washington being awarded the Medal of Freedom by President Johnson.

is made. Oxenburg manoeuvred Montserrat into position and, as the polite applause for the opening sequence rapidly fizzled out, withdrew in order to permit her to make her entrance. She took a deep breath, held her head up high and took several firm paces forward. But one of the heels on her ill-advised stilettos caught the edge of the large rectangular carpet that had been laid down as the effective acting area, and as a result she suddenly shot forward and literally burst into the spotlight. The manner of her entrance had thus been decided for her; and although she did not know it yet, she had just made the most fateful trip of her life.

The opening line of her recitative follows a gentle rocking orchestral introduction and is itself unaccompanied. Lucrezia sings 'Tranquillo ei posa' ('He is peacefully asleep'), but given the perfectly poised, lambent tone quality with which Montserrat projected the line, she could just as easily have been referring to her own voice. Lucrezia continues with her sad self-communing, trusting that her son, who is unaware that she is his mother, may never know of the tormented nights she spends locked in her own murderous guilt. The last line of sung recitative commences with a simple, slow ascent to a soft high B♭, held briefly, then descending, all set to the monosyllable 'Ah!', before rounding out with a cadential full close. During the ascent Caballé's tone, already an exquisite *pianissimo*, imperceptibly refined yet further. At the moment at which the audience, knowing neither the score nor the singer, thought that the ascent must have reached its highest point, she continued the vocal line without taking a breath and alighted upon the B♭, producing a sound which no one in living memory had ever produced.

Al Oxenburg remembers looking around him at the faces of people sitting nearby, and observing the odd mixture of incredulity and delight that was spread all over them. Then, with the aria 'Com'è bello', Caballé had an opportunity to exhibit the full power and range of her voice, ending with another *pianissimo*-capped cadenza. The audience erupted. Accounts differ, but Oxenburg believes that the applause lasted nearly five minutes, which is longer than most performances are accorded at the very end. By the end of the forty-five-minute Prologue which opens the opera the audience was verging on the hysterical. The Vice-President and General Manager of RCA records, George R. Marek, was in its midst and during the interval fought his way backstage to get to a telephone. He rang Roger Hall, RCA Victor's Artists and Repertory Manager, with a simple instruction: get here immediately. Bob Hermann, Rudolf Bing's right-hand man at the Metropolitan Opera House, was also present and similarly keen to inform the powerful and autocratic intendant of the sensational event.

After the interval, seats which had been empty during the Prologue were mysteriously filled as the operatic grapevine went to work. Drawing inspiration from the wildly enthusiastic audience, the whole performance took wing and ended with an increasingly abandoned Caballé emitting a blood-curdlingly loud scream at Gennaro's death, which sent the entire house into a frenzy. The final crashing chords vanished altogether under a torrential burst of yelling, clapping and cheering, which continued unabated, according to Oxenburg, for fully twenty-five minutes. Caballé had arrived in time-honoured New York style: the overnight sensation. Yet from her point of view, the performance was only just beginning, since the aftermath backstage was at least as eventful and lasted almost as long as the opera itself. The management of RCA Victor was present *en masse* and really did have blank contracts with them: the Metropolitan Opera House wanted to talk about arranging the earliest possible début; and a delirious Allen Oxenburg needed to sort out future dates and repertory. In case all this activity seems improbably telescoped, it should be borne in mind that everyone present had learnt that the Spanish soprano was flying out of New York the following morning, bound for England, in order to fulfil her already delayed contractual obligations at Glyndebourne. For the first time she found herself in demand at the highest international level and, back in Barcelona, Carlos soon found himself having to negotiate offers and propositions on her behalf. Montserrat and Oxenburg were up all night celebrating, ringing home to Barcelona to give the family the great news and, in traditional fashion, waiting for the press reviews to be published. The following morning Caballé was practically a household name in New York and her future career was assured. She especially treasures a telephone call she received from Marilyn Horne in which the American mezzo, besides congratulating Montserrat on her triumph, announced that she herself would never now consider singing the role of Lucrezia since Caballé had sung it to perfection.

The reviews were uniformly enthusiastic and, in the fashion of the day, highly detailed, apart from one piece of sub-editorial hyperbole which blazoned the following headline on the front page of *The New York Times*: CALLAS + TEBALDI = CABALLÉ. This much was the province of the news desk, but Raymond Ericson's considered opinion appeared on the Arts page:

Miss Caballé had only to sing her initial romanza . . . and it was apparent that here was a singer not only with a beautifully pure voice but an outstanding command of vocal style . . . [She] can soar effortlessly to high *pianissimos* which she has under complete control, and at its loudest her voice has a fine, bright edge. It is not particularly large but it is remarkably supple, and the soprano used it with all kinds of dramatic changes in volume, sometimes with exquisite floating tones in the middle register.

John Gruen, writing in the New York *Herald Tribune*, was particularly effective in evoking the atmosphere of the event:

No amount of advance publicity could have foretold the extraordinary impact that this stately Goyaesque woman would have on an audience already spoiled by the likes of Callas and Sutherland. When Caballé sang her first aria . . . there was a perceptible change in the atmosphere. It seemed for a moment as if everyone had stopped breathing. What registered, of course, was an acute awareness that here was singing of a most unusual sort. It had, to put it simply, the quality of greatness . . . If Callas has been dubbed *La Divina* and Sutherland *La Stupenda*, then Montserrat Caballé must henceforth be known as *La Superba*.

The critical ripples caused by Caballé's performance continued to fan out steadily across the whole of the American press: the only dissent that has come to light appeared in *Opera*, where there are some mystified musings as to the reasons for the audience's ecstasies. Evidently, even in Paradise, there is always at least one serpent.[1]

Despite all the heady acclaim and the obvious temptation to remain in America to cash in on it, Caballé boarded a plane bound for London in order to honour her pre-existing contract with Glyndebourne. As she discovered, she was thereby exchanging a world of neon-lit showbiz for the more austere pleasures of the Sussex Downs. What must have been rather more difficult for her to accept was that within twenty-four hours she progressed from being idolized as the new star to being admonished as an ill-prepared new recruit. The first rehearsal took place on Thursday, 22 April in the old Organ Room and took the form of a *sitzprobe*, piano-accompanied but with the conductor, John Pritchard, in attendance. The rehearsal had not been going for more than ten minutes when Pritchard proposed a break and asked to have a word with the soprano in private. He ushered her into one of George Christie's reception rooms and solemnly closed the door. As Montserrat recalls, he lost no time in coming to the point:

'Madame, you are not prepared.' I replied, 'No, sir, you know I was having to learn Lucrezia Borgia in the month I was supposed to learn Marschallin.' 'But the première is in just over three weeks! We'll have to postpone.' I said, 'What do you mean? Postpone the performance?' Pritchard said, 'No, not the performance: postpone you!' 'Postpone me!!?' 'Of course you. For the Marschallin you need two or three years to have the role inside you.' Now, I am not saying he wasn't right because really to understand a role like this, it's true, can take years. But I was so angry, and said, 'No, sir. Not me. I'll have it much sooner. Please be kind: give me one week, only one week, I don't ask very much. Just seven days. I will go home, and after seven days if I don't know the part you can replace me.' He accepted this, but looked at me and I'm sure that he was thinking, 'She's mad.' I learned it day and night that week, sleeping with the tapes, the score, everything. So on the eighth day I went back. I was sitting without the score. We began to rehearse and I think I made two or three mistakes, but this was nothing because the other singers were making more than me. And afterwards Pritchard came to me and said, 'You lied to me. You knew the part!' 'No! it was like I told you.' He said, 'Admit it, you were just too tired and didn't feel like rehearsing.' I don't think he ever believed me.

Caballé regards these performances with a fond memory: rather over-fond in fact, since although she has always spoken of the immense satisfaction she received from the glowing reviews, the latter prove on close inspection to be decidedly mixed. This is not altogether surprising since in 1965 the Marschallin was still active Schwarzkopf territory, and one only has to turn to the pirate recording of Montserrat's performance on 14 August, at the end of the Glyndebourne season, to hear how little she owes to the Central European tradition of *parlando* cerebration in singing the role. There is also the fact that she had learnt it unaided by those guardians of the Strauss style at Glyndebourne: both she and Carlos had been scandalized when, many months earlier, she had been approached by a senior *répétiteur* deputed by the house to teach her the role, who had demanded payment for his services. Hence her decision to go it alone. Among her detractors was the then editor of *Opera*, who found her insufficiently aristocratic and was evidently greatly put out by the fact that 'she has come to Glyndebourne with an enormous reputation from New York, where her *Anna Bolena* [sic] has "sent" most of the critics and public . . .'[2] Harold Rosenthal might at least have got his facts right. In any event, the Caballé family soon rallied. Carlos, who had been temporarily invalided out of his military service with a broken leg, somehow managed to drive his mother all the way from Barcelona to Lewes laden with stage costumes and provisions and to leave her there so as to be able to look after Montserrat during the long Glyndebourne summer season.

A little later, Caballé sang the Countess in *Le nozze di Figaro*, with – excepting Gérard Souzay as the Count – an uninspiring cast. These performances were hardly any better received than those of *Der Rosen-kavalier* and were dogged throughout by bad luck and ill-health. Souzay did not make it past the first night, and Caballé cancelled several performances due to the onset of severe hay-fever, a condition from which she had never hitherto suffered and which had been diagnosed by a doctor in Brighton. This led to blocked sinuses and, worse, inflamed vocal cords which would thereafter dog her during the spring and summer periods throughout her career. (Caballé is in good company: Grace Bumbry, Jon Vickers and Hans Hotter are amongst eminent fellow-sufferers and were similarly prone to last-minute cancellations as a result.) But there was another, ulterior, motive underlying these cancellations: Caballé simply could not bear what she and several of her colleagues regarded as the conductor's – Vittorio Gui's – leaden *tempi*. In retrospect it seems a shame that her one and only Glyndebourne season should have been marred in this way: the management had already viewed her delayed arrival with some disquiet and had been scandalized to discover that she barely knew her début role; the cancellations were an additional blow. Despite subsequent invitations both to repeat the role of the Countess and to sing Donna Elvira, she never reappeared on the Sussex Downs in a stage role.*

Immediately after the end of the summer festival in mid-August, and following some hastily arranged recording sessions in London (of which rather more later), Montserrat returned home to Barcelona for the first time since her triumph in New York nearly four months previously. Her reception by her father was emotionally overwhelming: the last time he had seen his daughter she was still only a promising young talent. Now she returned a fully fledged star, the subject of endless coverage of the local-girl-made-good variety in the Spanish press and television. But there was no time to sit back and bask: there was the pressing need to find new accommodation and to sort through the increasing number of offers with which she was being deluged. One upshot of her new-found fame was the need to regularize her representation which hitherto had been conducted on a relatively relaxed, piecemeal basis by whoever felt like making the necessary arrangements. Carlos had already proved his worth in steering a reasonable course

---

* Amends were made at the end of the 1992 season when Montserrat – originally envisaged in tandem with Glyndebourne's other superstar débutant Luciano Pavarotti – was invited to sing in the gala commemorating the closure of the old house. Ironically, it was Pavarotti who withdrew.

through the complex deluge of offers which had rained down since Carnegie Hall. Henceforth, he was to function as her personal manager and to this end established an office just off the Diagonal (in those days still called Generalisimo), Barcelona's principal and smartest thoroughfare. During his sister's sojourn in the Sussex Downs, Carlos had been busy sorting through the stream of propositions and had spent hours on the telephone to Montserrat discussing future plans. Suddenly, a woman whose greatest commitment had not up to now extended beyond eighteen months into the future was being made offers some three years hence: equally, there were many tempting propositions in the immediate short-term to make solitary concert or recital appearances in order to cash in quick on her new-found fame. All these were duly considered by Montserrat and her brother with a view to establishing the ground plan of a comprehensive and coherent career. But one thing was already quite clear: it would be centred in North America in general, and New York in particular.

The Metropolitan Opera House at this time was in a period of great upheaval and change. The 1965–6 season, which was about to start in September, was the last that the company would give in the old house on 39th Street since the new house in Lincoln Center was already structurally complete and was in the process of being fitted out. The all-important 1966–7 inaugural season there was already finalized in all essentials, particularly the details relating to the nine new productions – four of which were to take place in the opening week alone. Rudolf Bing was well aware of the furore which Caballé's New York début had caused and was keen to secure her services in the new house at the earliest opportunity. But Montserrat knew that the old house was scheduled to be demolished shortly after the end of the current season, and, displaying an historical awareness not always manifested by singers of her breed, made an impassioned plea to be allowed to sing at least once on the boards which had been trodden for the whole length of their careers by such giants as Rosa Ponselle, Enrico Caruso, Lauritz Melchior and Kirsten Flagstad. From the Met's point of view, this was touching but tricky, since the final season had been completely mapped out for the past two years. But perhaps it might prove possible to squeeze the new diva into a solitary performance of something suitable around the Christmas 1965 period when she was due to return to New York: and there was always the closing gala on 16 April 1966 at which everybody – stars former, current and future – would be appearing.

America was still the focal point of Caballé's career when she set out again on her travels with her husband in late August. But this was to the South not the North, and was in fulfilment of obligations contracted in the previous year. She was to return to the Palacio de las Bellas Artes in Mexico in October still singing, as at Glyndebourne, what one might characterize as her old-style repertory: Elisabeth in *Tannhäuser*, Mimì in *Bohème* – with Bernabé as Rodolfo – and the Countess in *Figaro*. On 23 October she undertook a single performance of *Madama Butterfly*, not in Mexico City itself, but in the town of Puebla. Ironically, given that her husband was singing Puccini with her throughout this Central American trip, the Pinkerton at this single performance was not Bernabé Martí. Instead, it was an up-and-coming fellow-Spaniard in his late twenties who coincidentally enough was also in the last year of professional obscurity: Plácido Domingo. This was the first occasion on which the celebrated partnership of Caballé and Domingo sang together, and both retain fond memories of the experience. Perhaps not surprisingly, Cio-Cio-San hardly figured in Montserrat's stage repertory once she had achieved fame, and it is amusing to note that in these last handful of years when she was still performing the role, this Puebla *Butterfly* was the only occasion on which she sang without Bernabé by her side.

But before this eagerly awaited reappearance in Central America, Caballé was scheduled to make her stage début at the historically important Teatro Colón in Buenos Aires, singing Liù to Birgit Nilsson's Turandot. All did not go well, however. From the very first rehearsal, Montserrat came into conflict with the conductor, Fernando Previtali, who, as a former pupil of Franco Alfano, was keen to point out the special nature of his insight into how the work should go.* Of course, as Montserrat might have pointed out – but did not – Alfano had nothing whatsoever to do with the composition of the role of Liù, whose music right up to the point of her death was composed by Puccini, shortly before his own. Previtali kept insisting, however, that she sing her Act I aria 'Signore, ascolta' in a more demonstrative and full-voiced fashion. She tried to compromise and sing a little more loudly, but the conductor stopped the orchestra and yelled, 'No! Not like that. Voice! Voice! Voice!' Upset, she replied, 'Maestro, this is how I sing the role', to which he brusquely responded, 'Not when I'm conducting you don't. You will sing it as it ought to be sung or not at all.'

The stormy rehearsal finished as best it could and Montserrat repaired to her hotel room with her husband who was with her throughout this important trip, not least because she was already pregnant with their first child. A telephone call was suddenly put through from the Directorate of

---

* Franco Alfano: 1876–1954. Not, as is so often presumed, a pupil of Puccini but a successful composer in his own right, whom Toscanini persuaded to complete the final scene of *Turandot* based on Puccini's sketches.

the Colón informing her that the conductor was insisting on her removal from the cast and that she was therefore to be replaced in the role. She was free to leave Buenos Aires. Montserrat received the shattering news with as much dignity as she could muster, but the minute she put the phone down, collapsed in tears and became inconsolable. She was sadly packing her bags when there was another telephone call, this time summoning her to the director's office. When the Martís arrived, they were ushered in to find not just the general administrator and the conductor but also, wholly unexpectedly, Birgit Nilsson. The director said immediately: 'We have a problem: Madame Nilsson has informed us that if you do not sing Liù, she will not sing Turandot.' The conductor seemed to bow to the inevitable and muttered his assent to Nilsson's *force majeure*; but with astonishing lack of grace and tact, he then said to Montserrat: 'Although I accept you back in the production, you will sing it as I want it to be sung.' Nilsson, calm and authoritative, spoke up to relieve the impasse into which Montserrat was being further manoeuvred. 'Maestro, you are committing an error of judgement. This young lady sings the role in a way you will wait an entire lifetime to hear repeated, if then. I think she is extraordinary. If she is not permitted to sing the way she wishes, then I am leaving the production.' At this point the conductor's stance wholly collapsed: replacing a relative newcomer as Liù was one thing; but to replace Nilsson as Turandot was unthinkable.

After this stormy meeting, the Swedish soprano invited the Martís back to her hotel suite and told Montserrat: 'In my opinion you are a splendid singer who has an extraordinary career ahead of you. You will undoubtedly become a star.' This was praise indeed from a singer of Nilsson's stature. Montserrat thanked her profusely both for this and for her selfless action. But, Caballé continued, she was unable to understand the conductor's ingrained animosity towards her conception of the role of Liù. Nilsson replied: 'Are you really trying to understand it, Montserrat? Then don't waste your time! When one is a musician and a personality, automatically we are criticized, but thank God we don't understand the reasons for it, because otherwise we would not be the personalities we are.' This encounter served as a great lesson for Montserrat: through Nilsson's words, she came to realize that the uniqueness of certain individuals will always disturb those poorly formed personalities for whom distinction of any kind, or even mere difference, is somehow perceived as a threat. As Caballé says:

> You break the unwritten rules, you don't do something as it has always been done, and a conductor who cannot follow a musical personality at this level will automatically say that this person is

unmusical and difficult. Nowadays it can be just the same when you have a talk with a stage director. You have only to ask them, 'Why?' and they look at you as if you were already the enemy. The moment you say, 'Please give me a reason for this', then you are being impossible and temperamental.

This Argentine *Turandot* was a triumph, in spite of the conductor's glowering presence in the pit. But joy at such a success was soon wiped from Montserrat's mind when shortly afterwards she suffered a miscarriage during the eighth week of pregnancy. It was fortunate that Bernabé was with her to offer comfort and support and it is worth noting that, for a singer so often criticized for whimsical cancellations, she proceeded in spite of this personal misfortune to fulfil all her subsequent engagements in Mexico, including further performances of *Turandot* with Nilsson.

After a brief period of recuperation, Caballé left for Dallas where she was scheduled to make her North American stage début as Violetta, with Franco Bonisolli as Alfredo and Mario Zanasi as Germont. The performances were conducted by Dallas Civic Opera's co-founder and music director, Nicola Rescigno, who is best known for his collaboration with Maria Callas, both on stage and, more particularly, in the recording studio late in her career. A rather dim and distant pirate recording of one of these Dallas performances survives and gives a clear indication of the extent to which Caballé had rapidly captured the imagination of the American opera-going public.

This had been exploited by a particularly shrewd piece of marketing by RCA, who had lost no time in buying into Montserrat's unexpired recording contract with Vergara following her Carnegie Hall triumph. It was clear that some of the Spanish company's existing back-catalogue of ten or so Caballé recordings could be repackaged for international distribution under RCA's own label in due course: but none of them seemed to capitalize satisfactorily on the specific repertory with which she had made her reputation. What was needed immediately was a début disc of *bel canto* plums, preferably including something from *Lucrezia Borgia*. On such short notice even RCA had been unable to set up recording sessions utilizing its own preferred studio forces in Rome, so instead what was effectively another Vergara recital disc had been hastily planned and recorded in London, by Decca engineers, after she had finished her stint at Glyndebourne in August. With the exception of 'Casta diva' from Bellini's *Norma* – the acknowledged touchstone of *bel canto* excellence – the repertory was either little or utterly unknown, including arias from Donizetti's *Roberto Devereux* and *Maria di Rohan* as well as the closing scene from Bellini's *Il pirata* and, inevitably, Lucrezia's 'Com'è bello'. The master tape had been whisked off to New York for processing and the publicity machine set to work. The resulting disc was entitled 'Presenting Montserrat Caballé' and the artwork on the cover consisted simply of a black and white charcoal sketch of the Spanish diva subtly altered around the eyes and the mouth in order to make her look uncannily – and from the ethical point of view rather questionably – like Maria Callas (see illustrations). It was rush-released in December 1965 in the USA where, in the first five days of its availability, it sold 75,000 copies.

In the midst of this veritable Caballé mania, Montserrat returned to New York, this time accompanied by her brother. She had long since agreed to Allen Oxenburg's proposed series of *bel canto* sequels to *Lucrezia Borgia*, and the first of these, Donizetti's *Roberto Devereux*, was due to take place in Carnegie Hall on 14 December, with a much-needed (from the box office's point of view) repeat performance two days later. The Metropolitan had also managed to reschedule one of its performances of the season's opening new production of *Faust* to take place on 22 December, at which the original Valentin and Marguerite were to be replaced by two house débutants, Montserrat Caballé and Sherrill Milnes, alongside the Faust and Méphistophélès of John Alexander and Justino Diaz, conducted by Georges Prêtre. The year had therefore come full circle as Caballé returned to the scene of her first triumph and found herself being fêted all over again. If anything, the accolades this time were even more fulsome:

> Since Miss Caballé had created such a sensation in concert performances of opera here, there was considerable anticipation in the capacity audience as to how she would make out in a full-fledged production and how her voice would sound in a house the size of the Met . . . [Her] voice in all its pure loveliness projected beautifully in the auditorium. The exquisite *pianissimos*, the delicate colorations of phrase, the gleaming high tones were as much a delight to the ear as always. There is more to the soprano's singing than just gorgeous sounds. She is a musicianly singer, and instinctively at least, a sincere and tasteful actress.[3]

For *Opera* magazine, a review was supplied by its occasional New York correspondent, John Ardoin, a Callas expert and author of the standard work on her recordings, *The Callas Legacy*. Having missed the *Lucrezia Borgia* earlier in the year, he attended the Carnegie Hall concert performances of *Roberto Devereux* in a somewhat sceptical frame of mind. He was soon won over:

> It is difficult to assess Miss Caballé's accomplishment with complete rationality and calm, so overwhelming was its impact . . . [She] has been compared to Maria Callas, and her use of voice, musicianship and temperament in *Roberto Devereux* gave justification to the comparison. The two voices, however, are totally different, and for this reason there is only one Callas as there is only one Caballé . . . At least the fans of Maria Callas who succumb to Montserrat Caballé will not have to alter their monograms.[4]

Given this level of public and critical acclaim and the all-important factor of having had a successful début in front of a Met audience, it is not surprising that Montserrat was immediately called into detailed negotiations with the Metropolitan Opera House concerning her future commitments. Rudolf Bing had been in the house on the night of 22 December, and no sooner had the Jewel Song in Act III been tumultuously acclaimed by the audience, than Carlos Caballé found himself being summoned to his office. The Austrian autocrat was direct and to the point: he wanted to open immediate discussions geared to presenting Montserrat before the New York public on as regular a basis as possible. He invited Carlos to return with his sister the following morning. When they did so it was to be kept waiting in an outer office as a strained, high-pitched and multilingual dispute was heard emanating from within. After a while Franco Corelli emerged beaming from Bing's office, and the Caballés were ushered in, only to find Mr Bing playing nursemaid to an exquisitely coiffured poodle which the Italian tenor had left behind.

From Rudolf Bing's standpoint, there must have been considerable attraction in having a new star soprano to hand with whom to cement the success of the new opera house in Lincoln Center. His ploy was to offer her the title-role in *Norma*, to which, if she would be gracious enough to perform it without insisting upon a new production, he would add engagements in the already planned new stagings of *La traviata*, *Il trovatore* and *Die Zauberflöte*. Apparently, the man who expected Caballé to be the answer to his prayers apropos *Norma* thought nothing of simultaneously offering her Pamina; Desdemona in *Otello* was already taken for granted; and he was very keen she should tackle *La gioconda*, a long-time favourite with the Met audience.

Retrospectively, we may wonder how many of these extraordinary propositions were motivated by near-panic on Bing's part, since it is exactly at this juncture in the Met's fortunes, with the removal to the new house mere months away, that he found himself lord and master of an alarmingly shrinking roster of star sopranos. Callas had already sung her last in the house with just two Toscas in May 1965; Zinka Milanov would sing her farewells as Maddalena di Coigny in the course of the current season; Renata Tebaldi had been going through a vocal crisis, and was in any event insisting upon a revival of *Adriana Lecouvreur* – a work Bing detested – as the price of her return; the glorious but shamefully taken-for-granted Eleanor Steber, back-bone of the Met's soprano casting for over twenty years, would be summoned out of enforced retirement one last time to replace an ailing Dorothy Kirsten; and the magnificent Leontyne Price was very reluctant to sing at all, so great was her fear of over-exposure. With these limitations to a free hand in casting lead-soprano roles, it is perhaps not so surprising that Bing made such extraordinary offers. And yet he was by all accounts a shrewd judge of voice who had been in the business for decades and whose early taste and standards had been formed by the legendary Vienna ensemble of the 1920s. The conclusion seems inescapable that, even at the highest level of critical perception, there was always an underlying belief that Montserrat was capable of singing pretty much anything. 'I remember Rudolf Bing always used to say to me, "You don't need to be so cautious, picking and choosing. With your voice you can sing whatever you feel like."'

On one occasion she sat in Bing's office listening to an extraordinary range of glamorous star roles being laid out for her delectation and feeling utterly horrified as Carlos politely dismissed the various propositions one by one. She herself was not prepared to consider *Norma* as yet, though the inclusion of 'Casta diva' as part of her début recital disc had raised clear expectations that she would undertake the role at the earliest opportunity. But as for La Gioconda and Pamina, Carlos ruled these out of court on vocal grounds, sensibly enough since it would be hard to call to mind any soprano who, in the course of even a thirty-year career had successfully progressed from one of Mozart's lightest roles to Ponchielli's heaviest, let alone one who was expected to sing both roles within the course of the same season. A somewhat taken-aback Rudolf Bing rummaged in his desk and produced a copy of the schedule for the 1966–7 season in the new house. He simply handed it to Carlos and said, 'All right, read this list and tell me what your sister should be singing.' Of all the possibilities for her immediate future appearances at the Met, only the Verdi roles – Violetta, Desdemona and Leonora – were acceptable. The 1967–8 season at the Metropolitan would be a rather different proposition, however, since here Bing still had sufficient lead-in time to offer Caballé *carte blanche* choice

of nearly twenty different roles. On the strength of just one performance, and that in the old house, it looked as though the Met already
had a new queen.

Back at home, Caballé's immediate task was to begin rehearsals for
performances of *Il trovatore* at the Liceo in January 1966. The three
performances were completely sold out in advance, not surprisingly
since these were the first appearances that Caballé had made on the
Liceo stage since her New York triumph, which had been exhaustively
reported in the Spanish press. (Such was her level of new-found prestige
that at this time she was awarded the Lazo de Dama de Isabel la Católica,
Spain's highest civilian honorific.) The days before the first night on
13 January were somewhat fraught, since the scheduled Manrico, Carlo
Bergonzi, had withdrawn very late in the day – concerned at the thought
of being upstaged by the obvious house favourite, according to some
press reports, though this seems implausible. In the event, despite an
undistinguished substitute, the performances were a triumph: the third
and last (on the 18th) produced an interminable ovation. But Montserrat
had no chance to rest on her laurels since she was already rehearsing
the next production, *Tannhäuser*, in which she was to sing the role of
Elisabeth. These three performances were not nearly so well received,
but this seems to have had more to do with the otherwise mediocre
cast and conductor than with any shortcomings on Caballé's part. Certainly the Liceo lost no time in organizing an *homenaje* for its local star
diva, which occurred after the first performance of *Tannhäuser* and took
the form of the presentation of the Medalla de Oro del Gran Teatro del
Liceo.* And as if this were not satisfaction enough, Montserrat now
discovered that she was again pregnant.

After no more than a short break at home with Bernabé, she departed,
this time to fulfil a long-standing engagement to make her début in
Brussels at the Palais des Beaux Arts, singing *Salome* in concert. At the
end of March the Martís travelled to America where Montserrat had a
busy schedule of important engagements ahead of her. First was her
début at the prestigious Academy of Music, Philadelphia's opera house,
in what was a new role for her: Maddalena di Coigny in *Andrea Chénier*,
with Franco Corelli as the revolutionary poet. The rehearsals went well
up to and including the full dress, which took place the day before the
opening night. Caballé who, as usual, had brought her own costumes
and accoutrements, left them in her dressing-room overnight. When
she and Bernabé returned two hours before curtain up the following
day, it was to walk into a screaming row between Corelli and the opera

---

* The first of six such presentations in homage across the period 1966–87.

house's administration – ironically, Philadelphia's general manager, Aurelio Fabbiani, was the tenor's US agent – concerning cash pre-payment of fees. Since Montserrat had contracted through Columbia Artists' Management (CAMI), she was momentarily alarmed as to whether the tenor knew something she did not concerning their prospects of payment. Bernabé therefore went off to gather reassuring words from Fabbiani, leaving Caballé to prepare for Act I. She opened the wardrobe door and discovered that all the elaborate lace trimmings had been ripped from her crinoline, and the black velvet of the plain dress she wore for the other three Acts had been hacked about with scissors. In addition, her powdered white wig had been cut into pieces. The soprano was traumatized, and was found by her husband and Fabbiani collapsed in tears. Evidently, someone wished to 'nobble' Caballé before she had even sung a note. All manner of speculation ensued as to who may have been responsible for the sabotage and their motives in so doing. Montserrat refused to follow the easiest line of reasoning, which seemed inexorably directed at the dressing-room next door, until Corelli and his wife, Loretta, came to see what the commotion was all about. Signora Corelli advanced solicitously upon the vandalized wig, and to this day Montserrat bridles at the reminiscence of the strange tones with which the woman stroked the object, cooing '*povero perruchetto*' – 'poor little wiggy' – the while.

The curtain went up twenty minutes late that night as the wardrobe staff frantically restitched the black dress and found a stock replacement for the crinoline, and Bernabé rushed back to the hotel in order to grab his wife's dark *Traviata* wig and bring it back for spraying. Madame Corelli meanwhile danced attendance backstage on her increasingly hysterical husband, rubbing a crucifix up and down his throat to repeated cries of 'Madonna, Madonna'. None of which could be described as conducive to producing the settled conditions of calm and concentration from which one imagines most great performances emerge. But this is to reckon without the motivating force of a high octane mixture of anger and adrenaline. Caballé remembers: 'People misunderstand how this kind of thing affects me. When I am angry I am not a person who loses my temper for everyone to see. Instead, I keep it bottled up inside me and somehow manage to channel it into my performance.' As a result, her Maddalena met with a most enthusiastic reception. But more than one reviewer drew attention to the fact that, exquisitely as she had sung, this kind of verismo war-horse was not the sort of work to show her off to best advantage. Indeed, she evidently thought so herself, since after the last performance she gave a press interview during the course of which she mentioned, with great firmness, that she would never sing the role again.* Immediately after the last performance, she and Bernabé departed for New York.

On 16 April 1966 the old Metropolitan Opera House held its closing gala. Among the sopranos taking part were Renata Tebaldi, Zinka Milanov, Birgit Nilsson, Leontyne Price, Régine Crespin, Eleanor Steber and Montserrat; the tenors included Jon Vickers, Nicolai Gedda, Richard Tucker, James McCracken and Franco Corelli. Evidently the vocal thrills on offer during the course of a long evening were plentiful, Caballé's particular contribution taking the form of the Act III trio from *Der Rosenkavalier*, with Rosalind Elias as Octavian and Judith Raskin as Sophie, conducted by Georges Prêtre. But surely the most frisson-inspiring moment must have belonged to Leopold Stokowski who, at the age of eighty-four, launched into a fiery speech from the orchestra pit protesting against the immediate demolition of the historic old house, which the management had sold off as a real estate to finance the construction of the new.†

The real substance of this further American expedition was another concert performance given under the auspices of the American Opera Society in Carnegie Hall on 25 April, this time of Bellini's *Il pirata*, in which Caballé was to sing the role of Imogene, and her husband the role of the titular pirate Gualtiero. Up to now Montserrat's performances in *bel canto* repertory had avoided immediate comparisons: but *Pirata* was still relatively fresh in the memory of AOS devotees, having been performed as recently as 1959 in the same hall with, as we have seen, no less than Maria Callas as the heroine. Comparisons may well be odious; but they are also unavoidable and, quite frequently, illuminating. Moreover, in deciding to mount the work at all, the AOS was actively inviting them, since it was Allen Oxenburg's private contention – which he wished to see fully vindicated in public – that in Montserrat Caballé the opera-going public had a fully worthy successor to Maria Callas. All very provocative, although it is surely significant that John Ardoin avoided the issue altogether in his review:

> The role of Imogene seemed tailor-made for [Caballé] with its long-lined legato phrases and ample opportunities for bursts of temperament. Her voice soared with ease without relinquishing an iota of the score's excitement. The coloratura passage-work was dashed off

---

* In fact, Caballé did sing the role again, both on stage and in a studio recording, but not until many years later.
† Stokowski protested in vain: the house was demolished within the year, and the old gold front curtain chopped into thousands of small pieces of cloth to accompany RCA's release of the farewell recording.

with greater clarity and *brio* than that in *Roberto Devereux* last autumn, and her voice, for some strange reason, seemed larger and more opulent. Miss Caballé has an undeniable and cherishable way with the *bel canto* repertory, and she illuminated *Il pirata* with radiant singing while making its heroine a fleshy, rather than cardboard, character. Bellini would doubtless have been pleased.[5]

It is unfortunately impossible to verify Ardoin's assessment of Caballé's performance since, unusually amongst these AOS revivals, no recording has ever come to light, whilst Callas's 1959 performance has latterly been widely available. Even so, it is probably right to adopt Ardoin's stance in treating each singer as an individual phenomenon rather than lamenting the impossibility of direct comparison. Perhaps the most significant point to emerge from his review, beyond the expected appreciation of an obviously superlative voice, is the emphasis upon 'temperament' as a notable feature of Caballé's performances. In England, in particular, this has always been discounted, principally one suspects because of the familiar prejudice which sees large people – particularly women – as, *de facto*, figures of fun, incapable of emotional depth. It is therefore interesting to discover in what light Montserrat's earliest international audiences saw her.

By this time, RCA's hastily assembled recording plans were about to come to fruition in the shape of Caballé's first complete opera recording. Not surprisingly, the work chosen had been *Lucrezia Borgia*, of which this would be its first-ever studio recording. The sessions had been arranged to take place during May in the company's studios in Rome, with the RCA Italiana Opera Orchestra and Chorus. As in New York, the conductor would be Jonel Perlea, though in the event he and the soprano were the only survivors of the Carnegie Hall performance, since Alfredo Kraus replaced Alain Vanzo as Gennaro and Shirley Verrett was to sing Orsini instead of Jane Berbié. The recording, which took place in tandem with RCA's *Un ballo in maschera* with Leontyne Price, progressed smoothly except for some problems experienced by the entire cast as the result of the hot weather, and it stands as the first of the series of thirty-four complete commercial opera recordings which Caballé has made to date.

Mindful of the unhappy conclusion to her first pregnancy the previous year, Montserrat was told to do nothing which would place her unborn child at risk. With Carlos's help, she progressively withdrew from most of her stage commitments and, by June, was undertaking only occasional concert work. The major exception was a concert in Paris, given in the Salle Pleyel on 21 June as part of the weekly radio series

Le Prestige de la Musique and which effectively constituted her Parisian début. The programme was calculated to cement her reputation as the new queen of *bel canto* and comprised Elisabeth I's final aria from *Roberto Devereux*, the closing scene from *Anna Bolena* and the mad scene from *Il pirata*. Interspersing all this furious vocalism were extracts from *La vida breve* and Granados' *Goyescas*. The sold-out auditorium, which was characteristically reported by the press of the day as containing any number of social luminaries, was roused to frenzies of enthusiasm. Several of the reviews made the same point: Paris had seen nothing like it since Maria Callas had made her belated début at the Palais Garnier in 1958.

Montserrat spent most of the remainder of the summer at home in Barcelona resting. However, she was perversely determined to honour one last contractual obligation, a series of five *Manon Lescaut*s to be given at the Teatro Colón in July, impracticably enough during the sixth month of her pregnancy. Her des Grieux for the first three performances was a tenor with whom she would soon be forging a close partnership at the Metropolitan, but with whom she would now be singing for the first time: Richard Tucker. Bernabé, who was already at the Colón singing Enzo in *La gioconda*, was due to take over for the last two. The opening night was an immense success, most of the reviewers marvelling at how a singer they had last heard just months beforehand as an ethereal Liù could now manifest such power and *spinto* tone in the new role. But she started to suffer from back and intestinal pains during the second performance and at the third only just managed to get through the Act II duet without fainting. She was terrified that she was about to lose the child she was carrying, less than a year after she had lost her first in exactly the same location. The fourth performance – the first with her husband – she withdrew from, but managed to perform on the last night.

In fact, the remainder of Montserrat's pregnancy was fraught: her blood pressure was high and her weight increased inexorably. The baby was due on 10 October but this date came and went without result. The doctors became increasingly concerned, not least because of the mother's physical condition. A further fortnight passed, at which point Montserrat was admitted to the Clinica Bona Nova for tests and observation. Finally, on 29 October she went into labour. This continued for forty-eight hours until the frantic doctors made the discovery that due to malformation of her bone structure, the baby was wedged and, like the mother, in a very parlous condition. They decided to intervene surgically, and Caballé's son was therefore delivered by Caesarean section. In deference to the long-standing family tradition, the baby boy was named directly after his father, Bernabé. But though the baby was fine, Montserrat was in a bad way: the musculature she regarded as the basis of her technique had been sliced open and painfully restitched; and she had reached a greater body weight than she had ever carried before. But these were considerations which only really impinged upon Caballé the singer; Montserrat the woman was oblivious to them, at least in the short term. She was too busy coping with the new role for which she had spent so much time preparing: motherhood.

CHAPTER SEVEN

1967–1969: Yankee Doodle Diva

The demands of motherhood are as nothing compared to the incessant claims of New York-style stardom: scarcely had Caballé become familiar with her new baby than she was required to pack her bags and return to the centre of her professional activity, America. The whole of Christmas/New Year had been spent *en famille* in Barcelona, with Montserrat's parents happily coming to terms with their new responsibilities as grandparents to the infant Bernabé Aurelio. With Caballé's career in full swing, it was inevitable that the baby's day-to-day care would increasingly be entrusted to her parents during her prolonged periods of absence, particularly when, as on this occasion, she was to be accompanied professionally by her husband. The couple were due to depart for Philadelphia for the first of a whole series of engagements arranged by the man whose very name had been given to Montserrat's son and to whom he was now godfather: Aurelio (Ray) Fabbiani. At the time Fabbiani was one of the most important figures in American opera by virtue of his connections both with the Philadelphia Opera and Franco Corelli. The Martís first appeared together towards the end of January in a solitary performance of *Tosca* at the Academy of Music (following Tebaldi and Richard Tucker in the same roles earlier in the season). Then, at the beginning of February and in between commuting to rehearsals at the Metropolitan Opera House, Caballé appeared in a gala concert for the benefit of the Orchestra's pension fund with Gianfranco Cecchele, conducted by Seiji Ozawa, with a programme calculated to remind Philadelphians of her *bel canto* credentials. This was probably a Pyrrhic victory in the light of the frosty reviews accorded her Tosca and subsequent Cio-Cio-San, where the hoary old argument was revived that a singer capable of all the necessary *bel canto* refinements is automatically wasted in *verismo*.

In any event, Caballé was on much safer ground, at least in terms of repertory, in the performance which marked her stage début at the new Metropolitan Opera House in Lincoln Center on 6 February. This was a revival of the previous year's production of *Il trovatore* in which she was partnered by the Met's tenor and baritone stalwarts, Richard Tucker and Robert Merrill. An extended commentary appeared in *Opera*, where Herbert Weinstock mused:

> . . . having heard her several times and having listened to her record-ings carefully, I do not know what sort of singer she really is . . . On the existing evidence, she has not the temperament, accuracy or agility for Donizetti or Bellini; and her acting so lacks excitement that, like Victória de los Angeles, she is perhaps really a concert artist. The Metropolitan audience . . . showered approval on everyone con-cerned.[1]

Weinstock was similarly unimpressed with the performances of *Otello* which commenced a run at the Met on 27 February 1967. In addition to Caballé's début in the role of Desdemona, Zubin Mehta was also making his début conducting the work. Neither met with much approval, which was reserved for Tito Gobbi's Iago. James McCracken in the title-role was generally felt to be wanting. However, from the evidence of the pirate recording made from a Texaco broadcast, Gobbi – grey-toned and desiccated – is well past his prime. Caballé is quite clearly in hers; McCracken gives an overwhelmingly committed per-formance, and Mehta's conducting is electrifying, very much in the Carlos Kleiber mould.

There was a rather touching prelude to these performances, which concerns Elena Doria, the young soprano who had befriended Mont-serrat in Rome in 1955. After Caballé had made her début at the old Met in *Faust* she had returned to Barcelona taking with her piles of Metropolitan programmes and leaflets to peruse at leisure. One day she had been reading all the names of the ballet, orchestra and chorus at the house. Suddenly she stopped dead in her tracks. There in the list of chorus singers she had found the name of someone for whom she had been searching many years – Elena Doria. As Caballé recalls:

> The next time I came to the Met, rehearsing *Otello* in 1967, I searched among the faces of the chorus to find her. In Italy she had looked like Veronica Lake, but there was no one like that in sight. So I went to the chorus-master, Kurt Adler, and told him I was looking for Elena. Right away he pointed to a woman with red hair. I ran to her and said: 'Eléna, don't you know me? I am Montserrat.' She looked shy and said, 'Oh yes, but many years have passed and now you are a great star, and I thought you would not remember me.' I was very moved.

Montserrat's performances at the Met continued well into March, but from mid-month – ominously enough, the Ides – she was also engaged in rehearsals for the AOS's next Carnegie Hall concert presentation, Handel's *Giulio Cesare*. At a time when baroque opera had fallen into near-total oblivion in the principal operatic centres, it is strange to reflect upon New York's continuing obsession with this one work. The AOS itself had already given a performance of it less than two years previously; and the (ill-fated) opening of the new Metropolitan Opera House had been rather overshadowed by the adjacent New York City Opera's staged production of the work which, conferring belated stardom upon Beverly Sills, had been counted the highlight of the autumn/ winter period of 1966–7. In any event, Caballé's Cleopatra, given on 21 March 1967, was enthusiastically acclaimed by the capacity audience in Carnegie Hall that night, as the old pirate LPs in increasingly scarce circulation confirm.

Immediately afterwards she left for New Orleans where she was to make her début singing the title-role in Massenet's *Manon*, with John Alexander as her des Grieux. As with the Handel, the score was much cut: the Cours-la-Reine and Hotel Transylvania scenes vanished altogether. Even so, she was much applauded and admired in the role, especially for her dramatically intense and committed account of the Saint Sulpice scene in which the lovestruck and shameless Manon pursues her former lover to the very threshold of his ordination as a priest, hoping (successfully, as it transpires) to seduce him back. Apparently, the orchestral brass – and in particular the horns – had a bad evening and compounded their delinquency by laughing loudly amongst themselves every time one of them cracked a note: perhaps this Manon should have chased some of the orchestral players instead. But these New Orleans performances were not the end of Caballé's travails with the opera, since she was scheduled to make her important début with it at the end of April, together with *La traviata*, in Madrid at the city's only functioning opera house, the Teatro de la Zarzuela.

The cast, apart from Violetta, was undistinguished, but *Manon* was a different proposition, since des Grieux was no less than Alfredo Kraus. These would be the Spanish soprano and tenor's first stage appearances together following their collaboration in the recording studio the previous year. The meticulous Kraus duly rehearsed as directed, but Montserrat remembers that, in performance, he was reluctant to enter into the spirit of the tempestuous *folie à deux* which we are to imagine binds the lovers through thick and thin. On the opening night, during the Saint Sulpice scene, Montserrat was feverishly pursuing Kraus around the set on her knees, imploring him to return to her. His unwritten response to these attempts at supplication was to hiss through clenched teeth: 'Get back! For God's sake stop trying to touch me!' so loudly that it even blocked out the sound of the prompter. This, of course, is reasonably in character while des Grieux is resisting Manon's last-ditch assault on his religious resolve, but must have become hilariously inappropriate when he is supposed to capitulate and flee his own ordination entwined with his lover. In retrospect, Montserrat regrets that her impetuosity on stage should have so disturbed the eminent tenor. Nevertheless, he was not to be appeased, and what was their first appearance together on stage also turned out to be their last.

Conversely, the pairing with the now largely forgotten Flaviano Labò in that year's Florentine Maggio Musicale went well. Caballé had been engaged to sing Imogene in *Il pirata* and the performances were to mark her effective début in Italy as a principal. The production was by Mauro Bolognini and rehearsals had been progressing smoothly for over three weeks when, somewhat to the soprano's surprise, a new man presented himself and began to reblock extensive parts of the stage action. Montserrat let it go for a while but eventually had had enough of this interference. She stopped, walked forward and said, 'Who are you and what do you think you're doing?' She was mortified to learn that the man was none other than Bolognini himself. He had been busy elsewhere for the first weeks of rehearsals and an assistant had been taking his place. Completely unabashed, Caballé then inquired whether the director thought it reasonable to treat his own *mise-en-scène* and the artists involved in it as some kind of musical cash-and-carry, making what seemed like arbitrary changes to everybody's hard work. She said: 'I think your assistant has done a wonderful job, and as far as I'm concerned, he is in charge of this staging. Please leave us to get on with our work.' For the sake of musical peace, he did so, and was soon rewarded as a genuine admiration and affection sprang up between him and the soprano, which endures to this day. Most of the performances were conducted by Franco Capuana, a seasoned veteran who had made some recordings for Decca with Renata Tebaldi. The critical response was overwhelmingly favourable and, to judge from the different pirate performances which have emerged in recent years, the audience reaction was ecstatic. If there had been any tendency on the part of the Italians to regard with a certain scepticism the talents of a woman whose reputation had been made elsewhere, these performances single-handedly swept them away. In many ways these *Pirata*s were the acid test of Caballé's acceptance: to sing a demanding key role of the Italian *bel canto* school in front of an Italian audience and, as a foreigner, still achieve a triumph would be proof of her new status as *prima donna assoluta*. Her achievement was chronicled by Brendan Fitzgerald, writing in the Milan *Daily American* on 16 June, the morning after the first night:

> . . . if the chance to see this rarely performed and very early work by the 'Swan of Catania' were not enough to bundle the cognoscenti into Florence's Teatro Communale, the presence of Montserrat Caballé as the prima donna would be. A young singer but already legendary, she is appearing for the first time in Florence in a role that allows a leisurely display of her singular gifts, after bringing New York to its knees in the same part last year . . . [She] is the stupendous revelation to the Florentine public. What a voice, incredibly smooth in texture and of an unbelievable ease in transition of register, like a glowing pearl rolling on velvet, it is the perfect vocal counterpart of Bellini's moonlit, shadowed genius. Her commanding presence and enormous dignity are a pleasure in themselves. A large woman, she is not given to large gestures, but her economy of movement is intelligently applied to superb effect. Marvellous eyes and their telling deployment complete a memorable style. It is very like being able to see one of the great prima donnas of the culminating moment of *bel canto* and romanticism.

And at precisely this moment, fast approaching the zenith of her powers, Caballé re-entered the studios of RCA in Rome in order to record her second complete opera, *La traviata*, as well as the first two recital discs to be made under her new contract, miscellanies of rare Verdi and Rossini arias. We live in an age when all twenty-eight of Verdi's operas (including the reworked *I Lombardi/Jérusalem* and *Stiffelio/Aroldo*) are available on compact disc, so that it is worth remembering that in 1967 barely more than half the composer's output had then been recorded. The plight of Rossini on record was even worse: of his thirty-nine complete operas (including substantial revisions) less than one quarter were available in 'complete' – actually invariably incomplete – recordings. In choosing to commit to disc arias from *I due Foscari*, *Attila*, *Alzira*, *Il corsaro*, *Armida*, *Otello*, *La donna del lago* and *Tancredi*, Caballé gave the RCA management the fright of their lives, since they considered the sales potential to be negligible, whilst the costs of transcribing orchestral material and parts was exorbitant. A determined diva is not easily deterred, however. These were records she wanted to make, acting principally out of a belief that in these long-buried operas there was much beautiful, undeservedly forgotten music. Already, with little more than two years' stardom behind her, Caballé was using her new-found position and power not to further her own glory – though that would prove an inevitable concomitant of success – but as part of her genuine campaign on behalf of the *primo ottocento* composers. Such was the artistic and commercial success of the recordings when they were released the following year that Montserrat found herself in the ironic position of being pursued by RCA to make more recordings of *bel canto* rarities on more or less any financial terms she cared to name.

Following these extended recording sessions in Rome she returned home for what was effectively becoming her annual holiday period, variously covering late July, August and early September. Certainly this year – 1967 – with a nine-month-old baby son to consider, she had been reluctant to accept any engagements during the peak months of the numerous summer music festivals in Europe. Her next major undertaking was not therefore until the middle of September when she departed for America once again, this time accorded the honour of having been chosen to open the Metropolitan Opera House's new season. This brought her back in front of the New York public in one of her handful of favourite roles, Violetta, which she increasingly chose as her preferred 'calling card' when making significant house débuts. On the opening night gala – a revival of the old Alfred Lunt/Cecil Beaton production – her partner was Richard Tucker, who more than one observer has noted bore an uncanny resemblance to Montserrat's husband.

Performances continued well into October, with several changes of Alfredo, by which time the house was firmly in the grip of Karajan fever. The Austrian maestro was rehearsing his own new production of *Die Walküre*, in the process making his Metropolitan Opera House début at the age of fifty-eight. Everyone was in a state of mild panic.* Karajan found time to slip into one of the performances of *La traviata* about which people were waxing so lyrical. The first Caballé knew of this was when she received a contract from the Salzburg Festival authorities inviting her to sing the role of Donna Elvira in the following Summer Festival's new production of *Don Giovanni*, with Nicolai Ghiaurov in the title-role, Gundula Janowitz as Anna and Karajan both directing and conducting. This was an unsought but very attractive honour which Caballé had every intention of accepting, but before formalizing contractual arrangements she received a further proposition which rather complicated matters. Karajan, as was his wont, had decided to extend the project beyond the already expansive confines of the Grosses Festspielhaus and to produce a recording which would be used as the soundtrack

---

* Sir Rudolf Bing charts the progress of this extraordinary operatic ordeal in his sometimes unreliable but always entertaining autobiography, *5000 Nights at the Opera* (Hamish Hamilton, London, 1972).

of a film he intended to direct in a Munich studio in the spring of 1968. Caballé was indeed to be the Elvira for this extended plan. But there was a condition attached to the proposed contract: the soprano was required, within six months, to shed a minimum of fifteen kilos (thirty-three pounds). Furthermore, she had to present herself at the Munich studios the following February for preliminary screen tests. The recording would take place some time thereafter, and filming shortly after that.

Caballé was worried about this proposition on a number of fronts. She had been slowly gaining weight throughout the 1960s, but had seen a fairly dramatic increase following the birth of her son. She was by no means sure that the stipulated weight loss was at all feasible for her, let alone one set to a timetable. And she was already contracted at the Metropolitan to sing Luisa Miller during the time she was expected to make herself available in Munich. In the event, although she had already been announced for the 1968 Salzburg Summer Festival, the project fell through for reasons which at this remove Montserrat no longer remembers. Certainly no recording took place, nor was any film made, though the Salzburg Festival duly had its *Don Giovanni* with Teresa Zylis-Gara as Elvira.

The stint of *Traviata*s at the Met marked the beginning of a five-year contract Caballé had agreed to sign at Rudolf Bing's behest, the culmination of which was to have been his cherished realization of what was referred to as the 'Tudor Ring', comprising new productions – all Metropolitan firsts – built round her appearances as Donizetti's queens in *Anna Bolena*, *Maria Stuarda* and *Roberto Devereux*.* But her next port of call, following a mixed bag of recitals and concerts in the deep South, took her for the first time to Venezuela and a solitary performance of *La traviata* at the opera house in Caracas, with Bernabé as Alfredo. With their combined fees Montserrat decided to engage in her first real diva's caprice: a glossy limousine. She subsequently arranged to purchase a silver Mercedes, still her preferred mode of transport. On numerous occasions, Bernabé has tried to persuade her to get rid of the ageing vehicle, but Montserrat will have none of it: even the suave and stream-lined replacement which was acquired in 1993 sits more or less unused in the garage. It was her first car, and she seems determined to keep it at all costs.

She immediately returned to Dallas where she had successfully managed to persuade an initially reluctant management – who understandably enough would have preferred the latest *bel canto* novelty – to mount

---

* The project was, alas, never realized, falling victim to some ugly rivalry between the two Lincoln Center Opera Houses.

instead performances of *Le nozze di Figaro*, thus affording her an opportunity, increasingly rare, to sing one of her beloved Mozartian roles.
The cast was of a comparably high calibre, with Sesto Bruscantini in
the title-role and Graziella Sciutti as Susanna. On the opening night,
during the complicated plottings in Act IV when the Countess and her
maid exchange costumes the better to deceive their men-folk, Caballé
was perched on a bench which progressively became more crowded.
She had already moved along several times, and with the newest arrival
shifted herself into empty space, landing on the stage floor with a loud
thump. As Montserrat points out, in those days she was sufficiently
adept to need no assistance in righting herself, though both she and the
rest of the cast suffered acutely from the giggles as a result. Perhaps
some of this evident good humour underpinned John Ardoin's subsequent review: 'Caballé deserves a special word: here was some of the
most convincing work she has done to date . . . She was pert and
charming, as naturally acted as sung.'[2]

The Dallas performances continued until the end of November, at
which point Montserrat returned to New York to begin rehearsals for
yet another AOS Carnegie Hall presentation, her début in the title-role
of Donizetti's *Maria Stuarda* with the glorious and as yet unreconstructed
mezzo Shirley Verrett as Elisabetta. This, as New Yorkers are wont to
say, was evidently a hot night. One makes allowances for some permiss-
ible chauvinism on the part of the Spanish press, but the reports which
appeared soon after the performance on 6 December contain entire paragraphs dedicated to explaining how impossible it would be for mere
words to express the unprecedented scenes of yelling and screaming
which greeted Caballé at the end of Act II. Even the previously unimpressed Herbert Weinstock observed: 'The really encouraging and surprising exception was Montserrat Caballé in the title part. Here was a
new Caballé involved in story and character . . . visibly and audibly
engaged. She was properly rewarded by the audience.'[3]

Back home in Barcelona and before beginning her Christmas/New
Year vacation she sang just two performances of *Tosca* at the Liceo,
with her husband as Cavaradossi and, following the late withdrawal of
Sesto Bruscantini, Cesare Bardelli as Scarpia. On the opening night –
16 December – while Caballé was edging her way nervously around
the fictive interior of the Palazzo Farnese, avoiding the loathsome Baron
Scarpia's advances, she chanced to lean over the back of an elaborately
carved chair. It gave way and to the accompaniment of some sniggering
from the groundlings, the soprano attempted to set it upright. She
succeeded and continued in her nervous progress around Scarpia's
domain. Unfortunately, she arrived back at the chair, which this time

collapsed altogether, to the audience's amusement. In a rare public display of temper, Caballé picked the offending item up and flung it with all her force upstage where it crashed into the back wall of the set and broke into pieces. The audience instantly fell silent as the blazing-eyed soprano strode forwards, leaving many, doubtless including Signor Bardelli, wondering what possible chance any poor Scarpia would stand against such a Tosca.

After a brief family holiday at home, Caballé resumed her professional activities in 1968 with a gala concert at the Liceo on 10 January celebrating the thirtieth anniversary of Spanish Radio. In the second half she sang duets with her husband but, prophetically enough, also included 'Casta diva'. Given her recent forays into ever more recondite *bel canto* repertory, the Barcelonese public – and they were not alone – must have been wondering when she would finally confront the one work that everybody did know and which has always been regarded as the summit of any soprano's ambition – *Norma*. But all those opera houses that had asked her already knew the answer: not yet. Even so, Montserrat's inexorable progression towards the role was to take a decisive step forward at the end of her forthcoming trip to America. She returned to New York at the end of January to begin rehearsals for the Metropolitan's new production of Verdi's *Luisa Miller*, which had not been given in the house since 1936 and which Bing had decided to mount especially for her – courtesy of a large donation from Mrs John Rockefeller – as part of her new contract. Bernabé travelled with his wife but did not stay in New York, where she was to be partnered by Richard Tucker. Instead, he continued to Philadelphia where he was contracted to sing the role of Pollione to Joan Sutherland's Norma in the Academy of Music. In all senses, this was to prove an eventful trip.

The rehearsals proceeded smoothly. After one of them Montserrat was wandering around the labyrinthine corridors of the Met's backstage when she walked into Renata Tebaldi. The two divas had met briefly on two previous occasions: once after Montserrat's old Met début in December 1965 when they had been formally introduced; and again during the course of the Met's closing gala in April 1966, at which both had performed. On this last occasion, Caballé had taken the opportunity of thanking Tebaldi in person for all the great performances she had given in Barcelona while Montserrat was a student and recounting how she used to queue for both tickets and autographs. Now, the Italian prima donna had been promised her desired *Adriana Lecouvreur* and was therefore back in the house, preparing first for a series of performances of *La gioconda*. There and then the two women made arrangements to attend at least one of each other's performances. Caballé's opening night took place first, on 8 February 1968, and though the work was a considerable rarity for the Met audience, *Luisa Miller* met with a resounding success. Herbert Weinstock reported that 'Montserrat Caballé, in complete control of her luscious voice, acted the best performance of her Met career.'⁴

But this was New York in early February: freezing cold and very bleak. Shortly after the première Caballé caught a head cold, one of the many dozens with which she has been afflicted throughout her career. The obvious solution was, of course, to cancel, but the next scheduled performance – the matinée on the 17th – was part of the famous Texaco Metropolitan radio series and was therefore to be broadcast live throughout the USA. No singer, and particularly an ambitious soprano, willingly passes up the opportunity of this kind of nationwide exposure, and from the first symptoms Montserrat placed herself in the hands of the Met's principal physician who had a reputation for nursing singers through their various medical mishaps.

It so happened that La Tebaldi herself felt slightly under the weather and shortly afterwards visited the same doctor, who wondered aloud whether he had the beginnings of an epidemic on his hands. Finding out that Caballé was already unwell, Tebaldi swung into action, got hold of the Spanish diva's number from the Met's personnel office and immediately telephoned her younger colleague. 'We'll have to do something about this and *pronto.*' Shortly afterwards, she arrived together with her inseparable companion, Tina, at Montserrat's suite at the Mayflower, laden with pots, potions and inhalations. She put her straight to bed, since she was running a temperature, and stayed with her for two days, sleeping in the adjacent room. Caballé began to wonder whether Tebaldi might not be jeopardizing her own performances of *La gioconda* by such solicitude: did she not need some time for herself in order to prepare for her role? Tebaldi soon dispelled Caballé's fears: 'Oh, *Gioconda*'s nothing: you just scream a bit and behave melodramatically and you get through it!' Right up to the time of Montserrat's live matinée broadcast Tebaldi was to be found backstage plying Caballé with lozenges and gargles, while at the same time readying herself for her own performance that evening. Pirate tapes of the Verdi performance survive and only go to prove the efficacy of La Tebaldi's nursing: there is no evidence that Caballé is performing at anything less than full voltage. Not surprisingly, this episode cemented a close friendship between the two sopranos.

It was after the recovery period of this admittedly minor but, for a singer, significant illness that Montserrat travelled to Philadelphia in order to hear her husband and Sutherland in *Norma*. As the Australian soprano tells the story,[5] this involved some surreptitious 'moonlighting' on Caballé's part from Chicago (*sic*), cancelling a performance and pleading illness as an excuse. Apparently, after *Norma*, Caballé partied the night away, her elaborate bouffant coiffure steadily collapsing, fortifying herself the while with occasional platefuls of spaghetti despite an earlier claim to have lost her appetite. Some of this may well be true; but the suggestion of brazen Callas-style truancy needs to be corrected. Montserrat was *not* scheduled to sing in Chicago throughout this period: she did not make her début at the Lyric Opera until 1971. In fact, she remained constantly in and around New York since she was contracted to sing eleven *Luisa Miller*s at the Met over a two-month period. Furthermore, she was already scheduled to be in Philadelphia because on 5 and 8 March she gave performances of *Il pirata* there, with Bernabé – who was already rehearsing the role of Pollione with Sutherland – singing Gualtiero. And none of the Metropolitan performances was cancelled. Even the rather more extended excursion to New Orleans for a brace of *Il trovatore*s with Domingo fell harmlessly within a precisely organized schedule.

Sutherland's anecdotal error is, at worst, only benign mischief-making. Certainly there has never been any trace of professional rivalry between the two women. They may have met when they were both singing Bellinian heroines, and even shared tenor and conductor husbands to whom they were married, but there was no hint of friction between them. Ultimately, they had something else in common: an irrepressible and, at times, girlish sense of humour. Moreover, something very positive came from this new-found friendship: Sutherland gave Caballé her score of *Norma*, saying, 'You should look at this. I know you're doing Imogene, but this is the role you ought to be singing.' Caballé duly took the score away but was very doubtful. Not because she was in any way daunted by the legendary demands of the part – she has always been of the opinion that Imogene, at least in terms of *tessitura*, is much harder – but because she was unable to imagine how she could master the altitudinous flights of coloratura she had heard at Sutherland's performance. Then, of course, on reading the printed score closely she discovered that very little of this actually appears in Bellini's vocal line. She delicately broached this with Sutherland, who was typically forthright. 'Montsy, you've got to adapt it to your vocal means. I couldn't make much of it so I do what I'm best at with it. So must you, and that way make it your own.' And, in fairly short order, she did.

At the end of her ten-week period at the Met, Caballé arrived at an enforced hiatus in her career, since she had set aside the period of April, May and early June for Karajan's *Don Giovanni* project. Left with time on her hands, she thus returned home – as always – to Barcelona, enjoying the unexpected opportunity to spend time with her baby son. She remained there until mid-June, at which point she travelled to London in order to fulfil her most cherished recording project to date and the one for which she had had to fight hardest: Strauss's *Salome*. Incredibly, in 1968 this was only the second stereo recording of the work: even so, RCA was reluctant to enter into open competition with the luridly Sonicstage Culshaw 1961 production for Decca with Nilsson, conducted by Solti, which had set new standards in production and recording values. There was also the fact that Caballé was primarily regarded by the record-buying public as a *bel canto* specialist – an impression which her recorded repertoire to date did nothing to dispel. But such was her influence within the classical recording industry, particularly with a view to her popularity in America, that her wishes in the matter could simply not be denied. Thus it was that RCA gathered together in the improbable surroundings of Walthamstow Town Hall's assembly room a wonderful cast including Sherrill Milnes as Jokanaan, Richard Lewis as Herod, the inimitable Regina Resnik as Herodias and James King as Narraboth, conducted by Erich Leinsdorf.

It was during these sessions that the final arrangements were made concerning Caballé's already long-overdue London début. But these were not with the management of the Royal Opera House, Covent Garden, which then as now was notoriously dilatory in bringing the majority of exciting new vocal talents before the London public. It had been left to the private enterprise of the London Opera Society – which had been set up in 1967 in direct emulation of Allen Oxenburg's New York organization – to enter into successful negotiations to present Montserrat in London for the first time. The LOS had been financially underwritten by a flamboyant South African soprano, Denny Dayviss. A designer friend of the latter's, Alan Sievewright, had drawn her attention early in 1967 to the 'Presenting Montserrat Caballé' LP and had soon found himself flying to Florence – where Caballé was singing in *Il pirata* – in order to open negotiations. His abiding memory is of seeing the diva backstage in her dressing-room with her son, Bernabé, tucked up in an improvised carry-cot, fashioned out of a shopping bag. The work she wanted to perform was more or less self-selecting: what else but the *Lucrezia Borgia* that had brought her such success in New York? But back in London the venue proved rather more problematic. The Society had already experimented with London's gargantuan Royal Albert Hall when presenting its inaugural concert performance of *Les*

Huguenots with Joan Sutherland, and would later settle happily into the altogether more congenial Theatre Royal, Drury Lane. But the *Lucrezia Borgia* had been booked into London's premier concert venue, the Royal Festival Hall, which, if acoustically problematic in the orchestral repertory, was thought to be little short of disastrous for the human voice. Montserrat was made aware of this problem and went to the hall in the company of the LOS's directors in order to test the sound. After some experimentation it was decided that things would go best with the singers not, as anticipated, lined up in front of the orchestra, but as they would be in the opera house, behind and higher up, with which arrangement Caballé declared herself satisfied.

After the successful completion of the *Salome* recording, Montserrat again found herself with time on her hands, since the whole of the July/August period had been set aside for her Salzburg performances. On such short notice, only opera houses in Spain, which in those days operated largely outside the international opera circuit, could contemplate mounting performances from scratch. As a result, the only significant work which Caballé undertook before returning to London was a bare handful of performances of *Roberto Devereux* in Bilbao and Oviedo during the second half of September, with her husband in the title-role, conducted by Manno Wolf-Ferrari.

For the duration of her stay in London, Caballé was accompanied by her brother Carlos, who regarded the London début as second in importance only to New York. Preliminary piano rehearsals were held in Denny Dayviss's Grosvenor Square apartment where the diva soon became a household fixture. As the night of 4 October approached, Caballé's composure started to desert her: it is, in a way, rather touching to imagine Montserrat, who for three years and more had already been the toast of New York, standing backstage at the Festival Hall in a state of extreme tension, feeling like a tightly wound spring. She had the unconditional support of all those around her, and the fact that the performance was being conducted by Joan Sutherland's husband, Richard Bonynge, gave her further reassurance since Bonynge was a noted singers' conductor. In the fashion of the New York AOS presentations, the opera was semi-staged to the extent that characters made entrances and exits and generally tried to manage without recourse to the two or three judiciously placed music-stands at the front of a raised acting area. Montserrat's voice was in particularly responsive form and she soon began to relax into the performance, the more so given the audience's manifest enthusiasm. At one such outburst she looked up into the nearby boxes to discover Sutherland beaming broadly back at her. As a contemporary review put it:

Caballé aroused the same degree of enthusiasm here that she had inspired in New York three years ago singing the same role. The hushed audience hung on her every note, marvelling at the lustrous quality of her voice and the flawless brilliance of her florid singing.[6]

Another point which emerged to a greater or lesser extent in all the reviews was the debt the London public owed the LOS for bringing the finest contemporary singers to London at a time when the Royal Opera House was evidently either unable or unwilling to do so. (The cast included another London débutant, Ruggero Raimondi, whose birthday this was.) The celebratory party afterwards took place at Denny Dayviss's apartment, where Caballé was moved to tell Sutherland how much she had enjoyed singing under the latter's husband, thereby repaying a compliment that Sutherland had paid her back in Philadelphia at the time of the *Norma* with Bernabé. It was a pleasure, Caballé observed, to perform under a conductor who seemed to be breathing and phrasing in sympathy with the singers, and who had such mastery of the *bel canto* style. She hoped that she would be able to work with him many times in future. At which point Sutherland interjected, 'For that, Montsy, you will have to go out and marry one of your own.' Giggling and wide-eyed, Caballé retorted, 'But I'm already married to a tenor!' Sutherland said, 'I know, Montsy. Bad move.'

Immediately after this performance Montserrat flew to the south of France in order to perform the same role in a house for which she had developed special affection, the Opéra de Marseille. But this was a fully staged production, directed by the very man who had effectively been responsible for making her New York début possible, Bernard Lefort. Montserrat then returned home to Barcelona, partly to be with her family in preparation for Christmas, and partly to give three performances of *Roberto Devereux* at the Liceo, which opened the 1968–9 season on 9 November, with her husband in the title-role and Piero Cappuccilli as Nottingham. In a recent book on the artistic history of the Gran Teatro del Liceo, this season is regarded historically as 'la consegración definitiva de la Caballé'.[7] The opera had not been given in the house since 1860 and had been mounted specially for the soprano despite some mutterings from the subscribers who were not familiar with the work and, worse, could not even go out and buy a recording since none then existed. In the event, the performances had, as the house's Spanish biographers put it, a most spectacular success, at which Caballé demonstrated that vocally she could do anything she wanted, combining coloratura, fine-spun lyrical lines, heroic declamation, exquisite *mesa di voce* and, of course, the by now legendary high *pianissimi*. And whilst in London, she had already entered into negotiations with EMI with a view to remedying the lack of a recording. Indeed, this latter proposition became the basis upon which her hitherto exclusive contract with RCA was to come to an end in order to encompass a whole series of major opera and recital projects with the rival English company.

At the heart of her hopes for this new contract was Caballé's desire to commit the 'Tudor Ring' of Donizetti's English queens to record. But just as she and Rudolf Bing were frustrated in their attempt to stage the 'cycle' at the Metropolitan by the New York City Opera's precipitate rush to do them first with Beverly Sills, so the recording project soon foundered when EMI found it more expedient (and certainly cheaper) to 'buy in' a ready-made American Westminster recording of *Roberto Devereux* made in London in the summer of 1969. But these disappointments lay some way in the future. For the time being it was one untrammelled success after another. During the first half of December 1968 Caballé returned to the Teatro Communale in Florence where, together with Richard Tucker and the now unfairly forgotten Mario Zanasi, she sang a series of performances of *Il trovatore* under the baton of Thomas Schippers. That given on the 11th would appear to have been broadcast; certainly a very tolerable pirate recording of the event has survived which provides us with a clear idea not only of the sensuous beauty of Caballé's voice at this time but also its sheer amplitude and stamina. William Weaver wrote of the first night (which took place on 3 December):

> I have never heard 'D'amor sull'ali rosee' sung more beautifully or more movingly. It was an answer to the critics who have attacked her for being a cold or lazy artist. Though every sound she made was lovely, there was nothing abstract about the singing. The sounds had meaning and emotional power. She also acted with noble dignity and conviction. Now she must record this opera.[8]

Alas, Weaver's imperative went unfulfilled. Although the *Trovatore* Leonora was one of Caballé's greatest roles, she was destined never to make a studio recording of it. Indeed, the obvious opportunity for this to happen was soon to pass her by: in the late summer of 1969 RCA made a new recording of the work, with Plácido Domingo in the title-role – his first complete opera recording – conducted by Zubin Mehta, two colleagues with whom Montserrat had already established the closest and most cordial of working relationships. But the Leonora was Leontyne Price, who remained under exclusive RCA contract and thereby came to make her second *Trovatore* for the company.

Caballé returned directly to Barcelona after these performances in order to begin rehearsals for what was rapidly becoming the regular Caballé Christmas/New Year slot at the Liceo. This year's novelties were twofold: a new production of Massenet's *Manon*, a role which she had been keen to repeat ever since her triumph in the work in Madrid; and Donizetti's *Maria Stuarda*, at least as much of a rarity in those days as the preceding *Roberto Devereux*. The three performances of *Manon* took place around Christmas, thus allowing Montserrat to pass most of the time at home with her family. Her des Grieux was the stylish French tenor, Alain Vanzo, and the performances met with great success notwithstanding the feeling that the skittishness of the character had been slightly overplayed in the early Acts. But the real triumph came with the opening of *Maria Stuarda* on 5 January 1969, in a new staging by Bernard Lefort, conducted by Reynald Giovaninetti. The Liceo's loyal and regular audience had only just finished their ovations for Montserrat's *Manon* when she had made even more friends by standing in for an indisposed Anja Silja and singing the role of Elisabeth in *Tannhäuser* on the evening following her own daytime dress rehearsal for *Maria Stuarda*. The Donizetti opera then received three performances in the space of one week to progressively more rapturous acclaim. After the last performance on 11 January, the management of the theatre made a second formal *homenaje* presentation to her, and her ovations continued, as the archivists of the house record, for over twenty-five minutes in an ever-deepening mountain of flowers.

Not surprisingly, Juan Antonio Pámias, the impresario acting on behalf of the *proprietaros* (private owners) of the Liceo entered into immediate negotiations concerning Caballé's future plans with the theatre. Following such stupendous successes in then unfamiliar *bel canto* works, it was surely time that she tackled the acknowledged summit of its repertory, Bellini's *Norma*. Montserrat still harboured – and for some while continued to harbour – misgivings with regard to her suitability for the role. This had led her to defer offers from both Paris and Milan. But she had also come to see, thanks to Sutherland's prompting, that sooner or later she would have to sing the role. Where else could she possibly contemplate so doing than in front of the loyal and enthusiastic Barcelonese audience, to whom – in deference to José Antonio Bertrand's wishes – she had always determined to offer her newest assumptions? She therefore agreed to the proposition, and in order to give them a Caballé Christmas show they would never forget, performances of *La traviata* and then *Otello* would precede it. She was now, indisputably, the queen of the Liceo.

*   *   *

With the exception of an extended excursion into the Milanese studios of RAI (Italian Radio and Television) to record *Ernani* for subsequent transmission with Bruno Prevedi, Peter Glossop and Boris Christoff, conducted by Gianandrea Gavazzeni, Caballé's next major project did not take place until March when she returned, yet again, to New York and began rehearsals for Allen Oxenburg's latest AOS presentation, Bellini's all-but-forgotten *La Straniera*. During these rehearsals for the performance on the 26th she whisked backwards and forwards almost daily to Philadelphia, together with the conductor Anton Guadagno, rehearsing there for a new production of *Lucrezia Borgia* which was due to open two days later. The Carnegie Hall concert had a by now wholly predictable triumph and a surviving recording offers ample proof of the reasons; not least Caballé's off-stage *pianissimi* roulades, seamless and ravishing, with which we are to imagine the character of Alaide drawing closer as she rows herself across a lake. Bearing in mind how often Caballé triumphed in New York during this period, one wonders whether she was not setting an unrealistic level of expectation amongst her audiences. When vocal miracles become commonplace, there is a danger that people's responses to them become dulled; and at this point in any great performing artist's career there comes a subtle but drastic shift in underlying critical response. No longer praised for what one can uniquely do – since this is now taken for granted – there is instead an increasing tendency to carp over relatively unimportant details in the artist's performance; much as one might stand before the Sistine ceiling and complain about Michelangelo's treatment of the trees in the landscape backgrounds.

In fact, Caballé had not yet reached this peak of critical saturation, either in New York or Philadelphia, as the contemporary reviews attest. But there is a sense in which, if not *hubris*, then certainly justifiable pride was coming before a fall. On 9 April Montserrat returned from Philadelphia to New York to give her first-ever solo recital there, in Lincoln Center's vast and acoustically inhospitable Philharmonic Hall. It set the pattern for what was to become, from her audiences' point of view, the most characteristic and, indeed, preferred form of contact. *The New York Times* gave extensive coverage to this major event:

Those who have thrilled to the singing of Montserrat Caballé in her many opera and concert performances here will probably be pleased, if not particularly surprised, to learn that a Caballé recital is like one long ravishing melody interrupted only by applause . . . Miss Caballé was in marvellous voice from the moment she began the Italian group that opened her programme . . . The soprano sang the old war-horses all right, but with embellishments and interpretations that renewed them almost miraculously and gave them the refinement, elegance and loveliness one might associate with fine porcelain. This began the evening's long melody, touched with the familiar Caballé graces: evenly matched tones, exquisite pianissimos, smooth crescendos and diminuendos. The audience – so big it overflowed on to the stage – was transported, and after Strauss's 'Wiegenlied', for example, it seemed the applause would never stop.[9]

The following morning, Montserrat was basking in the reviews in her suite in the Mayflower Hotel when Allen Oxenburg, who had been present at the recital, rang to invite her and her retinue to lunch. In addition to her brother and husband the party also included Miguel Zanetti and Denny Dayviss, who had not actually met the New York impresario. Oxenburg's apartment was only two blocks away facing Central Park, so the Caballé entourage set out on foot for their lunch appointment. After a couple of hours of conviviality Montserrat announced that she was tired and that, since she was flying back to Philadelphia the next day for an orchestral recital, she was returning to the hotel. Dayviss remained behind to talk operatic shop while the other three set out on the short walk back to the Mayflower. Half an hour later Oxenburg received a telephone call from Carlos: Montserrat had been injured in an accident. Dayviss and Oxenburg flew round to discover the diva in bed with her left leg propped up on a pile of pillows, crying piteously. Apparently she had started to cross the road when she had seen a taxi rapidly approaching, and so speeded up her step: but in so doing she had missed her footing and tripped, landing on her left knee, hitting the high metal-edged kerbstone. In agonizing pain, Montserrat immediately insisted that nothing on earth would get her into an American hospital: if she had to go to one, it was going to be in Barcelona.

In the event, a doctor friend of Oxenburg's from a nearby hospital came and made a preliminary diagnosis: Caballé had severed the lower tendons which hold the patella (or knee-cap) in place, and the patella itself was fractured. Arrangements were made to transfer her back to Barcelona, where surgery would be imperative. In the meantime, the wound was dressed and the whole leg set in a temporary plaster cast. Within a matter of hours, Caballé – inevitably leaving a string of cancellations behind her – was taken by ambulance to Kennedy airport, from where she caught an Iberia Airlines flight home. The plane was met at El Prat airport by an ambulance from the Clínica Quirón which whisked the soprano off to hospital. Five hours later she was undergoing surgery to replace the irreparable tendons and clamp the knee-cap back together again. After this procedure, the leg was again plastered and she remained in traction for the next three weeks, until a second minor operation was conducted during which a small metal plate was inserted underneath the patella and clamped by means of iron rods into the newly inserted tendons. In total, Montserrat spent just over six weeks in the clinic and remained in plaster for a little more than three months. The major casualty of this occurrence was her eagerly awaited début at La Scala, Milan, where she should have been rehearsing a new production of *Luisa Miller* from the end of April onwards, with a first night scheduled for 15 May.* She had no alternative but to withdraw, thereby setting the unfortunate pattern that marked her career at La Scala, which has borne the brunt of her cancellations through serious illness.

Thus far, Montserrat had turned her enforced inactivity to good advantage and had been busy studying the role of *Norma*. But her next major engagement was looming, a semi-staged concert performance of *Il pirata* for the London Opera Society, this time at the Theatre Royal, Drury Lane. This was due to take place on 22 June, but by mid-month Caballé had decided that although the one-off performance would not make the same physical demands on her as a run that was fully staged, she was not well enough to undertake the engagement. She therefore notified Denny Dayviss of her intention to cancel. The impresario, in desperation, flew to Barcelona and had prolonged discussions with both Montserrat and her brother: she could be spared most of the rehearsals, she could sit throughout, she would not have to make entrances and exits as dictated by the drama; anything, in fact, so long as she would simply come and sing. Dayviss's persuasive advocacy won the day, abetted by increasingly panic-stricken telegrams from EMI who were scheduled to start the first recordings under Caballé's new contract soon after the concert performance, as well as RCA, who had already booked the studio space for a recording of Donizetti rarities to be made in July. And, of course, the Caballé support system would be there in force, Carlos having decided to attend the performance and Bernabé singing Gualtiero.

In the event, Montserrat was very glad she had decided to come. She was thrilled with the theatre, whose operatic history is in fact far longer and more distinguished than Covent Garden's, and on the night found an audience responding to her every turn of phrase. At the start of the

---

* Technically, of course, these performances would not have been her house début, since she had already sung there in *Parsifal* in 1960. But they would undoubtedly have been regarded as such by the Milanese, given that Luisa would have been her first appearance in a principal role.

closing scene, having sat throughout the performance with her crutches discreetly at her side, the diva hauled herself to her feet, steadied herself against the music–stand and flung the crutches to one side. Arthur Jacobs wrote in *Opera*: 'she rose triumphantly over her disability: in sensuous quality, in power, in variety of expression, in phrasing and in distinct articulation of notes, her voice was thrilling.'[10] Frank Granville Barker was even more enthusiastic:

> Montserrat Caballé brings to Bellini every quality his music demands – a voice of ravishing radiance and warmth, flawless clarity and poise in fioriture, the ability to shape every phrase both elegantly and mean-ingfully, and a sense of vocal colouring that makes every word tell. She scaled heights of pathos in the Mad Scene which no other soprano could touch today . . .[11]

From this triumph Caballé flew straight to Rome where, in the space of four days, she made a recording of *Un ballo in maschera* with Flaviano Labó and Mario Sereni under Bruno Bartoletti for RAI. She then returned to London to begin sessions for a third disc of rarities – this time comprising long *scene* from Donizetti's *Belisario*, *Torquato Tasso*, *Gemma di Vergy* and *Parisina* – for RCA. Some jolly promotional material from RCA told us: 'Montserrat Caballé has discovered some of the most exquisite melodies you have never heard. [She] had a marvel-lous time. She could use her greatest asset: that *pianissimo* which tastes like angel cake.'*

In fact that *pianissimo* was even more conspicuous on the disc of Puccini arias, conducted by Charles Mackerras, which Caballé made shortly afterwards as her first recital record for EMI. Meanwhile there was the small matter of her début at the Arena di Verona to consider. She had recently been cut out of the plaster that had encased her leg for over twelve weeks and not surprisingly was obliged to use crutches in order to manoeuvre herself around. The whole leg had been badly wasted, and she had been informed by a physiotherapist that there was a danger of her losing full use of the quadriceps, as well as the possibility of circulatory problems arising at some point in the future. Even so, after her London triumph, she was no longer minded to regard her temporary physical disability as an insurmountable barrier to perform-ance; but this was reckoning without the Arena's vast tracts of space

---

* A second disc of Donizetti rarities was subsequently planned, and Montserrat remembers recording long *scene* from *Marin Faliero* and *Fausta* for it. But the disc was never completed and the two arias have remained unissued, presumably sitting in RCA's vaults in New York.

which all performers, even the fully fit, have difficulty negotiating. There was also the question of the audience's willing suspension of disbelief: should the youthful French princess Elisabeth de Valois really be hobbling around on crutches in an opera which already has one character – the Grand Inquisitor – doing just that? As a result of these considerations Montserrat reluctantly decided to cancel: but the Verona administration were extremely loath to take this on board. Every day they bombarded Carlos's office with renewed requests. In the end it was left to the persuasive powers of Jean Vilar to change Montserrat's mind. The legendary producer, together with his assistant Piero Faggioni, had been entrusted with these first-ever performances of Verdi's *Don Carlos* at the Arena. He believed all would be well and did what he could to abbreviate Elisabeth's entrances and exits (her first, a full-length perambulation of the whole stage, was entrusted to a double); and the designer, Luciano Damiani, provided a series of costumes whose long, flowing, almost floor-length sleeves went some way towards masking the soprano's otherwise all too visible means of support. Furthermore, the French princess's ladies-in-waiting were in fact two nurses from the hospital in Verona deputed to accompany the soprano on stage throughout the performance.

The performances have passed into operatic legend. This is hardly surprising when one considers the cast, which, apart from Caballé, included Plácido Domingo in his local début, Piero Cappuccilli as Rodrigo, Marquis of Posa and Fiorenza Cossotto as Princess Eboli. A pirate tape of the opening night has survived and reveals quite clearly what drove the Veronese (and tourists) to such ecstasies. But the final seal on what was clearly Caballé's night was set by her outrageous and, one would have thought, vocally impossible prolongation of Elisabeth's – and the opera's – final note from a climactic but brief high B to a sustained *fortissimo* which sees out the whole of the thunderous brass-laden ten-bar coda. During the rehearsals, Caballé had hinted to the conductor, Eliahu Inbal, that she would like to prolong this particular note somewhat, but he had advised her against so doing, pointing out that she would soon be out of harmony with the orchestration unless she was capable – which obviously no one was – of holding the note to the very end. On the opening night, to the conductor's amazement, she proved her point. The audience went mad, as they were to do at the Met some three years later when she did the same thing, but it is noticeable that in between times when she recorded the role under Carlo Maria Giulini she was obliged to be on better (if less thrilling) vocal behaviour.

Domingo sheds an amusing sidelight on the first performance when he recalls the scene which took place after it had finished. Apparently an egregious old claqueur had done the rounds of all the principals' dressing-rooms before the performance had started, with a view to securing guaranteed approval in exchange for hard cash. He was well known for this and harmless insofar as he wielded no influence with a genuine claque, the organized protestations of which have been the bane of most professional singers' lives. Evidently, Domingo as much out of charity as from any ulterior motive, slipped him some money; Cappuccilli refused, as did Montserrat; which left Cossotto, who alone would appear to have been lavishly generous. As the artists rolled out one by one for their curtain calls each was greeted with a salutation suitable to their emolument. Cossotto was greeted with screeches of approbation – 'Divina! diva!'; Cappucilli with 'Magnificent, but such a miser!'; Domingo with the oddly ambiguous (given that he had paid for it) 'Plácido, you're always placid.' But as Caballé awkwardly shuffled along the length of the footlights on her crutches, the claqueur fell momentarily silent and thoughtful. Then suddenly he yelled, 'Montserrat, go to Lourdes!'

Immediately after the run of five performances ended, Caballé flew to London, where she was to take part in further EMI recording sessions. The work was Verdi's *Requiem* and reunited her with Cossotto and Ruggero Raimondi. The tenor, perhaps a surprising choice for this work, was the powerfully intense Jon Vickers, and the conductor, Sir John Barbirolli in one of his last excursions into the recording studios. Montserrat found singing alongside Vickers a memorable experience and one which she was keen to replicate on stage; but the extraordinary rapport which sprang up between soprano and conductor was, like Barbirolli himself, destined to be short-lived. The principal memento of this is, of course, the recording itself. But the original brochure which accompanied the LP set contained a photograph of Caballé and Barbirolli together, in profile, facing each other, with the soprano's out-stretched arms resting on the conductor's shoulders, whilst he, in a wholly spontaneous and paternal gesture, holds her chin in his right hand. Bearing in mind that he had only recorded *Otello* less than two years previously, and that Montserrat never did in fact commit her Desdemona to disc, it is frustrating that their careers did not intersect earlier.

Back home in Barcelona, Caballé began preparing for the arduous schedule she had set herself for the Christmas/New Year period at the Liceo. In the immediate short term, she was still having to deal with the consequences of the severe wasting of the muscles in her left leg. It is from this residual handicap that all her subsequent problems of balance – and, in particular, climbing stairs – ultimately stem. Indeed, the forthcoming performances of *Norma* would be the first appearances she had made in public without the use of crutches in over nine months. By chance, she had even more time on her hands to devote to preparing her forthcoming début *Norma*s than Carlos's already leisurely schedule had originally allowed, since in September 1969 the orchestra of the Metropolitan Opera House went on strike, and Montserrat, who was contracted to sing more than a dozen performances of *Un ballo in maschera* and *Luisa Miller* there, suddenly found herself at a loose end. Rudolf Bing informed her that although she was formally released from her contract, he would ensure that her stipulated fees were nevertheless paid and subsequently sanctioned Caballé's hastily arranged performances of *Don Carlos* in Lausanne in mid-October.

Beyond these commitments, there was practically no professional work to act as a distraction from a period of intense musical preparation as well as gradual physical recovery. As a result she only finally appeared in *La traviata* on 21 December and with a not especially distinguished cast. *Otello* opened two nights later, with James McCracken in the title-role and Peter Glossop as Iago, thereby re-creating the Met's line-up from earlier in the year, this time under the baton of Anton Guadagno. According to Carlos the applause at the last performance continued for over one hour. Even so, there was a sense in which both soprano and audience alike were marking time, awaiting with bated breath the main event which everyone knew was in the immediate offing. Once the Liceo had closed its doors after the last performance of *Otello* on 30 December, the theatre went dark, but not inactive. The old house, its loyal public and its star soprano were all looking forward to launching a new operatic decade with a new production of the opera whose title role embodies the very concept of diva: *Norma*.

CHAPTER EIGHT

1970–1973: *Prima Donna Assoluta*

On 8 January 1970 Montserrat Caballé stood backstage at the Gran Teatro del Liceo in Barcelona, about to face the greatest artistic challenge of her career. The house was packed to overflowing with an audience – itself nervous with anticipation – many of whom had travelled from abroad simply to see this new production of Bellini's *Norma*. There was a general feeling that Caballé might just prove to be the true successor to Maria Callas in the role, which the Greek soprano had last sung right at the end of her stage career, at the age of forty-one, in March 1965. It is of course true that in the interim other sopranos had come forward to essay the role, notably Joan Sutherland and Elena Suliotis. But the one lacked temperament just as surely as the other suffered from an excess of it, shortcomings which effectively prevented either from giving the kind of fully rounded performance that Norma demands. As written, the role is not especially taxing in terms of *tessitura*: indeed, Caballé has always maintained that from this point of view the role of Imogene in Bellini's *Il pirata* is harder. What distinguishes it, however, from virtually all other contemporary tragic heroines is the sheer length of the part and the astonishing variety of emotional and dramatic situations it embraces.* No matter how familiar one becomes with the score, in the theatre just how long Norma actually *sings* never ceases to amaze: there always seems to be one more vocal hurdle to surmount. This is an impression reinforced by the dramaturgy of the stage action, which delays the heroine's first appearance for half an hour but then has her singing at the end of the opera for an unbroken forty minutes.

The opera is set during the Roman occupation of Gaul, the local inhabitants of which are governed by a caste of Druids, chief among whom is the high priestess, Norma. The loathed Romans are led by

---

* The great nineteenth-century soprano, Lilli Lehmann, was of the opinion that all three 'Ring' Brünnhildes, which she herself sang, were easier to perform than one Norma.

the proconsul, Pollione, whose task is to keep the natives in order. The latter, however, are only waiting for a signal from Norma to rise up against the occupying forces. What no one knows is that the supposedly chaste priestess has had a long-standing affair with the Roman leader and has already secretly borne him two children. And now, as Norma's people are clamouring for action, Pollione's affections have turned elsewhere: unknown to the heroine he is pursuing one of the novitiate priestesses, Adalgisa. As the opera unfolds we see Norma in a multiplicity of guises: authoritative religious leader calming her fractious people; devoted but guilt-racked mother; potential infanticide; rejected lover; and, in the memorable scene where she learns of Adalgisa's dereliction, sympathetic mother-confessor turned wrathful avenger. The emotional range of the role is therefore remarkably wide and Bellini's score reflects this emotional intensity at almost every turn, from the prayer-like invocation, 'Casta diva', to the baleful gloating of 'In mia man alfin tu sei'; from the coloratura optimism of 'Ah! bello a me ritorna' to the impassioned heroic declamation of 'Dormono entrambi'.

In recent memory, only Maria Callas had been thought to qualify as a great exponent of the role. And in some quarters there had even been reservations about her performance, focusing not surprisingly on the extent to which this pinnacle of the *bel canto* repertory should really be sung by an unequivocally beautiful voice. Moving deeper into the mists of vocal history, it is notable how few sopranos in the earlier twentieth century have risen successfully to the challenge of Norma. Only Rosa Ponselle would seem, by general consent, to have been fully worthy, although Giannina Russ and Ester Mazzoleni were both much admired. Evidently, then, this is a role which not only sorts out the girls from the women, but, from among the latter, the real *prime donne*.

As we have seen, Caballé had taken her time in coming to the role and, courtesy of her knee and the Met strike, had enjoyed a more than adequate period of preparation for her début performance. Nevertheless, she was worried as to how things would go. Apart from any musical considerations, these would be the first performances that she had given for more than eight months without the aid of crutches, and in which she would be obliged to move her still painful leg around the stage without the possibility of so much as a walking stick coming to her assistance. Nor did the last-minute defection of the scheduled Pollione, Mario del Monaco, ease the situation. Bruno Prevedi was hastily imported to sing the role, which certainly imposed no problems from Montserrat's point of view but rather unbalanced the vocal relationship between Pollione and his confidant, Flavio. Flavio had been carefully cast to afford a significant but untaxing début to Carlos Caballé's latest discovery, José Carreras, and even at this stage of his career, the great honking bronze of del Monaco's voice would have contrasted sharply with the silvery lyric tones of the twenty-three-year-old Carreras.

In the event, Montserrat had an unreserved triumph, which a pirate recording of the night noisily confirms. Even so, she was not entirely happy and she set about a revision of the role in time for the second performance three days later. If this seems an implausibly hasty time-scale, Caballé herself has spoken of how she approaches new roles and the priorities which enable her to make radical changes on a more or less spontaneous basis.

Whenever I prepare a new role the first thing I do is take the score and read it as if it were a book. Then the music is immediately inside me. Only after that do I go to the piano and play the score through. At this stage I only read the music, but just from that I know more or less what the words will be. If the composer is good, his music alone will tell me what the words that inspired him are. So if I read a piece of music for the first time and later hear it in the theatre or on a record there is never a difference between how it sounds and how I heard it inside me. You see, I *need* the music to speak to me in order to discover what a new work is like. I cannot begin my approach from the libretto, through the words. Of course poetry speaks to me, but in a different, more limited way. It is particular and specific, whereas music goes beyond that and deals with feelings, with the infinite. So I form my impressions of a new work not according to what a libretto tells me, but according to what the music, the composer's line, the whole sound tells me. After all, I am only an interpreter, a tool in the realization of a masterpiece, and I have to be inspired by the music if I am to serve it well. When a singer truly feels and experiences what the music is all about, the words will automatically ring true. This is logical because the meaning of the words is there, written into the music. Maria always said so too, both publicly and on the occasions when we spoke in private.

From these comments, two things emerge quite clearly. Firstly, for a singer so little given to the literary aspects of opera, there is obviously no need to establish 'concepts' of dramatic presentation: the music has become so 'interiorized' that a change in interpretation can be manifested simply by a change in vocal performance. Secondly, and perhaps most obviously, Caballé's views place her apart from virtually all the singers of what one might loosely term the 'post-Callas generation', most of whom, at least in interview, advocate a primarily text-based method of research and learning. The current fashion is to treat nineteenth-century

Italian opera as drama which happens to be sung, rather than as the more historically authentic phenomenon of a vehicle for singing which happens to convey drama. All of which leaves Montserrat as a proud survivor of an earlier operatic civilization. Yet unlike the dinosaurs this calls to mind, she can be a singer of lightning-fast musical reflexes and responses: hence the ability to rethink a role as demanding and complex as Norma within little more than seventy-two hours.

The second performance of the work at the Liceo on 11 January 1970 has unfortunately not been preserved, but a detailed contemporary review gives some indication as to the nature of the transformation:

> The first [performance] was certainly impressive, starting with a 'Casta diva' revealing perfect emission of tone and the most sensitive control of phrasing. The scene in which Norma contemplates killing her children was powerfully yet touchingly expressive, and there was tragic dignity in the final scene of self-sacrifice. As an interpretation, however, this Norma was not all of a piece: at times it was Caballé's own, but at others the undertones of Callas were too close for comfort. In 'Oh non tremare', for instance, where Norma taunts the faithless Pollione in fearsomely descending scales, Caballé seemed to be striving for the tigress qualities of Callas which are alien to her own artistic nature. As a result, she overweighted her tone and lost her usually impeccable sense of line. At the second performance she made it clear that she had completely rethought her approach to the role, and the result was a revelation. Here was a Norma presented in Caballé's own terms as a singer, a wholly *bel canto* Norma whose music was poured out in a seamless flow of tone, with *fioriture* that were unforced and always meaningful . . . With this second performance, Caballé left no doubt that the Norma of the 70s had arrived on the scene.[1]

Throughout the 1970s it was her portrayal of Bellini's Druid priestess that set the seal on her worldwide fame; as the new decade progressed it was the one role which she sang in all five of the great international opera houses – the Palais Garnier, La Scala, the Metropolitan, the Vienna State Opera and Covent Garden, in that order – as well as in innumerable other theatres and concert halls. And it was on 20 July 1974, in the Théâtre Antique at Orange, that she gave what she herself regards as the greatest single performance of her career.

In late January Montserrat returned to London for a further concert opera performance given by the LOS, as well as recording sessions for a disc of operatic duets for EMI with her husband. The opera was *Roberto Devereux* and was given at the Theatre Royal, Drury Lane, on the 29th of the month, with Bernabé in the title-role and Tatiana Troy-anos as Sara, conducted by Charles Mackerras. (The last time tenor and mezzo had met – in a New York City Opera *Carmen* the preceding year – Bernabé had broken poor Troyanos's nose, such had been the force with which he had thrown her to the floor at the end of Act III). With the exception of Domingo replacing Bernabé, this was the line-up which had been intended to form the basis of the commercial EMI recording of the work. In the event, Caballé's fans had to content themselves with the disc of duets from *Un ballo in maschera, Les Huguenots, Andrea Chén-ier, Manon Lescaut* and Donizetti's *Poliuto*, with not even so much as a bar of *Devereux* by way of compensation. Some critics reported that Caballé's concert performance began uncomfortably with signs of vocal strain (an assessment the soprano flatly refutes). But even for them the evening obviously picked up considerably as it went along, and by the end we read: 'her fiery delivery, her complete command of colour and dynamics were matched by absolute histrionic conviction: one really believed Elizabeth I had abdicated'.[2] The London Opera Society there-fore had good cause to be grateful for the close ties which had been forged between its management and the Caballés and which would continue for a further five years.

Sadly, the same could not be said of its progenitor across the Atlantic. The American Opera Society, which had already enjoyed a five-year connection with the Spanish diva and which could justly regard itself as having been instrumental in launching her international career, was suffering a terminal decline in its fortunes. The highlight of the AOS's 1969–70 subscription series of concert operas in Carnegie Hall was scheduled to be Rossini's *La donna del lago*, with Caballé as the lady of the lake, Elena. This was to have taken place on 21 January 1970, but was cancelled for financial reasons. Instead, a gala concert was offered, starring Caballé, as a consolation to the subscribers. So far, so good: but then things started to go wrong. In an unsigned circular dated 9 April the following text was sent to all the AOS's subscribers:

Late in January, Madame Caballé felt she would be indisposed on February 6th and her appearance was rescheduled for March 19th. Disinclined to come to the United States, once again Madame Caballé cancelled – and this time only two days before the performance and, as fate would have it, on the eve of the only postal strike in the history of the nation. Added to our humiliation was the frustration of not being able to reach our subscribers, despite an immediate mailing. The effect of this last cancellation was utterly demoralizing to our fund-raisers and was financially ruinous.

Ruinous indeed, though it is not clear why, with a postal strike looming, it should have been thought more expedient in the land of Bell Telephone and AT & T to have recourse to the US Mail. A thinly attended performance of Goldmark's *Die Königin von Saba* on 26 March (not involving Caballé) provided the *coup de grâce*. The proceedings of the AOS were formally wound up, but the extent to which the responsibility for this could be laid at Caballé's door is highly debatable. The *Donna del lago* performance had, after all, been cancelled from underneath her for 'financial reasons', clearly indicating that the AOS was already in serious trouble. But whatever the reasons for this, it is clear that Montserrat's non-appearance coupled with the losses sustained on *Die Königin von Saba* proved fatal for the AOS. Even so, New Yorkers did not have to go for long without its operatic novelties, since within less than two years Eve Queler had founded the Opera Orchestra of New York concert series, which dedicated itself to performances of rare repertory in Carnegie Hall, often with Montserrat Caballé in the principal role. And, over the succeeding years, Caballé and the Society's president, Allen Oxenburg, remained on the closest possible terms: he would accompany her on a La Scala tour to the Bolshoi; stay many times on her farm at Ripoll; and, in the summer of 1989, attend the Martís' silver wedding anniversary celebrations.*

The next in her planned long line of important European débuts duly took place in February 1970 when, on the 24th, she finally appeared at La Scala, singing the title-role in Margherita Wallmann's new production of *Lucrezia Borgia*. Probably the most significant long-term feature of this début was the collaboration between Caballé and Wallmann: the two established an immediate rapport, and were to work together again on many new productions in Milan, Paris, Barcelona, Nice and Orange. Following further performances of *Lucrezia Borgia*, this time at the Teatro della Zarzuela in Madrid, Caballé returned to Italy where, within one week, she recorded two performances for RAI: *La donna del lago* in Turin and Spontini's *Agnese di Hohenstaufen* in Rome.† Caballé's conquest of Italy continued, this time at the Teatro Costanzi (better known as the Rome Opera House), where she had a great success in May 1970. Local critics not only heaped praise upon the soprano but also manifested their gratitude for what was, astonishingly, the first-ever

---

* Allen Sven Oxenburg died prematurely in 1992, never having read this account of his dealings with Caballé. Of all the extraordinary people active in the world of opera, he was surely one of the most significant.
† The Spontini was conducted by Riccardo Muti, who was then at the very outset of his international career. It was the first collaboration of what was to prove a decade-long and very fruitful partnership.

performance of *Maria Stuarda* in the Italian capital. It so happened that one of the performances was attended by the famous Italian film director Luchino Visconti who, at least in Italy and England, was equally well known for his sumptuous and often controversial opera productions. His companion for the evening was Queen Frederika of Greece, mother of the present Queen of Spain, who was then resident in Rome. After the performance the couple presented themselves backstage in the diva's dressing-room where Caballé – no cinephile but very aware of Visconti's stage work with Maria Callas – proceeded to make self-deprecatory remarks about her acting skill by way of pre-emptive defence. Visconti brushed these aside and told her that her greatest assets were her remarkably expressive face and hands: so long as she used those to best effect, it was wholly unnecessary for her to engage in histrionics, for with a voice like hers, a look, a gesture were all she needed.

The performances in Rome continued until the end of the month, after which Caballé proceeded to Paris to begin rehearsals for her first performance there of Norma, due to be given in concert on 9 June in the Théâtre des Champs-Élysées with Bernabé as Pollione. On the afternoon of the performance, less than an hour before the Martís were due to depart for the theatre, Montserrat received a telephone call in her suite at the Hotel Raphael. It was Maria Callas, who had been unobtrusively attending several rehearsals, sitting at the back of the darkened auditorium unbeknownst to the performers. The two women had in fact first met two years earlier over a leisurely dinner in New York at Trader Vic's, attended also by Peter Andry of EMI and Callas's then constant companion, Pier Paolo Pasolini.

The Greek diva's message was simple: would Caballé and her husband care to come to dinner? At that very instant Bernabé was prostrate with nerves at the thought of the performance that lay ahead and, imagining that he was thereby staving off a fever, was propped up in bed under several layers of blanket and with damp towels wrapped round his head. In any event the Martís had other fish to fry and Montserrat politely declined, pointing out that she and her husband were about to depart in order to give a performance. Callas replied, 'But do you mean to say that you haven't been informed? The chorus has gone on strike and the performance has been cancelled.' Caballé accepted Callas's offer without a moment's hesitation now that her evening was so unexpectedly free, and on the instant Bernabé leapt out of bed, miraculously recovered.

That evening the couple enjoyed a superb meal at Callas's apartment on the Avenue Georges Mandel: then, after dinner, Montserrat and Maria fell to discussing musical matters, in particular the treatment and weight of voice necessary in some of the trickier coloratura passages in

Norma. By way of demonstration, both sang a passage from the trio finale to Act I. They listened intently to each other, and Callas went on to observe that the Spanish soprano in singing the line had strictly observed the letter of the score. She went on to echo exactly what Caballé had already been told by Joan Sutherland a couple of years earlier. 'You are exactly the right voice type for this role and for you much the best thing to do is simply to follow Bellini's line. You find your own way to the musical heart of the drama, just as I do, but through your own unique vocal qualities.'

Following a further round of recitals, with which Caballé increasingly interspersed her principal stage engagements, she returned to Rome in early July, together with her husband, to begin a series of intensive rehearsals with Gianandrea Gavazzeni in preparation for EMI's première recording of *Il pirata*, with the forces of RAI Rome. These sessions, which took place in the newly built Auditorium Foro Italico, were spread over an entire fortnight and proved a focal point for both Roman and visiting high society. Queen Frederika attended them, together with the Spanish Infanta Beatriz (King Juan Carlos's aunt), whilst another distinguished visitor was the eminent Turkish soprano, Leyla Gencer, who came partly out of interest in the work and partly because of her regard for the performers.* The recording studio, though functionally ugly in the modern manner, at least had the benefit of air-conditioning which was found to be vitally necessary in the sweltering Roman summer. Tempers inevitably became frayed from time to time, not least given the orchestra's characteristically unruly behaviour. Gavazzeni, very much a gentleman of the old school, found this difficult to deal with. At one session, with everybody in attendance, the orchestra refused to stop eating ice-creams and reading newspapers, despite the maestro's repeated calls to attention. The atmosphere was becoming extremely tense and unpleasant, and the singers – minus Montserrat who was sitting out in the auditorium with the royal visitors – looked on with mounting alarm. One of the male singers had already been noted for having an insouciant habit of 'adjusting' his groin periodically: in the current fraught situation, this had become incessant. Queen Frederika, meanwhile, was observing the whole proceedings avidly through her opera glasses. Suddenly, Gavazzeni, who was wearing a high-buttoned summer jacket, ripped at it with a yell of frustration, sending a shower of buttons into the orchestra. The tension, as the delinquent players stared on in disbelief, was palpable. Queen Frederika turned to

---

* Gencer and Caballé had in fact first become acquainted during the summer of 1965 when both were working at Glyndebourne.

Montserrat and inquired rhetorically, 'Do you think he does that often?' The soprano replied: 'I don't know, Your Majesty. But I'm sure the one I'm looking at always does *that*.' The session collapsed altogether when a member of the orchestra went round picking up the maestro's buttons and with mock ceremony offered them back to him. Gavazzeni instantly stormed out of the hall and it took the better part of a day's tough negotiations between the recording producers and the orchestra's union representatives before the sessions could resume.

The recording was nevertheless completed on schedule by 31 July, and after a barely two-week holiday back home, Caballé set out for London where she was due to record the role of Elisabeth de Valois in the full five-Act version of Verdi's *Don Carlos* for EMI. The conductor of this recording was Carlo Maria Giulini who, more than anyone else, had been responsible for the work's restoration to the repertory in the late 1950s. The opera was recorded in Walthamstow Town Hall with an all-star cast that included many of the newest operatic luminaries. In addition to Caballé there was Domingo (making only his second complete opera recording and the first with his compatriot), Sherrill Milnes, Ruggero Raimondi (in his first principal role on record) and Shirley Verrett (with whom Montserrat had most recently collaborated on a disc of operatic duets made for RCA the preceding year). The Royal Opera House Orchestra was engaged for these sessions at Giulini's behest, as the sole survivors of the ensemble with which he had first performed the work to such acclaim at Covent Garden in 1958.

Given the scale of the undertaking, it is perhaps surprising that the sessions proceeded as smoothly as they did and that the work was fully recorded on schedule by 31 August. When the resultant recording was released the following year the set became a best-seller and from the outset was accorded 'classic' status. Montserrat's principal remembrance of the event is the – alas – sole opportunity it gave her to work with Giulini, whose knowledge and love of the score and care and concern for the singers she regards as almost unparalleled. Although not readily drawn on the subject of the relative merits of her recordings, Montserrat nevertheless regards this *Don Carlos* as something quite exceptional – less on her own account, however, than for the overall standard of excellence which Giulini inspired.

During this period in London, Caballé entered into preliminary negotiations with the Royal Opera House with a view to making her already long-delayed début there. As ever when making an important first performance in a foreign house, she suggested that *La traviata* be given. Fortunately, Covent Garden had been planning a revival of the controversial Visconti production to round out the 1971–2 season, and so this time it looked as though Londoners would finally get to hear the Spanish diva in her natural environment. In the meantime, of course, it was left to the initiative of Denny Dayviss to give the adoring London public something more than future promises. For her forthcoming season of presentations at the Royal Festival Hall, Miss Dayviss had arranged, with the enthusiastic collaboration of Carlos Caballé, for Montserrat to appear not only in *Maria Stuarda* but also, most importantly, in *Norma*. And it was during this same period of negotiations that Caballé, with the permission of both her recording companies, was allowed to 'moonlight' and make a disc of French opera arias for Deutsche Grammophon with the New Philharmonia Orchestra conducted by Reynald Giovaninetti.

Then it was back to America, where on 3 October she returned to the Metropolitan Opera House in order to sing Amelia in *Un ballo in maschera*, with Plácido Domingo as King Gustavus. As with the Met *Traviata*s three years previously, Caballé found herself singing opposite a different tenor at each performance: Domingo was speedily followed by Carlo Bergonzi – whom Caballé remembers fondly for his ability to calm the nerves of all those around him by his relaxed stage demeanour and effortless vocalism – and Richard Tucker, among others. On the other hand, the baritone Robert Merrill was a permanent fixture: he sang the role of Renato to Montserrat's Amelia at every one of her numerous Met performances, as well as being her frequent Conte di Luna and Germont Père. Montserrat recalls him as having probably the most sheerly beautiful baritone voice of any of her collaborators, although both Milnes and Cornell MacNeil were more accomplished stage performers. Merrill's problem was remembering the words: one night in *Il trovatore*, during the Act IV duet, Caballé was astonished to hear the baritone singing the cabaletta to the words 'L'ho dimenticato, l'ho dimenticato' ('I've forgotten it'). And on one occasion, having boasted to the young Carreras, who was singing Alfredo, that he had sung the elder Germont more than 300 times at the Met alone, the tenor was convulsed to hear Merrill sing the opening words of 'Di Provenza il mar, il sol' on virtually every single line of the first verse.

Caballé's stay in New York was this time punctuated by a major stint in Chicago where, on 22 October, she made her belated début at the Lyric Opera in – inevitably – *La traviata*.* The new production by Giorgio De Lullo was designed by Pier Luigi Pizzi and described by

---

* She had originally been contracted to début at the Lyric Opera in October 1966, singing Desdemona in *Otello*. In the event, this coincided with the ninth month of her pregnancy, and therefore never took place.

Roger Dettmer – the music critic of the *Chicago American* and a long-term Callas fan who had covered all the Greek diva's performances in that city in the 1950s – as 'stupefyingly sumptuous'. He was equally impressed by the star soprano's performance.

> Montserrat Caballé made her Lyric début as Violetta in a conception so thought out and at the same time so spontaneous, that one must recall Callas of the period 1954–8 for comparison. The dedication that Caballé now brings to her characterization is new since I saw her in Dallas as the Countess Almaviva two years ago; she can have no peers today, surely, as the world's leading *lirico-spinto*.[3]

The enthusiasm was not shared, however, by the Chicago-based contributor to the New York Metropolitan's magazine, *Opera News*, Claudia Cassidy: 'Miss Caballé . . . has ballooned to proportions no costume can modify. The lovely face and glossy hair remain, but that glossy voice of such rare beauty was not in full estate, not in song and not in crucial recitative.'[4] This reviewer also berated the production for extolling bad taste – 'typical of the staging is that papa Germont keeps his hat on in the garden scene' – and complained that Act I resembled nothing so much as a 'Second Empire brothel'. It is worth remembering though, that Cassidy was the critic whom Michael Scott describes as 'an abject fan' of Maria Callas.[5] And, given that Verdi wished the opera to be set in contemporary (i.e. 1853) Paris, it's fair to ask what else should Violetta the courtesan's salon be but a *Deuxième Empire* bordello? Even so, Cassidy's critique raises an interesting question, and one which, though unspoken, underpins the reviews of many critics, including some of those written on the occasion of Caballé's Covent Garden début in the same role, namely: is it acceptable for large, statuesque women to appear on the operatic stage singing consumptives or fey romantic heroines?

What this polarized critical debate centres around is the question of verisimilitude and how it stands in the delicate critical balance with an audience's presumed 'willing suspension of disbelief'. Those who have trouble accepting on stage a fat Violetta or Mimì should logically balk at the idea of a black Cherubino or a six-foot Alberich. Perhaps there are some who do. But surely the relevant criterion is not one of cinematic plausibility but the ability of any singer to incarnate the role through his or her singing of it. In what way should it aid an audience's involvement in Violetta's plight that the singer convincingly resembles a consumptive? The terminally ill do not sing. It is left to the artistry of the individual to convince simply by the power of singing. This, after all, is why opera is opera and not some other art form, least of all spoken drama with added music, as certain musically ignorant producers today seem to regard it. In this context, it is worth recalling Bellini's words to his inexperienced last librettist: 'Carve in your head in letters of adamantine, "the opera must draw tears, terrify people, make them die, *simply through singing*".'

It is also worth positing the modern-day feminist standpoint, expressed at its most combative and pungent by Catherine Clément.[6] She, nauseated by the posthumous Callas bandwagon of endless books, compilation discs and fan clubs – 'leave this woman alone, whose job it was to wear gracefully your repressed homosexual fantasies' – suddenly recalls that there is an alternative.

> I am remembering . . . the image of a fat woman. A tremendous pile of meat that sings for us, and is *alive*. She is tremendous, a fat lady who knows how to turn her weight into opera. Her name is Montserrat Caballé . . . fixed superbly in her song, attentive to vocal perfection alone, she sings as if she sought to banish the memory of the one who sacrificed her voice to the perfection of a body that finally conformed to death. Oh, Caballé . . . never get thin. Stay buried in life . . . Thank you for being so, in the midst of those masculine wings flapping their useless hands, their empty hands all around you. Never will there be anyone like you.

If hardly the last word in graceful compliment, Clément's admiration is nevertheless sincere, as the rest of her book makes clear. Less than twenty years separates the review of Caballé's Chicago Violetta and the above quotation, but the underlying philosophical standpoints belong to different worlds. Today we seem to be coming full circle in our appreciation of what it is that makes opera singers unique: first and foremost, they sing opera. And those who sing it best are a distinct and select breed. Effectively they define what the genre is all about and practise it in such a way that if, for example, an audience were to find something intrinsically amusing in the sight of Caballé's Mimì in Act I, one can be certain that it would not be giggles that were being stifled by the end of Act IV. For this kind of musical magic, the verisimilitude thought to be demanded by an audience conditioned by cinema and television is a poor alternative.

Christmas 1970 was as usual spent in Barcelona, allowing Montserrat not only to be with her family but also to offer the Liceo regulars an extended conspectus of her repertory. For the first time she performed the opera which had made her famous, *Lucrezia Borgia*, in her home house. Predictably she had a triumph, but it was one which was shared with José Maria Carreras (as he was then styled) in the role of Lucrezia's son, Gennaro – his first-ever performance as a principal. He remembers:

> I look back on the Barcelona première of *Lucrezia Borgia* on 19 December 1970 as my real début. I cannot forget just how much Montserrat trusted in my abilities. Simply that a soprano of her status had expressed a desire to sing with a total unknown was so news-worthy in itself that great interest focused on me even before the performances. I felt wonderful because a truly great artist like La Caballé believed in me and it was her belief that gave me strength. Since then, I have appeared with her on stage more than 250 times and on every occasion I have fallen under her spell. I just fall in love with her right there on the stage and whenever I sing with her I'm a lost man. Of all the prima donnas I have worked with, she more than anyone *becomes* the person she is portraying. In this she is simply incredible. Perhaps the best example was the *Adriana Lecouvreur* we did together in Tokyo in 1976. No one before that, and certainly no one ever since, has sung with me so perfectly in character as she did that night.*

The *Lucrezia* was only one of a hat trick of 'home' performances given by Caballé across the Christmas and New Year period. *Il pirata* opened on 3 January 1971 and can lay claim to having been the ultimate family show, since in addition to Montserrat as Imogene and Bernabé as Gualtiero, Carlos Caballé's eight-year-old eldest daughter, Isabel, made her stage début in a mute role as Imogene's son. At the final curtain after the mad scene, by all accounts a further one ensued in the audience, with wave after wave of deafening cheers and yelling greeting the performer. Even now, however, Caballé's total enslavement of the Liceo audience was not yet over, for on 10 January she gave the first of a series of four performances of *La bohème*. The tenor who sang Rodolfo opposite her for the first time was also making his Liceo début. His name was Luciano Pavarotti, well known even then, though mainly for his association with Joan Sutherland. Montserrat retains fond mem-ories of his collaboration: although she undoubtedly worked more extensively on stage and in the recording studio with both Domingo and Carreras, there is perhaps a sense in which the pairing of Pavarotti and Caballé recalls the great *monstres sacrés* of nineteenth-century opera such as Grisi and Mario. So it is all the more frustrating that their

---

* Happily this was broadcast by NHK television and has been widely circulated in pirated copies. The flirtatious interplay between the two principals bears out the truth of Carreras's assertion.

recorded joint legacy should feature none of the great *bel canto* works of the early nineteenth century.

In reviewing Puccini's work for *Opera*, Gilbert Price came down firmly on the musical side of the operatic debate when he wrote: '*La bohème* had in Caballé a Mimì whose singing was so touchingly beautiful that her physical unsuitability for the role seemed unimportant.'[7] The third performance, on 14 January, must have been an unusual event, since the evening was styled 'Beneficio con Bandeja a favor de los empleados permanentes, porteros y acomodadores' (or, 'Benefit, with tray, in aid of the full-time staff, doormen and ushers'). This takes a little explaining. It has to be borne in mind that at this time and, indeed, right up until 1981, the Liceo was a privately owned and unsubsidized theatre. The consortium of owners had many years previously appointed Juan Antonio Pámias as impresario, and all decisions relating to repertory, casting and staging were left to him within the overriding stipulation that at no time was the opera to incur a deficit: if it did, he himself was financially responsible to make good the shortfall. The permanent front-of-house staff were not well paid under this arrange-ment and the temporaries functioned on more or less the same basis as the notorious *ouvreuses* – box-openers – at the old Paris Opéra who relied for their income on gratuities, forcibly solicited if necessary. On this night, a table was laid out in the centre of the Liceo's main foyer and on a ceremonial cloth, flanked by a pair of ornate candelabra, an enormous tray was set for the purpose of receiving large-denomination bank notes from the circulating audience. It would be a brave man or woman who, under the watchful eyes of the staff, failed to make the necessary gesture.

Evidently the singers thought so too, since they also donated their fees, although this gesture would not have much helped to swell the coffers. Throughout the thirty-odd years of the Pámias regime, the world's greatest singers performed regularly at the Liceo for a fraction of what they could expect to earn in Italy, Germany or America, partly out of regard for Pámias and the impossible juggling act he was expected to perform economically, and partly out of love for the beautiful and historic theatre. Montserrat, who in 1968 had reputedly been paid $10,000 for a single New York recital, sang at the Liceo from 1962 to 1981 (the Pámias years), never once receiving more than 40,000 pesetas (or £200) for any of her performances, with the exception of the one night previously mentioned when she miraculously doubled her earn-ings by being paid Anja Silja's fee. Indeed, for some other performances, Montserrat agreed to be paid the contractual sum applicable to daily manual workers agreed at union minimum rates: 600 pesetas. For the entire batch of Mimìs, Caballé was paid the equivalent of £100. When stories are told of the legendary greed of star sopranos – not to mention that of the agents who promote and exploit them – it is salutary to contemplate the astonishing example set by both Caballés in their dealings with the Liceo.

Continuing the steady, planned progress by which she was making her débuts as a principal in all the major European houses, Caballé next travelled to Naples, where she was due to sing in a new production of *Il trovatore* at the Teatro San Carlo, with Ludovic Spiess as Manrico, Peter Glossop as Count di Luna and the appropriately named Biserka Cvejic as Azucena, conducted by Giuseppe Patanè. Unfortunately, the Neapolitans took against the tenor and greeted his rendition of 'Ah si, ben mio' with jeers and catcalls. Spiess, already unnerved by the sepulchral silence that had greeted his every utterance, was devastated and began to signal desperately to Caballé that, though still in mid-scene and with the potential catastrophe of the cabaletta – 'Di quella pira' – still to come, he proposed to leave the stage. She tried to reassure him, but the wall of booing only continued, at which point the soprano lost her temper, strode forward to the front of the stage and held up her arms in an imperious command for silence. On the instant the 3500-strong audience fell quiet and, as Montserrat tells the story, she realized for the first time the genuine power which, as a diva, she held – quite literally – in her own hands.

She peered out into the now stonily silent auditorium and said, 'You have paid for your seats, so of course you have every right to protest at our performance, but not until the scene has finished. You will let him sing the rest of this scene.' She motioned to Patanè to continue the performance, whereupon the conductor launched into the fiery introduction to the second half of Manrico's aria. Spiess was horror-stricken and, facing Montserrat upstage with his back to the audience, said, 'But they don't want to listen to me.' Caballé replied, 'Never mind about them. I shall stay on stage for the rest of the scene so you can sing "Di quella pira" to *me*.' He did so, and capped the single verse given with a resounding top C which he even managed to prolong until cut off by the descending curtain. Vulgar, no doubt, but guaranteed to win applause, especially in Naples, where the audience erupted in cheers. Spiess was grateful to Montserrat, and she herself had learned a valuable lesson in the mysterious and potentially dangerous art of direct confrontation with a volatile audience. This would stand her in good stead in the years to come.

After a handful of miscellaneous concerts and recitals, Montserrat returned to Barcelona so that she could spend some time with her infant son. Fortunately, Bernabé was not engaged to perform at this time either, so that, until Caballé's journey to Milan in early April, she had the rare and welcome opportunity of living *en famille*. The return to La Scala was for a much-heralded new production of *Maria Stuarda*, mounted, like the previous year's *Lucrezia*, specifically for the soprano. And again the stage director was Margherita Wallmann, this time working with designs by La Scala's resident scenic magician, Nicola Benois. The opera had in fact been premièred at La Scala in 1835, having been banned the previous year in Naples where, according to legend, the two *prime donne* – Anna del Serre and Giuseppina Ronzi-de Begnis – had brawled violently during the scene where Mary Stuart forcibly reminds Elisabeth of her illegitimacy ('figlia impura di Bolena', etc.). No such controversy surrounded this production, though looking at the picture taken backstage (see illustrations) one might be forgiven for wondering if history was not about to repeat itself. Again, one of these performances has survived on pirate disc, but in sound so distant and murky that it is hard to draw positive conclusions. Even so, the great confrontation scene between the two queens – surely the reason for this otherwise unremarkable work's return to the repertory – seems relatively underpowered, for all Caballé's evident attempts to bolster her tone and intensify her declamation. One has only to turn to either of her two slightly later concert performances in London and Paris to hear the authentic frisson missing in Milan.* Even so, the Callas authority, Stelios Galatopoulos, evidently thought highly of the occasion:

> In moments of noble humility, tenderness and melancholy, she has an extraordinary sensitivity that never fails to touch the listener's heart. It is because of this that I feel that Maria Stuarda is Caballé's best Donizetti role . . . It was in the confession scene [at the close of the opera] that Caballé became incomparable. Her voice had all its purity all the time, and never for a moment became merely a beautiful voice in isolation, as it sometimes does. Here Caballé achieved with her own means what as a rule only genius can do.[8]

It is all the more sad, therefore, that in the on-going saga of bad faith exhibited by EMI, Caballé never recorded this, one of her greatest roles, and that in the same year the recording company again preferred, at no

* Or indeed to continue listening to the fill-up included as a comparison on the discs, in which a clearly axe-mad Leyla Gencer so vehemently demolishes her Elisabeth that the audience breaks into spontaneous applause mid-sentence.

cost to themselves, to distribute a ready-made *Maria Stuarda* starring Beverly Sills.

After this reconquest of La Scala, Caballé's next assault on a major European operatic bastion was her effective début as an acknowledged prima donna (rather than the young aspirant who had sung there in the late 1950s) at the Vienna State Opera House. But before the opening night of the chosen work, *Il trovatore*, on 15 May, the Caballés made an excursion to London in order to sing a one-off concert performance of *Norma* at the Royal Festival Hall, presented by Denny Dayviss. Almost as a private joke, she had cast the opera for two married couples: Montserrat as Norma with Bernabé as Pollione, and Fiorenza Cossotto as Adalgisa, with her husband Ivo Vinco as Oroveso. The good-natured London operatic public was not bothered by this blatant nepotism, even if the distaff side of the relationships was felt to be much the more distinguished, in stark contrast to the Parisian public some eighteen months later who took exception to this and manifested their displeasure in no uncertain fashion. In London, however, Montserrat's triumph was complete.

Montserrat Caballé has become the Norma of the 70s. The reception which she received at the concert version of Bellini's opera at the Festival Hall on April 26 could only be compared to those once accorded to Callas at moments of similar triumph. Caballé does not have the dramatic presence of the older artist . . . On the other hand, [her] voice has none of the ugly tone and uncontrolled vibrato which marred Callas's singing . . . Caballé is in the same class as Callas because she acts with her voice as Callas did – and what a fine instrument it is! . . . Technique is the basis of *bel canto* singing, but the great divas have always given something more, and Caballé has the ability to thrill by the harder sound and to melt with the beautiful *pianissimo* note. Such qualities make her the foremost interpreter of the role of Norma today, a great experience to hear . . . 'È manca la diva?' it was recently asked. Not while Caballé is still singing Norma.[9*]

It was in this spirit of critical euphoria that she should have been wafted to Vienna in order to win over the notoriously recalcitrant Viennese. Unfortunately, she became unwell and, though hoping right up to the last rehearsal to be able to appear, she felt so nauseous on the eve of the *Generalprobe* that in the event she was obliged to cancel. Such

---

* In fact, far from *still* singing Norma, this was only Caballé's sixth-ever public performance.

was the disappointment amongst the Staatsoper audience that the hastily summoned replacement became the object of some boorish behaviour after her first aria, leading the management of the house to the desperate expedient of lowering the safety curtain in mid-scene. Caballé, meanwhile, consulted a doctor and soon discovered to her delight that she was pregnant. Thus reassured as to the grounds of her malaise, she was free to return at the end of the following month, when she was accorded the honour of singing at a State gala which consisted of a single performance of *Don Carlos*.

Caballé spent most of July and August commuting between Barcelona and London. At home, she and Bernabé had recently completed negotiations for the purchase of a derelict farm property some 100 kilometres to the north of Barcelona in the pine-forested foothills of the Pyrenees, close to a town called Ripoll. Parts of the farmhouse dated back to the sixteenth century and there was a large abandoned granary within view of the house for which the couple had their plans. They instructed an architect who had come to their attention while he was supervising the refurbishment of the Liceo, to draft designs for the conversion and extension of the buildings. When these were completed some two years later the farm would become the focal point of Montserrat's domestic existence.

The trip to London involved a further concert performance presented by Denny Dayviss (this time with Carlos Caballé's collaboration) at the Festival Hall – *Maria Stuarda*, again with Shirley Verrett as Elisabeth and introducing José Carreras to the London public for the first time. The rehearsals for this performance were slotted in and around the sessions for Caballé's recording of Puccini's *Manon Lescaut* for EMI with Plácido Domingo; and this in turn was followed by the recording of an all-Verdi recital which concentrated, in contrast to the earlier 'Verdi Rarities', on the composer's popular, mainly late repertory. Montserrat was, of course, mindful of the fraught progress of her last pregnancy and was keen to avoid any obvious strain or overwork which might cause complications. After all, she was in her late thirties and indisputably overweight. As a result, scheduled commitments for the rest of the year were, where possible, deferred. But two she was determined to fulfil. The first was the recording of *Pagliacci*, which duly took place in London's Walthamstow Town Hall in August for RCA, with Domingo (as Canio) and Sherrill Milnes; and the second was the honour of again being asked to perform in New York at the opening night of the Metropolitan Opera House season on 20 September, this time in *Don Carlos*. But her doctors in Barcelona, where she had returned after the London sessions, were strongly against any further professional exertions, and the by now seven-months-pregnant Caballé had to cancel her appearances.*

Unfortunately, by early November all the signs were that history was about to repeat itself, and she was admitted to a clinic in Barcelona for continuous observation. By mid-month the doctors were sufficiently worried to suggest that a further Caesarean section be performed. As a protracted period of labour showed no signs of coming to an end, the doctors intervened on 15 November and Montserrat was thereby delivered of her second child – and only daughter – who was promptly named after her mother. This now effectively brought the tally of Montserrat Caballés in the family to three: the diva herself; her own daughter; and her brother Carlos's second daughter, born in 1965 and destined to become her aunt's personal secretary. To avoid confusion, the soprano remained Montserrat, her niece became known as Montse, and her daughter as Montsita. No such fine distinctions of nomenclature, however, have ever come to the rescue to help sort out the problem of a family which even today contains three Carlos Caballés – father, son and grandson.

But there was one sad aspect to this addition to the family, given that Montserrat had always cherished the ambition of having three children. The consultant gynaecologist and obstetricians were quite adamant: this was to be her last child.

Caballé was not scheduled to sing again until the première of a new production of *Luisa Miller* due to open at the Liceo in the first week of January 1972. She spent the whole pre-Christmas period at home with her children attempting daily exercises to restore the function and strength of the abdominal muscles, inevitably weakened by the Caesarean. In the event, she was called upon to put her powers of recovery to the test sooner than anticipated since the Liceo ran into a crisis at Christmas when, with less than forty-eight hours' notice, Katia Ricciarelli – another of Carlos's artists – cancelled what would have been her house début in *Don Carlos*. Caballé agreed to Pàmias's desperate plea to take on the four scheduled performances, which reunited her with Shirley Verrett as Eboli and so gave the Liceo regulars an unexpected seasonal gift. And if any of those present worried as to how the surgery might or might not have affected Caballé's vocal projection, they were soon reassured: 'her fans were delighted to find that the safe delivery of her second child had left the singer's voice completely unharmed'.[10] In fact, these unscheduled appearances served a useful turn in preparing

---

* Caballé was replaced by Martina Arroyo.

her for the subsequent *Luisa Miller*, which had not been seen at the Liceo for more than a century. Together with Carreras as Rodolfo, she celebrated her return to full performing health.

In the on-going series of début performances in European houses, 1972 was the year in which the majority of those that had yet to see Caballé were duly won over. First in sequence was the Teatro la Fenice, the exquisite principal house in Venice where Rossini's *Semiramide* and Verdi's *Ernani, Rigoletto* and *La traviata*, among others, all had their premières. Strangely, however, given her preference for making débuts in the last opera, Caballé chose instead to sing *Roberto Devereux*, perhaps out of a desire to establish unequivocally her *bel canto* credentials with the historically aware Venetians. If, indeed, this was her motivation it was not ill-advised, since the press reviews were amongst the most adulatory – and detailed – she had ever received.* And it took the Italians, who could afford to take their own repertory on trust, to ignore the *sense* of Caballé's singing and to concentrate instead on its qualities as pure sound. Thus, under the title 'Il miracolo della Caballé', the critic of *Il Gazzettino* wrote:

> Caballé's singing is extremely emotional . . . But this is an emotional-ism that has nothing to do with sentimentality – rather, it is inherent in the very sounds she makes, such as today one only hears in the 'interiorized' or self-communing tones of Sviatoslav Richter.[11]

After this it was off to the São Carlo in Lisbon – scene of her earliest international guest appearances whilst still at Bremen – in order to sing a series of *Normas*. Thereafter, on 26 March, she appeared for the first time in a full-length opera in Paris. Admittedly, this was still not at the Palais Garnier nor, indeed, even in a staged performance. Instead, she sang *Maria Stuarda* in concert at the Salle Pleyel, again with Carreras but this time with the tempestuous Michèle Vilma in place of Shirley Verrett. A recording of this performance has survived and, as conducted by Nello Santi, shows all the flair and dramatic vehemence otherwise lacking at La Scala the previous year.

Most of the following two months was spent back in America where the Met had scheduled further performances of *Don Carlos* as a conso-lation to Montserrat for having missed the opening night of the season. The cast included Franco Corelli in the title-role, Sherrill Milnes as Posa, Grace Bumbry as Princess Eboli and Cesare Siepi as King Philip,

---

* Caballé has never been one of those artists who affects indifference to press reports and criticism. After every first night the coffee table wherever she happens to be staying groans under the weight of newsprint.

with Francesco Molinari-Pradelli conducting. The matinée on 22 April 1972 – a live Texaco broadcast – became very fraught by the last Act. As usual, Corelli was in an advanced state of hysteria from habitual stage-fright. Montserrat was already standing in the wings waiting to go on stage for the soprano's principal aria, 'Tu che la vanità', when Corelli suddenly rushed blindly across the backstage area and shot past the soprano, in the process striking her fiercely in the stomach with his elbow. She staggered backwards and was caught by Cesare Siepi who, while supporting her, actually broke one of his fingers. Completely winded and in considerable pain, she imagined that she would be unable to go on: but it was too late, for the beautiful orchestral introduction was already well underway. Groggy, she was manoeuvred on to the stage and only then realized that she was expected to deliver her great set piece feeling sick and disorientated. A perfectly decent pirate record-ing of this performance is in circulation and reveals that the soprano got through it without the least mishap. She herself attributes this recovery to the sudden access of fury she experienced at the tenor's unexplained and unapologized-for behaviour. This adrenaline high – if physical low – is presumably what prompted her to repeat her old Veronese trick of hanging on to the climactic high B throughout the opera's closing bars. The effect on the audience in the theatre may be imagined. The listeners to the live relay on the radio were no less moved, if the response of Renata Tebaldi is anything to go by. The Italian soprano immediately rang the Metropolitan's switchboard and had her-self put through to Caballé's dressing-room where, after paying fulsome compliments, she had one burning question: 'How ever do you manage to sing that note? The next time we meet up you are going to show me how to do it!'

In between these *Don Carlos*, Montserrat commuted to Philadelphia where she sang in the production of *Norma* originally mounted for Joan Sutherland with Caballé's husband, though ironically she herself was now singing with Pedro Lavirgen, with Richard Bonynge conducting. The doyen of opera critics in America, Irving Kolodin, wrote about these first-ever Caballé US Normas in the *Saturday Review*:

It was reasonable to expect that a singer of her vocal fluency would find Bellini's florid line congenial to her. What is unexpected is the serious effort she has expended to make something unusually credible of the characterization. She earns her place with the greatest Normas of all time not only by some ethereally beautiful singing, but also by her disposition to the mother rather than the priestess in Norma's nature.

This last raises an interesting point, perhaps connected with the fact that Caballé, unlike most of her great predecessors in the role, actually did have 'miei figli' to consider in real life.

Between these commingled *Don Carlos* and *Norma*s Caballé managed to fit in, on 11 April, what had long since become one of the hottest events in the New York musical calendar: her annual appearance at Carnegie Hall. And she remained in New York right through to the end of the 1971–2 season at the Metropolitan Opera House, for this year, 22 April was not just the end of the season but also the end of an era. A very special gala was mounted in order to honour the retirement of the lately knighted Sir Rudolf Bing, who had almost single-handedly guided the fortunes of the Met, its singers, conductors and directors, for virtually the entirety of the post-war period. The tall, patrician, Viennese-turned-English intendant entertained no very high opinion of the majority of those around him, particularly the singers, and occasionally voiced his feelings on the subject. During one such diatribe he described star singers – perhaps with a certain Italian tenor particularly in mind – as no better than waiters and horse thieves who, because of a throat deformity, had some claim on our attention; but who remained horse thieves none the less. Exceptionally, however, he seems to have had the highest regard for Montserrat. Bernabé remembers sitting with Bing during a rehearsal of *Un ballo in maschera* when the latter turned with tears in his eyes and said, 'That is the most extraordinary sound I have ever heard from a singer. It is a miracle. No one has ever sung like this before and no one will ever sing like it again. Think yourself lucky to be hearing it.' In fact, Bernabé recalls thinking at the time, 'But she always sings like this!' It was only with the passage of the years that he came to appreciate the truth of Bing's assertion.

Had a bomb dropped on Lincoln Center on the night of Bing's fare-well, the world of opera would have ground to a halt for at least a decade: indeed, scanning the list of performers, one wonders how houses in Milan, Paris, London and Vienna managed to stay open. Amidst an unending procession of great singers, Montserrat rightly took her place as one of the newest. She deliberately declined the offer of a solo aria, contenting herself instead with the Act II duet from *Manon Lescaut* with Plácido Domingo. In so doing, many people present felt that they were witnessing the renaissance of that rare operatic phenomenon, a great soprano/tenor partnership, such as had been seen in the 1950s with Callas and di Stefano and in the 1960s with Tebaldi and Corelli. Already the Spaniards had recorded three complete operas together and were about to commit two more to disc during the coming summer. (In the summer of 1973 they would record two more.) They had appeared together on stage on numerous occasions, stretching as far back as 1965. And Carlos Caballé was now handling all Domingo's Spanish contracts and sundry other European engagements. As Montserrat said in interview: 'I have sung many things with Luciano, and even more with José. But with Plácido I sang everything.'

She remained in North America giving a series of recitals, one of the most notable of which took place in Vancouver in May, where Irving Guttman, artistic director of the Vancouver Opera Association, had persuaded her to donate her services for the benefit of the VOA. The reviewer in the local newspaper, evidently a star turn in his own right, reported that she:

> gave a shamefully small audience at the Queen Elizabeth Theatre . . . a superlative object-lesson in ear-ravishment, spine-tinglement, sock-frying and sheer vocal perfection . . . Those who weren't there missed the vocal experience of a lifetime – it really was, you know. Caballé is at the very height of her powers and she was obviously at the very top of her form . . . Five – can you imagine it? – five standing ovations. At least . . . If they hadn't turned on the house lights the only way to clear the theatre would have been to call the fire department to bring their hoses and wash them out.[12]

Whatever else, this certainly conveys the genuine enthusiasm engendered by the event. (If only 1000 people attended in a concert hall seating 2800, this was because – according to the reviewer – that figure represented the sum total of opera lovers in Vancouver.)

The flight from Canada direct to London where Caballé was due to begin rehearsals for her next engagement was anything but uneventful. During it, one of the passengers had a heart attack and the anxious cabin crew were unable to provide much by way of medical help. In the absence of a qualified doctor happening to be on board, Montserrat came forward and, out of her own hand-luggage, produced a bottle of cafinitrin tablets, placing one under the blue-lipped man's tongue. She plied him thus with vaso-dilators until he began to show signs of recovery, whereupon she began to administer coramine drops which she also invariably carried with her. It was this story – itself unreported in the interview – that persuaded a feature writer for the *Gramophone* magazine to report that Caballé had trained as a nurse. In fact, she had picked up both the knowledge and the medicine from her long-time association with Dr Alfredo Rocha and the ever-present necessity of dealing with her father's condition. An ambulance greeted the plane at Heathrow and whisked the passenger off to hospital. He survived, and to this day regards Montserrat as having saved his life.

The London critics, when reviewing Caballé's long-awaited début at the Royal Opera House as Violetta in June 1972, were not inclined to be so grateful. Much irrelevant commentary was devoted to the fact that she had brought her own costumes, a state of affairs to which everyone had been alerted by the Royal Opera House's peculiar decision to broadcast the matter on the title-page of the programme. Indeed, her sartorial deception would probably have passed unnoticed in any other production, but London had the Visconti staging which relocated the work in the 1890s and had enormous, entirely black-and-white *art nouveau* sets, with a restricted palette of costume designs to match. Particularly unfortunate from this point of view was found to be Caballé's dress in Act II, scene 1 – an elaborate billow of powder-blue, with matching snood, set against the only black and white garden ever seen outside the drawings of Aubrey Beardsley. But what was critically written off as a diva's caprice was, in fact, a simple physical necessity: two of Vera Marzot's original costumes were designed around the wearing of arm-length evening gloves which Montserrat was simply too self-conscious about the size of her arms to countenance wearing.

Much space was also devoted by the critics to reporting that at the end of Act I, with the concluding flourish of 'Sempre libera', the diva held a champagne saucer above her head and proceeded to empty it down her *décolletage*. This piece of admittedly not very spontaneous and messy *joie de vivre* was, in fact, Caballé's attempt to provide a frisson at curtain-fall, and had been approved by the revival's producer, John Copley. As she recollects, 'I had no high E-flat' – not that Verdi wrote one, though its interpolation has become traditional – 'so I thought I ought to do *something*!' And again, mention was made of the fact that, at the start of Act III, this Violetta recited Germont's letter without any document being visible. But this was a matter of deliberate artistic choice, echoing Sarah Bernhardt's famous gesture in *La dame aux camélias*. In all this, it can be seen that her actual singing passed largely without comment, perhaps because it was simply taken for granted. All cognoscenti present would have been familiar with her recording made five years earlier. It is likely that there was some underlying feeling that in the flesh she did not quite manage fully to recapture the exalted standard she herself had set. Certainly, there was only one verse of 'Ah fors'è lui' and only one of 'Addio del passato' (standard theatre cuts both), although they had of course been sung complete on her RCA recording. The problem may have been that in the course of the years since that recording, Caballé had come to sing more overtly dramatic, *lirico-spinto* repertory and had in some ways vocally out-grown the role. On the other hand, the rather distant evidence provided by a pirate recording of one of these performances reveals that the soprano was in good voice and fully capable of doing the role justice. Perhaps the memory of Mirella Freni, upon whom the original costumes had been designed, was too recent to allow for a balanced judgement. In any event, although it was still one of her five favourite operas, it is noticeable that Montserrat sang few *La traviata*s on the main operatic circuit after these Covent Garden performances, and dropped the work from her repertory altogether two years later as she increasingly took on new, heavier Verdi roles.

All this was doubtless unfortunate, but would have been relatively unimportant had it not set the regrettable pattern of Caballé's entire Covent Garden career, which in retrospect can be seen to have consisted of too little, too late. Never once did she sing so much as a bar of Donizetti in the Royal Opera House, notwithstanding the fact that during her career the house has managed to stage productions of *Maria Stuarda*, *Lucrezia Borgia* and *Anna Bolena*.* But then this was a house whose casting director at the time of Caballé's first international triumphs – Joan Ingpen – could sit in on a rehearsal of *Lucrezia Borgia* in October 1968 and observe publicly that the soprano had a wonderful voice but was not remotely suited to *bel canto*. And one of her long-serving successors at Covent Garden felt that Caballé was no better suited to anything else either, an artistic policy which effectively kept her out of Hamburg in the 1970s and the Royal Opera House in the 1980s. During twenty-five years of an internationally celebrated career Caballé was never given a single new production at Covent Garden until her cameo role in Rossini's *Il viaggio a Reims* in 1992, a full twenty years after her début. (Across the same period, Domingo was given ten). Undoubtedly Montserrat sensed the unspoken *froideur* at senior management levels with which she was treated. After her belated début at Covent Garden in the summer of 1972, she did not reappear there in a stage role until three years later: and she only sang *Norma* there a full eight years after it had first entered her repertory.

In interview, Bernard Haitink – before he became music director at Covent Garden – described Caballé as a 'very special animal. You have to give her what she needs, but then, what she does with it is fantastic.' The simple truth is that Covent Garden never met her artistic needs, and that at the end of the day – almost certainly subconsciously – she responded by never meeting theirs. The situation was most aptly summed up by Denny Dayviss who observed:

* These works were all sung by Joan Sutherland in new or borrowed productions specifically mounted for her, and were never revived.

Covent Garden never made a fuss of Montserrat: it was just factory-
line opera and she was just another singer to be given the occasional
revival. That is why so many people here came to the conclusion that
somehow she was better in concert performances. Actually, this isn't
true, since I have seen her give astounding performances in the opera
house, particularly in Barcelona and New York.

The real reason why Caballé appeared to greater advantage in concert
performances in London was due to the extent to which Denny Dayviss
made certain that each event *was* something special and that the diva
was made to feel special too. To the unsympathetically inclined, this
doubtless appears as little more than pandering to a singer's vanity; but
one can only judge by results, and if, in Montserrat's case, this is what
it takes to get the very best out of her, then the London public owed
more gratitude to Denny Dayviss than to the Royal Opera House. It
was at her promotions that people were able to hear one of the greatest
sopranos of this century at her absolute best.

The point is made with ironic economy when one observes that,
during the fourth and fifth performances of Caballé's run of *La traviata* at
Covent Garden, on 10 July she sang the title-role in Donizetti's *Caterina
Cornaro* at the Royal Festival Hall. Of a singer who was then being
indifferently received by the critics in the Verdi, Harold Rosenthal could
write apropos her Donizetti: 'she was in fabulous vocal form, and her
singing of the beautiful, slow arias that Donizetti gave to his heroine in
the Prologue and each of the two Acts, displayed her artistry and technique to the full; one seldom hears such wonderful singing as in the last
Act prayer, "Pietà, Signor".'[13] One of the present authors was at this
performance and remembers vividly the magnificence of the *preghiera*,
during which time and space seemed to stand still. If her reception at
the Royal Opera House had been muted, at least on the part of the
critics, that at the Royal Festival Hall was jubilant. And in spite of the
cavils, the London public reaffirmed its utter devotion to Caballé during
this, her first extended stay in London.

This was just as well, because she remained in London for virtually
the whole of the next two months, though not singing in public. During
her stay she recorded the role of Mathilde in the first-ever complete
recording in French of Rossini's *Guillaume Tell* for EMI; Liù in *Turandot*
for Decca; and the title-roles in Verdi's *Giovanna d'Arco* – again for
EMI – and Bellini's *Norma* for RCA. And, in between the latter two
recordings, she even returned to Barcelona for five days in order to
record a *zarzuela*, *El pajaro azul*, which was never released outside Spain.
This unprecedented and subsequently unmatched level of activity drew

some harsh comment from Andrew Porter, who complained of 'assembly line opera',[14] though as more than one observer has pointed out, we should be glad enough of such an assembly line being in operation today. Three of the four opera recordings acquired more or less instantaneous classic status; only about the *Norma*, unfortunately, is it possible to voice reservations such as might justify Porter's comment. RCA evidently felt that more work needed to be done, since the recording was withheld from release for over three years while various 'patching' sessions were held. But these never involved Caballé, whose role had been recorded complete in eleven days. Not that there is anything drastically wrong with the recording, one or two moments of surprisingly fudged ensemble towards the end of the work apart: it simply fails to convey the full vocal splendour and dramatic impact of which Caballé was capable in the role on stage.*

If this was evident at the Palais Garnier, where Montserrat finally completed her 'Royal flush' of major European house débuts in October 1972, it has been largely obscured by the scandal which surrounded the event. As in London some two years previously, the four principal roles were sung by the two married couples: Caballé and Martí, Cossotto and Vinco. But the Parisian public did not take kindly to this arrangement any more than they were ever prepared to accept Richard Bonynge's conducting as the price of having his wife sing. Montserrat was already nervous about the occasion: her first intended Parisian *Norma* had foundered due to the chorus strike, and her début as a recitalist at the Palais Garnier on 8 May 1972 had ended with her fainting on stage during her last item. The immediate background to these new Paris *Norma*s – the first revival of the production Franco Zeffirelli had created for Maria Callas eight years previously – was even more fraught. Though the extended run of ten performances had been contracted long before, it so happened that they constituted the opening of Bernard Lefort's last season as director of the Opéra de Paris before the inauguration of the eagerly awaited new regime of Rolf Liebermann, hot-foot from Hamburg. Even while she was still labouring in London during the summer of 1972, Montserrat was visited by the renowned impresario Sandor Gorlinsky – a close friend of Liebermann's – who turned up at the Westbury Hotel and told both the soprano and her brother that she

---

* For the best of Caballé in the role, one needs to see the video of the solitary performance given in July 1974 at Orange. There is an odd parallel here with Maria Callas, neither of whose studio recordings made in 1954 and 1960 capture the essence of which she was capable but which is audible in two pirate recordings from 1952 (London) and 1955 (Milan).

should cancel the forthcoming Paris run. In return, she would be given two new productions under the new administration, *I vespri siciliani* and one other of her own choosing. She would, of course, have to plead a fictitious illness in order to avoid the ten *Norma*s, but she was not to worry about the substantial loss of earnings this would entail, since – at a judiciously distanced future date – she would be assured of ten replacement performances in Hamburg at a suitably enhanced fee. Shabby deals like this have never interested Caballé, who turned it down flat and, no doubt, had a word with her old friend Lefort, who could rest easy in the knowledge that his star soprano would turn up as scheduled. It is a matter of public record that Caballé thereafter never sang at the Paris Opéra during the entire eight-year directorship of Herr Liebermann, uninvited by the man who had, presumably, once been so very keen to secure her services.

But Montserrat's demonstration of good faith was not, in the event, properly rewarded. With only two days to go before the gala opening night of the Paris Opéra season on 28 September 1972, she recounts that Bernabé was stricken at the dress rehearsal – a starry pre-première gala in its own right – with severe chest pains. No immediate diagnosis was forthcoming and the theatre's own doctor prescribed medicine which only seemed to make matters worse. The tenor was therefore advised not to sing. The Martís informed the Opéra directorate of this, but Montserrat recalls being told that since the Ministry of Culture had insisted on economic cut-backs being made during this, Lefort's last season, the Opéra had been obliged to abandon the practice of retaining 'covers' (or understudies) for the principal roles. Bernabé was therefore begged to sing the opening night as scheduled, which would at least give the theatre some extra time to try to find a replacement, if necessary. But poor Bernabé was no better on 28 September and only just got through the duet with Adalgisa. In the ensuing interval he was given pain-killers and after a quarter of an hour agreed with his wife to see how the rest of Act I, including the fearsome closing trio, would go. Montserrat remembers seeing him on stage in evident distress, drenched in sweat, singing with only a fraction of his customary power. There followed another interval devoted to panic-stricken consultations between the Martís, the doctor and Lefort, after which it was decided that Montserrat would go out and sing the next scene (during which Pollione is not required – the opening sequences of Act II beginning with 'Dormono entrambi'). Perhaps Bernabé would have recovered in the interim. But in the brief pause before the closing scenes of the work it was finally clear that the tenor was unable to sing as he was now bringing up small quantities of blood. Both the doctor and Montserrat forbade him to go on, and she accompanied a nervous Lefort on to the stage for the necessary announcement. After the administrator had told a groaning audience that the performance was at an end, Caballé herself added, 'I'm fine, but one of our colleagues is ill and you cannot perform a duet on your own!' (which Lefort, extraordinarily, had tried to persuade the soprano to do).

The French press, naturally enough, had a field day, reporting apocalyptic scenes such as had not been witnessed at the Palais Garnier since Callas's withdrawal from the same opera roughly ten years previously. Montserrat was reported to have refused to accept her fee, suggesting instead that it be used to finance refunds. But again, in interview, she denied this, stating that instead she had offered to sing an additional performance some time later during the contracted run of ten. None of this, however, ever came to pass. Bernabé was replaced on medical grounds for the remaining performances, finally properly diagnosed as suffering from an hiatus hernia, and Montserrat – who by this time must have been convinced that there was a jinx on her attempts to perform *Norma* in Paris – developed an indisposition after the fourth performance, cancelling the remaining six. She rejoined her spouse in Barcelona where some fiery press denunciations appeared concerning the perfidy of the Paris Opéra. Caballé did not set foot on its stage again until 1981, by which time Bernabé had retired from singing and Bernard Lefort was once again the artistic administrator.

Just as her recording schedules hardly allowed her time to breathe, so Caballé's performance schedules admitted of no opportunity to brood. In November she gave four performances at the Liceo of a role which she had never before undertaken and which no one expected any soprano to sing while still at the height of her career: Adriana Lecouvreur.* Taxed about this in interview, Montserrat's reply was engagingly straightforward: it was such a beautiful role, in such a well-crafted opera, why ever should she have to wait ten or twenty years before singing it? She wanted to perform in *Adriana Lecouvreur* while still at her peak and able to exploit to the full the opportunities that the role offered her rather than wait until it was simply a vehicle in which, vocally, she could 'get by'. The opening night on 7 November was yet another in the unbroken line of her Liceo triumphs and one which she

---

* The *tessitura* of the role is, to put it mildly, obliging, and therefore much favoured by sopranos whose range no longer comfortably extends much above the stave. Since Adriana is a temperamental actress the part automatically appeals to ex-Toscas who can no longer manage Puccini's more fearsome vocal demands.

again shared with José Carreras, surely ideally cast in the role of
Adriana's dashing lover, Maurizio. At the third performance, during
the Act I love duet, Montserrat nuzzled a little too assiduously against
Carreras's chest, so that her silver wig became entangled in the braids
on his military tunic. Despite the frantic efforts of both to disentangle
themselves, the wig remained resolutely caught, which accounts for the
strange spectacle to which the Liceo audience was treated that night as
the lovers retreated momentarily off-stage, glued head-to-chest.

Such mishaps would, however, probably have passed unnoticed during the mayhem which surrounded Montserrat's next stage appearance.
She had originally been approached by La Scala with a view to opening
the 1973–4 season, but had made a counter proposal: she would prefer
to appear a whole year earlier in a new production of *Norma*. This, in
the days when only works by Verdi could open the hallowed Milanese
season, effectively denied Montserrat the chance of singing on 7
December, the traditional opening night. The theatre had agreed, and
as a result the first new production of the 1972–3 season opened on 22
December. The cast was the same as in Paris, with the exception of
Gianni Raimondi as Pollione. The performances were to be conducted
by Gianandrea Gavazzeni and the production had been entrusted to the
Italian film director, Mauro Bolognini, who had commissioned sets
from a noted *avant-garde* artist, Mario Ceroli. But trouble started from
the very first stage rehearsal, at which Caballé belatedly discovered the
nature of the production. In a rare example for this era – at least outside
Eastern Germany – of what is now termed 'deconstructionism', the
whole opera was played out in front of an enormous, skeletal Rubik's
cube, with what looked like large packing-cases dotted about the stage.
Not surprisingly, Caballé was profoundly unhappy, and particularly so
with a piece of chorus blocking that left her fighting through the crowds
as if in a market place. At the end of a three-hour rehearsal she asked
to have a word with the director on stage. He arrived, beaming. 'Tell
me, in your opinion is what we have just rehearsed artistically acceptable?' she inquired. The director replied, 'Almost perfect.' 'I see,' Montserrat nodded, 'thank you very much.' With this she returned to her
dressing-room, collected her few belongings, left the theatre and, on
arriving back at her hotel, rang a horrified La Scala management to
inform them of her withdrawal from the production.

A crisis meeting was immediately convened at which Caballé, who
had been persuaded by the Milanese management to remain in the city,
was asked to make known her reservations. She did so and concessions
were made, but about the set there was no turning back: the better part
of a ton of Russian wood had already been carpentered and was sitting

backstage. In the event, the production was reblocked and most of the 'packing-cases' duly dispatched. Vocally, however, Caballé had an overwhelming triumph in an opera that had not featured in La Scala's repertory since Callas's palmy days in the 1950s. No sooner had the orchestra played the two soft chords at the end of 'Casta diva' than the audience – whom we may presume, in this of all works, to be almost impossible to satisfy – simply exploded in cheers and bravos. After several minutes of this, Gavazzeni made two determined attempts to carry on with the scene, but the orchestra was drowned out by the ceaseless clamour of the enthusiastic throng. Only when Caballé signalled to the increasingly grumpy conductor to continue did the crowd finally fall silent and the opera proceed. Happily, this would prove not to be a unique event at La Scala since Caballé returned to sing the role on an almost yearly basis, including the legendary performances with the company on tour at the Bolshoi in 1974. What was characteristic of her assumptions was perhaps best summed up by Lorenzo Arruga, the noted musicologist, in his chronicler's overview of La Scala's operatic history:

> Her *Norma* . . . so lyrical, so immobile, so completely summed up in the internal tragic line of the song, never remotely metallic and never fiery but always wrapped in the shadow of mystery, seemed to be connected directly with the original Bellinian sensibility and at the same time seemed to respond to certain feelings of our time which question the perennial music drama.[15]

And it is surely significant that though divas have come and gone ever since, La Scala has never revived this opera after Caballé last sang it there in 1977. So this chapter ends as it began, with a triumphant *Norma*. In the intervening three years Caballé had sung the role in many of the world's great venues, and in the next three would continue to sing it virtually everywhere else. In the process she had grown from the artist who, in interview with Bernard Levin filmed for the BBC in 1970, could say that she was really only the daughter of Norma rather than Norma herself, to the one singer in the world who was universally recognized as capable of doing the role full justice. Even so, the consequent strengthening and darkening of her voice had not been without its disadvantages – of which her Violetta was probably the most significant casualty. And her final arrival at the pinnacle of success had not been without spectacular controversies. As the decade unfolded, Montserrat was to learn the essential truth of Shakespeare's dictum: 'Uneasy lies the head that wears the crown.'

She would be fortified from time to time by remembering a piece of advice that Maria Callas had given her in the earliest days of their

friendship. The essence of this was: 'The day you stop arousing controversy, Montserrat, pack your bags and go home. Until then let the cat
fight the dogs.' But Caballé, although a woman of comparably steely
resolve, had never shared Callas's passion for direct confrontation, nor
her fundamentally 'driven' temperament. The Spaniard was, after all,
both a happily married wife and a devoted mother, and she had always
believed herself willing to give up singing if the needs of her family
were felt to be suffering.

In fact, as the Christmas/New Year period of 1972–3 unfolded, it was
Montserrat herself who was suffering. She was, of course, scheduled to
return to La Scala for several more performances of *Norma* stretching
well into January, but she had felt unwell on Christmas Day and even
worse the day after, with a sore throat and a muzzy head. One of the
army of family doctors was called to attend, and made an immediate
diagnosis: mumps. Bernabé and the children were confined to another
part of the flat, which was relatively easy given that the Caballés had
recently acquired and incorporated the flat next door where her parents
had been installed. Meanwhile, Carlos informed La Scala that his sister
would not be returning during the present run, which meant that her
first Milanese Norma would, at least for the time being, also be her
last. Gavazzeni received the news with horror and a certain degree of
suspicion. He contacted Montserrat in Barcelona and said, 'You're afraid
to come back. You know perfectly well that the performance you gave
last week was historic and you don't dare return because you're not
sure that you can live up to it.' Montserrat was vastly amused by his
challenging flattery, whilst Carlos immediately arranged for her to be
photographed propped up in bed, her swollen neck glands visible for
all to see. The resulting polaroid was duly dispatched for the management of La Scala's inspection who thereupon resigned themselves to the
inevitable and set about finding a whole series of replacements. Gavazzeni, on the other hand, picked up a copy in person after presenting
himself unannounced at Carlos's flat at seven o'clock in the morning *en
route* to his Christmas destination.

This left Montserrat in a uniquely frustrating position in that, whilst
she was unexpectedly and agreeably reunited with her family, she was
effectively unable to have any contact with them. Moreover, with the
prospect of making her début in the same role at the Metropolitan in
little more than six weeks, the pressures were beginning to build. As
she convalesced, she thumbed through an engagement diary by now
filled several years into the future, featuring an ever-lengthening list of
planned recordings. She might have been forgiven for wondering, at
least momentarily, if her life was her own any more.

❧ IV ☙

'Croce e Delizia'

La traviata

—————————— ⟶✦⟵ ——————————

CHAPTER NINE

1973–1976: Triumphs, Troubles and Transition

In the early part of 1973 several newspapers carried reports that Caballé, unable to bear the lengthy periods of enforced separation from her family, was going to retire. It is certainly true that at about this time she had already turned down an offer made during the closing weeks of Rudolf Bing's managership of the Metropolitan Opera House which would have offered her undisputed *prima donna assoluta* status at that house, with the pick of repertory and new productions, for a period of ten years. But as she was to reveal later, the reason for this was that she simply could not contemplate taking up near-permanent residency in New York or indeed anywhere away from her beloved Barcelona, a condition which the contract would effectively have imposed. Even the London *Times*, not a paper normally given to reporting operatic hearsay, reported that Caballé's retirement was imminent. In fact, she had no such intention, nor indeed ever has had at any point subsequently. Wryly, she recalls numerous occasions on which, during the course of an interview, any expression on her part that she was missing her children was interpreted as an intention to retire. The truth of the matter is that although she was undoubtedly devoted to her family, she was married to her music and destined to go the distance.

The year began (after Montserrat's recovery from mumps) with her first-ever performances in partnership with Plácido Domingo at the Liceo, when they sang together in three performances of *Un ballo in maschera*. These were immediately followed by four performances of a revival of *Norma*, beginning on 25 January, with Bruno Prevedi as Pollione. After the last performance on 3 February at which the ovations continued for more than half an hour, Caballé was the object of the theatre's fourth formal *homenaje*, commemorated in the form of a medal presented to her on stage as flowers rained down from the boxes on either side. She interrupted the applause to tell the emotional audience that she wanted to make them a promise: so long as she had a voice, she would sing for them every year without fail.

After no more than a day's rest she set out for New York and a week's intensive rehearsal for a revival of *Norma* at the Metropolitan. The work had been most recently heard there with Joan Sutherland and Marilyn Horne as the priestesses, and an interesting comparison was drawn between them and Caballé and Fiorenza Cossotto in the *New York Times* review:

> This *Norma* had an aspect that the previous [team] lacked. Radiantly as those two great singers sang the two big duets, their voices were, paradoxically, too well matched. In this new cast the creamy voice of Miss Cossotto contrasted beautifully with the more vibrato-free, instrumental-like Caballé sound.[1]

Caballé remained at the Met until 24 March, interspersing half-a-dozen Normas with four *Il trovatore* Leonoras, where her Manricos included James McCracken, Plácido Domingo and Richard Tucker. At the end of the month, she went to Miami to sing four further Leonoras, this time for the Opera Guild and with her husband as Manrico. The reviewer in *Opera* wrote apropos Bernabé's performance: 'He is an intelligent artist and had nature endowed him more generously he would surely be one of the celebrated stars of our time.'[2] Alas, nature had not; the basic middle-voice, medium-volume timbre of Bernabé's tenor was rather gruff and monochrome, which reduced the sheerly pleasurable aspects of listening to his singing by a margin. On the other hand, he possessed a stentorian and effortless top: high Cs came naturally to him; and even these were not the end of the story. Denny Dayviss remembers sitting in a car with Montserrat, Bernabé and Carlos driving through the Catalan countryside when the latter challenged Caballé's husband to sing as high and loud as he could. The result was a high E♭ above C, which was not only ear-splitting but actually shattered the windscreen, necessitating some emergency DIY on the part of the embarrassed but secretly proud tenor. In fact, this was nothing unusual: Montserrat remembers her husband singing the role of Raoul in Meyerbeer's *Les Huguenots* during rehearsals at the Liceo, firing off a whole fusillade of ringing high E♭ s.

There was a bare handful of further *Trovatore*s back at the Met – three tenors in three performances – before Montserrat finally left North America at the end of April *en route* to Naples where she was to give five performances of *Norma* during the course of May, partnered by Viorica Cortez as Adalgisa and Pier Miranda Ferraro as Pollione. After a brief return home, she flew to Hamburg at the end of the month to give two performances of *Don Carlos* and one of *Il trovatore* at the Staatsoper, thereby making her belated German stage début as an internationally famous soprano. In fact, though extremely popular in Germany – her records sell in abundance – the number of her operatic appearances there barely extends into double figures, and it is somehow symptomatic, for example, that she has never sung an opera on stage in Munich since 1962, despite the Bavarian capital's status as one of the country's three most important opera houses. Perhaps the memory of the Bremen years was simply too strong ever to allow Montserrat to sing in Germany frequently enough to satisfy German audiences, who remain amongst her most loyal and enthusiastic.

After half-a-dozen miscellaneous recitals throughout Europe during June, Caballé returned to London in July to record the role of Margherita in Boito's *Mefistofele* for EMI, with Plácido Domingo as Faust and Norman Treigle in the title-role, conducted by Julius Rudel. The day after the sessions in the much-lamented Kingsway Hall were completed, Montserrat travelled in a royal limousine to Leeds Castle in Kent, where she had been specifically invited to give a private recital for the British Royal Family and at which she was introduced to Prince Charles, who was a keen fan, for the first time. The following day she returned to London, this time to Walthamstow Town Hall, to begin rehearsals for the RCA recording of *La bohème*, again with Domingo.

The opera was conducted by Sir Georg Solti, on loan from Decca, whom Caballé had met only once at an unsuccessful audition in Frankfurt many years earlier. The preliminary rehearsal took place in the conductor's home in St John's Wood, to which the principal singers had been bidden with strict instructions to bring their scores with them. Once Domingo, Caballé, Milnes, Raimondi and Judith Blegen had arrived, an assistant of Solti walked in carrying a large cardboard box. The conductor then asked each of the singers present to hold up their

scores and went round gathering them up, while his assistant issued
pristine copies of the Ricordi edition. The old scores were put in the
box and the singers were told that they could have them back after
the sessions were finished: in the meantime, they were to forget all the
slovenly old routines and 'traditions' to which they had become falsely
attached. There then followed a painstaking disquisition from Solti concerning Puccini's intentions, which provoked Sherrill Milnes to inquire
with a deadpan expression, 'You been talking to the guy, then, maestro?'
When the singers filed out later that afternoon, it was in a thunderstruck
silence, broken only by Domingo turning to Caballé and saying, 'Montserrat, isn't it nice to breathe some fresh air?'

The first full recording session took place in Walthamstow Town
Hall the following day, comprising the whole of Act IV which had
both the soprano and tenor in despair, feeling as if they were being
treated as sardines to be squeezed into a can. They approached the
project's producer, the industry veteran Richard Mohr, and begged him
to intercede on their (and, they believed, Puccini's behalf) with the
unyielding conductor. An uneasy *modus vivendi* was worked out,
whereby the singers – under a degree of sufferance – were given rather
more licence to expand their phrasing than would otherwise have been
the case. Even so, Caballé remains utterly unconvinced when contemplating the finished product:

> With all respects to the maestro's view of Puccini, in my opinion you
> cannot conduct him à la Bartók. *Bohème* is not a score to submit to
> a laboratory experiment, each piece cut up and inspected. The music
> must soar freely through the air: it should not be treated as an aca-
> demic exercise, put together for the pleasure of musical snobs. But,
> for them, it is, of course, the perfect *Bohème*.

Immediately after completing the recording on 4 August 1973,
Caballé returned home for a few days' holiday, before travelling back
to the same venue in London in order to begin the sessions, again for
RCA, for the first-ever studio recording of Verdi's *I vespri siciliani*. She
was due to sing the role of Elena, with Domingo as her lover, Arrigo,
Milnes as his father, Montfort, and Raimondi as the Sicilian villain,
Procida, with the London Symphony Orchestra conducted by James
Levine. But on the third day of her Spanish sojourn, Montserrat and
her husband were involved in a car accident: one of the tyres on the
family Mercedes burst, sending the car skidding across a road and crashing into a tree. Fortunately Montserrat and her husband were wearing
seat-belts, but both of them had to be fitted with neck braces as a result
of the 'whiplash' spinal injuries they had sustained. Caballé had no

option other than to cancel the recording. Haggard RCA executives flew to Barcelona to see if there was any way in which they could persuade the diva to attend, but once they saw her and her doctors they remained under no illusions. An elaborate plan was evolved to record the opera in London as scheduled minus Montserrat, who would then be dubbed on later once she had recovered. But in a work as long and as full of complex ensembles as *I vespri*, this was soon discounted as impracticable, and Martina Arroyo was hastily imported as a replacement.

At the beginning of September 1973 Caballé returned alone to Chicago to begin rehearsals for a new production of *Maria Stuarda* which Carol Fox, one of the Lyric Opera's founder directors and its general manager, had arranged to have mounted specifically for her, by borrowing the recent production from the Rome Opera. Six perform-ances were scheduled, all with Viorica Cortez as Elisabeth and Bruno Bartoletti conducting. Midway during the two-week rehearsal period, Montserrat, who wherever she was always rang home every single day, learned that her son was unwell. A doctor had been in attendance and was of the opinion that the child simply had flu. But from one day to the next Bernabé junior's health worsened. He began to complain of severe headaches and, without warning, succumbed to a very high fever.

I was very worried because apart from anything else I was so far away, and no one seemed to know what the problem with Bernabé really was. I attended the dress rehearsal [on 19 September] but really I remember nothing about it. I was so upset. I knew the production already because it was the one by Giorgio De Lullo which had been mounted for me originally in Rome. I spoke to Carol Fox about the possibility of being released from my contract but she said this was simply not possible – all six performances [3600 seats per night] had been sold out on the strength of my name. And then on the day after the first night I rang home to discover that they knew what it was: my son had contracted salmonella, which in children can be very dangerous. I told Fox that I was leaving immediately, but the opera house refused to release me just because he was ill and made it clear that they would only do so in the event of real emergency. What more did they want? I said to them, 'Fine, you will only let me go if he dies. But if he dies, he doesn't need me then. He needs me now!' So I contacted the Spanish ambassador in Washington and explained the situation to him. He sent me an American doctor from New York attached to the Spanish Consulate there who, when he arrived after the next performance, was prepared to say that I had an acute intestinal inflammation which needed twenty days' bed rest. I flew straight home to be with my son.

Soon after Montserrat's arrival home, Bernabé developed blood-poisoning and fell into a coma which lasted for three days. The doctors, juggling with hit-or-miss administration of various antibiotics, felt he had little chance of recovering. Fortunately, on the fourth day, the young boy slowly began to regain consciousness and recover from his life-threatening illness. But Montserrat was subsequently sued for breach of contract by the Chicago Lyric Opera. Her American agents, Columbia Artists' Management Incorporated (CAMI) and, in particular, Ronald Wilford, arranged for one of the members of the board of Directors at the Met in New York, who was a lawyer, to intervene on Montserrat's behalf. She was advised to write a letter standing on the medical evidence that had already been submitted, rather than – as the diva would have much preferred – arguing the moral considerations of the real situation. In any event, Carol Fox's intransigence backfired since the Lyric Opera lost the law suit.

In fact, it backfired twice. Soon afterwards Renata Tebaldi, in the twilight of her stage career, was obliged to cancel performances of *Manon Lescaut* in Chicago through illness. Caballé's EMI recording of the work had just appeared in America to rapturous acclaim and so Fox personally contacted Caballé in New York where the latter was singing at the Metropolitan to see if she would fill in for Tebaldi. Montserrat's first reaction was to decline, but as Fox (who had done her homework) pointed out, Montserrat's dates were free. Caballé, mindful of her own experiences with the Lyric, contacted Tebaldi to establish why she had cancelled. Had there been any trouble with either the production or the management? It transpired that Tebaldi – though she did, in fact, think the production was dreadful – was genuinely ill. But even with the senior diva's blessing, Montserrat still did not feel much minded to help the Chicago Lyric Opera in its own hour of need and refused to sing. This whole episode served to strengthen Caballé's resolve always to put the welfare of her family first and to sharpen her ingrained mistrust of so many opera house managements. In consequence, as the 1970s progressed she became less and less prepared to spend months at a time away from home. And in the immediate short term, the principal upshot of this affair was the building of the small votive chapel dedicated to the Virgin Mary halfway up a hill on her farm at Ripoll, in gratitude for the recovery of her son.

*   *   *

The 1973–4 season at the Gran Teatro del Liceo opened on 8 November with a new production of the last opera which Donizetti saw staged in his own lifetime, *Caterina Cornaro*. This work, which deals with the troublesome affairs of the eponymous and real-life, fifteenth-century Queen of Cyprus, had remained unperformed between 1845 (only its second-ever production, in Parma) and 1972, when it was revived at the San Carlo in Naples with Leyla Gencer in the title-role. Montserrat rapidly espoused Caterina's cause and had, in fact, already sung the work in concert in London:* indeed, as soon as the four performances at the Liceo were over, she was due in Paris to undertake a further concert performance at the Salle Pleyel, with the forces of ORTF (Orchestre de la Radio et Télévision Française), which effectively ensured that the work, in being set down for subsequent transmission, thereby received its first professional recording. The stage performances at the Liceo – in a rough-and-ready amalgam of anonymous sets – were the usual tumultuous success with the Barcelonese audience.

Immediately after this she flew to Rome where, once again for the local forces of RAI, she was to take part in a recording/broadcast performance, this time of Strauss's *Arabella*. As so often when dealing with Wagner or Strauss performances given in the Latin countries, the opera was cast to the teeth: Siegmund Nimsgern sang Mandryka, René Kollo Matteo, with no less than Kurt Moll as Count Waldner. One can only salute the enterprise of RAI at this period under the direction of Francesco Siciliani, who showed themselves endlessly prepared to mount performances of rare (at least for Italy) repertory.† Nevertheless, it is a pity that this particular revival was not mounted some years earlier: Caballé's voice is now unmistakably that of a mature woman which no amount of ethereal *pianissimo* can disguise. When this *Arabella* lets fly, it is quite clear that we are listening to a Medea in the making.

Perhaps something of the same problem affected Caballé's next scheduled appearances. She was due to sing the first of four Violettas at the Liceo, commencing on 6 December, with José Carreras as Alfredo.

---

* It is a pity that no one at the time thought to escort Caballé just across the Thames to the National Gallery, where Titian's portrait of Caterina Cornaro hangs. In this authentic painting – unlike the egregious fake in the Uffizi – the resemblance between Queen and diva is very striking.

† In addition to the *Agnese di Hohenstaufen* and *La donna del lago* in 1970, RAI had also mounted for Montserrat a broadcast performance of Strauss's *Salome* in 1971, with Nimsgern as Jokanaan, conducted by Zubin Mehta. Unfortunately, this latter performance – which by all accounts was sensational – is the only one of Caballé's quartet of RAI operas from this period never to have materialized on pirate disc.

Unfortunately, during the later stage of rehearsals, she caught a bad cold which affected her opening performance adversely. Having acquitted herself of a most distinguished 'Ah, fors'è lui' – the first verse of which ends with the words 'misterioso, altero, croce e delizia al cor'* as Violetta muses on the idea of love – Caballé launched herself into the transitional passage before the cabaletta, comprising the two coloratura statements of 'Gioir!' and 'Sempre libera' which frame Alfredo's off-stage romantic credo. In Verdi's score, both cries of 'Gioir' are written to high D♭, which the soprano has never in her career sung in downward transposition. As a recent book about the Liceo recounts,[3] the high note turned out to be a *gallo* (or as we would say in English, a 'frog in the throat'). Apparently the audience gave her an ovation at the end of the Act, though certainly no one in Barcelona had ever heard Caballé crack on a note before. Notwithstanding the audience's warm response, however, she refused to take a solo curtain call, not on the grounds that she was afraid of adverse reaction but simply because on this occasion she did not feel that she had merited one. The rest of the performance – one of the best Violettas she recalls singing – took place without further incident but the following day Caballé contacted Pámias and informed him that she was withdrawing from the three remaining performances as she felt unwell.

All in all, by mid-December, she would have been justified in regarding 1973 as having been fraught: she had begun the year suffering from mumps; had a disagreeable brush with the Chicago Lyric Opera; and seen her son fighting for his life. If the Liceo regulars were inclined to view her recent *Traviata* mishap indulgently, they did so with good reason: it was Caballé's seventy-eighth performance since her début there in January 1962, and she had sung twenty-two different roles in the house, all of them without any meaningful remuneration. She repaid their indulgence no more than a few days later, when, having as usual spent Christmas with her family, she reappeared at the Liceo on 29 December in a new production of *Aïda* where not only was the exposed high C in 'O patria mia' in place, but everything else as well.

> . . . she offered an Ethiopian princess that was the result of a highly intelligent approach to the score. One could sense in advance that her lyrical voice would be ideal for Acts III and IV, but she achieved great drama in 'Ritorna vincitor!' and power in the Act II ensembles. Caballé's Aïda, much more than interesting, turned out to be really first-class.[4]

---

* 'mysterious, elevated pain and pleasure of the heart'.

The Radamès, Plácido Domingo, felt even more strongly about the quality of Caballé's performance, since within mere days he was on the telephone to the management of EMI in London begging them to put together a commercial recording of the work at the earliest possible opportunity. As he himself put it, brushing aside the fact that he had already recorded the role of Radamès just two years previously with Leontyne Price for RCA, Caballé's singing was the stuff of operatic legend, and had to be immortalized on disc, the sooner the better. EMI had entertained no plans to record the work in the foreseeable future, having not that long previously issued a recording with Birgit Nilsson and Franco Corelli under Zubin Mehta. But Domingo's persistent advocacy won the day, and for once it is to EMI's great credit that the team which they so hastily assembled in order to make a recording no more than six months later contained not a single weak link and remains, as Domingo predicted, a classic.

Meanwhile the last performance of *Aïda* at the Liceo took place on 5 January 1974 under circumstances which, though giving a very clear indication of the sensational nature of the performance, must nevertheless been quite a trial for all concerned. As was by no means unusual at the time, Pámias had run out of money, even for the purposes of paying the corporate fee of 500,000 pesetas (or approximately £2500) for the services of Caballé, Domingo, Bianca Berini and Giampiero Mastromei. The impresario decided to exploit the extent of public clamour for tickets at all four performances and instructed the besieged box office to pack people in by selling them hand-written tickets. According to a contemporary report, boxes that should normally have seated four held eight, all the corridors and passageways were packed with standees, and those who had not been able to manoeuvre into even these fringe positions deposited themselves ten-deep in the stalls aisles. The net result was that a theatre which seats a little under 3000 had more than 4000 paid admissions that night, the additional revenue being used to pay the singers. The response accorded to these *Aïda*s – Caballé's first in well over a decade – was more than fit recompense for the disappointment of the cancelled *Traviata*s. In truth, the surprise is that she had taken so long to return to the former role: after all, she had already been singing Norma for three years, and Amelia in *Un ballo in maschera* for even longer. In the heavy repertory stakes, the role of Aïda is surely less onerous than those she already sang. But perhaps Caballé regarded Aïda as a decisive shift in her repertory which would inexorably lead towards the transition into heavier roles such as Gioconda and Turandot as the voice both amplified and darkened.

*   *   *

In mid-January 1974 Caballé made yet another of her excursions to the south of France in order to sing two staged performances of *Caterina Cornaro* in Nice. She has always found the Côte d'Azur a highly congenial performing locale and estimates that she has spent well over 500 nights ensconced in the Hôtel Negresco in what is now called the Montserrat Caballé Suite, overlooking the Promenade des Anglais. But the secret of the area's attraction went beyond its glorious climate and luxurious accommodation: rather as with the Liceo and Pámias in Barcelona, the running of the Municipal Opera House in Nice – together with those in Toulon and Nîmes – was entrusted to a lone entrepreneur whose seemingly impossible task it was to provide audiences with star attractions on a strictly limited budget. Ferdinand Aymée accomplished this with such skill and charm that all the singers of the Caballé circle, and in particular Montserrat and José Carreras, found the proposition of singing in his houses irresistible, even if the fees were not. Both could have employed their time far more lucratively in the world's front-ranking venues, but there was more than enough compensation to be had out of the old-world courtesy and consideration Aymée lavished upon his favourites.

Then it was back to America and business as usual. In fact, this trip turned out to be perhaps the most extraordinary of all Caballé's New York triumphs. She immediately began rehearsals for a new production at the Metropolitan of Verdi's rarely performed *I vespri siciliani* in which she was to sing the long and involved role of the Duchessa Elena who acts as the dramatic catalyst between not only rival suitors but even rival peoples. The work had never been given at the Met before, and was produced by the highly regarded English director, John Dexter, and designed by Josef Svoboda, whose contribution characteristically took the form of an enormous, stage-wide staircase rising into the dim distance. The conductor was the relatively newly appointed music director of the Met, James Levine, working here for the first time with Caballé on stage. Her other colleagues included Nicolai Gedda as Arrigo, Justino Diaz as Procida and Sherrill Milnes as Monfort.

In the fashion of the house, an enormous amount of pre-publicity was generated through the medium of its magazine, *Opera News*, and the inevitable Texaco broadcast of a Saturday matinée performance has ensured that although Caballé had been prevented from taking part in the RCA recording under Levine the previous year, we still have a document of what she herself regards as one of her greatest stage roles. Certainly she views this Metropolitan production as one of the two or three greatest of her professional career, despite the fact that she was always unsure of her footing on the endless steps, and countless times during rehearsal – and once in actual performance – collapsed in a giggling heap. At one point during the pre-production preparation there had been some wrangling as to whether the steps would or would not be carpeted. Dexter wrote a letter to Montserrat saying how much he looked forward to their working together, going on to state a belief that it would be nice to think all those in the same line of business espoused: 'The most important thing in directing an opera is to make the singers feel comfortable.'[5]

The opening night of *I vespri siciliani* on 31 January was a sensation. After Caballé's singing of Elena's Act IV aria, 'Arrigo! Ah parli a un core', the performance was stopped dead in its tracks as the audience clapped and cheered for a continuous seven minutes. In fact the ovation would have gone on even longer had not Caballé made clear signals to Levine to continue with the performance. As Harold C. Schonberg wrote in the *New York Times*:

> . . . the sounds were beautiful indeed: not particularly intense, but possessed of an instrumental purity and a haunting color. Her famous *pianissimo* singing was never heard to better effect than in the third Act* . . . which was exquisitely delivered, with perfect control. The audience responded with one of the season's longest ovations.[6]

The run of performances of *Vespri* continued throughout February and into March, and as had long since become Caballé's custom, they were interspersed with guest appearances around the eastern seaboard, most notably a further return to the Hartford Opera in Connecticut, where she sang in performances of *Un ballo in maschera* with her husband as Riccardo. But perhaps the single shining jewel in the crown of this, her tenth extended New York visit, was the concert performance in Carnegie Hall on 6 March of Donizetti's totally forgotten *Parisina*. Caballé had of course already recorded the closing scene in 1969 as part of her rarities disc, but the pirate tape which survives of this complete performance – for once in excellent sound – permits us to hear that, in spite of her undertaking heavier repertory in the intervening years, Caballé's voice remained clearly at its peak.

She rounded out the end of her North American stay by touring Canada, including a return to the by now Caballé-mad Vancouver with

---

* In fact, Elena barely sings at all in Act III, which consists almost entirely of the long father–son confrontation between Monforte and Arrigo, followed by the half-hour long ballet. But the Metropolitan had chosen to give Verdi's five-Act work minus the ballet and with the other Acts regrouped around two intervals. Hence the confusion.

not a seat to be had, and even ended up performing in Anchorage. Back in Spain she returned to Madrid, where she had already made one complete *zarzuela* recording a few months earlier – Vives' *Maruxa* – and proceeded to set down another: *La Villana*.

In the midst of this whirlwind of activity, she took time off to see her doctor. She had been increasingly worried about abdominal pains and irregular periods. A biopsy was recommended and this revealed that she was suffering from a tumour, still quite small and probably benign. The doctors advised her that in the immediate short term she was in no danger, but that she should be carefully monitored, particularly if she became aware of any changes in her physical condition.

Caballé then returned briefly to Milan to finalize the details of a revival of La Scala's production of *Norma*. This time, however, the performances were scheduled to take place not in Milan but in Moscow, as part of La Scala's historic exchange with the Bolshoi. It was during this tour that Montserrat performed the heroic feat of singing three Normas in the space of just five nights to the overflowing and rapturous Russian audience. At the end of the last performance the house manager was obliged to come out and instruct the audience not to applaud and cheer quite so noisily, as the theatre's vast antique chandelier was thought to be in danger (not to mention those sitting underneath). The entire trip was a triumph for La Scala, but the evident feeling of the people was that Caballé had enjoyed an even greater personal one. Though she was not to return to Russia for fifteen years, it is clear from the reception she then received that the Moscow public had come to regard her as a national treasure, an impression only intensified by her celebrated return in the winter of 1992 when she was greeted simply as 'Tsarina'.

Caballé's next port of call was London where she was scheduled to record the first of a whole series of complete operas under the terms of a new contract which her brother Carlos had negotiated the year before with Philips, the Dutch-based arm of the international conglomerate Polygram. The work was *Così fan tutte*, part of Colin Davis's on-going cycle of Mozart's seven mature operas. Montserrat was thrilled to be taking part in this particular recording since it was the first – and as it transpired, the last – Mozart opera she was to set down. In the middle of these *Così* sessions, she was also due to give a concert performance on 29 May 1974 in the Royal Festival Hall of *Adriana Lecouvreur* with José Carreras as Maurizio. Fortunately, since the work was part of the current repertory of both principal singers, it was not necessary for too much rehearsal time to be devoted to this one-off concert. But the Mozart required a great deal of hard work and concentration, particularly the recitatives. Caballé was therefore horrified to discover that on

Montserrat's parents, Ana and Carlos, on their wedding day.

Aged about eight, at around the time of her first lessons at the Liceo.

As a baby.

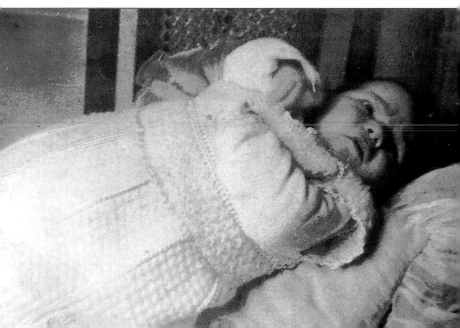

At a restaurant in Barceloneta, aged about eighteen.

A musical soirée at the home of Montserrat's patron, José Antonio Bertrand (second from left), with Alicia de Larrocha at the piano, c.1954.

With Eugenia Kemmeny, the teacher responsible for instilling Caballé's formidable technique, taken after the soprano's début at the Liceo in 1962.

With Pablo Casals and Conchita Badía on the occasion of the French première of *El Pessebre* in Toulouse, October 1962.

Montserrat's professional début as a principal, singing Mimì on 17 November 1956 in the Stadttheater, Basel.

Her first performance of *Salome*, Basel, February 1958.

Her début at the Palau de La Música, Barcelona, in 1963: with Alfonso Sanz (the Director of the Associación de Cultura Músical) and Carlos Caballé, her brother and artistic manager.

Her début at the Liceo on 7 January 1962, in the Spanish première of *Arabella*.

Madama Butterfly, with Bernabé Martí
as Pinkerton, in 1962. *(Guirau)*

Montserrat and Bernabé at their wedding
in S. Maria de Montserrat, 14 August
1964.

Leaving Carnegie Hall in
triumph with Allen Sven
Oxenburg after *Lucrezia
Borgia*, 20 April 1965.

Above: The RCA cover for Caballé's first internationally released LP.

Above left: Recording *La traviata* in Rome, June 1967, with Georges Prêtre.

Left: Montserrat's British début in May 1965, singing the Marschallin at Glyndebourne.

Below: Visiting her husband and Joan Sutherland singing together in *Norma*, Philadelphia, March 1968.

Belated début (as a principal) at La Scala in February 1970, singing Lucrezia Borgia.

Backstage at La Scala with Renata Tebaldi after the first night of *Norma*, 22 December 1972.

Two divas about to relive history? Caballé and Shirley Verrett backstage at La Scala during the first night of *Maria Stuarda* in April 1972, with Antonio Ghiringhelli and Margherita Wallmann.

As Elisabetta in *Roberto Devereux* in February 1972, Caballé's only stage performances at the Teatro La Fenice, Venice.

As Violetta, making her Covent Garden début in June 1972. On this evidence, it is a mystery why Caballé's own costumes should have aroused such controversy. *(Donald Southern)*

the very first day of recording, instead of some relatively undemanding passages of *secco*, or the anticipated ensemble work, she was expected to begin by recording her formidable Act I aria, 'Com'è scoglio'. This rearrangement of schedules had been necessitated by the unforeseen absence of Ileana Cotrubas – the Despina – whose mother was daily expected to be allowed out of the iron-fisted dictatorship that was then Ceaucescu's Romania.

In fact, it took several days for the promised visa to materialize, and the Romanian soprano was in such a state of nervous prostration at this turn of events that the sessions were continually rescheduled to take account of her absence. Hence the need for Caballé to record her major aria cold. Although she understood the reasons for this well enough, this did not prevent her from being furious at the way in which it had been sprung upon her, and she sang the first take in a considerable temper. The producer Erik Smith's attitude was that Caballé could always retake the aria later if she wanted: but in the event she listened to the playback of the first take and declared herself completely satisfied; there would be no need for any retake. It is this performance, without subsequent edits, that appears on the finished recording. Some while later, the Dorabella of this set – Janet Baker – gave an interview during the course of which she stated that, in her opinion, Montserrat Caballé, together with Dietrich Fischer-Dieskau, constituted the yardsticks by which great singing should be judged – no mean tribute from one of the finest singers England has ever produced.

The concert performance of *Adriana Lecouvreur* that took place in the midst of all this was a triumph for all concerned. The reviews were uniformly enthusiastic and Stelios Galatopolous was obliged surreptitiously to extend his list of works in the Caballé pantheon: 'Adriana, the tragic tragedienne, together with Maria Stuarda and Caterina Cornaro, [are] Caballé's best roles. Today in these roles she is incomparable. (I hope the recording companies are listening and will act on this whilst the iron is hot.)'[7]* It is all the more unfortunate in the light of these reviews that this performance was the last complete opera which Caballé gave under the aegis of Denny Dayviss's concert promotions. They folded the following year after a typically brave but financially ruinous performance of Ernest Bloch's *Macbeth*.

In early June, Caballé travelled to Madrid where she sang two performances of *Adriana Lecouvreur*, again with Carreras. She then returned to Barcelona where she was due to make her first recordings as a star

---

* Unfortunately they were not and did not. Caballé never made studio recordings of any of these operas.

singer for Spanish Columbia which, despite its name, was actually a subsidiary of the Decca Record Company in England. Decca had agreed to Caballé's demands that a proposed series of recordings for them should be made in Spain, thus sparing the soprano at least some of the necessity of having to travel too far from her family during the summer months. The disc comprised a juicy selection of operatic excerpts divided neatly between items from Montserrat's current repertoire – *Vespri siciliani*, *Ballo in maschera*, *Trovatore* and *Adriana* – and works which she had never sung (and never would sing) on stage – *Rigoletto*, *La sonnambula*, *Suor Angelica* and *La Wally*. The Orquesta Sinfónica de Barcelona was conducted by Gianfranco Masini, and when the disc was released in England,[8] the editor of *Opera* wrote: 'The most ravishing piece of singing on this recital is . . . "D'armor sull'ali rosee", which quite eclipses Milanov's famous performance.'[9] Other equally eminent critics all managed to find superlative examples of the art of singing on the disc, although – surely indicative of the quality of the disc as a whole – each chose a different aria as his personal favourite. The Earl of Harewood, a life-long friend of Maria Callas and the editor of *Kobbé*, wrote apropos the Act IV extract from *Vespri*, ' "Arrigo! Ah, parli a un core": . . . Montserrat Caballé . . . demonstrates exquisite sensibility throughout and a *pianissimo* top C just before the end of the aria which is one of the loveliest I ever heard on record. This 1974 performance is nothing less than perfection.'[10] And the recording of Angelica's aria became the enthusiastic object of a detailed review by John Steane in *The Gramophone*: 'Caballé has the perfect voice for [this] aria: fine body and warmth in the middle range and a heavenly *pianissimo*. A heartfelt performance, it often calls to mind the legendary record made by Ponselle in retirement, and Caballé gains in the comparison by being less openly emotional.'[11]

But Montserrat was beginning to feel unwell: her abdomen was swelling and it was fast becoming clear that surgical intervention would in all probability be necessary. She was, however, determined to fulfil a final clutch of engagements first, one of which was the recording of *Aïda* under the baton of Riccardo Muti that EMI had arranged earlier in the year. All opera lovers have good cause to be grateful for this postponement, since without it two triumphs of Montserrat's career might never have materialized. The recording of *Aïda* has been regarded since the day of its release as a classic of the gramophone. In the later context of reviewing a compilation album entitled 'Great Sopranos of Our Time' (containing arias sung by de los Angeles, Callas, Cotrubas, Freni, Gruberová, Schwarzkopf, Scotto and Sutherland, as well as Aïda's Act III aria extracted from the above set), John Steane wrote:

what is in some ways best is kept till last – Caballé's Aïda, sounding gloriously full-bodied . . . [She] strings the phrases of 'Oh patria mia' on a miraculously held line of breath, the high C *dolce* (as Verdi must have dreamt of it) and the final *pianissimo* floated and sustained to perfection.[12]

And within ten days of the conclusion of the sessions for this recording she gave the magnificent Norma at Orange already mentioned. In fact, it came within a hair's breadth of being cancelled, since both the dress rehearsal and the day of the actual performance on 20 July were disrupted by the Mistral, the unruly Atlantic wind that habitually strafes the south of France. With an expectant audience of 8000 already in position in the open-air Roman amphitheatre and an estimated 2000 camped around the perimeter, the starting time was delayed for well over an hour on the off-chance that the unpredictable gusts – up to sixty miles an hour – would subside. They did not, and blankets borrowed from a nearby army base were distributed amongst the audience, many of whom had turned up in evening dress and were bitterly cold. At 9 p.m. the director of the Festival, Jacques Bourgeois, decided that cancellation was inevitable. But Montserrat, busy tucking sheets of newspaper underneath her costume, instead suggested that they just go ahead and start and then cancel if it became absolutely necessary later in the performance. The film director, Pierre Jourdan, who had an army of cameramen poised to take up positions on stage, was duly notified. At 9.15 the performance began.

The orchestral players, on loan from the new opera house in Turin, were obliged to fix the music to their stands with clothes-pegs and the audience had to reconcile themselves to the spectacle of the principals' costumes billowing uncontrollably behind them. Under these circumstances, it is miraculous that any kind of performance was possible: that it should have turned out to be probably Montserrat's greatest simply defies belief. Yet the evidence of Jourdan's film remains for all to see. There is no trace of operatic routine; every vocal measure, every stage movement, seems to arise from the compelling urgency of Norma's desperate plight. From a flawless 'Casta diva' in which Caballé's otherworldly absorption in her prayer to the chaste moon goddess seems to hang weightlessly in a kind of elevated spiritual plane, to a snarlingly ferocious 'In mia man alfin tu sei' in which one actually fears for Vickers' safety as this dagger-wielding Norma circles ever closer like some vengeful bird of prey, no aspect of this ultimate operatic role escapes her. This performance gives the lie to all those who have ever regarded her as uninvolved or unconvincing on stage.

When the film was shown commercially in Paris early the following year, Jacques Bourgeois invited Maria Callas – then resident in the city – to attend the opening night as his personal guest. She accepted and sat through the screening in uncharacteristic silence. At the end she turned to her host and simply observed, 'You have made her look too beautiful.' One wonders what thoughts must have been going through Callas's mind; at the time she had not sung on stage for ten years and might reasonably have expected never to see her undisputed supremacy in the role seriously challenged. In any case, both Jourdan and Bourgeois noted that she was disconsolate for some time afterwards, but within two days of the première she telephoned Caballé in Barcelona to congratulate her. In the Italian that the two singers habitually used in conversation, Callas remarked upon 'la grandezza del tuo servizio, alla musica e al personaggio' ('the greatness of your service both to the music and the character').

Some while later, Montserrat unexpectedly received a pair of earrings through the post: they were from Callas, who had been given them to wear by Luchino Visconti on the occasion of her La Scala performances of *Norma* in 1955 and which she had worn in all subsequent assumptions of the role. Maria Callas died less than two years later, and this simple gesture perhaps marks an unspoken acknowledgement on her part that the torch had already been passed on. Certainly, Callas herself seemed to have come to think so. Her last-ever press interview took place mere days before her death and during it she responded to Philippe Caloni's provocative question as to whether, in her estimation, she had any real successors. She replied unequivocally: 'Only Montserrat Caballé.' Be that as it may, Montserrat, whilst cherishing the friendship and the mutual respect that lay behind the gift, could never bring herself to wear Callas's earrings on stage. As she acknowledges: 'There was only one Maria.'

After her début at the Aix-en-Provence Festival on 25 July 1974, happily preserved in a recording from the French National Sound Archives and which ended by all accounts with an emotional farewell speech, Caballé returned to Barcelona as promised in order to rest in preparation for the forthcoming surgery. It was now envisaged that she would need to have a complete hysterectomy as the tumour had actually grown to the point where she was beginning to appear pregnant. Faced with the inevitability of yet another bout of abdominal surgery, this time more grave in its implications than her previous Caesarean sections, Montserrat submitted to the necessary arrangements and agreed that the operation should take place on 13 September. This modicum of delay enabled her not only to record the role of Amalia in Verdi's *I masnadieri* for Philips in London during August, as long since scheduled, but also to repay an outstanding favour in the process. During the first week of September she took part in recording sessions (for Spanish Columbia) for a disc of opera duets with Giuseppe di Stefano. Ten years previously, when Montserrat had been singing as an almost total unknown in Mexico City, it was di Stefano who had been responsible for alerting his extensive network of friends and colleagues about this new and, in his opinion, sensational young soprano. It was he who had first spoken to Rudolf Bing at the Metropolitan (though the latter needed evidence on his home ground to be convinced); and, more importantly, he had so enthused to the music director of the Dallas Opera, his old friend and Callas-collaborator Nicola Rescigno, that the latter had decided to cast Caballé as Violetta in what would have been her North American début in November 1965, had not the *Lucrezia Borgia* in Carnegie Hall unexpectedly intervened.

But by 1974 the position of tenor and soprano had been completely reversed. Caballé was now the toast of the musical world and in the tenth year of her operatic stardom: di Stefano, on the other hand, had been in progressive vocal decline for many years, had just finished the punishing and profoundly ill-advised last concert tour with Maria Callas and was in financial difficulties occasioned by his eldest daughter's terminal illness. Montserrat wanted to collaborate again with the man who, when it had been in his power to do so, had wholly unselfishly helped her. And so the sessions took place. In order to minimize the vocal risks of such a partnership, the repertory had been carefully chosen from either stylistically neutral or unknown works, half of which were French – *Manon*, *Werther* and *Les pêcheurs de perles* – and the other half Italian, including Zandonai's *Francesca da Rimini* and Carlos Gomes' *Il Guarany*. The one operatic mainstream exception was the Act I duet from *L'élisir d'amore*, which might be thought to find both soprano and tenor oddly employed but which in fact works out very well – he intense and emotional, she brusque and skittish.

One week later Montserrat was finally undergoing surgery. The whole family was at the hospital and as the hours dragged on – well past the time the doctors had estimated – Bernabé was in such a state that he decided to go and see what was happening in the theatre. However, he had insufficient courage to go on his own and insisted that his brother-in-law accompany him. Carlos was not keen on the idea and tried in vain to dissuade him, but Bernabé's wishes prevailed. Carlos remembers arriving at the viewing window of the operating theatre in time to witness two doctors, one on either side of Montserrat, pulling apart her abdominal walls, while a third struggled to lift out a tumour the size of a football. Both men stared on in horror and utter disbelief as the doctors continued to wrestle with an object that clearly weighed many kilos. In fact, they were so overwhelmed that they fled the scene almost immediately, returning to the waiting room where yet more nerve-racking time passed. They were informed that the operation was proving unexpectedly complex, since in addition to the large benign tumour, the doctors had discovered two smaller, malignant specimens, which they had also had to remove. Both Bernabé and Carlos were plunged into gloom, but were cheered shortly afterwards when they were informed that the surgery had been successfully completed.

After a routine recovery, Montserrat was discharged from hospital in mid-October and returned to her apartment in Infanta Carlota. But the immediate problem soon became clear: how to re-establish full abdominal muscle tone which, as we have seen, from the earliest days of her Liceo training Montserrat has always regarded as the very foundation of her singing technique. She consulted several specialists, one of whom gave a novel piece of advice – try standing like a man and arranging your bodily support accordingly. In the event, with Bernabé in solicitous attendance, she set about a programme of exercises designed to restore her damaged musculature. She adhered to this regime for an unbroken period of six weeks, working, in her own words, 'like a mad woman'. Even so, she was not well enough to undertake the revival of *Anna Bolena* which was being mounted specifically for her and which was due to open two days after the start of the 1974–5 season at the Liceo.* Pàmias managed to secure the services of a not especially eminent soprano from London, who was announced to the audience as coming 'direct from Covent Garden'. After a first Act received in glacial silence, a woman shouted from the fifth tier – home of all the true *mélomanes* – 'From Covent Garden? What is she there, the door-keeper?' Evidently, it is no easy matter to replace an indisposed Caballé, least of all in her native Barcelona.

In the event her return to the stage took place on 24 November when she unexpectedly undertook the scheduled *Norma*s in Marseilles, which no one in the opera house there had imagined she would actually be well enough to perform. The loyal audience was even more apprehensive than Caballé herself, but although, not surprisingly, her perform-

---

* This was already the second of Caballé's on-going series of non-appearances in this particular work. She came to believe that she was simply cursed in all her attempts to sing the role.

ance was somewhat uneven, by the end of the evening the old stamina began to assert itself and she was duly accorded an emotional reception.

Her next appearances were much less demanding and effectively came as light relief: a series of five performances of *Adriana Lecouvreur* in Trieste. After this it was back home to Barcelona for Christmas, though the whole of the period from 23 December onwards was devoted to rehearsals at the Liceo for the new production of *I vespri siciliani* which was to open on 2 January 1975. The work had not been seen in Barcelona in over a century, and the management obviously hoped to repeat the success of the preceding year's *Aïda* by again pairing Caballé with Domingo, a hope that was duly realized. Montserrat remained at the Liceo in order to rehearse and give three performances of *Don Giovanni*, a most welcome return to her old-style repertory but nevertheless taking full account of her new-style vocal developments: instead of Elvira she essayed for the first time the more obviously dramatic role of Donna Anna and, as the recorded evidence reveals, was fully equal to its demands. Immediately after these performances, she returned to La Scala where she spent virtually the whole of the next two months. After giving a recital there on 22 January, she began rehearsals for a revival of *Norma* at the end of the month. The first night was only the second performance of the role which Caballé had given in the house: she had sung just one performance in December 1972 before contracting mumps; the stupendous performances she had given with La Scala in 1974 had taken place at the Bolshoi Theatre in Moscow. The question was, after her definitive assumption of the role in Orange, could she repeat the unrepeatable for the Milanese? The review which appeared in *Corriere della Sera* left no doubt: after two whole columns of phrase-by-phrase vocal analysis under the headline 'Stupenda Norma della Caballé', we learn that her performance was: 'una lezione stilistica della quale non si può immaginarne una assolutamente più perfetta'.*[13]

Barely a fortnight later occurred the opening night of a prestigious revival of Zeffirelli's production of *Un ballo in maschera*, not only with Caballé as Amelia, but with José Carreras making his house début in the role of Riccardo. The performances were an outstanding success – Carreras recounts that they were the greatest of his career thus far – and had two very important repercussions for both artists in the short term. A pair of Herbert von Karajan's closest associates, including his right-hand man Andrea von Mattoni, were at the performances, and Carlos Caballé found himself being asked on behalf of the Austrian conductor

* 'One could not imagine a more absolutely perfect lesson in style.'

whether Carreras would be free to sing at the Salzburg Easter Festival the following year in performances of the Verdi *Requiem*. This was obviously an astute career move for Carreras; and Carlos was even more delighted when subsequently the maestro himself rang him in Barcelona to request that Montserrat make her début at the Salzburg Festival in the same performances. To cap it all, representatives of Philips, to whom Carreras was now exclusively contracted, immediately decided to press ahead with a whole series of Caballé/Carreras recordings, beginning with *Ballo* in Dresden in June.

After only a few days in Barcelona the soprano was off again, performing a series of miscellaneous recitals in Sabadell, Trieste and Paris, as well as two stage performances of *Andrea Chénier* in Nice conducted by Gianfranco Masini. At this point she embarked upon a schedule which in the event – and notwithstanding two quite serious illnesses – kept her working continuously, virtually without so much as a day's break, for the next six years. Not that there had been many gaps in the preceding six, but at least there had been some, and a pause in which she could draw breath had occasionally punctuated her major engagements in the past. From now on it was an endless round of tightly dove-tailed stage performances in the major operatic centres, interspersed with studio recordings of complete operas.

Nor was it simply a matter of hawking the familiar roles around at greater frequency – this had never been Montserrat's style: an increased workload for her *de facto* implied a whole new repertory. In her current state of voice there appeared to be no very pressing reason why she should not undertake more or less any role that took her fancy. After all, she was in the twentieth year of her professional career and had sung her way up from Pàminas and Mimìs to be the undisputed reigning Norma. Doubtless many would feel this to be a more than adequate summit of ambition; but this would be reckoning without Caballé's self-confessed musical curiosity. In the process, she would tackle many of the repertoire's real monsters, including Turandot and La Gioconda, and provoke any amount of head-shaking as to the advisability of so doing. Real vocal risks were of course involved, as Caballé herself was well aware. But as we have observed before, a determined diva is not easily deterred, least of all one who by the mid-1970s had acquired such clout. And if some things were sacrificed, others would be gained in the vocal profit-and-loss account.

In mid-April 1975, after a stage absence of nearly three years, Caballé returned to the Royal Opera House, Covent Garden, to sing a scheduled eight performances in a revival of Visconti's production of *Il trovatore*.

Again the reviews were mixed, just as again the costumes were her own (they were actually the ones she had worn for the solitary performance at Orange in 1972). Certainly it did her no favours that the previous year's recording of the Act IV aria should have been released at exactly this moment: nor did the circulation of the news that in between performances she was singing Elisabeth de Valois in Frankfurt and Mimì in Valencia. The first night performance was, by all accounts, patchy, but the second fared much better, with Caballé in lustrous form: particularly memorable was the entire Act IV sequence crowned by the great soaring phrase of her death scene 'Primo che d'altri vivere' – and the subsequent chromatic descent – sung on a single breath, *pianissimo*, sprawled flat on her back on a flight of stairs. On the same evening at a hastily assembled midnight gala she sang the most impressive 'Tu che le vanità' heard in house history. It was all the more unfortunate that the projected run of eight performances did not materialize, and punters attending the last three were treated to the efforts of Liliana Molnar-Talajic, whose principal achievement was to make Montserrat seem both tall and slim.

In between the third and fourth performances of *Il trovatore* Caballé gave a solo recital at the Royal Festival Hall on 2 May 1975. Because of this extended sojourn in London, she was spending an increasing amount of time as Denny Dayviss's guest at her apartment which overlooked Regent's Park. This was a convenient arrangement from all points of view, not least Montserrat's, who had come to regard Denny as family. There was one small matter that had been urged upon Miss Dayviss by the local police: it was inadvisable for the two women to linger in the kitchen unaccompanied, since the female residents of flats facing on to the park had recently been subjected to the attentions of an exhibitionist or 'flasher'.

The recital on Friday, 2 May was a typically varied programme: a group of Handel opera arias was followed by a set of Strauss *Lieder*, including 'Cäcilie', 'Allerseelen' and 'Morgen!', whilst the second half included extremely rare Donizetti arias from *Betley* and *Adelia*, and concluded with a mixed group of Spanish songs. But the performance – Caballé's first London recital in over five years – had barely commenced when one of the spotlights in front of the enormous acoustic canopy silently emitted a blinding burst of light and went out. Caballé faltered and, turning to Zanetti who was just completing a Handel *ritornello*, evidently asked him to stop. The audience, most of whom had witnessed the real cause of the problem, were mortified to see the soprano walk forward and hold up her hands in a plea for attention, in so doing revealing the full width of the floor-length cope she was wearing over her black gown, which was otherwise hidden from sight. In a small, rather inappropriately girlish voice and approximate English, she said, 'Please, my eyes are no so good, and it no help to sing if there is flash in audience. So please, no flash.' Three thousand people sat squirming with discomfort, each of them dying to tell Montserrat that no one was actually taking pictures of her, that it was simply a blown light-bulb; but it was of course impossible to say anything. In a suddenly charged atmosphere, Caballé returned to the piano and motioned to Zanetti to recommence the introduction. But as he did so, the audience watched amazed as Montserrat's shoulders began to heave up and down, and sounds suspiciously like stifled giggling began to emanate from the platform. Head lowered, the soprano turned to Zanetti, who fell silent a second time. She then walked forward again, wreathed in smiles, and said, 'Please, when I say *flash*, I not mean . . .' and completed her sentence with a piece of mime, delicately opening wide the panels of her cope with both hands.

As bursts of disbelieving laughter erupted throughout the auditorium, a stricken Carlos Caballé said to Denny Dayviss in the wings, 'My God, she doesn't know what she's saying!' Denny replied, 'My dear, I'm afraid she does.' The audience buzzed and hummed, and Montserrat, by now hiding her face in her hands and emitting high-pitched hoots, tried (and failed) to compose herself back at the piano. When she finally managed to do so, the whole evening went on to be a triumph, though a few punters were scandalized and went home in high dudgeon. But for the vast majority of those present, this evening served to confirm Caballé's reputation as the diva not only with a smile, but also the most infectious giggle as well as an unexpected grasp of the finer points of English vocabulary.

At the end of the run of Covent Garden *Trovatore*s, Caballé returned briefly to Spain giving two performances in Zaragoza – one *Norma* and one *Butterfly* – before commencing a five-day return to the Hamburg State Opera for two *Trovatore*s. She then returned to London in mid-June for recording sessions for Decca. The work was Verdi's *Luisa Miller*, which reunited on disc Caballé with Luciano Pavarotti as Rodolfo and Sherrill Milnes as her father. With her staple performance diet now consisting largely of Normas, Aïdas and Amelias, Montserrat's assumption of the role of Luisa seems retrograde: yet by courtesy of her prodigious technique, she contrived to lighten her voice convincingly in Act I and rose in fine style to the challenge of the Act II *scena* and the whole of Act III. She had not yet sacrificed flexibility to power: and the two vocal features which one might have thought largely incompatible were brought into even sharper contrast less than a year later when, at

La Scala, she sought to sing Luisa back-to-back with her début in the role of Turandot.

In fact, Caballé spent the greater part of summer 1975 in the recording studios. No sooner had the *Luisa Miller* been finished than she flew to Dresden to take part in the recording of *Un ballo in maschera* for Philips with Carreras. Colin Davis had been rehearsing the Staatskapelle in the Lukaskirche for some days, but the engineers were experiencing difficulties in balancing the sound, which only worsened with the addition of the voices. According to Carlos Caballé, three full days of sessions took place before it was decided at an emergency meeting of the technicians, producer and conductor that the recording would have to be abandoned. As a result, the singers were simply paid off with their expenses thus far and given a promise that the recording would be rescheduled as soon as practicable.

At this point Montserrat flew home to Spain, gave a recital in Figueras, and on 3 July departed for Aix-en-Provence, where her friend and former agent Bernard Lefort was now the Festival's artistic administrator. The work which had been chosen for her stage début there was Rossini's *Elisabetta, Regina d'Inghilterra* – a considerable rarity, though, as so often, one already given by Leyla Gencer. Gøsta Winbergh sang the role of Leicester, Queen Elizabeth's *inamorato* (who is secretly married to Mathilde (Valerie Masterson)). The performances were given in the open air arena in Arles under rather disagreeable circumstances for the performers, since the *ad hoc* arrangements for dressing-rooms in this improvised theatrical space took the form of army tents which proved no deterrent to the mosquitoes that swarmed in from the nearby river. As a result, the singers went about smeared from head to foot in insect repellent. After the first two performances, the conductor, Gianfranco Masini, and cast – with the exception of Winbergh – removed to St John's Smith Square in London in order to record the work for Philips. (José Carreras had always been envisaged for the role of Leicester on the recording and would have sung it at the Aix Festival had not scheduling problems intervened.) The sessions went smoothly but had not been completed when everyone was required to return to Arles for a single further stage performance of the work that had been arranged by Lefort specifically for the purposes of a television relay. Unfortunately, on the day itself – 28 July – the technical crew were instructed by their union to withdraw their labour and as a result the performance was cancelled. Caballé was furious at the loss of the televised performance, though she was later pleased to learn that a videotape of the dress rehearsal exists, which was filmed in order to practise the various camera angles.

The day after this débâcle, she and her colleagues returned to London in order to complete the Philips recording. She had with her, neatly arranged inside a large hat box, the elaborate and convincing stage props representing the royal regalia of England (including Elisabeth's crown, orb and sceptre) which had been made for her by Jordi Suriña. At Heathrow airport she was stopped by Customs officials and asked if she had anything to declare. She said, 'No.' One of their number then asked what she was carrying in the hat box, to which she replied, 'My crown jewels.' The officials humoured her until they removed the lid, whereupon their expressions suddenly became very serious. Despite her explanations, she was detained for a while until the English Customs were satisfied that they were not in fact dealing with a particularly brazen smuggler. And even then she was lucky not to have her personal props confiscated.

It was only a matter of days before she was off again, giving recitals in Marbella, La Coruña and Santander. She then returned to London where this time she recorded *Il corsaro*, with Carreras and Jessye Norman, of whom she retains fond memories. After completing a further recital schedule which embraced several cities in Spain as well as a trio of guest appearances in Germany – Mannheim, Saarbrücken and Stuttgart – she returned to the clinic in Barcelona for a routine check-up following the abdominal surgery she had undergone the previous year. This revealed that, in the interim, although she had recovered fully from the hysterectomy, she was now suffering from polyps, which would require excision and cauterization. She was admitted to hospital and operated on immediately, which of necessity entailed the cancellation of what would have been her début at the War Memorial Opera House in San Francisco in a new production of *Norma*. In the event, Rita Hunter sang in Caballé's stead and enjoyed a personal triumph.

Nevertheless, Caballé was back on stage barely one month after what she remembers as a very painful business (and one that would necessitate several follow-ups). Admittedly this took place well away from the mainstream operatic circuit, in Tenerife, and allowed her to judge the state of her vocal recovery in the only forum that matters, in front of a public. But the role was Norma, in which there is no real margin for error. In the event, this Tenerife performance gave her sufficient courage to fulfil an obligation to which she had committed herself earlier in the year, again at Giuseppe di Stefano's behest. Following the latter's Far Eastern tour with Maria Callas, which had ended in Sapporo, Japan, in November 1974, it had been arranged at the tenor's urging that the two veterans would return to Tokyo exactly one year later in order to give fully staged performances of *Tosca*. For a few months, at the beginning of 1975, Callas had worked seriously on this project, going so far as to obtain the covert use of the Théâtre des Champs-Élysées in which to rehearse. Unfortunately, word of this leaked out, and a journalist managed to inveigle his way unnoticed into the auditorium whilst she was practising. An article appeared in *France-Dimanche* detailing the piteous state of her voice, which by this time was in all probability no more than the perfect truth. Nevertheless, Callas was justifiably scandalized at the breach of faith, sued the newspaper and (posthumously) won, but came to a much more significant decision: she would never sing in public again. This left di Stefano with a crisis on his hands – scheduled *Tosca*s in Japan in less than six months' time, with sold-out houses which had been achieved on the strength of the Japanese being able to hear, no matter what the condition of her voice, the most famous soprano in the world. In desperation, di Stefano contacted Caballé who, having been assured of Maria's blessing in so doing, agreed to sing in her place. Callas herself came on the line and said, 'We both love Pippo' – di Stefano's pet name – 'so I want you to sing in my place, partly for my sake but, more importantly, for his.' Caballé's consent necessitated her agreed withdrawal from scheduled performances of *Le nozze di Figaro* at the Liceo. It is a measure of Caballé's standing in the operatic world that, by the time the three *Tosca*s took place, not a single ticket had been returned and, moreover, there was a clamour – unfulfilled – for additional performances.

Thereafter Caballé plunged into an intensive period of rehearsals at the Teatro San Carlo in Naples, directed by the Italian *metteur-en-scène*, Alberto Fassini, for a new production of an opera that she was about to undertake for the very first time: Donizetti's *Gemma di Vergy*. It was in a television interview screened during this run of performances that Caballé, questioned about her motivation in having this forgotten work revived, replied:

> I believe that singers have a certain obligation to offer 'new' works alongside their familiar repertory. Maria Callas was the first to make a stand on this and Joan Sutherland and I have both been doing it for many years. Joan once said to me, 'Montsy, if you and me don't do it, who will?'

She might have added that she had already, some six years previously, recorded the great Act I *scena* as part of her Donizetti rarities recital, and that in her opinion – paraphrasing and extending Lilli Lehmann's famous dictum – singing just one *Gemma di Vergy* was the equivalent of three *Norma*s. Certainly no one was better placed to know, since, as William Ashbrook records in his definitive Donizetti biography,[14]

Caballé was the first singer in the twentieth century to tackle the role, the dramatic substance of which is essentially a reworking not only of the composer's own earlier *Anna Bolena* but also of Bellini's contemporary *Beatrice di Tenda*.

The last performance in Naples was on 21 December – sensationally, it included an encore of the whole Act II *concertato* – and the following morning Caballé returned to Barcelona in order to begin stage rehearsals for a revival of *Don Carlos* at the Liceo, which opened for a run of three performances on 28 December, with Giacomo Aragall – Montserrat's next-door-neighbour in the Avenida Infanta Carlota – in the title-role and Gwynne Howell as Philip II. After a brief excursion to give two more performances of the same opera in Nice, Caballé returned to the Liceo in order to give three *Gemma di Vergy*s with the same cast as in Naples, including Juan Pons (in a small role), recently promoted from the Liceo chorus and a discovery of Carlos Caballé, as well as the house début of another of Carlos's finds, the Argentinian tenor, Luis Lima.

After the last performance on 20 January 1976, Caballé immediately departed for La Scala where she was due to sing six Aïdas: doubtless her recent excursion into the heaviest end of the *bel canto* repertory was an appropriate prelude to these performances. But she already had her sights set on her scheduled return to Milan, where she had been invited by La Scala's managing triumvirate of Paolo Grassi, Francesco Siciliani and Claudio Abbado to take the title-role in the performance commemorating the fiftieth anniversary of the première of Puccini's *Turandot*.

CHAPTER TEN

1976–1979: Heavyweight Contender

In mid-February 1976, Caballé, together with her husband, left for New York for what was by now her regular annual two-month stint at the Metropolitan Opera House. This year she was to offer an unusual conspectus of her repertory, including her first performances of the title-role in an opera that was also a return to her first love: *Ariadne auf Naxos* by Richard Strauss. The other two works in which she was to sing were *Norma* (with Bernabé who, replacing Carlo Cossutta at the last minute as Pollione, would thereby be making his Met début), and *Aïda* – which saw Caballé being paired for the first time with the singer whose indisposition had paved the way for Montserrat's New York début eleven years previously: Marilyn Horne. She had occasionally encountered Caballé in performance during her years at the Met, but the *Aïda* rehearsals were the first time the two women had actually met. Although Horne was, and perhaps still is, best known for her vocal partnership with Joan Sutherland dating back to 1961, the American mezzo-soprano had long since established an outstanding career of her own. Famed for her feisty plain-speaking, there was some initial apprehension at the Met as to how Horne and Caballé would actually get on. In fact, the two hit it off immediately. Each artist genuinely admired the extraordinary technical abilities of the other, but in addition to musical considerations, Horne fell in love with Caballé's giggly sense of humour, whilst Montserrat fell under the spell of Jackie's – as Horne is known to her friends – sheer vivacity. Out of this a new and significant operatic partnership was born, which has taken the form of numerous stage and concert performances throughout America and Europe, though undocumented in terms of commercial recordings. Horne looks back on their partnership with the greatest pleasure:

> I never worked with Montserrat until the *Aïda*s in 1976, but I'd heard her several times at the Metropolitan: she was tremendous in *I vespri siciliani*, and her *Adriana Lecouvreur* was perfection. What really

distinguishes the few great singers from the merely good is the quality and the beauty of their voice, and in particular their middle register. Montserrat's is simply remarkable. She can spin those incredible tones and they just come right out to your ear. There's no one else around today who can do that. At one of the joint concerts we sang together, she did a piece from Donizetti's *Sancia di Castiglia* – utterly unknown – and she just took it and made the whole thing come alive. The audience went crazy, it was so wonderful. And on top of being a fabulous singer, she is a very great and funny lady. I love her very much.

Just how capable Caballé could be of sending up her own perceived image as a very grand diva indeed was shown clearly in her assumption of the title-role in *Ariadne auf Naxos*, revived on 20 March under the baton of James Levine in the old Glyndebourne-derived Oliver Messel sets dating from the 1950s. These Strauss performances were sung in tandem with the performances of *Aïda* which, if allowing her no scope for any humorous displays, certainly allowed a different and increasingly noticeable aspect of her voice to come to the fore: '[She] sang the first two Acts with an almost Nilsson-like power; the way her voice dominated the ensemble in the triumphal scene was astonishing.'[1]

Montserrat flew straight to Salzburg on 10 April in order to rehearse the Verdi *Requiem* in which she was due to sing with Cossotto, Carreras and José van Dam. Thus at long last she was to make her début at Salzburg, albeit at Karajan's own Easter Festival and not the main Summer one. The first rehearsal took the form of a *Sitzprobe* in Karajan's office for Caballé and Carreras only, with the conductor inquiring of them exactly how they planned to phrase each sequence and exactly where they were proposing to breathe. Only subsequently, after the immediately following full rehearsal, did the Spaniards discover from José van Dam that Karajan did this not as some kind of test but so that he knew precisely where he needed to make any necessary allowances in the orchestral accompaniment. Montserrat had had a particularly funny time of it, nevertheless. Karajan had kept saying, 'You will need to breathe here, no?' And Montserrat, whose phrasing has always been of legendary length, kept answering, 'No, maestro.'

'Here?'

'No.'

'Here, surely?'

'No.'

Karajan's response was a lopsided smile and repeated exclamations of 'Fantastic, fantastic!'

In the event, her combination of vocal poise and breath control proved rather too fantastic for her own good, since as Carreras remembers, Caballé gave the performance of a lifetime and drove the 2000-strong audience in the Grosses Festspielhaus into frenzies. Unfortunately Montserrat never reappeared at the Easter Festival, and only made her début at the Summer Festival – in the form of a recital – in 1987.* Perhaps the final word on the whole business of her relations or, indeed, nonrelations, with Karajan is best summed up by Caballé herself who, characteristically refusing to be drawn in public on a potentially controversial subject involving a colleague, said in interview: 'Let's just say he's got my photograph, and I've got his. In a nice frame.'

From Salzburg, Caballé flew to Paris where on 20 April 1976 she gave a concert performance of *Gemma di Vergy* in the Salle Pleyel. In common with her other appearances in the venue, this was given in association with French National Radio and survives in the archives of the Institut National de l'Audovisuel (INA). There was just time for the two scheduled performances of *Don Carlos* in Madrid before she departed for Milan and her first-ever appearance in the title-role of Puccini's unfinished masterpiece, *Turandot*. This was to be a gala celebration of the fiftieth anniversary of the work's first performance at La Scala on 25 April 1926, although no one at the Milanese house seemed to be much bothered that the work had been scheduled some three weeks behind the actual date of the anniversary. In fact, Montserrat was due to arrive in Milan on the 28th, begin rehearsals for a new production of *Luisa Miller* scheduled to open on 5 May, give a solo recital in the house during this first batch of rehearsals on 1 May, and then have a week of rehearsals for the new production of *Turandot*, which was to open on 13 May. In a properly organized opera house this programme would have been adhered to: but this was La Scala, and everything from managerial incompetence and duplicity, to an act of God conspired to frustrate these plans, with a double-dose of diva indisposition thrown in for good measure.

La Scala had originally announced that the new *Turandot* would be directed by Luigi Squarzina with designs by Pier Luigi Pizzi. But with less than a month to go, they decided instead to revive their old Margherita Wallmann/Nicola Benois production, and on this degree of short notice asked the original director to direct her own work. She accepted, despite misgivings about the short rehearsal time, only to

---

* Leaving aside all possible questions of artistic animosity, it is noticeable that many of the leading post-war sopranos never sang in Salzburg, Maria Callas, Renata Tebaldi, Joan Sutherland and Renata Scotto among them.

discover in May that the work had been entrusted instead to Sonja Frisell, Jean-Pierre Ponnelle's assistant and head of production at La Scala. Wallmann immediately withdrew, demanding a disclaimer in the programme (which she did not get). In the meantime, Caballé had fallen prey to toothache and had been obliged to have an upper back molar extracted, which led her to cancel the recital. As she once observed, 'You can sing without proper technique, you can even sing without a voice, but you can't sing without teeth!' La Scala wanted to postpone the première of *Luisa Miller* to 12 May, the night before the opening of the *Turandot*. But Caballé understandably objected to this telescoping of her performances and therefore the Puccini work was shifted back to 16 May. At that point, Mirella Freni became indisposed and withdrew from the role of Liù. This revised schedule would at least allow Caballé to sing on both opening nights but it meant that the Luisa Millers would then run into the period of her one-and-only Turandot. As a result of this, other singers were imported to sing Luisa, principal among whom was Adriana Maliponte.

And then, on 10 May – the day Zubin Mehta finally managed to begin stage rehearsals for *Turandot* after Caballé's dress rehearsal of *Luisa* – there was an earthquake in northern Italy which was felt throughout Lombardy, the Veneto and Piedmont. Caballé, holed up in her suite at the Marino La Scala, started to telephone everybody she could think of, including her parents back in Barcelona 'and her brother. Carlos, detecting the incipient tone of panic that was coming down the telephone line from his sister, rang Carreras who was in Turin with Katia Ricciarelli at the Teatro Regio – coincidentally also for performances of *Luisa Miller*. Abandoning his operatic partner, Carreras gallantly drove the 150 kilometres to Milan in order to reassure the terrified Caballé, who insisted on piling all her luggage into his car and driving back to Turin with him at five o'clock in the morning. Nevertheless, the *Luisa Miller* opening night at La Scala passed without mishap, and both Caballé and Luciano Pavarotti as Rodolfo were triumphantly received.

In the meantime, La Scala had recast the role of Liù in the shape of Elena Mauti Nunziata and Mehta had managed to squeeze in three orchestral sessions before the dress rehearsal of *Turandot* on 14 May, which went very well.* The theatre had gone out of its way to evoke as festive an atmosphere as it could for the *Turandot* gala on the 16th. The

---

* It was estimated that this much-touted 'gala commemorative new production of *Turandot*' received approximately ten hours' stage rehearsal, in contrast to Giorgio Strehler's production of *Macbeth*, which had opened the season and had enjoyed more than ninety hours.

Nobel prize-winner Eugenio Montale had agreed to make a welcoming speech and Mehta had decided to emulate Toscanini's original gesture and end the performance with the death of Liù (the point at which Puccini's own death had intervened). But the glittering gala audience who had taken their seats and opened their programmes experienced disappointment right from the start: not only had they expected Freni as Liù but there had been a persistent rumour that the Calaf was to have been Franco Corelli, for whom Gianfranco Cecchele was not thought to be much of a substitute. Nevertheless, Signor Montale's speech went down well, heaping praise on both Puccini and Caballé, and giving a vivid account of the 1926 première. Mehta duly appeared in the pit, acknowledged the warm applause and proceeded to conduct a character- istically intense first Act. There was, however, surprise amongst the cognoscenti when Turandot made her first – non-singing – appearance half-way through the Act, since the princess seemed to bear no physical resemblance whatsoever to Caballé. Perhaps, some concluded, this was just another diva caprice: if she was not actually required to sing then a stage extra could do duty for her.

In fact, Montserrat was sitting in her hotel room opposite fully made- up and in great distress. Before the performance had started she had discovered that she was bleeding and immediately thereafter had begun to suffer the most excruciating back pain. Francesco Siciliani, La Scala's artistic director, had rushed to Caballé's suite where he found her being comforted by her brother Carlos. Siciliani summoned Paolo Grassi, the theatre's Sovrintendente, as well as Grassi's doctor, who soon cleared the room. His preliminary diagnosis was quite clear, based upon the familiarity he had acquired in dealing with Grassi himself, who suffered from the same complaint: Montserrat was in the process of passing a large kidney stone. Mehta rushed to her room the moment Act I had finished, only to discover the diva in obvious pain and clearly incapable of performing. A scene ensued in which the several forces of La Scala's management each tried to shuffle the responsibility of informing the audience on to the other. In the end, doubtless to their relief, Mehta himself volunteered for the thankless task. The conductor Carlo Rizzi, then a student, was present in the audience, and vividly recalls the Indian-born conductor's handling of the situation, which unfortunately culminated in a monumental *faux pas*. Having explained the nature of the crisis to a rowdy and sceptical auditorium, Mehta tried to allay any suspicion that Caballé might simply be running scared from a role for which many thought her to be ill-suited by reassuring those present that the dress rehearsal had been a sensation and that Montserrat had sung tremendously. They really should have been there. Not surprisingly, he was greeted by a barrage of groans and jeers, which in no way abated with the further announcement that the performance would continue with the hastily summoned Emma Renzi in the title-role. By this time most of the audience must have decided that Mehta's planned laying down of his baton after Liù's death could not come soon enough.

This was scandal such as only the Milanese know how to manufacture, and the often wildly inaccurate press coverage of Caballé's sensational non-appearance continued for days. Montserrat, meanwhile, declined to be removed to the Milan City Hospital despite medical advice: instead she remained in the hotel for nine days while the agonizing process of ridding herself of the kidney stone took its course. As the doctors had pointed out, she obviously had a predisposition to this ailment and would in future have to be careful about what she ate and drank.

Caballé's first major engagement after a brief convalescence was in Hamburg where, in the space of eleven days in mid-June, she sang the greater part of her surviving Verdi repertory in the shape of two Aïdas, an Amelia and an Elisabeth de Valois. Via a solitary recital in Lyon, she then flew home to Spain where she was to commence her annual round of opera recordings during the summer months. This was unusual given that nearly all her opera sets were recorded in London: but the first project was something special, very dear to the soprano's heart, and one which she had held out for over a number of years. She had been set to record *Madama Butterfly* on at least two previous occasions, one of them with Pavarotti, but had always withdrawn on the grounds that for her it would almost be like committing an act of infidelity: *Butterfly* was the opera which she owed to Bernabé. As we have seen, the work formed the *leitmotif* of the Martís' courtship in the early 1960s, and Montserrat had always privately vowed that, if she was ever in the position of being asked to record the work, it would be with the man whose Pinkerton had won her as his wife. The major international companies had proved resistant to this proposition, but Spanish Columbia were rather more amenable. And so it was that across the period late June to early July 1976, Caballé's Cio-Cio-San, which had scarcely been in her stage repertory during her years of fame, was finally committed to disc.

No sooner was this completed than she flew to London, where in the space of eight days she recorded *Tosca* with José Carreras and the forces of the Royal Opera House, Covent Garden, conducted by its then music director, Colin Davis. If there was an increasing number of voices being raised querying the suitability of the heavier repertory which Caballé was undertaking, this recording certainly gave them the lie, as did the recital disc of *verismo* arias, including Turandot's 'In questa Reggia', which she recorded the following week, back in Barcelona, under the baton of Anton Guadagno. On the other hand, her recording of the facsimile manuscript edition of *Lucia di Lammermoor*, which took place at the end of August (following a brief summer vacation on the farm), was a decisive, if unexpected, shift back into the heartlands of *bel canto*, albeit in this case oriented in a more dramatic direction because of the restoration of the original keys and the elimination of so many ornamental accretions. Caballé is especially proud of this recording, since she regards it as the only musically truthful rendition of Donizetti's original intentions as revealed by the manuscript with which the grateful Donizetti authorities in Bergamo supplied her.

After completing this *Lucia* for Philips – again with Carreras – in London on 25 August, Caballé left for Strasbourg where, over a period of two weeks, she recorded the role of Marguerite in Gounod's *Faust*. This was her début recording for the French company, Erato, and featured Giacomo (Jaime) Aragall in the title-role. In fact there had been some surreptitious plottings behind the scenes to have the latter removed and replaced by a more starry tenor and, in the process, to have the whole project transferred to EMI. Caballé remained loyal to the contract she had signed and to the conductor, Alain Lombard. But it is a pity that the plotting bore no fruit, since the recording is ill-focused, the contributions of both chorus and orchestra mediocre and the conducting leaden. In making the recording, Caballé had bowed to the fervent wishes of those concerned and certainly – with the exception of some laboured coloratura – her contribution is technically accomplished. But Marguerite had never really featured much in her repertory – she had last sung it on stage in her début at the old Metropolitan Opera House in December 1965 – and by this stage she sounds disconcertingly mature for the role. The French musical authorities evidently did not think so, however, since her interpretation was awarded the Grand Prix du Disque when it was released in France the following year.

During a scheduled four-day gap in the sessions, Caballé and Aragall went to Vienna in order to sing in the opening night of the 1976–7 season at the Staatsoper in a revival of *Don Carlos*. This took place in front of a predictably glossy audience, including Elizabeth Taylor whose arrival upstaged that of the new intendant and artistic director, Egon Seefehlner. He was hoping, above all, to dazzle the difficult Viennese on this all-important first night. He – and they – were not disappointed:

This was a gala performance all right, and lasted an hour longer than usual because of the frequent and noisy ovations by the standees

. . . Montserrat Caballé delighted everybody with her portrayal of Elisabeth. [She] can sing rings around most lyric sopranos practising today; she was just great.[2]

Caballé spent the whole of the second half of September and the first half of October on tour in the Far East. The first two weeks were taken up with staged performances of *Adriana Lecouvreur* in Tokyo's NHK Hall. It was of these performances that José Carreras, the Maurizio, retains such a vivid memory.[3] As already noted, one of them survives both on pirate disc and video, the latter containing a delicious piece of spontaneous stage business between soprano and tenor. During the Act I love duet, one of Montserrat's heavy pendant clip-on earrings becomes partially detached during a clinch with Carreras, and when the two separate, it falls straight down the soprano's amply displayed décolletage. To her quizzical but in-character amusement, her partner delicately retrieves the item, handing it back to her with a silkily raised eyebrow and a barely suppressed smirk. Caballé's face is wreathed in smiles as she impulsively covers her partner in a kiss. As he leaves, she trips gaily across the stage, belying both her years and size in the process. No other preserved performance captures the diva so evidently enjoying herself, with the possible exception of her outrageous mugging in the 1988 Vienna production of Rossini's *Il viaggio a Reims*.

Thereafter, it was a round of concerts and recitals, taking her to Manila, Osaka, Fukuoka, Hiroshima and to the place where Maria Callas had bid her final farewell to the stage two years previously, Sapporo. By the end of the month she was engaged in a brief tour of the south of France, giving recitals and concerts in Avignon, Alès and Bordeaux, as well as three stage performances of *Un ballo in maschera* in Nice, with Carreras as Riccardo. Their partnership continued the following week back in Barcelona where they sang together in three performances of *Tosca* at the Liceo, with Ingvar Wixell as Scarpia, thereby reuniting the Philips recording cast. There followed an absolute rarity: a Caballé trip to the UK which did not involve either performance or recording in London. Instead, she gave a recital in the New Theatre, Cardiff – home of the Welsh National Opera – on 28 November 1976. The programme was a mixture of German, French and Spanish songs, with an opening group of *arie antiche* this time being drawn exclusively from works by Handel, including *Ezio, Ottone* and *Atalanta*. By all accounts Caballé was in superb voice, although during the singing of Strauss's 'Morgen' the audience was perturbed to witness her flailing her arms around like a windmill and, at one point, seeming to choke. She finished the song without the least interruption to the vocal line, but held up her hands to forestall the audience's applause: she went on to explain that half-way through the song a fly which had been buzzing continuously about her head had flown into her mouth and, not surprisingly, flown straight out again. The audience's laughter was redoubled when, during the silence which preceded a Spanish song, the sound of illicitly whirring machinery was heard throughout the auditorium, at which the soprano cried out, 'Aha! Watergate!'

Seefehlner's new regime in Vienna had obviously decided that Caballé had hitherto been insufficiently heard in the Staatsoper and that this was the season in which amends were to be made. Thus it was that in the space of the first three weeks of December the Viennese were treated to a comprehensive display of her current repertory when she sang one performance each of *Don Carlos*, *Trovatore*, *Tosca* and *Ballo*. If it seems strange that *Norma* did not figure in this list, that is simply because a new production of the work had already been scheduled for the end of the following March. Meanwhile, Montserrat's Christmas show at the Liceo was in some ways the hardest test of all, since no one in the post-Callas period had ever managed to make a success of Cherubini's *Medea*. The attractions of the role are obvious, at least in terms of dramatic opportunity. Bellini's *Norma* is basically only a rewrite of the central situation, with the important, Romantic distinction that Norma cannot bring herself to kill her own children in revenge, and goes so far as to forgive the woman who has supplanted her in her lover's affections. Medea, on the other hand, murders her children and poisons her rival before taking to the skies in her chariot and leaving mayhem behind her. The problem is that for a modern audience accustomed to the musical evocations of mania and vengeance such as Strauss's *Elektra*, Cherubini's musical language can appear anodyne, especially when, as increasingly happens nowadays, the work is restored to its original form as an *opéra comique*, sung in French and with yards of spoken dialogue. Indeed, Callas's very success as Medea, attested to by endless reviews and pirate recordings, does rather raise the question of the extent to which her gifts in this particular role were more theatrical than musical, and whether her achievement in it was not principally due to a broodingly intense and malignant stage presence. All of which is to say that Montserrat, like almost everybody else, finds it very hard to make any kind of effect in the role as it is written, even making allowance for the fact that life is made easier by singing the recitatives composed by Franz Lachner some fifty years after the work's première in place of the spoken dialogue.

According to a recent history of the Liceo, the audience felt that Caballé's voice was simply too lyrical for the role and that she lacked the necessary ferocity and vindictiveness (although the opening night was greeted with nearly 30 minutes' applause). There is some reason to believe that Caballé herself agreed with this view, since the work promptly vanished from her repertory and only reappeared in 1989. The correspondent of the Metropolitan's *Opera News*, however, thought otherwise: after praising Margherita Wallmann's début production in Spain (incidentally the début of any Cherubini stage work in that country) and the contributions of Luis Lima as Giasone and Christine Weidinger as Glauce, he wrote: '[Caballé] impressed as Medea, grasping the dramatic content of the role more with each performance. Her high notes were stunning, and she very cleverly sang her way in and out of Medea's (for her) uncomfortable *tessitura* below the stave.'[4]

The latter comment touches on an interesting point about the development of Montserrat's repertory towards the heavier roles. Much of the 'heaviness' in the *verismo*, late-Verdian and heroic *bel canto* roles stems not from any emphasis on the top end of the voice but, conversely, on the sheer amount of writing which can only be effectively encompassed in the chest register. Looking through the scores of such diverse roles as Amelia, Gioconda, Aïda, Santuzza and Norma it is striking how the vocal line barely creeps above the bottom of the stave for whole paragraphs of music, at the end of which, as likely as not, the singer is required to execute a cadenza across a range of over two octaves. It is this emphasis upon a dark, inherently baleful vocal quality that constitutes the real risk: not for nothing did the German conductor Hans von Bülow dub Verdi – a particular offender in this respect – 'der Attila der Kehlen' or the Attila of the throat. It is very difficult for any soprano who has been honking around in her chest register all night to 'refocus' the voice in its upper reaches and to project the necessary purity of timbre. The trade-off usually takes the form of some hardening or loosening of tone above the stave. In Callas's case it was very definitely the latter, whilst with Caballé – and over a much longer time-scale – it was the former; and in both cases the different vocal registers between head voice and chest became more separated. Many have thought that in Caballé's case this was too high a price to pay. Others, however, who witnessed her Geneva Giocondas in 1979, or even more extraordinarily her Paris Turandots in 1981, would not be likely to agree. And even if in the process she perhaps shortened her peak vocal longevity somewhat, it is also important to realize that, at the time of writing, she is still singing past the age of sixty.

Caballé returned to La Scala on 9 January 1977 in order to give a recital and sing in an entire run of performances of *Norma*. It is hard to know whose forbearance and indulgence one admires the more following the débâcle just seven months previously: Caballé's towards the theatre, or La Scala's towards her. In any event, the recital on 10 January found her in high holiday humour: in one of the numerous encores – Obradors' 'El vito' – the soprano became so caught up in the infectious rhythm that she volunteered some fancy foot-work as an additional accompaniment. Unfortunately, she also became caught up in the hem of her floor-length gown and, following a moment's awkward equipoise, she fell over in mid-aria with a loud crash. She ended up singing the rest of the aria squatting on the false stage which covers the orchestra pit at such functions without so much as batting an eyelid or missing a note. The audience erupted in delighted applause and, though prone, Caballé was doubtless left to reflect on the power of her personality and presence to get her through any situation, no matter how potentially embarrassing, and to turn it to her advantage. With a mischievous smile and an infectious giggle, Montserrat has achieved more throughout her career than most divas normally do by resorting to the traditional methods of snarls, threats and tantrums. And it is noticeable that whilst it has been the lot of practically everyone else at La Scala to be booed as a result of actually performing, the only real booing Montserrat ever received there was for her *non*-appearances, unfairly vented *in absentia* on her replacements.

The revival of *Norma* opened on 18 January and was televised live throughout Europe. On the opening night the need to pad out the interval with some relevant material for the live television relay audience provided the opportunity for a decorously phrased cat-fight between two divas past and present. The sight of Gina Cigna and Leyla Gencer upstaging each other with regal condescension was probably the visual highlight of the entire evening.* After the fourth performance, on the 28th, Montserrat flew to London in order to give what was fast becoming one of her regular annual recitals at the Royal Opera House, which this time involved a real novelty for the London audience. Unfortunately, it also proved to be the parting of the ways as far as its more po-faced members were concerned. After a brilliantly executed first half of Handel and Schubert, she concluded her customary Spanish second half with a group of *zarzuela* arias for the performance of which she had enlisted the help of a noted Spanish dancer and virtuoso castanetist, José de Udaeta. While the lean, bronzed performer preened himself in

---

* According to Cigna's own testimony in Lanfranco Rasponi's *The Last Prima Donnas*, Gencer made the fatal mistake, just before going on camera, of casually asking whether Cigna had ever sung the role of Norma. Cigna's frosty response was, 'Yes, Madame – only over 500 times.'

silent readiness, Caballé explained in her inimitable English the finer points of interpretation in the matter of wood- and bone-banging. This left most of the audience intrigued. The real show started when Montserrat perched herself delicately on the edge of a mock antique chair and proceeded to mime her wide-eyed relish of Udaeta's flauntings to the audience. She capped the event with a whole string of exquisite encores and sent the majority of her public home in raptures. As one reviewer remarked:

> the quality that most impressed was the singer's lovely sense of humour and it does seem a pity that there are not more opportunities for her to show off her comic talent in opera . . . her studied appreciation and exaggerated response to Udaeta's castanet solo was a minor masterpiece of comedy at its best.[5]

But there were a few who left the auditorium muttering darkly that the altarpiece of high art – a *Lieder* recital – had been desecrated, for which they would never forgive her (conveniently forgetting that they were not in an intimate salon but a 2000-seat opera house). As Montserrat herself was to remark many years later on another occasion when her vivacity got her into trouble: 'I thought the English were supposed to be famous for their sense of humour.'

The following day she returned to Milan to resume her performances of *Norma*. But she need not have bothered, since the last performance had to be cancelled when a short circuit in the stage electrics set fire to the house's venerable front curtain, which burned to a cinder. At least one critic was heard to bemoan the fact that the blaze had left Ceroli's sets largely unscathed. In fact, there would have been nothing but a chorus of approval, both from critics and public alike, had a fire consumed the sets of the next production of *Norma* in which Caballé sang. This took place at the Staatsoper in Vienna on 17 March amidst a level of pre-publicity unprecedented for the generally unoperatic mid-1970s, even making allowances for Vienna as an exception.

The ingredients certainly looked not so much promising on paper as a positive guarantee of fulfilment: apart from Montserrat, there was Cossotto as Adalgisa, the much underrated Carlo Cossutta as Pollione, the principal players of the Vienna State Opera Orchestra – in effect, the Vienna Philharmonic – under the baton of Riccardo Muti, and a brand-new production by Piero Faggioni with designs by Ezio Frigerio. Unfortunately, the promise was not fulfilled in practice: the rehearsal period was dispiriting, with endless rows between all concerned, particularly the conductor and the director. Montserrat was approached by Muti with a view to singing at least the second duet with Adalgisa in the original, higher key, to which the soprano tentatively agreed subject to Cossotto's consent. In the event, Cossotto, who felt she had been pressured into agreeing, experienced difficulty with the piece in a rehearsal and left the stage in distress, only to discover from Montserrat that in her absence the conductor had nonchalantly informed the Vienna Philharmonic that the piece would have to be played in 'downward transposition' – this, in a house where $a = 445$ Hz, the second highest in Europe – otherwise the mezzo could not cope.* Thereafter, poor Cossotto could do no right, and felt she had been utterly undermined by the conductor.

It was in this spirit that the production reached its opening night, at which the conductor had his own personal triumph. Happily, this was shared with the heroine, though none of the rest of it even began to work. Indeed, the opening night was, to quote Bellini, 'fiasco, solenne fiasco!' Cossotto, not surprisingly, sang below par, Cossutta was booed, and even Caballé found herself having to sing her opening recitative and aria without any of the familiar *appoggiature* and embellishments, all of which had been banished by the conductor. One has also to consider the details of the production. Caballé's costume for Act I had her dressed as an up-market relative of Papageno, covered in feathers. Joseph Wechsberg, writing in *Opera*, noted:

> If Mr Faggioni thinks he can produce opera in 1977 in *ancien-régime* style in the city of Vienna, he is mistaken. The citizens may never have had much appreciation for the pleasures of *bel canto* . . . but they will not accept ridiculous sets and costumes and they will laugh at precisely the moments when they should be moved. Ezio Frigerio's sets and costumes had to be seen to be believed.[6]

Against such a background, perhaps more was read into the sporadic shortcomings of the singers than would otherwise have been the case: nevertheless, the audience reserved the most unforgettable roasting for Signor Faggioni, whose befeathered production got the bird it deserved. The last word on the première can be left with Wechsberg: 'there was the sort of noisy confusion that many first-nighters love more than the opera itself. Split into fractions and factions, the audience cheered and booed until many no longer knew whom they were for and whom against.' Happily, none of this affected Montserrat, who immediately after the performance made her way out of the back of the opera house

---

* Standard concert pitch is $a = 440$ Hz pretty much throughout the world, except in Vienna's rival, Berlin. This effectively renders all vocal music almost a semi-tone higher than elsewhere.

and straight into the Hotel Sacher where a reception was held in her honour. And all five subsequent performances went very much more smoothly from the musical point of view, with Caballé approaching the levels expected of her in this, of all operas. On the other hand, despite being the most expensive that the Staatsoper had ever staged, Faggioni's production was rejected by the audience and never once revived. With it died Egon Seefehlner's hopes that he would open Vienna's hitherto closed doors to the glories of *bel canto*.

It gives some idea of the pressures of Caballé's workload at this time when one notes that in the fortnight before commencing Faggioni's rehearsals she had sung three *Salome*s at the Liceo* – the last of which on 22 February 1977 had been her 100th performance in the house – and two rapturously received concert performances in the Palau de la Musica of *Die Walküre*, with Birgit Nilsson and Thomas Stewart. The *Salome*, where the size and power of her voice in the closing scene had left the audience stunned, culminated in yet another on-stage *homenaje*. She then gave a week's worth of daily recitals in the Théâtre de l'Hôtel de Ville – the former Théâtre Sarah Bernhardt – in Paris; recording the closing scene from *Salome* as well as Strauss *Orchesterlieder* under Leonard Bernstein – their first collaboration – for DG following public performances in the Théâtre des Champs-Élysées; touring Germany; and singing *Norma* and *Ballo in maschera* in Valencia.

Unfortunately her next major project – *Aïda* at Covent Garden – fared scarcely better than the *Norma* in Vienna less than two months before. As in Vienna, Riccardo Muti, whose Covent Garden début this was, had drilled the orchestra to the nth degree of precision and, presumably mindful of recent events surrounding *Norma*, had taken a leading hand in the actual restaging of this by now anonymous revival. With the exception of the Amonasro, Peter Glossop, the musical line-up replicated that of the recent EMI recording which had set a perhaps unreal level of expectation among the audience. Certainly, none of the principals – with the possible exception of Cossotto – were thought to have produced the goods, cowed as they all seemed to be by the conductor's now noticeably brisker tempi.

Presumably for the same reasons that had led to her business with the champagne at the end of *Traviata*, Act I five years previously – the

* Press speculation had been rife as to whether Caballé – as had been announced at the beginning of the season – would actually perform the Dance of the Seven Veils herself. She did, replicating the choreography she had been taught back in Basel by Vaclav Orikowsky, which was reported as having thwarted certain sections of the public who had turned up in expectation of some sure-fire sniggering.

need to do *something* – Caballé ended Act III with a most extensive perambulation, practically into the wings, only to rush back into stage-centre with her enormous train billowing for untold yards behind her, and executing a perfect lunge at the knees of a horror-stricken Peter Glossop as the curtain rapidly descended. But the performance had more in store. Much of Muti's restaging had been geared towards eliminating the gaps between the scenes in Acts I, II and IV so as to preserve musical continuity. This meant that Amneris' great confrontation with, first, Radamès, and then the High Priests in Act IV was to be dove-tailed – with no lights up and no applause – straight into the closing scene. It is uncertain whether Fiorenza Cossotto had agreed to this piece of self-sacrifice on the mezzo's part, given that Act IV scene 1 is her golden opportunity for display. In the event, the audience was treated to the spectacle of Madame Cossotto, who had ended the scene prostrate, clambering around the extinguished footlights on all-fours, desperately attempting to take a curtain call in the pitch dark and stony silence, broken only by Muti's widely misinterpreted hisses of 'Basta! Basta!'

Caballé duly completed this run of performances as programmed, bringing her tally of roles at Covent Garden to a mere three – all Verdian – and the total number of stage performances to a paltry twelve. By this time she had sung eleven different roles in nearly 100 performances at the Metropolitan, and at the Liceo, as we have seen, her recent Salomes had constituted not only her 100th performance in the house but also the assumption of her twenty-eighth role there. Even the haphazard arrangements at La Scala had afforded her seven different roles, nearly all in new productions, including *Norma* which had been given four different sets of performances. She must have wondered if it was worth her while singing at the Royal Opera House at all. But, as usual, her schedules left no time for much introspection since she was immediately due in Aix-en-Provence to commence rehearsals for a new production of a work which had latterly vanished from her repertory: Donizetti's *Roberto Devereux*.

The public dress rehearsal, which was televised in France, and the last performance (pirated on sound only from in-house sources) both reveal very powerful and committed performances in progress, both on the part of Caballé, who was generally felt to be in stupendous form, and on that of her colleagues, who included José Carreras in the title-role. But a problem cropped up in between when one night torrential rain had caused mayhem in the open air theatre. Bernard Lefort, the Festival's director, was absent on this particular occasion, attending a funeral. A functionary decided at the last minute that the performance, instead of being cancelled, would be transferred to the cathedral. The principals, who were already in make-up and costume, were informed of this and quickly convened a meeting. No one was happy with this new arrangement: the cathedral had been used for an oratorio during the Festival and its impossible acoustics had been the cause of some damning reviews. There was also the question of whether the singers were happy, giving what would effectively become a concert performance of Donizetti's drama in ecclesiastical surroundings. They decided unanimously not to perform, but to offer instead an additional stage performance after the scheduled run had ended. But when Lefort returned from the funeral, a heated debate ensued which resulted in the Festival authorities issuing a writ for breach of contract against Caballé. This never came to court and indeed was never even surreptitiously settled out of it, since Aix had not a leg to stand on: the case was just quietly dropped. But in one man's heart the imagined outrage seems to have burned on inextinguishably: the functionary, one Sergio Segalini, has used the pages of his magazine *Opéra International* to carry on an almost obsessive vendetta against Caballé, either under his own name or through the agency of others, ever since.*

There followed an extended series of recording sessions in Strasbourg. First there was a complete *Turandot*, with José Carreras as Calaf and Mirella Freni as Liù for EMI, in which Caballé finally graduated to the title-role. Unfortunately, the set fell victim to some erratic engineering, which no amount of post-production and patching could ameliorate. And then for Erato, she recorded Strauss's *Four Last Songs*, like the *Turandot*, conducted by Alain Lombard. It was at these latter sessions that the veteran producer Michèle Garcin, together with Lombard, arranged for Montserrat to sing the closing scene of *Salome*, which was not scheduled to be recorded and for which there was not even any unused session time left to spare. Amazingly, the Strasbourg Philharmonic musicians willingly agreed to stay the extra time without payment and to play magnificently for an audience of precisely three for no better reason than that everybody present wanted to hear Caballé sing it. After a brief summer break, she returned to London to rehearse the revival of Zeffirelli's famous production of *Tosca* which had been originally mounted in 1964 with Maria Callas. It had also been in the

---

* To take just one example: in the review of the Covent Garden production of Rossini's *Il viaggio a Reims* in July 1992, in which Caballé sang the role of Madame Cortese, Segalini wrote of: 'cette poissarde des Ramblas de Barcelone' [*Opéra International*, no 161, September 1992, p. 39] ('this vulgar fishwife from Barcelona's Ramblas'). Montserrat's response to this, based on a rather deeper knowledge of the Mercat de la Boqueria, is to be flattered: 'Our fish-sellers are wonderful women with extraordinarily rich and powerful voices.'

first revival of this production in July 1965 that Callas had sung her last-ever performance in a staged opera. Montserrat was therefore thrilled to be taking part in these performances at the Royal Opera House, with which, in tandem with José Carreras, she would be opening Covent Garden's 1977–8 season.

On 16 September 1977, however, the news flashed around the world: Maria Callas was dead. Even though she had hardly sung on stage for thirteen years, the opera world was stunned and grief-stricken. Montserrat herself wanted to postpone the performances, but Covent Garden was equally determined to proceed: in consultation with the principal artists, they decided to present them in honour of Callas's memory, which burned brighter in that house than in any other save La Scala. The Greek soprano's death had left Caballé devastated, and of all those pursued by the media in search of instant response, her tearful tribute – filmed backstage in costume and make-up – was thought to be amongst the most moving and unquestionably sincere. Many years later she spoke at greater length on the subject:

> The admiration and respect for her is something I will always keep in my heart. She will never die; she is always with me. I remember hearing the news – it came as such a terrible shock I refused to believe it. Looking back, the real thing I learned from her was not so much musical as personal: the truth of her expression. She didn't try to be expressive, she simply *was*. And this you cannot copy. I remember the first time I went to her beautiful apartment in Paris. I just sat there on the sofa beside her listening for hours, talking not about herself, or colleagues, or gossip, but about music. I can still hear her voice. During the last two or three years of her life I spoke to her quite a lot. Remember, she sent me her *Norma* earrings, and there was the time, quite late, when I sang the Tokyo *Tosca*s. In the very last year I rang her often, wherever I happened to be and she would say to me, 'My God, Montserrat, what are you singing now?' We would laugh. And to me she always seemed to be perfectly all right. She said it was as if we had known each other for many, many years, and I felt that too – we became close because we valued the same things. She opened the way for all of us who, in our own ways, have followed after her.

In fact, notwithstanding the unhappy circumstance of the revival, the *Tosca* performances were among the most successful that Caballé ever gave at Covent Garden. Like Pavarotti in the same opera many years later, she brought with her an entire armoury of carefully thought-out stage business which she had accumulated throughout her career and which brought genuine illumination to the role. This devout Tosca, having consented to Scarpia's sexual proposition in order to secure her lover's release, was evidently quite prepared to go through with her half of the bargain. At a point in the action when most Toscas stand at Scarpia's dining table whiling away the moments with refreshment until they are required by the drama – and Puccini's music – to discover the knife, Caballé instead began robotically to unfasten the buttons on her sleeves, undo her dress at the back and remove her jewellery. The necklace was placed in her purse, but as she removed the second of her earrings, she dropped it, and the audience heard the faint metallic ring as – dead on cue – it landed on the knife. Only in retrieving it could one finally see that the idea had been born in the diva's mind and that Scarpia's fate was sealed. It so happened that on the first night, during the ensuing struggle, one of the two candelabra was overturned and extinguished: it was noticeable that when this Tosca performed the prescribed ritual placing of the candles on either side of Scarpia's corpse, she somehow found the time within the tightly organized musical sequence to relight it and thus complete the stage picture. On top of which she sang magnificently.

There followed a brief trip to France during which she sang in orchestral concerts in both Paris and Marseilles. Then it was off to San Francisco to begin rehearsals for her much-delayed War Memorial Opera House début. But it was not in the role of Norma, which her operation two years previously had obliged her to cancel, that she was to be heard: it was in the other pinnacle of the Italian heavyweight repertory, Turandot. Not that anyone in San Francisco, mindful not only of Caballé's previous local cancellation but also of the mayhem surrounding her first *Turandot* at La Scala in 1976, could quite bring themselves to believe that they were finally going to hear her, despite the management's frequent press-releases detailing the progress of the rehearsals of Jean-Pierre Ponnelle's production. In fact, Caballé was not the only débutant: surprisingly, these performances were Luciano Pavarotti's first stage Calafs, and the conducting had been entrusted to the twenty-four-year-old Riccardo Chailly. In the event, the anticipatory excitement of the opening night on 29 October was further heightened for an American audience by the presence of HRH Prince Charles, the Prince of Wales.

Ponnelle's production attracted criticism, though on questions of detail that would probably arouse little comment today. But the soprano had an undisputed success. Dale Harris (one of the most difficult American music critics to please) wrote:

she enjoyed a triumph, one of the greatest of her American career. Although to begin with she was understandably nervous, nowhere was there a sign of the basic vocal insecurity that had plagued her in *Aïda* at Covent Garden last summer . . . From the icy authority and subsequent rage of the Riddle Scene to the unfolding tenderness of the Third Act duet there could be no doubt of her vocal command . . . In her final triumphant acknowledgement of love, Caballé's voice streamed through the theatre like sunlight.[7]

Evidently, and as the pirate recording of one of the performances reveals, the increase in the sheer scale and volume of Caballé's voice was here shown off to best advantage. And if it had sometimes been thought in the past that she had had excessive recourse to her virtually patented *pianissimi* in order to avoid problems of singing high in full voice, they were nowhere apparent on this occasion. Indeed, in both expressive power and security of tone these live performances in San Francisco actually outshine the EMI recording made only two months earlier. But the pleasure she took in this triumph at the time must have been diminished in the space of a single afternoon when Bernabé, who had accompanied his wife on this trip and was returning on foot to their hotel perched on one of the city's steep hills, suffered a heart attack. He was immediately hospitalized and eventually, following extensive tests, fitted with a cardiac stimulator. He was never to sing professionally in public again.

This is not to suggest, however, that he retired completely. On the contrary, he threw himself whole-heartedly into an ambitious programme to transform the ever-increasing acreage of the Martís' farm at Ripoll. The old manor house was, under his supervision, converted into an enormous holiday home for the reception of as many as 140 children at any one time – many from the poorest areas of Barcelona – who would thereby be given an opportunity of enjoying holidays in pleasant country surroundings. And a little later, a substantial amount of money was raised and put into a project for the reconstruction and on-going support of a medical centre dealing with both research into and the care of infants born with Down's syndrome, which coincidentally had always been known as the 'Centro Montserrat para el Sindrome de Down'.

Back in Barcelona a sorry saga was beginning to unfold. Caballé and Domingo were scheduled to sing together at the Liceo in late November/early December 1977 in a revival of Meyerbeer's last opera, *L'Africaine*, which had not been given at the Liceo since 1949.

Domingo's own account of events centres around his increasing dissatisfaction with the standards of presentation and musical preparation at the Liceo, which he felt to be insufficiently professional. (The recording sessions in Munich for DG's *La traviata*, conducted by Carlos Kleiber, to which Domingo commuted in between performances at the Liceo doubtless acted as compensation.) He was so unhappy with the Meyerbeer staging that, on being informed by Pámias that one of the performances was to be televised live, he instead insisted on it being filmed in highlight version, only to discover subsequently that the whole performance had been televised as originally planned. At this point he refused to sing at the Liceo again and absented himself from the house for many years. Caballé and Domingo have never, to date, sung an opera together on stage again.

Into the 1980s there would appear to have been various behind-the-scene attempts to effect a stage reunion but these foundered following a particularly unpleasant bout of double-dealing concerning Covent Garden's planned new production of *Andrea Chénier*, which was to have starred Domingo and Caballé under Riccardo Muti. The consolation is that a musical reunion was finally effected in 1990 and sealed the following year when an enthusiastic Domingo, at Carlos's request and with Montserrat's approval, conducted her contribution to the opening Gala of the Teatro Maestranza in Seville. And they finally sang together again in January 1993 in the Auditorio Nacional in Madrid.

In December 1977 Caballé sang in two consecutive revivals of *Parisina*, the first in Nice and the second immediately following at the Liceo with another of Carlos's finds, Dalmacio Gonzalez, as Ernesto. As in New York, Eve Queler conducted, but the whole project ground to a halt when the orchestra, taking advantage of the political liberty in a country where almost forty years of dictatorship had only recently ended with the death of Franco, decided to go on strike. The last performance was therefore postponed until after Christmas, when Caballé's singing was said to have been more impressive than ever before. Perhaps this was as a result of the recent decisive, albeit temporary, return to *bel canto* repertory – a policy which took her to Hamburg at the beginning of 1978 for three concert performances in the Staatsoper of *Roberto Devereux* with Carreras and Alicia Nafé, conducted by Julius Rudel. Thereafter, it was back to America for an unprecedented ten-week stint in which she was scheduled to sing the title-role in *Adriana Lecouvreur* at the Metropolitan with Carreras as Maurizio, perform several recitals in and around the Eastern seaboard – including her traditional Carnegie Hall outing – and end the trip in some style with the most *recherché* operatic exhumation which even Caballé had ever undertaken: a concert performance of Mercadante's *Virginia*, a work which had originally been brought to her attention by Francesco Siciliani. Unfortunately this fell victim to the collapse of the planned sponsorship and so was never performed in public. But the Met *Adriana*s were a real triumph for all the principals, including Fiorenza Cossotto as a maniacally imperious Princesse de Bouillon.

After recitals in Las Palmas and Lausanne, Caballé returned to the Teatro San Carlo in Naples for six performances, again of *Adriana*, in the second half of April 1978. Her Maurizio was, as always, José Carreras, but this time the Princesse de Bouillon was Maria Luisa Nave. Of all the great roles which Caballé sang frequently on stage, this, together with her Desdemona and *Trovatore* Leonora, forms the most significant omission in her commercial discography. Unfortunately, Erik Smith, the senior Philips recording producer, disliked the work intensely and declined ever to schedule the opera as part of Caballé and Carreras's recording contracts. What was in the immediate offing for the pair were the refixed recording sessions for *Un ballo in maschera* which had been hastily arranged to slot in and around Caballé's forthcoming performances of *Norma* at Covent Garden. This was already a burdensome workload, given that she had spent most of May and June in Italy giving recitals at La Scala, the Maggio Musicale in Florence and La Fenice, as well as five performances of *La forza del destino* at the Milanese theatre.

The Scala *Forza*s had taken place at the end of the theatre's bicentennial season and had been given a new production by Lamberto Puggelli, with an all-star cast including Carreras as Don Alvaro, Piero Cappuccilli as Don Carlo, Sesto Bruscantini as Melitone and Nicolai Ghiaurov as the Father Superior. With the energetic and suitably rough-hewn conducting of Giuseppe Patané – replacing at the last minute Zubin Mehta, who was suffering from tendonitis – the performances were considered the high point of the season, and Caballé was enthusiastically reviewed. The general opinion was that the role of Leonora enabled Caballé to reveal the full range of her voice; and the Act II aria 'Madre, pietosa Vergine' brought the entire proceedings to a halt as the audience cheered for several minutes while Caballé in vain tried to carry on with the scene, ringing the monastery's bell over and over again. According to the reviews, few sopranos have been able to float so ravishing a *pianissimo* in 'Pace, pace, mio Dio' and then thrill the audience with the dramatic power of the final B♭ at the end of the same aria. For a work which the La Scala management had initially been extremely reluctant to mount and which Caballé was here singing for the first time, the entire run of performances generated tremendous enthusiasm and turned what can frequently seem a rambling and incoherent work into a genuine popular success.

The Covent Garden *Norma*s were, by contrast, highly problematic. Caballé arrived in London in June 1978 in order to begin rehearsing for the eight performances she had been contracted to perform. At the very first rehearsal, Grace Bumbry (the announced Adalgisa) enthused to Montserrat about this, their first collaboration in Bellini's opera, which would surely re-create the splendours of the original Guiditta Pasta/ Giulia Grisi pairing, with them singing the two principal female roles turn and turn about. This came as a complete bolt from the blue to Caballé who had in her pocket an unambiguous contract for eight performances – at $6000 each – in the role of Norma at the Royal Opera House. There was also the fact that she had never sung and had never learned the role of Adalgisa, which the American mezzo seemed to think Caballé would be singing to her Norma in half the performances. As it also rapidly emerged – although the conductor, Carlo Felice Cillario, knew nothing of this – Bumbry expected to sing the Act II duet for the women at Bellini's manuscript pitch, a tone higher than the standard printed edition. Montserrat had at first thought Bumbry was joking, but soon realized that the American was in deadly earnest and had contractual support for her beliefs. Bumbry was all for talking the situation through with the management but Caballé's reply was unequivocal: 'I don't have to talk to anyone. I have a contract signed by John Tooley to sing the title-role in eight performances of *Norma*.' Caballé immediately realized that both she and Bumbry had been the victims of managerial duplicity. Both had been offered the same role in the same set of performances. Outraged, she referred back to Carlos and the two of them had discussions with John Tooley who explained that Covent Garden had been obliged to offer Bumbry a certain number of performances in the title-role, otherwise she would never have agreed to sing Adalgisa in the first place. This admission paved the way for the traditional British compromise, whereby Montserrat would sing Norma in the first five performances with Bumbry as Adalgisa – in the customary keys – whilst Bumbry would take over the title-role for the last three, with a hastily imported Josephine Veasey filling the vacant role.

Although Caballé agreed to this arrangement, she was bitterly disillusioned by the theatre's double-dealing, which their clumsy offer to pay her just the same for her three unsung Normas did nothing to alleviate, since she has never been prepared to accept money for performances she did not give. She would comply with the revised arrangements but informed Tooley by letter that these performances would constitute her farewell to Covent Garden: she would also be withdrawing from the *Tosca*s on the Royal Opera's forthcoming Japanese tour, which had formed part of the same contract. Tooley wrote back in considerable alarm, first apologizing for the disagreeable situation in which Montserrat had blamelessly been placed, and then going on to beg her to reconsider her decisions, not least because they would in all probability spell the ruin of the Japanese tour. In the end Montserrat relented, but possibly would never have done so had she seen the posters which the Royal Opera stuck up outside the theatre 'explaining' to the audiences for the eight sold-out performances what had necessitated the rearrangements. The punters, already smarting from having to pay the highest ticket prices that Covent Garden had ever charged, were informed that the singers had unfortunately arrived having prepared irreconcilably different versions of Bellini's score (news that caused some head-scratching among the musicologically well-informed), as a result of which performances had been rescheduled. In an act of uncharacteristic generosity but wholly characteristic diplomacy, it was simultaneously announced that prices for the last three performances with Bumbry as Norma would be at a lower tariff, and that patrons who had paid to hear Caballé at them would be given a partial refund. It would be hard to know who should have been the more insulted by this proposal: Bumbry, whose fee was exactly the same as Caballé's and who would hardly be thrilled to be thought of as coming cheap; or Montserrat, who thereby stood implicitly accused in the eyes of the paying public of having caused the inflated prices in the first place by her extortionate demands.

Caballé, meanwhile, was busy recording *Un ballo in maschera*, fighting against the effects of hay fever for which she was receiving daily injections from Covent Garden's renowned house doctor, Alfred Alexander. In the event, the opening night of *Norma* on 6 July met with a lukewarm critical response and a general sense of expectation unfulfilled. The jaded notices, however, provoked an extended course of correspondence in *Opera* magazine from members of the public who, in the vast majority, were keen to point out that the experience of hearing Caballé as Norma was a privilege. As had occasionally happened before, once past the opening night, Montserrat began to strike form and by the third and fourth performances she gave a commanding account of the extended closing scenes of the opera where her sheer stamina seemed boundless. But evidently the critics had expected more from the Norma of the 1970s, and were inclined to blame her recent excursions into heavy repertory and, in particular, her assumption of the role of Turandot. In retrospect, the problem on the first night would seem rather to have stemmed from a combination of being overworked and under the weather. As the reviews – and the pirate recording – of her run of performances of *Turandot* in San Francisco make clear, the role certainly did not overtax her vocally.

In that summer of 1978, Caballé did not even pause for so much as two days in order to take a break. She left London to give a recital in Monte Carlo and then immediately flew to the West coast of America where she was due to make her début with two consecutive concerts in the Hollywood Bowl, given with her true mezzo partner, Marilyn Horne. One of these performances survives, and whatever problems Caballé was suffering from in London have evaporated in the jet-stream of her flight, an echo of which can be heard buzzing over the open-air venue during the *Semiramide* duet.

She remained in North America for the greater part of August, singing one of her rare performances of the Verdi *Requiem* in Saratoga,* with the Philadelphia Orchestra under Eugene Ormandy, as well as giving concerts in Cleveland, San Francisco and Minnesota. Thereafter she returned to Spain for a five-week period which took the form of a busman's holiday, including performances of *Luisa Miller* in Bilbao and Oviedo with Luciano Pavarotti as Rodolfo. But first she was due to sing in the beautiful, albeit reconstructed, Romanesque basilica in Ripoll, close to the Martís' farmlands, where she gave her usual annual recital, the benefits of which would be used to endow the Down's syndrome institution she was supporting. These recitals had been taking place in Ripoll since 1973, and were now a regular feature in the town's festival calendar. Ever since 1975, when the family's three-storey house on the farm had been finally completed, Ripoll had become the centre of their summertime leisure. Here, in the crystal-clear, unpolluted mountain air, everyone was at liberty to pursue their favourite pastimes. Bernabé ensured that, by careful management of the livestock which he had introduced, and lumber, the farm was financially self-supporting. Carlos senior, having suffered from sporadic ill-health for over forty years, found refreshment in the change of scene and climate. Montserrat's mother found Ripoll an ideal place in which, finally in her life, to take some hard-earned rest. Although the past decade had seen an unbelievable transformation in the family's fortunes, Ana was scarcely in a position to benefit from this since her health had been seriously declining for some time. Montserrat herself had taken to painting both as a form of recreation and self-expression. Already, her canvases

---

* Caballé has in fact only performed the work in public on five occasions: with Karajan in 1976 (Salzburg); this Ormandy performance; Muti in 1980 (Verona); Mehta in 1980 (New York); and Abbado in 1985 (Milan).

covered the walls of the farmhouse and were about to become the object of some unexpected admiration.

That summer, the famous Catalan painter Joan Miró paid a social visit to the Martís' farm. Left alone for a few moments, he started looking closely at the paintings on the walls. No sooner had Caballé materialized than Miró inquired who had painted these works. Montserrat answered vaguely that they were the work of a young student. Miró asked if she would be good enough to contact him and find out if he would be prepared to sell one of his canvasses or perhaps, if he had no special need of the money, would he like to take one of Miró's own paintings in exchange? This left the soprano in a quandary: would it be better to own up to the subterfuge or would she have to see it through? She chose the latter course and duly contacted Miró, giving him the news that the young man had been flattered by the older master's interest but felt that his apprentice work was unworthy of the artist's attention. Other members of the family upbraided Montserrat in no uncertain terms. Was she mad? She had passed up the opportunity of having any Miró of her choice. The soprano replied simply: 'But I much prefer my paintings to his.'

After this sojourn it was back to America: first to the East coast and a series of three concerts in New York's then Philharmonic Hall at which Caballé sang a mouth-watering programme of Strauss's *Four Last Songs* and the closing scene from *Salome*, under the baton of Zubin Mehta; and then to San Francisco where she was to appear in an illustrious revival of *Tosca* with Pavarotti and Giuseppe Taddei as Scarpia during the opening weeks of the 1978–9 War Memorial opera season. In fact, this cast sang the first five performances from 14 October through to the 25th, after which Gwyneth Jones sang just one, and the legendary Magda Olivero a further two. The San Francisco audience, used to its stars, nevertheless accorded this revival an excited ovation. And the local press enthused, though in a manner which one would have imagined the women's movement in America would have rendered inadvisable by this date: 'Caballé – her voice flawless even while her weight is simply out of control – provided a wonderful musical/dramatic counterpoint [to Taddei] . . . "Vissi d'Arte" went beyond a beautiful musical performance; it was a moving experience rooted in but not consisting of the voice alone.'[8] When one sees both the rehearsal and production pictures from these performances, the wonder is that any man would dream of writing so personally about Caballé's size when she is so clearly dwarfed by the tenor. But the most interesting commentary was provided by the then sixty-eight-year-old Magda Olivero, who had already had one career and was now enjoying the closing years of her second. Privately, she expressed her opinion about Caballé to Reuel Sherwood, a young Californian who had been to see both singers in the role and who would, in time, become part of Carlos Caballé's agency administration. Olivero was forthright and uncompromising: 'I think we should get down on our knees and thank God for a voice like hers.' Her words prefigured a *leitmotif* that runs throughout Lanfranco Rasponi's book, *The Last Prima Donnas*. No matter how lamentable the state of singing has become after the various divas have retired, Caballé provides a frequent exception. Thus Giulietta Simionato: 'For me the greatest living singer is Caballé. Not only is the instrument superb in quality, but the technique is prodigious. Some criticize her for not having enough temperament, but don't they realize she wouldn't be so astoundingly perfect if she had that too?'[9] And Renata Tebaldi: 'Tell me – with the exception of Caballé and Domingo – who is there? Montserrat is the last prima donna, capricious at times, but she obtains what she wants because she knows what is right for her.'[10]

Montserrat returned to Europe at the end of October 1978, giving recitals and concerts in Cologne, Gerona, Munich and Hamburg. She also gave two concert performances at the Hamburg Staatsoper of *Roberto Devereux* in mid-November as part of the theatre's 300th anniversary celebrations. Then, following a further anticipatory return to her *bel canto* roots in the shape of two performances of *Maria Stuarda* given in Nice, she spent the greater part of December singing Tosca, first in a single guest appearance at the Staatsoper in Vienna, then in a series of gala performances with which the newly refurbished Théâtre Municipal in Avignon reopened on the 15th. Apparently, the diva and her Cavaradossi – this time Giacomo Aragall – arrived from Vienna not long before the dress rehearsal of the new Avignon production, which probably accounts for Caballé's much commented-upon departure in Act II through one of the floor-length windows in Scarpia's room rather than through the more usual exit. Indeed, such was the relish with which the soprano reblocked all her moves from one performance to the next, to the despair of the lighting designer, that the crew amused themselves by placing bets as to where she might be found at given moments in the score, as well as how she might choose to make her exit. (They all invariably lost.)

The Christmas period was spent at home in Barcelona and this year's appearance at the Liceo took the form of a new production of *Maria Stuarda* in which Montserrat had last sung locally nine years previously. The staging by Giuseppe de Tomasi had been brought in from Nice and was apparently of great spectacle and brilliance. But this did not serve to over-shadow the voices, since both Caballé in the title-role and Bianca Berini as Queen Elisabeth received thunderous ovations from the Liceo audience. Nor had Montserrat quite finished with her annual Christmas show, though it was evidently running rather late this year. Following further recitals in the South of France and a brace of *Tosca*s in Nice – in which she sang for the first time with the burnished baritone of Matteo Manuguerra – she returned to the Liceo at the end of January 1979 for a series of performances of *La forza del destino*, again with Manuguerra and with José Carreras as Don Alvaro. In the latter's company, she then returned to Nice for performances of *Don Carlos*, given this time in the Italian translation.

The next six months were taken up by a relentless schedule of mainly concert and recital appearances throughout Europe and North America, which took her to Miami, Atlanta, Los Angeles, Philadelphia, Syracuse, Puerto Rico, Geneva and Valencia, amongst other places. Unfortunately this furious round of activity prevented her from taking part in February 1979 in the Philips recording of *La bohème*. She had provisionally agreed to sing the *seconda donna* role of Musetta to Carreras' Rodolfo and Ricciarelli's Mimì, under Sir Colin Davis, but the scheduling was impossible, and she was replaced by Ashley Putnam. In Paris Caballé gave a joint concert with José Carreras in the Salle Pleyel on 19 March at which her renditions of 'Pace, pace, mio Dio' and, above all, 'Depuis le jour' from Gustave Charpentier's *Louise* were wildly acclaimed, as the commercially issued recording demonstrates. She also returned to Paris the following month in order to make a pair of recordings for French EMI – Pathé Marconi – with Alexis Weissenberg: the first was a disc of Strauss *Lieder*; and the second comprised Turina's *Canto a Sevilla* coupled with some songs by Montsalvatge. In between these Parisian jaunts, Caballé somehow found the time to give two performances at Carnegie Hall: her usual recital, followed a few days later on 8 April by the first performance in New York of Verdi's *Aroldo*, the 1857 rewrite of his earlier work, *Stiffelio*. This was recorded live by CBS and issued as a commercial recording the following year. The Spanish press had a field-day in reporting the scenes of Caballé's triumph in the role of Mina, and the recording certainly confirms the committed theatricality of her performance. William Weaver wrote:

> paradoxically, she does more acting when she is not in costume, not framed in a set. Her Mina was thoroughly understood, intensely portrayed. At times she sacrificed beauty of tone to characterization, but in so doing, she made a persuasive case for the tormented adultress.[11]

Her only notable stage performances during this period were a series of *Salome*s at the Teatro de la Zarzuela in Madrid in mid-May, with Norman Bailey as Jokanaan and Josephine Veasey as Herodias. One of the performances, conducted by Julius Rudel, was televised live in Spain and survives as a pirate video. This not only reveals Caballé to be in stupendous voice, easily capable of surmounting Strauss's tropical orchestration, but passionately caught up in Salome's character: she seems on the point of devouring the Baptist's severed head, and a similar fate threatens the lion-skin rug on which she lolls while enduring the sexual snub of John the Baptist's voluntary return to the cistern. Indeed, it is the lion's head that seems to give her an idea . . .

Caballé gave two performances of *Norma* at the Opera House in Cologne at the beginning of June and followed this with three operatic concerts in Florence as part of the Maggio Musicale. Following a recital in Rome she flew to London for the first of her two scheduled recordings there that summer, both of which were to be made for EMI under the baton of Riccardo Muti. This was Bellini's *I puritani*, which at this stage of Caballé's career – with *Turandot*s already behind her and *La gioconda* imminent – might be thought a peculiar piece of casting, were it not for the critical success of the recording. Even so, for a meaningful parallel we would have to look back almost thirty years to the point in Maria Callas's career when the Greek soprano was singing the same roles, more or less alternately. The difference, of course, was that Callas was doing this at the very beginning of her career when she was still in her mid-twenties, assiduously encouraged in this insane regime – which more than any theories about weight-loss accounts for her early vocal decline – by the very man, Tullio Serafin, who so many regard as a great voice expert. Caballé, conversely, was in her late forties, had been singing for over half her life, had rarely taken the advice of conductors seriously, and knew exactly how far she could push her own voice. As a result, her Elvira falls into place as the last of her great Bellini roles on disc (setting aside her subsequent Adalgisa as a special case).

Before commencing work on her next recording project – the role of Santuzza in Mascagni's *Cavalleria rusticana* – she made three appearances in late July at the Munich Festival, giving a solo recital and two concert performances in the National Theater of *Maria Stuarda* with Brigitte Fassbaender as Elisabeth. No matter how implausible, at least in theory, these returns to *bel canto* roles may seem, particularly with a Santuzza looming, it is always noticeable that her performances in them meet with great acclaim. Thus James Helme Sutcliffe in *Opera*:

[She] was in complete control of that matchless instrument of hers despite the fact that one is aware of a slight shifting of gears between the ravishingly taken *pianissimos* (with well-managed, floated crescendos) and the transition to passages sung *con forza*. The spine-tingling confrontation between the two queens . . . fairly crackled with excitement.[12]

So too did the scenes between Santuzza and Turiddu in the Muti recording of *Cavalleria rusticana*, which took place in the Kingsway Hall, London during the first week of August. Despite the conductor's insistence upon strict observation of the printed vocal notation – which at least in the case of *verismo* opera, as documented by 'authentic' recordings, is evidently a chimerical pursuit – both Caballé and Carreras manage to generate the necessary tension, even carried over into the diva's curse, 'A te, la mala Pasqua!' where only on the last word is she finally allowed a touch of traditional *verismo* histrionics.

Caballé's next major engagement brought her back to the Royal Opera House, though not in front of the London public. In fact, Covent Garden, for only the second time in its history, was going on tour, this time to the Far East, with a repertory comprising *Die Zauberflöte*, *Peter Grimes* and *Tosca*. *Tosca* would be given not only in Tokyo, Osaka and Yokohama but, somewhat controversially from a political point of view, in Seoul. The Royal Opera had been terrified, as the English always are, at the prospect of suffering diplomatic embarrassment in foreign climes. They had even produced and distributed among the 300-strong company a little red book which contained, among other pearls of wisdom, the dictum 'The Second World War is not a topic of conversation in Japan these days.' Montserrat found this so funny that throughout the tour she never ceased to produce the book – much to the management's mortification – and quote from it for the 'enlightenment' of her endless interviewers.

Such had been the clamour for seats, principally for the *Tosca*, that extra performances had been scheduled. And an additional problem had been encountered in the shape of the characteristic desire of the Japanese to have an exact replica of the cast on the Philips recording set before them. Caballé, Carreras and Ingvar Wixell were no problem in the main roles, but the Japanese insistence on hearing Domenico Trimarchi as the Sacristan and Sam Ramey as Angelotti were obvious stumbling blocks. (In the event, they got Trimarchi, but not Ramey.) And there were occasional mishaps: whilst the *Zauberflöte* and *Grimes* were being performed in the newer Bunka Kaikan, the *Tosca*s were given in NHK Hall. One afternoon Montserrat was required for rehearsal in the Bunka where she had never thus far set foot. When she had not appeared after an hour the rehearsal was abandoned and frantic efforts set in motion to locate her, for despite the fact that she was the only member of the company to have sung in Tokyo before, she had shown an engaging confusion about local geography. At which point the telephone rang: 'Here is Montserrat Caballé. I am in my room in the Hotel Otani. For one hour and twenty minutes I drive around Tokyo in a taxi: then I say to the driver, "Well, you no know Bunka Kaikan. You know Hotel Otani? Good, we go Otani!" So here I am. What you want I do now?' In the event, all went well; one of the Tokyo performances was televised in Japan and subsequently shown on British television, revealing the by now almost intuitively subtle interplay between the principals, allied to superb vocal form. The performances in Seoul went just as well, for all that Carreras had to commute at the last minute since he was unavoidably detained in Berlin recording parts of the same role under Karajan for DG, and arrived to find his diva partner half-starved, too afraid to eat having seen vans trundling round the city with dead dogs for sale.

While the Royal Opera company flew home, Caballé stayed behind to make her long-awaited series of début appearances in Australia, giving two recitals in the Sydney Opera House – one in each auditorium – and in Adelaide and Melbourne between 5 and 11 November. In the process, she received the kind of adulation that had hitherto been reserved only for Joan Sutherland in her native country. Indeed, the Australian materialized at Caballé's hotel during the Sydney performance and secretly arranged for an elaborate box of watercolours to be left in her room as a gift for the increasingly prolific amateur painter. She also left two pieces of needlework, one a large sampler still to be embroidered and, as an encouragement, a second smaller item finished by Sutherland herself. Meanwhile, Carreras winged his way home, taking with him, at Caballé's request, the sizeable quantity of cash she had accumulated while in Japan and which she had no desire to take with her to Australia. Unfortunately, Japan had strict exchange control regulations at the time, and the amount that Carreras was bearing on Montserrat's behalf was considerably in excess of what could legally be taken out of the country. Undaunted by this, however, he had told Montserrat that he would simply go through Customs with the money: surely no harm would come to him. Nor did it, except that when he rang Caballé from the airport to inform her that he had successfully completed the tricky part of his mission, she immediately interrupted with the question, 'Where are you?' His reply, 'Inside', was greeted by howls of anguish from the soprano who automatically concluded the worst.

After this brief tour of the Antipodes, Caballé flew straight to San Francisco where she was due to commence rehearsals in mid-October for a new production of *Roberto Devereux* at the War Memorial Opera House. She had been suffering increasingly of late from pain in her left leg, which had been damaged in the fall some ten years previously. During the rehearsals the pain became worse and began to restrict her mobility to the point where she decided to seek medical advice. Some X-rays were arranged and revealed that she was suffering from thrombo-phlebitis: treatment was urgently required. In the event, Montserrat determined to go through with the opening night on 26 October but bowed to medical inevitability thereafter and so reluctantly cancelled the remaining five performances. She flew home to Barcelona and was immediately admitted to the Clínica Corachán for observation and tests. Dr Rodriguez-Arias recommended that Heparin treatment be first administered for the dissolution of the blood clot. This took place at the beginning of November and Caballé returned to the hospital on a regular basis for most of the rest of the month, which unfortunately impinged on the rehearsal period of her next engagement.

This was a new production at the Grand Théâtre de Genève of Ponchielli's blowsy melodrama, *La gioconda*, in which Caballé was scheduled to sing the heroine for the first time in her career. In undertaking this horrendously written role, she was probably taking the greatest vocal risk of her career: certainly more so than with the role of Turandot, which at least is unequivocally written for a soprano. As Puccini's heroine one might fail to make the requisite effect in terms of steely brilliance, but the half-hour role hardly calls for infinite reserves of stamina, nor is it really likely to lead to irreversible vocal damage. Ponchielli's heroine, on the other hand, can and usually does. With its relentless concentration on stentorian declamation in the lowest reaches of the chest register, coupled with the need to dominate large-scale climaxes on endlessly prolonged high Bs, the listener can almost hear the effect of Ponchielli's vocal writing acting like a rusty blade sawing back-and-forth across the soprano's diaphragm. Given that the integration of the chest register is always likely to be a major source of technical difficulty for sopranos – at least those few who truly have one – it is extraordinary that Ponchielli should have chosen to write the role of a girlish ballad singer in such a way as to maximize any inherent vocal inequalities. It is surely the role of Gioconda that hastened the end of both Elena Suliotis' and Anita Cerquetti's careers, and did nothing to prolong those of Callas, Tebaldi or Scotto. The surprise is that sopranos nevertheless queue up to sing the work in the only two countries where it survives in the repertory – Italy and America.

And here was Caballé about to sing the role for the first time, having only just emerged from hospital.* But a lot was riding on these performances. Not only was the cast of a uniformly high level, with Carreras making his stage début in the role of Enzo and Manuguerra as the scheming villain, Barnaba, but the work was receiving only its second-ever production in Geneva, as the high point of the theatre's gala centenary season. For Montserrat there was also the additional factor that in giving these performances she was returning to the country of her operatic apprenticeship for the first time in twenty years. And representatives from Decca were in attendance, since they had plans to record the opera with Caballé in 1980. These are precisely the sort of pressurized circumstances in which she flourishes. It is almost as if the tension, uncertainty and very often the physical strain only serve to put her on her mettle and elicit from her notably more intense singing and acting. Certainly this is evident in the broadcast performance of the opening night on 2 December, which is powerful and surprisingly effortless. The curtain calls after Act I alone involved a standing ovation, and the applause which followed Caballé's singing of 'Suicidio!' in Act IV brought the performance to a prolonged halt.

Unexpectedly, therefore, with this last major venture into a new role from what may be called 'killer' repertory – her own term for it is *massacrante* – Montserrat achieved a tremendous success. Nor was it a one-off, since she would give further performances of both *Gioconda* and *Turandot*, as occasion arose, for the next couple of years. She had even reached the point at which she was minded to accept the proposal from DG to record the role of Abigaille in their forthcoming *Nabucco*, to be conducted by Giuseppe Sinopoli, who assured her that it would be treated lyrically and sung rather than shouted. After all, this was only a recording, not a series of stage performances, and Callas's advice when Caballé had first been offered the role ten years previously – 'Your voice is like a Baccarat crystal: put it in that shaking-box of a role and it will shatter' – was perhaps no longer the truth about Caballé's instrument. But the proposition that subsequently came attached to the recording offer, whereby three staged performances were to be given with Caballé at the Deutsche Oper in Berlin, finally decided her against the project.

Apropos of the general direction of her repertory at this time, she observes:

---

* This was the third time this kind of thing had happened: two previous major operations had been immediately followed by staged *Normas*. A fourth was to occur in 1982 when, following hospitalization for kidney trouble, Caballé sang Turandot.

By the later 70s, my voice had become much darker, much heavier and with more volume. I would not have undertaken these roles in the first place if I did not think I had the voice to do them justice. Besides, in the past they had always been sung in a certain way, let us say by the very biggest voices, which is nice but does not leave room for much light and shade, or subtleties of expression. The big heroic voices are so often sexless, not man, not woman, just big. I wanted to do some of these roles, not the helpless little girls of some *bel canto* works, and to sing them as a *woman* and bring into them the kind of ideal I had when singing, for instance, *Devereux* or *Norma*, the roles of powerful women but somehow gentle too, with lots of feeling.

There were even repeated rumours that she was about to undertake Isolde. These all proved unfounded, though it is true that both Zubin Mehta and James Levine had expressed a desire to conduct her in the work. Indeed, *Tristan* was actually announced for the Opéra du Rhin's 1980–81 season at Strasbourg under Alain Lombard, with Caballé as the heroine, directed by Jean-Pierre Ponnelle. But she seems to have decided, at least for the time being, that it was a case of 'thus far, and no further', so that the project went unrealized.* Instead, she was hatching a plan to return to her *bel canto* roots in spectacular fashion and thus reverse the general trend of the past few years. Rather than use her *bel canto* vocal skills – as far as she could – on the war-horses of the *verismo* repertory, she would now use the darkened dramatic scale of her voice to enliven Rossini's last truly Italian *bel canto* opera: *Semiramide*.

---

* This decision on Caballé's part had wider ramifications, for had she sung in Ponnelle's production, the French director had every intention of taking her with him to star in the revised staging he was already contracted to mount at the 1981 Bayreuth Festival. This is probably the greatest lost opportunity of her entire career.

CHAPTER ELEVEN

1980–1982: Plain Sailing: Sudden Shipwreck

By now, it will come as no surprise to learn that Caballé spent the Christmas/New Year period 1979–80 at home in Barcelona, where her roles at the Liceo this year fully reflected her latter-day enthusiasm for heavyweight, *verismo* repertory. In addition to three Turandots, Caballé gave three performances of a work she had publicly renounced more than ten years previously: *Andrea Chénier*, in which she sang the role of Maddalena de Coigny. Unusually, the first performance of the latter took place on Christmas Day, and the closing duet between Caballé and Carreras apparently roused the over-capacity audience to near delirium. Her Turandot was no less ecstatically received, though some critics lamented that a singer so gifted in the *bel canto* repertory should wish to join the ranks of Turandots, as if successful exponents of the latter were commonplace.

Caballé then returned to North America, singing four *Tosca*s at the Metropolitan between 17 and 31 January. Her recitals during this stay took her to both extremes of the country: for in addition to her by now traditional Carnegie Hall recital on 14 February, she also sang in Los Angeles, San Francisco and Miami. The next four months were equally divided between stage appearances in short runs, for the most part away from the first-rank houses, and miscellaneous recitals here, there and everywhere. Probably the most significant appearances were in Hamburg, where in March she sang *Roberto Devereux*, again in concert performances; and in April/May staged performances of *Ariadne auf Naxos*. Other than this, her tireless schedules took her from *Forza del destino* in Avignon, and *Ballo in maschera* and *Roberto Devereux* in Las Palmas to an extended run in Nice, which in the space of three weeks saw her sing two performances in the title-roles of *Maria Stuarda*, *Luisa Miller* and *Tosca* – the last two operas both with José Carreras. Her recital schedule embraced Nîmes, Malaga, Limoges, Valencia, Ghent, Cannes, Hamburg and Cologne as well as La Scala and the Teatro dell'Opera in Rome. This period of what in retrospect seems to be almost random hyperactivity culminated in Madrid with three performances of *Turandot* at the end of May, followed, after a fortnight's break and some relaxed rehearsals, by three performances of *Maria Stuarda* in which the role of Queen Elisabeth was taken by Bianca Berini.

Montserrat's customary summer holiday this year had largely been sacrificed, first to the Decca recording of *La gioconda* which took place in London at Walthamstow Town Hall in June, and second to one of the most important operatic projects in which she had ever taken part. In Bernard Lefort's final year as director of the Aix-en-Provence Festival, it had been decided to mount an all-star new production of Rossini's rarely staged *Semiramide*, in which Caballé had been invited to sing the title-role for the first time in her career. Her colleagues were similarly outstanding exponents of the Rossinian repertory, and included Marilyn Horne as Arsace, Francisco Araiza as Idreno and Samuel Ramey as Assur, with the performances conducted by Jesús López-Cobos and produced and designed by Pier Luigi Pizzi.

The scale of the undertaking was enormous: by a considerable margin *Semiramide* is much the longest of all Rossini's Italian operas. At the time of writing no one has ever performed or recorded the opera in its entirety, so it is hard to make judgements, but the concert performances at Covent Garden in 1986 were described by their conductor as 'minimally cut' and still contained just over three and a half hours of music. It is clear that the 'grand' operatic style, which these days Rossini is credited as pioneering as a result of his exposure to French influences, was already manifesting itself before his removal to Paris in 1825. What is certain is that the title-role was fashioned with the vocal means of the composer's own wife, Isabella Colbran, particularly in mind, though there is plenty of evidence to suggest that by 1823, when the opera was first staged in Venice, she was no longer up to the demands that the music made on her and soon withdrew from public performance. The only other latter-day exponent prior to Caballé was Joan Sutherland, who had recorded the opera with Marilyn Horne in 1965, with a much-cut text and wholesale transpositions, up, down and sideways. The Aix Festival production, on the other hand, had been intended from the outset to be as complete as possible: Act I alone ran for an hour and fifty-two minutes. Unfortunately, at this remove, there only remain much-hacked-about pirate videos and recordings to act as evidence, totally belying the fact that in performance the work ran for just a little under four hours.

The production was thought to be sensationally controversial, dressed and set as it was virtually entirely in white, which extended even to the characters' wigs and make-up, with all the singers other than the two female principals done up as monochrome crosses between bits of architecture and playing cards. Of the Hanging Gardens or anything suggestive of the legendary Queen of Babylon's decadent court there was no trace. But the real *raison d'être* of the evening, as Rossini would have expected, was of course the singing. Here, the 1500-strong audience at each of the six performances in the courtyard of the Archbishop's palace was held enthralled. The music critics lavished superlatives on Caballé and Horne, and such was the stir created by the entire event that it was even reported beyond the confines of the purely musical press: thus the *Nouvel Observateur* in France ran a long article by Maurice Fleuret which ended, 'At this exalted level of execution, singing ceases to be a means of expression, much less an entertainment. It puts us in touch with the very essence of things.'[1] *The Times* in London carried an entire article devoted to the phenomenon by the noted columnist and critic, Bernard Levin. And Charles Pitt, *Opera*'s French correspondent and an erstwhile producer at Covent Garden, wrote:

> the roles of Semiramide and Arsace attracted the finest *bel canto* exponents throughout the nineteenth century . . . I wonder if these singers of the Golden Age were really superior to Aix's Caballé and Marilyn Horne? In their two big vocal encounters . . . their voices intertwined quite perfectly. And how brilliant each lady was alone.[2]

The last performance took place on 2 August, after which one might have assumed that Caballé would finally take a summer break: instead she gave recitals and concerts in Monte Carlo, Perpignan, Bregenz and S'agaró, as well as squeezing in a two-day excursion to London in order to record the role of Elena – Helen of Troy – in Decca's recording of Boito's *Mefistofele*. But at least the final recital (S'agaró) was in Cataluña, which allowed Montserrat to take a break towards the end of the month before returning to New York. She was due to commence rehearsals on 25 August for a new production of *Turandot* which would open the Metropolitan's 1980–81 season on 22 September, conducted by James Levine and with Luciano Pavarotti as Calaf. All in all, this was probably the most spectacular honour that the Met had ever accorded her. John Dexter, still at this time the Met's Head of Production, had decided that it was no longer artistically feasible to revive the old Cecil Beaton staging and instead proposed a new, radically spare *mise-en-scène*, cannibalizing the staircase set from *I vespri siciliani* and proposing to treat Alfano's ending in a stylized, black-draped fashion so as to distinguish it visually from Puccini's work. Then, just as in 1969, when she had been balked of her opening night *Luisa Miller*, the Metropolitan Orchestra went on strike. The opera house administration decided to play tough, and as a result all ten contracted performances of *Turandot* were abandoned, as were all the other performances during the opening months of the season. Bitterly disappointed, Caballé was given permission to return home to Barcelona on the understanding that she would return to New York on Concorde were the strike to be resolved speedily. Alas, it never was, and the eager New Yorkers were deprived – permanently, as it transpired – of the chance of hearing Caballé in this fabulous role.

The latter part of October 1980, which should have overlapped with her last three *Turandot* performances, was occupied with rehearsals and performances of the Verdi *Requiem*: in addition to being televised live from Avery Fisher Hall, it was also subsequently recorded by CBS for commercial release. The New York Philharmonic Orchestra was conducted by Zubin Mehta and, apart from Caballé, the soloists comprised Bianca Berini, Plácido Domingo and Paul Plishka. These performances were the last time Caballé and Domingo appeared together for over a decade, in an arrangement which had been carefully negotiated by Mehta and the recording company. No matter what strains her recent roles may have imposed upon her, Caballé's singing throughout this performance reveals her voice to be in pristine condition, culminating in a perfectly poised high B♭ in the 'Libera me'. In the course of a long and detailed comparative review of all the available recordings, Alan Blyth wrote a few years later that: 'Montserrat Caballé surpasses even her lovely singing for Barbirolli some twelve years earlier.'

Before leaving North America entirely, Montserrat made a brief journey northwards to Montreal where she gave a solo recital: thereafter she returned to Europe and immediately sang in two staged performances of *La forza del destino* at the Théâtre de l'Opéra in Nice. On 11 November she travelled to Hamburg where she gave a recital the following day in the Konzerthaus and subsequently appeared in three performances of *Tosca* at the Staatsoper. From there she returned to the south of France, first to Avignon where she sang three performances of *Norma* in the Théâtre Municipal; and then returned to Nice for two *Bohème*s with Luciano Pavarotti. The Avignon performances evidently caught her in less than best voice, since her coloratura seems to have been sketchy, but as one reviewer noted: 'what she may have lost in that respect has been compensated for by a gain in dramatic power: she is undeniably a great lady of the stage.'[3]

This year's commitment to the Liceo took the form of three performances of *Manon Lescaut* immediately before Christmas, with Nicola Martinucci as des Grieux, and a revival of *La bohème* shortly after, with José Carreras as Rodolfo. In the filmed extracts that have survived, one of the most striking features of what might on theoretical grounds be considered Caballé's by now inadvisable appearance as Mimì is the extraordinary intensity with which she both looks at, and listens to, every gesture and utterance of her Rodolfo.

A few days after the last performance on 3 January 1981, Caballé flew to London to rehearse a revival at the Royal Opera House of *Un ballo in maschera*. This was a very grand affair indeed, since the Riccardo was Pavarotti, and the eight performances were to be conducted by Bernard Haitink, then music director at Glyndebourne. Used as he was to the endless rehearsals possible at Glyndebourne, Haitink must have been taken aback by the conditions attaching to his house début at Covent Garden, where the star tenor managed to arrive even later than the star soprano. With everyone at last assembled, the real trouble began. In the breathlessly fast and difficult trio which follows on from the love duet in Act II, Pavarotti insisted on making a *ritenuto* which, although not marked in the printed score, he regarded as an integral part of the work's performing tradition. The conductor refused to permit its inclusion: the tenor insisted. In the face of the resulting musical *impasse*, neither Caballé nor the third voice of the trio, the baritone Matteo Manuguerra, knew where they stood or what to do. Haitink made it clear that if Pavarotti chose to sing the phrase his way at the first performance on 15 January, the prolongation of the orchestral accompaniment required to accommodate him would not be forthcoming: the orchestra would simply roll on into the notated entries of the other singers.

Montserrat was on the horns of a dilemma here, torn between a proven loyalty to a tried and tested tenor partner, and her understandable desire to follow the conductor's instructions. She and Manuguerra simply hoped that someone would see sense on the opening night and accommodate the other. No such luck. Pavarotti's lengthy caress of the phrase rang out simultaneously with the orchestra racing ahead: this had the effect of putting all the subsequent vocal entries out of kilter. For a more highly strung or perhaps less experienced artist, this would have been the worst kind of musical nightmare. Caballé just turned her back on the audience and faced up-stage in the hope of concealing the fact that she could not stop laughing. Poor Manuguerra had no idea what to do and just stood his ground. It was now effectively impossible for anyone to sing other than Pavarotti, who managed to catch up with his own vocal line and finish his phrase, then promptly walked off stage. As Montserrat watched him go she thought to herself that there seemed no point in her staying, so she walked off into the opposite wing. This left the utterly confused baritone at the end of a largely voiceless trio on an otherwise deserted stage, peering frantically to his left and right to see if he should follow his colleagues. The matter was decided for him when the curtain was rung down in mid-scene before the arrival on stage of the conspirators for the ensuing quartet.

A bemused audience hummed and buzzed as the house lights were half turned up. Backstage, there was pandemonium. John Tooley, then general administrator of the house, found the tenor incommunicado and rushed in desperation to Caballé's dressing-room, only to find her highly amused at the entire proceedings. Her response to Tooley's not entirely rhetorical question, 'But what shall I tell the audience?' threw him a much needed life-line: 'Tell them I'm sick. They'll believe that. They wouldn't believe the truth.' Thus it was that Tooley went out and announced that Madame Caballé had suddenly been taken ill and that the performance would resume as soon as possible. (There was, in fact, a further delay, since poor Manuguerra had been seized with diarrhoea and clamoured for an announcement craving indulgence on his behalf, which Tooley declined to make on the grounds that he had no desire to face a lynch-mob.) Thus Caballé sang her demanding part in Act III, Scene 1, including her aria 'Morrò', ma prima in grazia', with an audience wondering at the whims of a diva who sounded perfectly well, while frantic efforts were being made backstage to ensure that the piqued tenor would sing the rest of Act III after the second interval and that the baritone could be liberated from the lavatory.

The authorized version of events was, of course, widely reported, giving any number of people who were not present an opportunity to expatiate on the decline which Caballé's latter-day, heavyweight assumptions had caused to her basically lyrical instrument, and so on and so forth. As always in similar circumstances, she remained philosophical about the entire episode: 'People always believe what they want to believe. It was convenient, an escape for all concerned. What else can you do in a situation like that?' It probably helped that after the last performance she returned to Spain and gave a recital at the Palau de la Musica in Barcelona: on home territory, with a native audience, and in familiar repertory.

Much the same sense of returning to her roots marked Montserrat's next enterprise, which took her back to New York for an all-star gala on 17 February 1981 and three subsequent dates in Avery Fisher Hall with the New York Philharmonic under Mehta. These concerts included her first-ever public performances of Brünnhilde's immolation, the mighty climax of Wagner's *Götterdämmerung* with which the whole 'Ring' cycle concludes. Her colleagues in America, with Mehta principal among them, had been encouraging her for some while to tackle the Wagnerian heavies, and though she was proving reluctant actually to commit herself to stage performances, she was at least amenable to performing major extracts in concert. And of course there was no reason why she should not entrust these interpretations to disc, CBS having decided to record her in a conspectus of Wagner arias in between the performances.

She remained in America for most of March, giving recitals in Palm Beach, Pasadena and Torrance as well as a double bill of performances back in New York, in Carnegie Hall. The first of these, which took place on 2 March, was her annual solo recital, whilst the second, some nine days later, took the form of a concert of operatic excerpts, conducted by James Levine. This period was rounded out by a gala performance at the Metropolitan Opera on 19 March and was devoted to operatic arias and duets based on Spanish subjects. The house orchestra was conducted by Jesús López Cobos, and Caballé shared the stage with Carreras, the pair appearing in concert together for the first time in New York.

At the end of the month she returned to Europe to give a private recital in Paris on 23 March at the Palais de l'UNESCO at which the programme wholly comprised Spanish music, including works by Toldrà, Mompou and Granados. Montserrat's accompanist for this special occasion was the distinguished pianist Rosa Sabater who tragically died just a few years later in a plane crash. Thereafter, with the exception of a brief excursion to Las Palmas in order to sing in two performances of *Manon Lescaut* and a recital at the Grand Théâtre de Genève, she remained in France more or less without a break until the last week of June. This was the longest period she had ever spent in France – notwithstanding her previous forays to the Aix Festival and her numerous appearances at the opera houses in the South – and nearly six weeks of this were spent in Paris, which hitherto had only figured in her schedules on an occasional, one-off basis. It is fair to say that from this time on, if Caballé could be regarded as having any artistic home other than Spain, then it was the French capital: though she would continue to appear regularly in New York throughout the 1980s, one has only to examine her schedules to see how her centre of artistic gravity across this period shifted to France in general, and to Paris in particular.

At the end of March she undertook probably the most bizarre and unlikely project she had ever contemplated. For just two performances in the Théâtre de l'Opéra in Nice, she sang the role of Rosina in *Il barbiere di Siviglia* without upward transpositions, but with any amount of crazy coloratura. Not surprisingly, opinions are sharply divided about the results: many of the local audience regarded her performance as a comic revelation; others have spoken sombrely of the favour they have done the soprano's reputation by keeping the pirate recording of one of the performances under lock and key.

But even this was not the end of the story in terms of bewildering vocal diversity, for within ten days Montserrat was to be found back in Paris (after the Las Palmas *Manon Lescauts*) singing Brünnhilde at the Salle Pleyel in two concert performances of *Götterdämmerung*, Act III under the baton of Zubin Mehta, before returning to Nice and a brace of Maddalena di Coignys in *Andrea Chénier*. However, at the recital she gave in the Palais Garnier just two days later she was suffering from laryngitis. This recital was her first appearance on the stage of the Paris Opéra in nearly ten years, where she had not sung since the ill-fated *Norma*s in 1972. Evidently, both her vocal condition that night and the widespread knowledge of her most recent repertoire led to a great deal of press speculation and headshaking. This provoked Gérard Mannoni to write his review of her recital less on the strength of that particular performance than on placing her in a wider context. Under the headline 'Montserrat Caballé at the opera – to hell with the sanctimonious moaners', he wrote:

There is no one else today who possesses a comparable technical mastery of vocal means. She does with her voice exactly what she wants, even in physical conditions as difficult as those of this recital. From *forte* to the most long-drawn *pianissimo*, the voice is under control; responsive, flexible, always musical. And as for her breath control, it is perfection itself. Who else, apart from her, could – in the space of one month – and on a comparable level, sing *Götter-dämmerung* (Act III), *Il barbiere di Siviglia, Andrea Chénier* and a *Lieder* recital just before beginning a series of performances of *Turandot*? People always talk of Lilli Lehmann's vocal exploits, alternating Wagner and Mozart roles just a few days apart as if this was a kind of miracle. But is that any more astonishing than what Caballé has been doing for our gratification these many years past? And then, what joy in singing, what art in laughing at herself, of creating a complicity with the audience. Is she the greatest singer of the day? Absolutely![4]

In fact, this recital had fortunately been given at the very beginning of the rehearsal period for the new production of *Turandot* that was due to open for a run of nine performances on 15 May, thus affording the diva an opportunity to recover her form as rehearsals progressed. The conductor was Seiji Ozawa, and the production had been entrusted to an old colleague of Caballé's, Margherita Wallmann, who had commissioned utterly spectacular designs and costumes from Jacques

Dupont. The Liù was the wonderful Leona Mitchell and Calaf was sung by Franco Bonisolli. One of the performances – at which, due to indisposition, Bonisolli was replaced by Giuseppe Giacomini – was televised live by Antenne 2 and, judging by the number of copies in circulation, tens of thousands of domestic video-recorders were switched on that night. Despite the fact that the grandiose staging placed Caballé at what one would have thought would have been a considerable disadvantage during the Riddle Scene – at varying degrees of altitude up a soaring staircase and always miles back – her voice rang out loud and clear. One listens in vain for the least sense of strain, for any feeling that a note is under pressure or not given full weight of tone or length of breath. Not since Birgit Nilsson had the role ever been sung as effortlessly, and no one could pretend that the great Swedish soprano matched Caballé's range of tone colour, or security of intonation. The splendour of her performance that night must have come as a surprise even to her most ardent admirers.

M. Mannoni reviewed this *Turandot* for *Le Quotidien de Paris*:

> . . . the words which come to mind seem almost worthless when it comes to describing what [Caballé] gave us in this performance. The surly spirits have been busy telling us in advance that the role is not for her, that after Birgit Nilsson she would not stand a chance . . . However, not for a moment was she in difficulty. The voice showed infinite expressive inflection, founded on a solid chest voice and launched itself to resplendent heights. In the last Act when the staging finally allowed her to perform on the same level as her partners, Caballé proved that now no role can be considered outside her *fach*. For all those who are sensitive to the human voice, this is truly one of the most absorbing operatic experiences.[5]

Anybody fortunate enough to get hold of a decent copy of the transmission will witness not just a commanding piece of singing, but also one of the most intensely characterized and committed impersonations ever captured on video. Together with her Orange *Norma* from 1974, this Paris *Turandot* is her greatest 'recorded' performance.

Nor was this set of *Turandot*s in any way a freakish one-off, as the San Francisco performances of two years earlier had served to confirm. The last Paris performance took place on 13 June and, following a pair of gala recitals given on consecutive evenings in Menorca and Ludwigsburg, she again sang the role in two performances at the Théâtre Municipal in Avignon. These drew an encomium from *Opera*'s correspondent, Tony Mayer, who had actually been present at the Parisian première of the opera in 1928 with Maryse Beaujon and Georges Thill:

Turandot triumphed then. It has triumphed ever since. A series of performances was given – with wild success – in Paris and more recently in Avignon. In both cases Montserrat Caballé sang the title-role. Strange and formidable woman: a *prima donna* 'comme on n'en fait plus' . . . After years of acrobatic feats – and triumphs – Caballé seems set to conquer a fresh field. At the end of the performance, the audience went mad, stamping its feet and shouting itself hoarse.[6]

One can only wish in retrospect that Caballé had continued with this role and sung it in more places than she actually did.

Much of the rest of the summer of 1981 was taken up with performances of *La forza del destino*, first at the Vienna State Opera in late June (in the context of the Wiener Festwochen) and then, in late July, in the Roman amphitheatre – the Arena Sferisterio – at Macerata, where Caballé made her local début on the 25th. This was a new production given in sets by Giò Pomodoro imported from the Verona Festival, and reunited the soprano with José Carreras (in the role of Don Alvaro) with whom she had last sung little more than a fortnight previously in a joint concert given in the southern French town of Perpignan. The 6000-strong audience in Macerata accorded both singers a thunderous ovation, and though the local festival had in fact been in operation since the 1920s, it was these – and subsequent – Caballé performances that brought the festival wider international recognition.

Her only other major engagement this summer was a set of performances of *Tosca* given in the open air in Ravenna, the beautiful and artistically important watering-hole for the holidaying Byzantine emperors in the Veneto. The stage had been erected in the ruins of the fortress Roca Brancaleone and, in order to minimize traffic noise, the whole area had been closed to cars. Caballé, meanwhile, because of the makeshift conditions of the theatre, had elected to don wig, costume and make-up back in her hotel before being chauffeured to the performance. But with half a kilometre still to go, her limousine was stopped at a large pair of metal barriers by a *carabiniere* who flatly refused to let the vehicle through. After much heated debate in Venetian dialect between the chauffeur and the policeman, Montserrat got out of the car, strode to the barriers and flung them out of the way. Back in the car, she gave an imperious gesture of the arm and the command 'Va!' Not surprisingly, this display of Tosca temperament left the dumbstruck *carabiniere* paralysed as the car sped past him.

After these performances she was due to come to London where from mid-August she was to record the role of Maddalena in *Andrea Chénier* for Decca, with Luciano Pavarotti in the title-role, conducted by Riccardo Chailly. However, emergency distress signals had already been sent out by the Italian recording company Fonit Cetra, which, with little more than days to go before the commencement of sessions in London for its new recording of Rossini's *Il turco in Italia*, had been confronted by the withdrawal of Renata Scotto from the principal role of Fiorilla. It so happened that this opera was also being conducted by Chailly, who had his own suggestion to make as part of the desperate hunt which had been mounted for a soprano who could rescue the project. Carlos Caballé's office in Barcelona duly received a number of telephone calls from Alberto Zedda, whose sister Bianca was the artistic director of the Italian company, and, following the briefest of negotiations, Montserrat agreed to take on the role, which therefore involved her in repeated commutings from Ravenna to London. There was even the necessity of re-arranging some of the *Chénier* sessions in order to accommodate this other recording, which was made in EMI's Abbey Road studios, the scene of so many of Caballé's earlier recorded triumphs.

The *Chénier*, on the other hand, was made in Walthamstow Town Hall, but the recording was not satisfactorily completed by the end of the scheduled sessions because Riccardo Chailly had fallen ill and extra ones had to be arranged for the following year. In any event, Caballé was expected in San Francisco in order to begin rehearsing the inaugural production of the 1981–2 season at the War Memorial Opera House, *Semiramide*. This, though new to the Californians, was actually a re-creation of Pizzi's marmoreal Aix staging, here beginning the first of its numerous reproductions throughout the operatic world in the 1980s. It also served to reunite Montserrat with Marilyn Horne, although the role of Assur was on this occasion taken not by Samuel Ramey but by another native American soon to become famous in a very different kind of repertory, James Morris. The performances were conducted by Richard Bonynge, the first time he had collaborated with Caballé in over a decade. It almost goes without saying, however, that the real reason for his presence in San Francisco was that he was also scheduled to conduct performances of *The Merry Widow*, with his wife in the title-role. In fact, it was Sutherland who more than anybody else had been responsible for the restoration of *Semiramide* to the repertory, having sung the role throughout the 1960s, including at La Scala and the Maggio Musicale.

Inevitably, the three *prime donne* spent much of their time in one another's company either rehearsing, performing or holed up in the Huntington Hotel on top of Nob Hill. *Semiramide* opened on 11 September and was accorded a tumultuous reception: Arthur Bloomfield, the senior San Franciscan music critic, noted that 'The production boasted a more extensive yardage of vocal virtuosity than almost any performance on local record.'[7] The nearest to a hiccup was, in fact, no such thing, and indeed was taken by the audience as proof positive of the emotional involvement of both women. After the big duet in Act I – 'Serbami ognor si fido il cor' – had ended with an entire flurry of intertwined cadenzas, the two divas embraced as directed. The audience erupted with cheers and applause, but Caballé was momentarily non-plussed. She whispered in Horne's ear, 'I can't remember my next line!' In fact, since a whole march and chorus had been cut, this was 'I vostri voti omai', but Horne, mischievously taking advantage of Caballé's oft-noted confusion of 'b' and 'v' in Italian pronunciation – they are indeed reversed in Spanish – whispered back 'I bostri boti omai'. As intended, this completely 'corpsed' Caballé, who proceeded to shake uncontrollably with laughter in Horne's arms: and laughter, as anyone knows who has ever set foot on stage, is alarmingly contagious. Thus the audience, still roaring in tribute, were treated to the spectacle of what they believed to be two women overcome with emotion at their reception, rather than the reality of two seasoned performers giggling helplessly in each other's arms.

These performances became one of the hottest tickets in San Francisco's operatic history, and a free operatic concert given by Horne and Caballé in the Golden Gate Park between *Semiramide*s did nothing to assuage demand. The concert took place on a glorious Sunday afternoon and featured the Opera Orchestra conducted by its veteran music director, Kurt Herbert Adler. The event, which attracted a throng of 25,000, was filmed for transmission the following day and found everybody in the best of spirits, not least Caballé, who sang some real rarities amongst her solo items, including Giulietta's Act I aria, 'Oh! quante volte' from Bellini's *I Capuleti e i Montecchi*. Between the last two performances of the run in the War Memorial Opera House she gave a recital in Seattle, and then, at the beginning of October, crossed the entire breadth of North America in order to perform at a gala in Avery Fisher Hall, New York, conducted by Zubin Mehta, in which she sang 'Al dolce guidami', Anna Bolena's last-Act lament, and the final scene from *Il pirata*.

She spent the rest of the month singing in Hamburg, the longest run of performances she had ever given in Germany since her apprenticeship in Bremen. There were no fewer than four concert performances of *Norma*, with Alicia Nafé as Adalgisa, followed by three staged *Tosca*s. Then, at the beginning of November, it was back to France, first for a brace of *Manon Lescaut*s in her beloved Théâtre de l'Opéra in Nice, and then on to Paris where she was scheduled to star in an exact replica of the *Semiramide* given at Aix in 1980, with Horne, Araiza and Ramey, conducted by López Cobos. The first performance took place on 25 November and constituted the official opening of the 1981–2 season at the Paris Opéra. However, since the Palais Garnier was undergoing one of its periodic refurbishments, the performances were given instead in the Théâtre des Champs-Élysées (oddly named, since the theatre is in the Avenue Montaigne). These met with no less success than the previous revivals, with the added cachet that they were taking place in the French capital. This time Charles Pitt was moved to observe that 'Only superlatives could describe the vocal performances and the give and take between [Caballé and Horne].'[8]

Then it was back to Barcelona for the Christmas show at the Liceo, which this year was to take the form of three performances each of *Adriana Lecouvreur* and *Anna Bolena*. The rehearsal period of the latter was very fraught: Margherita Wallmann, whose second Liceo spectacular this was, suffered a heart attack; the original conductor – Armando Gatto – was replaced by Eugenio Marco; and Montserrat was suffering from an acute recurrence of the kidney trouble which had first plagued her at the time of the La Scala *Turandot* in 1976. This was the third occasion that the Donizetti opera had been scheduled expressly for Caballé at the Liceo, and much the most prestigious, since Wallmann's production had cost a fortune and the rest of the cast was distinguished, including Cesare Siepi in the role of Henry VIII, Alicia Nafé as Jane Seymour and Luis Lima as Percy. But on the second night of the new production on 5 January 1982, Montserrat was stricken with agonizing back pain and only just made it through the performance.

Caballé had been driven to tempt fate for this third time with the work, since earlier in 1981 La Scala had decided for budgetary reasons – or so they claimed – to cancel the scheduled new production of Gluck's *Alceste* which the soprano had already agreed to sing in May 1982, and to offer her instead the first-ever revival of *Anna Bolena*, which had last been heard in the house in 1958, sung by Maria Callas. This was then brought forward to February as part of a despicable bout of double-dealing behind the backs of three of the world's leading mezzo-sopranos – Agnes Baltsa, Elena Obraztsova and Marilyn Horne – whereby each was offered roles promised to the other. In the event, Obraztsova took the role of Jane Seymour, which had originally been intended for Baltsa. One may wonder in retrospect precisely what motivated the La Scala management to offer the revival to Caballé in the first place, since, as they were only too well aware, the Callas 'widows' actively opposed the presentation at the Milanese theatre of any work which they considered to be the artistic property of their idol.* However, Caballé had accepted this poisoned chalice voluntarily, while deciding that a run-in period with the role with which she had previously had so much bad luck was advisable. Hence the new production at the Liceo.

But if she had thought along the lines of 'third time lucky' she was sorely mistaken, since she was unable to give the last of her scheduled performances, instead being operated on in hospital for the removal of a kidney stone which had been found to be too big to be successfully passed through the urinary tract. It therefore became necessary to cancel an appearance in Hamburg and performances of *Gemma di Vergy* scheduled for mid-January in Nice. Thus began what Montserrat herself looks back on as the worst year of her professional life, when many people came to the conclusion, on the strength of her numerous cancellations, that her career was at an end. Many believed that the reasons for such a series of sequential indispositions, necessitating so many withdrawals, must be fundamentally psychological and/or vocal. But, in fact, they all had readily explicable physical causes.

As usual, Montserrat did herself no favours by returning to the stage at the earliest possible opportunity, which on this occasion took the form of the other performances she had been contracted to give in Nice one week after the *Gemma di Vergy*s. Thus it was that after a bout of surgery, Caballé's first outing was as Turandot, of all things. She remembers the occasion with a wry grimace:

> I had absolutely no power behind the voice. I could not support it properly. No volume, no strength, no nothing. I had thought I was going to be alright. After all, the surgery had not been too extensive, just a low incision at kidney level. But this time I misjudged how it would affect me and by the end I was practically finished.

It was in this condition that she travelled to Milan to begin rehearsing the revival of *Bolena*. Sandro Sequi had been entrusted with the probably thankless task of reviving Luchino Visconti's original production in Nicola Benois' sets. But before serious work got underway, Caballé gave a solo recital with Zanetti in La Scala on 1 February which, although a success with the audience, left her feeling shattered. The rehearsals went well enough in the absence of the conductor, Giuseppe Patanè, who was otherwise engaged in Rome, and there was a general hope that even the 'widows' would be appeased. In the midst of all this,

---

* It was this that effectively kept *La traviata* out of La Scala's repertory for nearly twenty-seven years, despite an attempt to revive it with Mirella Freni, until Riccardo Muti defiantly programmed the work in the 1991–2 season.

Caballé flew back to Barcelona in order to take part in a joint concert with Carreras at the Liceo, at which the repertory included duets from *Poliuto* and *Chénier*. This was tumultuously received, which makes the subsequent turn of events all the more regrettable.

Caballé delayed her return to Milan by a day because her seventy-year-old mother was unwell, having complained of miscellaneous symptoms for some time. It was decided that Ana would go into hospital for some tests, as a result of which Montserrat's brother Carlos would remain behind in Barcelona to watch over their mother's progress. Back in her suite at the Duomo, however, Caballé began to feel unwell. This was on 11 February and the first night was scheduled for the 14th. As the hours passed, she felt progressively worse: she began to vomit continuously and to suffer intestinal problems. It so happened that Denny Dayviss, together with her then associate Alan Sievewright, had flown to Milan specifically to see *Anna Bolena*, and so it was under these adverse circumstances that an old association was revived. Denny made arrangements for La Scala's doctors to attend, as it was only too clear that the soprano was in no position either to dress-rehearse or perform. The Scala medical team duly materialized and advised rest and calm. But the following morning a doctor from Milan's principal hospital, who had been summoned at Bernabé's insistence, took a sample and within the hour had diagnosed salmonella poisoning. At which point, on 12 February, it became quite clear that Caballé was not going to perform on the opening night as announced. Indeed, when La Scala's own doctors heard the result of the tests, they were keen to make arrangements for her to be admitted to hospital immediately. The artistic administration of La Scala was therefore duly notified both by its own medical staff and Caballé's office in Barcelona – as well as by the diva herself – that she was unwell and unable to perform.

The Opera House had had a cover on standby from the outset of rehearsals in the shape of the young American soprano, Ruth Falcon. She was informed of the situation and placed on alert for both the dress rehearsal and the opening night. But, just as we saw in the matter of *Turandot* in 1976, no one in the hierarchy of La Scala's management was prepared to take the responsibility of informing the public of Caballé's withdrawal. Unfortunately this characteristic inertia backfired badly. At 8 p.m. on 14 February 1982, a packed gala audience was told after some ten minutes' delay – and then by a disembodied voice coming over the theatre's Tannoy system – that Caballé was indisposed and that her place would be taken by Ruth Falcon.

The house erupted. To continual jeering, catcalls, whistles and screams Patanè walked out into the orchestra pit and mounted the rostrum as the house lights dimmed. Amidst the mêlée could be heard repeated cries of 'Let that clown Badini [La Scala's Sovrintendente] come and tell us himself!' As the minutes passed with no sign whatsoever of calm being restored, Patanè made a few half-hearted attempts to begin the overture (which would at least have been an absolute novelty for the Milanese, since it had never been played during the Callas performances). But he was unable to do so and, noticing that members of La Scala's management had all withdrawn from their several boxes, himself left the orchestra pit. In fact, Francesco Siciliani had slipped unnoticed into the box occupied by Giulietta Simionato – the Jane Seymour to Callas's Bolena – and, astonishingly, had persuaded her as a venerated old house favourite to do Badini's dirty work for him. So the audience was treated to the spectacle of the retired mezzo-soprano appearing before La Scala's curtain, arms upraised, trying to make her cries of 'Amici! Amici!' heard above the unremitting din. Far from acting as the calming influence that had been intended, it was apparent that brawls and scuffling were breaking out in various parts of the auditorium as different factions came to blows. Simionato was obliged to withdraw, shaken by the sight of elegantly dressed dowagers in the expensive stalls boxes standing up and baying for Badini's blood.

The mayhem continued for at least a further ten minutes, despite the raising and lowering of the house lights, at which point the anonymous voice again rang out through the theatre's loudspeakers duly informing the audience that the performance had been cancelled and that moneys would be refunded: the patrons should kindly leave the theatre immediately. Pandemonium followed: fist-fights were observed throughout the theatre and the sheer volume of howling voices was deafening. *Carabinieri* entered the premises and began to enforce the evacuation of the theatre. At least one group of protesters, having been ejected into the pouring rain, made a bee-line for Caballé's hotel and proceeded to scream abuse at the diva from the street. Bernabé was both distressed and enraged: Montserrat was in too feverish a condition even to register what was happening. Another, larger band of protesters besieged the theatre's stage door, thus ensuring that the departing members of La Scala's management required police protection in order to effect their escape. The disturbances went on for many hours, which afforded the Italian media in general and television in particular the opportunity to turn up in force and to record the sensational events.

Needless to say, Caballé was hounded in her hotel by dozens of journalists all demanding interviews. Bernabé fielded much of the preliminary flak, but as it became clear over the following days just what incredible scenes had transpired at the theatre, Montserrat felt increasingly obliged to explain the circumstances of her cancellation. It is fair to say that for at least a week afterwards, every major newspaper and news bulletin, both on radio and television, carried extensive reports of what had happened and why. Caballé seems to have responded with remarkable composure and good humour to the frequently provocative manner of her interrogators, going out of her way to praise her under-study, Ruth Falcon, and to soft-pedal the evident culpability of La Scala's management. She merely pointed out – time after time – that she had informed the authorities of her enforced cancellation through illness a clear forty-eight hours before the first night.

In fact, La Scala's trials were not at an end; nor were Caballé's. The next performance was scheduled to take place on 16 February, but there was no question of the soprano yet being well enough to take part. Unfortunately, Ruth Falcon had now fallen prey to a virus and was herself obliged to withdraw, which led to the cancellation of the per-formances on both the 16th and 19th. Meanwhile, La Scala had resorted to the desperate expedient of posting outside the theatre daily bulletins charting the medical progress of the Spanish diva, who was, in effect, being blackmailed by the theatre into returning to the run of perform-ances. As she recalls:

> With the food poisoning I had caught, I should have been in bed for a fortnight. Probably the theatre's doctors were right when they said I should have gone to the hospital, but I never go to hospital unless it is in Barcelona and I wished to stay in Milan to show that I was serious in wanting to sing the role. So many people had said that twenty-five years after Callas had done the role I must be so scared of her ghost in it. But this was not true and it never has been. And then the theatre said to me after the third performance I had missed – all within six days – that either I sing the next performance or they would cancel the whole production and say I was too afraid to sing. I did not want to sing that night but La Scala put it in a way that I could not refuse.

This finally took place on 21 February, in a distinctly fraught atmo-sphere. No one was happy: the management had been repeatedly pillor-ied in public; the diva had come in for more than her fair share of criticism and was both extremely apprehensive and still not fully recov-ered from her food poisoning; and the audience contained many who had come simply to vent their displeasure, irrespective of the quality of Caballé's performance. Not surprisingly, the 'pirates' were out in force, and numerous recordings of this one performance survive. They bear witness to the testimony of Denny Dayviss and Alan Sievewright among others who were actually there that Montserrat sang extremely well; only her visible indisposition towards the end of the opera momentarily compromised the level of her performance when, in the recitative that precedes the aria 'Al dolce guidami' she sang a high C which took the merest fraction of a second to acquire full amplitude and resonance. Yet in that split instant, a handful of voices in the upper tiers broke out in a commotion, as if they had been poised to pounce, waiting for the slightest pretext to cause trouble. Until then, she had been enthusiastically received after both Acts I and II, including an ovation for her interpolation of a – for her – rare high D in the ensemble following 'Giudici! Ad Anna!' The final curtain saw another contretemps between various parts of the audience, to which Montserrat remained oblivious since she had decided not to take a personal bow.

At this point she had clearly had enough: in any event her mother was seriously unwell back in Barcelona and, using this as a convenient pretext, she left the city on the morning of the 22nd and flew home, vowing never to sing this unluckiest of all her roles again.

> There was more scandal from people who had come only in the hope I would be bad. So I thought to myself afterwards, perhaps I shouldn't sing in the theatre any more and just think of myself. But that would have made no difference, since those people always say that I think only of myself anyway. It was hopeless, and I went home.

The final comments can best be left with Cecilia Gasdia who, at the age of twenty-one and totally unknown but for having recently won the Callas Competition, was brought in to sing the role in Caballé's place at the remaining performance.

> I was at the performance which Montserrat gave . . . She had an enormous success. Papers very frequently write inaccuracies which bear no relationship to the truth. [She] had a tremendous ovation, and even if there had been a momentary weakness, for the rest it was a magnificent evening . . . She sang the aria 'Al dolce guidami' like a goddess, and the theatre erupted in applause. I was there and I saw it . . . There are always those whom we call 'the unknown soloists' up in the galleries, those for whom nothing seems to be any good.[9]

Caballé cancelled all her engagements for the remainder of February and the whole of March, partly to allow herself a full recovery period and partly to remain at home with her mother who had just undergone a mastectomy. It was during this period that she consulted a specialist at a hospital in Barcelona who had long been familiar with the entire catalogue of the singer's various operations. He had become convinced that the only way she could regain full muscular control was to practise yoga. This set off an automatic train of association in Caballé's thoughts, leading her to contact her long-term collaborator and noted yoga practitioner, Zubin Mehta. He was all enthusiasm for the idea and came up with suggestions as to who Caballé should contact. With Bernabé's help and guidance, she soon began to follow a regime of yoga-based exercises prescribed by the experts which were designed to restore her full physical strength.

Unfortunately and lamentably as usual when following a bout of major illness, she decided to pick up the threads of her temporarily suspended career at a point of maximum effort and inconvenience to herself. She was due to sing *Norma* in South Africa as the first major operatic artist to have sung there for many years. As part of her formal contract for performances at the Civic Theatre, Johannesburg, she had insisted on performing before non-segregated audiences. But what she had failed to take into account was the city's altitude, some 6000 feet above sea-level. She had been virtually floored from the time she had stepped off the plane and found it almost impossible to rehearse, such was her wheezing and general shortness of breath. She had not apparently suffered similar symptoms when singing in Mexico City: but this was nearly twenty years, thousands of performances and many additional kilos later. On the opening night – 2 April – Caballé fainted backstage immediately after the conclusion of the cabaletta to 'Casta diva'. According to Emma Renzi, the South African soprano who had replaced Caballé as Turandot at La Scala in 1976, Caballé only got through with the assistance of an oxygen bottle strategically placed in the wings. Notwithstanding these problems, the performance received a standing ovation and Montserrat looked set to conquer her recent run of medical misfortune.

The following day she departed for Pretoria where she was to give a recital in the newly opened State Theatre that evening. The packed audience was somewhat apprehensive, having read all about Caballé's breathing difficulties in their Sunday newspapers. But Pretoria is at a much lower altitude than Johannesburg, and the soprano evidently encountered no difficulties. Indeed, she went on to give a comprehensive display of her art, including no fewer than eight encores. One of these was the so-called Swiss folk-song 'G'schätzli' which the Pretorians accurately heard the soprano introduce as an encore piece given to her during her years in Switzerland by Elisabeth Schwarzkopf in Geneva, rather than what so many members of the London audience *think* they heard Caballé say on one occasion was in imitation of her German colleague.[10] But back in Johannesburg, Montserrat's problems multiplied: the breathing difficulties persisted and, worse, she developed tonsillitis. The grand ensemble which ends the opera found the soprano almost voiceless at the third performance, as a result of which Caballé declined to take a curtain call. Many people backstage, Renzi included, encouraged her to do so, but, as usual, it turned out to be on her own terms. She went out and immediately silenced the ovation by raising her arms: she then proceeded to apologize to the audience for her singing, which of course had the effect of redoubling the applause. Three days later, however, the performance had to be abandoned altogether after the trio which concludes Act I, since Caballé suffered a collapse backstage, causing her to withdraw from the two subsequent performances which in the event were sung by Emma Renzi.

Montserrat thus returned home to Barcelona rather earlier than expected and instantly felt much better on returning to normal atmospheric pressure at sea level. After just a few days' break she left for Madrid where she duly sang all four scheduled performances of *La forza del destino* with Giuseppe Giacomini in the role of Don Alvaro and Juan Pons as the avenging brother Don Carlo. This went a long way to mollifying the Madrilenans who had originally expected to hear Caballé in a revival of an opera by Vicente Martin y Soler, *El árbol de Diana*, but from which she had withdrawn by agreement with the theatre, feeling herself to be unsuited to the very light soprano principal role. After the *Forza*s, she sensibly decided to take things relatively easy and allow herself plenty of time in which to prepare for the first new production that had ever been mounted specifically for her at the Liceo other than at the Christmas/New York period, Handel's *Giulio Cesare*, which was scheduled to open on 8 June. This change of routine had come about primarily as a result of the death in the previous year of Juan Antonio Pámias and the wholesale reconstitution of the theatre's administrative and economic structure that was occurring as a result.

The *Proprietarios* – the Liceo's wholly private owners – had come to be replaced by the *Consorci*, or consortium of interested parties, including not only the owners but also representatives of both local and national government which for the first time were to make a contribution towards the theatre's economic upkeep. There was also a need to modernize the whole Liceo operation, from its antiquated stage to its non-existent administration. Pámias had never had the money to establish what might be called an operatic infrastructure: all his efforts had been geared towards the presentation of the finest singers, irrespective of such sundry considerations as the quality of orchestral and choral support, much less production values. Caballé had never been much minded to worry about these shortcomings, which for years effectively barred Barcelona from being taken seriously on the international operatic circuit, if not by the singers themselves then certainly by the critics. But with the death of the genial, cigar-smoking impresario, following on so soon from that of the operatically indifferent Franco, whose forty-year regime had been artistically philistine, it was time for a long overdue change. As Carlos Caballé observes: 'If music is to be regarded as part of the culture of a nation, then it deserves to be subsidized by its elected governments, rather than being left to scrape around on its hands and knees, scratching for its very existence.'

As a first move, Lluís Portabella had been appointed as the Liceo's new intendant and one of his initial tasks was to extend the theatre's season beyond its usual November–March run by inviting Pro Música, a non-profit-making, nationwide musical sponsor, to put on a season of its own in the May–June period when the house would normally be closed. Thus came about the three performances of *Giulio Cesare* in a very elaborate production borrowed from the Deutsche Staatsoper in Berlin which combined spectacular quasi-baroque effects – Caballé, mounted high on an enormous, twenty-foot diameter bronze shield tilted up at forty-five degrees, gliding towards the audience, became the most photographically famous – with odds and ends of Bauhaus-style angularity. The work was savagely cut and had the baritone Justino Diaz in what was originally an alto-castrato title-role. Even so, the show evidently carried the day, and a great success was enjoyed by all, particularly Patricia Payne as Cornelia. And Caballé, in an amazing array of elaborate wigs and costumes, was thought to have recovered her best vocal form, as the television relay of the last performance serves to confirm.

Unfortunately this did not extend to the following week when the special season was brought to a conclusion with three performances of *Don Carlos*, starring Caballé, Carreras, Obraztsova, Simon Estes and Bernd Weikl, conducted by Charles Vanderzand. A problem that had already manifested itself during the performances of the Handel now became almost insuperable, as the average daily temperature in Barcelona soared into the mid-30° C, with 100 per cent humidity. As audiences and soloists alike sweltered in the non-air-conditioned theatre, many doubtless came to realize why the Liceo's season had historically never extended beyond the middle of April. Montserrat, in particular, was prostrated by this combination of heat and humidity, which turned the house into a steam-bath, and at the last performance was unable to sing her principal aria in the last Act. Not until she found herself in the altogether more salubrious atmosphere of Vienna for two performances of *Andrea Chénier* on 23 and 27 June did she feel her best form returning.

Thereafter she travelled to France where, after an absence of eight years, she sang again at the Théâtre Antique in Orange – the scene of her triumphant *Norma* in 1974. Presumably this extended absence had not been unconnected with the rift that had opened following the disputatious *Aïda* of 1976, when the Festival administration (including Jacques Bourgeois) had advertised Caballé in the title-role although she had declined to confirm the performance. But this directorate had now been severally dismissed from its post and Raymond Duffaut had been installed direct from Avignon where Caballé had latterly been highly active. The occasion of this return to Orange was a new production of *La forza del destino* in which the seventy-nine-year old producer Margherita Wallmann had decided – as she confessed to Montserrat with tongue-in-cheek insouciance – belatedly to join the ranks of operatic desecrators by relocating the work to the period of the Spanish Civil War, trucks, tanks, Gatling guns and all. Montserrat's role of Leonora was supremely unaffected by all this, as Wallmann had always intended, but the producer's cynically indifferent flirtation with modernism in the event backfired: although her avowed attitude had been one of 'this is the kind of rubbish they expect these days, so we may as well give it to them', the audience proved unresponsive to the production and booed it loudly. Both Wallmann and Caballé were secretly pleased, although perhaps for slightly different reasons.

The performance was televised in France (with, not surprisingly, a cosmetically adjusted curtain call) and reveals the soprano to be in fine voice, particularly in the awkwardly written intervals of the first Act aria, 'Me pellegrina ed orfana', and, rather more expectedly, in 'Pace, pace mio Dio' and the final scene, despite an otherwise patchy cast conducted by Miguel-Angel Gomez-Martinez.

After this solitary performance on 13 July, Caballé made her way to another Roman amphitheatre, this time at Macerata, where she sang in what transpired to be two sets of farewell performances: the first was the role of Norma; and the second (and by this stage one might have thought overdue) that of Mimì. Both were well received, particularly the *Norma*s, though ironically her Mimìs were thought to have been better sung. In fact, it is a miracle that no performances were cancelled, since Caballé was greatly disturbed by the news that her fifteen-year old son had broken his collar-bone in a car accident in Barcelona. As she admits,

I was so worried during rehearsals, I was on the phone the whole time. At first all I knew was that he had been in a bad car crash and was in hospital. Of course, I wanted to leave, but the family in

Barcelona kept telling me that Junior was being well looked after, so I decided to stay in Italy and do all the rehearsals and performances. But the first Norma [on 21 July] I know I sang badly because my mind was elsewhere. So between performances I went home after all, and once I had seen my son, though he looked terrible in plaster, I felt better and went straight back. Then I sang better, too. But really 1982 and the beginning of 1983 was such a bad time for me. It was difficult to know what to do. I had all these commitments months, years into the future, and I was going from one illness to another. If I cancelled, there was a scandal. If I sang at anything less than 100 per cent, there was a scandal. Drama if I sing, drama if I don't sing. What do you do?

Of course, she was now a complete victim of her own fame as well as of the audience's expectations with regard to the fast-approaching fifty-year-old's performances. There was the inevitable problem that she was increasingly in competition not only with her own recordings in the mainstream repertory, but also with individual audiences' memories of former glories. It must, after all, be distressing to read litanies of criticism penned not so much in anger but in sorrow, where the comparison is with one's former self. As she herself was to say later, 'You cannot sing in your fifties the roles you sang in your thirties. The intelligent thing is to know what roles you *can* sing in your fifties.' With this in mind, she began a comprehensive evaluation of her repertory and, at the same time, began to map out a preliminary list of new works which would serve to satisfy her own voracious musical appetite.

In the meantime, she stuck to her guns and fulfilled most of the engagements which had long since been planned for her, covering the remainder of 1982. She sang Elisabeth de Valois in Ravenna, and then in Vienna where she had been accorded the great honour by the State Opera's new intendant, Lorin Maazel, of opening the 1982–3 season with a performance of *Tosca*, together with Carreras, Juan Pons and no less than Walter Berry as the Sacristan. But thereafter, it was straight into more trouble. Montserrat was scheduled to sing seven performances of *Un ballo in maschera* at the War Memorial Opera House in San Francisco, where Terry McEwen had just taken over as the general director. Pavarotti was to be the Riccardo (or Gustavus III in this particular staging), with Ingvar Wixell as Renato (or Anckarstrøm). In the event, the only members of the cast to sing all seven performances were Kathleen Battle as Oscar and Ruza Baldani as Ulrica (Mme Arvidson). Wixell withdrew before ever singing a note. On the opening night – 10 September – both Pavarotti and Caballé sang as scheduled, but the tenor immediately fell ill with a cold which, so he is reported to have said, he had caught from the soprano during rehearsals. He therefore cancelled all subsequent appearances, including the concert in the Golden Gate Park which he and Montserrat had been due to give on the 12th. (He seems to have recovered sufficiently to complete the filming of *Yes, Giorgio!*)

Montserrat, meanwhile, was suffering from gastroenteritis which had plagued her sporadically ever since the salmonella infection earlier in the year in Milan. She got through the first four performances, although the fourth, with Vasile Moldoveanu, was a trial for all concerned. At the fifth, on 22 September, she barely managed to get past her opening lines in Ulrica's dwelling before withdrawing from the performance altogether. This sparked off any amount of press coverage, some of it centring on the known and shameful practice of certain divas notorious for their performances of just one Act of any work, having had it formally written into their contracts that that is sufficient to ensure payment of their full fee. In fact, as the War Memorial itself took the step of announcing, Caballé had refused to accept the fee they had offered her. She became afflicted with an eye infection which had rendered one eye completely bloodshot and had obliged her to wear dark glasses even on stage. As a result, she cancelled the last two *Ballos*. Terry McEwen told the press that he felt as if he had been the general director not for nine months but for forty years.

After just a few days' rest in Barcelona, Montserrat set out again on her travels, this time on a further tour of Japan – sponsored by the *Yomuri Shimbun* – during which she gave recitals in Tokyo, Osaka, Kanasawa and Fukuoka. The tour terminated back in Tokyo when on 1 November 1982 she gave a concert of operatic arias in the Bunka Kaikan. Just days later she was due back on stage at the Liceo in a revival of *Un ballo in maschera* but late in the day the Liceo administration decided to change the opera and instead mounted *Don Carlos*, which had already been given earlier in the year. At least this afforded the soloists the opportunity of performing the work in something other than a steam bath.

After the three performances at the Liceo Montserrat departed immediately for Vienna where, seemingly getting back into her vocal stride, she gave further performances of *Tosca*. By mid-December she was safely installed back home, preparing as usual for the family's Christmas by going on extended shopping sprees for presents and supervising the setting up of the traditional *Pessebre*, or Nativity Scene, complete with animals and Magi. By this time, the immediate family for whom it was necessary to get presents comprised Caballé's own parents (both living with their daughter in the enlarged Infanta Carlota apartment), her own children (Bernabé junior and Montserrat), Carlos and his wife, Brigitte, together with their four children, Isabel, Montserrat, Ana and Carlos junior. In the midst of all this activity rehearsals began at the Liceo for a new production of Spontini's rarely-performed *La vestale* in which Caballé was to undertake for the first time the role of the vestal virgin, Giulia. The first of four performances took place on 26 December and, as usual, Caballé remained in Barcelona until Epiphany (Twelfth Night) on 6 January.

The following morning she flew to New York in order to begin rehearsals for a concert performance of *Semiramide* which was to be given as the second offering of a new concert opera series sponsored jointly by Carnegie Hall and Columbia Artists Management Incorporated (CAMI). The promoters had taken the precaution of engaging as a cover the still then largely unknown June Anderson, whose attitude was sporting; she reasoned that it could do her no harm to hang around because even if Caballé did sing she would at least have had the experience of watching her idol in rehearsal. In the event, Montserrat attended all the rehearsals, and everyone – Anderson herself, Marilyn Horne (who was singing Arsace), and the conductor Henry Lewis – fully expected her to have her anticipated New York triumph in the role that she had made unmistakably her own.

But on the evening of 9 January 1983 Montserrat felt unwell, and by the following morning, the day of the performance, was suffering from a viral infection that made her incapable of croaking a note. Knowing full well just what such a late cancellation might unleash amongst the increasingly sceptical New York audience, she nevertheless had no alternative but to withdraw. The performance that did take place that night effectively made June Anderson's reputation in a city where she had hitherto only functioned as a second string at the New York City Opera, very much the plaything of Beverly Sills's whims as director of that organization. Anderson's success replicated some eighteen years on the situation that had once thrust Montserrat into the limelight, and in the same venue. But the precipitate nature of the replacement proved too much for the New York public, who jeered the announcement made in the hall that night. Caballé was no better two days later, and was also forced to cancel a recital in Avery Fisher Hall. The bitter disappointment of the respective audiences was taken up by the critics themselves. Peter Davis, writing in the *New York Magazine*, concluded that her singing career was probably at an end since, most major organizations are no longer willing to take a chance on her . . . [Is she] a pitiable creature constantly riddled with disease or a very capricious woman who actually enjoys disappointing audiences and giving impresarios heart failure? . . . The last of the old-time prima donnas may have made her final dishonourable exit.

Strong words, indicative of the disappointment that is caused when any great artist cancels. The truth of the matter was that Caballé was neither a 'very capricious woman' nor a 'pitiable creature': she was simply suffering from the effects of a sudden change of climate which took her from a mild Barcelonese winter in which she had enjoyed a tremendous personal success in the Spontini work, to a paralysingly cold New York where she had fallen ill, all within the space of just four days. Even so, the New Yorkers were not inclined to see matters in this light and thanks to some manipulative journalistic copy, of which Davis's is merely the most hostile example, Caballé's 'worst year of my life' drew to a slightly belated close on a note of sour-toned scepticism. But as she observes of this episode:

I have always made impresarios a lot of money across my career and have never, so far as I am aware, given any of them heart attacks. Nor, if I am able to sing, have I to my knowledge disappointed audiences. I would wish this gentleman good health but better intelligence. I did not go all the way to New York and rehearse for days just so I could have the 'pleasure' of cancelling.

All of this was a great shame, since otherwise Caballé's health – admittedly dire in the first half of 1982 – had improved greatly as the year had progressed. She had reportedly been in fine voice throughout the Japanese tour and for the Liceo *Vestales*: New York was simply unlucky, as Milan had been in the past. But there was no denying that a great deal of bad feeling had been engendered by this abortive trip and that the Americans, unlike the more explosive but more forgiving Italians, found it difficult to come to terms with Caballé's unreliability. Like the Italians, however, and in the teeth of Peter Davis's prediction, the major organizations actually did remain prepared to take a gamble on the likelihood of future performances, which gives some idea of just how important Caballé was. As Marilyn Horne was to observe some years later, surely it is better to schedule Caballé for x number of performances on the assumption that she might at least perform half of them and have a decent standby ready for the rest, than refuse to have her and thereby get no Caballé at all. In any case, something of this line of reasoning must have informed artistic planning at the highest levels, since within the year Montserrat was back in force in Lincoln Center.

With the benefit of hindsight, we can now see that an 'experimental' phase in Caballé's career had drawn to a fairly abrupt close, foundering upon the rocks of ill-health. The period during which she consciously tackled many of the heaviest dramatic roles of the soprano repertory was about to give way to an altogether more unexpected exploration of the *terra incognita* of nineteenth-century opera. As she approached her fiftieth birthday, she began to put into effect her own previously quoted dictum that you cannot sing in your fifties the operas you sang in your thirties. More important still was the fact that these new discoveries would take her away from the operas she had sung in her forties. Looking back over her repertory and the nature of the relationship star-performers forge with their audience, she observes:

I always sang heavy repertory, right from the very beginning. Operas like *Salome, Tosca, Manon Lescaut* are a very hard sing. *Turandot* was different, and I only approached that many years later, but the other three I had been singing for twenty-five years. They are roles which, if you are not prepared, will finish you off. If your voice is delicate or just purely lyrical and needs looking after, then you shouldn't sing any of these roles because you would have to force it to do so and in forcing you can damage it. *Semiramide* is one of the longest operas I have ever sung and it was very difficult for me because I came to it after *Gioconda* and *Turandot* and suddenly found I had to adapt the scale and darker timbre of my voice to a role with all this coloratura. And I was never a coloratura: rather a *lirico-spinto*, with coloratura, which is not the same thing. But with this kind of voice you can sing almost anything in the soprano repertory. This made it much easier for me to start singing new roles all over again, this time in the 1980s. For instance, I loved learning the role of Giulia in *La Vestale* – to learn a new work like that is to have a new lease of life. What never gets easier is the business of performing in front of a public. Every time I sing it is getting worse. Before even beginning to sing, to receive an ovation like I get these days makes me tremble all over. I think to myself, 'They're expecting something very special indeed.' And what can I do? I can only be me – and today, maybe not *even* me. You go out on stage and the public sees a myth. They don't see me, they see La Caballé, something not quite real. And I look out into this hall and say to myself, 'What can I give tonight?' And I always hear the answer in my own head, 'Just give them the truth.' It is the only thing you can offer and I think it's the only thing they understand.

As the 1980s unfolded, until she was laid low by the most serious and frightening medical condition with which she had ever been confronted, Montserrat's swashbuckling attitude towards the repertory inspired not only a revitalization of her reputation, but also a remarkable expansion of her personal popularity.

V

'Zu Neuen Taten'

Götterdämmerung

CHAPTER TWELVE

1983–1985: The Undiscovered Country

Caballé's career had made a decisive shift into a new phase with the opening on 26 December 1982 of *La vestale*. The opera, a considerable rarity, had originally been written by Gasparo Spontini in 1807 almost as a gift for Napoleon's Empress, Joséphine. It had of course been composed to a French libretto, which no less a figure than Beethoven had considered ideal. But such circulation as the work had ever achieved in the twentieth century, at a time when this and similar late-classical, pre-Romantic operas had fallen into oblivion, was in the form of an Italian translation, whereby the eponymous heroine Julia became Giulia. In this guise the work had been revived for Rosa Ponselle at the Metropolitan Opera House in 1925 under the direction of Tullio Serafin. With Ponselle's precipitate retirement, the work again disappeared from the repertory until it was given a sumptuous production by Luchino Visconti at La Scala in 1954, with Maria Callas in the title-role. Latterly, as so often was the case in the immediate post-Callas generation, Leyla Gencer had been the first to take on the challenge, so that once again Caballé became the latest in the royal line of succession.

The problem is that the opera itself – like Cherubini's *Medea* – is couched in a notably austere and undemonstrative musical idiom, with the characteristic addition of vast, static choral tableaux which do little to advance such action as the work possesses. It is undoubtedly finely wrought, but at all points obstinately unmemorable, even including the *lieto fine*, or happy ending, indicative of the work's classical orientation. A pirate recording of the broadcast of the performance given in the Liceo on 1 January 1983 survives and provides a clear enough reason as to why the greatest prima donnas are drawn to the work: the opportunities for an extended display of their vocal prowess in the lengthily written arias which punctuate the work, particularly in Act II. Montserrat was much applauded by the audience who had greatly enjoyed the spectacular production, with sets and costumes by Beni Montresor, which had been borrowed from the Théâtre du Capitole in Toulouse. In the event, however, these four performances were the only ones which Caballé ever gave: not because she was unhappy with the role, and certainly not because it was thought to have been unsuited to her, but simply because no other opera house was remotely keen to stage the work.

This was a problem which increasingly would bedevil Caballé's efforts to revitalize the repertory: she would find herself learning new roles in old operas, the possibilities for the singing of which almost never extended beyond a bare handful of performances. In one sense this scarcely mattered since she was already a seasoned veteran of one-off concert performances, many of which had never been repeated. But her new preoccupation was to show the stage-worthiness of the operas she wished to revive, as opposed to their purely musical attractions. And here she ran up against the same insurmountable barrier which has always confronted all adventurous star sopranos; the fact that, with only a handful of exceptions, unfamiliar works thus revived never actually do re-enter the repertory. They simply enjoy a very brief period of glory more or less exclusively attached to the soprano who revived them, and then vanish with her passing from the scene. To this extent, the whole concept of the '*bel canto* revival' is a misnomer: it would be more appropriate to speak of an ongoing series of temporary exhumations. But even if no star soprano has particularly managed to reshape the configuration of the international repertory, it stands to their great credit that this has never stopped some of them at least from trying. And here Caballé stands in the vanguard.

Not that in the immediate short term there was much possibility of exploiting further *terra incognita*: such things take a great deal of time and pre-planning. In consequence, Caballé's return to the stage after her New York illness in January 1983 was in an old favourite, *La forza del destino*, which was given four performances in Bari. She then proceeded, by way of a recital at the Royal Opera House in mid-February, to the Staatsoper in Hamburg where she once again sang the title-role in *Semiramide* which, extraordinarily, was given four concert performances. In fact, all her operatic appearances over the next six months were in this role: first in Las Palmas in March, with Lucia Valentini-Terrani as Arsace; then a week later in Avignon, with the same Arsace and John Tomlinson as Assur. In May she gave two concert performances at the Deutsche Oper, Berlin, which reunited her with Marilyn Horne and Sam Ramey under the baton of Jésus López-Cobos. And in mid-June she began rehearsing at the Teatro de la Zarzuela in Madrid for a new production of the work by Gianpaolo Zennaro – the first time she had ever appeared in it without the Pizzi staging. This was conducted by Eugenio Marco (who had been in charge at Las Palmas), and brought Caballé into contact for the first time with a new Arsace, the excellent French mezzo Martine Dupuy.

These sundry *Semiramide*s were pieced out with an extended recital schedule which took her to Annécy, Toulouse, Brussels, Dijon, Rome, Bonn, Oviedo, Monte Carlo, Alicante and Valencia, amongst other places. But undoubtedly the most significant of these recitals took place on 26 March when, with what must have been extreme trepidation, Caballé set foot again on the stage of La Scala, Milan for the first time since the débâcle of just over a year before. Although Italian audiences are as temperamental as any diva, they did not appear to be great grudge-bearers, and Montserrat was given an overwhelmingly noisy and warm welcome back. Her programme was typically all-embracing, and also as usual included any number of rarities. The first half opened with a chronological survey of Italian arias from the classical period: Gasparini, Niedermeyer, Lotti, Benedetto Marcello, Spontini ('O Nume tutelar' from *La vestale*), Cherubini ('Ahi, che forse ai miei dì' from *Demofonte*), Bellini ('Dopo l'oscuro nembo' from *Adelson e Salvini*) and 'Di tanti palpiti' from Rossini's *Tancredi*. After an ovation that most artists could not reasonably expect to receive even at the very end of a recital, she reappeared in the second half to sing a group of five Brahms *Lieder* and concluded her official programme with five arias by the Catalan composer, Amadeo Vives. The ovation which ensued took even Montserrat by surprise: there was an eternity of cheering and – surprisingly, from many of the women present – unrestrained yelling, before she could settle into her invariably improvised routine of encores. By the fourth – 'Me llaman la primarosa' from a Spanish version of *The Barber* *of Seville* – the entire audience was on its feet, utterly abandoned, as the RAI telecast reveals. With this single performance, all memories of the previous year's misfortunes were swept to one side and, at least as far as the Milanese and the diva were concerned, their rehabilitation was now complete.

An unexpected change to Caballé's schedules occurred towards the end of May 1983 at a time when she had otherwise decided to take some well-deserved rest. She was not due to sing at the Liceo again until the very end of the year, when another piece of arcana – Massenet's *Hérodiade* – was to be revived at her request, but in the meantime a sudden series of crises had afflicted the theatre's planned new production of *Tannhaüser*, which was being given as part of a season celebrating the centenary of Wagner's death. The sets, which were being borrowed from the Vienna State Opera House, had been intercepted by a picket-line of French farmers at the Spanish border, and the production had perforce to be given almost in concert form, the empty and darkened stage space relieved only by occasional clumps of horticulture. Elisabeth was to be sung by Gundula Janowitz, belatedly making her Spanish début. But the conductor, Heinrich Hollreiser, took a dislike to the singer scheduled to sing Venus and insisted on her replacement. This left the administration with a problem: how to cast the work with two days to go before the dress rehearsal. Following frantic calls to the Caballé agency office from Lluis Andreu, the Liceo's recently appointed artistic administrator, Montserrat agreed to the desperate proposal, at the shortest possible notice, to sing Venus at all three performances, although, as she pointed out, she had never sung it before and was not even familiar with the role.

In the event Caballé's prodigious sight-reading skills proved supremely useful here and the already attenuated staging was adapted to allow the inclusion of a black-draped console which would function as a music-stand and effectively hide her score from the audience. The performances were a great success and the soprano's sporting acceptance of this most unlikely challenge was duly appreciated by both the Liceo's audience and management.

Following her annual recital in the monastic church at Ripoll for the benefit of the Fundación, she travelled up through the Pyrenees to Orange where she was to give a recital and spend ten days rehearsing the solitary performance of the new production of *La gioconda* given on 23 July. The conductor was scheduled to be the up-and-coming Bulgarian, Emil Tchakarov, but at the very last moment he cancelled, and, at Caballé's suggestion, the veteran Eugenio Marco was instead brought in to conduct the Orchestre National de Lille. Uniquely amongst

At her home in Barcelona, with husband Bernabé and their children,
Bernabé junior and Montsita, 1979.

With José Carreras as Maurizio in their first-ever *Adriana Lecouvreur*, Liceo, 1972.

Below left:
In rehearsal with Luciano Pavarotti for a production of *Tosca* at the War Memorial Opera House, San Francisco, October 1978.

Below right:
Recording *Aïda* with Plácido Domingo in Walthamstow Town Hall, London, July 1974.

THE THREE TENORS

THREE GREAT MEZZOS

Above left:
With Marilyn
Horne as Arsace
in Pier-Luigi
Pizzi's famous
staging of
Semiramide, Aix-
en-Provence,
August 1980.

Above right:
With Fiorenza
Cossotto as
Adalgisa in
Norma, Paris,
September 1972.

With Brigitte
Fassbaender as
Brangäne in
Tristan und Isolde,
Barcelona,
February 1989.
(A. Bofill)

One of her many triumphant performances of *Norma* at La Scala.
(E. Piccagliani)

Tosca at Covent Garden, September 1977, during the run of performances dedicated to the memory of Maria Callas.
(Clive Barda/ London)

Above: Backstage with Zubin Mehta before her one and only performance of *Turandot* at La Scala in the shape of the dress rehearsal, May 1976. *(E. Piccagliani)*
Below: As the Duchessa Elena perched on the steps of the Met's first-ever production of *I vespri siciliani*, February 1974. *(J. Heffernan)*

Above: Listening intently at a play-back session.
Below: Probably the most famous, and certainly the most widely used, of all Caballé's specially posed publicity stills, wearing one of the Russian sables carried off in triumph following her Bolshoi *Normas. (Mayer)*

Four new roles at the Liceo in the 1980s
Above left: In one of her greatest roles as a particularly hieratic and sharp-clawed Turandot, January 1980. *Above right:* Dressed to kill as Cleopatra in *Giulio Cesare*, June 1982. *(A. Bofill) Below left:* As a wistful Marschallin in Act I of *Der Rosenkavalier*, December 1984. *(A. Bofill) Below right:* As the persecuted Silvana – her last role in the old theatre – in Respighi's powerful opera about medieval witchcraft, *La fiamma*. December 1989. *(A. Bofill)*

Sumptuously draped as Rossini's
Ermione in Pesaro, August 1987, the
opera's first staged performances since
1819.

Backstage at the Mérida Opera Festival,
dressed as Salome in Massenet's
Hérodiade, with Montsita and Bernabé,
July 1990. *(A. Bofill)*

Enjoying her finest moment in the otherwise fraught production of *Salome* –
her farewell to the role – at the Liceo in December 1988. *(A. Bofill)*

Caballé's appearances on stage at Orange,* no video is known to have survived of this performance. Indeed, none of her stage *Gioconda*s have been preserved, which is a great shame when one considers the impact she invariably made in the role.

> It is one of her best parts. She moves from happiness to jealous torment to a state of magnanimity with vocal conviction, a fair amount of *spinto* force (although ideally perhaps not enough for these huge surroundings) and a decent chest register.[1]

She continued her summer sojourn performing in vast Roman arenas by returning to Macerata where, for a period covering late July through to 13 August, she sang in four performances of *Don Carlos* and two of *Tosca*, the latter with José Carreras and Silvano Caroli. The Verdi fielded a starry cast, including Grace Bumbry as Eboli, Giorgio Zancanaro as the Marquis of Posa and the veteran Cesare Siepi as Philip II, with Giuseppe Giacomini in the title-role. Under the baton of Michelangelo Veltri the performances were enthusiastically received by the capacity audiences. Rodney Milnes – eventually to become the magazine's editor – wrote in *Opera* that Caballé brought 'an exquisitely floated line in the Farewell to the Countess d'Aremberg (both verses) and a great deal of beautifully shaped singing elsewhere . . . [The performance] scaled heights of eloquence in the final duet.'[2]

Before taking the second half of the month of August as her annual holiday – in fact just an extended period of idleness spent at the family farm in Ripoll – Montserrat performed two recitals in Spain, one in Santander on the northern coast, and the other in Perelada, a small but historically important town in Cataluña. Caballé's experience of singing in Perelada would in due course prove to be of considerable significance: four years later her brother Carlos became the first artistic director of the newly constituted International Festival of Music, based in and around the medieval castle.

Montserrat's 1983–4 operatic schedule got off to a most unusual start on 11 September when, as part of the 38th Sagra Musicale Umbra – Francesco Siciliani's old foundation, where Caballé had first sung nearly thirty years earlier – she sang the role of Hypermnestra in Salieri's utterly forgotten *Les Danaïdes*. Written at the same time as Mozart's *Le nozze di Figaro*, Salieri's opus gives a very clear idea of what made Mozart's work so special. *Les Danaïdes* is a grotesque farrago whereby fifty

---

* Starting with *Il trovatore* in 1972, continuing with *Norma* (1974), *La forza del destino* (1982), *La gioconda* (1983), *Don Carlos* (1984) and concluding with *Simon Boccanegra* in 1985.

daughters marry their fifty male cousins under the strict injunction of their father to murder their husbands on the nuptial night. One of the fifty, however – the eldest, Hypermnestra – has taken rather a shine to her intended, Lyncaeus, and instead of murdering him, urges him to escape. His soldiers locate the other forty-nine sisters, who are engaged in a Dionysiac orgy of blood lust, having killed their husbands and put the lot to the sword. The final edifying scene is set in Hell where molten fire rains down upon the sisters and their father has his entrails plucked out, Prometheus-fashion, by a vulture. This is the sort of subject matter that a Prokofiev or a Strauss might have made much of; but Salieri's suavely crafted musical platitudes hardly serve the turn. What we are left with is one very good role surrounded by yards of *recitativo accompagnato* and slow-moving choral tableaux.

The Perugia performance was given in concert – thereby depriving the work of probably its only claim to theatrical interest – under the direction of Gianluigi Gelmetti, and as pirate tapes of the European Broadcasting Union relay confirm, Montserrat enjoyed a tremendous personal success as the daughter torn between love and duty. The long sequence of declamation, arioso and aria in Act II, the great *scena* in Act IV, and the tempestuous outburst in Act V all found her in powerful and responsive form.

Caballé began the new opera season proper back in Hamburg with two performances of *Un ballo in maschera*, immediately progressing to Oviedo in the north of Spain where she sang two performances of *Otello*, with Gianfranco Cecchele in the title-role. One of these performances survives on a pirated, fixed-camera, in-house video and shows that of all Verdi's great soprano roles Desdemona in many ways suited Caballé's voice the best of all. Certainly, the Act IV *scena* is exquisitely sung, with no trace of wear-and-tear. This is all the more remarkable given that she had not sung the role for over thirteen years. When asked why she never sang what was obviously such a great role for her more frequently, the answer is a simple, sad 'Because no one ever asked me.' Perhaps this was less to do with any perception that she was unsuited to the role vocally than the simple assumption that it was ill-suited physically.

It is certainly true that by this time Montserrat had become a very large lady indeed as her weight inexorably spiralled upwards. Although it is extremely ungallant to speculate, we may be sure that Caballé herself was being unduly modest when bewailing in print the fact that her *avoirdupois* had exceeded 200 lbs (or approximately 100 kilos). The reasons for this had never been particularly clear: everybody's automatic assumption was that she must of necessity be a compulsive eater. Yet no one who was or is close to her has any tales of untoward gluttony to tell. Nor was there any question of alcohol playing a part in her weight gain: in former years, whilst not teetotal, she had never drunk more than the occasional glass of wine or spirits. It was simply a mystery, written off to that all-purpose shibboleth, glandular problems. But as unexpected events would later prove, this was no more than the literal truth.

The end of September and the first three weeks of October 1983 were taken up with a leisurely programme of recitals in Vienna – Caballé's début in the Grosse Saal of the Konzerthaus – Elda, Benidorm and Valladolid, as well as a trip to Paris in order to record an interview with Eve Ruggieri for French television as part of the series *Musique au Coeur*. Thereafter it was back to North America, first of all to New York where on 22 October she sang at the Metropolitan Opera House's Centennial Gala, conducted by James Levine. In a programme characteristically stuffed with stars, it is noticeable that the ovation accorded Caballé and Carreras after the conclusion of the final duet of *Andrea Chénier* – sung with glorious scenic inconsequence on the set of *La bohème*, Act II – is one of the two loudest and longest of the whole evening. The partnership continued in New York for the next two evenings when, in the Grand Assembly Hall of the United Nations Building, the two Spanish stars sang together in concert performances of de Falla's *La vida breve*, with Caballé as the lovelorn Salud and Carreras as her faithless lover, Paco.

At the end of October, she travelled the breadth of the country to the Pacific seaboard where she was due back in San Francisco at the War Memorial Opera House for the third year running, this time to sing the title-role in a revival of the production of *La gioconda* which had been mounted in 1979 with Renata Scotto and Luciano Pavarotti and which had provided the live television audience with such a genuine thrill when the Italian diva had been filmed backstage fulminating about the *gente di merda* who had taken more curtain calls than herself. Certainly, with Franco Bonisolli in the role of Enzo, Montserrat herself might have needed to look to her laurels, if not some choice Catalan, Bonisolli being noted for nothing so much as the athletic zeal with which he leaps into the limelight. But in the event – and doubtless much to Terry McEwan's relief – the revival went smoothly and was a great success. Caballé remembers that on the opening night Matteo Manuguerra, who was singing the role of the villain, Barnaba, made a rather unfortunate mistake. At the conclusion of the last Act, the baritone believes he has struck a bargain with the heroine whereby she will submit to his vile lusts as the price of his having released her former lover. He turns up at her home on Giudecca island to claim his prize. But, as the audience have already been made aware by Gioconda's aria 'Suicidio!', she has no intention of honouring her promise: Barnaba's reward will be her lifeless corpse. Montserrat duly stabbed herself and sank lifeless on to a couch, artfully covering herself with her voluminous cloak. Unfortunately, Manuguerra was otherwise occupied in signalling to the audience his displeasure at this turn of events and failed to notice how Montserrat had disposed herself. His final act of revenge, accompanied by the stage direction 'bending over Gioconda's body and screaming in her ear', is to say that he has drowned her mother. But she, of course, is already dead. The baritone finally turned round, only to be confronted by an amorphous, black-draped mass: he promptly picked up the corner of the drapery nearest to him and in so doing exposed the diva's lower quarters to an amazed audience. With considerable presence of mind – and no less diagnostic skill – he cried out 'Morta!' and, as prescribed, made his exit, leaving Gioconda's inert body shaking with laughter as the final chords of the opera rang out.

Caballé returned briefly to Spain at the end of November, taking part in an operatic concert in Madrid at the Teatro Real in the presence of the King and Queen of Spain and giving a recital in La Coruña. She then travelled to Vienna in order to rehearse briefly for a revival of *Andrea Chénier* which was due to begin a run of four performances on the 10th, with Cappucilli as Gérard and Nicola Martinucci in the title-role. On the opening night, all went well until Act III, the trial scene set inside the revolutionary tribunal. There is an extended duet during which Caballé's character, the aristocratic Maddalena di Coigny, appears in disguise in order to plead for the life of her lover, the poet Andrea Chénier, with the man who, mere months beforehand, had been one of her household servants. During the course of the duet Montserrat began to feel faint, was convinced that her heart had missed a beat, and suddenly realized that it was, instead, beating very rapidly indeed. She remembers somehow making her way off-stage, though still in mid-scene: her next memory is of staring at the ceiling, flat on her back on the floor of the corridor outside her dressing-room, hearing the theatre's doctor say 'I think she's had a heart attack.' This is indeed what was reported in the Viennese press and on television the following day, and was rapidly picked up by the Spanish media. But instead of being transported immediately to hospital, Caballé insisted on returning to the nearby Hotel Imperial where an army of medical attendants soon materialized, including a cardiologist summoned by the theatre's own doctor. It was established that the soprano was suffering from greatly raised blood pressure – thus discounting the possibility of her having had an actual heart attack – and had probably experienced a bout of lipidaemia. Two days later, together with her husband, she returned to Barcelona where further medical tests were performed. These all proved negative and Montserrat was simply placed on medication and ordered to take a week's complete bed-rest.

Immediately after this, she began rehearsing for the new production of Massenet's *Hérodiade*, which was due to open on 30 December. This rarity had been premièred originally in Brussels in 1881 and was the composer's first notable success, some three years before *Manon*. The work is not so much based upon the biblical story – which was later to act as the inspiration for both Oscar Wilde's play *Salomé* and Strauss's opera – as on Gustave Flaubert's novella. This basis in late nineteenth-century French sentiment accounts for the wholly different slant of the work, which has Salome unaware of her parentage and virtually adopted by the Baptist, whom she adores. The heart of the opera is what one can only describe as two extended love duets for John and Salome before the former is led off to execution at Hérodiade's command. In the final scene Salome seeks revenge and attends a celebratory orgy simply in order to murder the evil Queen: but upon being informed that she is, in fact, her long-lost mother, Salome turns the knife upon herself instead.

All this gave Massenet ample opportunity to write the kind of quasi-religiose, quasi-exotic music that so frequently characterizes his best scores, together with large tracts of ballet music and two very juicy and taxing parts for the 'lovers' (Herod and his wife do not get quite so much of a look-in, despite the work's title). As a video of the television relay in Spain which was filmed at the last performance on 8 January 1984 amply demonstrates, Caballé as this 'other' Salome was in sumptuous voice, evidently fully recovered from the episode in Vienna. The high-lying vocal declamation is thrillingly despatched, and there are some chandelier-rattling high Cs from both Montserrat and José Carreras as John the Baptist. Nor was this the end of the attractions in what was evidently a triumphant run, with the theatre more than sold out at each of the four performances, since the conducting of Jacques Delacôte was much admired, as was the Herod of Juan Pons and the remarkably intense Hérodiade of the unpredictable but exciting Dunja Vejzovic.

Caballé remained *in situ* after the run had concluded in order to rehearse a revival of *Ariadne auf Naxos*, which was given three performances between 12 and 18 January, with Alicia Nafé as the Composer, Celina Lindsley as Zerbinetta and Klaus König as the tenor/Bacchus. The production by Mario Krüger had been borrowed from the

Staatstheater in Braunschweig specifically to accommodate the star soprano, who increasingly wished to get back to her greatest musical love – Richard Strauss – whenever the faintest opportunity presented itself. Montserrat enjoyed herself hugely in the title-role, not least the opportunities for displays of *grande-dame hauteur* in the opera's Prologue. And when the real singing started, it was felt that no one in living memory had produced such an exquisitely coloured, immaculately sustained account of 'Ein schönes war', Ariadne's first great musing monologue in the opera proper.

She departed for Paris shortly afterwards where she was due to give her first recital at the former Théâtre Louis Jouvet, which had, under the ownership of Pierre Bergé, the director and partner of Yves Saint Laurent, been renamed the Théâtre de l'Athénée. Bergé's principal innovation had been to inaugurate in the intimate auditorium lengthy seasons of recitals given, always on a Monday, by the world's greatest singers under the generic title 'Les lundis musicaux de l'Athénée'. Within this context, it is fair to say that every opera and concert singer of note appeared before the Parisian public. Montserrat's performances became the most eagerly sought after and much the most regular: until obliged to relinquish proprietorship in accordance with his new-found status as Director Designate of the Opéra de Paris in general, and the new Opéra de la Bastille in particular, Bergé ensured that Caballé reappeared there every season. In this fashion, an already immensely popular singer graduated to the status of much-loved artist. The French music critic André Tubeuf wrote at length on this subject and in so doing summed up much of what constitutes Montserrat's perceived appeal.

In this little world in which artists – for fear of not seeming sufficiently 'artistic' – swathe themselves in grand postures, you just rely upon your voice, your natural sympathy, your very presence. The jealous will never forgive you for it. Popular? You are absolutely without precedent. As an artist? You have just two predecessors: Callas and Schwarzkopf, both of whom have rehabilitated singing whilst revolutionizing expression . . . Caballé was the first and remains the only one whose voice had as its primary function, and charismatic power, being beautiful. She has devoted her art to the beauty of sound. This genius of sonority has revived it for us at a time when even the pianists no longer bother. And behind this genius there is a power-house, all-conquering but elusive: breath control. Caballé's least sound is inconceivable without the totality of her breath control and her greatest achievement is much the least audible: her *pianissimi* . . . The whole of her voice is in [these] and her breath, and hence her soul –

and almost nothing which as yet belongs to the composer. The stage has never known a more pure singer . . .³

Following a brief return to Las Palmas in February for two performances of *Tosca*, Caballé made her way to Belgium where she gave two concert performances of *Semiramide*, with Martine Dupuy as Arsace, first in Antwerp and then at the Théâtre de la Monnaie in Brussels. The latter drew superlatives from the local press under the headline 'Triomphe du *bel canto*'. She then returned to North America at the beginning of March when, with the exception of a recital given early in the month in Miami, she otherwise remained in the city of New York for an unbroken period of seven weeks during which she sang in half a dozen performances of John Dexter's austere production of *Don Carlos* at the Metropolitan, gave two recitals at Carnegie Hall, and one at Avery Fisher Hall, and even sang in Radio City Music Hall, with Pavarotti, Diana Ross and Frank Sinatra. This would seem to have been Montserrat's complete reply to the sharp criticism her cancellations the year before had provoked. The reviews also prove that the common assumption that these non-appearances were due to vocal decline was unfounded. The first outing to Carnegie Hall took place on 11 March, just before the extended period of rehearsal at the Metropolitan began. The recital programme took the form of Caballé's characteristic admixture of *arie antiche*, classical pieces, some Rossini and a second half largely devoted to Spanish items. Oleg Kerensky, writing in *Music and Musicians*, reported that:

> She was in her finest voice. Her rendering of an aria from Rossini's *Elisabetta, Regina d'Inghilterra* ['Bel alme generose'] held the house breathless . . . Forty-five minutes of encores included arias from *Adriana Lecouvreur, Gianni Schicchi, Tancredi* and *Mefistofele*, as well as more Spanish songs. When Madame Caballé sings like this it is easy to forgive her . . . past non-appearances.⁴

Then, little more than a month later, she returned to the same venue for a further recital when on 16 April, under the patronage of the Instituto de Cooperación Ibero-Americana and the Consulate General of Spain, she gave a programme of works by Alberto Ginastera, Enrique Granados, Joaquin Turina and Joaquin Rodrigo, amongst others. Tim Page writing on the all-powerful arts page of the *New York Times*, observed:

> The age of the diva is not over, and Montserrat Caballé is the proof. [This] was a musical event in the grand manner, combining fine singing, rapturous audience enthusiasm and the quick-silver operatic

glamour that one associates with the careers of such artists as Melba, Garden, Farrar and Callas . . . The voice is the main event at any Caballé concert. And what a miraculous voice it is! Miss Caballé's seamless legato, and her ability to float soft, stratospheric phrases across a concert hall of any size have rightly attained the status of legend . . . [She] has been presenting recitals at Carnegie Hall for almost twenty years, but only once or twice during Monday's concert was there any sign of diminishing power. For the most part, the tones were perfectly centered, the breath control all but incredible, the *pianissimos* ravishingly beautiful . . . the hysteria quotient throughout the evening hovered around fever pitch.[5]

Caballé crowned her New York sojourn with her first-ever appearance at the legendary Radio City Music Hall. This was the centennial charity gala given by the Memorial Sloan-Kettering Cancer Center and was billed as 'A Once-in-a-Century Evening of Entertainment' at which Buddy Rich and his orchestra accompanied Sinatra and Ross, and John Williams – he of *Star Wars* fame, not the guitarist – conducted the New York Philharmonic as backing group to the two opera stars, Caballé and Pavarotti. This trip was rounded off with a recital in Montreal, following which Caballé returned to Barcelona in time to take part in another charity gala, this time at the Liceo in aid of the local Red Cross, during which she sang a long and taxing tripartite programme.

It is quite clear that by this time Caballé recitals had become events in themselves. Audiences would turn out – and indeed continue to do so – irrespective of the scheduled programme, always assuming the latter was made public much before the eve of the recital itself. Some critics deplored a state of affairs whereby the performer was now considered in preference to any musical material she might choose to perform. But this was to ignore the blindingly obvious: there comes a point in the career of all great performers at which their personality, as perceived by the public, simply outgrows the appeal of whatever performance material they have to hand. In a sense, the skill and artistry of such people, their ability to mould the material to their expressive powers, is taken on trust: one attends simply in order to see and hear these phenomena at work. There is, of course, a danger that the work in hand is overpowered or, worse, becomes an irrelevance. But Montserrat is only too well aware of the problem.

I am only a singer. Someone who is there to serve the music, to give expression to what the composer was trying to say. People talk about Callas's Norma, Caballé's Mimì, but what is important is Bellini's Norma and Puccini's Mimì. The style of the different composers, their work, needs love, not demonstration or exhibition. You feel all this inside you and you try to bring it to the audience through your sound. But I am not doing it for them: I do it for the composers. It is a wonderful feeling when you sing a musical line and feel that, through you, the audience has contact with the music. The danger for us is that we might come to believe our own, shall we say, mythologies. When you start to believe the claims made about you in publicity, it is the beginning of the end.

True, but Caballé's own thoughts fail to take into account the power, not of her voice, but of her character. Ultimately, beyond the matter of musicianship, it is this which draws capacity audiences to this day. She may believe that in singing before a public in 1994 she is still primarily serving the composers; but that public has long since committed to memory the glorious musical service she has given in the past, and is now content simply to bask in the warmth of the woman's personality.

Evidence of this state of affairs proliferated throughout the 1980s, even before her later spectacular 'cross-over' to a much wider audience in the company of Freddie Mercury. At the end of May 1984, she sang in the Hayarkon Park in Tel Aviv with the Israel Philharmonic and Zubin Mehta to celebrate the seventy-fifth anniversary of the founding of the city before an audience that was estimated by the mayor as numbering between 400,000 and 500,000. According to reports the crowd was such that it completely overflowed the open air amphitheatre and spread out over the grass in all directions for as far as the eye could see. At a time when it is popularly supposed that only Pavarotti is capable of attracting such audiences, it is as well to remember an example like this, achieved without the backing of a large multinational media conglomerate and with no more personal publicity than Caballé herself can generate, given that she has never at any time employed press or PR people on her behalf.

With the exception of a revival of *Giulio Cesare* given five performances at the Teatro de la Zarzuela in Madrid between 22 June and 4 July, the peak summer months were taken up with miscellaneous recitals given, as was becoming Caballé's wont, in ever more recherché Spanish locations, including Cadaques, Cambrils and Benalmedena. She had never been the kind of diva to insist upon great pomp and ceremony, willing only to appear in a select handful of the world's most agreeable and prestigious – not to mention high paying – venues. Indeed, it became a fetish with her to find places in which she had never sung and proceed to give a recital in them, however inauspicious the surroundings or circumstances. Basically, this is just another manifestation of the same restlessness which impels her to seek out new repertory, and arises out of genuine curiosity and a lively, active imagination; but one should never underestimate the potential for boredom that can arise in such an extended career. After giving almost 4000 public performances, there must come a point at which it all becomes a job like any other, with its own inherent rewards, rigours and routines. New repertory in new places was Caballé's strategy for survival.

Not that her return to Orange in early July in order to commence rehearsals for the new production of *Don Carlos* on the 13th constituted anything other than business as usual. The cast was of a uniformly high level, including Grace Bumbry as Eboli, Renato Bruson as Posa, Simon Estes as Philip II and Giacomo Aragall in the title-role. The solitary performance was conducted by Thomas Fulton following the withdrawal of James Conlon and was filmed for a television broadcast in France. The production – increasingly the norm at Orange – was roundly booed by the capacity audience, but the singers were cheered to the echo, and rightly so, given the superb quality of both the solo and ensemble singing.

After barely a week's summer holiday, inevitably spent at the farm in Ripoll, Caballé returned to America, this time directly to the Western seaboard where on 22 August she gave a solo recital in the Hollywood Bowl in front of an audience of at least 10,000. The following day, she began rehearsals for an all-star revival of *Ernani* in which she was to sing the role of Elvira, for the first time on stage in her career, with Sherrill Milnes as Carlo, Paul Plishka as Silva and Luciano Pavarotti in the title-role, under the baton of Lamberto Gardelli. Following her misfortunes with the preceding *Ballo in mascheras* in San Francisco, it must have come as a great relief to the management that she sang all seven contracted performances as scheduled, beginning on 7 September 1984. Unfortunately, the problem this time focused on the tenor, who withdrew after the first night when one of his daughters was taken seriously ill back in Italy, and was replaced by Nunzio Todisco.

At the end of this run of performances, Montserrat returned to New York where on 7 October she gave a joint operatic concert with José Carreras, conducted by Garcia Navarro in Avery Fisher Hall. The next month was taken up with recitals given in Strasbourg, Turin (at the Teatro Regio), Bologna (at the Communale), Lisbon (at the São Carlo) and a concert in Parma, as well as a brief return to Paris for a concert at the Salle Pleyel on 12 November.

A few days later, Caballé visited London, this time accompanied by her newly appointed personal secretary/minder, her nineteen-year-old niece, Montse Caballé, brother Carlos's middle daughter. But this was not for the purpose of public performance: rather, it was in the nature of a personal favour to an old colleague. Decca had had in mind for some time to do a second recording of *Norma* – technically their first, since the original one had been made by them for RCA – with Joan Sutherland in the title-role. It was a foregone conclusion that Pavarotti would sing Pollione; but who would be the Adalgisa? Every other recording of the work and indeed virtually all stage performances had always cast the role with a mezzo. But it has always been clear from Bellini's manuscript and the distribution of the original cast – Giuditta Pasta as Norma, Giulia Grisi as Adalgisa – that the youthful temple virgin was meant to be sung by another soprano who as often as not takes the top line in the duets for the two women. Sutherland's husband, Richard Bonynge, came up with a suggestion which Decca, mindful of the triumph enjoyed by the same cast's *Turandot* some twelve years previously, were only too keen to see realized: try to secure the services of Caballé as Adalgisa. Montserrat had been both honoured and intrigued by the proposition and had accepted with alacrity as a kind of tribute to her colleague. What neither Caballé nor any of her colleagues can have known at the time was that this was to be the last complete opera recording that the Spanish diva would make.

The sessions which involved Caballé took place in the last week or so of November 1984 in Walthamstow Town Hall and have since proved to be a fertile source of 'Caballé stories'. One of the producers, the late Peter Wadland, told how Caballé arrived a little late for a scheduled recording session bearing the most enormous bouquet of flowers. Smiling sweetly, she threaded her way past Bonynge sitting on his conductor's rostrum, through the ranks of the orchestral violins, and finally arrived at the base of the hall's raised platform, looking up at Sutherland who was leaning over her music-stand observing the proceedings. The Australian diva said, 'How nice of you, Montsy. Flowers for the *prima donna.*' Caballé, laying them ceremoniously at Sutherland's feet, smiled even more sweetly, intoning, 'No, Joan. Flowers *from* the *prima donna.*'

Sutherland herself tells another story concerning the recording of the duet 'Mira, o Norma'. Two takes had already been satisfactorily completed in the course of the late afternoon session, but the producer, in consultation with Bonynge, thought that a third would be advisable in order to clarify one or two points of orchestral accompaniment. Sutherland was ready to oblige but Caballé pulled a long face. The former tried her powers of persuasion: 'Let's go through it one more time, Montsy – you know what they're like, they love having three or four lots of everything.' But Caballé's reluctance became outright refusal: 'I no think I can sing any more. Anyway, no better than I sang already. I am so tired.' There was much consternation in the control room, and Bonynge's telephone was evidently glowing red as the decision was taken to bow to the inevitable. Following the termination of the session, Montserrat sidled over to Joan and whispered conspiratorially, 'Good. I was worried because Harrods will be shut in half an hour.'

The return to Barcelona for Christmas – presumably laden with Harrods' finest goodies – took place at the beginning of December and Caballé immediately threw herself into rehearsals for the new production – borrowed from La Scala – of *Der Rosenkavalier*. This was one of those rare opportunities for Montserrat in her mature career to undertake on stage one of her beloved Strauss roles, which in this case set her Marschallin – not otherwise performed since Glyndebourne in 1965 – amongst a seasoned cast of Strauss regulars, including Hans Sotin and subsequently Günther Missenhardt as Ochs, Helen Donath as Sophie and Tatiana Troyanos as Octavian. The conductor, who had recently débuted at the Liceo, was Uwe Mund; within a few years he would be appointed the house's music director. The first night took place on 9 December and met with tumultuous success; but the third and last performance six days later ran into real difficulties when Troyanos withdrew, and a desperate hunt for a replacement brought in a singer who had never sung the role on stage before, with less than an hour to go before curtain up. And this on what was to have been the television relay. The production pictures show Montserrat looking thoroughly at home in the role, playfully indulgent in the early scenes of Act I, and suitably pensive as she examines her face in a hand-mirror, contemplating the passage of time at the end.

Before the Christmas break, she managed to squeeze in two recitals – one in Zaragoza and the other in Valencia. 1985 should have started very early indeed with her removal to Berlin on 2 January in order to rehearse for two concert performances of *Semiramide* reuniting the original Aix-en-Provence cast, including Marilyn Horne and Sam Ramey. But Montserrat had felt unwell throughout the Christmas/New Year period, this time rather unusually having contracted a bad head-cold, apparently *in situ*. She held on until the last moment, hoping at least that her nose would stop running and that she would therefore be able to perform in Berlin as scheduled. But the cold showed no sign of improvement and in the end Caballé was obliged to cancel. She remained at home for the next two weeks, and though not feeling any worse, by the end of the fortnight she certainly felt no better, and was still plagued by this oddly persistent cold. This did not, however, prevent her from riding to the rescue of the Teatro dell'Opera in Rome when they discovered, at the last minute, that they were without a Cleopatra for their new production of *Giulio Cesare*. Few enough singers have the role in their repertory, so what at first had seemed to be an impossible task of finding a replacement turned into a casting director's dream when Caballé agreed to perform the role which she had sung as recently as 1982 in Barcelona. Unlike all previous performances of the work in which Montserrat had taken part either on stage or in concert, this production was geared to a more 'authentic' presentation of Handel's score. Thus Caballé found herself not only singing all eight of Cleopatra's arias, but doing so in the presence of a Julius Caesar sung not by a baritone but by Margarita Zimmermann at alto castrato score pitch. The performances lasted for four hours, which gives some indication of the fullness of text employed. A contemporary review of the single performance Caballé gave on 1 February 1985 noted:

> Caballé's mastery in 'Se pietà di me non senti' and 'Piangerò', enhanced by ornamentation, an exquisite use of *mezza-voce* and phrases springing directly from the heart, was unforgettable. Acclaimed by public and critics alike, it was a triumph such as Rome has not known for ages.[6]

Prior commitments in New York prevented Montserrat from doing any more than this first performance, leaving one Beatrice Haldas to complete the run. The New York dates comprised her annual Carnegie Hall recital, followed by half-a-dozen performances of *Ernani* at the Metropolitan Opera House, with Luciano Pavarotti, conducted by James Levine. No sooner had she arrived in New York on 8 February than her cold symptoms, which had been irritatingly persistent, became more severe. But there was no question of her cancelling the Carnegie Hall recital, since it had been specifically mounted in order to celebrate the twentieth anniversary of her début there. She received a standing ovation before having sung a note and as she stood on the platform she looked out into the auditorium:

> I was so happy to see that round shape of lights, looking just like a little crown hovering overhead. I looked up there and said to myself, 'Well, I have that over my head once again; so I am still here. I can hardly believe it!' The whole recital was my way of saying thank you for twenty years of affection, of loyalty to the New York public who had made my career.

After a full two-hour programme, she proceeded, against a mounting tide of hysterical applause, to give a record-breaking thirteen encores, one of the last of which was 'Casta diva'. This emotional atmosphere continued for over an hour, and after the last encore Montserrat raised her arms for silence. To an instantly quiet throng she simply said that she had no more left to sing, but that for once she had something to ask of them. Would they care to sing for her? 'Happy birthday' might, after all, not be inappropriate. The audience erupted in cheers, rose to its collective feet and gave a roof-raising rendition which reduced the soprano to tears.

In all this Caballé was still unwell: but the sheer adrenaline rush of such an occasion had safely seen her through. She was now hoping that the two-week rehearsal period before the run of *Ernani* would allow her to recover fully. As previously agreed, on 12 February she broke from rehearsals in order to travel to Washington, DC where she had been invited by President Reagan and his wife Nancy to sing at the state dinner in the White House being given in honour of King Fahd of Saudi Arabia. At this glitzy gala Caballé gave a brief programme of Italian baroque opera arias, Spanish songs and a Rossini piece at which, unusually, she was accompanied by the twenty-three-year-old nephew of Joaquin Turina, Fernando, and applauded by the likes of Donald Trump and Pearl Bailey. The following day she received by special courier a letter from the White House stating: 'Dear Madame Caballé, Nancy and I are delighted that you and Mr Martí could be with us . . . Your performance made the evening an especially memorable experience for all who attended. Thank you for sharing your wonderful gift with us. With our appreciation and warm regards to you and Mr Martí, sincerely, Ronald Reagan.'

Back in New York, Caballé resumed rehearsals, but her poor health persisted. Levine was amazed to see her sitting through them using up box after box of paper tissues. After four days of this, he decided to have a word with the soprano, who dolefully recounted how she had been suffering from her wretched cold continuously for seven weeks. He pointed out that no one suffers cold (or indeed flu) symptoms for that length of time: there must be something wrong; she should consult a doctor immediately. Montserrat had a brief discussion with one of the Met's physicians to whom, by now, she was no stranger, and he recommended that she have a few basic tests done at the New York City Hospital. One of these consisted of a swab of the nasal discharge. Analysis rapidly revealed that this was not, as everyone – Caballé included – had assumed, simple catarrh: it was cerebro-spinal fluid.

The implications of this were serious in the extreme, given that such fluid finds no external outlet except in cases where something has gone wrong within the cranial area. Further tests were urgently arranged involving brain scans, which revealed that Caballé's hypothalamus – a small gland at the rear base of the brain which controls the pituitary and thence all hormonal and metabolic function – had split into three lobes, two of which were wholly inoperative with only a fragment of the third in working order. The net result of this was that for an unspecified number of years past, whenever the problem had originated, she had been operating on less than 25 per cent of this all-important gland's capacity. And the prognosis, should what was left functioning of her hypothalamus itself become tumorous, was grim indeed.

At this point Montserrat immediately discharged herself from hospital and flew back to her family in Barcelona, leaving behind the usual rancorous press reports of impossible diva behaviour. Everyone at home was devastated: in particular Montserrat's mother, Ana – by now herself seriously ill – felt crushed by her own helplessness and, as throughout times of crisis in the past, put her trust in her profound faith. Husband Bernabé was more practical and arranged for her to be admitted to the Clínica Quirón in the Carmelo district of Barcelona, close to the Parc Guëll and, appropriately, situated in a street called Virgen de Montserrat. A team of no fewer than seven doctors (including Jaime Pujadas, Manuel Subirana and Dr Alfredo Rocha, the Caballés' medical attendant since the days of the Bertrands) were deputed to conduct further tests, assess the results and come up with a plan of action. This they duly did. To Caballé's horror, their considered advice was that she should immediately undergo brain surgery: they produced a series of sketches which showed in great detail not only the nature and location of the trouble, but also how they proposed to operate. The general idea was to insert a metal plate at the base of the *sella turcica*, or 'Turkish saddle', and bolt the gap which the expanding tumorous hypothalamus had caused in its housing, allowing the cerebro-spinal fluid to escape via the sinuses.

The details of the proposed surgery had terrified Montserrat, who was far from convinced that it would be of any use: if she was destined to die of what may loosely be termed a brain tumour, then she was minded simply to let things take their course rather than become involved in complex and dangerous surgery. Her brother Carlos shared her opinion and took the extraordinary step of contacting Herbert von Karajan at his home in Anif in order to ask the Austrian maestro's advice. Karajan, it had been known for some years, was suffering from progressive spinal degeneration and had already undergone several painful operations to relieve incidental symptoms such as the clawing of his feet. He suggested that Carlos should contact directly the Turkish specialist, Dr Yasserghyl, with whom Karajan consulted in the Kantonal Hospital in Zürich. Carlos did so and, not surprisingly, met with a request to view the medical records compiled in Barcelona. Montserrat's brother was reluctant to antagonize the home team by this recourse to a second opinion, and therefore 'arranged' for copies of the relevant material to be spirited out of the clinic. It was at this point that he saw for the first time, in addition to the test results, the preliminary drafts outlining the surgery, which was due to be conducted by drilling through the upper jaw at the top of the gum and progressing through the nasal septum, thus arriving eventually at a slight diagonal at the underside of the *sella turcica*. There was also the question of the introduction of the metal plate and the bolts. Carlos was utterly horrified.

In the event, Dr Yasserghyl's advice was reassuring: he advocated 'masterful inactivity', at least so far as surgical intervention was concerned. Provided Montserrat pursued a course of preventive medication, he was inclined to minimize the potential danger of her contracting meningitis, which had been much elaborated in Barcelona. Medication could also be used to stabilize the problem of the leaking fluid. The basic difficulty would, of course, remain: an only part-functioning and possibly entirely fallible hypothalamus. But then the surgery proposed in Barcelona would not have been addressed to this problem either, the resolution of which would remain essentially in the lap of the gods. In any event, a further referral was given, this time to Dr Kürsten in Vienna, whose prognosis and advice coincided exactly with that of his Zürich colleague. As a result of all this second-hand medical consultation, Montserrat decided that she would not undergo surgery. Apart from anything else, she was not at all convinced – despite assurances to the contrary – that the surgery would be successful. She might just as well go on singing for as long as was left to her.

She underwent some preliminary laser treatment during March 1985 with a view to preventing the further spread of the tumour within the fragmented hypothalamus; and after responding to drug treatment, unexpectedly discharged herself from the clinic at the end of the month. Immediately after leaving the Quirón, she contacted the homoeopathic doctor who had always treated the family, Honorio Giménez, and gave him copies of all the medical documentation that had been accumulated so far. She then entered his clinic for a three-week period of treatment. Meanwhile, her illness had necessitated the cancellation at the Liceo of a new production of Pacini's *Saffo*, which would have been only the latest in her long line of musical reclamations within the *terra incognita* of early-nineteenth-century operas. In the event, the 'undiscovered country' which Montserrat had come closest to exploring had been that of which Hamlet speaks in his famous Act III soliloquy, 'To be, or not to be . . .'.* But she was determined to return to the stage at the earliest possible opportunity, and after a single press conference in which she tended to underplay the seriousness of her condition by making no reference to its cause, she departed for Madrid where she commenced rehearsals for a new production of Gluck's rarely performed *Armide*.

Privately, she was terrified. People who knew the truth had been speculating out loud as to what effect the strains and resonances set up by full-voiced singing, particularly in the highest register, might have upon the evidently delicately balanced state of her hypothalamus. She herself had been cautiously practising her way back to full vocal projection and it was perfectly true that the voice, as such, had been unimpaired by the latest developments. Indeed, the enforced hiatus in the otherwise continuous pursuit of her career had probably done it some good, though this was not a state of affairs that Caballé herself would much credit, believing, as she always had, that rest in no way benefited her singing. She speaks of her return to the stage on the evening of 16 April in the Teatro de la Zarzuela as one of the most momentous in her whole life. Not only was there a public to convince that her health was not an insuperable barrier to the continuance of her career at the highest level: she needed convincing herself. In some ways the work offered her no easy recipe for success: a sober and, indeed, sombre neo-classical tragedy of fairly unrelieved gloom, with few obvious opportunities for vocal display. Nevertheless, the vein of dark melancholy which pervades Gluck's score obviously touched a chord and the performance – conducted by Ileana Cotrubas' husband, Manfred Ramin – enjoyed a clamorous success with the Madrid public. Four further performances followed through to the end of the month, by which time Montserrat had become fully reassured as to her stage-worthiness: she would simply carry on, as always.

> I have come to believe that, just as I was gifted with a voice, so I was gifted to recover my health naturally. I have talked with Bernabé about how it could be possible, because really, after so many operations, so many illnesses, I don't understand it myself. It is something I cannot explain – a strength, a will, I do not know. It has to be something in the body, not in the mind. But then doctors have said to me that it is the mind that makes you go on and live again. I suppose they must be right.

* *Hamlet*, Act III, Scene 1, ll.76–82: '. . . death/The undiscover'd country, from whose bourn/no traveller returns . . .'

It must indeed have been Caballé's 'will to live' that got her through the next few years, because as contemporary photographs of her testify, she looked in bad shape. If it is possible for a very large lady to look haggard and drawn, then that is certainly how she appeared during the middle and later 1980s. And undoubtedly her precarious medical situation was responsible for her progressive withdrawal from commitments to performances on the wider operatic stage, almost as though she had consciously decided that if she was going to die in harness, then at least it would happen in her native Spain. And to this end, she would keep herself busy, concentrating upon her career and the continuous expansion of her already legendary repertory. In retrospect, we can see quite clearly that although Montserrat did indeed survive these years, they were nevertheless a period marked by a diminution in her natural ebullience. How could it be otherwise, given that from one day to the next she had it in mind that at any time nemesis might strike? Nor did she have the immediate consolations of wide-spread public support, since she had decided from the outset that this was not a matter for common knowledge and the public need not be party to what was a very private concern.

Within just a few years, however, she would reap the benefits of her courageous stance and – wholly unexpectedly – make the breakthrough into the realms of mass-media popularity enjoyed by few artists in her profession. By which time, looking back over a thirty-five-year-long career, she could afford to smile impishly and say: 'You know the Phoenix? It's me.'

CHAPTER THIRTEEN

1985–1988: Mercury Rising

In 1985 the British-based rock group Queen toured Europe and in the process played in Barcelona at the football club stadium. After their Spanish sojourn, the group's founder and lead vocalist, Freddie Mercury, appeared on a television news magazine called 'Informe Semanal' and astonished the many millions of viewers by announcing that of all the great Spanish institutions he admired, Montserrat Caballé was the greatest and the person he most longed to meet. This was widely reported in the Spanish press and was drawn to the soprano's attention not only by friends, but by her brother Carlos. In the immediate short term, of course, nothing came of the matter, since Montserrat was engaged in an unbroken schedule of appearances in Hamburg (three concert performances of *Semiramide* under Henry Lewis, with Marilyn Horne, Francisco Araiza and Sam Ramey), a recital tour of France, and a series of five performances of *Andrea Chénier* covering the first half of June at the Teatro de la Zarzuela in Madrid. But on the 22nd she came to London in order to give a recital the following day at the Royal Opera House, at the end of which a personal introduction between Caballé and Mercury was effected by Mike Moran, who was now one of the rock star's musical entourage but who in the 1970s had worked at Covent Garden as a chorus répétiteur.

It transpired that Mercury had been a passionate admirer of the soprano for many years and, as and when possible, had attended several of her performances. And there was a further link in that his personal assistant, Peter Freestone, had for many years worked in the wardrobe department at the Royal Opera House. Montserrat viewed the entire proceedings as an unexpected but pleasant tribute from one musician to another, but it evidently served to sow a seed of a rather more practical nature in Mercury's mind, and one which would soon bear spectacular fruit.

The recital tour of France which had occupied the latter half of May 1985 took Caballé to Orléans, Bordeaux and Toulouse where, as usual, the French press devoted columns to high-flown rhetorical rodomontade, the gist of which was that Caballé sang very well indeed. But undoubtedly the most important of these French outings took place on 20 May, when Montserrat took part in one of the jolliest romps of her entire career and one which clearly pointed the way forward to her renewed involvement with the Rossini revival later in the decade. The occasion was billed as the Gala Rossini and was held in the rococo jewel of an opera house built for Louis XVI at Versailles, the tiny Théâtre Gabriel which is, alas, rarely used for public performance. The Chamber Orchestra of Europe were in the pit; an English actor, Paul Brooke, was imported to impersonate Rossini in whose honour the performance was being given; and Claudio Abbado was in charge of the music.

The event was filmed for television and shown throughout Europe. In it, the cream of Rossini singers lined up for a series of solos, ensembles and party pieces, all to be greeted by the composer himself as they made their vocal offerings. Among others, Ramey sang Lord Sidney's long *scena* from *Il viaggio a Reims*; Marilyn Horne sang Arsace's second aria, 'In si barbara sciagura' from *Semiramide*; Ruggero Raimondi sang 'La calunnia' from *Il barbiere di Siviglia*; and Montserrat delivered a flawless account of 'Sombre forêt' from *Guillaume Tell*. The ensemble pieces included an hysterically over-the-top rendition of the sextet from *Cenerentola*, capped by the onomatopoeic finale to the first Act of *L'Italiana in Algeri*. Together Horne and Caballé sang a duet from *Tancredi*, recalling the splendours of their work together in *Semiramide*. In so doing, Montserrat was engaging in a personal première, since the only music she had sung from *Tancredi* in the past was the hero's 'Di tanti palpiti', whereas she was now singing for the first time music written for the heroine Amenaïde. She also sang for the first time in the great prayer from *Mosè*, which united Horne, Araiza, Raimondi and the chorus, though this was not in fact performed in the theatre but filmed earlier in the Palace chapel. Montserrat was even given one particular indulgence: during the chorus of girls bearing lilies which punctuates Lord Sidney's aria, she appeared in a stage box in a bejewelled blue gown in order to play the castanets, much to everyone's amusement. For a woman who merely weeks beforehand had been undergoing laser treatment for a brain tumour, the complete assurance of her stage demeanour – grand and flirtatious at the same time – and the remarkable poise of her voice came as an enormous relief.

Following the Madrid *Chénier*s of which no evidence survives other than favourable press reviews, her next stage engagement took her back to Orange where, from 6 July onwards, she was rehearsing for a new production of Verdi's *Simon Boccanegra* in which she was to sing for the first – and as it transpired, only – time in her career the role of the Doge of Genoa's kidnapped daughter Maria, known as Amelia Grimaldi. The production was by Jacques Karpo and conducted by Maurizio Arena, with Piero Cappuccilli in the title-role, Paul Plishka as Fiesco and Lando Bartolini as Amelia's hot-headed lover, Gabriele Adorno. Although Caballé had never sung the role before, it was noticed that at one point in the Act I duet with the tenor, she turned her back to the audience in three-quarter profile in order to deliver a prompt to her colleague who had lost his lines. Reviewing this performance, Tony Mayer wrote:

> she may have neither the youthfulness nor the figure for Maria, and she may also pay more attention to her technique than expressing the gamut of emotions that successively pervade Boccanegra's daughter, but so fabulous still – even in the highest register – is the purity and transparency of her voice that (especially when she is in top form and does not have to fight against the Orange Mistral) she still keeps the audience spellbound and deserves all the fantastic enthusiasm she arouses.[1]

Montserrat managed to fit in a week's holiday after this solitary performance and returned to the farm at Ripoll before giving a series of recitals in small Spanish towns. She broke this regime twice, first in order to give her annual recital at the monastery church in Ripoll itself, and second to sing at the Arena di Verona. The former event turned into quite an occasion: for some time Caballé's children – Bernabé junior, now nearing nineteen and Montsita, fourteen – had been bewailing the fact that both of them were too young ever to have seen their parents singing together on stage. Indeed, the earliest conscious memory either of the children had of seeing their mother sing was the *Semiramide* performances at Aix-en-Provence in 1980. As a result, for some time they had been exerting gentle pressure on their father to sing with Montserrat just one last time in public, basically for the children's benefit. This recital in 1985 therefore became the vehicle of both Bernabé's comeback and final farewell to the concert platform in the company of his wife. He sang three arias – 'Recondita armonia', 'Ch'ella mi credi' (from *La Fanciulla del West*) and 'O Paradiso' – and, following Montserrat's solo numbers, they sang together duets from *La bohème*, Marchetti's *Ruy Blas* – a characteristic rarity, even in the context of a family recital – and an encore piece from Caballero's *L'Africana*. Not only were the Martís' children thrilled by the experience, but so were her parents, for whom this would be one of their last public outings together in over fifty years of marriage.

The trip to Verona was for a performance which took place on 4

August, a charity gala entitled 'Opera for Africa' in which Carlos, at José Carreras' prompting, had gathered together most of the numerous singers with whom he had enjoyed professional contact, to provide the operatic equivalent of Bob Geldof's triumphantly successful Band Aid given at Wembley Stadium in aid of Ethiopian famine relief the previous year. Together with Carreras, Caballé sang the 'Brindisi' from *La traviata*, Act I, in which the audience were exhorted to fill in for the missing chorus, and later in the programme delivered a 'Casta diva' marred only by a slight loss of breath which prevented the correct resolution of the final trill. This did not stop the audience of 20,000 from erupting in applause, perhaps as much to acknowledge Caballé's stature as her actual singing. In fact, the general level of singing was much higher than usual at such affairs.

Montserrat's next major project reunited her with Claudio Abbado, for whom she had already developed a strong liking on the basis of the Rossini gala. Indeed, it was the success of this collaboration that had led to the present invitation from the Italian maestro. The forces of La Scala, Milan, of which Abbado was then still in charge, were to give a performance of the Verdi *Requiem* not, as usual, in the theatre itself, but in the location of the work's original performance in 1874, the Milanese church of San Marco. The other soloists were Lucia Valentini Terrani, Peter Dvorsky and Samuel Ramey. It was noted in a review which somewhat surprisingly appeared in *Opera* that 'Montserrat Caballé's angelic voice counterbalanced theirs in perfect intonation, reaching Verdi through the purest solvent of Bellini *bel canto*'.[2]

Two days later Montserrat flew back to New York in order to continue rehearsals for probably the starriest and certainly the most grandiose production in which she had ever appeared at the Metropolitan Opera House in New York. Once again she had been accorded the ultimate honour of the opening night of the season: the fifth such occasion in her New York career, although, as we have seen, her three previous opening nights had all failed to materialize due once to her pregnancy and twice to the Metropolitan being on strike. The work was *Tosca*, which had just been given a sumptuous new production earlier in the year directed and designed by Franco Zeffirelli, in which the principal roles had been sung by Domingo and Hildegard Behrens. This opening night revival was to star Caballé and Pavarotti, and to add to the inherent glamour attendant upon any Met opening night – this was the house's 102nd season – the French fashion house of Chanel had arranged to preface the performance with a gala dinner to celebrate the launch of their new perfume, Coco. This was combined with a ball and fashion parade, for which Karl Lagerfeld had designed a whole new series of frocks, and the entire glitzy proceedings were conducted out in the Met's capacious foyer. A seat in the stalls for the opera itself that night cost $1000: and the price of attending the preceding dinner-dance was $10,000. The revenue from all this was intended to swell the coffers of the Met, which was attempting to raise $5.5 million on a dollar-for-dollar challenge grant from the National Endowment for the Arts. In the event, this one night more than half met the target figure, since the supper netted $1.5 million, Chanel donated $250,000, and the box office takings amounted to $600,000. Such is the drawing-power of genuine stars. Michael Redmond was one of the very few critics to attend this performance on 23 September, and wrote at length of the experience:

> It was an event as much as a performance, and the stuff of the legend of which the Met is made. For weeks now, the most important question on the opera scene has been, 'Will Caballé actually sing?' It is a measure of her stature as 'the last of the prima donnas' . . . that this engagement could so dominate everybody's attention. It remains to be said that yes, she did sing, and gloriously . . .[3]

At just about the same time as this run of performances was drawing to an end, *Diapason*, the principal French magazine devoted to the review of recordings of classical music, published the results of a poll it had been conducting amongst its readership with a view to establishing the most popular and respected artists. The readers had been confronted with a list of conductors, singers and instrumentalists, and asked to mark their favourite. Karajan came first, Caballé came a close second, and Rostropovich third. Montserrat observed that it was nice to be sandwiched between two eminent conductors, even if she was not thin enough to work with one of them. Coincidentally, her next engagement was in Paris at the Châtelet where she gave a recital accompanied by Miguel Zanetti. Two days later, on 23 October, she gave a joint concert with José Carreras in Antwerp, and the following day left for Brussels where she was due to give another concert performance of *Semiramide* at the Théâtre de la Monnaie on the 29th, with a repeat performance in Lille two days later. But on the evening of the 26th, she played a little permitted truancy and flew to Milan where she gave a recital to a packed and enthusiastic La Scala audience.

Virtually the whole of November 1985 was taken up with yet another of Caballé's pet projects: this time a resurrection of Cherubini's utterly forgotten *Démophoön*, in a new production by Luca Ronconi, with spectacular sets and designs by Gianni Quaranta, at the Teatro dell'Opera in Rome. The work was largely written during the composer's sojourn in London in 1788 and premièred the year after in Paris, where it was the first Cherubini opera to be heard. The libretto – originally by Pietro Metastasio – is set in classical Thrace and concerns the plight of Astor's daughter, Dircé, who has been secretly betrothed to the king's son and heir, Osmide, and has borne him a child, yet finds herself being selected by his father, King Démophoön, as the annual virgin sacrifice. This new production in Rome – the work's belated Italian première – scored a considerable success, largely on account of some extremely distinguished singing from a cast also including Veriano Luchetti as Osmide, Giuseppe Taddei in the title-role and Jean-Philippe Lafont as Astor, purposefully conducted by Gianluigi Gelmetti. But the production itself must have been a contributing factor to this success since, within the static conventions prescribed by the libretto and, indeed, Cherubini's music, Ronconi contrived some very striking stage pictures, with the omnipresent chorus mounted vertically against the outer edges of the proscenium.

At the centre of the production shone a star, Montserrat Caballé, an excellent Dircé in the first two acts and sublime in Act 3 because of the intensity of feeling in her *legato* and her musical *mezza voce* singing. She provided an authentic lesson in the *bel canto* style of eighteenth-century opera and Cherubini in particular. All the artists earned a triumphant ovation which was repeated at the five later performances.[4]

Caballé's next engagement was back in Spain, where on 3 December she gave a recital in the Teatro Real in Madrid. This was in aid of the Fundación Reina Sofía in the Queen's presence and was by all accounts an emotionally charged evening. Accompanied, as ever, by Miguel Zanetti, the soprano sang arias from Handel works including *Rinaldo*, *Joshua*, *Theodora* and *Jephtha*; and in the second half devoted herself entirely to Rossini, comprising arias from *Tancredi*, *Elisabetta*, *Maometto II* and *Armida*. Apparently the royal protocol attaching to such an occasion precluded the singing of any encores, but such was the clamour of the public that Queen Sofía arranged to have a message conveyed to Caballé on stage that she effectively had royal assent to continue.

The middle of the month was left free so that Montserrat could make arrangements for the family's Christmas, but from 21 December onwards she was engaged in rehearsals at the Liceo for what should have been her Christmas show but which in the event turned into a set of concert performances. The work was once again *Semiramide*, here receiving its first performances in Barcelona in the twentieth century – it had last been heard in 1885 – and, much more extraordinarily, Caballé's first-ever performances of a Rossini work in her home theatre. The original plan had been to import Pier Luigi Pizzi's Aix-en-Provence staging, but fairly late in the day the Liceo pleaded that it was beyond their technical resource to mount it. Since Pizzi's production takes place in an unvarying white box, we may safely conclude that the Liceo's objections were financial rather than technical. In any event, the performances duly took place, starting on 26 December, and were simply given in concert with Caballé in the title-role, Valentini Terrani as Arsace and Jean-Paul Bogart as Assur, conducted by Alessandro Siciliani (Francesco's son). Roger Alier wrote in *Opera* that: '[Caballé] was in excellent voice and her "Bel raggio lusinghier" was one of those wonderful memories to treasure. Her successive duets were also exquisite.'[5] All of which makes it the more sad that within a mere handful of days of the last *Semiramide* on 3 January 1986 Montserrat should have run into serious trouble in New York, and a trip which should have set the seal on her complete rehabilitation as a reliable performer instead turned into a nightmare of disillusionment. She was due to take part in a performance of the Verdi *Requiem* in Carnegie Hall on 12 January in aid of the Richard Tucker Memorial Foundation, with two days of rehearsals beforehand. But she did not attend these, informing the promoters in New York that she had unavoidable commitments in Spain, and that she would instead arrive in New York as early as possible by Concorde on the morning of the final rehearsal. She did so, only to be greeted by Richard Tucker's son who informed her that her absence had upset her colleagues and that she had therefore been replaced. She retired to her hotel, but had little enough time to brood since she was required the following day at the Metropolitan to do a 'walk-through' rehearsal of the *Tosca* in which she was due to sing four performances during the period 15–25 January. She sang in the semi-public dress rehearsal the day after to considerable acclaim but was, by her own account, already feeling unwell. The following day it was clear to her that she had once again caught a bad cold in New York and she informed the opera house that she would be unable to perform. The Met therefore replaced her in all four *Tosca*s. She has never – at least to date – sung at the Metropolitan since.

Caballé remained in North America, first recuperating at her hotel in New York and then departing as scheduled for San Francisco on 26 January to begin rehearsals for a joint operatic concert to be given with Marilyn Horne in the War Memorial Opera House some three days later. This show then went on the road, playing next at Avery Fisher Hall back in New York's Lincoln Center before moving on to Missouri, the Kennedy Center in Washington, DC, and ending up in Miami. The backbone of the repertory sung by the women in duet was drawn, not surprisingly, from *Norma* and *Semiramide*, with the 'Barcarolle' from *Les contes d'Hoffmann* thrown in as an encore. Thereafter, and as if to prove her indestructibility, Montserrat returned to New York where in mid-February she gave a recital at the Brooklyn Academy of Music, following that a few days later by three performances at Avery Fisher Hall of Pergolesi's *Stabat Mater* with Lucia Valentini Terrani and the New York Philharmonic under Zubin Mehta.

She returned to Barcelona at the end of February with a handful of recitals – in Cologne, Barcelona and London as well as a concert performance of *Les Danaïdes* in the Grosse Saal of the Konzerthaus in Vienna – scheduled for March, before beginning rehearsals for a run of stage performances of *Hérodiade* at the Teatro dell'Opera in Rome throughout April. This reunited most of the cast that had given the work to such great effect at the Liceo in December 1983: Carreras, Caballé and Pons, although Agnes Baltsa who was originally announced to take the title-role did not sing and was replaced by Ana Paglianos. Apparently the performances ran for more than four hours, not because of any excessive length in Massenet's well-crafted score but because of three yawning intervals which the producer, Antonio Calenda, decided to place between the Acts, despite the objections of both cast and conductor (Gianluigi Gelmetti).

At the end of the month Caballé returned to New York to take part in a very glamorous and prestigious Benefit Gala in aid of the Philharmonic's Pension Fund, conducted by Zubin Mehta, with Itzhak Perlman and Isaac Stern. The two violinists played a Vivaldi double violin concerto whilst Montserrat contributed yet another rarity, this time an aria, 'Sola son io . . . Al figlio tuo la morte', from Donizetti's *Sancia di Castiglia*, as well as the more familiar 'Tanti affetti' from Rossini's *La donna del lago*. If the Met administration was still smarting over the cancelled *Tosca*s, that of the Philharmonic was thrilled beyond measure. At a private ceremony after the performance, the soprano was made an honorary member of the New York Philharmonic, the first singer ever to receive such an accolade.

Her return to Spain brought her back to one of her earliest loves: *Die Walküre* was to be given a run of five performances at the Teatro de la Zarzuela in Madrid between 12 and 24 May 1986. In a Madrid season – cast throughout by Carlos Caballé – that had already witnessed Ruggero Raimondi in Piero Faggioni's staging of *Boris Godunov* and would go on to have Carreras in *Pagliacci* and Domingo in *La bohème*, this *Walküre* was something very special: Caballé and Siegfried Jerusalem sang Sieglinde and Siegmund; Hans Sotin, Wotan; Johanna Meier, Brünnhilde;

Brigitte Fassbaender, Fricka; and Kurt Moll, Hunding. Gustav Kuhn conducted, and the only fly in the ointment seems to have been the set designs and staging by Hugo de Ana, which were of monumental high-tech irrelevance to the work and, some four years later would prove quite literally to be the stumbling-block upon which Caballé's by then soured relations with the Liceo administration would finally founder.

There was a lot of press speculation in Spain as to how Caballé would fare in such experienced Wagnerian company, but as usual she saw the overall musical context of this move quite clearly and was under no illusions as to the nature of the role she was undertaking.

I first sang Sieglinde in 1977 at the Palau de la Música in concert, with Nilsson as Brünnhilde and Thomas Stewart as Wotan. There were just two performances, but at that time I really did not have enough vocal weight to get through the complete opera. I was then in the third decade of my career and the voice had generally become much stronger at the bottom and the volume quite excessive for certain little-girl, lyrical roles, so I thought that Wagner would be an obvious move to make. But I only just made it, a fact which no one at the time noticed. By the mid-1980s it was no longer a problem for me – I had the stamina and if I was losing a little at the top I had gained much at the bottom. And always at the back of my mind there was Isolde, which so many people had asked me to do but had never come about.

With the exception of a pair of recitals in Paris – one at the St Étienne Festival and the other at the Théâtre de l'Athénée – Montserrat remained in Spain for most of late May and June, to accommodate her pre-existing schedules which entailed recitals and television recording in Barcelona and Madrid. But the trip to the French capital, though brief, was momentous: between the two recitals, she was invited to the Ministère de la Culture et de la Communication where she was informed by the Minister, François Léotard, that she was to be honoured later that month by the French Government. On 27 June 1986, he formally presented her with the insignia of *Commandeur de l'Ordre des Arts et des Lettres* at the Ministry's rue de Valois address. In the speech that accompanied the ceremony, M. Léotard showed just as much flair for *le mot juste* as Caballé herself. Apropos of the award, he observed: 'Montserrat Caballé doesn't need it, but France does in order to tell her that we love her . . . It has been twenty years since she entered the hearts of the French and with this honour we want to bind her to us even more closely.'

Her next major international engagement did not take place until July when, after an absence of seventeen years, she returned to the Arena di Verona in a staged opera, this time a new production of *Andrea Chénier* with Carreras in the title-role and Renato Bruson as Gérard, conducted by Gelmetti. Out of the total of twelve performances scheduled for the Festival, Caballé had been contracted for the first four and the last two, though indisposition prevented her from returning for the latter and also obliged her to cancel what would have been her début at the Edinburgh Festival. But there remained the first four which were a triumph, not least on account of Attilio Colonello's sumptuous sets and production, and saw Caballé accorded an overwhelming ovation after singing a bare handful of notes.

She resumed her activities at the very end of August when she gave a concert in the Teatro Rossini in Pesaro as part of the Rossini Festival which had increasingly put the obscure coastal town – the composer's birthplace – in the Marche on the musical map. It was here that *Il viaggio a Reims* had received its first-ever staged performances in 1984 with an astonishing cast under Claudio Abbado, and in this 1986 season, apart from giving the first modern stage performances of *Bianca e Falliero* with Katia Ricciarelli and Marilyn Horne, there were recitals by Horne, June Anderson and Luciano Pavarotti, all of which, together with Caballé's, were filmed for Italian television. Just a few days later, Montserrat arrived in Buenos Aires for the first of two recitals at the Teatro Colón, and followed these with a grandiose, open-air operatic gala given in Luna Park.

In mid-September, Caballé travelled to Paris in order to commence what was for her an extremely lengthy rehearsal period for a new production of Strauss's *Ariadne auf Naxos* to be given at the Salle Favart, better known as the Opéra-Comique. The director was the intendant of the Opéra de Paris, the critic-turned-producer Jean-Louis Martinoty, who had expressed some trenchant views in the past concerning the 'star system' which he was quoted as describing as: 'no more than a procession of princes who sing without rehearsal and alter a production to suit themselves'. In theory he should have been the last man on earth with whom Caballé would wish to collaborate (and vice versa). In the event, after some preliminary skirmishing, the rehearsals went well, and the production, though hyperactive in the modern fashion, was a considerable success, not just in Paris but also in London where the Royal Opera House gave the work two series of performances, neither of which involved Caballé. This was a great pity since the Paris production showed her to particular advantage. As she observed:

I have done many *Ariadne*s and, after all, been honoured by Vienna for my singing of Strauss. So I think I know this repertory really well. *Ariadne* contains this great ocean of music, a kind of conceptual grandeur which unites both the wonderful lyrical inspiration on the one hand and the knock-about humour on the other. The Paris production was not at all Viennese, but very French indeed, with any amount of activity going on around me on stage. At first I was taken aback and felt I stuck out like a sore thumb, but what M. Martinoty said made sense and I tried my best to realize his intentions.

The director was also evidently impressed, and went so far as to say so in print, obliquely praising himself as having been instrumental in extending her theatrical range.[6] The truth of the matter is that Caballé, with her sense of comic timing, found a ready-made outlet for her talents in the Prologue of the opera, where she played the *grande dame* rearranging the allocation of the on-stage dressing-rooms with infinite glee and *hauteur*. In the opera proper, her enormous, expressive eyes spoke volumes as she stared fixedly sideways in barely disguised contempt at the *commedia dell'arte* outrages going on around her. The French – and in particular the Parisians – who had had better opportunities than most to witness the diva on stage, in concert and in recital, and were already therefore well acquainted with her individual sense of *drôlerie*, responded wholeheartedly: the run of just five performances in the intimate Salle Favart became the most sought-after ticket in Paris.

Immediately after this she travelled to Rome, where she was due to begin rehearsals for her first-ever stage performances of an opera which she had performed in concert as long ago as 1970, but which no opera house had previously shown itself willing to mount: Gaspare Spontini's *Agnese di Hohenstaufen*. The work had been originally premièred in 1829 at the Royal Opera House in Berlin, where Spontini had been the court composer to Frederick III of Prussia throughout the decade. Set in the late twelfth century during the period of the Guelph-Ghibelline feud, the opera was originally written to a German text, telling of the attempts of Heinrich von Braunschweig to marry the eponymous heroine in the teeth of political and familial opposition. In this, his last stage work, Spontini aimed to achieve a summation of his personal style, based as this was on long, static choral tableaux and the regular interpolation of spectacular *coups de théâtre*. Although his subject-matter and its stage treatment can be seen, therefore, strongly to prefigure French Grand Opera as exemplified by the works of Meyerbeer (who took over his job in 1842), the musical style remains resolutely neo-classicist and not readily distinguishable from the works of his contemporaries such as

Cherubini. Needless to say, there is a plum role for the soprano who, like her predecessor Giulia in *La vestale*, needs to be submissive and imperious by turns and is given *arioso*-style monologues of great length and even greater tedium. Even in his own time Spontini had the reputation of being a voice destroyer (but then, so did Rossini) and certainly one can see why the role should appeal to someone whose repertory had increasingly come to focus upon blazingly dramatic roles. However, a video pirate survives of a television relay of one of the six performances in the Teatro dell'Opera during November 1986 and, impressive outbursts from the soprano apart, makes for very stodgy viewing and listening.

Caballé ended 1986 by returning to Barcelona and giving four performances of Gluck's *Armida* at the Liceo in the stage production borrowed from the Teatro de la Zarzuela with which she had made her return to the stage following the alarming medical developments of the previous year. The opening night – 6 December – was just one month and one day short of the twenty-fifth anniversary of her Liceo début back in 1962, and marked the assumption of her forty-second new role in the house. As in Madrid, the work was conducted by Manfred Ramin and the cast included both Veriano Luchetti and Peter Lindroos. It seems hard to imagine any Gluck opera – *Armida* in particular – creating a real sensation with an audience, but such ensued on the opening night, the cast unexpectedly finding themselves having to take an endless series of unrehearsed curtain calls. The scenes which greeted the end of the last performance on 14 December were even more extraordinary: but for these there was definitely an ulterior motive. By this time it was known to the hard-core aficionados in the upper tiers that the house had not scheduled any formal celebration on 7 January 1987 in order to commemorate Caballé's silver anniversary. The reasons offered for this in print concerned the theatre's lack of modern equipment and scene-changing facilities, which meant that the sets for an *Aïda* that was due in the house in January could not be removed to accommodate a one-off gala concert. No one was much impressed with this line of argument, however, least of all the occupants of the fourth and fifth tiers, who took the opportunity of unfurling an enormous banner that ran round two-thirds of the tier's horseshoe and which read in Catalan: 'Montse: Estem amb tu' ('We are with you'). The evening's programmes were dismembered in order to provide the wherewithal for an impressive shower of ticker-tape, and flowers rained down to carpet the forestage. After a fifteen-minute standing ovation the banner and its bearers duly reassembled on Las Ramblas facing the entire width of the theatre, awaiting the diva's emergence into a vast throng foregathered outside the house's unassuming exit. It is safe to say that following this exhibition the management of the Liceo was evidently obliged to have second thoughts: the *Consorci* hastily contacted the soprano with a view to arranging an appropriate gala on the exact date.

This duly took place, but in case it is imagined that a silver anniversary homage would at least allow its recipient to put her feet up and bask in the accolades and tributes, it must be noted that Spanish versions – at least on this showing – are labour-intensive in the extreme, since that night Montserrat sang 'Porgi amor', the 'Willow Song' and 'Ave Maria' from *Otello*, 'Casta diva', the Act I duet from *Otello*, 'Già nella notte densa', and the closing scene from *Salome*. Montserrat was so overcome with emotion that the Mozart at the beginning almost defeated her; not surprisingly, she struck form in the long Verdi *scena*, and came into her own for the extract from *Norma*, sung with the participation of the Liceo's chorus. As the applause and cheers died away, the orchestral cellos could be heard outlining the opening melody of the love duet from *Otello*, at which point José Carreras walked on to the stage, provoking a further outburst which stopped the music dead in its tracks as the two singers embraced.

The musical content of the second half was much shorter, consisting only of the orchestral Intermezzo from Puccini's *Manon Lescaut*, conducted by the evening's presiding maestro, Carlo Felice Cillario, and the *Salome* Schlussgesang. After this came a series of speeches, the longest of which was given by the President of the Catalan Government, the Hon. Jordi Pujol. A number of musical organizations made formal presentations – medallions, statuary and honorabilia – and then Señor Pujol introduced 'the man who made it all possible', Montserrat's husband, Bernabé. Finally, on a stage that was by now packed with admirers, including her own children, Montserrat herself made an emotional and very dignified speech, looking back over her career and thanking the audience. White doves were released in the auditorium and flew everywhere, including one which with a fine sense of theatrical effect landed at the diva's feet and which to the audience's amazement she scooped up, pressed to her bosom and held aloft. In all, a complete triumph, scarcely undermined by the theatre's horrified discovery over the following days that the doves had taken up residence in various inaccessible nooks and crannies and had taken to performing on some of the audience during the rescheduled *Aïda*s.

However, there was absolutely no time for Caballé to sit back and bask in the afterglow of public euphoria. La Scala had a crisis on its hands, and, ironically, had turned in desperation to the woman who usually sat at the heart of their crises to resolve this one. A new production of *Salome* by the avant-garde American stage director Robert Wilson was due to open at the Milanese theatre on 11 January 1987, but the intended heroine – Eva Marton – was ill. After some frantic telephone calls between Milan and Barcelona, Caballé came to the rescue for the all-important *prima* at just forty-eight hours' notice. The costumes had been designed by Gianni Versace, the orchestra was to be conducted by Kent Nagano, and Helga Dernesch and Hermann Winkler were singing the Herods, with Bernd Weikl as Jokanaan. The entire affair was one of those events much patronized by high society and its latter-day media replacement, the jet set. (Bianca Jagger was photographed not so much embracing as engulfing Caballé after the performance.) And the audience had what it likes best – a real scandal: whilst the singers were uniformly applauded and Caballé showered with flowers, the production team was booed off stage as the auditorium erupted in jeers and whistles.

Montserrat thought this was particularly unfair: she knew that Wilson had been rehearsing the work for the better part of six months, first in America and latterly in Italy, and if she found his approach unconventional, she was utterly convinced of his dedication both to Strauss's score and Oscar Wilde's original play. In the frantic last-minute rehearsals she had with the director, she noted that all Wilson's ideas and suggestions were directed from the score, with movements synchronized with specific bars. By the first night, an unexpected rapport had sprung up between Caballé and Wilson which was in no way compromised by the poisonous reviews that the *mise-en-scène* received from the Italian press. Two years later, when she was asked to sing the role at the Liceo, Montserrat did so on the understanding that it would be in the Wilson staging. And it was the theatre's failure to meet this requirement, and the problems encountered with its home-grown replacement, that marked the beginning of the rift in the relationship between Caballé and the Liceo at the end of 1988. Immediately after this solitary *Salome* – Eva Marton soon recovered – Montserrat departed for Vienna where two concert performances of *Semiramide* were given in the Grosser Saal of the Konzerthaus, with Kathleen Kuhlmann as Arsace and Boris Martinovic as Assur. On one of the evenings an ardent fan had himself introduced to the soprano backstage after the performance: the pianist Ivo Pogorelich immediately suggested that she should give a recital as part of his festival in Bad Wörishofen.

Caballé's next major project constituted both a stage première and a return to the past. The work was Boito's *Mefistofele*, in which she had recorded the role of Margherita for EMI fifteen years earlier, but had never sung on stage. Now, thanks to the Teatro de la Zarzuela in Madrid and the planning of its intendant, José Antonio Campos, she had the opportunity of remedying the omission in a new production by Emilio Sagi, designed by Toni Businger with Giorgio Merighi as Faust and Yevgeny Nesterenko in the title-role. *Opera* magazine noted: 'Caballé delighted everyone with a tender, beautifully controlled performance which reached real pathos in her unforgettable delivery of "L'altra notte in fondo al mare".'[7]

In the latter part of February and for most of March, Caballé once again went on tour in America, this time South as well as North, embracing recitals and concerts in New York, Miami and Caracas, as well as giving a joint concert with Marilyn Horne in Dallas. At the end of the month she returned to London for what was by now her annual recital at the Royal Opera House. Any feeling that she might be running out of new material to set before her London audience was soon swept aside on opening the evening's programme: six arias from Vivaldi's opera *L'Olimpiade*; two pieces by Spontini – one from his opera *Nurmahal*; Ravel's three *chansons hébraïques* – only one of which is actually in Hebrew, the others being in Yiddish; a group of four songs called *Recuerdos de juventud* by L. Martínez Palomo; and three songs by Fernando Obradors. As the soprano explained to the audience at the outset of the recital, she proposed to sing the comprehensive selection of arias from *L'Olimpiade* in order to honour the announcement made at the end of 1986 that her home city of Barcelona would host the 1992 Olympic Games. And the Ravel items were offered to mark the fiftieth anniversary of the composer's death. But the rarities did not stop with the printed programme: after two reassuringly familiar encores, Caballé reappeared, not with Miguel Zanetti, but with a different pianist, much younger and more informally dressed (tails plus trainers). She proceeded to explain that the next encore was a piece that had been written for her by a long-time admirer who was present that night in the audience and whom she encouraged to take a bow: Freddie Mercury. For a large percentage of the audience, this information offered no enlightenment whatsoever, since Caballé's characteristic English had clipped the surname, which had sounded therefore more like Murray. And it is a moot point how many of the audience recognized the rock star by sight. Most people there only realized what had happened the following day, when they read their newspapers which were full of the 'sensational' collaboration at the Royal Opera House. Only then was it generally realized that the piece concerned was called 'Exercise in Free Love', since the diva had performed it, as written, as a vocalise. Nevertheless, all this media attention was a foretaste of things to come.

In fact, matters had been very active on the Freddie Mercury front for the whole of the preceding six months. In October 1986 Caballé had formed part of a deputation, including the President of Cataluña and the Mayor of Barcelona, which had descended upon Lausanne for the purpose of some last-minute lobbying on the Spanish city's behalf in the matter of the forthcoming selection of the 1992 Olympics venue. Up against stiff competition from Paris, amongst others, one of the principal platforms upon which Barcelona's bid was based was that this, for the first time in modern history, could well prove to be not just a sporting affair but a cultural Olympics as well, thus giving the city an opportunity to show off to best advantage its wealth of talent. To this end, Caballé gave a recital in Lausanne Cathedral in which she sang items in ten different languages. The following day she acted as guide to a group of wives of members of the International Olympic Committee, conducting them around a new exhibition celebrating the work of great Catalan artists, including Dali, Picasso, Miró and Tapiés. In the event, this sending in of the cultural heavyweights proved effective, and the President of the Olympic selection committee, Juan Antonio Samaranch, duly announced that Barcelona had been selected. The Mayor of Barcelona, Pasqual Maragall, suggested to Montserrat that, given their city's success, she had something to sing about. This gave her food for thought:

> Once I was back home after the Paris *Ariadne*s – I had had to sneak away to Lausanne between performances – I spoke to Carlos who I know had many discussions with Pasqual Maragall, our Mayor. Then one day Carlos rang me from London and said, 'I want you to have a meeting with Freddie Mercury.' I was very surprised, even though I knew that Freddie had for some time been an admirer, but apparently Maragall had said to Carlos that what we needed to get the idea of Barcelona as the Olympic city really launched was a theme song, and as Carlos had already had contacts with Freddie in London it was his idea to ask him. So a meeting was fixed for early 1987.

Due to pressure of work this was put back for a month and finally took place in March, after Caballé's return from America, at the Ritz Hotel in Barcelona. Montserrat was rather nervous that day, not knowing quite what to expect, and was duly ushered into the enormous Garden Room of the hotel to find Freddie Mercury looking even more anxious than she was. With him were Mike Moran, Jim Beach – the latter's manager – and Peter Freestone. Between them they had installed an impressive array of hi-fi equipment as well as a concert grand piano, and ensured that a large buffet table was piled high: this was just as well since Caballé had arrived at one o'clock in the afternoon, left after three hours in order to attend an orchestral rehearsal at the Palau de la Música, returned at 8 p.m. and remained until three the following morning.

> We spent the whole time listening to music, eating and improvising. Freddie had many pieces of music he wanted to play to me which he had recorded in his studio in London. I particularly liked the song which became 'The Fallen Priest' because it was very dramatic, almost operatic. And another thing I heard that day was 'Guide me Home', which touched me deeply. 'Barcelona' as such did not exist at that time – it was only a musical sketch of just a few bars which Freddie sang. But I liked it and he promised to develop it for me to celebrate the Olympic success. At the end he gave me another cassette which was of music from his new solo album, 'The Great Pretender'. There was a piece on it called 'Exercise in Free Love'. He told me, 'I was trying to imitate your voice in this piece, with all its high lying phrases and *pianissimi*. But I didn't succeed. I hope one day you will sing it for me, properly. I give it to you as a present.'

Mercury had worked rapidly on the 'Barcelona' song over the following week and telephoned Montserrat to say that it was nearing completion. Her suggestion was that they meet up some time after her Royal Opera House recital which would be bringing her to London at the end of March. Meanwhile, Caballé had been busy preparing a surprise for him: with the evidently none-too enthusiastic support of Miguel Zanetti, she had been rehearsing 'Exercise in Free Love' with the intention of working it into her Covent Garden recital as an encore piece (ever assuming, as she herself insouciantly added, that the public demanded any). Thus it was that the London public that night witnessed the first manifestation of what was soon to catapult Caballé into a wider fame beyond the confines of the rarefied world of opera. And later that evening the vehicle with which she would do so finally came into definitive being as, after the recital, she was escorted back to Mercury's Kensington mansion. There, until six o'clock the following morning, the diva and the rock star hammered out the final shape of what, in the event, unofficially became Barcelona's Olympic anthem. She appropriated the vocal line which, on the demonstration tape, Freddie himself had sung in falsetto, making numerous alterations and mixing a number of Spanish words into the otherwise English lyrics. These bear a moment's consideration, particularly since it has always been assumed that the text is a conventional paean of praise to Barcelona itself. Yet how could, 'The moment that you stepped into the room / you took my breath away'? and 'If God is willing / friends until the end' be said of a city? It seems clear on the strength of these and other sentiments that it is not a city that is here being apostrophized, but a human being: Caballé herself. It is self-evident that in the context of a homage to Barcelona, Freddie was also paying a loving tribute to his favourite singer.

The song was recorded at the beginning of May in Mercury's own studio in London after Caballé had spent the whole of the preceding month in Naples where she had given six performances of a new production by Antonio Calenda of *Semiramide* with Kathleen Kuhlmann, Rockwell Blake and Jean-Philippe Lafont, conducted by Alessandro Siciliani. A fixed-camera pirate video gives a reasonably clear idea of the proceedings, which if nothing else come across as a tumultuous riot of colour after Pizzi's monochrome astringency. Soon after the 'Barcelona' sessions in London, Caballé and Mercury had the opportunity of trying out the first fruits of their collaboration in front of a live audience of 2500 which gathered at the glitzy Club Ku in Ibiza for the first of what would prove to be a long series of galas celebrating (and also raising funds for) Barcelona's selection as the Olympic city, under the title 'Ibiza '92'.

Apart from miscellaneous recitals given in Zaragoza, Barcelona (at the Palau de la Música), Bordeaux, Geneva, La Rochelle and Jarnac (near Cognac), Caballé's next major project did not take place until mid-June when she began rehearsals at the Liceo for the new production of Pacini's *Saffo* in which she should first have appeared in Madrid in 1985 but had been prevented from so doing by the medical crisis she was then undergoing. Like Bellini, who was five years his junior, Giovanni Pacini was a Sicilian, born in Catania. His father had been a noted Rossinian *buffo* bass, and the operas belonging to the early part of Pacini's career all bear the stamp of Rossini. *Saffo*, however, was the product of a profound musical rethink on the composer's part, in which he sought to recapture something specifically Greek in the overall tenor of the music. Written to a libretto by Cammarano, author of *Lucia di Lammermoor* and *Il trovatore* among others, the work was premièred at the Teatro San Carlo in Naples in 1840 and enjoyed an instant success.

The story concerns the mythical poetess from the island of Lesbos who wins the Olympic song contest for her impassioned outburst against the yearly sacrificial leap of a virgin from the rock at Leucas, but who in so doing makes a deadly enemy of the Leucadian priest, Alcandro. The latter has his revenge by persuading Saffo's beloved, Faone, that the poetess loves another, and instead urges the affections of his own daughter, Climene. In Act II Climene and Faone are indeed married, but Saffo presents herself at the proceedings and desecrates the altar. In Act III, stricken with remorse, she resolves to take the Leucadian leap herself; the discovery that she is Alcandro's long-lost daughter and that her marital rival is, in fact, her sister does not seem to help matters much, so she goes ahead and jumps.

Caballé was quite clear about her reasons for undertaking the work, which she had first been offered as long ago as 1969 by the American Opera Society. But at that time she had not even sung Norma and had declined to take on what she regarded as the overwhelmingly dramatic title-role in the Pacini opera. As she observes:

> The tessitura of *Saffo* is rather like that of Sieglinde in *Die Walküre*, perhaps fractionally higher at the top. I think one of the principal reasons why the work is not performed these days is because of the voice type required, not so very high and not so very low, but of extreme density and needing great power to project across very thick orchestration. You need a great deal of volume, and in 1969 I didn't have that. By the early 1980s when the possibility of singing the role arose again, my voice had grown much bigger and I thought that now I would be able to serve this very dramatic music well.

In theory this should have been true. But Caballé was still a sick woman – the photographs accompanying interviews she gave at this time prove the point all too graphically – and the video which survives shows her having intermittent difficulty sustaining the demands of the role, especially at those points where Pacini's score is reminiscent of *Norma*: for example, the sudden outburst in Act II, 'Spose è già!', when Faone's perfidy is discovered, and the big trio in Act III. Even so, she gives a powerful performance of a work which seems eminently worth reviving; and it says much about her motivation that she not only undertook this challenge, but also – within less than a month – attempted an even more demanding role, that of Ermione.

But before leaving for Pesaro in order to begin rehearsals for Rossini's opera, there were two significant engagements to fulfil: one was the inaugural concert of her brother Carlos's new summer music festival held in the courtyard of the medieval castle at Peralada in northern Cataluña, at which Montserrat sang in a performance of Mozart's *Requiem* conducted by Antoni Ros-Marbà; the other was her first appearance at Salzburg since 1976, comprising her first-ever solo recital at the Summer Festival. Both these events took place against a background of great anxiety, not on account of Montserrat's own health problems, but on those of her close friends and family. On the day of the Peralada performance – 18 July 1987 – José Carreras entered the Hospital Clinico de Barcelona, having returned by air ambulance the day before from

Paris, where he had been informed that he was suffering from advanced leukæmia. Montserrat returned to Barcelona the following day, like her brother distraught at this turn of events, and immediately went to see Carreras who was due to start on a course of chemotherapy within a matter of hours. Manifesting the same kind of work ethic-oriented stoicism which was seeing her through, she reassured the tenor that their next major project together – the world première of *Cristobal Colón*, newly commissioned from Leonardo Balada – would go ahead just as soon as he was well again: they would be back on stage together in no time. But in fact this was so much bravado on the soprano's part. Like most people, she thought of leukæmia as a fatal disease, and with Carreras suffering dreadfully from the grim side-effects of the treatment, she left for Salzburg with a very heavy heart. Nor was there any consolation on the home front, since Caballé's mother Ana was sinking rapidly into the final stages of the pancreatic cancer that would soon kill her.

In the event, Salzburg provided some light relief. The programme was almost an exact replica of the one which Montserrat had given earlier in the year at the Royal Opera House, although one of the six Vivaldi arias from *L'Olimpiade* had vanished in the meantime. The sophisticated Salzburg audience expressed delight when the soprano returned to the platform to sing her final group of Spanish pieces wearing an elaborate black mantilla. At the end of the official programme, Caballé and Zanetti settled into their usual improvised routine of encores, after two of which they retired from the stage for a moment or two's respite. Montserrat was immediately approached by the Grosses Festspielhaus's manager, who informed her that because of union regulations and the need to avoid running into overtime, she must not continue performing and should simply take one last bow. Evidently he was unaware of the protocols involved in dealing with any diva, let alone this one, and was probably misled by the non-committal response he obtained before Caballé sailed back on stage with Zanetti. Once installed at the piano, she advanced to the front of the vast Festspielhaus stage and proceeded, in time-honoured imperial fashion, to throw the dissenter to the lions. She told the audience, 'There is a man in the wings who tells me I am not allowed to sing for you any more, because of the rules about overtime. I am happy to sing for you more pieces, if that is what *you* want.' The audience's response left the unfortunate official in no doubt whatsoever that if he insisted on ending the performance he would undoubtedly face a lynch-mob: he quietly made good his escape, leaving Caballé to another half-hour's-worth of encores.

*　　*　　*

Then it was off to Pesaro, for all that Caballé went with many gloomy forebodings as her mother's health rapidly deteriorated and Carreras fought for his life back in Barcelona. (In the event – and with official permission – Caballé commuted back to Barcelona, via Ancona and Rome, after each public performance, so as to be with her mother.) The opera, *Ermione*, was receiving its first stage performance in modern times, and indeed only its second-ever, since it had failed miserably at its première in Naples in 1819. The opera's libretto is closely based on Racine's *Andromaque* which, being written to conform to the classical French – and Greek – unities of time, place and action, provides a concise and watertight framework for Rossini's music. As is evident from the change of name, the opera shifts the focus of attention in this Trojan War endgame to the character of Hermione, who is loved by Orestes, but does not reciprocate his affection, being instead betrothed to Pyrrhus, King of Epirus. The latter has now, however, turned his feelings towards Andromache, the widow of the Trojan hero Hector, but she is wholly dedicated to the memory of her dead husband and his living embodiment in the form of her young son Astyanax. Put simply, then, A loves B, who loves C, who loves D, who loves E, who is dead: an unbroken chain of unrequited love.

Philip Gossett, the doyen of Rossini scholars and moving spirit behind the Pesaro Festival, spoke of the work at a press conference before the opening night as 'a major accomplishment which must be reckoned one of the finest works in the history of nineteenth-century Italian opera'. And Richard Osborne, one of Rossini's more recent biographers, has repeatedly written of *Ermione* as being one of the composer's very greatest scores. Clearly, therefore, Caballé had taken on a considerable responsibility in agreeing to perform a role for which there was simply no performance tradition and in which the full weight of the composer's inspiration on behalf of his wife, Isabella Colbran, fell squarely upon Montserrat's shoulders. Certainly the character of Andromaca provides no competition for the singer of the title-role, and indeed, Marilyn Horne only undertook it – replacing Valentini Terrani at short notice – because of the opportunity it afforded her to work with Montserrat once again. As usual with Rossini's Neapolitan operas, there is a clutch of tenors, incarnated in these performances by Chris Merritt (Pirro), Rockwell Blake (Oreste) and Giuseppe Morino (Pilade). And for once the production, by Roberto De Simone, was dignified, intelligent and above all appropriate in the handsome neo-classical set designs and costumes of Enrico Job.

RAI had set up their cameras in order to televise the opening night on 22 August live. The dress rehearsal two days earlier in front of a packed and enthusiastic audience had been both filmed and recorded in its entirety as part of the technical preparations for the première. In the event, this was just as well, since an anti-Caballé claque of less than a dozen had bought tickets with the intention of manifesting displeasure that their preferred soprano, June Anderson, had not been given the role instead. Act I's seven-movement structure, lasting eighty minutes or so, went smoothly and was well received by the audience. But at the heart of the second Act sits an extraordinarily extended and variously interrupted *scena* for the heroine which passes from her rejection by Pirro, through her crazed demands to Oreste for revenge, to bitter remorse and imprecation when he duly obeys her. As the recorded evidence of the first night suggests, Caballé was audibly beginning to tire towards the end of what for the heroine at least is a long evening. Although she gave a performance of remarkable commitment, authority and power, the canary-fancying claque greeted her curtain with cat-calls and whistles. This provoked the majority of the audience to intensify their applause, which in turn provoked yet more jeering. In the midst of this mayhem, Caballé leaned over the orchestra pit and managed to have the conductor's full score passed across to her. She brandished it aloft and, above the tumult, eyes ablaze, hollered in Italian, 'I sing the score exactly as Rossini wrote it': a claim which the booers could hardly refute, given the non-performance of the score during the preceding 168 years.

At this juncture the evening's conductor, Gustav Kuhn, appeared on stage, and he fell to his knees at the diva's feet. This only served to increase the partisan racket on both sides of the house, which did not begin to die down until the safety curtain was lowered. Ugly scenes then took place in the foyers and street outside, and Salvatore Accardo, the Italian violinist who was conducting the season's other offering, *L'occasione fa il ladro*, was seen leaving the theatre shaking his head in disbelief. The immediate controversy did not stop here, however, since once it became known through news broadcasts and press reports the following day what had transpired, the television audience clamoured to know why none of the brouhaha had been visible on the supposedly live relay. Indeed, those Italians who had attempted both to watch and listen to the performance as a simulcast – with pictures from the television but the sound taken from a simultaneous radio relay – had been upset to discover that what they were watching did not synchronize with what they were hearing. The head of RAI 3 revealed that the stage director, Roberto De Simone, had, at the last moment, refused to allow the use of television lighting which he believed would have impaired the visual quality of his all-important opening night, and that, without telling the television audience, RAI had simply transmitted the videotape of the dress rehearsal, whilst the radio relay went out live from the theatre. In this fashion the scandals simmered on for days, with all manner of accusations and denials. Once again, 'La Caballé in Italia' had provided plenty of theatrical incident for the media.

The English critics, who had turned out in force for the event, gave a less sensationalist slant to their reviews. Richard Osborne wrote in *Opera*:

> There is so much in the role [of Ermione] in Act II principally, that we must hope that other sopranos will come to it to illuminate its many-sidedness but Caballé remains a Rossini singer of much subtlety and refinement and, as the world's second Hermione, she has made a further distinguished mark in the annals of opera . . . A small anti-Caballé claque was in the house (how grandly she routed them at the curtain call!).[8]

In *The Times*, John Higgins noted:

> Mme Caballé moved around the stage with a regality that would have made Queen Victoria appear servile, and she delivered the notes. On the opening night she dealt summarily with a small faction in the house who presumably would have preferred another soprano in the part . . . Hell hath no composure like a Caballé scorned . . .[9]

It is worth adding that at the subsequent three performances, not only was Caballé in stronger form, she also – despite her understandable apprehensiveness – met with unanimous audience acclaim.

But the most intriguing aspect of the entire affair did not emerge for almost two and a half years, when Sergio Segalini's magazine *Opéra International* printed in its December 1989 edition an open letter to the administration of the Pesaro Festival, written by 'nine spectators from the gods'. Though the magazine nowhere mentioned the fact, this letter had originally appeared at greater length and in Italian in the correspondence columns of the October 1989 issue of *L'Opera*: presumably the French editor simply had the piece truncated and translated. The nine worthies had turned out to the opening night of that year's Pesaro Festival, a performance of *La gazza ladra*, which had starred Katia Ricciarelli. They claimed that they had turned up on the morning of the première queuing for cheap tickets. Apparently, they were photographed and had their names taken by men they described as either hired-hands or relatives of Ricciarelli, 'gorillas with Catanian accents,' who then proceeded to keep a beady eye on them during the actual performance. The essence of their complaint was that they were thereby prevented from booing the Italian soprano who, in their view, should never have been employed in the first place. The reason they go on to give for this in Monsieur Segalini's publication is that Rossini is ill served by the willingness of the present Pesaro administration to cast the composer's works with singers 'at the end of their careers, with clapped out voices and disastrous technical control. Montserrat Caballé's Ermione two years ago started this new tendency . . . but the case of this *Gazza Ladra* is even worse.' The truly amazing thing, beyond people being prepared to admit in print that their sole motivation in going to a performance is to disrupt an artist's reception, is the fact that this dreary piece of self-justification on the part of frustrated booers gets half a page under the historiated rubric 'Letter of the Month' in a magazine that never carries any correspondence.

There was to be no respite for Montserrat on her return to Barcelona. Ana Caballé was bedridden, nearing the end. Even so the soprano honoured her contracted tour of Scandinavia, giving both concerts and recitals in Stockholm, Helsinki and Copenhagen during the first half of September. Following her performance in the Finnish capital, she received a phone call from Carlos telling her that their mother had taken a turn for the worse and that she should come home the following day. But on her return to Barcelona, she discovered that her mother had already died: Carlos had simply been trying to spare her feelings the day before. The funeral took place on 14 September in the Church of Santa Maria Medianera close to the Caballés' residence, attended by the whole family. The rest of the month was devoted to the inevitable processes of grieving, coupled with the practical necessities of rearranging the flat in Infanta Carlota and adjusting to a regime without the family's undisputed mainstay. Montserrat herself fell prey to a recurrence of the leg trouble that had plagued her ever since 1969: at her current weight – effectively out of control as a result of her illness – the pressure on her left knee was enormous.

It was fortunate, therefore, that her schedules for the next two months comprised nothing more arduous than a reasonably well-spaced series of concerts and recitals which would take her from San Francisco to Warsaw, and Miami to Monte Carlo. Even so, at many of these she was obliged to use either a walking stick or crutch, to the audiences' consternation. But the first professional work she undertook after her mother's death did not entail public performance at all: instead she came to London in the first week of October and in the course of two days filmed the video at Pinewood Studios which was due to accompany the forthcoming release of 'Barcelona'. The one really noteworthy event of her touring schedule during the remainder of 1987 took place on 31 October when she gave a gala concert at the Stadttheater in Basel celebrating, rather late in the day, the thirtieth anniversary of her operatic début there. As often at these special galas, the high point of Montserrat's offerings was the closing scene from *Salome*, which many in the audience that night claimed to retain a vivid memory of her having sung in the same theatre during the late 1950s.

At the end of November she began rehearsing for the first presentation at the Liceo of the production of *Mefistofele* in which she had appeared in Madrid earlier in the year. In the event, she was the only survivor of the original cast, since Faust was now sung by another of Carlos's new discoveries, Antonio Ordoñez, and the title-role taken by Bonaldo Giaiotti. The opening night on 4 December was televised live, to which we owe the existence of the pirate videos in circulation. Ordoñez certainly made an impression with some vibrant, ringing tones; and Giaiotti rather less of one, the voice now grey and woolly. As in Madrid, the whole opera benefited from the committed conducting of José Collado. Montserrat sang a tremendously impassioned account of Margherita's prison scene, including the famous aria, 'L'altra notte'. This brought the opera to a complete halt for an ovation which the soprano did her best not to encourage, draped as she was up against the prison wall, with her back to the audience.

From mid-December onwards she had cleared her performance diary, not only allowing her time to prepare for this first Christmas without her mother, but giving her a chance to study her next new role, Madame Cortese, in the Vienna State Opera House's most expensive new production, Rossini's *Il viaggio a Reims*, due to open on 20 January. Not that the expense was due solely (or even principally) to the costs of rebuilding Luca Ronconi's original Pesaro production in Gae Aulenti's designs: the total of nearly three-quarters of a million pounds sterling included the wages of the singers, who were: Caballé, Cecilia Gasdia, Lella Cuberli, Lucia Valentini Terrani, Raquel Pierotti, Chris Merritt, Frank Lopardo, Enzo Dara, Carlos Chausson, Ferruccio Furlanetto – later Sam Ramey – and Ruggero Raimondi, with very much the first division of the Vienna Philharmonic conducted by Claudio Abbado. A show that had already been fairly wild in Pesaro became positively deranged during its two seasons in Vienna. The opening night was televised live throughout Europe and beyond, though needless to say the exception was the UK, where it was not shown for more than five years.

In restaging the work for Vienna, Ronconi, who had recently worked with Caballé on the Rome *Démophoön*, took the decision to reconstruct the production around the idea of 'La Caballé' playing the hostess Madame Cortese as herself. Accordingly, the paraphernalia of her Golden Lily Hotel, where the motley group of travellers wishing to attend the coronation of Charles X in Reims Cathedral are all staying before the last stage of their journey, was littered with joky references to Caballé the Diva. Her first entrance on stage was greeted by languid youths who rushed from the wings and were duly rewarded with autographs over which they swooned. The hotel linen was brought on for her inspection, the sheets turning out to have enormous ten times-life-size publicity photographs of Caballé plastered all over them. The diva was directed to deliver her opening aria, 'Di vaghi raggi adorno', with one such sheet draped over her shoulder, executing a little bump-and-grind routine the while. For the cabaletta, she repaired to a cash register thoughtfully attached to her personal sedan and barked out instructions to her staff while furiously totting up the guests' accounts. And all this within the first ten minutes of the opera. What took so many members of the viewing audience by surprise was the overwhelming relish with which Caballé flung herself into the proceedings, including taking over the conducting of her colleagues in the complex finale to the fourteen-voiced 'Gran Pezzo Concertato' at the end of Act I.*

Throughout, although Madame Cortese is supposed to be Swiss, reference was made to Caballé's Spanishness, which extended from her Velasquez-style jet-black costume, replete with lace trimmings and mantilla, to her alarming outbreak of the castanets during Don Alvaro's contribution to the multinational celebrations forming the finale. By the end of the evening, at which Charles X and his coronation retinue materialized in the Staatsoper itself, the audience was punch-drunk with delight; and the subsequent six performances became one of the hottest tickets in the house's history, notwithstanding unprecedently high ticket prices. The last performance was on 3 February 1988 and the following day Montserrat returned home to Spain, where she would remain for the rest of the month giving concerts and recitals in Valencia, Bilbao, Mataró and Malaga, as well as filming both in Madrid and Barcelona for Spanish television.

On 27 February, amidst a blaze of media publicity, José Carreras returned to his native Barcelona, having left the hospital in Seattle where he had been undergoing agonizing treatment for the replacement of his own irradiated bone marrow. Caballé was among the very first to greet him on his arrival, although she, like everyone else, found their joy in

---

* In fact, the end of Act II, given that – notwithstanding the performance protocol in front of royalty in 1825 – Rossini's musical structure is clearly in three Acts.

seeing the tenor again mitigated by his appearance, which bore all-too-evident signs of the ordeal through which he had been. And at this stage, however keen people may have been to know how Carreras' voice might – or might not – have withstood months of treatment, no one actually asked: it was enough that he himself had survived.

Almost immediately, Caballé was back on her travels, first to Munich where she was required to do some filming for ZDF as part of a forthcoming documentary devoted to her, and then on to London, where she recorded several more tracks with Freddie Mercury for the *Barcelona* album. More recitals back in Spain followed before she departed for Madrid on 6 April to rehearse a new production by Hugo de Ana of *Ermione*, designed by the director. Fine as the Pesaro production had been, this newly conceived Madrid staging was on an altogether higher level, with some of the most striking stage pictures ever seen in the Spanish capital. The only survivor of the 1987 cast apart from Montserrat in the title-role was Chris Merritt as Pirro: Margarita Zimmermann sang Andromaca, Dalmacio Gonzalez, Oreste, with Justin Lavender as Pilade. And the fervent, impassioned conducting of Gustav Kuhn in Pesaro yielded to the more phlegmatic pulse of Alberto Zedda. (Kuhn had been the intended conductor, but was unfortunately unavailable.) In the extended passages of heroic declamation, Caballé's voice rang out freely and was clearly unimpaired. She also did her best to involve herself wholeheartedly in the stage drama up to and including the decision to replace Rossini's swooning heroine at the end with a full-blooded suicide in keeping with Racine's original.

The Madrilenan public manifested nothing but enthusiasm for the performances, the third and fourth of which framed a homage to Caballé in celebration of the silver anniversary of her début in Madrid. Unlike the comparable event the year before in Barcelona, Caballé was not expected to provide all the singing herself this time. In an extended first half, she was serenaded by colleagues including Giuseppe di Stefano in a Tosti aria, Fedora Barbieri singing Mistress Quickly's 'Reverenza' from *Falstaff*, Ileana Cotrubas in the 'Mirror' aria from Massenet's *Thaïs*, and Chris Merritt in arias from *Guglielmo Tell* and *La fille du régiment*. Only in the second half did the diva sing for her supper, with a series of Spanish songs fleshed out with arias by Mozart, Pacini and Rossini.

Immediately following the run of *Ermione*s in Madrid, Caballé departed for Naples, where she gave a further six performances at the Teatro San Carlo in the original Pesaro production from 1987, with yet another new Andromaca in the shape of Kathleen Kuhlmann, and Douglas Ahlstedt as Oreste. One of Carlos Caballé's newest artists, Luca Canonici – who had substituted at short notice for the stricken Carreras in the film of *La bohème* the previous year – undertook the small but significant tenor role of Pilade. Montserrat remembers listening to him from the wings of the theatre and thinking to herself, 'What a voice! He sounds just like the young Pavarotti.' Just a few days after the last performance on 18 May 1988 she departed once again for America where, in the space of just six days, she performed in Costa Mesa, San Francisco and Los Angeles, before departing for surely the most exotic venue in which even she had ever performed: the Forbidden City of Beijing (formerly Peking). The concert hall there, otherwise known as the Great Hall of the People, holds a staggering 10,000 spectators. The event had been organized by the Association for the Upkeep of the Great Wall of China, and the performance, which also involved contributions from Mireille Matthieu and Maya Plisetskaya, was televised live in China under the title *The Return of Marco Polo*. Caballé, the only artist to perform three items on the programme, was described as 'one of the greatest artists and most important cultural icons of our time'. Her contribution comprised 'Casta diva', Pablo Casals' 'Cant dels Ocells' ('Song of the Birds') and, appropriately and one supposes inevitably, Turandot's 'In questa Reggia', performed in the costume designed for her in the 1981 Paris production. As with all these gala benefits, she accepted no fee, viewing her work in the broader context of forging stronger political and cultural links between nations. Her success was such that she was immediately invited to return the following year in order to give two solo recitals in the city. And in the interim, a ceremonial plaque bearing her name was set into the Great Wall by decree of the People's Republic of China.

In mid-June she spent several days at home in Barcelona filming a documentary for French television. This nearly two-hour marathon formed part of Jacques Chancel's on-going series *Le Grand Echiquier* and featured a number of musical items recorded before an invited audience in the Palau de la Música, as well as an extended interview – in French – with Caballé. This two-way discourse was enlivened by one of the very first appearances on television of José Carreras since his return from Seattle. Clearly moved, the tenor told at length of the debt he felt he owed both Montserrat and her brother, and went on to make a very public promise: in response to Chancel's question as to when he would return to the stage, Carreras simply replied that he did not know at that time when this would happen, but that when it did, it would be in partnership with Montserrat. In his own words, 'When you have come as close to the edge as I have, you cannot play with the sheep any more: you have to run with the lions.'

After some long-overdue holiday spent on the farm, Caballé took part in her brother Carlos's second International Festival at the Castle of Peralada. The opening concert on 15 July was scheduled to have been a gala entitled 'The Garcia Sisters: Maria Malibran and Pauline Viardot' at which Montserrat and Marilyn Horne would have tackled the warhorses from their illustrious nineteenth-century predecessors' repertory. Unfortunately Horne was ill, abandoning her entire European tour, and the much-amended programme took place, incongruously enough, with Luca Canonici as Horne's replacement. Later that month, following two performances of Mozart's *Requiem* given back in Barcelona, Caballé returned to Peralada in order to form one of the 'Quintet Vocal de Cataluña' which, with some additions and young professional soloists, was due to give a benefit gala performance of Rossini's *Petite messe solennelle* in the original instrumentation. Then, following a brief excursion to Verona in order to take part in yet another fund-raising gala – this time the inaugural benefit for José Carreras' newly formed Leukæmia Foundation – it was back to Peralada in order to rehearse for a staged production of Purcell's *Dido and Aeneas*, in which Caballé sang the role of the Carthaginian Queen for the first time. In one sense it was just bad luck that Montserrat should have done so in the context of an otherwise wholly English team of singers, musicians – the English Bach Festival Baroque Orchestra and Chorus – and producers. Two prospective biographers innocently inquired of Caballé in what language she was performing her role, only to be answered with withering scorn: 'You do not know your own language?!' In the embarrassed silence that followed, the essential truth – at least for this singer – of the dictum *prima la musica, dopo le parole* struck home.

Caballé's next port of call was Dubrovnik in the then Yugoslavia. On this first visit she renewed her acquaintance with the eminent (if controversial) pianist Ivo Pogorelich, and enjoyed such a personal success with the Croatian audience that, as in Beijing, she was immediately re-invited. After a handful of recitals in Spain, including Pamplona and Trujillo, Caballé returned to France where she was due to perform in what was effectively the world première of Bizet's cantata *Clovis et Clotilde*, which the young composer had written in 1857 while still a student at the Paris Conservatoire as his attempt – which was successful – to secure the much-coveted Prix de Rome. The generic set text, of the usual formulaic banality that had so exasperated Berlioz, at least offered a variant on the usual single soloist. Here Clovis, King of the Franks, is converted to Christianity in the fifth century and is impersonated by a tenor, whilst his consort, Clotilde, enjoys two passages of fiery declamation which frame a very beautiful, somewhat Gounodesque prayer. The two performances took place on consecutive evenings in Soissons Cathedral, with the Orchestre National de Lille under Jean-Claude Casadesus (who had discovered the manuscript in the Bibliothèque Nationale) and Gérard Garino as Clovis. The whole affair was treated as a media event in France, with a live radio relay of the second performance on 17 September and cameras from both satellite television and FR3 in attendance. The work had already been recorded by Erato the preceding week back in Lille, a level of overkill which this slight piece hardly merited.

Unfortunately, Caballé took away rather more of a souvenir from this experience than simply the appearance of the cathedral's outstanding architecture: just a few hours after eating some fish at a formal reception dinner given by the Mayor of Soissons, she became nauseous and dizzy. Food poisoning was diagnosed, and the soprano was confined to bed back in Barcelona for the rest of the month. She soon recovered from the immediate symptoms but in the midst of all this she had to commence rehearsals for one of the starriest galas in which she had ever appeared. Entitled 'La Nit', 'the Night' had been planned as the formal celebration of Barcelona's selection as the Olympic city. That day the Olympic flag had been passed on from Seoul to the holders-designate, and the gala sought not only to raise funds for the forthcoming Games but also to inaugurate a four-year 'Cultural Olympiad' running up to the Games themselves.

Caballé kicked off with the un-Toscaninied version of Verdi's 'Inno delle nazioni', originally written for the Great Exhibition in London in 1851, accompanied by the augmented chorus and orchestra of the Liceo spread out on the terraces halfway up the mountain of Montjuic. The enormous, elaborately lit fountain formed the centrepiece, and the artists, among them Dionne Warwick, Rudolf Nureyev, Spandau Ballet and José Carreras as well as Montserrat and Freddie Mercury, played to the 40,000-strong audience, including King Juan Carlos and Queen Sofia, ranged down the length of the fountain-lined approach route from the Plaza d'España. The culmination of the event was to have been the first public rendition in situ of 'Barcelona', sung by Caballé and Mercury, with a fine sense of timing given that the album was to be released throughout Europe the following week. Unfortunately, Freddie got cold feet, later pleading inadequate rehearsal time, and insisted on miming to a playback, at which he was considerably more adroit than Montserrat. The British press contingent pounced on this and indulged in some public scoffing at the singers' expense. They even went so far as to report that the audience was disappointed, which was unlikely since most of them remained unaware of the deception. In any event, a different measure of the evening's worth can be gauged from the fact that less than three months later the film of 'La Nit' won a gold medal in New York as Music Video of the Year. Caballé was clear about the attractions performing such music held for her:

> When I sing opera my voice is an instrument in the hands of the composer, so all my life my voice had been directed in very, shall we say, disciplined ways. It has big possibilities, but it has always been at the service of something else. Now for the first time ever I feel free. This has liberated my voice.

It certainly liberated her reputation: by the end of the month as both the single of 'Barcelona' and the full-length LP had been released virtually worldwide, Caballé watched with delight as they rapidly climbed the various international hit parades. In Britain, the single peaked at number seven in the pop charts shortly before Christmas; and in Spain, not surprisingly, went straight to the top. Two days after 'La Nit' Caballé came to London at Polydor's behest to take part in the UK launch of her and Freddie's disc. This took place in the Crush Bar of the Royal Opera House, and was widely reported by the British press – musical and otherwise – in the days that followed. Caballé was now set to join that handful of opera singers whose fame extends far beyond the confines of opera.

CHAPTER FOURTEEN

1988–1990: The Last of the Liceo

After a hectic ten days spent promoting the new *Barcelona* album, Caballé returned to Spain in order to prepare for the Royal Gala opening of the newly completed Auditorio Nacional in Madrid. The decision had been taken to commence not with the expected opera gala, but with a single work: Manuel de Falla's unfinished choral cantata, *Atlántida*. Of course, Caballé was no stranger to this work, having first sung it in Geneva – albeit in Italian – under Ernest Ansermet in 1963. On that occasion she had sung both the female roles in the work, which comprise the long arias in Parts I and III for Pirene and Isabella respectively. At this Madrid performance, however, Teresa Berganza sang Pirene, leaving Caballé to incarnate the Spanish queen. This performance inaugurated a week of furious activity in the new building, which comprised not only the main Berlin Philharmonie-style concert hall but also a smaller auditorium, holding approximately 400, for chamber ensembles. It was in the latter that Caballé, for the one and only time in her career, held an extended series of master-classes, which ran from 22 to 27 October 1988. She had refused all previous requests to conduct such classes, reasoning that they were more of a forum for ageing singers to score points off the impressionable young than a serious form of teaching. There was also her belief that matters of true musicality, such as interpretive response, cannot be taught.

However, the National Institute for Stage Arts and Music (a subdivision of the Ministry of Culture) had been arranging for some time to present an entire series of master-classes by the most eminent Spanish musicians. They were determined that Caballé should be the very first and so, in deference to the wishes of the project's patron, Queen Sofia, Montserrat had consented. As usual, she had done so on her own terms: entrance among those wishing to be participants was under no circumstances to be restricted to young career singers; she would not discuss any questions of interpretation; she would need a set of anatomical slides to be made up; she would introduce each of the six open-ended sessions by giving a lecture on the matters of technique to be covered; and she would accept no fee.

Those who arrived on the morning of 22 October expecting the kind of master-class which spends half an hour explaining the shades of meaning to be derived from different pronunciations of the word 'Blau' must have been pole-axed. Instead, microphone in hand, the soprano stood in front of a screen with a diagram of the human anatomy projected upon it and proceeded to give a 'naming of parts' as a preface to describing their individual functions and how they worked together as a whole. The lecture was entitled 'La Arquitectura del Sonido' ('The Architecture of Sound') and dealt at length with the basic nuts and bolts of voice production:

> Producing a sound is analogous to building a house: the foundations of both are hidden underground. A sound is built on an abdominal base which works as a foundation. Arising from ground level (the diaphragm), the sound takes on the architectural shape or style that one wishes to give it. The sound may be airy, as with the slender vaults of Gothic architecture or broad and strong as in Romanesque, based simply on our ability to employ the lower musculature (the foundations) and manifest a particular style – a mission entrusted to the diaphragm. It may seem odd to start with this description . . . [But] I personally think that through achieving a proper knowledge of ourselves and our physiology, we may be able to control certain parts of our own anatomy that are very important for singing, and allow us to achieve the sound we desire.

There followed an erudite analysis of specific muscles – the sternum-cleoid-mastoid was a real star turn – before the various participants were selected at random from the audience. Immediately, it became obvious that one of Montserrat's cherished concepts in theory – that anybody who had wanted to participate could do so – was awkward in practice, since it pitched amateurs of middling years and the simply star-struck up against highly talented young students and professionals. There was a minor scene when a young girl who had sung in an excruciatingly pure *voce bianca* – a vibrato-less hoot – burst into tears following Caballé's unarguable observation that such a voice had very restricted application in the opera house. The girl became almost hysterical, at which point a man in the audience, evidently her teacher, stood up and sprang vociferously to her defence. In this difficult situation, Caballé remained completely calm, merely pointing out that hers was not – as she had been accused – a mere personal prejudice against the voice type: it simply could not be relied upon for either power of projection or accuracy of intonation, especially in large halls. By this time the already uncomfortable audience was starting to voice its displeasure at this partisan interruption, whilst a few others rallied to offer support.

But the atmosphere was rapidly dispelled by the jocular interplay between Caballé and an American soprano who attempted, of all things, Adriana's 'Io son l'umile ancella'. In this multinational gathering their discussions were conducted in English, and Caballé began her habitual list of questions by saying, 'Well there are not many people here who speak English, I think, so you can tell me one woman to another, how old you are?'

'Forty-five.'

'Aha, forty-five, that is a wonderful age. I am fifty-five, a more wonderful age!'

The lectures continued under such headings as 'Breathing', 'Sound Formation', 'The Workings of the Larynx,* 'How to Emit Sound through the Controlled Emission of Air' and 'Singing as the Maximum Application of Diaphragmatic Development'. Throughout, Montserrat would demonstrate with the particular participants the points she was trying to make.

A young hopeful gave a wobbly account of Manon's 'Adieu, notre petite table', which put Caballé on her technical mettle. She had the girl sing vocalizes and stalked around her, examining her posture and feeling her musculature in action. Unexpectedly, she grabbed the girl's hand, saying, 'I am a big woman, but even so feel this' and proceeded to clasp the hand to her own abdomen. Caballé then emitted a loud clear note and said, 'Can you feel what happened?' The girl, much taken aback, nodded her assent, but her subsequent singing gave no hint of this, whereupon Caballé had her sing a simple middle A, *mezzo-forte*, for as long as she could sustain. The voice came and went in intensity and focus until Montserrat, who had been thoughtfully positioning a clenched fist at various points around the girl's abdomen, suddenly pushed hard and deep, to the accompaniment of the first truly steady note the girl had uttered. The audience gasped in amazement. Very few of those present had recognized the extent to which singing is a physical process, susceptible to manipulation at the hands of a master. Caballé, surprised at the audience's reaction, explained that she had often tried this approach, even with illustrious colleagues.

---

* This lecture was such a success that Caballé was invited by the professor of laryngology at the University of Madrid's medical school to lecture his students. After some hesitation, she declined.

And then there were the spectacular successes: Ismael Pons, for one, a young Spanish baritone who gave a distinguished account of 'Eri tu' from *Un ballo in maschera*; and Isabel Rey who, though clearly nervous, sang an immaculate 'Ah, non credea mirarti' from *La sonnambula*. By the end of the week, Rey was under contract to Carlos Caballé. In all, everybody had had a good time: there had been laughter, tears, the occasional drama, a wealth of insight and the overwhelming impression of Caballé, the supreme communicator, in her element. Many people observed that when (or if) she chose to retire, a ready-made career as chat show hostess lay before her.

Further proof of this proposition was on offer little more than a week later, when on 7 November Caballé returned to Paris for another recital at Pierre Bergé's Théâtre de l'Athénée. For the first time in public, she wore glasses, a fact to which she made reference at the end when sorting through tracts of sheet-music in order to select her encores: 'At my age, I have no choice.' A small bouquet of flowers whizzed through the air and landed at the foot of her music-stand. She peered over the top of her glasses and instructed the flowers to stay put for a moment; then, having selected her encore and given the music to Zanetti, she executed a slow motion arabesque, picking the flowers up with the very tips of her fingers. To the delight of the audience, she went on to announce: 'My husband once told me a very beautiful thing, so I always act upon it – flowers are like women: one should never leave them lying on the ground.' And after the seventh and final encore, most of those present immediately trooped backstage, where in the dilapidated corridors of the theatre the diva proceeded to hold court for longer than it had taken her to give the actual recital programme.

Not that there was anything unusual in this these days. Her fame, and the special regard in which she is held by her audiences, ensure that she is at least as much in demand for her personality as she could ever be for her singing. The rituals of her informally introduced encores bring the first tangible contact in the course of any evening with Caballé the person as opposed to Caballé the soprano; and this would reach its fruition in the scenes backstage, where some would come to see the possessor of one of the greatest voices of the twentieth century, but most to have a brief reunion with Montsy. Of course, this applies to a specialized audience, the kind that turns out to concerts or recitals. The non-opera-going public was generally unaware of Caballé's existence and would probably have remained so had it not been for the over-whelming international success of her collaboration with Freddie Mercury.

*   *   *

At the end of 1988, Caballé performed two of her favourite roles: in the space of three concert performances given in Stockholm, Göteborg and Copenhagen, she sang *Semiramide*; and on 27 December she sang the first of five performances of *Salome* at the Liceo. The rehearsals for this new production had been underway since mid-month and had already been the subject of a certain amount of press speculation. As we have seen, Montserrat had decided to sing this role on stage one more time as a result of the pleasurable experience she had had with the Robert Wilson staging at La Scala the previous year, and had been assured by the Liceo authorities that the Milanese *mise-en-scène* would be brought in for her. In the event, it would seem that they took fright at the rehearsal demands and costs involved, and decided instead that it would be cheaper and certainly more expedient to mount their own production. The Liceo administration had latterly been undergoing profound changes: the theatre had just appointed an Austrian conductor, Uwe Mund, as music director and had imported from Cologne an academic and critic, Albin Hänseroth, to act in an advisory capacity concerning both repertory and casting. Luis Andreu remained artistic administrator for the time being before his departure to look after the affairs of the new opera house in Seville. Hänseroth subsequently took over this position at the beginning of the 1989–90 season.

Having taken the decision to dispense with the Wilson staging – an unwelcome piece of news which initially displeased Caballé greatly – the theatre tried to procure a staging at least similar in spirit. Luis Andreu would appear to have deputed responsibility for resolving this problem to Dr Hänseroth, who turned to his familiar contacts in Cologne. As a result, the resident choreographer at the opera house, Jochen Ulrich, was appointed to take on the task. He decided, hardly surprisingly given his *métier*, to treat the work pretty much as a ballet, with all the principal singers doubled by dancers. This would at least obviate all problems concerning the diva and the Dance of the Seven Veils. But what had seemed novel and intriguing at the discussion stage when Caballé had first seen Katrin Kegler's designs, turned into a nightmare from the soprano's point of view once the set was actually built. At the first stage rehearsal, she discovered to her horror that she was expected to perform the role perched on top of a five-metre-high and very rickety tower, wearing a dress which, fastened around her shoulders, billowed down to the floor and spread out to form the whole of the stage-cloth. Since this object was forever being made to flap around by the dancers who moved in and out of its folds, not only were clouds of stage dust being fanned straight up into the soprano's face, but the movements also made the narrow tower on which she stood sway precariously. Then there was the matter of the moon, an enormous disc which in the original model had been at the back of the stage, behind the soprano, but which had now been hung from the fly-tower right in front of her. This left her singing her opening lines straight into a lump of cardboard just feet from her face, with no view of the conductor and choked by swirling dust.

There followed what would in diplomatic circles be termed a full and frank exchange of views. But the solutions available were strictly limited: one, to water the floor cloth to keep the dust down, was counter-productive, since this only served to increase the cloth's weight and thereby the soprano's storm-tossed tribulations at the top of her tower. Caballé ended the last stage rehearsal before the dress rehearsal in tears of both rage and frustration. She had managed to persuade the director to allow her to sing the closing scene at stage-floor level, which meant that her supporting tower sank slowly into the ground – albeit none too smoothly – after the Baptist's head had been delivered. This also gave her the opportunity at last to rid herself of the stage-cloth costume and to appear in a startling blood-red shift which came from her own wardrobe. But the need to deliver her great paean of love to John's head while dragging around the bundled-up floor-cloth had left her utterly dispirited, as had Herr Mund's conducting.

Both the local and national press had printed pages of polemic concerning the progress of the production before it had even opened. But the whole affair took on a new dimension when, with only three days to go, Caballé herself gave an interview expressing her dissatisfaction with the production. This was seized upon by the media as a 'denuncia' and reprinted *ad infinitum*. Meanwhile, Herr Ulrich held a press conference, together with the conductor and all the dancers (though – surely significantly – none of the singers) in which he defended both his production and his methods. In this highly charged atmosphere, the dress rehearsal took place before a restricted audience who saw Caballé stalk out of the theatre without so much as a word. In retrospect, it is clear that at this point she should have cancelled, and was indeed advised to do so by many of those closest to her. But, as she has always maintained, though she may have withdrawn from performances in other places for all manner of different reasons, she never cancelled in Barcelona. And although it would have been relatively easy to have pleaded indisposition, it was the case that over the previous two years she had been cancelling very rarely and then only under medical duress. She would just have to go through with it.

The atmosphere on the opening night was tense in the extreme: very few productions reach the stage with this degree of adverse and controversial pre-publicity. There had even been a dispute about the curtain calls, with Caballé minded to bring on stage neither the conductor nor the producer as expected. Instead, she said to her dancing counterpart, Darie Cardyn, 'Ulrich is your choreographer, you bring him on.' And when she did, it was to the accompaniment of stentorian booing from all parts of the house, which, despite the director's previously professed indifference to the public's response, left him ashen-faced and clearly unnerved. The last performance took place on 8 January 1989, the day after Caballé had returned from performing at the Gala in Madrid celebrating Spain's first Presidency of the European Community, and was scheduled to be televised live. She discovered, more or less by accident, that this would necessitate a complete reblocking of the final scene, since the cameras found it impossible to get a good close-up of the Baptist's head in its silver salver, perched as it was too high on the bundled floor-cloth. Caballé was requested to perform the scene lying flat on the floor with the head in front of her. In the event, she complied, and thus fortuitously gave the viewing audience a clear indication of how she had felt about the production. When, arranging the salver in front of her the better to savour Salome's prize, she chanced to lean with her elbows on either edge; the dish immediately broke in half, emitting a crack like a rifle shot. What was meant to be silver was revealed to be no more than a papier-mâché prop. A spasm of rage crossed Caballé's face and an audience of millions witnessed the diva pound the wretched object into fragments with her bare fists, before lifting the head aloft in eye-flashing triumph.

With the exception of two brief excursions at the end of January 1989 – one to Los Angeles in order to give a recital in the Dorothy Chandler Pavilion and the other to Amsterdam for a joint opera concert in the Concertgebouw with Jaime Aragall – the rest of that month and the whole of February/early March was taken up with what was arguably the greatest musical challenge of Caballé's career: her first performances of Isolde. She had been toying with the idea for many years, encouraged, as we have seen, by conductors such as Alain Lombard, James Levine and Zubin Mehta. Indeed, had it not been for Lombard's precipitate departure from the Opéra du Rhin in 1980, it is more than likely that the role would have been in Caballé's repertory throughout the decade. In the event, it was only now that she engineered the opportunity to sing it. Her reasoning seems clear enough: now or never. She was fifty-five, in the process of progressively withdrawing from stage commitments on the wider international scene, and yet had never sung this last, most testing of her five favourite roles.* As she herself said in a

---

* The others being Salome, Violetta, Norma and Semiramide.

press interview before the opening night, 'I am not afraid to die singing Isolde.' The venue was a foregone conclusion; where else would she sing her first Isoldes other than at her home house, the Liceo? For the occasion, a new production was to be mounted by the team responsible for the previous season's *Mefistofele*, Emilio Sagi and Toni Businger. And the cast was first-rate, with René Kollo as Tristan, Brigitte Fassbaender as Brangäne, Franz Grundheber as Kurwenal and Matti Salminen as King Mark, conducted by Peter Schneider.

Caballé had prepared Isolde thoroughly but, of course, found herself pitted against much more seasoned colleagues, all of whom had learned the hard way how to deal with the specific problems of Wagnerian performance. In particular, they had developed the crucial art of pacing themselves throughout Wagner's extended structures. In agreement with the conductor, Montserrat sang the dress rehearsal two days before the first night in full voice throughout, while her colleagues mostly marked. Her account of Act I was thrilling, full-voiced and imperious and went a long way towards recalling her own idol in the role, Kirsten Flagstad, though without the latter's marmoreal coolness. This Isolde was unmistakably a woman in an evil temper. Her colleagues, Kollo in particular, were amazed that with so little time to go before the opening night she had been so prepared to give it her all.

Unfortunately, Caballé's prodigious vocal expenditure at the dress rehearsal proved unwise: rather than living off her vocal interest, she had dug a little too deep into her capital. This was evident on the opening night – 22 February – where the first Act, though fine, did not quite recapture the fire of two days previously. Occasional passages in the – somewhat cut – second Act found Caballé labouring hard; and by the 'Liebestod' she was in evident vocal difficulty. She had obviously not yet mustered the necessary stamina to sustain her through such a role. Typically, she learned from this mistake, pacing herself better at the subsequent performances – themselves more considerately spaced at four day intervals – but at a certain cost to dramatic voltage in Act I.

Although there was no *a priori* reason why Caballé should not tackle the role of Isolde, undoubtedly she should have done so earlier in her career. Even so, the reviews of the Spanish press were enthusiastic. Roger Alier, writing in *La Vanguardia*, noted:

In the first Act, Caballé demonstrated that she was in excellent vocal form, phrasing with great strength, with perfectly even emission, and coping with the musical climaxes without resorting to screaming or falling prey to vocal deficiencies . . . The second Act was exquisitely lyrical as she brought the role to life with great sensitivity. In the third, however, we were perhaps expecting a little more from the 'Liebestod' which, although notable, was afflicted here and there with vocal unsteadiness, resulting in a level of accomplishment that did not quite match what could have been . . .[1]

This *Tristan und Isolde* was given six performances through to mid-March, though Caballé's concentration was compromised at the third by the fact that her father had been rushed to hospital that afternoon. Fortunately, it turned out to be nothing serious, and he was discharged within a day or so. The whole production was due to be repeated two months later in Madrid at the Teatro de la Zarzuela, whose restrictions of stage space had largely determined the static, boxy nature of the sets, if not the static, boxy production going on within them. But at least this production did not interfere with the meaning of the work or the ability of the singers to convey it. In between these two bouts of *Tristan*, Caballé returned to North America at the end of March and gave recitals in Miami, Atlanta and New York. The New York recital took place not in Carnegie Hall, but as part of 'The Great Performers' series in Avery Fisher Hall, and continued a trend whereby Caballé recitals are treated at least as much as a social phenomenon as a musical event. The reviewer in the *Daily News* captured the essence of the occasion:

. . . a concert by the soprano Montserrat Caballé has much in common with a showing of *The Rocky Horror Picture Show*. In both there are understood protocols, and both the performer and audience know their roles to perfection . . . As is always the case with Caballé, the real show starts with the encores. While endless waves of warmth and love flow to and from the stage, she talks to her audience, jokes, giggles and sings magnificently. She has lost nothing over the years: her *pianissimo* floated, her low notes were rich, the middle range glorious, her high shimmering. Her projected emotions were like Callas and she sang like a goddess . . . The house cheered, but it is quite likely that no one enjoys a Caballé concert more than the soprano herself.[2]

After a handful of miscellaneous recitals in Spain and France in mid-April, Caballé returned as promised the previous year to Beijing, where this time she gave two solo recitals, with Zanetti accompanying, on 27 and 29 April. She had taken the trouble to learn Mandarin phonetically in order to sing three authentic Chinese art songs as encores. President Pujol was in attendance as part of the plan to foster closer links between China and Cataluña. But whatever political gains might have been made on either side were almost immediately swept away: Caballé had arrived to discover a heady atmosphere of freedom and desire for democracy sweeping through the capital, and personally observed one of the many peaceful demonstrations that were becoming a daily occurrence in Tiananmen Square. Within a matter of days, the world was stunned at the ferocity with which this movement was brutally suppressed in the space of one night as the last Communist bastion slammed the door shut.

Two days after her return from China, Caballé departed for Madrid in order to rehearse the revival of *Tristan*, which was to be given five performances between 10 and 22 May. There were two major cast changes: Richard Versalle, a Canadian tenor, replaced Kollo; and Kurt Moll sang King Mark instead of Salminen. The penultimate performance on the 19th was televised live in Spain, and gives a clear impression at this, Caballé's tenth public performance of the role, of the extent to which she had mastered its demands. Isolde's curse in Act I rises to great heights of declamatory fervour and the voice rings out clearly above and beyond the orchestra. Only the Irish Princess's spiteful sarcasm escapes her, as it has escaped virtually all other exponents of the role, with the possible exceptions of Olive Fremstad (by repute) and Birgit Nilsson (on the evidence of records). The love duet goes especially well, the ample, weather-beaten frame of the tenor and his voice – much more focused than that of Kollo – blending well with the soprano. We even get a securely turned account of the *Liebestod*, though the concluding F# on 'Lust' – approached from an impossibly awkward interval and arriving plumb on the break in most sopranos' voices between middle and head register – is a little suspect. Otherwise, there is nothing here to suggest either that the soprano was operating at less than fully fit capacity or that the role would not become one of the mainstays of her repertory. It is very surprising, then, to note that the last performance in Madrid, on 22 May 1989, was also the last occasion to date on which Caballé sang Isolde. Doubtless this was principally due to the fact that no one asked her: she herself was perfectly prepared to take on the challenge again, preferably in more auspicious surroundings. But the major international houses simply did not think of her in connection with this kind of repertory – indeed, apart from her very earliest years in Basel and Bremen, she barely sang any Wagner on stage outside Spain, and in this particular instance no further opportunity arose.

Whether or not she would have made a world-beating Isolde is open to conjecture. But what is beyond dispute is that she must be the only soprano who has passed within the space of three days from the rigours of Wagner to the runaround of Rossini. On 26 May, she was back in Vienna for the all-star revival of *Il viaggio a Reims*. In fact, she had missed the opening night, which was the day after her last *Tristan*, explaining to Claudio Abbado, who had done his best to persuade her to come and sing anyway, that it was simply impossible. In the event, she was replaced at this one performance by the young Brigitte Poschner-Klebel, who sang well but not surprisingly left a void at the heart of the production. When Caballé finally appeared on the stage at the Staatsoper on the 26th it was to a burst of applause from the audience, not a common occurrence among the sophisticated Viennese. As Abbado said: 'She is a fine artist, quite one of the most important with whom I have ever worked. We have not performed together a great deal, but what work we have done has, I think, been truly memorable.'

Depending upon one's attitude to Ronconi's production, things had got even better (or worse) than the year before. One of the harpsichord players slid a 'whoopee' cushion under Cecilia Gasdia, whose improvised Roman poetess, Corinna, thereby improvised a sound never previously heard in the auditorium. Sam Ramey and Ruggero Raimondi 'corpsed' each other in their one brief dialogue, leaving the American bass spluttering to the audience, 'Ich bin nur ein Opernsänger!' When Montserrat made her second entrance, she was hidden from the audience by a crimson golf umbrella, corpsing everyone else on stage, then turning to reveal that she was wearing a green fright wig studded with white bows. It was at these performances that the text of the cabaletta finale to Act II was rewritten by the singers and projected on to a screen behind them, complete with bouncing ball, in which they apostrophized Abbado himself, thanking the conductor for having them all back. And the business concerning the various characters' suggestions at the end of the opera for the subject-matter of Corinna's final improvisation was hijacked by Enzo Dara's enthusiastic scream of 'Pappatacci!'*

The two (of three) performances in which Montserrat sang received an even noisier and prolonged ovation than the year before: that of the last night, 28 May, went on for over forty minutes, threatening to hijack the house record belonging to a Domingo/Kleiber *Otello*. Afterwards, the artists were besieged for autographs outside the stage door: Caballé in particular seemed to have attracted an enormous band of unusually young devotees. With characteristic directness, she inquired what had brought them to the opera house: the response was 'We are fans of Freddie Mercury, and we wanted to hear the woman who screams so high on "Barcelona".' Abbado, who throughout these performances invariably chaperoned Montserrat in person, turned to her and said, 'It's a good job we weren't playing *Parsifal*.' By the time the production

* The cod ritual undergone by Mustafà in the second Act of *L'Italiana in Algeri*, in which Dara, Lopardo and Raimondi had all recently sung at the Staatsoper.

and cast reached Tokyo five months later, things had got even worse (or better) as each member assiduously packed an entire skip of personal props with which to astonish and upstage each other, though what the Japanese made of it all can only be imagined, given that the other works on the visiting Staatsoper's agenda included *Wozzeck* and *Parsifal*.

June provided no let-up in Montserrat's busy schedule: there were two revivals of *Clovis et Clotilde* to perform, in Mérignac and the Cathedral at St Denis, as well as recitals in Toulouse and Paris proper. It was at the latter in the Théâtre des Champs-Élysées that Caballé stopped singing half-way through a group of four Spanish songs, simply standing on stage peering intently out into the audience. After a puzzling pause, she walked forward with a smile and announced: 'I must wait a moment because there is a man in the front row who is changing his tape over.' The audience guffawed, though many must have shifted uneasily in their seats, given the remarkable number of people who were doing exactly the same. Eventually she leaned forward and inquired, 'Is it working? . . . You're sure? . . . *Eh bien!*' and continued to sing. Nor was this an affectation on the soprano's part, since she is always keen to learn who, from amongst her most assiduous fans, had managed to capture the best recording. The same attitude underpins her feelings towards commercially available pirate recordings where, unlike so many of her colleagues whose first response is to call their lawyers, her invariable reaction is to say, 'Really? That exists? Can you get me a copy?'

Certainly, there ought to have been enough in circulation of the concert performance of *Saffo* she gave in the Viennese Konzerthaus on 17 June, since the abiding memory of looking down from seats in the balcony was of myriad red and green flashing lights parked on people's laps throughout the stalls. Paradoxically, however, no recording has ever appeared, despite an Austrian Radio broadcast of the performance. Perhaps this is a reflection of Caballé's relatively laboured singing that night, though considerations of quality alone have not normally been known to deter pirates. In fact, the work could do with a decent commercial recording, and if this concert broadcast was scarcely ideal, it would nevertheless be a lot better than having nothing.

The month of July 1989 had for some time figured prominently in the diaries of many opera-lovers as offering – all in the context of one event – a number of 'firsts'. The occasion was the first opera festival to be held in the Roman amphitheatre at Mérida; Caballé was to sing the title-role in *Medea* for the first time in twelve years; and José Carreras would be singing Giasone for the first time, in the process giving his first performances in a stage role since his recovery from leukæmia. On paper, then, the whole proposition was irresistible. But what no one had properly taken into account were the climatic conditions. Mérida – known in Roman times as Augusta Emerita – is a small town in the southern Spanish province of Extremadura. It had been built originally in the second century as one vast retirement home for the legionnaires and foot soldiers, and though little known, remains to this day the most complete example of Roman town-planning outside Italy. At the heart of the surviving monuments – which also include aqueducts and temples – is what one might term the town's leisure complex: two vast arenas sitting side by side, one of 14,000 and the other of 6000 capacity. The latter auditorium is of supreme architectural significance in that the actual Roman proscenium survives virtually intact, whereas those of comparable amphitheatres (such as Verona and Orange) have long since vanished. It must have seemed a wonderful idea to stage *Medea* there, and to have Caballé and Carreras as its stars.

But with an average mid-afternoon temperature of 45°C (113°F) life was virtually impossible for all those who made the journey, not least the singers. The blistering, bone-dry heat left even the fully fit prostrate; the effect on the soprano and the tenor can therefore be imagined. Caballé suffered a fainting fit during rehearsals and became a virtual prisoner in the cool, cloistered environment of the converted convent in which she was staying. But, of course, this was a media event, particularly in Spain, and the last performance – on 29 July – was due to be televised live. There was no real place to hide. Another problem emerged when it was discovered that until late-evening, one could fry an egg on the stone seating of the arena. In consequence the entire project became a nocturnal affair, with performances put back to commence at 11 p.m. and the daily routine adjusted accordingly. But even under these inauspicious circumstances, the three performances met with tremendous success, though partisan feeling and sheer relief at seeing Carreras back on stage no doubt played their part in this.

Certainly Caballé flung herself into the dramatic demands of the role with a vengeance, easily outstripping her more decorous portrayal at the Liceo in 1976. On the other hand, for all the increase in volume and darkness of chest register, the earlier account was more effortlessly (and accurately) sung. The high notes in Mérida were gratingly hard-edged and the deliberately ferocious attack wearyingly overdone. Still, Montserrat felt she had drawn closer to her own ideal in Mérida, but without believing even then that she had fully conquered the role. She plans to sing Medea again, this time in the location of the original myth, from which she hopes to draw inspiration for the dramatic and musical demands of the role.

*   *   *

There was a single repeat performance of *Medea* to open the third Festival of the Castle at Peralada on 4 August 1989, after which Montserrat remained *in situ* in order to rehearse for yet another personal première, her first stage performances in Puccini's *Le Villi*. Two days later, she flew to Edinburgh where, on the 16th, she finally made her début at the Festival with a recital in the Usher Hall. However late a début this may have been, those present more than made up for it by piecing out the soprano's occasional imperfections with their thoughts, effectively willing her out of the severe and sombre stance which the administration had advised her to adopt in front of a reputedly hard-to-please audience. As the *Guardian* reported in an article entitled 'Cult of the Definitive Diva':

> In the second half [the audience] went progressively mad, the intake of breath after each song becoming a heavy sigh, the cheering louder and longer; they threw flowers, adored her misunderstanding with her accompanist in the first of the encores, and finally awarded her the standing ovation . . .[3]

The enthusiasm was such that afterwards, backstage, the Festival's then director, Frank Dunlop, was moved to observe that he had never witnessed scenes like it, least of all in Edinburgh: whoever this Caballé was, she had better come back soon.

The following morning she flew home to Barcelona in order to keep a very important date: her silver wedding anniversary. The actual date was 14 August 1989 but at that point Montserrat was in transit between Peralada, Barcelona, London and Edinburgh, so that the celebrations were held over until Friday 18th. They took place at Las Lloses, the farm at Ripoll, where a formal garden party had been laid out for the 150 guests. After drinks around the swimming pool, a number made the trek across to the nearby hill where, in the small votive chapel that Montserrat had had built back in 1973 as a thanks offering for her son's delivery from salmonella, she and her husband had their marriage resolemnized. Bernabé was so overcome with emotion he could scarcely utter the words: it was left to Montserrat to get both of them through it. The officiating priest evidently expected that Caballé would lead the singing of the hymnal, but she declined, preferring instead to blend into the acoustic background. After which, it was back to a sumptuous banquet, while uninvited paparazzi hovered in the middle distance, snapping away.

Montserrat's next major engagement took her back, after an absence of fifteen years, to Moscow, where on 5 September 1989 she appeared in a gala recital at the Bolshoi Theatre with José Carreras. This had been arranged for the benefit of the victims of the Armenian earthquake which had occurred in December 1988. The reception accorded to both artists was so intense that they were given police protection, since they were mobbed wherever they went. As two of the first opera singers to appear in the Russia of *perestroika* under Mikhail Gorbachev, both felt they had a particular responsibility to the Soviet public, which manifested itself in a series of encores that went on for more than an hour. The event was broadcast by Russian television on deferred relay later that evening, and additional proceeds were expected to be raised by subsequent screenings throughout Europe.

When they arrived back in Barcelona, it was immediately to begin rehearsals for the much-postponed world première of Leonardo Balada's Columbus opera, *Cristóbal Colón*, in which Carreras took the title-role and Caballé created Queen Isabella. Both parts had been written by the composer with their respective performers in mind, and thus it was that the singers found themselves with roles – particularly in Montserrat's case – that fitted like a glove. The opera had been commissioned in the mid-1980s with a view to celebrating the forthcoming Columbus quincentenary, and the libretto had been written by the famous Andalusian poet and playwright, Antonio Gala. The composer, a native of Cataluña, was best known for a previous opera, *Zapata*, which had been dedicated to Sherrill Milnes and whose music, originally abrasive, had recently undergone a post-modernist sweetening process, rather like Penderecki. All this meant that the work was painless to listen to and very confidently laid out for both voices and orchestra. The conductor was Theo Alcántara and the staging a no-expense-spared effort, directed by Tito Capobianco with designs by Eduardo Urculo and Mario Vanarelli, which set the whole of the action in and around an enormous revolving metal astrolabe.

The impossibly fragmented dramaturgy of the piece – much of it told in flashback when not actually mingling past, present and future simultaneously – had Caballé as Isabella appearing at various intervals. She was first to be heard explaining her desire to prioritize the reconquest of Granada above all colonial projects in an extended *arioso* in which she tells the importunate Colón that the decision to support his voyage of discovery will be made not by her but by a Royal Commission in Salamanca. She then returns after scenes of Columbus's interrogation to inform him that she cannot help: the successful Granada campaign has left her coffers exhausted. Columbus departs dejected, leaving Isabella to be upbraided by her husband, King Fernando, for her lack of vision. Thus persuaded, Columbus is resummoned before Isabella, who authorizes his trip, and the pair join in the inevitable duet.

Most of the second Act is set at sea and revolves around endless squabbles between the hero and his arch-rival Martín Alonso Pinzón, sung by Carlos Chausson. But in a further flashback, Columbus recalls Isabella's words of encouragement to him before his departure, and the Queen duly reappears to sing her third extended piece, full of soaring cantilena and the occasional burst of cautious coloratura. Her last appearance is in a surreal epilogue, which takes place after Columbus has sighted land, and in which all the characters of the drama are brought on stage, together with a chorus of Indians, to give thanks to the Creator and sing of their hope for humanity. This seems a quaint way of completely rewriting history in order to provide an unnecessary happy ending.

During the four performances of *Cristóbal Colón*, Caballé was still suffering from leg trouble and was visibly very cautious when negotiating the various different levels of the set, particularly a circular ramp which spun her slowly upstage. Even so, the opening night on 24 September found her in fine voice, making the most of the many opportunities given to her by Balada's tailor-made music, as did Carreras, whose voice rang out with virile power. All in all, it was quite a popular success, cemented by the live television relay which went some way towards allaying the press speculation concerning the allegedly astronomical scale of the artists' fees.

Within a few days Montserrat was en route to Vienna in order to fit in a few hectic last-minute rehearsals and, more importantly, select a whole new range of props and paraphernalia for the Staatsoper's tour of Japan, where *Il viaggio a Reims* was due to open on 21 October in the Bunka Kaikan in Tokyo for a sold-out run of four performances. The Japanese were thereby confronted by a stage full of the most expensive opera singers in the world, much of the time unable to sing for laughter at each other's activities.

Caballé's next major commitment was her annual Christmas show at the Liceo, which would have brought her tally of works performed there in 1989 to four had it not been for the fact that at the last minute the theatre decided to mount two performances of Casals' *El Pessebre* at the end of November, in which Montserrat agreed to sing, bringing the total to an unprecedented five. The fifth work was another rarity, Ottorino Respighi's *La fiamma*, which Caballé had originally agreed to perform having been told that the production and design were to be entrusted to Piero Faggioni. Notwithstanding the débâcle in Vienna of their *Norma* in 1977, she had always held the Italian director in high regard, and particularly looked forward to working with him once again in a work whose historical setting, not to mention the religio-supernatural elements, demands the eye of an expert scenographer. The text by Respighi's habitual collaborator, Claudio Guastalla, tells of Silvana, the second wife of Basilio, the Exarch of Ravenna, her persecution by his mother, the Empress Eudossia, and the growth of her love for Basilio's son by his first marriage, Donello. The story is set in the royal Ravennan court in the seventh century AD and revolves around witchcraft: we see one practitioner dragged off to the pyre at the end of Act I and by the end of Act III the same fate awaits Silvana herself who has meanwhile seduced her own stepson and killed her husband with the power she has inherited from her mother – 'the flame' of the title.

Much of the time Silvana is a passive victim of circumstance, with music to match: but there is some powerfully heroic declamation required in her Act I reminiscence of childhood, and above all in the Act III confrontation with her husband at the end of which he drops dead. Yet she takes part in one of opera's most remarkable love duets, in which tones of Gregorian plain-chant mingle ecstatically with Monteverdian monody. In all, the work is tremendous, making a very powerful impression on stage and revealing Respighi to be in this, his penultimate opera, no less a master of form, local colour and pace than Puccini. It is a mystery why the work is not in the international repertory.

But the Liceo artistic administration was horrified by the costings for Faggioni's sumptuous set and costume designs and, worse still, his demands for rehearsal time. After some wrangling with the director, they decided instead to borrow a production from the Hungarian State Opera in Budapest. Caballé only learned about this very late and then by the sheerest of coincidences. She happened to be at the check-in desk at Zurich airport where she ran into the Liceo's general manager, Josep Maria Busquets, who was returning from Hungary. He told her there and then that the purpose of his visit had been to finalize a deal for the loan of the Budapest production that he was sure would be a more than adequate substitute. Since this was the second year running that Caballé's Christmas show at the Liceo had been handed over late in the day from directors whose work she knew and trusted to persons unknown without prior consultation, she was not at all pleased. Nevertheless, she attended rehearsals and the management was responsive (or felt guilty) enough to heed her complaint that the costumes were uniformly appalling, and had the lot properly remade. But unfortunately, such effort as had been expended was largely in vain. Throughout the rehearsals Montserrat had been suffering increasingly from chronic bronchitis and repeatedly warned by her doctors that singing was inadvisable. In the end, it became so bad that she reluctantly decided to inform the Liceo authorities that she was unable to perform. She may not have expected sympathy by way of response, but she was utterly flabbergasted by the reply she actually received:

> I was told that if I did not sing, the management would be unable to find a replacement for me as Silvana and would simply close the theatre for the five nights. Basically, it was just artistic blackmail, both unethical and ungracious. But there was nothing I could do about it.

In the event, she sang all five scheduled performances between 14 and 26 December, but in this context 'singing' is a relative term. She was in poor voice on the opening night and on the 20th was virtually hoarse. She looked terrible, and only a kind of fatalistic determination got her through the run. As soon as it was finished she collapsed completely and was confined to bed for a lengthy period, being monitored on a daily basis by her doctors, whose worst fears had been realized, since she had gone on to develop pneumonia. As a result, she did not sing in public for nearly two months, the longest period of enforced idleness she had ever endured in her entire professional career – longer even than the hiatus dictated by the discovery of her illness back in 1985. By the end of the fifteenth week of 1990 she had sung in public just four times that year, the starkest possible contrast for a singer who, in most years, would have thought nothing of despatching such a work-load within a week. This was primarily a reflection of her precarious state of health at the time: but in fact it involved very few cancellations, which indicates clearly that she had already some time previously resigned herself to this phased withdrawal from performance.

But Caballé is nothing if not a *bête de scène*. And the one thing worse than feeling unwell at home was her overwhelming sense of boredom. As the pneumonia slowly cleared up, she began again to respond to the lure of the spotlights. First it was Vienna, with a recital in the Konzerthaus; and then, by the end of April, she was in Munich, back in partnership with Marilyn Horne, singing for the first time in the newly built Philharmonie am Gasteig. As she gathered both pace and stamina, she began to accept those invitations to sing which had never stopped pouring in, and took to turning up on very short notice for recitals in Spain and the South of France. The exception to this were two outstanding commitments in Paris, the first of which took the form of a gala at the Théâtre des Champs-Élysées to honour the retirement of Régine Crespin; and the second, five days later on 19 May, marking Caballé's début in the new Opéra de Paris de la Bastille – the first operatic concert to be given in the new auditorium.

This latter event found her in stupendous voice, delivering an impassioned and vocally huge account of Manon Lescaut's dying aria, 'Sola, perduta, abbandonata', in stark contrast to her singing of Desdemona's Act IV *scena*, with its subtle colorations and half-tones. The wife of one of the founder directors of the Royal Shakespeare Company was present that night, and observed that never, in all her years of experience of 'straight' stage Desdemonas, had she heard anyone so capable of conjuring up the sadness and tragic foreboding of this scene. It was a mystery to her that Caballé could summon it 'cold', without having lived through the rest of *Otello* first. But this, of course, is what great singing is all about.

On 25 May 1990, Caballé returned to Madrid for a period of rehearsal preceding the first performances there of *La fiamma* in which she was to repeat the role of Silvana. This took place on 5 June, and found the soprano in infinitely better voice than in Barcelona. She did more than enough to impress both audience and critics, and enjoyed a real personal success throughout the run.

Montserrat managed to squeeze in a few days' holiday on the farm at the end of June, giving her a chance to spend some time with her children who were now grown up and forging lives of their own. At twenty-two, Bernabé junior was at the university in Barcelona studying social anthropology (which made a change from his teenage passion for astronomy) and Montsita – five years younger – was already dedicated to the life of dance, to which end she was studying with her mother's friend, Maya Plisetskaya, in Madrid. At the beginning of July the whole family, including Montserrat's husband, made their way across Spain for her eagerly awaited return to the Mérida Opera Festival, which was to open on 14 July. The problems which had been experienced with the weather the previous year had been taken into account when drafting rehearsal schedules and the spacing of performances, so that this excursion should have been trouble-free. And so it was up to and including the first night, when the 6000-capacity audience turned out at practically midnight (still 32°C) for a memorable production of Massenet's *Hérodiade*, with Caballé and Carreras as Salome and John the Baptist, Juan Pons as Herod and Elena Obraztsova as Herodias. The rather rough orchestra and chorus had been imported from Sofia, and the conductor, Jacques Delacôte, did what he could under the circumstances. But the performance as a whole was magical, deriving inspiration from the extraordinary setting. If there was an occasional harshness of voice amongst the soloists, no one complained.

The following night there was a performance in the adjacent amphi-theatre of Prokofiev's ballet, *Romeo and Juliet*, conducted by one of Montserrat's heroes and closest admirers, Mstislav Rostropovich. The entire Caballé family had been invited to attend the performance by the President of Extremadura and had been placed at the front of the specially erected stalls in the Teatro Romano. At the end of the ballet the spectators in the back rows got up to applaud, at which point the central dais collapsed. Bernabé junior sustained a broken ankle; his father, a broken rib; Montserrat simply plummeted through the three-and-a-half-metre drop to land face-down in the wreckage of the col-lapsed scaffolding. Every newspaper in Spain carried a front-page picture the following day of poor Montserrat being hauled upright by galvanized rescuers. In fact, she had been lucky – many others had been hospitalized – and, apart from the shock, sustained little more than bad bruising. Brother Carlos had responded immediately, repeatedly punching the Festival's director, Manuel Canseco, and yelling 'Asesino!' in front of the Minister of the Interior. Carlos's rage had been all the greater since, in his capacity as artistic administrator of the music – as opposed to theatre – festival at Mérida, he had by accident been billed for the rigging work undertaken in the Teatro Romano next door and had noticed that instead of the agreed sum of eight million pesetas, which had been authorized for the installation of the stalls seating, only three had been charged.

Needless to say, the bad feeling all this engendered completely over-shadowed the two remaining performances of *Hérodiade*. In fact, it was never satisfactorily resolved, despite the subsequent dismissal of Señor Canseco, and the following year's opera – a new production of *Semiram-ide* reuniting Caballé and Marilyn Horne in the principal roles – never took place. 1990 was therefore the year of the second, and last, festival of opera at Mérida.

Good humour was soon restored at the joint concert Caballé and Carreras gave as part of Carlos's fourth – and, for him, last – Peralada Festival on 28 July. Montserrat then spent the beginning of August rehearsing for a new production there of Donizetti's comic opera (composed to his own libretto), *Le convenienze ed inconvenienze teatrale*, here retitled *Viva la mamma*. When this opera was given many years ago in London at the lamented Camden Festival, it was under the title 'The prima donna's mother is a drag', which gives an idea of the plot's transvestite goings-on. The essential *donnée* is that the role of 'la mamma' – Agata Scannagalli – is sung by a baritone in drag, here the strapping Juan Pons, for once minus his beard and, in this production relocated to the 1950s, looking remarkably like Anita Cerquetti. Montserrat

played the part of the hysterical prima donna, Corilla Petronilla Scortich-
ini, with effortless ease, including the interpolation in Act II of a deliberately atrocious account of 'Di tanti palpiti' from Rossini's *Tancredi*. In a
Festival that also included a new production of *Samson et Dalila* with Carreras and Marjana Lipovšek, as well as an opera gala given by Domingo,
these performances were a highlight, perhaps as much due to the spectacle
of Caballé in voluminous white silk pyjamas, turban and crimson ostrich
feather, as to Juan Pons done up as Divine.

Montserrat's schedule for the next fourteen weeks consisted solely of
a widely spaced series of recitals in Europe and concerts in Spain: there
was no more stage work in the offing until she was due to commence
rehearsals at the very end of November for a revival of *Die Walküre* at the
Liceo, which she had requested be performed as her habitual end-of-year
offering. In the meantime, she returned to Dubrovnik and to the Edinburgh Festival, where for the second year running she galvanized a
capacity audience in the Usher Hall. There was a brief recital tour of
Scandinavia during September, and in October she came to London to
record a CD of choice operatic duets with José Carreras for Philips.
This was the first such 'purpose-built' duets project the pair had ever
undertaken: their previous recorded work together had all been of complete operas. The repertory was carefully chosen with reference to both
singers' careers, and comprised the mother/son duet from the Prologue
of *Lucrezia Borgia*, the Saint Sulpice scene from *Manon*, 'Già nella notte
densa' from *Otello*, virtually the whole of *Andrea Chénier*, Act IV and
the prison duet from *Hérodiade*. The Philharmonia Orchestra was conducted by Jacques Delacôte and the recording was produced in Black-
heath Concert Hall by the industry veteran Erik Smith. Unfortunately,
the disc has never been issued, since the quality of the sound recording
proved unacceptable on finally edited playback some months later, and
Carreras, in his then capacity as an exclusive Philips artist, declined to
authorize its release. Thus Montserrat's first operatic recording in five
years languishes somewhere in a vault.

In November 1990, whilst Montserrat was giving concerts and recitals
in Madrid, Lisbon and – against an ever-deteriorating political background – Belgrade, the Liceo was preparing for her Christmas presentation, a revival of the production of *Die Walküre* in which she had sung
in Madrid in May 1986. As on that occasion, she had opted to repeat
the role of Sieglinde, and the surrounding cast was of high quality, with
Simon Estes as Wotan, Robert Schunk as Siegmund, Marjana Lipovšek
as Fricka and Johanna Meier as Brünnhilde. The problem would come
to centre around director Hugo de Ana's stage set. In Madrid, this had

presented Caballé with no difficulties since although it was steeply raked, in Act I the inclination did not begin until the level of the ash tree some way upstage, which left the soprano with plenty of room in the flat forestage area. But at the Liceo, whose floor, unlike at Madrid, already incorporates a slight incline, the rake of the set commenced at the front, starting at the prompt box. During a production conference which had taken place in October between the director and the Liceo's stage technical manager, Josep Maria Folch, it had been pointed out that the increase in the stage floor's steepness could create difficulties for the soprano, as a result of which it was decided to build a sort of cat-walk running across the front part of the set so as to counteract the rake.

Caballé returned from filming sessions for a German ZDF documentary about her in order to attend the first orchestral rehearsal for the *Walküre* which she expected to take the customary form of a *Sitzprobe*.* But when she arrived at the theatre, she found the curtain up and the stage fully set with Hunding's hut, which she had to traverse to reach her dressing-room. In so doing, she became aware of the steep rake which the set now incorporated and discovered that she could only reach it from the wings by walking up a set of three steps. Discussions immediately ensued with the stage director who pointed out how a new piece of flooring had been added to smooth the soprano's on-stage progress. But Montserrat realized that the extensive alterations to the set – which must have necessitated the building of a whole new series of trestles with which to support the false floor – would make it impossible for her. However, this was supposed to be a *Sitzprobe* and she had no intention of getting into a protracted wrangle about the staging at this point: she simply had to concentrate on the orchestral rehearsal. And to this end, since it was now impossible for anyone to sit on the forestage in conventional *Sitzprobe* fashion, she went and sat in the front row of the stalls behind the conductor, Uwe Mund. The rehearsal of Act I took place, at the end of which de Ana returned, together with Señor Busquets, the intendant, in an attempt to persuade Montserrat of the practicability of the set: after all, it was just the same as it had been in Madrid. But she knew that it was not and said so roundly, pointing out that one would only have to refer to the video of the Madrid *Walküre* to see the difference. At which point, thanking her colleagues among the musicians, she announced to Busquets that she was withdrawing from the production, and promptly left the theatre.

* Curtain down, no costumes or make-up, the soloists simply sitting on a row of seats on the immediate forestage with the orchestra and conductor in the pit.

It had all changed, not just scenically but musically as well from how
it had been in Madrid, and none of it was for the better. The conducting in Madrid [Gustav Kuhn] was excellent, but in Barcelona
there was no colour, no nuance, no feeling. And then there were the
changes to the set. How could I sing the role of Sieglinde, so passionate and so involved, on a piece of metal work which was not even
wide enough to allow the Siegmund and I to be on it at the same
time? They knew all about the problems I have had with my left leg
ever since the accident in New York in 1969, and had always taken
my difficulty with slopes and steps into consideration in previous
productions. But now, after the problems and disappointments of
the *Salome*s in 1988 and *La fiamma* in 1989, this really upset me:
for three years running, inadequate stagings, creating unnecessary
problems. And I did not believe the promises, since none of those
previously made by the administration had ever been honoured. So,
finally, I decided to withdraw, the first time in twenty-eight years I
had walked out on a Liceo production.

The press statements immediately released by Señor Busquets
announced that Caballé had been obliged to cancel because of indisposition: but the soprano is fiercely proud of her almost unblemished track-
record in the house, and refused to be party to this piece of subterfuge.
Having read the reports in all the following days' newspapers, she felt
that she had been the object of some nasty double-dealing, and subsequently dismissed Busquets' claims in the press.

In 1962, when I was working in Germany, I nearly reached the point
of giving up my career altogether because I realized that all that was
being achieved there was dull, daily routine. I very much love the
Liceo and wish the theatre good fortune, but I have the impression
that the ambience prevailing [there] is very similar to that earlier time
in Germany.[4]

The theatre decided to stand its ground and instead announced that
Montserrat had been in no physical condition to undertake her role, an
assertion the Liceo was nevertheless unable to support with any medical
evidence (they never even requested Caballé to produce a certificate).
She took violent exception to this statement, believing it to constitute
a fundamental untruth.

On 26 May 1991 an article appeared in the Catalan daily newspaper,
El Periódico, featuring an interview with the soprano who was then in
London for an operatic concert at the Royal Festival Hall. Asked about
her relationship with the Liceo, she replied, 'No comment. Make what

you like of that.' Subsequently she confirmed that she would not be singing in the forthcoming season at the Liceo – she had been otherwise scheduled to repeat the role of Elettra in *Idomeneo* which she had sung in a new production in Madrid earlier that year – and that her reasons concerned a matter of 'sensibilidad artística'. She proceeded, with the recipient's permission, to read out the contents of a letter which she had originally written and sent on 28 May to Señor Busquets with copies to Jordi Pujol and Pasqual Maragall – the President of Cataluña and the Mayor of Barcelona respectively – in their capacities as President and Vice-President of the Consorcio del Liceo. In it, she had drawn attention to the fact that, during the preceding three seasons, three of her productions had undergone post-contractual changes, surely attributable either to bad faith or incompetence. It was up to Busquets as the general manager to do something about it.

All this media attention only served to stir up more trouble. The specific trigger this time was Carlos's activities as musical adviser to the forthcoming Olympic Games, a task which he had not sought but one to which he had simply been appointed, just as some while later José Carreras was nominated musical director. In accordance with the original intention of making this a *cultural* Olympics, a decision was taken by the ten-member Ceremonial Committee (referred to as the OBS) under the chairmanship of Lluis Bassat to include as part of the spectacular opening celebration a specially concocted medley to be sung by Spain's operatic stars. They decided upon a sextet and, in the event, chose Aragall, Berganza, Caballé, Carreras, Domingo and Pons. The veteran tenor Alfredo Kraus was scandalized, though his own well-publicized statements condemning the three tenors' concert which had taken place in Rome in 1990 as a vulgar prostitution of opera no doubt ensured his omission. This galvanized him – he had presumably revised his opinion of large-scale out-door opera junkets – into complaining to the press of his treatment at the hands of what he saw as the 'Carlos Caballé mafia': 'José Carreras has declared war against me . . . Naturally, I would ignore [him] if I were ever asked to mount anything similar.'[5]

In fact, Carreras came in for a surprising number of attacks over his directorship, all of which he treated with great dignity and to which he declined to respond, though he cannot have derived much encouragement from the silence of the OBS, which failed to exhibit the courage of its corporate convictions. Even so, Kraus's outburst did draw a robust response from the Olympic Committee, which even spoke about the scale of certain artists' financial demands (the stars of the sextet performed for one peseta apiece), whilst arranging to placate him with a solo appearance during the ceremony. And Carlos, for once replying directly, observed in the course of an interview given to *ABC*: 'If helping one's compatriots makes me a mafioso, then I am one, with great pride.'[6] A few days later, both Carlos and Alfredo Kraus took part in a live phone-in radio discussion in which Kraus delivered an on-air apology for his 'mafia' accusation.

In fact, this flurry of media activity on the subject of the Caballés' power brought forth further complaints, though all of them, significantly enough, were anonymous. Certain singers, who declined to be named, were to be found moaning to the media about their years of exclusion from the Liceo as a direct result of the Caballés' influence. It is at least as likely that what actually kept them out of the Liceo during the Pámias years was their own greed, to say nothing of their vocal condition. Obliquely, Montserrat herself touched on this in an interview with the French magazine, *Le Monde de la Musique*:

> I have always been willing to be paid much less [at the Liceo] than anywhere else because the director loved voices, and within a very limited budget wanted to bring the greatest singing stars. At the time most agents refused to work with the Liceo because financially they had nothing to gain from so doing . . . But in 1981 Pàmias died and the Liceo was reconstituted . . . and received for the first time a state subsidy. Agents suddenly underwent a profound change of attitude. Fees went up like a rocket . . . the opera house got itself into the financial big league, and the result of all this is that it is now 60,000,000 francs [£6 million] in the red. I wish to state clearly that my personal fees have not increased by so much as one centime.*[7]

Meanwhile, the business with the Liceo had taken a sudden turn. On 30 November 1991 a full-page article appeared in *El País* entitled 'El Liceo busca la paz con Montserrat Caballé' ('The Liceo seeks peace with Montserrat Caballé'). In it, Busquets went on record as saying that the theatre, mindful of the approach of the thirtieth anniversary – on 7

---

* She might have added that she had on occasion aided the crisis-ridden theatre herself. One such instance occurred in 1984 during the run of *Ariadne auf Naxos*. The tenor in the opera learned from his agent, Vladarski, that the house was in serious financial difficulties and unlikely to be able to pay the artists after the performance that night. He therefore refused to sing in the opera-proper unless he was paid in the interval after the Prologue. Montserrat quietly sent her chauffeur, Rafa, on a break-neck drive to and from her apartment in Infanta Carlota where the soprano knew she had some unbanked money to hand. Rafa returned with the necessary cash and the performance duly resumed. She was reimbursed by the theatre three days later.

January 1992 – of her début there, had offered the date as an *homenaje*; was asking her to keep a date free in July during the Olympic Games in order to give a solo recital; and that the theatre would continue to make offers to the diva. Dr Hänseroth added that although *Lohengrin* had already been scheduled in December – the period when Caballé traditionally performed at the Liceo – there were many days in between performances that had deliberately been kept free: if she wanted to sing, they would arrange the dates. The newspaper went on to observe that the soprano was uncontactable, being in Nice for a recital, but that the Caballé agency office had stated categorically that they had no record on file of any such offers or propositions.

The situation remained in a state of uneasy suspense for the rest of the year. And 7 January 1992 came and went at the Liceo – in darkness that night – without any Caballé. The following day, most of the principal Spanish newspapers published the complete text of a letter from Montserrat addressed to Señor Busquets, written by the soprano ten days previously, in response to a fax he had sent her on 27 December, formally inviting her to sing at the Liceo on 7 January. In it, she declined his offer on the grounds that she was previously engaged in recording work for the forthcoming Olympics. But she now had a further complaint: there had been recent press reports that the Liceo had been sending her invitations to appear both in this current and future seasons.

> This is not the case, Señor Busquets, and you know it perfectly well. You should not try to manipulate the media in this fashion. The concrete invitation has just come to hand in the form of a fax, for a performance in ten days' time. This cannot be taken seriously.

She ended the letter by requesting Busquets to stop feeding disinformation to the press and authorized him to publish her letter if he so chose.

This closed the door with a resounding slam: after such a letter, it was utterly impossible for anyone to imagine that there was still any room for manoeuvre. Strangely enough, the controversy did simmer on, with the Liceo's technical stage director, Josep Maria Folch, giving an inflammatory interview to *El País* without Hänseroth's knowledge or permission, in which he claimed to speak for the theatre in saying that Caballé would have to yield in this matter.[8] The first Dr Hänseroth knew of this was when his secretary alerted him to the *El País* article the following day. Presenting himself before the horrified artistic administrator, Señor Folch claimed to have acted out of loyalty to the beleaguered administrator. Hänseroth was mortified: as he said, 'This kind of "help" I can do without.' Perhaps there was a feeling that Caballé was merely engaging in tactics, or some form of brinkmanship with the Liceo: in fact, she was deadly serious. This was the theatre to which she had effectively dedicated the greater part of her performing career, her artistic home in which she had sung forty-seven different roles in 191 performances,* for an unbroken period of twenty-eight years. The strength and duration of this relationship between a *prima donna* and an opera house is effectively without parallel this century, a fact of which the Barcelonese are rightly proud.

But the performance of *La fiamma* that had taken place at the Liceo on 26 December 1989 became the last occasion on which she was ever to sing on the stage of the Gran Teatro del Liceo. A tragedy for Caballé, the Liceo and its audience alike.

---

* These figures exclude the two performances of Casals' oratorio *El Pessebre*, as well as the nine concerts/galas in which she took part.

CHAPTER FIFTEEN

1990–1993: Silver and Diamonds

The seeds of the ultimate rift with the Liceo had been sown at the end of 1990, when Caballé should have been singing in the revival of *Die Walküre*. Her last-minute withdrawal meant that, apart from two or three previously scheduled recitals in Spain and some recording sessions for a disc of contemporary Catalan songs by Antoni Parera Fons entitled 'Somnis i Records' ('Dreams and Memories'), her next engagement was not until the beginning of February 1991. This took the form of a new production at the Teatro de la Zarzuela in Madrid of *Idomeneo*, mounted as part of the Mozart bi-centennial celebrations in collaboration with the Liceo which would be offering the work itself later in the year. Caballé was to tackle for the first time the role of Elettra, the jealous and vengeful but no less love-struck daughter of Agamemnon. The cast included Diana Montague as Idamante, Gösta Winbergh in the title-role, and the 'discovery' of the Caballé master-classes two years earlier, Isabel Rey as Ilia, with Michael Schønwandt conducting. Alas, these five performances caught Montserrat at the lowest ebb in both her personal and professional fortunes. Throughout she had become progressively more withdrawn: she felt permanently unwell, and her thoughts were dominated by a bleak fatalism. At the last performance – on 3 March – she even declined to take a curtain call.

But an unexpected ray of light penetrated the gloom. Montsita, Montserrat's by now nineteen-year-old daughter, had been studying ballet with Maya Plisetskaya in Madrid since 1988. Whilst she stayed in the city, she had done so as the house guest of Cristina Ordovás, the Condesa de Ruiz de Castilla, who was a long-time fan and friend of her mother. It so happened that Cristina had heard Montsita singing about the house and had become convinced that the girl possessed a genuine voice. She had been thinking of telling Montserrat this for some time. But in the summer of 1990 Montsita sustained a tendon injury, as a result of which she was obliged to abandon her ambition to be a dancer. Cristina decided to speak to Carlos about the situation and between them they felt that for the time being it would be best to say nothing to the parents. In any case, Carlos was highly sceptical about Cristina's claims, that is, until he travelled to Madrid and heard his niece sing for himself. If at first she was virtually too shy to sing in front of him, he soon realized that he was dealing with genuine talent, and proceeded, over the next three months, to do some preliminary work with Montsita concerning the basics of breathing and the emission of sound. By the end of 1990, Montserrat's daughter had been placed with a noted teacher and former soprano, Isabel Penagos, in Madrid, with whom she continued to make significant progress.

Two months later, while both Montserrat and her husband were in Madrid for the performances of *Idomeneo*, Carlos decided to tell his sister and brother-in-law that there was a young singer he wanted them to hear and about whom he was keen to solicit their opinion. They were surprised at this request but, reasoning that it must be of considerable importance because otherwise Carlos would never have asked them in the first place, they agreed to turn up one afternoon at the rehearsal stage in the Teatro de la Zarzuela. On arriving, they discovered Montsita, Penagos, Carlos, Cristina and all three of the latter's maids in attendance. Everybody chatted for a while and then sat down. Montserrat inquired, 'So where is the audition?'

'Here,' Carlos replied.

'And where is the singer?'

'Here, too.' At which point Montsita walked forward, stood by the piano and began to sing Gluck's 'O del mio dolce ardor'. Her parents were flabbergasted, but by the time the young girl launched upon a securely turned and expressively phrased account of 'O mio babbino caro' everybody present was in tears, including Cristina's domestic staff. Montsita looked around her and said, 'Was it really that bad?' In fact, far from being bad it was the one wholly positive experience Montserrat had during this period.

The following month Caballé underwent further tests and treatment at the Clinica Quirón. By mid-April 1991 she was back in full swing, at least in terms of performance schedule, singing at a UNESCO gala in Paris and, later in the month, giving an operatic concert to celebrate the inauguration of the new auditorium in Athens. Less than a fortnight later she was doing exactly the same, this time in Seville, where in collaboration with all her Spanish colleagues, she participated in the Gala Lirica which opened the new opera house, the Teatro Maestranza. Her chosen solo, 'Pleurez, mes yeux' from Massenet's *Le Cid*, found her in far better voice than her recent efforts in Madrid, doubtless benefiting from what proved to be an emotional reunion. Whilst all the other items on the programme were conducted either by L. Garcia Navarro, E. M. Asensio or Edmon Colomer, Montserrat's contribution was conducted by another singer taking part that evening: Plácido Domingo. After so many years of professional estrangement, it was extremely touching to see – and, albeit in a rather different arrangement, hear – the pair performing together again. And in the final line-up for the inevitable 'Brindisi' from *La traviata*, Caballé was to be seen framed by Carreras on one side and Domingo on the other, a strictly forbidden glass of champagne held aloft toasting more, perhaps, than solely the new opera house. The public would have been even more entranced to witness the party that followed afterwards in the bar of the Hotel Colón, which went on until 6 o'clock the following morning and featured such unmissable musical treasures as Domingo playing the piano while Caballé joined in dancing a *sevillana*.

On the upbeat engendered by this *rapprochement* so long awaited by the public, Montserrat was wafted, first back to Paris for her annual recital under the umbrella of 'Les Lundis Musicaux', conducted now at the Salle Gaveau, and then on to London where she had two important 'firsts' ahead of her. On 18 May she sang three Rossini arias in the operatic half of a gala which had been arranged by Alan Sievewright, the impresario and former collaborator of Denny Dayviss, for the joint benefit of British Youth Opera and English National Ballet. The guest of honour was HRH Diana, the Princess of Wales and the event took place in the historic Banqueting House in Whitehall, designed by Inigo Jones, with its ceiling painted by Rubens. It was also, as Montserrat the staunch monarchist discovered to her chagrin, the location of King Charles I's public execution in 1649.

Five days later, Caballé returned to the Royal Festival Hall where she gave for the first time in London an orchestrally accompanied concert of opera arias. In a first half dominated by the 'Willow Song' and 'Ave Maria', Caballé also offered, as so often, some rarities, comprising this time arias from a student opera of Bellini's and Mercadante's *Le due illustri rivali*. *The Times*'s notice testifies to the form Montserrat was in that evening:

> The voice raised itself on a slow winch of portamento throughout Nelly's 'Dopo l'oscuro nembo' from Bellini's *Adelson e Salvini* and spun to a long, fine thread the little cadenzas of pathos woven through 'Dove sono' from Mercadante's *Le due illustri rivali*. For Verdi's setting of Desdemona's 'Willow Song', Caballé, now in perfect control of breath and pitch . . . dropped each note, each phrase, deep into the pool of memory. Her 'Ave Maria' was intensely private, yet ardently projected: this was the high point.[1]

Slowly, and for no readily apparent reason, Montserrat was beginning to feel somewhat better. She was regaining her performance powers and singing her way without mishap or cancellation through a leisurely programme of recitals in Spain. And then, in the latter part of July during a routine return to the clinic in Barcelona, she had a rewarding consultation with her doctors: on-going medical replacement therapy had suddenly found the right formula. There were definite signs that her glandular system was responding, producing a small but crucially significant weight loss. This was the first such loss she had experienced in more than ten years and it proved to be indicative of a general improvement in her systemic function. Not surprisingly, Montserrat was overjoyed, and as a cautiously adjusted medication continued, was thrilled to find herself losing kilo after kilo. A process of rejuvenation was set in motion that has continued to this day: she was beginning to enjoy both her life and art once more.

This dramatic improvement in health allowed her, for the first time in many years, to look to the future with some optimism and to plan accordingly. She lost no time in picking up the threads of a career that had been not so much interrupted as gradually run down. The first and most significant fruit of this was a new recording contract with her old company, RCA, now owned by the German giant, Bertelsmans Music Group. Accordingly, her first major engagement after the summer break saw her return to London where over a period of a fortnight in mid-September she made a series of recordings of songs and arias that were to be used, in conjunction with reissued archive material, as part of a planned series of CDs entitled 'Eternal Caballé'. Musically speaking, this was an extraordinary proposition since it is virtually unprecedented for newly recorded material to be issued cheek-by-jowl with material up to twenty-five years old. It is difficult to imagine any singer's voice standing comparison with itself across such an extensive period. Even so, the plan was to celebrate this silver anniversary association – and, simultaneously, Caballé's vocal longevity – by juxtaposing, for example, the very first recording of a *bel canto* aria she had ever made, 'Al dolce guidami' from *Anna Bolena* in 1964, with a brand-new recording of 'Com'è bello' from the work in which she had first achieved international fame, *Lucrezia Borgia*. Also included were a new version of an old favourite, 'O mio babbino caro', the first commercial recording of one of her favourite war-horses, the closing scene from *Maria Stuarda*, and excursions into new repertory, comprising arias from *Carmen*, *Samson et Dalila*, *Le Cid* and even *The Phantom of the Opera*. All in all, a risky proposition vocally, given the opportunities provided for the making of invidious comparisons. It is a measure of just how profoundly (and rapidly) Montserrat's health and whole outlook had been transformed that the new recordings stand up to them as well as they do.

The rest of the year was taken up with a widely spaced schedule of concert and recital work, the frequent gaps a legacy of her progressive withdrawal from performance during the latter stage of her illness. At the end of September she returned to Paris, this time to give an operatic concert at the Salle Pleyel. In October, she gave joint concerts with Carreras in Turku (in Finland) and in Stockholm, as well as singing recitals in Zurich and Spain. There was also, indicative of her post-'Barcelona' world fame, an ever-increasing amount of television work, which included her giving a charming account to the BBC of what the Palau de la Música had meant to her and her father at the outset of her career.*

Almost immediately after Christmas 1991, instead of celebrating her thirtieth anniversary at the Liceo, she found herself embroiled in the closing stages of her public dispute with the theatre's administration. Thereafter, she was required for three days of recording work at BMG's behest in order, together with her colleagues, to lay down the sound track of the fourteen-minute operatic medley which was to form part of Olympic Opening Ceremony later in the year. By the end of the month, when she was back in the Salle Gaveau in Paris, her performance schedule for the rest of the year had filled out to the point where it was difficult to see how she would manage to fit in some necessary rest. On 30 January she returned to Madrid in order to commence rehearsals for the kind of performance which was once her staple fare, but which latterly she had scarcely undertaken at all: a concert performance of a rare Donizetti opera. *Sancia di Castiglia* was given at the Teatro de la Zarzuela on 6 and 9 February, conducted by her now frequent collaborator, José Collado. After a slow start, the audience began to respond, and by the end of the opera, which concludes with an extended death scene for the Queen of Castille, they accorded Caballé a prolonged ovation:

> Montserrat Caballé deserved her welcome which, if initially had signs of reserve, had the advantage of increasing in fervour as the evening progressed and concluded with a personal triumph for the singer in a long and difficult role which she was singing for the first time . . . Montserrat, except for the hard edge to some of the *fortissimo* high notes (which these days she would do well to avoid) revealed admirably her qualities of colour, phrasing, sweetness and exquisite

---

* 'Barcelona', written and presented by Robert Hughes.

pianissimi. Any singer who, like Caballé, is able so deftly to modulate the intensity, expression and timbre of the confession aria 'L'adoro' is a singer par excellence who would deserve all the enthusiasm that Caballé herself aroused.[2]

Practically the whole of the following month was spent fulfilling engagements in connection with her new RCA/BMG contract. In the latter stages of February she came to London to record the two additional arias which each of the six artists participating in the brief Olympic medley were contributing to make up a full disc. All the singers had been asked to prepare one old favourite and something new to their recorded repertoire, so Montserrat obliged with 'Casta diva' on the one hand and 'Il est doux, il est bon' from *Hérodiade* on the other. Then it was off on an occasionally nightmarish round of promotions to publicize the release of *Eternal Caballé* which had her in London, Rome, Athens, Amsterdam, Paris and Seville all within nine days. Into all this she managed to fit a second operatic concert at the Royal Festival Hall (in celebration of the Rossini bi-centennial), recitals at the Rome Opera House and the Palau de la Música, and a joint recital with José Carreras at the Victoria Hall in Geneva given in aid of the tenor's Leukæmia Foundation which raised a staggering 500,000 Swiss francs (approximately £200,000).

Understandably enough, Montserrat took a week's rest after all this before returning, for the first time in three years, to North America for a brief tour, taking in Pittsburgh, Miami, Toronto and New York. But her schedules increasingly demanded her presence back in Spain, on whose behalf she spent 1992 'doing everything'. The Madrid *Sancia*s had appeared as part of that city's contribution to its status as the European Capital of Culture; now she was required in Seville to sing in the auditorium that had been specially erected as part of the city's enormous Exposition.

It was because of her non-stop commitment to the EXPO's inaugural week, performing every night, that she was unable to take part in the Freddie Mercury memorial gala at Wembley Stadium. The rock star had died of AIDS at the end of the previous November, and although it had always been envisaged that Caballé would form part of any musical tribute, the logistical problems proved insurmountable. Firstly she was engaged in performing the musical interludes in the nonagenarian Rafael Alberti's play *La Gallarda* on three consecutive evenings, which clashed with the Wembley event. And attempts to televise her live backstage during one of the intervals in the performance and beam her contribution via satellite direct to London were frustrated by the discovery that, since the Mercury memorial was itself being televised live worldwide from London, it was impossible to obtain a satellite link into the city. The unfortunate upshot of all this was that just as Freddie was denied the opportunity of appearing with her as planned at the opening of the Olympics, so Montserrat was unable to participate in his memorial gala. This saddened her, for his death had affected her deeply. Although she had known of his illness from the time of their first recording sessions together, she had never believed that it would overtake him so rapidly. Both, indeed, cherished plans for a future collaboration together, based upon a stage work Freddie wanted to write. In the event, the inexorable progress of his condition forestalled all such ideas and left Montserrat with a firm determination to dedicate much of her work to raising funds for AIDS charities. In future, she would frequently be seen in concert and recital sporting the simple looped red ribbon denoting AIDS awareness – an admirable stance from someone at the summit of a profession not normally noted for its concern with the problems of the real world.

At the end of April 1992 Montserrat was reunited with Marilyn Horne when the couple gave a joint concert in the Alte Oper in Frankfurt. Caballé then went on to give recitals in Oviedo, Rome, Lyons and in the cathedral at Chartres (in aid of Médecins du Monde), framing a pair of *zarzuela* galas given back in Seville at the Maestranza. At the end of May she attended the festival in Evian organized by the widow of Pablo Casals, at which she finally sang a piece which she had learned years previously, but had invariably cancelled all scheduled performances of, Berlioz's cantata *La Mort de Cléopâtre*, under the baton of Rostropovich. And then it was back to London where for the first time in more than eleven years she was to take part in a staged production at the Royal Opera House. It is even more remarkable that this was the first new production, as opposed to a revival, she had ever been offered by Covent Garden in a career which, even in London, extended back for more than two decades. The work was Rossini's Parisian *jeu d'esprit, Il viaggio a Reims*, here receiving only its second production, given that all previous performances – in Pesaro, Milan, Vienna and Tokyo – had been of Luca Ronconi's original 1984 staging. Of course, Montserrat had sung the role of Madame Cortese in this very *mise-en-scène* during the two sets of performances in Vienna in 1988 and 1989, as well as on the Japanese tour. She had, therefore, what we might call her 'preconceptions' as to how the role – and indeed the opera – should go. Surprisingly, Covent Garden had taken the decision to cast all the other roles in the work with débutants: as a result, Montserrat found herself as the only person with any stage experience in the opera. This left her in a rather unusual position, highlighted by the producer John Cox's decision to construct much of the scenic interest around Caballé as an operatic Queen Bee figure.

The rehearsal period under the conductor Carlo Rizzo went well, although she found herself the silent witness to a problem of musical coordination that had arisen between Sylvia McNair, who was singing the role of Corinna, and the harp solo that was meant to accompany her. The difficulty was that the singer's first verse was being sung, as marked, offstage, which meant the singer was unable to see her accompanist. Montserrat listened to the various solutions being proposed for as long as she could stand, then finally broke out, 'You sing. He just follows!'

The production opened on 4 July with a literal roll of drums and trumpet fanfares, celebrating the inauguration of the UK's Presidency of the EC. In the event, the reviews accorded this production turned out to be a presage of the UK's no less poorly received EC Presidency. No aspect of John Cox's staging, much less Mark Thompson's sets and costumes, went unexcoriated. After the ritual lambasting of the show, it was Montserrat's turn. She received some of the worst reviews of her entire career – most, admittedly, more in sorrow than in anger – tending to focus less on her singing of the role (which on the opening night was fairly approximate) than on her hyperactive stage antics. Adverse reference was made by all the critics to her running dialogue with the conductor and the prompter, though not one of them indicated the reasons behind this.

One of the *données* of Cox's production was that Madame Cortese's hotel was also a health farm. To this end, and textually supported by the libretto, apples figured everywhere in the stage action. The glass and steel revolving door to the hotel was topped by an enormous green specimen and, indeed, the first glimpse of Caballé in Act I was at her *toilette*, devouring her daily apple ration. Then, in Act III, while the various guests were lounging around the hotel's pool, Madame Cortese duly distributed a health-giving apple to each of her guests. At the dress rehearsal, Caballé had found herself with an apple left over in her basket and decided, quite spontaneously, to lob it at Carlo Rizzi. The packed house of friends and relatives enjoyed the whole business hugely. Not so the management. On the opening night, instead of the traditional good-luck message, Montserrat found an official letter awaiting her in the dressing-room, admonishing her for having placed orchestral players and their instruments at risk by her action, which she would be good enough not to repeat at future performances. Predictably enough, this piece of in-house discipline backfired completely. This time making deliberately sure she had a spare apple, in the apple-distributing scene of Act III Caballé suddenly came to the footlights, held up her hand and said, 'I was going to do something here but I have received a letter, so I will read it to you instead.' To the audience's amazement she read out the letter from the Musicians' Union, ending with a shrug, a comment of 'So . . .,' and threw the apple almost vertically into the air, where it was caught by an outstretched arm from the prompt box. The audience cheered, even as the critics cringed.

As one or two of them pointed out, the evening was in fact enormously enjoyed by the paying customers. It is equally true that once the reviews appeared, the audiences no longer felt permitted to enjoy themselves in the face of such stern judgement. Only at the last performance – on 17 July – was it finally possible to recapture the exuberant spirit that had marked the opening night. Indeed, in one important respect, it went one better: in the meantime, Montserrat had recovered her vocal form, and once past the vertiginous patter of her opening aria, proceeded to dominate the all-important ensembles not just physically but musically as well. The press had continued to have a field-day during the two-week run, one Sunday tabloid going so far as to manufacture an imagined scandal concerning a temper-crazed diva hurling apples at a hapless conductor under the headline 'It ain't over till the fat lady slings.'[3] This story had distressed Carlo Rizzi, who assured Montserrat that not only had he not the slightest objection to her apple routine, but was keen to extend it. Hence, on some nights during the course of the run, the conductor himself deposited pieces of fruit amongst the audience, asking for them back at the appropriate point. But at the last performance, both Montserrat and Rizzi had received word from the Royal Opera House that a claque would probably be in that night in order to generate some more newsworthy scandal. This put Caballé even more on her mettle: in addition to singing very well, she put into plan some pre-emptive defences, including the unfurling of a large, hand-written poster bearing the legend 'I love you', shown first to the conductor and then to the audience. And at the apple-throwing moment in Act III, Rizzi himself called out, interrupting Caballé's recitative, 'But Montserrat, where is my apple?' The empty-handed soprano looked momentarily non-plussed and then started patting various parts of her dress as if to check. Slowly, and with a shy smile, she lifted the front of her costume to knee-height, revealing an entire wall of apples hanging on strings. If anybody had turned out that night intending to boo, nobody dared amid the gales of laughter that pervaded the theatre.

The day after the last night Caballé, together with the members of her family who had come to London especially to see her in this favourite role, went home in order to start rehearsals for the opening ceremony of the Olympic Games which was due to take place on 25 July, televised live before an estimated audience of 3 billion in over 200 countries. But there was an outstanding commitment on Montserrat's part which, if it did not actually take precedence over the Olympic ceremony, nevertheless had to be accommodated within its schedule. On 24 July 1992 the opera house at Glyndebourne closed its doors, prior to demolition, with a farewell fund-raising gala at which many of its alumni had been asked to sing. Given that this was the theatre in which Luciano Pavarotti, Mirella Freni, Ruggero Raimondi and Samuel Ramey had all made either their UK or European débuts, one might have expected the final line-up to be rather starrier than in fact it was. None of these artists, in fact, took part. But Montserrat did materialize, even if the impending opening ceremony necessitated the hiring of a private jet to reassure the Olympic Committee that she would be back in Barcelona in time. She sang two items in the programme, which was televised live in Britain: the 'Willow Song' and Chimène's aria from Le Cid. The editor of Opera magazine, one of the sternest critics of the Covent Garden Viaggio, noted: 'Montserrat Caballé made her UK début here . . . her amazingly fresh account of the "Willow Song" and "Ave Maria" cheerfully effaced memories of less happy events at Another Opera House.'[4]

And then it was back to the Olympics themselves, and the elaborate razzmatazz that was witnessed by so many hundreds of millions around the globe. Early on in the proceedings, Caballé and Carreras appeared together to sing a newly composed sardana, the traditional Catalan dance set to a text of welcome: 'Benvinguts'. The whole Wagnerian-length ceremony went off without a hitch, culminating in the most spectacularly noisy fireworks display, the whole event proving to be a triumph for the precision and organizational spirit of which the Spanish could be so proud. And Carlos, who had been obliged to relinquish his artistic directorship of the Peralada Festival in order to devote himself for the better part of two years to the Olympics (for the princely fee of one peseta) was finally able to sit back and smile with quiet pride.

For Montserrat, it must have seemed strange that in a matter of days she was to be found, as usual, giving concerts and recitals far off the operatic beaten track: Perpignan, Antibes, Ajaccio, Marbella and Vic. But it was more in keeping with her new status that she travelled to Rome for a concert on 3 August in the venue made internationally famous by the three tenors event in 1990, Le Terme di Caracalla, where she was lionized by the 8000-strong audience in a programme of opera arias. Shortly after this, she made a fleeting reappearance at the Peralada Festival before returning to England. Her first port of call was Liverpool, where Alan Sievewright had devised a gala to celebrate the

Columbus quincentenary, introduced by Peter Ustinov and performed on the dock-side of the harbour in the presence of King Juan Carlos and Queen Sofia. Montserrat sang three arias: 'O mio babbino caro', 'Pleurez, mes yeux' and 'Casta diva'. Although it was mid-August, on the evening of the performance the temperature was 5°C, it having rained the whole of previous day during rehearsals. Montserrat had come to this event direct from Marbella where the temperature had been in the mid-30°sC. Needless to say, she had caught a cold in the transition, and this unsettled her performance, particularly of the Bellini. This was worrying, given that within thirty-six hours she was due to return to London in order to give a private recital in the ballroom of the Hyde Park Hotel which had been arranged by the producers of a documentary being filmed for British television. In the event, and although backstage barely able to utter a word, she produced a remarkable performance, with immaculate English in the aria 'O sleep' from Handel's *Semele* and some surprisingly nimble coloratura in 'Agitata da due venti' from Vivaldi's *La Griselda*.

There was a repeat of her appearance at the Olympics at the beginning of September, when she sang in the opening ceremony of the Paraplegic Games in Barcelona before embarking on a recital tour of Germany, which took her to Düsseldorf, Bielefeld, Mannheim and Hamburg. Thereafter, with the exception of a handful of recitals in Spain, she had an almost month-long break – well enough deserved in this her sixtieth year – before departing for Russia and a pair of recitals at the Bolshoi in Moscow and the Kirov in St Petersburg. Carlos, in his latter-day guise as media mogul, had ensured that the whole trip would be captured by the film cameras for the purposes of making a documentary video. Montserrat was treated to a level of attention by the Russian Government that one would normally expect to be lavished only upon visiting heads of state. Her tourist guides of both cities were conducted by motorcade: and everywhere she went she was mobbed by emotional throngs. Her arrival by train in St Petersburg at seven o'clock in the morning was greeted by all the local dignitaries, accompanied by a large military band oom-pah-pahing its way through the 'Triumphal March' from *Aïda*. And, most importantly, she was in splendid voice, as the resultant video, *Montserrat Caballé: From Russia with Love*, confirms.

She returned to London in early December to make a brief appearance at one of the institutions of British fund-raising entertainment, the annual Royal Command Performance, held that year at the Dominion Theatre in the presence of Prince Charles and Princess Diana. She was the first major opera star who had ever sung at this event, largely otherwise devoted to middle-of-the-road light entertainment Of course, in Spain she has frequently taken part in television programmes of a similar nature, but this was a new departure for her insofar as it was taking place as part of the popular culture of a foreign country. The first stage of this process had taken place earlier in the year, when she had been invited to participate in the last-ever edition of the thrice weekly chat-show which had been hosted by Terry Wogan for nearly ten years on the principal channel of the BBC. And the process would be continued later when she was invited by the noted balladeer, Michael Ball, to appear on his television show and sing a duet with him from Andrew Lloyd Webber's *The Phantom of the Opera*. It was on this occasion that Caballé gave a riposte worthy of standing alongside Ernestine Schumann-Heink's famous comment when asked to move sideways in order to avoid knocking over the violins' music-stands, 'Maestro, with me there is no sideways!' During the performance of the duet, both Ball and Caballé had been carried away by the emotion of the moment, to the point where Ball felt he had perhaps been overly tactile with the soprano. He apologized for having touched her so much. Surveying herself, Caballé replied, 'But darling, there are so many places to touch!'

Montserrat began the New Year in fine style. On 5 January 1993 she took part in the Gala de Reyes in the Auditorio Nacional in Madrid. This has become an annual event held, under the artistic direction of Plácido Domingo, to honour King Juan Carlos's birthday, featuring exclusively Spanish artists and repertoire. Domingo lost no time in seizing the opportunity of inviting Montserrat: in a concert that was televised live throughout Spain, the only two singers who appeared in the entire programme were Domingo and Caballé, singing both separately and, most importantly, in duet. This was the first time in over ten years, since the Verdi Requiem in New York in 1982, that the pair had sung together. Both were in resplendent voice, stimulating each other to give of their best. Montserrat gave a ravishing account of a piano-accompanied song by her fellow Catalan, Federico Mompou. There was also the thrilling power of her *forte* singing in the *zarzuela* pieces, sure and sustained. Domingo was, as ever, a pillar of vocal strength and seemingly ageless reliability. Together, they provided a poignant reminder not only of things as they once had been, but also of things which, through human fallibility, had been irretrievably lost. But at least we have this one precious example of their late collaboration captured on film. Domingo latterly was unequivocal in his admiration for the soprano:

I believe that Montserrat is one of the most important singers of all time. It is difficult to single out specific characteristics when there are so many things that make her great. But perhaps it is the beauty of her floating tone, which is simply unbelievable, and the control of her breathing in phrases – for instance, from the duet in Act III of *Aïda* – written in very oriental-sounding, sensuous vocal lines. That, nobody can do like her. Her breath control is impeccable and her phrases never end: you never know when she starts to breathe and when she is going to breathe again. I don't know how she retains the quality of tone and the beauty in her voice across such long, long phrases. I remember seeing her at La Scala once singing Norma. I was privileged to hear her because she was unbelievable, and the audience response was just as I imagine it was when Callas sang *Anna Bolena* or one of the other works for which she was really famous. On the other hand, I saw her in the production of *Viva la Mama* in Peralada a couple of years ago. And she was just screamingly funny, with her amazing sense of humour. We sang together on stage many times, but perhaps the *Aïda*s and *Ballo in maschera*s at the Liceo were the greatest performances. There were so many beautiful moments in all our collaborations, but those were the ones I particularly recall and I have a deep nostalgia for those magical times.

But, from Montserrat's point of view, perhaps the most significant tribute was that paid to her by the French who, though she was not much minded to celebrate her sixtieth birthday publicly, made her an offer she simply could not refuse. Acting on behalf of the French Government, M. Jack Lang, the Minister of Culture, formally extended an invitation to Caballé to celebrate her diamond anniversary amongst the Parisian public. The president of the Opéra de Paris, Pierre Bergé, was deputed to make the arrangements. He contacted the soprano to ask a simple question: in which of the numerous Parisian houses did she want to sing? She immediately chose the Palais Garnier, where she had made her stage début in 1972 as Norma and returned nine years later as Turandot. For her, the house was so full of operatic history that it was an automatic choice.

In her capacity as an honorary attachée of UNESCO (United Nations Educational, Scientific and Cultural Organization), she elected to give her recital as a benefit for La Fondation Mondiale pour Recherche et Prévention SIDA, the World Wide Foundation for Research into AIDS. The president of the organization, Professeur Luc Montagnier, had been the first scientist in the early 1980s to isolate and identify the human immuno-deficiency virus (HIV) as the causative factor in the development of AIDS, and since that time, all his efforts had been geared to further research. Montserrat felt that there could be no better way for her to celebrate her birthday than by contributing to a great cause.

During the interval, hordes of eager youngsters darted around the enormous foyers distributing leaflets explaining that at the end, just at the point when Montserrat thought she was going to begin her encores, her accompanist, Manuel Burgueras*, would instead play three preliminary chords; on the fourth, everyone should join together in a stirring rendition of 'Joyeux Anniversaire'. This duly transpired, with a surprisingly large percentage of the presumably French audience choosing to sing 'Happy Birthday to you' instead. Montserrat made a brave stab at composure, but was obviously on the verge of tears: she made a brief speech of thanks, gratefully accepting an elaborate crystal sculpture which had been specially commissioned, and tried to sing some encores. But she just managed to get through an account of 'Io son l'umile ancella' before acquiescing to the audience's desire to pay her homage. At this point in her life, at the climax of a great career that had already spanned thirty-five years, she no longer had any need to perform: it was enough for her public that for one more time Montserrat Caballé was there in front of them.

Six months later, it was the same story in the Royal Festival Hall in London. The occasion here was the silver anniversary of her London début which had taken place in the same auditorium on 4 October 1968. Although it is common for Caballé recitals in Europe to sell out solely on the strength of her name, in London at least it has usually been thought advisable to announce the programme in advance. Not so on this occasion. Billed simply as a celebratory recital at which surprise guests would perform, it was left to the public to decide whether they would subscribe 'blind'. That they did so – to overflowing – is one sure indicator of the regard in which Caballé is held by the London audience. They were rewarded by something entirely unexpected and quite exceptional. Not even the evening's printed programmes gave the least indication as to what Caballé would perform: a note simply said that 'she has chosen to introduce the programme personally, as she feels a deep affection for her London public and wanted to create an informal and more intimate atmosphere'. A hard task, one might think, in an auditorium the size of the RFH. But the soprano, hand-mike in hand, rapidly captivated her audience, explaining the reasons for including each item as she went along as well as providing a little musical commentary on the side. Better still, she was in fine voice and gave a thoroughly accomplished account of several Donizetti and Rossini pieces.

What no one had been prepared for in advance, however, was the point at which Montserrat announced that for the next item, which ideally

---

* The young Argentine pianist had first worked with Caballé in 1992 following Miguel Zanetti's withdrawal owing to illness.

required a younger voice, she would yield the stage to a young student, Montserrat Martí. She then added as a parting shot, 'Oh, by the way, she is my daughter.' As Caballé walked off, Montsita, tall and slender in an elegant white gown, fearlessly took up her place and sang Giulietta's Act I aria from *I Capuletti e i Montecchi*. Though her voice scarcely resembled her mother's in weight or depth of sonority, there were more than enough clues to show just whose daughter she was: in particular, the breath control was effortless and her phrasing had all the aristocratic finish which has distinguished her mother's singing. Another surprise followed in the shape of Marilyn Horne who, together with Caballé, brought the first half to a rousing conclusion with a spirited rendition of 'Serbami ognor' from *Semiramide*. Amazingly, this was the first time the two divas had ever sung together in London, though their partnership had long since been established in both opera and concert performances in Europe and America. Indeed the partnership continued to embrace Marilyn Horne's sixtieth birthday celebration in Carnegie Hall on 16 January 1994, as well as Caballé's own concert there later in the same year, when Pavarotti turned up for good measure. Montserrat herself was back in Carnegie Hall only four months later to mark the thirtieth anniversary of her début there with a recital that effectively set the seal on New York's canonization of her. And these days there is another performance relationship that is even more intimate: that between mother and daughter. It is rare now for Montserrat to appear on stage without Montsita sharing the limelight.

On 31 January 1994, a few weeks before the original manuscript of the hardback edition of this book was due to be delivered, the stage and auditorium of the Gran Teatro del Liceo were destroyed by fire. In the brief space of three hours, nearly 150 years of operatic history were reduced to ashes. Montserrat had not sung at the Liceo for over four years but, just as in real life death cancels all debts, the passing of such an historic building similarly brought about a spirit of reconciliation. The first she knew of the fire was when she was contacted by Carlos who, alerted by the press, had been watching with horror from the ninth-floor balcony in the Sarrià quarter of Barcelona as huge clouds of black smoke billowed into the clear sky. Just before noon, the roof of the theatre collapsed with an enormous crash, sending jets of debris many hundreds of feet into the air. Montserrat was numb with shock: the unfortunate events of the past few years were swept aside in the flood of emotion that overcame her as she contemplated her nearly thirty-year unbroken association with the house. In it, she had given some of her greatest performances and performed nearly fifty different stage roles, as well as spending her formative musical years listening to her idols.

The following day, at the express invitation of the Liceo's management, Caballé returned to the scene of devastation and, accompanied by
the principal cellist of the Liceo's orchestra, sang Casals' melancholy
'Cant dels Ocells' from one of the gutted boxes. As her voice floated out
into the now eerily day-lit auditorium, its brickwork still largely intact,
she was not alone in thinking that though the surface fabric had been
destroyed, the acoustic as determined by the underlying structure
remained unimpaired. But it is not an easy matter to evoke the necessary
political will, let alone the finance, to undertake so massive a task as the
rebuilding and restoration of one of Europe's greatest lyric houses, and
two and a half years on it is doubtful that the Liceo will be able to reopen
its doors in 1997, as originally hoped, to coincide with the 150th anniversary of the theatre's inauguration. What is certain is that Montserrat has
whole-heartedly co-operated in the various fund-rasing activities that the
Liceo management have initiated, including a spectacular gala on 17
March 1994 in front of 13,000 people in the former Olympic venue, the
Palau San Jordi, and a special event held at the Palau de la Música Catalana
on 22 April 1995, which marked the launch in Spanish of this book.

Caballé is one of the greatest singers, not just of the present era, but of the
whole history of recorded sound in the twentieth century. Her commercially recorded repertoire alone confirms as much. She has been profoundly admired by both her contemporaries and her distinguished
predecessors, best exemplified by Maria Callas' tribute mere days before
her death. Yet there is another, younger generation now occupying centre
stage for whom Caballé in turn represents a kind of ideal: June Anderson
has spoken of the debt she owes as a *bel canto* specialist to Montserrat's
tireless efforts to revive the repertory; while for Cheryl Studer – the closest to Caballé, at least in terms of breadth of repertory – Montserrat's
recording of *Salome* was the first operatic experience that really fired the
younger singer's ambition. Of course, Caballé has her detractors. In fact,
it is one indication of her stature that those who have disliked her have
done so intensely and for decades. But this is reassuring, since only the
greatest artists are capable of provoking such extreme responses: medioc-
rity invariably passes by. And moderation is foreign to the artistic credo
of a woman who has performed in public nearly 4,000 times and sung
nearly ninety different soprano roles in virtually every opera house
throughout the world.

And what of Caballé today? From the vantage point of mid-1996, it
seems safe to conclude that the diva's stage career has now, however
reluctantly, been set aside. Her last stage appearance – though no one
at the time expected it to be so – took place in London, on 17 July 1992

at the Royal Opera House in the shape of the final performance of the ill-fated run of *Il viaggio a Reims*. Since then, she has devoted herself exclusively to recitals and concerts, among which an interesting pattern has emerged whereby she returns only infrequently – annually at best – to the scenes of her greatest glories (North America, England, France and Italy), whilst giving an impression of making up for past omissions by touring extensively in places she only rarely visited in her prime, such as the Far East, Russia and the unified Germany. We could scarcely expect a woman in her sixties to manifest the kind of invincible technique she regularly displayed across the quarter-century during which she was at her peak, especially given the fact that she has sustained her public career now for more than forty years. Even so, on her night, it is surprising how few concessions have to be made in order to experience the Caballé voice of legend. Adapting herself with magisterial skill to the inevitable diminution of breath control and stamina, she has continued to find new life in her old warhorses, and to work her old magic into pieces new both to her and her public. This most certainly occurred on 15 June during the 1996 Hampton Court Festival, where Caballé – appearing for the fourth consecutive year – astonished her listeners with a flawless account of a long *scena* from Rossini's *Ciro in Babilonia*. Despite the fact that she had only recently spent six weeks in hospital undergoing yet more abdominal surgery, her singing was magnificent: the recitative bristled with dramatic inflections, the central cantabile flowed with the magical legato of which, in truth, only she has been capable, and the firework finale was dispatched with a triumphant ease and brilliance that, as so often in the past, drove the audience into frenzies. She knew how good it was too. A sly, shy smile of triumph shone in her eyes, much as to echo Luisa Tetrazzini's flashing riposte: '*Sono vecchia, sono grassa, ma sono sempre la Tetrazzini!*'

Not that Caballé's career or indeed voice is any way reminiscent of the extraordinary Italian diva's: the similarity rather stems from the fact that both are, in a way, throwbacks to the nineteenth century and perhaps beyond, to a time when the diva unequivocally ruled the roost. We hear much about the decline in standards of singing as if it were an inevitable fact of life; that it had to happen. And happen it has at a time when it might have been expected that material circumstances and modern convenience would serve to make things so much better. The truth is that opera and its musical practitioners are having a hard time adapting to the second half of the twentieth century. The only benefactors appear to be that *cadre* of stage directors whose principal qualification when directing opera is that they have neither seen nor heard of the piece before and have no specialist interest in operatic repertory. Today, we no longer talk of the current equivalent of Callas' Tosca or Tebaldi's Aïda but instead hear of Alden's *Simon Boccanegra* or Albery's *Nabucco*. If singing is in decline it is because singers are not what is wanted by those who now call the tune in opera houses. It is also noticeable that whilst large numbers of singers continue to be produced in every category, the burn-out rate, particularly among sopranos, is catastrophically high. It is now by no means unusual to hear of sopranos who in less than five years have passed through every stage of a forty-year career, from being the great hope of a generation to voiceless withdrawal. All of which is to say that circumstances today are no longer propitious for the production of artists who could stand in the places about to be vacated by, say, Caballé and Pavarotti. Divas and divos at this level are teetering on the edge of extinction. Some will doubtless welcome the change this represents: there may yet be a brave new world of ensemble playing, punctuality and polite professionalism; but of operatic star turns that pack out the auditorium and exert a charismatic power over their listeners simply by the greatness of their singing there will be no trace.

Without the likes of Caballé, the world of opera will be a poorer place. Her triumphs and scandals have been headline news for over thirty years, and her larger-than-life presence and personality shine as brightly today as they have ever done. Though it would be an exaggeration to say that her life has been wholly unaffected by the fame and riches her voice has brought her, there is an extent to which she remains at heart the somewhat withdrawn, somewhat melancholy character of her childhood, albeit one shot through with an unswerving iron will. She could live anywhere in the world but chooses to live in the same flat she occupied even before she became the toast of New York in 1965. And it is doubtless that same will that has enabled her to fight off an endless string of debilitating illnesses. Throughout her life, she has triumphed over a series of adversities; political, social, economic, personal, professional and medical. In the final analysis, Montserrat must be counted not so much a born, as a compulsive, survivor. Such people are rare and are to be cherished. The last words should be hers:

> When the day comes when I can no longer sing, no one need feel sorrow on my account. I will be perfectly happy. My career has been exciting, and to stand there with the feeling that, through me, the audience has had contact with great music has given me a sense of absolute artistic fulfilment. What is more, I have been given everything that anyone could hope for materially. But the things I have obtained this way are only a compliment to my life. In the end, what is truly important to me is my family: that is all I have ever needed.

Casta diva, indeed.

❧ VI ❧

'Qui la Voce Sua Soave'

I puritani

━━━━━━━━━━━━━━━━━━━━━━━━━━━━━━━━━

Critical Discography

INTRODUCTION

Discographies can take many different shapes and forms, ranging from perfunctory lists of works bereft of documentation or hard fact, to mind-numbing catalogues of figures and letters. Neither type holds much reader appeal, however, and in both cases it is hard to relate them back to the music and the artists concerned. The object here has therefore been to give a representative account of Caballé's recordings, commercial and pirated, together with an assessment of her performance in them. The principal limitations to this 'discussed discography' being complete are straightforward questions of space and availability. The former is an editorial decision of the publisher; the latter is dictated by the current state of the record market. Whilst no one could dispute the back-catalogue riches that the CD revolution has brought before us, the fact remains that, particularly in the case of the prime pirate labels like BJR, MRF and HRE, much still remains in LP limbo. Without specialist help and probably vast cost it would be impossible to acquire any of the pirate discs mentioned here, which is why there has been a conscious decision to concentrate primarily on those which have made the transition to CD. For the rest, we can only await the arrival of such gems as Caballé's 1968 Barcelona *Manon*, or her 1967 Metropolitan *Otello*, whilst signalling their one-time existence.

If anyone wonders why the pirated material has been included at all, it is simply because to omit it would seriously distort the image of Caballé's professional activity. True, she has made thirty-four complete studio opera recordings of thirty-four different roles, a non-duplicating tally which none of her forebears or contemporaries can match. But pirate recordings yield a further 50 complete operas, comprising 37 different works, of which 32 are of roles that she never recorded commercially such as the *Trovatore* Leonora and Adriana Lecouvreur. Considered together, they form probably the largest and most variegated body of work of any soprano on record. And there is the additional fact that Caballé herself barely draws distinctions between them in terms of relative value. If she never recorded *Adriana Lecouvreur* in the studio, no matter: the Tokyo pirate will do quite nicely.

In terms of method, the material has been arranged by what might loosely be termed 'schools', though this produces anomalies, such as Boito's *Mefistofele*, which sits awkwardly at the start of the *verismo* section but which would sit nowhere else at all. Within the successive schools, the recordings are discussed within the order of their making rather than on the basis of chronology of composition: it is, after all, Caballé's labours that are being discussed here, not those of the composers. Minor exceptions to this rule crop up in cases where a pirate performance survives which pre-dates a studio recording of the same role. These latter then take precedence. With single-composer recitals, the recordings have been grouped under the respective school. Miscellaneous recitals have been listed together in section VII. All recording dates are given where known, though it has not always been possible at this remove to ascertain precisely on which days out of an extended period Caballé was in attendance. All catalogue numbers quoted within the text may be taken to refer to CDs unless otherwise stated. Separate systems of national LP numbering in the pre-CD era have generally been omitted.

As a final point it should be mentioned that, whilst Caballé read and re-read the biographical chapters of this book, signing every page of the finally revised draft, she declined to exercise any control over the contents of this section of the book. All the opinions – as opposed to the anecdotal information – expressed in this discography are therefore the authors', and in several instances are known not to coincide with the soprano's own beliefs.

I: BAROQUE AND CLASSICAL
(i) WOLFGANG AMADEUS MOZART

Don Giovanni
Lisbon, pirate, i.1960: Legato CD (SRO-813-2)

This is a remarkable performance captured live (in decent and immediate sound) in Lisbon's Teatro São Carlos at the very beginning of 1960. It is the first performance by the then twenty-six-year-old Caballé to have become generally available, though this does not preclude the possibility that some of her earlier Basel performances between 1956 and '59 may yet see the light of day. The cast comprises the foremost exponents of every one of the principal roles drawn from the ranks of the Vienna State Opera. But there is one notable exception: instead of Elisabeth Schwarzkopf as Donna Elvira, we encounter instead the young Caballé. This is an important document not simply because it is the earliest evidence of the soprano's voice, but also because it presents her in a repertory with which she was not to be much associated in her glory days.

Although she is confronted by seasoned Mozartians such as Eberhard Wächter in the title-role and Erich Kunz as Leporello, Caballé sounds in no way outclassed or overparted. Indeed, she attacks the role with an astonishing – and some may think uncharacteristic – ferocity, quite literally from her opening line, 'Ah, chi mi dice mai quel barbaro dov'è?' At the end of the *recitativo accompagnato*, where she threatens to tear her seducer's heart out, all the repetitions of the word 'cor' are spat out venomously: and in the following – piano-accompanied – recitative she devours her way through the Italian text, relishing every last fricative and working herself up into a fine fury. The Handelian junketings of 'Ah, fuggi il traditor!', as Elvira implores Zerlina to avoid Giovanni's clutches, give us some idea as to how Caballé must have sounded in a genuine Handel role, such as Ginevra in *Ariodante*. But the crowning glory of the performance is her exquisitely shaded account of the notoriously difficult 'Mi tradì' and its preceding recitative, long-breathed, fulltoned, effortless and plumb in tune. All this, and a fair smattering of *appoggiature* for good measure.

Così fan tutte

London, studio, 22–31.iv.1974: Philips LP (6707 025); CD (416 633-2, reissued as 422 542-2)

This multiple-award-winning set is one of the best of Caballé's studio recordings, and would stand supreme in *Così* stakes were it not for the indifferent impersonations of the two male lovers sung here by Ganzarolli and Gedda. As it is, the distaff side of Cotrubas, Baker and Caballé taken together form the most distinguished and distinctive trio on record (with Klemperer's team of Margaret Price, Yvonne Minton and Lucia Popp the closest rival). The tone is set right from the outset of the sisters' first scene together, 'Ah, guarda, sorella', though it is not the one that most people – given the casting – would have expected. Caballé's Fiordiligi is astonishingly girlish – vivacious and almost kittenish compared with Baker's rather more sober Dorabella, a neat reversal of the sisters' characters as normally portrayed. Another surprise is the fact that the two women's voices, otherwise so different, blend flawlessly in duet and throughout the ensembles. The Act I trio, 'Soave sia il vento', has rarely sounded so lambently beautiful on disc, the voices floating effortlessly on the breeze the piece apostrophizes. Yet there is no lack of vigour or spine where needed: Fiordiligi's grandiose pledge to kill herself should she ever dishonour her conscripted lover – 'Lasciami questo ferro' – is sung with just the right amount of imperious and overblown fatuity. And that ultimate Mozartian test piece, 'Come scoglio', is dispatched with a technical address which mirrors Fiordiligi's single-minded *opera seria*-style reproach to the presumptuous 'Albanian' suitors. In Caballé's hands (or rather larynx) the two-octave leaps sound almost funny in their insolent ease – presumably Mozart's intention in writing them. Only the rather tremulous and shallow trills constitute a blemish.

In the Act II rondò aria, 'Per pietà', Caballé now puts the girlishness behind her and treats us to the real woman. If anything, Mozart's demands in terms of wide-ranging leaps are more extreme in this aria than in 'Come scoglio', albeit here at a more obligingly stately tempo. But she encompasses the descents below the stave – down as far as low A – without ever once compromising the legato singing with which she binds the first two slow sections together. (There is, however, the usual 'dead' pause between the two verses, where Mozart would have expected a discreetly ornamented vocal link.) By the end of the opera, Caballé's Fiordiligi has grown immeasurably in stature, passing from innocence to a kind of chastened, perhaps sceptical, adulthood. Throughout the performance, never once does she sacrifice the purity essential to the maintenance of correct Mozartian line: there is no trace here of the prima donna bringing early – much less, later – nineteenth-century vocal manners to bear. On top of which Colin Davis's conducting and the playing of the Royal Opera House's orchestra are a joy from start to finish, captured in impeccable sound. It is frustrating that this set remains Caballé's only studio recording of a Mozart opera.

(ii) MISCELLANEOUS

18th-Century Arie Antiche

Barcelona, studio, 1978: (Vivaldi: Vieni, vieni o mio Diletto, Chiare onde, Un certo non so che, Sposa son disprezzata, Da due venti, Agitata da due venti; **Lotti**: Pur dicesti; **Paisiello**: Nel cor più non mi sento; **Benedetto Marcello**: Quella fiamma che m'accende; **Pergolesi**: Se tu m'ami; **Costanzi**: Lusinga la speme; and **Giordani**: Caro mio ben) **Alhambra Decca LP (SXL-R 6936); Dischi Ricordi LP (OCL 16215); Forlane CD (UCD 10902)*; RCA/ BMG CD (74321 140732)**

The twelve songs making up this collection have had a lot of exposure on different labels and in different combinations, the fate which overtook all Caballé's recordings made originally in Barcelona for Discos Columbia S.A. during the latter half of the 1970s. They are now most conveniently to be encountered complete – together with her recordings of the *bel canto* masters' salon arias – on the two-disc RCA/BMG set issued in France in April 1993 specifically to commemorate the soprano's sixtieth birthday celebrations. In its original LP format, the recording consisted of one side devoted to half a dozen Vivaldi arias and a miscellany on the other of *arie antiche*, virtually all of which are to be found in the first volume of Alessandro Parisotti's late-nineteenth-century anthology of Italian song.

The recording is very close and airless, rendering the piano sound both brittle and tinkly, and lending an unwonted hard edge to the voice. These technical shortcomings are, alas, accentuated on the most recent CD transfer. Almost without exception the pieces are contained within the stave – only rarely venturing above it – and, at least as written, make no call on conventional virtuosity. Principally, they seem to be exercises in line and the tasteful projection of unexcessive emotions. Given their tendency to cleave closely to the bottom of the stave, they fall quite naturally within the range of a modern mezzo-soprano, and indeed probably the most successful latter-day practitioners have been

---

* The Forlane disc omits three items from the original recital programme – Vivaldi's 'Da due venti', the Lotti and the Costanzi – and adds ten items from Caballé's recordings of Bellini and Donizetti songs (see below).

Teresa Berganza (LP DG, 2531 192) and Cecilia Bartoli (Decca, 436 267-2). So what does an essentially nineteenth-century-style soprano make of them? In one sense the answer is, plenty. Caballé has a field day with verse repeats, liberally sprinkling ornaments, high notes and her beloved lightning-fast *pianissimo* chromatic ascents and descents wherever the opportunity arises. (The latter are heard to best advantage in the Pergolesi.) But an essential lightness of touch, and a close identification with the heroines' various plights – most of these arias are, after all, drawn from operas – are not much in evidence. She glosses over the onomatopoeic verbal wit of the Paisiello aria – 'mi pizzichi, mi stuzzichi, mi pungichi, mi mastichi' – in favour of some very grand, large-scale singing with plenty of florid embellishment. Similarly the coquetry which should inform the teasing of the love-lorn shepherd boy in the Pergolesi is given utterly strait-laced, though larded with decorative runs. Vocal virtuosity does duty for high spirits.

The principal criticism to be levelled at the Vivaldi arias is that the soprano is, paradoxically, too musically scrupulous to do the obvious thing and transpose them into higher keys which would suit her. Left in their originals, some of the faster runs are not so much aspirated as w-aspirated – the intrusive 'huh, huh, huh' sound replaced by 'wuh, wuh, wuh'. On the other hand, a fundamentally serious piece, such as the Marcello, taps unexpected depths of feeling and takes on, in Caballé's rendition, an oddly Spanish-sounding sensuality amidst the firm and powerful delivery. The finest things on the disc are the aria from Vivaldi's *Bajazet*, 'Sposa, son disprezzata', which offers a comprehensive display of impeccable *messa di voce* and seamless phrasing, and the well-known 'Caro mio ben', sung with an astonishing wealth of tone colours and dynamic shading. Perhaps this kind of more plain Baroque music does have something to gain after all when viewed, as here, through a strongly Romantic optic.

OTHER BAROQUE AND CLASSICAL RECORDINGS

Iphigénie en Tauride (C. von Gluck)
Lisbon, pirate, 3.ii.61: Voce LP (Voce-31)

Giulio Cesare (G. Handel)
(a) New York, pirate, 21.iii.67: Highlights LP MRF (.....); (b) Barcelona, pirate video, 12.vi.82 (transmitted in Spain on TV3)

Caballé sings Mozart – 1965–75
Various, pirate 1965–75: Historical Recorded Enterprises LP (HRE 363)

Agnese di Hohenstaufen (G. Spontini)
Rome, pirate, iv.1970: (a) Memories CD (HR 4104/05); (b) Myto CD (2 MCD 90215); (c) Foyer CD (2-CF 2029)

Medea (L. Cherubini)
(a) Barcelona, pirate, i.1977 MRF LP (....); (b) Mérida, pirate video (transmitted in Spain on TV1)

Démophoön (L. Cherubini)
Rome, pirate, xi.1985: Legendary Recordings LP (LR 215)

La Vestale (G. Spontini)
Barcelona, pirate, 29.xii.82: Legendary Recordings LP (LR 201-3)

Les Danaïdes (A. Salieri)
Perugia, pirate, ix.1983 Legato Classics LP (LC 002)

Mozart per Àfrica
Peralada, 18.vii.87: (Six Nocturnes (with the Quintet vocal de Catalunyà); Ave Verum; La libertà (KV 532); Wiegenlied; Vado, ma dove? (KV 583); Caro mio druck und schluck (KV 571a); Nun Lieber Weibchen (KV 625)) **Catalunya Música LP (60.1367); CD (25.1367)**

II: Bel Canto
(i) GIOACCHINO ROSSINI

Guillaume Tell
London, studio, 11.vii–1.viii, 7.ix.1972: EMI LP (SLS 970); LP Highlights on Pathé Marconi (290423 1); CD (CMS 7 69951 2)

This recording was made during the busiest period of Caballé's career, amid an endless round of performances in concert halls and opera houses throughout the world. Nevertheless she spent practically the whole of summer 1972 in various locations in and around London recording four complete operas, with a fifth – a zarzuela – made in Spain for good measure. Like the *Giovanna d'Arco* made the following month, this was an opera that Caballé had never sung (and never would) on stage. In retrospect it seems somewhat surprising that EMI took the decision to record the work in its original French, since insofar as it was known at all it was in Italian translation, as *Guglielmo Tell*. Even more surprising is the fact that the score was recorded uncut. Twenty and more years later, when the Rossini industry is in full swing and purist musicology in the ascendant, there has still not been a second recording of the work in its original form, which leaves this EMI release in sole possession of the high ground.

Technically, however, things are not quite so clear-cut, since the large-scale concerted passages in all four Acts suffer from a degree of aural congestion, which renders all the principal soloists almost inaudible at climaxes. The worst instance of this occurs right at the end where it is just possible to make out – score in hand and with the ears of faith – that Mady Mesplé and Caballé are singing; but this is hardly the pair of gleaming top Cs that Rossini evidently meant to crown the Hymn to Freedom and with it the whole opera. In gentler passages, however, the EMI recording serves very well, nowhere more so than in the magical scene at the beginning of Act II which introduces us to the Habsburg princess, Mathilde. On the heights of Rütli, overlooking Lake Lucerne, she has managed to separate herself from her hunting companions, and in accompanied recitative set to an agitated strings and woodwind orchestration, wonders whether or not she will here encounter her secret beloved, Arnold Melcthal. In the famous aria – 'Sombre forêt' – she contrasts the comforting solitude of the forests with the hollow glitter of the court life she so despises. The piece is simply enough written, making no great demands on a singer's technique apart from a flawless legato and an impeccable grasp of phrasing. In Caballé's performance the quintessential qualities of her voice are revealed: warm, feminine, fine-grained, fully rounded, with an almost fleshy but uncloying richness, yet still perfectly limpid and entirely effortless. The singing is also allied to a fine imagination, with the recitative being sharply characterized to suggest apprehension, whilst the aria proper – sung on what sounds to be no more than a handful of breaths – is regally shaped in terms of phrase and dynamic. Moreover, the high A♭s to which the aria repeatedly finds its way back seem to materialize out of nowhere: whether *pp* or *ff*, there is no trace of any scooping, lifting or even conscious 'placing'; the notes are simply *there*.

The following duet, an extended ternary structure with the outer fast movements set against fidgety running accompaniments, is not quite so successful, partly because here Caballé seems to be having more trouble articulating the French, and partly because of the low-lying nature of much of the vocal line. There is also the familiar problem where tenors and sopranos sing in sixths, which gives the tenor the dominant melody towards the top of his range whilst confining the soprano to little more than underlying counterpoint. But in Act III, the soprano comes into her own, and in the long interview with Arnold, which takes place in a ruined chapel, Caballé delivers the wide-ranging dramatic arioso of 'Pour notre amour' with tremendous fire and abandon. She also properly dominates the scene after Téll has been forced to shoot the apple from his son, Jemmy's, head by the tyrant Gessler. Mathilde sweeps on, immediately takes Jemmy into her protection, and denounces Gessler as a barbarian: 'Au nom du Souverain'. Here what is required is *spinto* declamatory power, and Caballé is equal to the challenge. Despite an unflattering sound balance she proceeds to inject a frisson into the scene, greatly helped by Gardelli's propulsive conducting. If she makes less impact in Act IV, this is principally a reflection of how the role is then written: Mathilde has nothing to do except restore Jemmy to his mother, Hedwige, which vocally takes the form of a brief solo, turning into a duet with Jemmy, finally developing into a trio with the addition of Hedwige's voice. Since Jemmy is sung *en travesti*, this trio is an all-female affair and very trickily laid out for the voices. It is compliment enough to say that the singers get through it without accident.

Elisabetta, Regina d'Inghilterra

London, studio, vii.1975: Philips LP (6703067); CD (432 453-2)

This was the first work that Rossini wrote for the Teatro San Carlo under the terms of his new Neapolitan contract in 1815. And it was the first opera the title-role of which Rossini wrote for the pre-eminent *prima donna* who was later to become his wife, the Spanish-born Isabella Colbran. Presumably not wishing to take unnecessary musical risks with both a new leading lady and a new public, Rossini re-cycled much of the music in this opera from an earlier work, *Aureliano in Palmira*. He also chose to deal with the vexed matter of added vocal ornamentation by writing all such passages into the score, leaving the star singers with little opportunity for improvised displays.

We first encounter Queen Elizabeth I in her throne room eagerly awaiting the return of the Earl of Leicester, who has successfully subdued the Scots in a military campaign. But the Queen's eagerness is more due to the secret love she bears the Earl than to his martial prowess. Accordingly, although the first verse of her *cavatina* is a stately apostrophe to the common good, the second is a palpitating depiction of the Queen's impatience to see her 'caro oggetto'. Rather unnervingly, this second verse is set to the same music as Rosina's 'Io son docile' from *Il barbiere di Siviglia*, and all interpreters of Elisabeth therefore have their work cut out making the passage sound suitably regal. Caballé certainly succeeds better than most, the tone at once commanding, clearly focused yet with an indication of emotional vulnerability. The one possible reservation concerns her treatment of the frequently recurring downwardly chromatic cascades with which Rossini lards Elisabeth's music, since she consistently softens the individual notes of which they are comprised, preferring a kind of rapid gestural 'smudge' across them. Admittedly, other singers who achieve needle-point clarity hereabouts – Cecilia Bartoli for one (Decca 436 075-2) – usually do so at the expense of some fairly flagrant aspiration.

But Caballé gets to grip with the character with the discovery that Leicester is secretly married and, worse still, to the daughter – such are the monstrous liberties taken with British history in Italian operas – of Mary, Queen of Scots. The English Queen's fury knows no bounds. Nor does her vocal line which, for all that Colbran was often described as a low soprano, repeatedly extends to high B, as well as making (presumably) more congenial excursions below the stave. The duet with the villainous Norfolk finds the soprano in fine fettle, the low B♭ on 'l'indegno' ('the unworthy man') positively spat out. She is no less impressive in the *recitativo accompagnato* that follows, where she bemoans her fate as both queen and woman ('Che penso desolata Regina…'). In the ensuing cat-and-mouse game she plays with Leicester – pretending to be unaware of his marriage and instead offering him the crown of England as her consort – Caballé could with profit be a little more sarcastic, though the murderously difficult written-out coloratura at this point probably precludes much by way of characterization.

On the other hand, anger is very much in this soprano's vocal vocabulary and both the *stretta* that ends Act I and the confrontation between Elisabeth and Leicester's wife at the beginning of Act II are superlative demonstrations of real vocal power. The formal duet ('Non bastan quelle lagrime') strongly foreshadows 'Mira, o Norma' from Bellini's much later opera, and is beautifully sung by both Caballé and Valerie Masterson, the latter deputizing for an indisposed Ileana Cotrubas. The Duke of Norfolk is duly banished with a piece of fine *spinto*-ish declamation, and Caballé delivers the scene when she descends to Leicester's dungeon determined to let him escape from his execution, and is instead saved by him from assassination at Norfolk's hands, with imperious command of the vocal line. 'Fellon, la pena avrai' seals the treacherous Duke's fate, repeatedly touching high B and with some very fast – if slightly cautious – triplet work. But all this is so much preparation for the highlight of the set, Caballé's delivery of 'Bell'alme generose', in which the Queen forgives the erring Leicester and his wife. This is a comprehensive display of the diva's skill, contrasting her almost intuitive sense of light, shade and tone colour with an entire armoury of vocal embellishments. Her singing is in the grandest possible manner, with a regal poise entirely suited to the character. Small wonder the recording is generally regarded as one of the crown jewels in the ever-expanding Rossinian discography.

Semiramide

Aix-en-Provence, pirate, viii.1980: (a) Historical Recording Enterprises LP (HRE 343), CD (1002-2); (b) Legato CD (SRO 509-2); (c) Highlights on Legato CD (LCD-112-1)

The pirate recording of the opening night of the Aix-en-Provence run of performances was happily preserved on both CD and video, having been simultaneously broadcast on French radio and television. Unfortunately, between the filming and the transmission date, the French television company, Antenne 2, got busy with the scissors and removed whole tracts of the accompanied recitatives which move the plot forward. The result is that, as televised and on disc, the narrative of the work is barely comprehensible, with the whole being got through in less than two and a half hours instead of the nearly three and a half taken at Aix.* Nevertheless, the document is of considerable importance, enshrining as it does the best evidence of the commercially undocumented partnership between Caballé and the amazing Marilyn Horne.

Things get off to a splendid start in the opening temple scene. Caballé does not have much to sing in this rather strange sequence – a *bel canto* heroine could usually expect an extensive entrance aria all to herself – but from the few phrases that she actually *does* utter it is apparent that she is on song. Nor is Caballé alone in this: both Marilyn Horne and Samuel Ramey are at the peak of their powers, as probably was Francisco Araiza as far as one can judge from what little is left of his singing after a double dose of cuts (Aix's, and then Antenne 2's). The heart of the title-role is contained in the cavatina, 'Bel raggio lusinghier' and three duets, two with Arsace – 'Serbami ognor se fido' in Act I and 'Ebben... a te, ferisci... Giorno d'orrore!' in Act II – and one with Assur that opens the second Act. The cavatina has been a happy hunting-ground for sopranos in the *bel canto* repertory in the post-War period: Callas sang it in recital as early as 1954 (EMI CDC 7 49005 2) and returned to it frequently during the remainder of her career; Sutherland sang it with breath-taking agility on her first recording, *The Art of the Prima Donna* (Decca 425 493-2) and then went on to record the work 'complete' (Decca 425 482-2); and in recognition of the role's origin as a vehicle for the vocally ailing Colbran, three mezzos with useful upward extensions have recorded the piece – Marilyn Horne (Decca 421 891-2), Teresa Berganza (Decca 421 327-2) and Cecilia Bartoli (Decca 436 075-2).

Without doubt, all of these are distinguished performances, each finding its own emphasis through musical and interpretative nuance. What makes Caballé's distinctive is its sheer narcissism. Where Callas is unmistakably the

---

* Even as performed at the Festival, however, the work was still cut. In 1992, as its major contribution to the Rossini bicentennial celebrations, the Pesaro Festival gave the first public performances of the uncut critical edition. There was three hours, fifty-six minutes of music, which means that *Semiramide* turned out to be Rossini's longest opera.

voice of a murderess and Bartoli capers with manic ferocity around some hyper-active embellishments, Caballé plays the Queen, ineffably serenading herself. Languid and sensuous, she spins the tone effortlessly (save for a few *fortissimo* bulges at the apex of rapid runs), and in her *dolce* ruminations upon the name of her intended lover, Arsace, she strikes exactly the right note of flirtatious decadence. The coloratura, furthermore, is precise and fully articulated: one can scarcely believe that this is a soprano who, on either side of this Aix run, was singing Turandot.

The duets with Horne provide an authentic frisson and at the same time afford us a glimpse of just how exciting these works must once have been when entrusted to real (as opposed to media-manufactured) divas. In fact, as the run of performances continued, both became increasingly inclined to impro-vise their coloratura in the second verses, yet never once – according to report – did they come unstuck. The two singers, notwithstanding their wholly dispar-ate techniques and timbres, blend beautifully, and it is small wonder that these performances became a by-word for vocal hedonism. The longer and rather more involved second duet, during which an amorous Semiramide learns with horror from Arsace just who he is, puts Horne and Caballé even more through their paces because of the wide emotional range the piece contains. Particularly fine is the soprano's distraught 'Ebben, ferisci', followed by an insinuatingly suave 'La madre rea punisce' (punish this guilty mother) which suggests that this Queen's objective in so saying is the reverse of her ostensible sentiment. And here, as throughout, the alert and athletic conducting of Jesús López-Cobos and the spruce playing of the Scottish Chamber Orchestra keep the dramatic temperature on the boil.

Perhaps finest of all is the confrontation at the beginning of Act II involving a long poisonous interview between the two partners in regicide, Semiramide and Assur. Here Ramey and Caballé spur one another to heights of scornful virtuosity, particularly during the cabaletta – 'La forza primera' – alas truncated to one verse. It is good news indeed that the French National Sound Archive has recently been seeking the permission of all artists concerned to release a commercial video of the transmission.

Il Turco in Italia

London, studio, viii.1981: Fonit Cetra, licensed to CBS Masterworks LP (CBS D3 36859); CBS CD (M2K 37859), reissued as Sony CD (S2K 37859)

Rossini wrote this opera in 1814 for the Teatro alla Scala in Milan as a follow-up to the work which had made his name and fortune the previous year in Venice: *L'Italiana in Algeri*. As the titles themselves suggest, the plot of the later work offers a kind of reversal of circumstances. This time, however, the usual collec-tion of stereotypes – senile and/or impotent husband, frustrated and flirty younger wife, lovers galore, some stupid, some exotic, some plausible – is enlivened by the introduction of a poet, Prosdocimo, who comments on the unfolding narrative. Thus, courtesy of Felice Romani (who would later become famous as Bellini's librettist) eighteenth-century *commedia dell'arte* meets twen-tieth-century Pirandello. It should be borne in mind that Rossini wrote the role of Fiorilla – the only fully developed part in the opera – for Francesca Maffei Festa, whose other major engagement in the La Scala season of 1814 was

Mozart's Donna Anna. From this we can tell that the composer would have found nothing *a priori* wrong in the notion of a Caballé singing the part, which involves a bored wife flirting with an Eastern potentate, dallying with numerous lovers, rowing with her husband, deciding to elope, being stood up and finally creeping back sorrowfully to her forgiving spouse.

The opera is a rich, ripe, rather unusual comedy. A great pity therefore that no one thought to tell this to the producers, Riccardo Chailly or any of the cast, for the performance comes over as a rather po-faced business. Perhaps at least some of the trouble stems from the fraught circumstances of the recording, with Caballé replacing Scotto at rather more than the eleventh hour. Given, then, that she is engaging here in some adroit sight-reading, it seems odd that the producer(s) did not seek to create the right ambiance in which she could deploy her undoubted gifts as a comedienne. Still, this does not detract from the set's musicological significance as the first complete recording of Rossini's score.

The Fonit Cetra/CBS recording catches Caballé in fair, if beefy, voice; hardly surprising when one considers that she had just set down *Andrea Chénier* and was commuting between these London sessions to Ravenna for scheduled *Tosca*s. But one has to search hard to find real signs of life in the impersonation. To hear what is missing one has only to turn to the fearsomely cunning battle-axe presented by Callas, or the pert but irresistible minx lightly sketched in by Graziella Sciutti (on a live pirate of an RAI Milan relay). Even so, Caballé's singing of what could be construed as Fiorilla's credo, 'No si da follia maggiore' (No greater madness than being faithful) is reasonably accomplished and, in the slow section of the duet with her husband, her rendition of 'No, mia vita, mio tesoro' is exquisite and deeply felt. The irony is that the piece is a bit of calculating effrontery on the part of the scheming Fiorilla and hence loses its dramatic (as opposed to purely musical) function if sung, as here, dead straight. In the subsequent outburst, 'Minacciarmi, maltrattami' (you threaten me, abuse me) Caballé makes little of the words. Indeed, whole tracts of the recitative pass by without significant inflection, even when the character is meant to be in a furious temper. On the other hand, her reading of the letter from her husband finally throwing her out is spoken in the blackest tones of a Lady Macbeth. The work, however, is supposed to be a comedy.

What ultimately undermines Caballé's performance is not the failures of imaginative response, but the pervasive vocal fallibility: triplets are smudged, runs are aspirated, there are some ugly bulges of tone, and throughout one has the sense of the soprano wrestling with a voice that will not completely obey her. Her reining in of her resources in order to lighten the tone is admirable in theory but rather less so in practice. The normally resonant middle voice is kept tight and compact, resulting in a loss of vocal colour. And at times it sounds as though she is picking her way gingerly across egg-shells. Given that she undertook the recording only as a mercy mission, it is churlish to be too critical, and it should be borne in mind that her contiguous commitments on stage and in the recording studio required her to concentrate on the demands of *verismo*. In such circumstances there are limits to what even a singer as versatile as Caballé can reasonably hope to achieve.

Ermione

(1) Pesaro, pirate, 22.viii.87: Legato CD (LCD-159-2); also transmitted live on Italian television

(2) Madrid, pirate video, iv.1988: transmitted on Spanish television

Unlike *Semiramide*, where the profusion of numbers leads to undeniable musical bloat, *Ermione* preserves a dramatic concision of surprising power and sweep. As always with Rossini's Neapolitan operas, the title-role was written for Isabella Colbran and is arguably, together with that in *Armida*, the most exigent of them all. What is quite clear from the outset in both the Legato CD pirate of the 1987 performance from Pesaro and the pirate video of the 1988 Madrid production is that, momentary weaknesses apart, Caballé has the absolute measure of the role in terms of both voice and temperament. In this she is immediately set apart from the handful of sopranos who have essayed some, or in Cecilia Gasdia's case all, of Ermione's music. The latter is to be heard on the only commercial studio recording of the work (Erato 2292-45790-2), a somewhat flabby affair with none of the requisite drive or passion, and though Gasdia sings very well, her light tone and girlish timbre are inappropriate for this grand tragedy-queen role. It is Caballé who truly confronts us with Racine's tragic heroine: the abrasive Act I duet with Pyrrhus, 'Non proseguir', establishes from the outset the scale of her performance. What it sporadically lacks in needle-sharp fluency of *fioriture* it more than compensates for in scorn and powerful declamation. In the unison section of the continued duet, 'Più straziata un'alma', the agonizings of the two desperate malcontents is depicted marvellously by Caballé and Merritt, with displays of *spinto* power giving way to softer tones, mirroring the deft modulations in Rossini's score. The duet effectively resumes after Pyrrhus' paralysingly difficult aria – here dispatched with brilliance by Chris Merritt – but now, with fine dramatic sense on Rossini's part, it ceases to be written for the voices in unison but for two independent and differently structured vocal lines. By this time, the soprano is well into her stride, although her subsequent duet with Orestes – sung in the Pesaro performance by Rockwell Blake, no less extraordinary than Merritt – suffers from some strident attack *in alt*. Nevertheless, by the end of the first Act we are forcefully reminded of who is the central character in this work when she ends the finale with a pair of ensemble-dominating high Cs set to a musical progression which Rossini later reused at the same point in the score of *Il viaggio a Reims*.

The heart of the role is to be found in the second Act where at last the soprano is allowed to make an effect in something other than duets and ensemble work. Her *gran scena* is marked by heroic declamation at the highest pitch of emotional expression: Ermione has just learned that she has been jilted by Pyrrhus, and is obliged to witness his nuptial procession. In a furious *allegro*, she instructs her hang-dog admirer Orestes to kill Pyrrhus, going so far as to give him the dagger with which to do the deed. This is accomplished offstage, although not by Orestes himself, and he returns in order to bask in his beloved's gratitude. Unfortunately for him, in the interim she has undergone a change of heart and rounds on Orestes for his part in the murderous assault. He exits pursued by the Furies whom Ermione has invoked, leaving her prostrate with horror as the curtain falls. (The Madrid production took the theatrically convincing – if mythologically inaccurate – decision to have Ermione stab herself at the end.)

In Caballé's performance, the dramatic recitatives in Act II are dispatched with temperament and haughty indignation. She also excels in her wealth of tone colour and dynamic variation, including an extraordinarily effective reading, numb-toned with disbelief, of the passage where she hears the nuptial march offstage. But the trade-off – at least on the opening night at Pesaro – is some approximate coloratura and a scramble through the triplet passages in 'Amata, l'amai', taken at a disobliging, if thrilling, *allegro* under the fiery conducting of Gustav Kuhn. The ensuing duet with Orestes certainly has its moments – did Rossini ever write more demanding and dramatically powerful music? – but Caballé is by now tiring and she reaches the end of the opera more by will-power than any remaining vocal resource. Later in the run she learned to pace herself better and encountered much less difficulty. By the time she came to tackle the role again the following year in Madrid she had mastered most of Ermione's pitfalls, as the later video pirate reveals. All in all, therefore, one of Caballé's most notable latter-day assumptions and one which will surely lead to the opera's restoration to the repertory as one of the truly great works of the nineteenth century.

Rossini Rarities

Rome, studio, vi.1967: (*La donna del lago* – Tanti affetti; *Otello* – O tu, del mio dolor...
Assisa a'piè d'un salice; *Stabat Mater* – Inflammatus; *Armida* – D'amore al dolce impero; *Tancredi* – O Patria dolce... Di tanti palpiti; *L'assedio di Corinto* – L'ora fatal s'appressa... Giusto Ciel!)
RCA Victor LP (SB 6771); BMG CD (GD 60941) (Issued in Spain on Ariola (9D 259273))

This recital disc was hailed as a classic from the first day of its release in 1968. It was, in effect, the first ever recital dedicated to Rossini, though one or two of the arias had been recorded by other singers as individual items before. The selection (carefully chosen to provide the widest possible contrast) was made by Caballé herself in conjunction with the musicologist Randolph Mickelson, and the recording was originally released to coincide with the centenary of the composer's death. Far from diminishing in significance with the passing of the years as the whole Rossini renaissance has flourished, the recording remains an absolute point of reference in the general discography. The Rossini authority Richard Osborne, when reviewing the long-overdue CD reissue for BBC radio, stated that if he were permitted to take only one Rossini recording to the proverbial desert island then it would undoubtedly be this recital, which contained the kind of singing that would have delighted the composer.

From the light-hearted coloratura fireworks of 'Tanti affetti' to the bronze-hued declamation of the 'Inflammatus', the exquisite *legato* refinement of 'Giusto Ciel!' to the heroic scale work in 'D'amore al dolce impero', one is confronted throughout by simple, flawless excellence. Nor is there any lack of interpretative insight, since each piece is persuasively characterized through the manipulation of vocal tone colour. It is hard to credit that the same singer who gives such monumentally powerful delivery of the extract from the *Stabat Mater* can go on to give such an awe-inspiring account of Armida's Act II variation aria, yielding not one iota in either tone or technique to the legendary performances of Maria Callas (EMI CDC 7 54437-2). It is possible to imagine a more naturally wistful tone of voice for Desdemona's lament (that of Frederica von Stade immediately springs to mind [Philips 432 456-2]); and the famous excerpt from *Tancredi* just misses the surreal level of virtuosity attained by Marilyn Horne (Decca 421 306-2). But then, von Stade could not have scaled the imposing heights of the 'Inflammatus' any more than Horne managed to spin the limpid soprano line of 'Giusto Ciel!' on her own superb recital (Decca 421 306-2). It is Caballé's achievement on this disc to have accomplished *all* these things with such prodigious skill.

(ii) VINCENZO BELLINI

Il pirata

(1) Florence, pirate, 13.vi.67: Nuovo Era CD (2207/8), reissued on Memories CD (HR 4186/87); Great Opera Performances CD (GOP 729 2)
(2) Florence, pirate, 15.vi.67: Melodram CD (MEL 27015)
(3) Rome, studio, vii.1970: EMI LP (SLS 953); CD (CMS 7 64169 2)

It was the success of this opera when it was premièred at La Scala in 1827 that made the reputation of the twenty-six-year-old composer, as well as marking the start of his collaboration with the librettist, Felice Romani. It also inaugurated that quintessentially Romantic feature of nineteenth-century Italian opera – the concluding mad scene for the heroine. With its numerous epigones, *Il pirata* became one of the principal vehicles of the great sopranos of the *primo ottocento*. The plot concerns Imogene, who has been coerced – as the price of keeping her father alive – into forsaking her true love, Gualtiero, and instead marrying Ernesto, Duke of Caldara. Gualtiero, a political refugee and regarded as a pirate by his enemies, is shipwrecked with his men off the coast where Ernesto's court is situated and, unrecognized by all save Imogene, tries to lure her back. But she is now a mother and, although torn by conflict, refuses. The couple are apprehended during an emotional *tête-à-tête*, Gualtiero and Ernesto fight a duel, the latter is killed, the former is led off to the scaffold, and Imogene goes mad.

Caballé undertook this, her first ever Bellinian role, in 1966 as part of the AOS series in Carnegie Hall; surprisingly (and ironically, given the work's title) no pirate of this performance has ever materialized. She evidently found the experience congenial, since the work featured regularly in her repertory over the following five years, in Philadelphia, Cincinatti, London and Barcelona, as well as the performances in Florence and the recording studios in Rome which comprise the surviving recorded sources.

Making what was in effect her Italian début, Caballé took the Florentines by storm in 1967 – as the Nuova Era/Memories pirate, taken from the Maggio Musicale's own archives, makes abundantly clear. She gives her all throughout the long and demanding part, including an astonishing number of high B♭ s, Bs and Cs, all sustained *fortissimo* as the score predicates. It is hard to imagine that she was ever heard in healthier voice – a condition which the excellent pirate recording on Nuova Era/Memories renders perfectly audible (rather more so than the rival Melodram edition, which was made two nights later when the conductor, Franco Capuana, fell ill and was replaced by a house répétiteur, Erasmo Ghiglia).

The EMI studio recording dates from just after Caballé's first assumption of the role of Norma. Not surprisingly, the voice sounds much more powerful throughout its range, but especially so in the lower register, which has in the interim taken on almost an excess of dark weightiness. As a result, the performance feels very grand indeed, with Imogene's opening word – 'Sorgete!' (Arise!) – sounding less like a compassionate request to a group of half-drowned sailors not to prostrate themselves than a full-blown injunction to get up immediately. Once past this misjudged opening, Caballé hits form and the characterization of the love-torn, put-upon Imogene, plaintive and woebegone, comes into complete focus through the subtlest manipulations of dynamic and tone colour. One would like to think that, at least in the two duets for soprano and tenor, this assurance was due to the subtle interplay between Caballé and her husband, Bernabé Martí, as Gualtiero. But, in truth, Flaviano Labò on the Florentine pirate makes the warmer, more even-toned impression. That said, there is no denying Martí's effortless and ringing power *in alt*, including a securely focused and long-held high D in the *allegro moderato* of his opening aria. As one would expect, the crowning glory of the set is the closing scene, which captures the soprano at her best, in turn imperious, distracted and pathetic. The hair-raising coloratura, stretched across two octaves between the Cs on either side of the stave, is flung off with tremendous panache, coupled with the sort of psychologically apt emotionalism that Beverly Sills used to find regularly in what otherwise looks in the score like pure display music. Caballé discreetly rewrites the literal repetitions of the cabaletta's second verse, a wholly authentic practice in which the original Imogene – the redoubtable Henriette Méric-Lalande – would definitely have indulged.

Norma

(1) Barcelona, pirate, 11.i.70: Melodram CD (CDM 27089)
(2) London, studio, viii.1972: RCA LP (SER 5658-60); CD (GD 86502(3))
(3) Orange, filmed live on 20.vii.74: Classic Video Dreamlife Laser disc (DMLB-21)
(4) Vienna, pirate, 17.iii.77: Exclusive CD (EX93T78/79)

For this – Caballé's greatest role – we have the evidence not only of her studio recording but also three live stage performances spread across the 1970s. The first pirate preserves her very first public performance in the opera; the second enshrines the legendary night at the Chorégies d'Orange when everything was remarkable, even the weather; and the third captures the opening night of a production which caused one of the biggest scandals at the Vienna State Opera in the post-War period. The sound on the Melodram – evidently a lap-top job recorded in the auditorium – is rough and ready, particularly so far as the orchestra is concerned but, when the voices move into the line of fire, one can hear with reasonable clarity all that is being sung. Unfortunately, it has not proved possible to sample the laser discs of the Orange performance, since these are currently only available in Japan and Italy in NTSC format. But videos are in circulation pirated from the original broadcast on French television, and a decent copy played on a stereo machine produces excellent sound and vision. The Vienna pirate is a real revelation, with sound that is virtually indistinguishable from a good quality studio recording.

The RCA studio recording was made in London at the end of a whirlwind of activity which had seen the soprano record three other complete operas in the space of a few weeks during the summer of 1972. This being the last in the sequence, it should have been the jewel in the crown, as none of the other three roles she recorded – Liù in *Turandot*, Mathilde in *Guillaume Tell* and Verdi's Giovanna d'Arco – could be considered significant in the way that the title-role in *Norma* indisputably is. Ironically, though, whilst Caballé's contribution to the other operas could in each case be described as 'definitive', the same cannot be said of her commercial recording of Bellini's masterpiece. Perhaps it is the single instance in her career where it would have profited her to break her own golden rule of never recording the same role twice. There are tiny flaws, such as the little 'hiccup' of placement on the high A♭ on 'mieto' just before the introduction to 'Casta diva' and the slightly awkward *gruppetti* at the start of the aria. In themselves, these are trivial details but disappointing nevertheless from a singer who, in live performance, came as close to vocal perfection as it is possible to come in this role. Even so, the RCA set has never lacked admirers. Writing in *Gramophone*, Richard Osborne noted: '[Caballé's] is singing of classical purity, whose very restraint moves one to tears... It is an interpretation of the opera, of the central role above all, which no lover of Bellini's great work (and no lover of great singing) can afford to miss.'[1] And perhaps if one takes the wider view, ignoring the odd passing blemish – as all admirers of Maria Callas's performances in this role choose to do – then Caballé does indeed come close to a notional ideal.

But no special pleading has to be entered in respect of the Orange performance. Here, her 'Casta diva' is so sublimely sung that the audience is swept up in a once-in-a-lifetime experience of simple, transcendental beauty. That one can also witness Caballé's imperturbable poise on the video adds a dimension to her assumption of Norma that is inevitably missing from audio recordings alone. One listens and watches enthralled as she sets off spectacular volleys of coloratura in the cabaletta 'Ah bello a me ritorna' before unleashing *spinto* ferocity in the concluding Act I trio with Pollione and Adalgisa (sung here by Jon Vickers and Josephine Veasey). But as with all her stage performances of Norma, it is in the second Act, beginning with 'Dormono entrambi', that Caballé delves deepest into her reserves of stamina and vocal power. Later in the Act, during the baleful confrontation with Pollione, 'In mia man alfin tu sei', she sings with astonishingly darkened chest tone – carried all the way up into the notional middle of the voice – that grimly conveys the contempt she has for her former lover. Her vain attempt to force him into abandoning Adalgisa is musically and thereby psychologically brilliantly portrayed: the first command of 'Giura!' is imperious, but the second, following Pollione's refusal, is more desperate, as if Norma's self-confidence has just for a moment deserted her. Yet, following her admission of betrayal before the assembled Druids, her voice sounds as if it had been purged of the weight of guilt and she returns to a pure, almost virginal tone in 'Qual cor tradisti', sung more in sorrow than in anger. Possibly the finest singing of all comes at the very end when she entreats her father to take care of her sons. The opening phrase, 'Un prego ancor', seems to suspend the passage of time, before the exquisitely shaped final plea, 'Deh! non volerli vittime', is floated on uninterrupted streams of tone. Here, stripped of her authority as a priestess by her own self-accusation, Caballé's Norma achieves full tragic stature as a woman and mother.

After this, the other performances on disc register less strongly, though each has its incidental beauties. It is, of course, interesting to hear Caballé's very first thoughts on the title-role in the Barcelonese performance, and a very accomplished piece of work it is. Certainly, no one who was in the theatre that night could have entertained the least doubts that one of this century's greatest Normas was before them. But the Melodram transfer is of such poor quality as to make this only sporadically apparent. On the Vienna transfer one can hear quite clearly that, whatever the inanities of Faggioni's production, by the second Act Caballé had got firmly into her stride on this most fraught of first nights, missed *pianissimi* and some bumpy phrasing apart.

Of the performances which find Caballé in best voice, the Orange pirate is the most distinguished; but in many respects the studio recording runs it a close second, ultimately lacking only the last element in theatrical abandon. Given that the RCA recording is generally available, and the Orange pirate is not, it is probably simplest to stick with the commercial set, not least because the supporting cast – Domingo, Cossotto and Raimondi – are so reliable. But there is an inescapable sense in which, one more time, Caballé's destiny is akin to Callas's in that neither of the Greek soprano's studio recordings fully captures the best of which she was capable in the role. Callas, perhaps, more naturally encompasses the vulpine aspects of Norma: the would-be infanticide, the commander of rebellious hordes. But Caballé's disposition towards the maternal side of Norma time and again brings its rewards in the shape of hauntingly beautiful phrases. Whatever else might be said of her interpretation, it is clear that she owes nothing to other interpreters and that, through her own unique way with the role, she elucidates for us in the late twentieth century the true meaning of early-nineteenth century *bel canto*.

I Puritani

London, studio, 19.vi–5.vii.79: LP (SLS 5201); EMI CD (CMS 7 69663 2)

I Puritani was Bellini's tenth and last opera. It was premièred at the Théâtre des Italiens on 24 January 1835 and was a spectacular success. Nine months later the composer died – of amoebic dysentery – at the age of thirty-four. For such a famous work, its recording and performance history is surprisingly scanty: in the entire post-war period there have been five studio performances, built around the talents of Callas, Sutherland (twice), Sills (on an American Broadcasting Corporation recording, made but never released in the UK) and Caballé. The latter is the only one never to have sung the role on stage. Callas's involvement always took the form of much-cut performances – there is over half an hour of Bellini's score missing from her 'complete' recording (EMI, CDS 7 47308 8) – and Sills avowedly disliked the part, singing it but rarely over a three-year period in the early 1970s. Astonishingly, Caballé set down the role back to back with that of Santuzza in Riccardo Muti's recording of *Cavalleria rusticana*. One would normally imagine that any voice that could sound right for the one role would automatically be wrong for the other: yet it is a measure of how virtually all the greatest sopranos are *sui generis* that

Caballé, like Callas before her, embraced a phenomenal diversity of roles.*
Certainly she makes a conscientious effort here to lighten her tone in order to
suggest the youthfulness that Elvira ideally requires – no mean feat when one
considers that her repertory on either side of these recordings included Normas,
Toscas, Salomes and Giocondas. And if her success here is only partial, none
of the other contenders (with the possible exception of Sills) sounds particularly
girlish either. In truth, it seems rather strange that in our own time the role
has fallen to such voices, when surely it would be much better served by a
genuine *leggiero* such as Kathleen Battle, or better yet, if such existed, the
modern equivalent of Olympia Boronat (HMV LP COLH 129) or Antonina
Nezhdanova (Court Opera Classics LP, CO 366).

Elvira's opening duet with her sympathetic uncle goes well, Caballé expertly
capturing the *mesto* (sad) quality referred to by her partner, but also revealing
a few hard edges and the occasional problem of transition between middle and
chest voice. Happily these blemishes are not in evidence during the ensuing
Polacca, 'Son vergin vezzosa', which captures Caballé in very fleet and nimble
form, adept at turning the corners of the chromatic runs and in the pin-point
staccati in alt. Only the ill-defined trill mars the overall impression, and even
here it is quite audible that she, as always, is at least doing something rather
than relying upon the expedient of many singers who just lean more heavily
on their natural vibrato to get them by. In the *largo concertato* of the first Act
finale, she spins ravishing phrases, evoking the virtually lost art of stylistically
authentic *portamento*; but the *stretta*, unfortunately, is a noisy scramble, violently
hard-driven by the conductor in which it is only occasionally possible to make
out which of the singers is actually singing.

The high point of Act II is, of course, 'Qui la voce sua soave' with its first
strains sung offstage, the whole aria reminiscent of the slow movement in a
mature Mozart piano concerto. Here Caballé's legendary breath control reaches
new heights, and the sense of shape she imparts to the music by her use of it
would incline any objective listener to believe that she had been singing this
music throughout her career. Small wonder that her singing of the aria has
been described as having 'a radiance and almost unspeakable poignancy that
make [her] the most sublime Elvira of recent years'.[2] Throughout her reading,
the detailed markings in the score – *pianissimi*, hairpins, accents, *tenuti* – are
scrupulously observed within the framework of a flexibly sustained and con-
siderate tempo, for here at least Muti gives his soprano a deal of expressive
freedom. The long duet in Act III focuses more upon the tenor than the soprano
and Alfredo Kraus, accompanying Caballé on disc for only the second time, is
in fine voice, with some ringing top Ds. However, he eschews the solitary top F
which the composer wrote into the score following the original tenor, Rubini's,
misreading of another high D, and which is such an amazing feature of Luciano
Pavarotti's performance on the second Sutherland set. During the duet, with
Elvira meandering in and out of insanity with alarming regularity, Caballé
characterizes her voice with great care, reducing her naturally lush tones to a

* When Callas first sang Elvira in 1949 she was in the middle of a run of *Walküre*
Brünnhildes. And Sutherland's second recording in 1975 (Decca, 417 599-2) was made
three years *after* her Turandot.

vibrato-less *fil de voce* as if the fragile line of sound is the thread by which Elvira's mental stability hangs. All in all, at what one might have thought was an improbably late date in her recording career to be singing a *leggiero* role, she turns in one of her most polished performances: more intensely felt and characterized than the superlatively sung Sutherland; and more beautiful and youthful than Callas, who, even in 1952, sounds too dark-toned and whose instinctive interpretative artistry cannot overcome her sheer vocal unsuitability for the role. Caballé, in many respects, really does offer the best of all possible worlds as enshrined on disc.

(iii) GAETANO DONIZETTI

Lucrezia Borgia

(1) New York, pirate, 20.iv.65: Voce LP (VOCE 7); Legato CD (SRO 801 2); Great Opera Performances (GOP 729 2)
(2) Rome, studio, v.1966: RCA LP (SER 5553-5); CD (GD 86 642(2))
(3) Milan, pirate, 2.iii.70: Myto CD (2 MCD 904.23)

Lucrezia Borgia is the opera that brought Caballé international fame, and the pirate on Legato/SRO preserves the very performance with which she achieved it. The RCA studio recording followed just over a year later when the soprano was six months pregnant, whilst the Scala pirate enshrines her postponed début in the house as a principal in February 1970. All three performances utilize slightly different texts. The work, derived from a play by Victor Hugo, was given at La Scala in 1833 when the Lucrezia – Henriette Méric-Lalande – drove the composer to distraction by her insistence upon a showy cabaletta at the end of the opera after the heroine has accidentally poisoned her own son. Oddly, this is omitted in the New York performance, Caballé preferring instead to emit a scream – the specified *grido straziante* – that would make a corpse sit upright. The other two sets both include the cabaletta and manage besides to incorporate material from Donizetti's later revisions. The RCA uniquely includes a further cabaletta for Lucrezia – 'Sì, voli il primo a cogliere' – which the composer bluntly tacked on to the end of her opening romanza, 'Com'è bello', probably at the behest of Giulia Grisi for the Paris première in 1840. Caballé herself never again performed this cabaletta for the simple reason that it is poor music and was never intended by the composer to be sung in addition to both verses of the preceding 'Com'è bello'.

Listening to the clearly recorded New York performance (transferred from LPs, clicks and all) it is impossible to believe that this was the very first occasion on which Caballé had sung in a *bel canto* work, much less that she had been labouring in obscurity for the preceding ten years. But the level of command exhibited throughout shows that her extended apprenticeship had been put to good use, marrying one of the most complete vocal techniques to an instrument of rare natural beauty. In the bare ten minutes it takes for her to sing the opening recitative and aria, one can actually hear the process by which a star is born. The ensuing ovation apparently took up nearly as much time as she had spent singing, and if there is a criticism of this set it is only that the applause, which historically considered is itself now part of the performance, has been crudely curtailed. Perlea, otherwise best remembered as the conductor of the Björling/Albanese *Manon Lescaut* on RCA, is perfectly competent if not especially dynamic: Caballé herself remembers being taken aback by the maestro's undemonstrative style, not having been told that, following a stroke, he had been paralysed down one side. And Vanzo in the role of Gennaro is mellifluous enough to make one regret that the extra music for the tenor was here excluded.

The RCA studio recording gives us Caballé in the two whizz-bang cabalettas that had been omitted in New York. Listening to these with hyper-critical ears, it is possible to detect an element of caution in her approach to the alarming pages of two-octave runs, trills and high notes that reveal her to be a singer whose coloratura technique, whilst impressive, is not quite on the same exalted level as her other vocal accomplishments, such as her sense of phrase, variety of colour, breath control and soft singing.* Perhaps the soprano's advanced pregnancy emerges as a critical factor in that here, for just about the only time on disc, her intonation is occasionally suspect, as in the second verse of 'Com'è bello'. On the other hand, the textually inauthentic but staggering nineteen-second *pianissimo* high A♭ which floats over the top of the ensemble finale of the Prologue, is just as astonishingly vocalized as in New York. As the live sets confirm, no knob-twiddling by RCA's engineers would have been necessary to make Caballé's *tour de force* perfectly audible above orchestra, chorus and half a dozen other soloists.

The 1970 Scala performance on Myto is fully on this level. The lap-top pirate sound, alas, relegates the principals to the permanent middle-distance, but the weight of tone and darkness of hue that Caballé had worked into her voice in preparation for her first Norma the month before is highly apposite. As is the way with live performances, the singers take risks they would not dream of taking (or be allowed to take) in the recording studio. Possibly the most spectacular of these is the diva's interpolated high D♭ at the very end of the Prologue. But then it is evident throughout that she is determined to make a total conquest of the prickly Milanese, to which end some notes are held for ages, both loud and, more often, soft. Indeed, she starts as she means to go on, since 'Tranquillo ei posa' is extended at least three times beyond its notated value. Lucrezia's poisonous interview with Alfonso goes particularly well, with Caballé relishing the menacing drollery of the Borgia's pointed reminders that he is her fourth husband. The final cabaletta – again both verses – is now flung off with a confidence and élan somewhat missing from the RCA set, and the final note reaches, indeed strains, out towards the audience for tumultuous applause. If the sound were any better, this would be the set to have as an adjunct to the self-recommending studio recording, even though Gianni Raimondi is not much of a match for Alfredo Kraus. As it is, the Carnegie Hall pirate is the safer bet in spite of its textual omissions, not least because it includes a large chunk of Caballé's *Roberto Devereux* for the AOS given later the same year. Aficionados, of course, will want all three.

---

* It was Callas's unique achievement to weld such a basically weighty and dark-timbred voice to really astonishing coloratura technique; but then she lacked Caballé's beauty of timbre and security *in alt*, whether loud or soft.

Roberto Devereux

(1) New York, pirate, 16.xii.65: MRF LP (MRF 82-S (3)); extracts on Legato CD (SRO-801-2)
(2) Aix-en-Provence, pirate, viii.1977: Legato CD (SRO-510-2), reissued on (HRE 1004-2); highlights on Legato CD (LCD 108-1)

The fortunes of the three works that comprise Donizetti's 'Tudor Ring' – *Anna Bolena* (1830), *Maria Stuarda* (1834) and *Roberto Devereux* (1837) – have fared pretty well in modern times. Maria Callas reawakened interest in *Anna Bolena* in 1957 and in so doing spearheaded a general revival of interest in the composer's serious operas. Leyla Gencer then took up the challenge with a determination that led to several of them being put on in theatres throughout Italy. From 1965, however, it was Caballé who did most to rehabilitate many of Donizetti's serious works, playing a central part in the restoration of ten of his operas (including the three of the 'Tudor Ring') throughout Europe and the United States.

Interestingly, her association with the Tudor works was conducted in reverse order of their composition, singing Anna Bolena for the first time in 1982 after having débuted as Maria Stuarda in 1967 and Elisabetta in *Roberto Devereux* in 1965. This is perhaps surprising given that the role of Elisabetta is generally regarded as being the most arduous, its demands equating in many respects with those of the title role in Bellini's *Norma*. And of all Donizetti's Queens, this Elizabeth is by far the most complex and fully rounded, forced as she is to deal with the betrayal of the man who, in historical reality, came closest to denying her the sobriquet of 'the Virgin Queen'. The plot tells of the conflict between love and duty caused by Elizabeth's love for Robert, Earl of Essex (the Roberto Devereux of the opera's title). When his emotional treachery is revealed, she orders his arrest, but is devastated by the chain of events that leads to his execution. In the closing scene, haunted by images of the blood-stained block on which Essex has been beheaded, she tears the ring of regal authority from her finger and announces her abdication.

The two available pirate recordings of *Roberto Devereux* date from December 1965 and July 1977. The earlier recording is, in fact, an American Opera Society concert performance in which Caballé marked her return to Carnegie Hall as an indisputable star, eight months after her sensational North American début in *Lucrezia Borgia*. From the moment she starts to sing, there seems to be a confidence, the radiation of a real personality – perhaps derived from an awareness of self-worth – that is reflected in the command with which she invests the music of Elizabeth. We deduce from the recitative preceding her opening aria this character's emotional turmoil, for Donizetti sets the words 'la mia vendetta' on an up-and-down scale that ranges from A above the stave to C below it, and Caballé expertly conveys the volatility that this flourish is meant to express. In the aria and cabaletta, the voice has a firmness and flexibility that equip it to deal almost effortlessly with the considerable demands of Donizetti's score. The upward leaps and the rapid alterations between the *cantilena* in which Elisabetta inwardly expresses her tender thoughts and the coruscating explosions of rage call for a singer with absolute security at both ends of her vocal range and who ideally is not forced to make awkward gear-changes in the middle. This is precisely what makes Caballé so impressive in 1965. The only deficiency is the generalized treatment of coloratura. In the cabalettas especially – and this is an opera littered with them – Caballé has yet fully to develop the necessary skills with which to invest ornamented passage-work with dramatic meaning. This is something which, at their best, both Beverly Sills (on the only commercial studio recording [HMV, SLS 787 (3)]) and Leyla Gencer were able to do when portraying the anguished Queen.

By 1977, when Caballé sang the role at the Aix-en-Provence Festival (from which the second pirate recording is taken), the supreme security at the top of the voice had temporarily deserted her. Right at the beginning, that same phrase 'la mia vendetta' which had been so effective in 1965 is compromised by an ungainly squall on the top A. And occasionally there are problems of equalization between the different vocal registers. But, for all this, even during the first Act where these problems are most apparent, Caballé achieves a grandeur that is entirely apposite to the matter in hand. A dark hue and suffocated tone pervades the voice during the *largo* passage of the second Act trio, 'Alma infida', which helps to convey Elizabeth's agonies. Here Donizetti's writing comes close to depicting the kind of naked fury expressed by Norma in the trio that closes the first Act of Bellini's opera. In the third Act, Caballé achieves the kind of full command that eluded her at the beginning of the performance. In the aria 'Vivi ingrato', she manages the breadth of phrasing and softness of voice that have always been a hallmark of her *cantabile* singing, and the final cabaletta, 'Quel sangue versato', is thrilling in its power. Here the high notes (touching several times on high B) give no cause for complaint. Although throughout the performance there are several instances of misplaced and cracked notes, these rarely distract from the general impression of total dramatic commitment. The Aix performance also survives as a pirate video of the television broadcast by Antenne 2. On the evidence of this Caballé gives what, in terms of dramatic voltage at least, is as fine a performance as was her Norma from Orange.

Maria Stuarda

(1) New York, pirate, 6.xii.67: MRF LP (MRF 13 S)
(2) Milan, pirate, 20.iv.71: Myto CD (2 MCD 911.37)
(3) Paris, pirate, 26.iii.72: (a) Foyer CD (2-CF 2093); (b) Legato CD (LCD-122-2);
(c) Memories CD (HR 4417/18)

This middle work of the Tudor trilogy is the one with which Caballé was most frequently associated, having sung it first in New York in December 1967 and thereafter on numerous occasions both in concert and on stage. It is surprising that, as yet, no CD transfer has been made of her New York début in the role and unfortunately it has been impossible to obtain the LPs released on MRF many years ago. Snippets of the American Opera Society concert have, however, found their way to various compilation pirate CDs, and these reveal – as with the 1965 *Roberto Devereux* – just how well suited to Donizetti's Queens Caballé's talents were. Possessed of an inherent nobility of tone, she also had the technical foundations to cope with the mixture of showy coloratura and seamless *cantilena* that the composer used to give voice to the fiery and poignant aspects of these tragic characters. The role of Mary, Queen of Scots, calls for a singer who can invest the long, plaintive lines of Mary's music with the necessary dramatic pathos. Yet we must have the feeling that this is a royal personage who can compete with the sharp-tongued Elizabeth in haughty pride. The encounter – historically inauthentic – between these two characters must boil with indignation, for unlike Verdi (and Puccini after him), Donizetti was not afraid to have two *prima donnas* confront one another on stage for a histrionic showdown. Whereas Aïda shies away from Amneris just at a point where a flare-up seems inevitable, the abuse exchanged between Elizabeth and Mary – culminating in the latter's scornful jibe 'Figlia impura di Bolena' – is not fore-stalled by any considerations of politesse and reserves of powerful chest tone have to be summoned up to bring off the volley of insults.

The two performances on pirate CD date from 1971 and 1972. The Myto transfer preserves the last in a series of five performances given by Caballé at La Scala in a production by Margherita Wallmann that she rated as one of the finest in which she had ever performed. Given her enthusiasm for the experience and the fact that she was well run in, one might expect Caballé to be at her best. Unfortunately, she is not. Her opening aria, 'Oh! nube che lieve per l'aria ti aggri', in which Maria reminisces about her beloved France, has a restless quality, a certain abstraction, that sounds as if she was finding it difficult to engage in the performance that evening. There is something perfunctory about her phrasing: line endings, for example, are not treated to her customary refinement and long finish. Though there is nothing particularly wrong about her singing, some of the usual ingredients seem to be missing, a state of affairs all the more apparent in comparison with the Legato/Memories recording of the concert performance given at the Salle Pleyel just under a year later. Here the soprano finds a wealth of tonal and dynamic variation in the aria's Bellinian simplicity; each time she sings of 'al suolo beato che dì mi nudrì' (that blessed land which once nourished me) she invests the music with subtle changes of colour and emphasis that serve to make each return to the phrase sound ever more achingly nostalgic.

Another aspect of the Paris performance that lends it a level of distinction which the Milanese one does not equal is the rapport Caballé has with José Carreras as Leicester. He brings to the role an ardour and youthful passion that Ottavio Garaventa just cannot match. The Act II duet, 'Da tutte abbandonata', finds the two Spaniards' voices blending perfectly, a world away from the nagging hardness of tone that pervades Garaventa's contribution and from the inertia in Milan that seems to afflict the soprano throughout the first half of the role. Even the great confrontation between the two Queens, which consti-tutes the dramatic highpoint of the work, lacks the intensity of the Paris pirate. The Scala set remains great theatre, and of course Caballé knows exactly what is required at this point to the extent that the audience is brought close to rapture. One or two details are even accomplished better than in Paris. For instance, when Maria rounds on Elizabeth, having endured the latter's humili-ation to the point where she can bear it no longer, Caballé manages to carry the chest voice so high that she has no difficulty with the savage line 'Meritrice indegno osena', which requires a sudden ascent from below the stave whilst still retaining the full dark quality of the lower voice. However, the Paris performance is, in general, the more remarkable. What may partly account for that impression is that the confrontation nearly always seems to go better when the two Queens are both sung by high voices. In Milan Caballé is pitted against Shirley Verrett who is no slouch when it comes to showing fiery temperament in the grand manner, but who is nevertheless an unmistakable mezzo. But at the Salle Pleyel a less accomplished singer – Michèle Vilma – electrifies; although she may not have Verrett's innate quality of voice, and her pitch occasionally sharpens in the middle register, she is undeniably more exciting and copes more easily with the high tessitura of the role.

The respective qualities of Caballé's two performances even out in the last Act, where she comes absolutely into her element. Having risen to the heights of dramatic fury in the second Act, the sympathetic side of Mary's character is now brought to the fore. In the long *scena* with Talbot, starting with an extended arioso and eventually leading to the aria 'Quando il luce rosea', Caballé on both sets portrays Maria in long, unbroken streams of velvet tone. In Paris, her breath control is amazing. Her trills on 'sorride' are not the vestigial efforts they sometimes are, and she phrases with fine imagination, for example singing *sostenuto* in order to link the two verses of the aria and finishing the piece with a simple cadenza that somehow encapsulates the essence of Maria's tragedy. Her final prayer, written like so much of the heroine's music in simple, undecorated long melodies, has exactly the kind of *mestizioso* Donizetti must have dreamt of. High above the voices of the chorus, Caballé floats the simple 'Ah' on a sustained G for the prescribed six bars before rising to B♭ in a finely judged crescendo, still all on one breath. Aided by Nello Santi's superb conducting, this is the crowning moment in what, on the evidence of both these performances, is the Donizetti role to which Caballé's gifts were best suited.

Parisina (d'Este)

New York, pirate, 6.iii.74: Legato CD (SRO 836-2); Great Opera Performances CD (GOP 771)

This was one of Donizetti's most popular tragic operas following its successful première in Florence in 1833, with Beethoven's favourite Carolina Ungher in the title-role. Within a handful of years it had been appropriated by such legendary divas as Eugenia Tadolini, Henriette Méric-Lalande and Giulia Grisi, which gives some idea of the role's attractions. The libretto by Felice Romani is derived from Byron and concerns the ill-fated love of the heroine for Ugo, the adopted son of her husband, Duke Azzo of Ferrara. The passion is reciprocal but unconsummated. This, however, does not stop Azzo from publicly accusing the pair of adultery. Indeed, he is only prevented from killing Ugo by the last-minute revelation that the young man is, in fact, his own son by a previous marriage. But his hand is not long stayed: as Parisina fearfully contemplates a most uncertain future, Azzo has the palace windows flung open to reveal Ugo's lifeless body on a bier. She dies of grief.

This pirate recording of a solitary concert performance given in Carnegie Hall on 6 March 1974 under the auspices of the Opera Orchestra of New York was the first time that Caballé had undertaken the complete role. She returned to it in fully staged performances nearly four years later, first in Nice and then

Barcelona, and on each occasion the conductor was Eve Queler. Of the staged performances, no audible document survives but it is hard to imagine that either could be better than this electrifying New York concert, captured in very decent stereo sound. From her opening recitative at the start of the second scene of Act I, it is clear that Caballé is in her most commanding form. She deploys an abundance of colours with which to characterize the unhappily married Parisina's plight, and proceeds to give the opening aria – 'Forse un destin che intendere' – an heroic vocal scale, whilst preserving complete control of the occasional passages of floridity which intersperse the vocal line. Better still is the following cabaletta, 'V'era un dì', where she sings a series of rapid ascending trills flawlessly and in the second verse manages to find a completely different range of expression to vary the repeat. At the end the audience erupts. This sets the pattern for the whole evening. In the Act I duet with Ugo, Caballé gives a display of truly great singing, including an unexpected sense of heady abandon in the faster coloratura passages of the cabaletta. In the ensemble that comprises the Act's finale she achieves some of the most concentrated tone captured on disc and dominates the *stretta* with powerful high notes and nimble *fioriture*. In Act II her beautiful lament, 'Ma fugace lampo', modulates most unexpectedly into 'Sogno talor di correre', a wistful *larghetto* containing some rather surprising key changes. The whole is crowned by a perfectly executed chromatic ascent and descent, capped in turn by a text-book trill and an immaculately sustained, ultra-*pianissimo* high B♭. The audience's reaction is frenzied; the two men nearest the microphone(s) can scarcely believe what they've just heard. Yet there is more to come. In the acrimonious duet that follows with her husband, who has heard her murmuring Ugo's name in her sleep, Caballé sounds at first tentative and fearful, but rallies in order to launch the defiant cabaletta when, goaded beyond endurance, she finally admits her guilty love.

Parisina's great solo *scena* effectively occupies the whole of Act III. (It is this sequence that appears on Caballé's *Donizetti Rarities* disc.) The aria 'Ciel sei tu che in tal momento' entails the same kind of unusual harmonic side-slips as enlivened Act II, causing one to wonder if this intrinsically difficult writing was crafted by Donizetti with the talents of the Viennese-trained Ungher in mind. In any case, the musical craftsmanship is of a high order, which certainly helps to avoid the sense of generic routine into which many of the composer's other works fall. Caballé relishes the opportunities that the score presents her to the full and sings her way invincibly through the final lament, which starts with powerful, tragic declamation and eases into an *allegro* full of cascading coloratura. The cadenza just before the second verse repeat is breath defying as, all in one breath, she takes a two-and-a-half-octave descent and then back up in steps to an infinitely prolonged high B♭ before returning to the centre of the stave. Small wonder that the closing bars are smothered by the sort of cheering normally only encountered in sports stadiums. This is Golden Age singing.

Lucia di Lammermoor

London, studio, vii.1976: Philips LP (6703 080); CD (426 563-2)

There has never been any critical consensus concerning Caballé's performance in the title-role of this recording. On the LP set's first release in the UK in September 1977 *Gramophone* found her hard-toned and dull,[3] whilst *Records and Recording* reported that she gave one of her best performances on disc.[4] The CD reissue in 1990 found the same *Gramophone* critic in revisionist mood, 'hugely enjoying' the set,[5] whilst the Editor of *Opéra International*[6] informed us all that Caballé was incapable of singing this repertory, written as it was for a 'dramatico d'agiltà'. In fact, the role was written for Fanny Persiani (*née* Tacchinardi) and premièred at the Teatro San Carlo in Naples in 1835. Donizetti's score, and the repertories of the majority of other sopranos who have undertaken the work, make it quite clear that the role was intended for a high soprano with plenty of flexibility: in other words, a coloratura. (Persiani's other big roles were Amina in *La sonnambula* and Linda di Chamounix: she was famous for her brilliant coloratura *in alt*, having a voice which extended effortlessly to high F). And for those many decades when this was the only serious Donizetti opera to survive in the repertory, it was the coloraturas who kept it there. Only in the post-war period has it fallen to much heavier, darker and – in terms of musical dramaturgy – unsuitable voices such as Maria Callas, Renata Scotto and Leyla Gencer. Lucia is, after all, an innocent, 'other-worldly' girl given to the Romantic vapours who goes mad when she is prevented by the political dictates of her brother from marrying the man she loves. If the voice is too obviously that of a *woman*, such credibility as the piece evinces simply collapses. So, in theory at least, the decision of Jesús López-Cobos (the conductor of this set) to revert to Donizetti's original higher keys for Lucia's music should make perfect sense in terms of presenting the character in its most girlish, virginal light. The mystery, then, is why Caballé was chosen to sing it, for the net result of the conductor's Urtext tinkerings is to put the tessitura out of the soprano's comfortable range, with a punishing insistence upon high Bs, Cs and even D♭s. Doubtless Caballé could have encompassed this at the outset of her career with no particular difficulty: but for a woman who had, by this time, embarked upon a wholly different and much weightier *spinto* repertory, the problems are audibly acute.

She starts well: both 'Regnava nel silenzio' and its preceding recitative are imaginatively sung, evoking Lucia's nervous uncertainty, and with some fabulous examples of her long, unbroken phrasing. But the trills are no more than approximations and those which pepper the cabaletta 'Quando, rapito in estasi' go seriously astray (the one on 'corre' doesn't even resolve on to the next note). We get both verses but perversely the soprano is tied to a literal repeat of the notes – wholly inauthentic performance practice – except for an ill-advised stab at singing the otherwise *legato* high Cs and Bs on 'il ciel per *me*' as *pianissimi staccati*. And if the other high Cs and Bs are screamy, on the three D♭s in the final bars of this cabaletta one can practically hear the voice bleed.

This is more or less the pattern throughout: something utterly treasurable, such as her first verse of the love duet 'Verrano a te' with Carreras (who is superb throughout), is followed by some very shrieky sounds *in alt*. The crowning glory of any *Lucia* is usually, of course, the mad scene. On this set we are spared the spurious cat-and-mouse cadenza for flute and soprano which seems to be so much a part of this opera's fundamentally trivial appeal. Caballé begins superbly with a ravishing 'Il dolce suono mi colpì', misjudging perhaps only the weight of chest voice she uses for the repeated cries of 'il fantasma'. She is wonderful in the section after 'sparse di rose' as Lucia imagines she hears her wedding music, and the singer performs prodigies of breath control in this snail's pace rendition of 'Ardon gli incensi', as well as realizing to perfection the score's marking of *rallentando e portando la voce* at 'pregherò per te al giunger tuo'. But the trills are poor specimens and the *acuti*, again, uncomfortably pressurized.

To hear what the right voice can achieve in this music, one must turn to the first Sutherland recording (Decca, 411 622-2) or the Gruberovà (Teldec, 9031-72306-2), or better still, search out Beverly Sills's 1970 recording (EMI, SLS 797), which manages to imbue the most routine coloratura with psychological depth. Great Normas, on the other hand, can bring little to this music.

Donizetti Rarities

London, studio, vii.1970: (*Belisario* – Plauso! Voci di gioia... Sin la tomba è a me negata!; *Parisina* – No, più salir non ponno... Ciel, se tu che in tal momento... Ugo è spento; *Torquato Tasso* – Fatal Goffredo!...Trono e corona; *Gemma di Vergy* – Lascia, Guido, ch'io possa vendicare... Una voce al cor...Egli riede) **RCA Red Seal LP (SER 5591); RCA/BMG CD (GD 60941)**

This was the last 'panel' of Caballé's legendary *bel canto* rarities triptych and the first to be made in London. A second disc of Donizetti *scene* was planned and two of the four intended items recorded. However, this disc was never completed, thus consigning the recorded extracts from *Marin Faliero* and *Fausta* to apparent oblivion. None the less, it would be churlish to complain, since what we have constitutes riches enough. This recording, unobtrusively excellent, catches the soprano at her absolute peak. No technical demands are beyond her powers here, and everything is dispatched with a seemingly total effortlessness. When the disc was first released it brought forth panegyrics and twenty-two years later, on the occasion of the disc's much belated CD transfer, the response was even more rapturous. Vivian Liff noted that 'The voice is used like a fine instrument, the phrasing is often awe-inspiring, and the music is brought to pulsing life wholly through an innate musicality and deep respect for the score... a shining example of the highest attainments of the authentic *bel canto* soprano in the second half of this century'.[7]

The *Parisina* and *Gemma* extracts – both works which Caballé went on to perform complete – are much stronger musically than the sequences from either *Belisario* or *Torquato Tasso*, which saddle the soprano with dismally banal cabalettas at the end of her big arias. This does not prevent Caballé from putting on an impressive show, infusing urgency into the blood-and-thunder closing section of the *Belisario* aria, as inappropriately chirpy a bit of nonsense as Donizetti ever penned. The *Torquato Tasso scena* depicts Eleonora d'Este's longing for death if she cannot have the poet of her dreams in her arms. Caballé executes a pair of cadenzas – like most of those on this disc, especially written for her by the musicologist Michael Aspinall – on the words 'm'accendea' and 'necessità' that simply defy belief in terms of length of breath and refinement of *pianissimo* tone.

But it is undoubtedly in the two longer excerpts that she comes into her own. The *preghiera* from the *Parisina scena* – 'Ciel, sei tu' – contains flawless *legato* singing, the voice seeming to resonate in the mind's ear even in those passages where the singer is actually silent. The second verse is even more ethereally impressive, before the soprano breaks off at the sound of the offstage funeral march. In the ensuing confrontation with her husband, Azzo, she is imperious until confronted by her stepson's body, at which sight the voice fairly shrinks with horror. But in the fiery cabaletta, 'Ah, scenda, indegno', where Parisina unleashes wrath upon her husband's head, Caballé makes all the words bitingly clear, offering at the same time powerful attack and blazing delivery. The complete New York performance of some four years later might, as one would expect, manifest greater dramatic conviction, partly through the use of a much darkened chest register. But this performance of the closing scene remains a classic in its own right. In the *Gemma* extract the coloratura runs are magnificent, not so much diamond pinpoints as a string of opalescent pearls. The cry of joy on the word 'sposa' as Gemma looks forward to her husband's return is of a size and security unheard in the Italian repertory since the palmy days of Tebaldi; and in the lead-in to the second verse of the cabaletta, 'Egli riedi', she floats a cadenza of staggering virtuosity before polishing off the whole scene with a fusillade of perfectly secure *fortissimo* high notes.

Voice fanciers and the general operatic cognoscenti will need no convincing, but for anyone new to Caballé's art wanting to know where to start, there is no finer repository of her greatest performances than this RCA set which, on two mid-price CDs, also includes her superb Rossini and Verdi recitals.

OTHER BEL CANTO RECORDINGS

Presenting Montserrat Caballé

London, studio, viii.1965: (*Norma* – Casta diva; *Il pirata* – Oh! S'io potessi... Col sorriso d'innocenza; *Roberto Devereux* – E Sara in questi orribili momenti... Vivi, ingrato; *Lucrezia Borgia* – Tranquillo ei posa... Com'è bello!; *Maria di Rohan* – Infausto Imene...Havvi un dio.**) RCA LP (SB-6647); RCA/BMG CD (09026 61458 2); also available in Spain on Ariola Eurodisc CD (259272)**

La straniera (V. Bellini)

New York, pirate, 26.iii.69: LP (2 HOPE 216); Legato CD (LCD-134-2)

La donna del lago (G. Rossini)

Turin pirate, iv.1970: (a) LP (3 HOPE 206); (b) LP (BJR 116); (c) Foyer CD (2-CF-2028); (d) Legato CD (SRO-803-2); (e) Melodram CD (MEL 27074); (f) Myto CD (2 MCD 89012)

Caterina Cornaro (G. Donizetti)

(1) **London, pirate, 10.vii.72** Foyer CD (2-CF 2048);
(2) **Paris, pirate, 25.xi.73** Rodolphe LP (RP 12474/5); CD (RPC 32474/5)

Gemma di Vergy (G. Donizetti)

(1) **New York, live, 14.iii.76:** CBS LP (Masterworks 79303);
(2) **Paris, pirate, 20.iv.76:** Rodolphe LP (RP 12499/500); CD (RPC 32499/500);
(3) **Naples, live, xii.75** LP (UORC 282); Myto CD (MCD 952.126)

Canzone (G. Rossini, V. Bellini and G. Donizetti)

Madrid, studio, vi.1980: (Rossini: *La regata Veneziana:* I – Anzoleta avanti la regata;
II – Anzoleta co passa la regata; III – Anzoleta dopo la regata; Mi lagnerò tacendo (1); L'invito;
Mi lagrò tacendo (2); **Bellini:** Vaga luna che inargenti; Per pietà, bell'idol mio; Ma rendi
pur contento; Almen se non poss'io; Malinconia, ninfa gentile; L'abbandono; L'allegro
marinaro; **Donizetti:** Ah, rammenta, o bella Irene; Le Crépuscule; La zingara; Una lagrima;
Me voglio fà'na casa; Amore e morte) **Discos Columbia SA, issued on Dischi Ricordi LP**
(ARCL 227006); RCA/BMG CD (74321 14072 2)

Norma (V. Bellini) (in the role of Adalgisa)

London, studio, xi–xii.1984: Decca LP (414 476-1); CD (414 476-2)

Petite Messe Solennelle (G. Rossini)

Peralada, live, 29.vii.88: (Caballé in chorus – concert for the benefit of the Fundacío
Internacional José Carreras per la lluita contra la luecémia) **Catalunya Musica LP**
(63.1383/4)

III: GIUSEPPE VERDI
(i) THE LYRIC ROLES

La traviata

(1) Dallas, pirate, 13.xi.65: Melodram LP (MEL 476(2))
(2) Rome, studio, vi.1967: RCA LP (SER 5564-6), LP highlights (SB 6779); CD
(RD86180(2))
(3) London, pirate, 28.vi.72: Foyer CD (2-CF 2049)
(4) Philadelphia, pirate, 13.iv.73: Melodram CD (CDM 270106)

The role of Violetta – inspired by Alexandre Dumas *fils*'s autobiographical
novel and play, *La dame aux camélias* – has attracted an astonishing array of
sopranos, from those (like Callas, Caballé and Scotto) who have all been successful Giocondas, to Queens of the Night, such as Sills, Studer and Gruberovà.
This diversity of the role's practitioners has led to the odd idea that no 'one'
soprano can hope to do it justice, on the grounds that Act I ideally requires a
coloratura, Act II a *lirico-spinto*, and Act III an unalloyed lyric. The fact is that
this is how Verdi wrote most of his soprano roles in the first half of his career,
presumably with a reasonable expectation of performers coping single-handedly
with their various demands. Caballé on the RCA set – only the second absolutely complete recording in the work's history – is notable for the general air of
dignified command with which she infuses Verdi's most sympathetic heroine.
When, after the party, Violetta considers Alfredo's declaration of love, she sings
both the prefatory recitative and both verses of 'Ah fors'è lui' full of inward
musing. The repeated cries of 'Gioir!' which preface the cabaletta are extraordinary not only from the point of view of needle-sharp accuracy but also dynamic
variety. And the high Db on the third statement of the word appears out of
nowhere in a perfectly placed *pianissimo*, without any need for the voice to
'find' the note, and on an unbroken breath from the preceding middle Eb. This
is unobtrusively supreme virtuosity.

In both scenes of Act II there is no lack of *spinto* power either to fuel the
intensity of utterance needed for 'Amami Alfredo', or to ride the big ensemble
in the casino scene. Indeed, the dramatic voltage generated between Caballé

and Sherrill Milnes as Germont *père* would register all the more strongly as great singing were it not for the execrable conducting of Georges Prêtre, which reveals the most peculiar approach to *rubato*, full of arbitrary and ill-motivated lungings and swoonings that momentarily unsettle all the performers at various points. Even so, the grief-stricken tone with which she sings 'Dite alla giovine' and then numbly asks of Germont what she must do is one self-evident highlight of the performance. Act III is the quintessence of early Caballé on disc: limpid, yet rich-toned, with a wealth of colours at her disposal, and a naturally affecting quality of voice. And, to do justice to the *pianissimi* that made her famous, the high As that terminate both verses of 'Addio del passato' are quite miraculous. When a highlights LP was issued at the end of 1968, no less an authority than Andrew Porter wrote: 'Caballé's Violetta is one of the most beautiful things put on record for a long time ... One could write an essay on the heroine's interpretation: moving, unaffected, warmly emotional but always controlled ... The finely spun soft high notes, the delicate portamentos, the free, sensitive use of *rubato* – all these sound spontaneous, not like "applied" expression.'[8]

The other three sets which preserve various live performances of Caballé's Violetta really only form interesting pendants to the studio recording, since all of them are in poor, 'in-house' sound and feature the usual round of abridgements and cuts. Yet all three are of some historical interest, if only because of extraneous factors. The Dallas recording – never thus far transferred to CD – contains the performance which, had not *Lucrezia Borgia* in Carnegie Hall unexpectedly intervened, would have made the soprano's reputation on the international circuit, according to Carlos Caballé. And certainly, her vocal form – from what one can discern of it – sounds every inch that of a fully fledged and confident performer. The London pirate comes from a run of performances that constituted Caballé's début at the Royal Opera House, and although, as is outlined in detail in the biographical text, her appearance met with lukewarm notices, her singing gives no justification for such a response. In fact, her vocal performance as such was largely overshadowed by the critical column inches devoted to detailing the diva's oh-so-shocking decision to wear her own costumes. Yet one only has to listen to any of these recordings to appreciate that Caballé's Violetta is on a level of finish that evokes the legendary divas of the nineteenth century. And one can scarcely imagine any of them being criticized principally for their frocks.

The Philadelphia pirate turns out to be a real collectors' item. Following an immaculate, one-verse only, 'Ah fors'è lui', Caballé floats an exquisite high D♭ on 'Gioir!', extending the note for one of those hushed breathless eternities for which she was famous live in the theatre. But in the rapid scale figuration of 'Sempre libera' – immediately before Alfredo's offstage interjection – she omits the last downward run, leaving a startlingly bare vocal gap in the proceedings. The high Cs and D♭ of the subsequent linking cadential flourish are all in place, but in the second verse of the cabaletta things really go astray: two whole bars vanish, and virtually all the scale passage work is replaced by stony silence. None of this deters the audience from giving her an ovation. All strange enough, but what sounds even more peculiar is Caballé's reappearance in Act II after Carreras's superbly sung Alfredo has swept offstage. She barely manages to utter a note before members of the audience start cheering and unleashing a torrent of applause. The innocent ear might well wonder what could possibly merit such a response: the answer is that she had simply reappeared. Between Acts I and II there had been an extended interval during which the audience was informed that Caballé had been stricken by 'abassimento di voce'. The Philadelphian public were simply voicing their relief that the performance was to continue.

Luisa Miller

(1) **New York, pirate, 17.ii.68: Nuova Era CD (013.6329/30), reissued on Memories CD (HR 4331/32)**
(2) **London, studio, vi.1975: Decca LP (SET 606-8), highlights on LP (SET 623); CD (417 420-2)**

Luisa Miller is a transitional work in Verdi's output, moving away from the rousing *Risorgimento* manner of his earlier works in favour of an altogether more sensitive approach to style and subject matter. The work was written for the Teatro San Carlo in Naples and premièred there in 1849. The libretto was an adaptation of Schiller's play *Kabale und Liebe* and, at least in terms of setting, marked a significant departure from the composer's stock-in-trade. The story concerns the ill-starred love of Luisa, a humble maiden who lives with her father in a small Swiss village, and Rodolfo, the innocent son of wicked Count Walter, who has murdered his way to power. The Count has a dynastic marriage in mind for his son and is determined to thwart the boy's love for a mere peasant. To this end, Luisa is persuaded – as the price of saving her father's life – to repudiate Rodolfo. He, believing her to be faithless, poisons himself and his former beloved. As they die, the truth emerges and they are reconciled.

In the opening scene, there is no appreciable distinction to be observed in the condition of Caballé's voice between the 1968 live stage performance and the 1975 studio recording. The principal difference is the numerous minor cuts to which the text is subject at the Metropolitan. Technically, the cavatina 'Lo vidi e'l primo palpito' does not present her with any problems: the triplets are cleanly executed, the trills are in place where marked and are plausible enough examples of their kind. There is also in 1975 a conscientious attempt to lighten the voice. Even so, it is hard to hear Caballé as an ideal Luisa at this stage of the opera, where the essential impression needs to be one of provincial innocence: her tone quality in both recordings sounds very womanly. On disc, perhaps only Moffo [RCA, 86646-2] sounds really right here.

But the world of pastoral trilling depicted in the opening scene is a long way off from the slow moving reserves of *spinto* tone required by the soprano later in the Act, when in a dramatic ensemble her vocal line barely descends below the top of the stave. In the studio recording, Caballé's voice is beautifully poised, settling into the naturally warm tones of her middle voice. Only at the dramatic high B natural on 'non m'abbia l'oppresor' ('let not the tyrant take me') does she fail to dominate the ensemble, vanishing into the cavernous Kingsway Hall acoustic. In the same passage in the live 1968 performance Caballé takes a risk in singing the opening phrase 'Ad immagin tua creata, o Signore' *pianissimo* and yet succeeds triumphantly in remaining audible. As for the climax of the ensemble, such is the level of distortion in the off-air tapes that it is difficult to tell who is singing what, but the audience – who were presumably better placed to hear – seem duly impressed. It is only at the beginning of Act II, when almost half of the opera has already elapsed, that the soprano can make a real effect with her principal aria 'Tu puniscimi, o Signore', even though, from a dramatic point of view, Verdi's musical means and the tone it implies become improbably grand. It is as if the simple Swiss miss of Act I has turned into a Tyrolean Tosca.

During the aria's prefatory recitative, Caballé's high B on 'invano' in the studio recording shoots out like a steel bolt, skewering the note dead centre, and pinning it in place until the octave drop. Considered as pure voice this is thrilling, though it rather seems to set the tone for the *andante agitato* that follows in terms of grandeur and power of utterance. The conductor, Peter Maag, takes it at a relatively brisk tempo and the fussy syncopated accompaniment is played with unswerving rhythmic accuracy. Perhaps taking her cue from this, Caballé delivers the aria in correspondingly strict and clipped fashion: there is more a sense of God being given a piece of the soprano's mind than being asked for help. Since the singing, as such, is magnificently assured, this might seem to be carping, but we have only to turn to the live performance to hear the difference: the tone is softer, more evidently supplicatory, and the impression much less one of a star diva intent on delivering the goods. Ironically, therefore, the live performance before 4000 people maintains a greater sense of intimacy than the very 'public' statement chez Decca. Or at least until the *andante*'s cadenza, where the newly famous soprano treats the Met audience to her speciality: an infinitely long drawn *pianissimo in alt*. The cadenza in 1975 is altogether simpler in dynamic outline, thereby eschewing this element of vocal over-sophistication. The rather determined assault that Caballé makes upon 'Tu puniscimi, o Signore' in the later performance finds a fitting outlet in the cabaletta where her stentorian declamation is better suited both to the lunging rhythm and the dramatic situation.

In Act III – surely Verdi's finest achievement as a composer to date – both these performances touch the sublime. It is not showy music; indeed, virtually the entire Act is articulated in ensemble form, comprising two extended duets involving Luisa – the first with her father and the second with Rodolfo – and a final trio for all three. In the first duet (with Milnes, very fine as her distraught father) Caballé manages the tricky reversion to little-girl *staccati* in 'La tomba è un letto' with great skill. But the real challenge comes in the sustained singing required in the headlong 'Ah! In quest'amplesso' and then in the *andante* 'Adrem, raminghi e poveri' as father and daughter resolve to leave the village. Caballé sings the latter with a mere fraction of her full voice, the better to characterize the sad, wistful nature of the piece. On the Decca recording it would be sublime but for the high C followed by a trill at the very end, neither of which is up to much (this fares altogether better in the live performance at the Metropolitan). The second duet (with Pavarotti in prime form on Decca and Tucker just a little stentorian on Memories) is even better as music and elicits a comparable performance. Her singing of 'Ah, piangi' comes as the most soothing of antidotes to the poison that Luisa has unwittingly taken, Caballé caressing each line almost as if in solace. The cabaletta 'Ah! maledetta' goes like the wind and is thrillingly delivered. The beautiful closing trio, 'Padre, ricevi l'estremo addio', is launched by Luisa as the poison starts to work, and here in both performances Caballé blanches her tone, introducing deliberate momentary weaknesses into her singing by ironing out her natural vibrato. It is powerfully affecting as a performance both live and on the studio recording. Small wonder Luisa was, perhaps unexpectedly, one of her great roles.

Giovanna d'Arco

London, studio, vii–ix.1972: EMI LP (HMV SLS967); CD (CMS 7 63266 2)

It is often the case that attempts to revive recondite works flounder because the singers engaged have neither the status nor the security of technique to make the best case for them in front of a paying public. However, nobody could justly accuse the post-war revivals of Verdi's seventh opera of undercasting: its two generally available recordings star Renata Tebaldi and Montserrat Caballé in the title-role (partnered respectively by Carlo Bergonzi and Plácido Domingo). During the last twenty years, other notable singers have also taken up the challenge of Giovanna, including Katia Ricciarelli, Margaret Price and, perhaps most memorably, Susan Dunn. Yet despite their advocacy, the work has failed to enter the general repertory. Why this should be so is made plain on both the pirate of Tebaldi's 1951 live performance with the RAI Milan orchestra and chorus, conducted by Alredo Simionetto (Melodram, MEL 27021) and Caballé's studio recording for EMI, conducted by James Levine in his first-ever opera recording. *Giovanna* simply fails to repay the effort expended vocally upon it, which in Tebaldi and Caballé's case is considerable. Instances abound of almost comical ineptitude in the musical setting, of which the chorus of demons and their wheezing harmonium accompaniment is merely the most bizarre. On the other hand, the title-role imposes considerable demands on the soprano, and to the extent that *Giovanna* contains any development in Verdi's style, it does so through the music given to the heroine and the way in which it portrays her two facets: the humble country girl and the warrior maiden. The former is defined melodically by the kind of long-breathed, slow-moving cantilena at which Bellini was so adept; and the latter, characterized by driving rhythms, leaping intervals and powerful declamation.

Here, in this recording made in Abbey Road studios in August 1972, at the height of her vocal powers, Caballé genuinely possessed what it takes. In Giovanna's cavatina in the Prologue, 'Sempre all'alba ed alla sera', where she pleads to the Virgin Mary to be given the sword and helmet that will help her to defeat her country's oppressors, all the soprano's customary ability with extended melodies is in evidence; and when, in the space of one bar, Giovanna becomes battle-hungry, the words 'spada' and 'cimier' are sung with that distinctive attack that marks out the true Verdian soprano. In the Act I romanza, 'O fatidica foresta', the contemplative side of the principal character comes again to the fore: appropriately, therefore, the tone is sweet and girlish, with the triplets lightly touched in. In the soprano/tenor duet that follows – which incidentally comprises the best music of the score and points towards the epic scale of the love duet in Act II of *Ballo in maschera* – Caballé and Domingo are every bit a match for Tebaldi and Bergonzi on the live pirate. Caballé suddenly finds an urgency in her voice as she struggles to resist Carlo's entreaties, and in the phrase 'La mia mente... va smarrita' (My wits... are wandering) the character's desperation is caught by singing the first part of the phrase on a *fil de voce*, and the second with an incisive plunge into the chest register. The top Bs and Cs that are dotted throughout the score cause her no difficulty at all, as when – just as in *Ballo* – the ecstatic 'T'amo, si t'amo' is eventually wrung out of the reluctant heroine. The struggle of the character to overcome her feelings for Carlo, prompted by admonishments from the chorus of angels, keeps the propulsion of the duet at a high level. In the passage that starts 'Pur dessi gli angeli', it is as if tears have welled up and are having to be restrained; the repeated command 'lasciami' conveys simultaneously Giovanna's serious intent and her lingering reluctance; and when she despairs at being accursed ('Son maledetta!') the simple cadence in the score is transformed into a heart-piercing cry that is attacked *forte* and then shrinks in volume as if, through despair, all the girl's will to live had evaporated. These are the moments that make Caballé's Giovanna particularly treasurable. Even when the music makes no special claim on our attention either in terms of its quality or technical demands, Caballé – and, it should be said, her colleagues Domingo and Sherrill Milnes – perform so passionately that the triviality is easily overlooked. If there is a fault in her performance, it is that she does not quite dominate the ensembles as the soprano should. But then even Tebaldi would have had difficulty overcoming the furiously driven, loud and sometimes brash musical direction of James Levine.

The critical enthusiasm for this set has always ultimately centred on Caballé's performance: indeed, it is one of her most admired achievements. Even those who feel that she is sometimes not always properly alive to the meaning of what she is singing, or vocally suited to the matter at hand, could not fail to be impressed with the intelligence and quality of her singing here. Even the Editor of the French journal *Opéra International*[9] who, as we have seen, is no great admirer of her art, awarded the set on its CD reissue the magazine's 'Timbre de Platine', normally only reserved for performances in gaslight mono by the long-since dead.

I masnadieri
London, studio, viii.1974: Philips LP (6703 064), highlights on LP (6570 067); CD (422 423–2)

This was the opera written to a commission from London – one of only two such given to European composers in the entire nineteenth century* – and premièred there in 1847 at Her Majesty's Theatre in the Haymarket. The opera failed at the time, despite the presence in the cast of the Victorians' favourite songbird Jenny Lind, whose oft-advertised personal piety normally kept her away from the fleshpots of the opera house (money overcame her religious scruples). The work has never established itself in the repertory at any time since, probably due as much to its egregious plot – faithfully adapted from Schiller's first play *Die Räuber* – as the manifest weakness of Verdi's music. One specific problem is that, in accommodating La Lind, Verdi was obliged

---

* The other was Weber's *Oberon*, given at Covent Garden in 1826.

to write the part with her light, high, flexible voice and old-fashioned musical tastes in mind, which accounts for the odd figure the soprano cuts in this otherwise no-holds-barred melodrama. The story is a convoluted recycling of the Gloucester/Edmund/Edgar sub-plot from *King Lear* (here named Massimiliano, Francesco and Carlo) with the addition of an orphaned niece – Amalia – who is beloved by both brothers, though she herself, of course, is devoted solely to the good one of the pair.

Caballé recorded her role in August 1974 in St John's Smith Square, London, just a few weeks after setting down her Fiordiligi for the same company, and mere days after her legendary Norma in Orange. In retrospect, it seems strange that the world's ranking Norma should be assigned a Jenny Lind role, for which either Sutherland or Sills would have been a more obvious latter-day counterpart. But then neither of these sopranos was under contract to Philips (which was embarked upon a whole series of rare early Verdi) or had recently made a real splash with the recorded première of another Verdi rarity, *Giovanna d'Arco*. Probably, as so often, there was the old feeling that if it appeared in the treble clef, then Caballé could – and probably would – sing it. And she does, superbly, despite the numerous passages of canary-fodder that would have sounded *passé* even in a Donizetti opera.

Amalia's entrance scene is distinguished by some fabulous vocalism, not least in the recitative where Caballé's account of the long, high *melisma* on the word 'corrucciarmi' is simply stunning. The aria proper, 'Lo sguardo avea degli angeli', ripples and prances along and the soprano's matchless *legato* manages to lend it greater coherence than it actually possesses (listen to Sutherland on the rival Decca set (433–854–2) where the coloratura sauce instead becomes the meat and two veg). And the closing cadenza – a rapid, *sotto voce* straight up-and-down scale – is so extraordinary as sheer sound that one pushes the replay button to confirm what one has just heard. Her soft singing in the ensuing duet with Ruggero Raimondi (superb as Massimiliano) is very lovely, tapping a silvery vein of melancholy not often heard in what is, after all, a naturally golden toned voice. This timbre carries over into the fairly banal quartet that brings Act I to a close. The whole of the first scene of Act II belongs to the soprano who has come to mourn at Massimiliano's tomb, only to discover that he and her proscribed lover, Carlo, are not dead, as she had been told by Francesco. The latter materializes and forces himself upon our heroine, first with threats and then physical force until she repulses him with his own dagger. (There are a lot of daggers in this work.) The 'tomb aria' – 'Tu del mio Carlo' – exhibits Caballé's technical control when singing almost an entire piece, as here, in considerably less than half voice, together with an amazing chromatic descent on the merest feathers of tone. It is hardly her fault that the subsequent cabaletta should be such a piece of drivel, a shameless variant of 'Ah non giunge' from *Sonnambula* (though this much may have been at Lind's insistence). Still, the coloratura brilliance is accomplished, if not quite flawless, in the fastest, highest-flying passages, where Sutherland of course comes into her own. Nor can Caballé be blamed for not making much of what should be the high-powered duet between Amalia and Francesco when the unison passage of mutual threats and recrimination is set to an imbecilic, 'oom-pah-pahing' little waltz tune. The duet cabaletta, after she has snatched the dagger, is scarcely any better as music. Even in Caballé's hands, no alchemy occurs and Cappuccilli as Francesco sounds as if he could hardly be bothered to sing: some dross is destined to remain dross no matter what effort is put into it.

Act III opens with Amalia, who has escaped, bumping into Carlo, whose merry band of brigands and their chorus of 'Pillage, rapine, arson and death' give the heroine a nasty turn. Unfortunately, at the moment of the lovers' reunion, a brash, brainless *allegro* erupts. Hearing singers of the refinement and skill of Caballé and Bergonzi in this stuff is a dispiriting experience. Matters musical improve somewhat for the joint passage 'Ma un 'iri di pace' over which the soprano floats some heavenly high notes. But the duet cabaletta is another stinker, the trills of which catch out both soprano and tenor in each of the most unnecessarily repeated two verses. Amalia reappears briefly at the very end of Act IV for the general reunion, only to be stabbed – at her own request – by her beloved (so as to prevent her from the horror of loving him). Small wonder that London never again invited a commission from an Italian composer.

Rarities

Rome, studio, 1967: (*Un giorno di regno* – Ah! Non m'hanno ingannata! ... Grave a core innamorato; *I Lombardi* – Qual prodigio! ... Non fu sogno!; *I due Foscari* – No, mi lasciate ... Tu al cui sguardo onnipossente; *Alzira* – Riposa. Tutte, in suo dolor vegliante ... Da Gusman, su fragil barca; *Attila* – Liberamente or piangi ... Oh! nel fuggente nuvolo; *Il corsaro* – Egli non riede ancora! ... Non so le tetre immagini; *Aroldo* – Oh, cielo! Dove son'io! ... Ah! dagli scanni eterei) **RCA Victor LP (SB-6748); RCA/BMG CD (GD 69041)**

The first two items on this recital are not especially suited to Caballé's voice. The comic aria from *Un giorno di regno* is uncertain in expression, and the weak trill undermines the progress of the very jaunty cabaletta, whereas the tragic one from *I Lombardi* is decked out with streams of Jenny Lind-type coloratura flicks and ticks, which ideally require a voice of far less substance and weight than Caballé's. But the *scena* from *I due Foscari* is another matter: the opening recitative is tremendous, with one of her great arching *pianissimi* phrases; and in the aria proper there is one of the finest examples on disc of her incredible '*ppp*' high notes floating weightlessly over the accompanying chorus. The *Alzira* aria – a dream scene – is an unusual, rather fine piece which suits her down to the ground and in which she carefully lightens her tone to suggest the fanciful imaginings the aria describes, even though the cabaletta is indescribably banal as music. Odabella's superb Act I aria from *Attila* gets a performance to match, sung not only with the most meltingly beautiful tone but also a miraculous *legato* which gives the impression that the entire piece has been performed with just one unbroken breath. (Incidentally, and despite RCA's booklet notes in the CD transfer, there is no solo cabaletta to this piece.) The aria from *Il corsaro*, in which Caballé essays the role of Medora (she is, of course, Gulnara on the complete recording for Philips) is lambently beautiful, with a ravishing cadenza. Then, in the *gran scena* from *Aroldo*, Caballé deploys an altogether more dramatic timbre that would produce any amount of excitement were it not for Guadagno's dismal conducting which undermines the piece. Even so, there is a real Caballé rarity at the end of the recitative, a prolonged *fortissimo* high D on 'soccorri' which considerably raises the temperature. Although subsequent performances of this *scena* by Caballé (in 1974 and 1979, for instance) achieve a higher level of dramatic voltage, she did not venture this note again for the public's delectation.

(ii) THE 'DONNA DI FORZA' ROLES

Il trovatore

(1) New Orleans, pirate, 14.iii.68: Melodram CD (MEL 27047)
(2) Florence, pirate, 11.xii.68: (a) Hunt CD (2-CDLSMH-340380); (b) Legato CD (LCD 123-2); (c) Melodram CD (MEL 272035); (d) Nuova Era CD (2280/81), reissued on Memories CD (HR 4521/22)
(3) Philadelphia, pirate, 1.xii.70: MRF LP (MRF-134(3))

All three of these pirate recordings of Caballé's *Trovatore* Leonora manifest the kind of authentic Verdian singing that was once by no means exceptional but which, in the space of the subsequent twenty-five years, has become virtually extinct. Turn to any of the recordings preserving Caballé's live performances, in New Orleans (1968), Florence (1968) and Philadelphia (1970), and one will experience a taste of that tradition of *lirico-spinto* singing which once supplied the world's opera houses with Amelias, *Forza* Leonoras and Aïdas. To meet the requirements of these roles, the soprano's voice must unmistakably be that of a woman, not matronly but rich and strong, suggesting experience rather than innocence.

This quality is apparent in Caballé's Leonora. The breadth of phrasing in 'Tacea la notte' is superb throughout, and is perhaps at its most spectacular in the performance from Florence where, aided by Schippers' sensitive conducting, she is given all the room she needs to make phrase after phrase memorable. The burnished tone with which she invests 'dolci s'udiro e flebili gli accordi d'un liuto' conveys the sense of melancholy which pervades much of this character's music, though the velvet can turn into silk at will, as on the high B♭ to which Leonora's outbursts of ecstasy ('e versi me lan conconci' and 'la terra un ciel') are set. The single verse given of the ensuing cabaletta, 'Di tale amor', presents few problems for a singer so experienced in dealing with the demands of *bel canto fioriture* (though ironically it is Schippers' marginally slower pacing compared to that of the other two recordings that leaves the soprano breathless for a brief moment). It is the combination of lightness and heft that gives Caballé the edge over such illustrious Verdian singers as Milanov and Price: for great as they are in the more stately passages, they lack the agility (in a way that Caballé and Callas do not) to negotiate the faster moving parts of the score with ease.

The level of Caballé's singing is maintained throughout the second and third Acts on all three pirate recordings. But for the soprano, everything is leading to the fourth Act. And here one can only admire the subtle differences in the details of Caballé's singing between these three performances whilst marvelling at the overall consistency she achieves throughout. In the Philadelphia performance (alas never transferred to CD), almost every phrase of 'D'amor sull'ali rosee' is framed with a hushed *mezza voce*, indicating that this is no public expression of love for Manrico but the private thoughts of a tortured soul. The ache in the repeats of 'le pene' with the ascent to the *tenuto* high C, sung with the soft plush of eiderdown, is heart-rending. Only the 'glitch' at the end of the final cadenza and the wobble on the too-long-held final note spoils an otherwise faultless rendition. The 'Miserere' which follows finds Caballé's Leonora more urgent and panic-stricken than on the two other performances, and the single verse of the cabaletta, 'Tu vedrai', is so fluently dispatched that one regrets its cut (following traditional live-performance fashion) in the two performances preserved on CD.

The particular features of the New Orleans Act IV begin to reveal themselves in the 'Miserere', which admittedly gets off to a grim start as what sounds like a group of hungover monks bemoan their condition. But Caballé is above such matters and gives, if anything, a finer account than in Philadelphia, one very much in the Met tradition of stentorian full chest voice à la Zinka Milanov. The interpolated top Cs on 'di te scordami' are superbly focused and powerful, setting off yet another volley of applause just as at the conclusion of the preceding aria. In the absence of the cabaletta, matters then proceed swiftly to the duet with Conte di Luna; and swift is the word, for despite the frenetic conducting of Knud Andersson, never once do Caballé and the admirable Enzo Sordello (the man Maria Callas had sacked from the Met for holding on to a note longer than she did) fall behind the beat. In fact, they seem to revel in this melodramatic account, which reaches its height in the duet-cabaletta, 'Vivrà! Contende il giubilo', taken at almost twice the speed of, for instance, Mehta on the set with Price and Milnes (RCA RD86194). Such speed serves a musico-dramatic purpose, lending Leonora's comments a manic intensity. In the euphoria of saint-like martyrdom, she rejoices in the thought of telling Manrico as she dies (by having poisoned herself) that 'Salvo tu sei per me!'

Yet despite the qualities of great Verdi singing in the pirates of the New Orleans and Philadelphia *Trovatore*s, Caballé's performance from Florence can lay claim to being her finest. This is not simply because it has the best sound, but also because, in the absence of a commercial recording, it comes closest to the kind of Leonora one imagines Caballé would have set down under studio conditions. Nowhere is this more apparent than in the fourth Act. The vocal magic begins right from the start in the recitative preceding 'D'amor sull'ali rosee' when the entire phrase 'deh pietosa gli arreca i miei sospiri' is sung, unbelievably, on a single breath. The *dolcissimo* high B♭ at 'pietosa' in the midst of this is so delicate it sounds almost translucent. In the aria, she exploits every technical ability at her command in terms of dynamic variation, breath control and tone colour. A singer without her incomparable *legato* could never hope to prevent the piece collapsing altogether, so slowly is it taken with the conniv-ance of Schippers. Yet it is precisely this *legato* that somehow manages to provide a forward momentum during the most ethereal of long-held *pianissimi* or even across moments of silence. In singing such as this one understands precisely what André Tubeuf meant when he described Caballé's as 'a slow voice, spreading out like a becalmed sea'. And small wonder that the Florentine public erupt with ear-splitting applause and yells of 'bis' which, on the Melo-dram set, continue for three full minutes. When order is restored the 'Miserere' follows, and we immediately hear a different vocal colour as the tone changes from a golden muscat to the colour of cassis, suffused with the character's despair as she is brought back to reality by the monks' funereal chanting and the ominous tolling of the bell. She treats each cry of 'di te scordami' with a different emphasis and weight of tone, so that the numerous repeats each convey something different about Leonora's plight. As only the greatest artists can, she manages to find a new way of expressing music that is so familiar.

Un ballo in maschera

(1) Rome, pirate, RAI recording 23–28.vi.69: Melodram/GDS CD (GDS 21016)
(2) London, studio, vii.1978: Philips LP (6769 020); CD (426 560-2)

This, of all Verdi's operas, suffered most at the hands of the ever-vigilant Italian censors who were unhappy at the depiction of a frivolous and libertine court and the regicide dénouement. As a result, the work was not performed in Naples – for which it had been intended – and was instead premièred on 17 February 1859 at the Teatro Apollo in Rome. The role of Amelia, torn between duty to her husband and her love for the king, makes all the familiar Verdian demands of a soprano, taking her across a range of more than two octaves (from high C to low A♭), with a generally low *tessitura* and a marked disparity between its *spinto* and lyrical extremes. Her two solos are characterized by one or other of these, and given their different vocal and dramatic demands, it is not surprising that few sopranos on record have shown themselves to be the mistress of both.

Amelia first appears (and then only briefly) towards the end of Act I. We are at the fortune-teller, Ulrica's, where she has come in search of a cure for the love that torments her. Under Bartoletti's stolid direction on the 1969 RAI recording, the emotion is somewhat generalized: though there is resolve in Caballé's 'si, qual esso sia' ('yes, if it must be'), and terror in her singing of 'Mio Dio qual loco' ('O God what a place'), it is all so much more sharply realized nine years later under Davis's more propulsive baton. Although by 1978 Caballé's tone has become noticeably heavier, she nevertheless shapes the arch of Verdi's melodic contour with precisely matching dynamics, so that as the line climbs the volume gradually swells, and as the former descends the latter diminishes. With only a little less vocal wherewithal in 1978 she achieves a good deal more.

At the beginning of Act II, Amelia appears at the foot of the gallows to which Ulrica has sent her to gather the herb that will cure her guilty love. This is one of the most heavily written of Verdi's soprano *scene* and in the 1969 recording Caballé is in resplendent voice throughout, coping effortlessly with the low tessitura of the recitative and clearly conveying the anxiety of the character's agonized self-communings. But it has to be said that some of the drama of the recitative fails to penetrate the cool *bel canto* to which she – with the conductor's indulgence – treats us. This is not the case in the studio recording, where Davis in no sense indulges his soprano but instead makes exigent demands of her in terms of tempo and dynamic. The recitative is fast to the point of fluster, and Caballé finds herself hard-pressed simply to get the notes out. So it is only when the tempo broadens at the self-command 'S'inoltri!' ('Press on!') that her performance begins to settle and a sense emerges of the voice being brought under full control. The terror of 'Perire!' is memorably evoked through a stark juxtaposition of registers. Then, in the aria proper, 'Ma dall'arido stelo divulsa', Caballé finds scope within the longer note values for a more varied range of tone and dynamic, thereby producing an atmosphere more properly suggestive of a soliloquy than the same passage in the earlier performance.

In the dramatic highpoint of the *scena* – the passage following the chimes of midnight – Davis unleashes such a tornado of speed and volume that the soprano is forced to resort almost to *sprechgesang*. She lets fly with a series of half-sung, half-spoken yelps of terror, climaxing in a resounding top B. Perhaps for some this method of delivery is to be faulted irrespective of whether it is used as a matter of interpretative choice or vocal necessity. But what is surely undeniable is the sense of primal fear that the performance communicates. The concluding prayer in the RAI performance is exquisitely launched, climbing effortlessly through the first two phrases ('deh, mi reggi, m'aita, o Signor...') reaching a climax on the third with a rock steady and ringing top C. On the Philips set this top note has a hard, glassy quality, but Caballé makes amends with the (unmarked) *portamento* descent to the middle D, which is flawlessly negotiated.

The famous love duet follows immediately with Riccardo's arrival ('Teco io sto'). On the 1978 studio recording one is aware of the deeper insights which stem from Caballé's long acquaintance with her role, not to mention her altogether greater rapport with an artist of Carreras's calibre (Flaviano Labò on the earlier set was by 1969 somewhat overparted). She sings her final attempt to repel him ('va, Riccardo!') with a mixture of regret and wavering resolve, barely able to let go of the notes. Then, after the reluctant avowal ('Ebben: si t'amo'), her appeal 'Ma tu nobile...' is floated on an arching span of warm tone, whilst the repeat of 'mi difendi dal mio cor' is sung on a single breath, its melodic contour growing fainter with each repetition. The phrase ends on a perfectly poised middle E held to the double bar just at the threshold of audibility. Carreras launches 'O qual soave brivido' with infectious rhythmic brio but the actual emotional climax of the duet – at Amelia's cry of 'si, t'amo!' – is simply enormous, both vocally and orchestrally. The unison repeat of the main duet theme blazes with passion, though Caballé's last high B is less focused than in her earlier recording and the top C – by her own standards – is screamy. But these are the only blemishes in an otherwise inspiring performance of the duet.

In the plaintive Act III aria – 'Morrò, ma prima in grazia...' ('I shall die, but first a favour...') – the challenge for any soprano is to 'paint' with imaginative vocal *chiaroscuro*. In the RAI recording Caballé experiences no technical problems with the piece and her prodigious breath control allows her to sing across whole phrases which most others are obliged to chop up into more manageable segments. It is all effortlessly sustained and as a piece of singing it is magnificent; yet there seems to be some failure to identify with Amelia's predicament: the emotion is generalized, the voice monochrome. But by 1978 her interpretative stance has been entirely re-thought, as has much of the detail she chooses to emphasize. Immediately apparent is a striking change in tone and volume. Whereas the 1969 performance was delivered at a fairly unvarying *mezzoforte*, on Philips the aria is begun in a withdrawn half-voice, dignified yet resigned. The end-phrases of the first two lines are sung *diminuendo*, fading away in sorrow. 'L'unico figlio mio' is even more delicately drawn, as if the very act of mentioning her only son causes Amelia untold pain. Despite the stresses and strains that are occasionally audible on the Philips set, Amelia remains one of her most notable Verdian assumptions and one which has never been accorded its critical due. It is even more surprising to note that it is the last Verdi role she ever recorded.

Don Carlos

(1) **Verona, pirate, 2.vii.69: Melodram CD (MEL 37057)**
(2) **London, studio, viii.1970: EMI LP (HMV SLS 956); CD (CDS 7 47701 8)**
(3) **New York, pirate, 22.iv.72: Foyer CD (2-CF 2092)**

Caballé made the EMI recording of Verdi's most ambitious opera in the Abbey Road studios in the summer of 1970, the year after her sensational performances in the role in the Arena di Verona (preserved on Melodram) and a year before singing it at the Metropolitan Opera House (preserved on Foyer). Her naturally limpid soprano is perfectly suited to Elisabeth's early utterances, in particular the exquisite Act II romanza 'Piangere, mia compagna' when she consoles her lady-in-waiting who has been humiliatingly dismissed by the King. She sings 'Ti seguira mio cor, ah ti seguira' all on one breath despite a rise to *pianissimo* heights half-way. And then, just to show she is not a creature of fixed habit, in the second verse she phrases completely differently, with altogether greater power and volume, and caps it all with one of the most beautiful *pianissimi* captured on disc. In the preceding duet with her now stepson Don Carlos – 'Io vengo a domandar' – the soprano has to cope with some of the lowest writing for her role. On the phrase 'Nel'oblio' (in oblivion) she executes a perfectly drawn-out *diminuendo*, her inability to let the words go functioning as a vocal emblem of the infinite regret she feels.

In Verdi's revision the Queen takes no solo part in Act III; and her contribution to Act IV consists mainly of providing a dramatic launching pad for the mezzo's 'O don fatale'. But Act V belongs to the soprano. It opens with what is arguably Verdi's greatest single aria, 'Tu che le vanità', in which Caballé's voice is powerfully reinforced with the rich *pastoso* tone that had been the hallmark of her recent début in the role of Norma. In the aria she marks the sharpest possible dynamic contrast between the first subject – her apostrophe to Charles V's tomb – and the second – a general plea for her lament to be heard in Heaven. The word 'Francia', is sung on a downward *glissando*, like a feather lightly brushed against the cheek; yet at the end, for 'La pace del avel' (the peace of the grave), Caballé finds a jet black chest tone, full of contemptuous loathing. In the handful of bars that constitute the aria's coda her unique ability to place a high note *pianissimo* without any 'finding' of the note whatsoever, much less a scoop up to it, has never been heard to greater effect. In the ensuing duet with Carlos the music from Act I is briefly reprised before taking on a martial strain, all rippling harps and arpeggiated trumpets, in which *Aïda* begins to peep out at points. But with the start of what may be thought to be the duet proper, 'Ma lassù ci vedremo', in which Elisabeth dreams of meeting up with her beloved in a better world, Caballé sings throughout in a half voice full of noble resignation as well as the expected sadness. The floated high B♭ on 'Il sospirato ben' is simply heart-stopping.

The worst that one can say about this set has nothing to do with the performances, but simply with EMI's CD presentation of it. One would mind rather
less having to pay full price for a recording approaching its silver anniversary
if the accompanying booklet did not scramble the running order of the Acts
almost beyond comprehension, and if the side break between the first and
second discs was not the most brutal and incompetent piece of butchery ever
perpetrated by hacks in a hurry.

Aïda

**London, studio, vii.1974: EMI LP (SLS 977), LP highlights (ASD 3292); CD (CDS
7 472718)**

From its Cairo première in 1871, Aïda has always been among the most popular
of all operas, though with the current dearth of genuine *lirico-spintos* to do
justice to the title-role, it may yet join the ranks of those works like *Norma*
which are rapidly vanishing from the international stage. If it does, then we
shall at least be able to refer back to this recording to hear how it could be
sung. Certainly none of those who have committed the role to disc subsequently
have such comprehensive wherewithal to bring it off as Caballé had, though
Maria Chiara, if recorded earlier in her career, might have done so. And of
those who came before, only Leontyne Price and Renata Tebaldi are on comparable levels of achievement.

The EMI recording was made in the summer of 1974, within weeks of
Caballé's epoch-making Norma at Orange. Given the vocal form she was
exhibiting at this time it is quite extraordinary to reflect, retrospectively, that
she was in fact far from well and shortly to undergo surgery. From her first
utterances in the Act I trio to the final magical bars of the Act IV duet, her
Aïda is one of the truly great assumptions. She even manages to make something vocally positive of the Ethiopian princess's excessively passive character:
'Pavento' (I am afraid) in the Act I trio is treated to one of her classic long-drawn
diminuendi ending on the threshold of audibility, which Caballé herself acknowledges as being derived from the practice of Miguel Fleta. More obviously
Verdian is the cry of 'Sventurato!' in the recitative preceding 'Ritorna Vincitor!',
where she produces the real *spinto* goods. But the highlight of this is 'numi
pietà', the repetitions of which are effortlessly floated on seamless strands of
legato as one might examine pearls from different angles, first one way, then
another. In the Act II duet with Amneris – Cossotto, superb throughout –
Caballé summons the most fabulously soft tone colour when, instead of standing up to her rival, she instead opts for the ploy pathetic. And she easily rides
the cruelly written big ensemble which crowns the triumph scene.

But it is in Act III that any Aïda finally comes into her own. In the recitative
'Qui Radamès verrà', Caballé really lets fly as she considers her emotional
options in the scene to come, and the sheer range of dynamics she employs is
unequalled on disc. Yet in the aria itself, 'O patria mia', she resists the temptation to overplay the pathos of the repeated 'mai più's': no little gulps or sobs
disrupt the immaculately sustained line. And, of course, there is the famous
high C in the second verse which has so terrorized successive generations of
sopranos but which Caballé sings as if it was the easiest, most natural thing in
the world. (Indeed, one supposes that in a sense it must have been, since she

holds the note, *dolce*, in timeless suspense and then phrases all the way across until the end of the following 'vedrò' on a single breath.) As if all this were not enough, the very last bar of the aria beggars belief in terms of vocal poise, refinement of tone and expressive power. She sounds properly crushed by the end of the bruising duet with Amonasro, but gets her own back when Radamès materializes, and sounds every inch the woman scorned. Yet when she needs to get her own – or rather her father's way – she spins the most seductive tones imaginable in 'Là ... tra foreste vergine'. In the final scene as the lovers expire in each other's arms in the airless tomb, Caballé's verse of 'Morire! Si pura e bella!' captures with its ethereal unbroken phrases the essence of Verdi's direction 'vaneggiando' (as if in a delirium); and 'O terra addio' is a heartrending farewell. As Riccardo Muti – whose first opera recording this was – observed many years later: 'I believe that in this century, voices like Caballé's are of the highest degree of rarity. For this reason alone, I would like to thank her for all she has given to the world of music. But beyond this, I would like her to know how much I love and admire her.'

OTHER VERDI RECORDINGS

Otello
New York, pirate, 11.iii.67: Great Opera Performances LP (GOP 19); CD (GOP 761)

Ernani
Milan, pirate, RAI recording, 20–27.xi.68: LP (BJRS 110-2); CD (a) Nuova Era Reprints (2359/60); (b) Frequenz (043-018)

Messa di Requiem
London, studio, 18 and 30.viii.69 and 25.i.70: EMI LP (HMV Angel SAN 267-8, reissued on EMI CFPD 4144283; CD CZS 7 62892 2)

Verdi arias
London, studio, 8–11.vi.71: (*La forza del destino* – (i) Pace, pace, mio Dio†, (ii) La Vergine degli angeli; *Aïda* – (i) Qui Radamès verrá!... O patria mia, (ii) Ritorna vincitor!; *Macbeth* – Vegliammo invan due notti... Una macchia è qui tutt'ora†; *Otello* – Era più calma... Willow Song and Ave Maria†) EMI LP (ASD 2787); CD (CDM 7 69500 2) (only items marked †; the recitative of Lady Macbeth's Sleepwalking Scene is also omitted from the CD transfer)

I vespri siciliani
New York, pirate, 9.iii.74: Great Opera Performances CD (GOP 746)

I vespri siciliani
Barcelona, pirate, 2.i.75: Legato/Standing Room Only CD (SRO-837-2)

Il corsaro
London, studio, viii.1975: Philips LP (6700 098), highlights on LP (6570 067); CD (416 398-2), reissued on (426 118)

La forza del destino
Milan, pirate, 10.vi.78: Legato CD (LCD-141-3)

Aroldo
New York, live, 8.iv.79: CBS Masterworks LP (79328); CD (MZK 79328)

Canzone

Madrid, studio, vi.1980: (Lo spazzacamino; Nell'orror di notte oscura; La zingara; In solitaria stanza; Stornello; Ad una stella; Perduta ho la pace) **Discos Columbia SA, issued on Dischi Ricordi LP (ARCL 227006); RCA/BMG CD (74321 14072 2)**

Messa di Requiem

New York, live, ii.1981: CBS Masterworks LP (D2 36927)

IV: GIACOMO PUCCINI

Manon Lescaut

London, studio, 7–15.vii.71: EMI LP (SLS 962, reissued on EX-28-1175-3); CD (CDS 7 47736 8), reissued on CMS 764 8522

February 1893 was obviously a very good month for opera lovers, since it brought both a significant hail and a magnificent farewell. The latter was Verdi's *Falstaff*, unveiled at La Scala on the 8th; the former was *Manon Lescaut*, the opera which made Puccini's reputation and which saw the light of day on the first of the month at the Teatro Reggio, Turin. The libretto – the work of seven men, including the composer, his publisher, a rival musician and half the literati of Milan – was drawn from the same novella by Abbé Prévost that had furnished Massenet with his most enduring success just nine years earlier. It was probably the desire to avoid direct comparisons that dictated the dramatic structure of at least the inner Acts of Puccini's work, with unfortunate results. For if Massenet's opera is episodic and over-long, Puccini's work is positively telegramatic. Still, he manages to paint a reasonably rounded portrait of Manon, the proto-typical Puccinian heroine who loves (Acts I and II), suffers (Act III) and dies (Act IV).

This EMI recording was made in the summer of 1971 in Kingsway Hall, London, though technically it is disappointing, with muffled voices, congested climaxes and cavernous sound. We first encounter Manon at a coaching inn *en route* to a convent at her father's command. Instead, she elopes with the dashing Chevalier des Grieux, though already in Act II she is installed as another man's mistress. Caballé's opening lines are a wonderful mixture of innocence and calculation, light girlish tone allied to a highly seductive way of phrasing, such as 'Vo'ricordarvi. Il nome vostro?'. Already by the time of Manon's reappearance to keep her assignation with des Grieux, Caballé's voice has developed with the character, spinning webs of cool coquetry around Domingo's ardent suitor. This Manon's elopement is entirely by design rather than accident, as is her defection between Acts I and II to an older man. Installed in Geronte's palace, Caballé's Manon directs her *maquillage* with punctilious authority and endures the *divertissements* with barely concealed boredom. 'In quelle trine morbide' – Manon's attack of nostalgia for her former lover – gives Caballé her first real chance to show her Puccinian paces and is accordingly sung with rich, refulgent tone and an infinite sweetness. The big duet, 'Tu, tu, amore? Tu?' as des Grieux turns up unannounced for a bout of recrimination, is suitably highly impassioned, though the recording itself puts several layers of thick muslin over the singers' voices.

The character strikes her first truly tragic note when contemplating the jewels and riches she will have to leave behind as the price of renewing her association with des Grieux. This reluctance to depart occasions Manon's arrest and, in Act III, her deportation as a whore to America (where we are to presume there was a shortage). The most original part of this motley opera involves Manon having to do some heavy vocal duty in order to ride the ensemble in the embarkation scene, a task to which Caballé rises easily, even with the engineers evidently working for another company. But, as is usual with tragic heroines, it is in the last Act that the soprano comes into her own, having here a protracted death scene on the plains outside New Orleans (!). Fortunately, this coincides with the best music in the score, black-browed and fulsomely dramatic, which always catches out the lyrics who fancy their chances in this work. No problems for Caballé, however, even at this relatively early stage in her recording career a full-blown *lirico-spinto*, for whom 'Sola, perduta, abbandonata' might have been written. What is especially notable is the range of expression she brings to the piece based upon her *bel canto* skills of line, phrase and colour, rather than on the more obvious *verismo* expedients of gulps, sobs and screams. And her unsurpassed *pianissimo* singing makes the ever-diminishing dynamics of Manon's death throes musically convincing: Caballé really does expire gradually before our very ears.

Incidentally, EMI's art department appear to have been as derelict as their engineers on this set. The CD transfer is graced, on slipcase, jewel-box and libretto, with a picture of Caballé and Domingo entwined wearing mediaeval German dress – actually unused publicity material for *Mefistofele*. It serves to make them look as if they had wandered in from a performance of *Meistersinger*.

Turandot (in the role of Liù)
London, studio, 20–25.viii.72: Decca LP (SET 561-3); CD (414 274-2)

The character of Liù is really Puccini's last great creation: with her death the composer's interest in the narrative ceased. Alfano may as well not have bothered to stitch together a completion for Calaf and Turandot, about whose fates no audience could care less. So it is not entirely surprising that a top-notch Liù can usually steal a Turandot's thunder, although practitioners of either role scarcely grow on trees, and those – like Caballé – who can successfully encompass both are even rarer. This set was recorded, most spectacularly, in the Kingsway Hall, London, in August 1972 and marked Caballé's début on the Decca label. It also brought her first recorded contact with Pavarotti and Sutherland – exclusive Decca artists – both of whom, however, were colleagues she had known personally for many years. What with Nicolai Ghiaurov as Timur, Peter Pears as the Emperor and Zubin Mehta let loose on the London Philharmonic, Decca had obviously decided to produce the ultimate recording.

Certainly, Montserrat makes a magically beautiful thing out of her role. One knows one is in for something special right from the outset when she sings 'Perchè un dì, nella reggia, m'hai sorriso' in a love-struck half-voice and floats the high B♭ on such a prolonged and perfect *pianissimo* that people who have never heard this set before tend to sit staring in disbelief. She threads her way effortlessly through the pentatonic *chinoiserie* of 'Signor, ascolta!' and holds the final note for a full thirteen seconds of breath-defying *pianissimo*. (Actually, some new term should really be coined for singing of this degree of perfectly focused impalpability.) Yet she rises to crown the densely written ensemble leading up to Calaf's decision to bang the gong with no audible strain at all, which is why one knows she could just as easily have sung the title-role, even at this early stage.

In Act III, where Liù puts herself in the firing line of Turandot's wrath, Caballé finds exactly the right *voce soffocata* – on plentiful display elsewhere in this set – to phrase her pleas to be gagged lest her screams under torture disturb her blind master. 'Tanto amore segreto', in which Liù finally declares her love and willingness to die protecting it, is the point at which mere words start to fail: the passage 'Ah! Come offerta suprema dell mio morte' is sung as a single line, hovering weightless somewhere over the summit of Mount Olympus. It would need a more mettlesome princess than Sutherland to avoid being upstaged by all this, to say nothing of the subsequent aria, 'Tu che di gel sei cinta', where Caballé seems to dispense with the necessity of breathing at all, so unbroken is her phrasing. If this set continues to sell in its thousands because of Pavarotti's expansive 'Nessun dorma', there are other, equally great treasures to be heard on it.

La bohème
London, studio, 27.vii.73–4.viii.73: RCA LP (ARL2 0371); CD (RD8037(2))

Caballé's dislike of this recorded performance – set down in London in the summer of 1973 – has already been documented in this book. She is, of course, entitled to her opinion, one which was evidently shared by at least some of her distinguished colleagues on the set. But singers invariably manifest only a partial view of proceedings. The responsibility for the whole opera, the overriding dramatic cohesion of which any star singer's contribution forms just one part, ultimately rests with the conductor. But out of the sometimes belligerent factions that go to make up a commercial recording, a surprising synthesis can often emerge between the singers and conductor. And so it is here. Despite Montserrat's views, this is one of the two or three finest *Bohème*s ever committed to disc, precisely because of its inspired combination of great voices and great conducting.

From her very first utterances, Caballé lightens the voice to suggest the character's girlishness; and in the Act I aria – 'Mi chiamano Mimì – she provides a classic demonstration of Puccinian *portamento*, softening the bare outlines of the notes as written and binding whole phrases together with her legendary, seamless *legato*. It is also, like so much of her finest singing, a *tour de force* of dynamic variety and colour. By the time we reach the duet, 'O soave fanciulla', she sounds to the life like a young woman in love, and the sense of emotional surge is quite overwhelming. At the Act end, not only does she sing the most perfectly secure *pianissimo* top C of any recorded Mimì, but she does so without breaking for breath from the whole of the preceding phrase.

In Act III, one of the most notable features is her extremely convincing cough, presumably a memento of all those Swiss and German Mimìs in the late 1950s and early 60s. In her dialogue with Marcello detailing the pitiable state of affairs things have reached in her relationship with Rodolfo, Caballé sounds utterly desperate. But in the scene with her lover, 'Donde lieta uscì', she spins all her tonal magic on a web of the sheerest vocal beauty. Small wonder the lovers postpone their intended separation. In Act IV, once the reunited pair are left alone – 'Sono andati?' – Caballé's singing, despite (or because of?) the fraught nature of the sessions, is of fully achieved greatness, flawless in technique, ravishing as sound and profoundly involved. Her death-bed reminiscence of 'Che gelida manina' is moving in the extreme and her dying monotones, grey and racked with suppressed pain, set the seal on her performance. This is one of Caballé's greatest recordings.

Madama Butterfly

Barcelona, studio, 29.vi–2.vii.76: Spanish Columbia, issued on Decca LP (D68DR 3)

The critical reaction to this set when it first appeared in 1978 was almost universally one of praise for Caballé's portrayal and hostility to nearly everything else, particularly the conducting. The problem with Gatto is not so much the pacing as the general *ennui* that comes from a conductor determined never for a moment to draw attention to himself or to highlight any of Puccini's orchestration. First, last and in between he is there simply to dedicate himself to the soprano's greater glory. The irony is that this seems to have backfired, for it has allowed an otherwise remarkable performance from Caballé to pale into the background of recorded *Butterfly*s, leaving it as her only commercial opera recording not yet transferred to CD (though this may have something to do with contractual difficulties, since the set was made for Discos Columbia in Spain and only issued under licence by Decca).

No one would think of Caballé, any more than Callas, as a natural Cio-Cio-San. In Callas's case, the feat by which she could create the right kind of voice for a part is acknowledged as one of her great accomplishments. Caballé, too, was adept at finding the appropriate vocal colour, especially in Puccini (though perhaps to a lesser extent than Callas) and this recording is a classic instance of her ability. Through a lightening of tone and a sensitivity to the text, she presents from the outset a geisha of engaging flirtatiousness whose tragedy, as it unfolds, is wrapped up in the soft-grained *morbidezza* that characterize her voice in Puccini roles. When, just before the wedding ceremony, Butterfly tells Pinkerton that she is following her destiny by marrying him – 'io seguo il mio destino' – Caballé unfurls the phrase on one of those slow, languorous expanses of tone in which she loves to luxuriate. And even the ecstatic top A on 'Amore mio', though full of power, is nicely judged within the framework of the 'little woman' impersonation. In the great duet that ends the first Act – accompanied on this set by her real-life husband, Bernabé Martí – the long arches of sensuous phrasing spring, as ever, from the firm architectural foundation of her breath control.

The second Act is on a similarly high level, but just occasionally a nagging suspicion creeps up concerning the extent to which she is being hampered by having to keep the voice so slimmed down. For instance, 'Un bel dì vedremo' is nicely sung but comes across as somewhat under-characterized, too reined-in. The glorious singing on her Puccini arias disc (EMI, CDC-7 47841 2, see below) is not quite matched here, even though that rendition makes little concession to the 'child-bride' scale of the character. Also, once or twice Caballé allows the mask to slip, revealing the true dimensions of the real voice. This happens, for example, when she confirms with Sharpless that the law of America does not tolerate desertion as a ground for divorce. 'E il magistrato: "Ah, mascalzone, presto in prigione" ' is intoned with a dramatic intensity more suited to Medea. At moments such as this, where there is a chink in the art that conceals her art, one may feel that the role is more appropriately sung by lyrics – Freni or de los Angeles perhaps, both of whom show themselves to be preternaturally 'right' for Butterfly (albeit, in the latter case, occasionally strained by the role's tessitura).

But Caballé's performance in the final Act is stunning. One might have predicted that her treatment of a phrase like 'Tu sei con Dio ed io col mio dolor' would melt the heart, and indeed it does (the direction in the score that the vocalization of 'dolor' should die away into the distance is perfectly achieved). But what also impresses is that she finds a special way of dealing with other crucial episodes. Her repeated calls for Suzuki and the following 'E qui, è qui... Ecco il Console' sound hysterical, whereas other singers, like Callas, keep Butterfly in good humour. Caballé's interpretation is valid, for why should Cio-Cio-San be calm, believing that her long-absent husband has at last arrived? A stark contrast immediately becomes apparent in her voice with the crushing recognition that it is not Pinkerton who has come but his new wife, Kate. In the brief dialogue that follows, there is a resigned and noble dignity that comes naturally to Caballé and, moreover, a poignant, tearful quality in her tone. Then in the final desperation of 'Tu, tu, tu...piccolo iddio', she is at last able to throw off the shackles and unleash that flood of *spinto* force that has been not far beneath the surface all along. Clearly enunciating every word of some of the best text Puccini ever set, we can almost *see* the diminutive Butterfly grow before us to tower over the 'piccolo iddio' as she forces the child to take one last look at his mother's face. The scale of the *forte* singing here is superb: how well she marks the difference between the *allargando* phrase 'il materno abbandono', stretched out with agonized intensity, and the immediately following 'O a me, sceso dal trono dell'alto Paradiso' (sent to me from the throne of Paradise), sung with a king of searing lyrical ecstasy. It is a splendid end to a wonderful performance and whoever owns the rights should transfer the set to CD immediately.

Tosca

London, studio, 4–11.vii.76: Philips LP (6700 108); CD (412 885-2)

Caballé was originally supposed to record this opera in the early 1970s with Luciano Pavarotti and Peter Glossop under the baton of Herbert von Karajan. But, like the other Caballé/Karajan projects, this one failed to materialize for a complex variety of reasons. Pavarotti's Cavaradossi instead wound up shortly afterwards on Decca (with Freni, under Nicola Rescigno); Karajan's second recording of Puccini's opera – his first, with Leontyne Price, is much the better – was finally made at the end of the decade (with Ricciarelli and Carreras); and Caballé's Tosca went to Philips, who started to record the work in London in the summer of 1976 just two days after she had completed her commercial

recording of *Madama Butterfly* in Barcelona. The role had figured in her repertory from the earliest days and if anyone is minded to wonder how effective
Caballé was as Tosca on stage, they should badger the BBC to release commercially the telecast of the Royal Opera House performance in Tokyo in 1979,
which is tremendous.

In essentials, the Covent Garden *Tosca*s on tour replicated the line-up of this
Philips recording, though without such luxuries as Sam Ramey's Angelotti or
Ann Murray's Shepherd Boy. But what matters in this work are the three
principal roles and the conductor, which is where this set scores spectacularly,
with Carreras at his most fresh-voiced and ardent, Wixell at his most unpleas-
antly insinuating, Davis bringing characteristic care and intelligence to a score
often wrongly thought not to benefit from such virtues, and Caballé in one of
her greatest recorded assumptions. Less tigerish than many practitioners, this
Tosca is presented at the outset not so much a woman tormented by jealousy
as one utterly at the mercy of her larger-than-life emotions and with a very
grand sense of self. This is clear from the diva's off-stage cries of 'Mario', less
the usual siren-song than a peremptory summons to dance attendance. Only
with Caballé's melting tone at 'innanzi la Madonna', when Cavaradossi tries
to kiss her, does Tosca unbend. Thereafter, she alternates the extremes of the
character's emotions – kittenish seduction, fulsome religiosity and sharp-
tongued instruction – with consummate skill, toying with Carreras's hero just as
an exquisitely groomed cat might with a prospective meal. And the traditional
flashing-eyed jealousy gets a good look in when she spits out 'occhi cilestrini'
(sky blue eyes) upon seeing the Attavanti portrait. The duet proper, with its
shameless built-in reprise 'dilla ancora' (say it again) finds both protagonists in
magnificent voice, with a parting shot from Tosca – 'Ma falle gli occhi neri'
(But make her eyes black!) – which functions both as a caress and an argument-
clinching farewell. Yet her subsequent return, only to encounter the lascivious
Scarpia who plays on her just as she plays her lover, reveals the instability of
Tosca's emotions, rendered here perfectly through Caballé's analogous use of
the widest contrast of volume, colour and attack. 'Presago sospetto!' (just as I
suspected) is pure *grand guignol*, a diva to the life, oblivious to her self-
dramatizings. Even her tears are a piece of over-blown theatricality.

In Act II we again encounter Caballé playing Tosca for all she is worth in
terms of the famous lady of the theatre. Her reply to Scarpia's reassurance of
safety 'Sgomento alcun non ho' (I have no fear) is pure bluff, archly intoned
for maximum effect. But the real woman peeps through as the police chief's
repeated questions rattle her fragile composure: 'Solo! Si!' is a real outburst of
violent temper. The ensuing scene of diva-baiting somewhat underwhelms due
to Davis's rather too careful approach at this point, which robs the drama of
the necessary visceral excitement, and Philips's incomprehensible decision to
bisect the Act across the two discs, a piece of barbarism still perpetuated on
the mid-price reissue. But the sheer, sad beauty of Caballé's 'Vissi d'arte' is
more than fit compensation, though one could do without the sharp intake of
breath masquerading as an emotional sob after 'altar'. The high Bb-Ab-Gb
sequence at the end on 'Signore' is, as in all her recorded performances of the
aria, unbroken for breath and sung as a progressive *diminuendo* from the thrilling

fortissimo B♭ to a mere thread of tone on the G♭. The effect is not marked in the score but it is unlikely that Puccini would have objected.* Other performances sound disappointingly plain-jane after this. And Caballé's liberal use of chest voice as Scarpia dies at her feet provides a genuine vocal frisson (just as well, since 'E avanti a lui tremava tutta Roma', which can make such an effect when spoken, is here sung as marked in the score).

The Act III duet with Cavaradossi goes well, though the high C on 'lama' as Tosca recounts the night's events to her lover is a screechy specimen and might with profit have been remade. As Caballé paints a picture of the life the lovers will lead together after the 'fake' execution, she pours out her most honeyed tones: 'Nuvole leggere' sounds an almost plausible day-dream, and 'Mille baci' a guarantee of erotic fulfilment. But the tenor is, of course, shot for real. (Incidentally, the rifle fire on this recording, like the canon shots in Act I, is oddly mis-timed and ineffective: for the best sound effects, turn to the otherwise dismal Sony set [S2K 45847], of which they are the absolute highlight.) And Caballé's stentorian singing of Tosca's last words before jumping off the battlement – 'Scarpia, avanti a Dio' – suggests that the Baron is going to have to do a great deal of explaining in the hereafter.

Turandot

(1) Strasbourg, studio, 22–31.viii.77: EMI LP (HMV SLS5135); CD Highlights (CDM 7 63410 2)
(2) San Francisco, pirate, 29.x.77: Historical Recording Enterprises LP (HRE 226-3); Legato CD (LCD 188-2)

It is a pity that Caballé did not delay recording her studio Turandot by just a couple of months until after she had gained some stage experience of the role. It is also unfortunate that the EMI recording should have been entrusted to inept engineers unequal to the task of achieving an acceptable sound balance in the Palais de la Musique in Strasbourg, which emerges here sounding paradoxically both dry and cavernous.† These factors combine to deprive the commercial recording of the full splendour of which Caballé proved herself capable in this role. To encounter this, it is necessary to acquire the HRE San Francisco pirate (alas not so far transferred to CD), which preserves in excellent sound not only her first-ever stage performance as Turandot but also Pavarotti's as Calaf. She can also be seen and heard to great advantage on a pirate video of the French television broadcast of the Paris Opéra performance in 1981.

It would be wrong, however, to imply that there is anything inadequate about her singing on the EMI set. In truth, it is of a quality that was sufficient to disarm the critical speculation made in some quarters that she had little business attempting the role in the first place. Her performance was greeted in *Gramophone* as a 'superb, keenly memorable portrayal', and there is certainly much in it that marks out this Turandot from any other on disc. From her first utterances in the narrative opening of 'In questa Reggia', instead of the visceral

* Caballé's only recorded forebear in this practice appears to be Giannina Arangi-Lombardi in 1932 [Columbia GQX 10508 (BX 1119)].
† Things have picked up sonically somewhat on the CD highlights transfer. Apropos of the original engineering, which became the subject of numerous over-dubbing sessions in London, both Caballé and Carreras were convinced that it was an act of sabotage inflicted by disgruntled employees.

power associated with dramatic sopranos such as Eva Turner and Birgit Nilsson, Caballé sings in a reined-in half-voice. At decisive points, she uses ethereal *pianissimi* as a means both of 'interiorizing' the story and, at the same time, projecting a powerful impression of the intensity of Turandot's obsession. This first happens at the mention of 'Lo-u-Ling' and then again shortly afterwards when Turandot suggests that her royal ancestor now lives on through her: 'oggi rivivi in me'. The effect is to surround the character with a penumbra of mystery and other-worldly absorption, very different from the usual impression of a despotic ice-princess who rules by terror. As the piece progresses, and its vocal gradient becomes ever more steep, the studio recording catches a slight edge to Caballé's top Bs and C which is a pity, since neither in San Francisco nor four years later in Paris was there anything to be heard other than complete vocal assurance and effortless, pure-toned power. Still, this hardly detracts from the conviction of the whole which, under Lombard's leaden baton, is not so much impassioned as monumental, reaching a climax between Caballé and Carreras that sweeps all before them.

In Act III what is most notable about Caballé's Turandot – and this was equally true of her stage assumptions – is the sheer, brutal nastiness of the woman in her confrontation with Liù (here rather pallidly sung by Mirella Freni, no match for Caballé herself in the role). As the hapless slave-girl is tortured, this ice-princess only becomes ever-more malevolent and peremptory in her demands, the repeated cries of 'Parla!' taking on a manic intensity of utterance not heard since Callas forswore the role in the early 1950s. Then, in what usually comes across as one of the opera's biggest let-downs, Caballé manages not only to make 'Del primo pianto' sound beautiful – this much one would have expected – but also quite heartfelt, and actually convincing as the last stage of the ice princess's long-delayed thawing. In what is left, post-Toscanini's prunings, of Alfano's completion of the final duet, Caballé and Carreras between them make the most impressive recorded case for some very doubtful music since Nilsson and Corelli locked antlers at the Met in 1961. But such is the stunning splendour of the sounds made by Caballé and Pavarotti together in San Francisco, under Riccardo Chailly's thrilling direction, that for once one rather wishes that the whole of Alfano's efforts, including some crucifying excursions way above the stave for the tenor, had been performed. Really, whoever has inherited the amazing Rogues' Gallery of HRE's pirate tapes should get this one transferred to CD immediately. Until then, the EMI recording – itself only transferred to CD in highlight form and omitting all but three minutes of Alfano's ending – will have to do as second best.

Puccini arias

London, studio, vii.1969: (*Turandot* – (i) Signore, ascolta!; (ii) Tu che di gel sei cinta; *Madama Butterfly* – (i) Un bel dì vedremo; (ii) Tu, tu piccolo iddio; *Manon Lescaut* – (i) In quelle trine morbide; (ii) Sola, perduta, abbandonata; *Gianni Schicchi* – O mio babbino caro; *Tosca* – Vissi d'arte; *La bohème* – (i) Mi chiamano Mimì; (ii) Donde lieta uscì; *Le Villi* – Se come voi piccina; *La Rondine* – Chi il bel sogno di Doretta) **EMI LP (ASD2632, reissued on SXLP 30562); CD (CDC-7 47841 2)**

This disc was recorded in the Kingsway Hall, London, in 1969, a year in which, ironically, Caballé sang no Puccini on stage at all. The bare facts are worth setting out since the CD transfer, which was made by EMI's American subsidiary, Angel, bears no recording information whatsoever and gives only misleading production and copyright dates of 1987 (which is simply when the compact disc was issued). The programme opens with Liù's arias from *Turandot* in which Caballé sounds fuller voiced than on the complete Decca recording made three years later and a trifle more generalized in expression. But all the refinement of phrase and timbre are already present, including the high *pianissimo* B♭ at the very end of 'Signore, ascolta', which is held for a full fifteen seconds and here sounds like eternity. There is no attempt at the dreaded 'bamboleggiamente' posturings in the two *Madama Butterfly* arias, which are simply sung full-voiced, beautifully sculpted, and with an overwhelming vocal climax to 'Un bel dì vedremo'. The same warm and full-bodied lyric sound appears before us in the arias from *Manon Lescaut*, where again the soprano declines to evince the girlishness she successfully brings off in her complete recording, and instead prefers to give 'In quelle trine morbide' and 'Sola, perduta, abbandonata' large-scale public performances.

The aria from *Schicchi*, for all its beauty, misses any sense that Lauretta is indulging in histrionics merely to get her own way. (In fairness to Caballé, few performances convey this outside the comic context.) The *Tosca* item is distinguished by her virtually unique ability to sing the three-note sequence on 'Signore' without a break for breath. Her Mimi is an unusually full-voiced and determined young miss, quite sharp-tongued in her contextual aside 'Lei m'intende?' and with an absolutely huge vocal (and orchestral) climax at 'Ma quando vien lo sgelo'. But the two finest pieces of singing – and characterization – come in the least known items: the arias from *Le Villi* and *La Rondine*. In the former piece, Caballé makes something quite fabulous out of the otherwise tedious repetitions of the phrase 'Non ti scordar dì me', which ends with a note sung more quietly than anyone before her had ever managed, and well beneath the threshold of volume at which one would have imagined that a singer could still retain total control over the voice. And in the last item – 'Chi il bel sogno' – the length, purity and seamless transparency of her phrasing is simply staggering. In terms of sheer vocalism, this disc sets new standards. Sadly, though, the CD transfer has been poorly edited by EMI Angel, the final resonance of several arias being chopped off and the unexceptional level of residual tape hiss replaced by inadequate seconds of dead silence. It should be remastered by the parent company and restored to the catalogue immediately.

V: VERISMO

Pagliacci (R. Leoncavallo)

London, studio, 3–6.viii.71: RCA LP (SER 5635-6); CD (GD 60865(2))

The role of Nedda featured in Caballé's repertory from her very first season as a professional singer in Basel, and she went on to perform it in Vienna just a year or so later. Thereafter, silence, with the exception of this starry recording put together in summer 1971 in Walthamstow Town Hall. The original LP issue, in a boxed set of two discs, was a thoroughly commendable release, the opera taking up three sides and the fourth being devoted to arias from other, unknown, Leoncavallo works sung, two apiece, by the *Pagliacci* principals, Caballé, Domingo and Milnes. But now that record companies are controlled by accountants to whom product is product, the CD transfer omits the rarities and instead couples the work with Puccini's *Il tabarro*, a bite-sized piece of back-catalogue which BMG just happened to have lying around.

Nedda is not a grateful role for a soprano who has to do a fair amount of work in what will always remain a tenor opera, and is expected to make beautiful youthful sounds whilst portraying a low-life tart. Some adapt more readily to this challenge than others, and Caballé's innately dignified, indeed regal tone hardly qualifies her as an obvious contender. But the voice here is in prime condition and the sensuous beauty she can tease out of a line like 'O che bel sole di mezz'agosto', with magically tapered soft singing, puts her in a class apart from other recorded Neddas. Even the two little imitative bird-calls immediately preceding 'Stridono lassù' are ravishing simply as sound, whilst the aria sweeps forward with irresistible élan. The sour interview with the hunch-back Tonio reveals a cruel streak in Nedda's nature and Caballé's voice takes on the keen tones of mockery, archly poking fun at her unwanted suitor. And for once on disc, the laughs – both written into the music, and added – are thoroughly convincing. Courtesy of negligent producers, we do not hear the whiplash she inflicts on Tonio (Milnes, quite superb), but her voice provides it as, in the bitterest of chest voices, she describes him as 'difforme, lurido'.

The duet with Silvio is undermined by the rather parched tones of the baritone singing the role but, as throughout, Nello Santi's conducting works wonders. And Caballé pours out the tone, relishing the many passages of pre-Puccinian *sviolinata*.* She underplays the withering scorn of Nedda's second exchange with Tonio – exactly the sort of thing at which Renata Scotto excels – though she faces up to Domingo's towering Canio with steely power. As Colombina in the play-within-the-opera, she deploys the lighter, more girlish voice that she might have used for Nedda herself, except of course that it would have left her with nowhere to go vocally in this harlequinade, which in its earliest stages is exquisitely touched in. But as the piece lurches towards tragedy, the rich, full Caballé tones come to the fore, Colombina increasingly swept aside by a Nedda in fear of her life. Her final lines of defiance are delivered with the kind of voice one always hopes to hear from Brünnhilde about to jump on Grane, but rarely does. Nearing its silver anniversary, this *Pagliacci* is still the best all-round version in the catalogue.

Mefistofele (A. Boito)
London, studio, 16–25.vii.73: EMI LP (SLS 973); LP highlights (issued on HMV Greensleeve ESD 1027171); CD (CDS 7 49522 2)

This opera was first performed at La Scala in 1868 and was one of the most notorious fiascos in the house's history. According to reports the opera originally ran for nearly four hours and at a couple of subsequent performances was given in two parts on consecutive evenings. But Milanese hostility to the daringly modern piece, as well as Boito's avant-garde theorizings, led to its with-

---

* The exact doubling of the vocal line by the entire string band.

drawal. The work was only performed seven years later in front of the famously enlightened Bolognese in a revision which deleted whole tracts (and Acts) of the original. It is this 1875 version that has come down to us today and forms the basis of such performances and recordings as the piece receives. Since the work is not in the repertory of any of the world's major houses, we rely for our knowledge of the score on this and a handful of other recordings. But even the much-cut revision has its longueurs and passages of uneven inspiration, a fault which it shares with most other works based on Goethe's *Faust*.

Caballé, who only finally sang Margherita on stage in 1987, made this recording in July 1973 in EMI's Abbey Road Studios. (The great choral scenes which frame and punctuate the work, in which the heroine takes no part, were done in Kingsway Hall.) We first encounter her in Act II, the Garden scene, in which the rejuvenated Faust pays court to the young girl. Caballé's tone is rather womanly for the self-proclaimed 'fanciulla del villaggio' and the courtly mock-antique of the music hardly gives her anything to get her teeth into as the wooing couples come and go. But things pick up when Faust and Margherita begin their main interview – 'Dimmi se credi' – even if there is an odd thing to have left on a professional recording when Caballé momentarily falls off a note, not high, on the word 'filo' as she explains her domestic arrangements. Irrelevant, really, given the beauty of her singing as the brief passage continues, but there it is. There follows a most peculiar gabbled *prestissimo* quartet that makes all the singers sound like chickens running around in a blind panic. One really wishes that Boito had been capable of writing better – *much* better – music than in this lame scene with which to introduce the object of Faust's love. And what can be said of the dramaturgical skill of a famous librettist (Boito himself) who, having introduced us to Margherita in the nondescript garden scene as late as Act II, brings her straight back in Act III for her death scene in prison?

Still, at least the prison scene is much the best thing in the score, and finally gives the soprano something worth singing. The opening aria, 'L'altra notte', is a simple, slow two-verse piece with some vestigial coloratura appropriate to what is, in effect, a mad scene. And since the spinning of a sad, lyrical *cantabile* is Caballé's absolute forte, the results are predictably satisfying, even if she nearly runs herself out of breath in the discreet extension she inserts to the second verse's coloratura. Margherita's confession of sins when Faust turns up to save her is characterized with superb vocal imagination, her pale, bleached tones oddly suggestive of dementia and disorientation. This leads into the duet, 'Lontano, lontano', a haunting and highly unusual piece for an Italian opera in which Caballé and Domingo croon softly as they imagine a life together, far away. Their performance is almost unbearably moving. Her soft singing in the following 'Spunta... l'aurora pallida' (added as an after-thought for a revival in 1876) is truly miraculous: at least this Margherita goes to her death in fine style. If only she had been given a better part by the composer before so doing.

Cavalleria rusticana (P. Mascagni)
London, studio, 19–22.vi.79: EMI LP (SLS 5187); CD (CMS 7 63650 2)

The set was made in June 1979 in London's Kingsway Hall just before Caballé was due to record *I puritani* with similar forces under the same conductor, Riccardo Muti. She was not happy with how she was exhorted to sing the role of Santuzza, not just by the conductor but by his wife, who was full of eager suggestions. It is a role, of course, that Caballé never sang on stage but she was still clear in her own mind what the requirements were and how it should go. She arrived prepared to give it her dark-hued *verismo* all – Santuzza has often been sung by mezzos – only to find herself being told to lighten her voice in order to emphasize the character's girlishness. This makes a certain amount of dramatic, but not much musical, sense, and Caballé, who did her best to oblige, views the results with resignation. This is not how she thinks Santuzza ought to sound.

Having said which, most of the time she sounds fine, and the relatively light timbre with which she invests her voice at the outset leaves her with plenty of room for manoeuvre as the drama unfolds. As early as 'Sono scomunicata' she manages to inject some real heft into the voice and sound just the right edge of desperation without in any way disturbing the line or engaging in conventional *verismo* sins like crashing through registers. Her launching of the Easter Hymn is radiantly beautiful even if the subsequent development is very much at the mercy of the star conductor, moulding, moulding. In the set-piece aria 'Voi lo sapete', she covers the wide-ranging emotional territory with an appropriate variety of colour and intensity, all bound within her customary impeccable *legato*.

But the heart of the work is the duet between Santuzza and Turridu which immediately follows, and this finds both Caballé and Carreras in excellent form. The urgency of her repeated 'Debbo parlarti' leaves us in no doubt as to the nature of Santuzza's plight and, as she faces up to her former lover's rejection – Carreras impressively brazen – she sounds genuinely heartbroken. Santuzza's line 'gli diceva che oggi è Pasqua' is marked by the composer to be sung 'tetra' (grimly), and Caballé duly delivers, making this Easter sound more like a black sabbath. Strangely, however, her subsequent taunt to Lola is hardly 'con amarezza' (scornful) – for this type of sharp-tongued savagery one needs to turn to Renata Scotto (RCA, RD 83091). On the other hand, no one else manages the long-limbed *mezza voce* way she sings 'Santuzza piange e t'imploro', phrasing without any break into the following line. It is indeed a brutal Turridu who can turn this down. It is true she has occasional trouble in negotiating the ins and outs of the chest register – mainly in the interview with Alfio, 'Turridu mi tolse l'onore' – but even here there are delicate touches which a naturally darker voice could never achieve and which afford a greater dynamic relief to what is otherwise so frequently a one-dimensional role.

Adriana Lecouvreur (F. Cilea)
Tokyo, private, 21.ix.76: Historical Recording Enterprises LP (HRE 246); Legato CD (LCD-111-2)

Cilea's opera is much the best work Puccini never wrote, easily surpassing the thin and laboured efforts of hacks such as Giordano and, in at least one important aspect, even surpassing the work of the master since Puccini could never bring himself to write powerful mezzo roles, much less confrontation scenes between two adult women. It is astounding that a work that has attracted sopranos of the calibre of Ponselle, Muzio, Cigna, Caniglia, Olivero, Tebaldi, Caballé and Margaret Price, as well as a comparably starry roster of tenors, should bask in such critical disfavour; as a result the work is a rarity both on the stage – it has not been seen in London, for instance, in the entire post-war period – and in the recording studios, thereby depriving us of an opportunity of hearing Caballé and her usual Maurizio, José Carreras, in two of their best roles under optimum conditions. As it is, we must make do with this tolerable pirate in genuine, if muffled, stereo taken from a performance given in NHK Hall, Tokyo, in 1976.

As with the other great 'diva' opera, *Tosca*, Caballé is here clearly in her element, perhaps even more so given Adriana's higher level of intelligence and the ready wit she is capable of displaying in her working relationship with her colleagues at the Comédie. (Tosca is a lone-wolf *assoluta*, hard to imagine having friends, whereas Adriana is surrounded by them.) Just as the poor tenor in *Aïda* is thrown in at the deep end from the word go with his big aria, so is Adriana almost immediately brought before us to sing her best-known piece, 'Io son l'umile ancella'. This is prefaced by her speaking lines from the Racine play she is about to perform, a thoroughly effective device in opera (think of Lady Macbeth's entrance) as well as a homage to the great actresses – Bernhardt and Duse among them – who had made Scribe's original play famous. Caballé delivers them in a powerful *mezzo* speaking voice, full of authority, and goes on to sing her brief aria at an incredibly slow and lingering tempo, each phrase, each note, practically caressed to death within an amazingly smooth legato. (Though there is the odd matter of her habitual explosive stress on the last syllable of 'fedeltà', as if in English one might holler 'FAITHful'.) In the ensuing dialogue with the secretly smitten stage manager, Michonnet (excellently sung by Attilio d'Orazi), Caballé sounds so non-committal and languid in her responses that we know immediately that this Adriana is emotionally preoccupied elsewhere. Maurizio materializes – Carreras, the soul of youthful passion – and a brief duet follows in which Caballé's vocal languor begins to sound like real infatuation.

In the incident-packed second Act, Adriana finds out her lover's true identity (no mere subaltern but the Count of Saxony himself) and crosses swords with the powerful Princesse de Bouillon, who has her own designs on him. The short, highly charged duet for the lovers provokes a storm of applause mid-music (can this really be the undemonstrative Japanese?) and the confrontation between Caballé and Cossotto, each claiming Maurizio as her exclusive lover, generates enough electricity to keep Tokyo lit up for weeks. Alas, Caballé is miles up-stage by the end of the Act and too far from the microphones for her evidently stentorian denunciation of the Princess to register properly. The slanging match between the divas resumes in Act III: provoked by the Princess's taunts, Adriana recites a blazing speech from Racine's *Phèdre*, clearly turning the text against her humiliated hostess, though this turns out to be a Pyrrhic victory. The recitation is, as in Act I, spoken, but here amounts to a substantial fourteen lines of prime tirade, which Caballé delivers with shamelessly over-the-top, eye-rolling abandon, school of Magda Olivero. Only the last four words, 'che mai debba arrossir' (she should blush for ever) are sung, with a degree of *spinto* power that brings another spontaneous ovation.

Adriana's triumph is short-lived. In Act IV she receives an anonymous gift – actually from the Princess – of withered violets liberally doused with poison. Not realizing this and thinking instead they are an insult from the faithless Maurizio, Adriana sings her other principal aria, 'Poveri fiori'. Again, the piece is performed very slowly indeed, which makes Caballé's ability to sing the first three lines on one breath all the more incredible; as is her *diminuendo* on 'senza ritorno', where the volume of the voice is imperceptibly reduced from *ff* to *ppp* with completely undisturbed emission of tone. This stops proceedings dead in their tracks as the audience erupts, as well they might; such vocal control is a lost art these days. Maurizio arrives to clear up past confusions and to offer his hand to Adriana. But it is too late: a tender, rather beautiful duet of reconciliation breaks off as she begins to feel unwell. Caballé's singing hereabouts is of ineffable sweetness, tinged with melancholy. And 'Ei m'ama, ei m'ama' is scarcely believable in the context of a live performance so perfectly poised is the voice in its prolonged high-lying *pianissimi*. Yet this is immediately followed by authentic *verismo* histrionics as Adriana's mind starts to wander. Caballé declaims 'Scostati profani! Melpomene son io!' in accents that would raise the dead before singing her final strains in a progressive diminution of volume ending on the edge of audibility. It is very doubtful if the role has ever benefited from a comparable combination of uninhibited commitment and vocal refinement.

Andrea Chénier (U. Giordano)
London, studio, 16–24.viii.81: Decca LP (410 117-1 DH3); CD (411 117 2DH3)

Chénier is a characterless assemblage of second-hand musical scraps. However, its allure for star tenors is well-nigh irresistible because of the title-role's glamour and high-profile exposure, which for once puts the diva rather in the shade. Thus the piece survives in the repertory as a vehicle for whole-hearted *verismo* vocalism. Here on this recording it certainly gets it and, from the soprano at least, a measure of unwonted subtlety to boot. The main sessions took place in London's Walthamstow Town Hall in August 1982 although, for a variety of reasons (including conductor Riccardo Chailly's indisposition), the recording was not completed until June 1984. Caballé's contribution, however, as the aristocratic Maddalena di Coigny, was entirely set down in the earlier sessions immediately after completing *Il Turco in Italia* for Fonit Cetra, during what was the most difficult and disagreeable year of her career.

In Act I just before the French Revolution occurs, the Maddalena we first meet is a slightly spoiled and very self-possessed young miss. As the post-revolutionary narrative unfolds in the remaining Acts the principals pass through fear and suffering and the heroine emerges as an admirably decisive and mature woman prepared to mount the tumbril with her condemned lover. Even if the music is undistinguished, the potential for character development is beyond that of most paste-board heroines of the time, and something of a gift for a singer with a flair for powerful and vivid narration. At her first entrance Caballé stresses Maddalena's 'other-worldliness' and, indeed, weariness at the routines of preparing for a grand ball. She hardly sounds girlish but is shrewdly pitted against Astrid Varnay as the Countess, whose voice is not so much mature as extinct, thereby restoring the vocal balance between mother and daughter. But her baiting of the poet Chénier is dispatched with nicely judged drollery for all that his response – Pavarotti, rather unrelieved in expression – shames her into an apology. In Act II, set five years later, we are thrown headlong into the world of the Terror in Paris, with spies spying on spies and daily denunciations. Maddelena, now living in fear of her life and dressed as a poor seamstress, comes to beg for Chénier's protection (duet: 'Ecco l'altare'). 'Proteggermi volete?' (Will you protect me?) is sung in the kind of melting half-voice that no man could refuse. And the lovers' resolve – 'Fine alla morte insiem' (Together unto death) – provides the kind of vocal thrill that this work is all about.

Act III takes us into the Revolutionary Tribunal itself where Chénier is to be tried at the hands of Maddalena's former lackey Gérard, now the public prosecutor who has designs on her himself. She turns up to plead for Chénier only to discover Gérard's intentions to possess her and have her lover executed. But in her great narrative aria, 'La mamma morta', she paints such a vivid picture of both her sufferings and her new-found passion that Gérard relents (in vain, as it transpires). Caballé's singing of the single most famous piece in the opera is notable for its intense power of communicating the story: we seem to see with her the château in flames and the agony of the period that followed. 'Porta sventura a chi bene mi vuole' is exquisitely phrased with a pang of real recognition and there is more than a touch of manic abandon in her apostrophe to love, including a real snarl in the chest register at one point (immediately followed by angelic soft singing) as she imagines her own death. But the *raison d'être* of the whole work is the final Act when the lovers are reunited in prison and face execution together ('Vicino a te'). Her first verse sounds a little pinched and covered, at least compared to the open-throated approach of Pavarotti, but by the time of 'La nostra morte è il trionfo dell'amor' she has opened up nicely and really lets fly, whilst still finding space in which to phrase a beautiful account of the single line 'Col sole che le indova'. It is in exactly this fashion that Caballé puts her *bel canto* skills at the service of these *verismo* warhorses, considerably to their benefit.

OTHER VERISMO RECORDINGS

Andrea Chénier (U. Giordano)
Philadelphia, pirate, 5.iv.66: Historical Recording Enterprises LP (HRE 386-2); Great Opera Performances CD (GOP 766)

Adriana Lecouvreur (F. Cilea)
Barcelona, pirate, xi. 1972: MRF LP (MRF 100)

La gioconda (A. Ponchielli)
(1) Geneva, pirate, 6.xii.79: Legato CD (LCD 170-2);
(2) London, studio, 17–29.vi.80: Decca LP (D232D3); CD (414 349-2)

Mefistofele (A. Boito) (Caballé as Elena)
London, studio, 12–14.vii.80: Decca LP (D270230); CD (410 175-2DH3)

VI: OTHER REPERTOIRE
(i)GERMAN

Salome (R. Strauss)

London, studio, 21–30.vi.68: RCA LP (SER 5582-3); CD (GD 86 644(2))

Given the demands of the part (once Salome is on stage she never leaves it) and the colossal scale of Strauss's orchestration, the composer's own ironic assessment of what it requires – a sixteen-year-old with the voice of an Isolde – is no more than a literal truth. But many years and at least ten operas later, Strauss came to revise his opinion and deplore the big Germanic wobblers who had come to monopolize the role. He even hoped to lure Elisabeth Schumann into singing it with the promise of reduced orchestration. This never happened but it gives a clear indication of his final vocal preference in the matter: Brünn-hildes and hopeful mezzos need not apply.

Caballé recorded this favourite role by her favourite composer in June 1968 in Walthamstow Town Hall, London. (RCA would have preferred *Lohengrin*, which they continued for some years to try to record with Caballé as Elsa, in vain.) The cast is at a uniformly high level, with such luxuries as James King's Narraboth and Julia Hamari's Page. Only Leinsdorf's conducting and the slightly recessed orchestral image have ever come in for any criticism, valid in the latter case, much less so in the former. Caballé's princess is a petulant and demanding brat from the outset. Yet after roundly anathematizing the Romans and Jews present at Herod's table from which she has just fled, her voice softens to a chillingly innocent whisper as she notices the moon. Her shameless assault on Narraboth in order to get to see the imprisoned John the Baptist is a brilliant mix of matter-of-fact methodology – the outcome is a foregone conclusion on her part – and telling little touches of wheedling, girlish colour. When con-fronted by Jokanaan her immediate horror is starkly vocalized; but she soon melts, and Caballé's singing of 'ein Bildnis wie Elfenbein. Gewiss ist er keusch wie der Mond' (An ivory portrait. Surely he is as chaste as the moon) on a silver filigree thread of tone allows us not only almost to see the moonlight, but also to hear the nascent sexual obsession. But Jokanaan is a harder nut to crack than Narraboth, and Salome has to work overtime, making a threefold appeal first to his white body, then his black hair and finally his red mouth. By the time of her crazed apostrophe to the Baptist's hair, Caballé's voice positively bristles with sexual abandon, real *spinto* power entering her high notes and a kind of panting longing underlying her soft ones. The address to his mouth is perfectly controlled vocally but sounds utterly manic in effect, Narraboth's suicide in no way disturbing her insanely reiterated pleas – 'Lass mich küssen deinen Mund' (Let me kiss your mouth) – at a thrilling *fortissimo*. Her last cries before he returns to the cistern are positively deranged. The Baptist's fate is sealed, and by the time she informs Herod that she wants the head, in the sweetest little Shirley Temple voice, on a silver salver, the iron has entered her soul. As Caballé repeats her demands there is implacable resolve in her voice, unmoved by Herod's (the excellent Richard Lewis) futile attemps to buy her off. Her singing of the closing scene draws all these threads together. Nervous and hysterical at the beginning whilst waiting for the head to be brought to her; spiteful and ill-tempered when taunting it; and finally, trans-figured with a kind of triumphant, other-worldly joy. This Salome is one of Caballé's finest recordings.

Salome Closing Scene and Five Songs with Orchestra (R. Strauss)
Paris, studio, 5–7.v.77: DG LP (2530963); CD (431 171-2)

These Strauss recordings were made in the main studios of the ORTF building in Paris at the same time as Caballé and Bernstein were performing the *Salome* Closing Scene at a public concert at the Théâtre des Champs-Élysées. Made some nine years after her complete studio recording for RCA the first thing one notices is the much improved sound picture, the voice clearly focused within the overall image. The second factor, which makes its presence felt almost as quickly, is Bernstein's conducting, wayward and voluptuous even at this date, but bespeaking a level of interpretative creativity denied to most other maestri. As for Caballé, none of the incidental beauties of the earlier complete recording is sacrificed, but there is here an addition of raw power at both ends of the register, particularly the lower. And Bernstein's caressing of the main melodic outlines exactly matches his soprano's approach, now spit-fire quick, now dreamily languid. The post-orgasmic moments, humid with a shim-mering, luminescent after-glow, are quite the creepiest on disc. And the climax, with Bernstein evidently putting his foot straight through the podium, is really overwhelming.

The orchestral songs get a similar treatment, which leaves *Cäcilie* sounding rather stentorian and overblown. But *Wiegenlied* – sung more or less *piano* throughout – is a ravishing experience, all the more so for the relative sup-pression of the text in favour of *legato* tone which spins out the essence of this lullaby. *Ich liebe dich*, a lunging and manic setting of a rather peculiar poem, catches Caballé out in the first verse where 'nachtens der Blitz' goes astray in the orchestra *mêlée* and the top notes are snatched at. But with the inevitable *Morgen!* she is back in her element, with the high floated tones – 'Wogenblauen' – and the whole second half of the first verse sung on just one breath. The last song, *Zueignung*, was in 1977 a recorded première, though neither DG's original LP documentation nor that of the CD transfer makes any reference to the fact. It was originally written in 1883 as the first of Strauss's eight opus 10 songs. The orchestral version performed and recorded to this day is that by Robert Heger. But on this Caballé disc we hear for the first time the composer's own orchestration made in 1940 as a thank-offering to Viorica Ursuleac, whose labours on behalf of Strauss and his ill-fated *Ägyptische Helena* he wished to salute. Hence the additional line at the end 'Du wunderbare Helena' – which DG omits from the text and translation but which Caballé sings loud and clear – and the recomposed coda. It is a much more impressive piece in this guise and Caballé does it full-throated justice at Bernstein's slightly too relaxed tempo. Strange, though, that a Strauss first went unremarked in 1977 and still does, presumably because no one at DG has actually listened to what the com-pany refers to as 'product'.

(ii) FRENCH

Caballé sings French opera arias

London, studio, viii.1970: (*Faust* – Il était un Roi de Thulé ... Ah! Je ris de me voir si belle en ce miroir; *Mireille* – Voici la vaste plaine et la désert de feu‡; *Roméo et Juliette* – Je veux vivre dans le rêve; *Les Huguenots* – O beau pays de la Touraine; *Louise* – Depuis le jour; *Carmen* – C'est des contrebandiers... Je dis que rien ne m'épouvante; *Thaïs* – Ah! me voilà seule... O mon miroir fidèle‡.) **DG LP (2530 073); reissued on CD (431 103-2)** (with the exception of the items marked‡)

This interesting and unusual recital casts the soprano in half a dozen roles she never sang on stage. The only exception is the opening item, Marguerite's scene from Act II of *Faust* which, with Caballé in fresh, lustrous voice, sets the tone for the whole disc. She works hard at her French – only the *voyelles nasales* rather defeat her, as they do most non-Francophone singers – and lightens her tone as much as possible for most of the pieces, since five of the seven heroines are girls as opposed to women. Even so, it comes as a slight shock to hear this much richness of voice expended on pieces normally sung by characteristically thin and acidic French sopranos. Beautifully as the *Faust* item is sung, Caballé's creamy warmth and amplitude sorts ill with the kind of brittle glitter that seems predicated by 'Ah! Je ris de me voir' and which singers of much more modest endowment can bring off more naturally. This is also very much the case in the *Roméo et Juliette* aria, the vocal requirements of which make no demands on Caballé's unique gifts, whilst putting a savage spotlight on her technique in high-lying rapid coloratura, not all of which comes off with the necessary abandon (though the final cadenza is a dazzler). The Micäela aria from *Carmen* Act III fares better, though the sheer amount of *spinto* power with which she invests the central section rather suggests that the *contrebandiers* and general riff-raff up the mountain that night had better watch out; and, as often happens, with Italian(ate) voices singing in French, the language tends to distort the timbre on the all-pervasive 'en', 'an' and 'on' sounds.

The *Mireille* death scene – despite its atmospheric opening – turns into a rather martial piece before its melting and visionary central section with its solo trumpet *obbligato*. Caballé shapes the highly disparate musical paragraphs with great care, and even injects some narrative urgency before the reprise of the first verse, ending with a really huge high B. The Meyerbeer piece, complete with prefatory flute concerto, is a winner, sung with unflappable poise and line (despite the high *tessitura*), and one rather good trill where it matters most. The second half, a brilliant *allegro* display piece of no more musical worth than most Meyerbeer, comes off well, with a gloriously extended vocal *crescendo* on the penultimate note. The 'Mirror' aria from *Thaïs*, Massenet's Tristanesque paraphrase, is sung by the soprano at the start in an almost panting voice, as if the mere sight of her own reflection had left her sexually aroused. Caballé is often heard at her best in these self-communing pieces, but she brings any amount of dramatic power to the middle section, as well as the expected refinements of expression, (even, if, on this occasion, a decent trill is not one of them).

But best of all is the aria from *Louise*, sung here as if in some post-coital trance, with breath-defying mastery of endlessly floating soft phrases. The whole piece emerges with the most seductively sumptuous ebb-and-flow which has never been matched on disc. The final *pppp* on 'heureuse' has to be heard to be believed, and by the end the heroine is not the only one likely to be 'tremblant délicieusement'. That this is no studio fakery, or the product of hours of recorded labour, is there for all to hear a full nine years later, when Caballé does exactly the same – if anything even more daringly slow and tonally withdrawn – in 1979 in front of a live audience in the Salle Pleyel: (Rodolphe CD, RPC 32501). Incidentally, a plague upon DG, who in belatedly transferring the LP to CD as part of their catch-penny 'Grosse Stimmen' series, not only omit all documentation, texts and translations, but also unceremoniously dump the arias from *Mireille* and *Thaïs*. Even with the interpolation of the Bernstein closing scene from *Salome* – unnecessary, as it is available on another DG disc – this CD runs for under sixty-one minutes, leaving plenty of room for the omitted items, which are now presumably forever banished to LP limbo. (To add insult to injury, it was precisely these items that Alan Blyth in his original *Gramophone* review[10] thought were the finest on the disc.)

(iii) SPANISH

Canciones de Enrique Granados

Barcelona, studio, 1964: (*Canciones amatorias*: Descúbrase el pénsamiento; Mañanica era; Llorad, corazón; Mira que soy niña; No lloreis, ojuelos; Iban al pinar; Gracia mia. *Tonadillas*: La maja dolorosa Nos. 1–3; El tra, la, la y el punteado; El mirar de la maja; Callejeo; Amor y odio; El majo discreto; El majo tímido; La maja de Goya) **Vergara LP (11 0 003 LS); RCA Victor LP (SB6686) RCA/BMG; CD 09026-695392**

Romanzas de Zarzuela

Studio, Barcelona, 22–26.iv.74: (**Luna:** *El niño judio* – De España vengo‡; **Caballero:** *Chateau Margaux* – Romanza de Angelita‡; *Gigantes y cabezudos* – Romanza de Pilar; *El Señor Joaquin* – Ballada y aubada; **Giménez:** *El barbero de Sevilla* – Polenesa‡; **Barbieri:** *Jugar con fuego* – Romanza de la Duquesa‡; **Chapí:** *Las Hijas del Zebedero* – Carceleras‡; *La patria chica* – Canción de berger; **Barbieri:** *El barberillo de Lavapies* – Canción de Paloma; **Serrano:** *El carro del sol* – Canción Veneziana) **Spanish Colombia, issued on Anacrouse LP (UM 3925); Decca** (items marked ‡ only) **LP (7.302)**

Spanish Songs (vol. 1) (acc. M. Zanetti)

Barcelona, studio, viii.1977 (**de Falla:** *Siete canciones populares Españolas*; **Turina:** Anhelos; Farruca; Cantares; Si con mis deseos; **Granados:** Elegia eterna; La maja y el ruiseñor; Cançó d'amor; L'ocell profeta) **Spanish Columbia, reissued on Decca LP (SXL-R6888); Spanish Columbia CD (WD 71320)** (CD available only in Spain)

Spanish Songs (vol. 2) (acc. M. Zanetti)

Barcelona, studio, xi.1978: (**Granados:** La maja dolorosa Nos. 1–3; **de Falla:** Tus ojillos negros; Oración de las madres que tienen a sus hijos en brazos; **Albéniz:** Besa el aura; Del salón; **Obradors:** Del cabello más sutil; El molondrón; El vito; Aquel sombrero de monte; **Vives:** *Canciones epigramáticas* – (a) El amor y los ojos, (b) El retrato de Isabela, (c) Válgame Dios, que los ánsares vuelan; **Rodrigo:** *Cuatro madrigales amatorias*) **Spanish Columbia, issued on Decca LP (SXL 6935); Spanish Columbia CD** (available only in Spain) (WD 71327)

Songs by Turina and Montsalvatge (acc. A. Weissenberg)

Paris, studio, 27.iv.79–5.v.79: (**Turina:** *Canto a Sevilla*; **Montsalvatge:** *Cinco canciones negras*) **EMI Pathé Marconi LP (2C 069-16380)**

Montserrat Caballé à la UNESCO (acc. R. Sabater)

Paris, live, 23.iii.81: (**Granados:** Elegia eterna; Cançó d'amor; L'ocell profeta; **Mompou:** Damunt de tu només les flors; Aquesta nit un mateix vent; Jo et pressentia com la mar; **Toldrà:**

Canticel; Platxèria; Maig; Romanç de Santa Llúcia; Cançó de bressol) **PDI CD (80.0455)**
(released in Spain only)

The appeal which Spanish music now holds for audiences has been largely brought about by the great Spanish singers who have headed international opera during the past thirty years. The likes of Teresa Berganza, Pilar Lorengar, José Carreras and Alfredo Kraus have done much to promote awareness outside Spain of the diversity of Spanish vocal music, ranging from Sevillian monodies dating from the thirteenth century, through indigenous baroque and eighteenth-century *tonadilla*, to the remarkable profusion of twentieth-century art song. It is undoubtedly this latter, created by composers whose inspiration has been drawn from the rich vein of Spanish folksong, that has turned what might otherwise have remained a purely national feature into one appreciated and admired throughout the world. And in this process, two singers above all have been in the vanguard: Victória de los Angeles and Montserrat Caballé. They, like most Spanish (but not Italian) singers, have chosen to embrace the piano recital almost as their preferred form of public performance. The sheer scale of these two singers' recital work is legendary, and from the very beginning of their careers they carried the torch for Spanish song. If the *canción* cycles of Turina, Obradors, Rodrigo, Mompou, Montsalvatge and Toldrà are now enjoyed almost as much outside Spain as they are inside, then it is thanks in large measure to the advocacy of these two great sopranos on the concert platform and on disc.

But even the avowed commitment of singers like Caballé, Berganza, Domingo and Aragall has failed to achieve a 'breakthrough' for that quintessentially Spanish entertainment, the *zarzuela*. Resolutely, it refuses to come to life outside Spain. The arias, when extracted and sung in concert or on record, provide an entertaining *divertissement* for international audiences who respond to the appealing verve and easy lyricism of these works, but as a whole the form refuses to transcend national borders. Items from *zarzuela* have often been a feature of Caballé's concerts and recitals, and she recorded four such works complete. In addition, as early as 1964 she recorded two *zarzuela* recital discs, one of arias and the other of duets (with her husband, Bernabé Martí) which, unlike the complete works, were given international release. On both she is in fabulous voice, affording a luxuriously sung taste of the passion and humour which distinguish the works of the best *zarzuela* composers. Since none of these discs are currently available outside Spain – and many of them not even there – we can do no more than draw attention to their existence and hope that it will not be too long before an enterprising record company gives them international exposure.

Caballé's enduring – and most accessible – contribution to the music of her native country resides in the various song cycles she recorded both before her years of fame and in the latter half of the 1970s.* She invariably brings to these songs certain characteristics that are frequently thought to distinguish the

---

* Although she recorded many items from the Spanish song repertory, there are, of course, many more that she did not. In particular, it is a great pity that she has not recorded the four songs specially written for her by L. Martínez Palomo (b. 1938) under the title *Recuerdos de juventud*. Caballé premièred these on 27 February 1987 at a Carnegie Hall recital in New York.

Spanish voice from that of other Europeans. The warm, rich tone centred on a middle voice that conjures up an image of velvet rather than silk; a voice that throughout its range is suffused with a slightly darker hue than is usual in, say, the French or Italian soprano; and an almost imperceptible 'ictus' of not-quite-glottal attack for dramatic and emotional emphasis. This is a distinctive Iberian sound, often blurring the line that divides sopranos from mezzos. And its sound is one which is embodied in the works of composers like Granados and de Falla. What also comes naturally to Caballé is her responsiveness to the rhythms of Spanish dance and folksong whereas, in the hands of non-Spaniards, nuance and subtlety are often sacrificed to caricature of the flashing-eyed, picture-postcard variety.

Caballé's particular virtues are first encountered on the recordings she made in 1963 and 1964 for Vergara. These include a record dedicated to the *Tonadillas* and *Canciones amatorias* songs cycles of Enrique Granados (1867–1916), and recitals of songs by Eduardo Toldrà (1895–1962) and Frederic Mompou (1893–1987), the latter accompanied by the composer himself. It is amazing that not one of the ten different recordings she made in this period for Vergara has been transferred to CD for international release. Perhaps RCA/BMG, who now owns the rights to all these recordings, will see the light of day and reissue them as a collected edition (though it is hoped that a sampler of these *introuvables* will be issued to coincide with the publication of this book). Listening to any of the original LPs, what is immediately apparent is the sheer voluptuousness of the voice at that time, how well focused it was and how flexible. There is also a remarkable combination of creaminess and clarity in the actual timbre, heard perhaps most impressively in the Granados songs. In the *Tonadillas* cycle, which depicts the courtship etiquette of the eighteenth-century *majos* and *majas* – the Madrilenan proletariat – Caballé is superb at evincing the melancholy of these betrayed or lonely lovers. Particularly effective is the third of the 'Maja dolorosa' triptych, where just the right kind of lyrical shadings are applied to make the song profoundly memorable. And in 'El majo discreto' the soprano is vividly flirtatious and easily copes with the tripping rhythm of the second verse. When she sings 'Seriá indiscreto cantarlo yo' (It would be indiscreet of me to tell) she somehow imbues the voice with a kind of lascivious wink. But for all the glories of this 1964 performance, its drawback is that it is sung on a rather large, operatic scale. In 'Callejo', for instance, a nimbler, more word-conscious approach would have yielded better results, and in 'El majo timido' she misses the pertness and exasperation that Conchita Badía, for one, so adroitly used to convey this *maja*'s frustration with her too-timid lover.

For a more interiorized, involving performance of Granados's songs, one should turn to Caballé's 1977 recital (recorded by Spanish Columbia and issued in the UK on Decca SXL-R6888). Here the range of vocal colouring and vivid-ness is as apparent as before, but this time the rendition operates on a more intimate level, making it all the more effective. Also from the same sessions comes Caballé's recording of de Falla's *Siete Canciones Populares Españolas*. These date from 1914 and form an anthology of works from various regions of Spain inspired by different traditions of folksong and dance. In 'El paño moruno' the soprano captures the Southern Spanish sound, all suppressed fire, hinting expertly at the tragedy underpinning the surface brio. And she shows herself to be incomparable in the sad, short songs, written almost like vocalises ('Asturiana' for example) or in something like 'Nana' (Lullaby) where the depth of tone is astounding. In the latter, the ache is so profound that we are left in no doubt that this is no mere goodnight lullaby but the lament of a grieving mother. Fermenting under the surface of several of the seven songs has been the dark-hued, slightly throaty tone so characteristic of Southern Spanish singing: but at last, in 'Polo', Caballé gives full rein to the 'cante jondo' sound of absolute despair. Dominated by a mezzo chest tone, she articulates the vocal flourishes that give the piece its Moorish quality as expertly as any flamenco singer. The range of response displayed here between 'Nana' on the one hand and 'Polo' on the other proclaims artistry of a very high order.

Turning to Joaquín Turina's *Canto a Sevilla* (the seven sections of which comprise four songs and three instrumental movements), we travel a long way from the restraint of Granados and the easy lyricism of de Falla. Despite its fame, this is not the best of the composer's works, and on the evidence of Caballé's 1979 recording accompanied by Alexis Weissenberg (EMI Pathé Marconi 2C 069-16380), one gains the impression that they are pieces that have yet to penetrate beneath her skin. This is not to say there is any problem with voice or technique, for the former is in fine estate and though, technically, Turina's writing is complex, requiring the singer to make exotic modulations and to negotiate a higher lying *tessitura* than in most other Spanish works, these are not problems that trouble Caballé. In all four songs the composer's obsession with Seville is apparent, and 'obsession' here is not too strong a word, for there is a kind of neurotic tension between the texts and the music. 'Semana Santa', for example, portrays the celebrations of the Easter procession, and though the religious is mixed in with the carnival aspects, the music itself is highly wrought, often loud and unyielding. In the second song, 'Las fuentecitas del parque' (The Little Fountains in the Park), the lovely phrase 'O entre el mago silencio de la noche estrellada' (Or in the magic silence of the starry night) does not elicit the soft-grained musical response that the text would suggest. Caballé has all the power that Turina demands of the singer at this point. It is simply that, through no fault of her own, a delicacy is missing, perhaps sacrificed by the composer's over-ambitiousness.

One finds a much more appealing use of the *sevillianismo* that pervades Turina's works in the four songs on the recording made in 1977. 'La estrella de Sevilla' adopts a lighter mood than is customary for this composer, and that less brooding atmosphere is well captured by the soprano, whose tone becomes appropriately crystalline and bright. But the preceding three songs, 'Anhelos' (from the *Tres sonetos* cycle of 1930), 'Farruca' (from the *Tríptico* set of 1929) and the early composition, 'Cantares' (from *Poema en forma de Canciones*, dating from 1918) are full of brooding Andalusian passion. She may come from the north, but how well Caballé responds to the obsessive passions of these agonized southern lovers all of whom crave 'absolute oneness' with the object of their love. A kind of dark Latin 'angst' underlies these pieces, superbly hinted at by the singer who makes them all the more poignant by her restraint.

If the *Canto a Sevilla* cycle sounded less than fully absorbed by Caballé, her rendition of the Montsalvatge song cycle, *Cinco canciones negras*, on the same EMI 1979 recital disc could hardly be bettered. Inspired by the composer's interest in *habañeras* and other popular South American themes (which had been integrated into local folk culture as a result of the return of Catalan seafarers) the Caribbean manner found – in the words of Montsalvatge himself – 'a place at the periphery of our traditions as a new, vague and evocative manifestation of musical lyricism'. The first song, 'Cuba dentro de un piano' (Cuba inside a piano) is a favourite of the soprano's in recital. So sultry and languorous is her reading that it conjures up the image of a smoke-filled Havana bar where the colonial politicking fills the gaps between mid-day dozing and afternoon drinking. 'Chévere' has a forcefulness and menace that wholly contrasts with 'Punto de Habañera', where again the languor of Cuban life is beguilingly captured in a witty, flirtatious account of the pretty girl in a white dress who catches the eye of the sailors as she saunters past. The best-known song, 'Can-cíon de cuna', is moulded in gorgeous lines of sad tone, with dips into charac-terful Latin-American chest voice. Lullabies, whether they be by Mozart, Strauss or Montsalvatge, hold, it seems, a special appeal for Caballé. And then in the rumba-like 'Canto negro', it is left to the interpreter to decide what to make of a text full of onomatopoeic gestures. De los Angeles and Berganza keep matters light-hearted and upbeat. Caballé, on the other hand, opts for a much more serious reading. The spirit and fire is there; but so is a sense of danger.

Joaquín Rodrigo's attractive *Cuatro Madigrales Amatorias* draw their inspi-ration from Spanish music of the sixteenth century, being modern adaptations of songs by Juan Vásquez written in 1551. Caballé included this cycle in her 1978 recital (Decca SXL 6935) and at first it seems that the rich sound lavished by her on 'De dónde venís, amore?' is symptomatic of a general inappropriateness. Surely a more brittle edge on the voice is called for to deal with the bell-like tinklings of the musical setting. But such doubts disappear altogether in the face of the artistry she applies to 'Vos me matastes niña eb cabello' (You killed me, girl with the flowing hair) and 'De los álamos vengo, madre' (I come from the poplars, mother). The melancholy of the one is a world away from the vivaciousness of the other. The little coloratura flicks she brings off in this last song belie the size of the voice, and in general Caballé gives the impression less of an opera singer under full sail than someone completely absorbed in the sheer joy of the song's infectious rhythm.

Finally, something must be said about Caballé's recordings of three superb Catalan composers with whose work she has a special affinity. The items by Fernando Obradors (1897–1945) will be familiar to anyone who has attended the singer's recitals over the years. They embody – in a manner much less portentous than Turina – everything one associates with Spanish music. The songs on the 1978 recital are drawn from the first of four volumes compiled by the composer entitled *Canciones Clásicas Españolas*. 'Del cabello màs sutil' is sung with ravishing poise and gentleness in nice counterpoint to the rippling piano accompaniment. And 'El vito', which in a Caballé recital is often used as the flourish with which she sends the audience home on a high, has all the panache that one has come to expect. For a taste of her way with the exquisite miniatures of Frederic Mompou and Eduardo Toldrà, one could do no better (in the absence of the recordings she made of their songs for Vergara in 1963) than turn to the recording of the recital she gave for UNESCO in 1981 (PDI 80.0455). The lyrical grace with which she sings the three Mompou songs drawn from the cycle *Combat del Somni* gives pleasure enough. But what makes a deeper impression is the expressive power of the music, all the more surprising since Mompou's was 'an art in miniature', eschewing anything that was ostentatious. His non-virtuosic music calls for a delicacy one would hardly consider the province of a soprano who was at the time treading the boards as Turandot and Gioconda. But so captivating is Caballé's performance of these songs, inspired by the memories of the composer's childhood in his native Cataluña, that the live audience applaud as they might a sensational performance of some barnstorming Verdi piece. The five items she goes on to sing by her beloved Toldrà serve, like the Mompou, to remind us of something fundamental about Caballé: they are Catalan. And Catalan is, after all, the language she speaks at home.

OTHER RECORDINGS
(i) German

Armida (A. Dvořák)
Bremen, pirate, 19.ii.61: Foyer CD (2–CF 2015)

14 Lieder (R. Strauss) (acc. M. Zanetti)
Barcelona, studio, 1964: (Ich liebe dich; Ruhe, meine Seele; Ich schwebe; Traum durch die Dämmerung; Zueignung; Wie sollten wir geheim sie halten; Wiegenlied; Ich trage meine Minne; Freundlich Vision; Schlechtes Wetter; Morgen!; Befreit; Die Nacht; Cäcilie**) Vergara LP (715-STL), reissued on RCA LP; Available on CD in Spain only on Ariola 9D 25971**

Der Rosenkavalier (R. Strauss) (Marschallin's role complete)
Glyndebourne, pirate, 14.viii.65: Historical Recording Enterprises LP (HRE 356-2)

Ein Deutsches Requiem (J. Brahms)
Boston, studio, 17.ii.69: RCA LP (SB-6825/1-2); CD (GD 86800)

Arabella (R. Strauss)
Rome, RAI recording, 27.xi.73–1.xii.73: Historical Recording Enterprises LP (HRE 404-3)

Liebestod (from *Tristan und Isolde*) (R. Wagner)
Strasbourg, studio, 8.ix.76: Erato LP (reissued on Erato Presence 15538)

Vier letzte Lieder (R. Strauss)
Strasbourg, studio, 9.ix.77: Erato LP (reissued on Erato Presence 15538)

Lieder (R. Strauss) (acc. A. Weissenberg)
Paris, studio, 27.iv.79–6.v.79: EMI Pathé Marconi LP (2c 069-16381)

Scenes from Wagner Operas
New York, studio, 1–2.x.82: (*Tristan und Isolde* – Liebestod; *Der Fliegende Holländer* – Senta's Ballad; *Tannhäuser* – Dich, teure Halle; *Götterdämmerung* – Brünnhilde's Immolation**) CBS Masterworks LP (D 37294)**

(ii) French

Manon (J. Massenet)
Barcelona, pirate, xii.1968: MRF LP (MRF BARD 2(3))

Faust (C. Gounod)
Strasbourg, studio, 26.viii–7.ix.76: Erato LP (STU 710314); CD (2292-45682-2)

La Damoiselle Élue (C. Debussy)/*Poème de l'amour et de la Mer*
(E. Chausson)
London, studio, vi.1977: Symphonica LP, reissued on Collins CD (EL 1022-2)

Hérodiade (J. Massenet)
Barcelona, pirate, 2.i.84: MRF LP; Legato Classics CD (LCD 182-2)

Clovis et Clotilde (G. Bizet)
Lille, studio, 8–9.ix.88: Erato MusiFrance CD (245 106-2)

(iii) Spanish

Atlàntida (M. de Falla)
Geneva, live, 3.iv.63: Cascavelle (CD (VEL 2005)

Canciones de Eduardo Toldrà
Barcelona, studio, 1963: Vergara LP (11 0 002 L)

Canciones de Federico Mompou (acc. Mompou)
Barcelona, studio, 1963: (Damunt de tu només les flors; Aquesta nit un mateix vent; Jo et pressentia com la mar; Fes me la vida transparent; Aureana do Sil; Cançó de la fira; Pastoral; Dalt d'un cotxe; Margot la Pie; J'ai vu dans la lune; Aserrín aserrán; Petite fille de Paris; Pito, pito, colorito; Cantar del alma; Sant Marí; Neu; Llueve sobre el río) Vergara LP (701-TL)

Canciones de Xavier Montsalvatge i Joaquín Rodrigo
(acc. M. Zanetti)
Barcelona, studio, 1964: (Montsalvatge: *Canciones para niños*; Cançó amorosa; Oraçao; Rodrigo: Aire y donaire; La Espera; Coplillas de Belén; Coplas del pastor enamorado; Canción del grumete; Canticel; Muy graciosa es la doncella; Serranilla) World Records LP (CM87) EMI LP (ASDL 833)

Duós de Zarzuela (with Bernabé Martí)
Barcelona, studio, i.1965: (Guridi: *El caserío* – Buenos días; Vives: *La Generala* – Mi dulce sueño de adolescente; Soutullo: *Le leyenda del beso* – Amor, mi raza·sabe conquistar; Torroba: *Luisa Fernanda* – Caballero del alto plumero; Bretón: *La Dolores* – Dolores mía… Aqui tu; Caballero: *El duo de la Africana* – Comprende lo grave de mi situación)

Romanzas de Zarzuela
Barcelona, studio, 1965: (Serrano: *La cancion del olvido* – Marinela, Marinela; Chapí: *El Rey que rabio* – Mi tio se figuro; *El Barquilllero* – Cuando está tan hondo!' Vives: *Los Bohemios* – No quiero que aquí vengo yo; M. Fernandez: *El cabo primero* – Yo quiero a un hombre; Arietta: *Marina* – Pensar en él; Luna: *El niño judio* – De España vengo; Guerrero: *La rosa del Azafran* – No me duele que se vaya; Penella: *Don Gil de Alcala* – Bendita Cruz) Vergara LP (742-SRL); RCA Victor (RB6699)

El pajaró azul (R. Millán)

Studio, Barcelona, 26–29.vii.72: Spanish Columbia LP (CS 7248)

La Villana (A. Vives)

Studio Barcelona, 16–19.i.72: Spanish Columbia LP (CS 8618/9)

Maruxa (A. Vives)

Studio, Barcelona, 16–19.iv.74: Spanish Columbia LP (CS 8622/3)

Canço d'amor i de guerra (M. Martínez Valls)

Studio, Barcelona, 1974: Spanish Columbia LP (CS 8624); CD Alhambra (WD-71466)

Somnis i Records (A. Pereira Fons)

Studio, Madrid, 15–20.i.91: issued in the UK as *Dreams and Memories* on CshCD 663

VII: Recitals and Miscellaneous
(i)COMMERCIAL

Recital – XII Festival de Granada

Barcelona, studio, vii.1963: (Items by Schubert, Strauss, Debussy and de Falla) **Vergara LP (11 0 005 L)**

Duós de Amor (with Bernabé Martí)

Barcelona, studio, 1964: (Duets from *Madama Butterfly*, *La bohème*, *Manon*, *Don Carlos* and *Andrea Chénier*) **Vergara LP (781-STL)**

Los Encores de Montserrat Caballé (acc. M. Zanetti)

Barcelona, studio, 1964: (Items by Handel, Costanzi, Mozart, Beethoven, Schumann, Brahms, Wolf, Respighi, Castagnero, Ginastera, Gálvez, Montsalvatge, Rodrigo, Obradors and Padilla) **Vergara LP (775-STL)**

Great Operatic Heroines (orig. Arias de Opera)

Barcelona, studio, 28–31.xii.64: (**Verdi:** *Otello* – Willow Song and Ave Maria; *Un ballo in maschera* – Ecco l'orrido campo … Ma dall'arido stelo divulsa; **Donizetti:** *Anna Bolena* – Piangete voi? … Al dolce guidami*; **Charpentier:** *Louise* – Depuis le jour; **Puccini:** *Tosca* – Vissi d'Arte) **RCA LP (SER 5598)**

Great Operatic Duets (with Shirley Verrett)

London, studio, 1969: (**Rossini:** *Semiramide* – Serbami ognor . . . Alle più calde immagini; **Donizetti:** *Anna Bolena* – Sul suo capo aggravi un Dio; **Bellini:** *Norma* – Mira, o Norma; **Offenbach:** *Les Contes d'Hoffmann* – Barcarolle; **Verdi:** *Aïda* – Silenzio! Aida verso noi s'avanza; **Puccini:** *Madama Butterfly* – Flower Duet; **Ponchielli:** *La Gioconda* – L'amo come il fulgor del creato) **RCA LP (SER 5590); RCA/BMG CD (GD60818)**

Great Opera Duets (with Bernabé Martí)

London, studio, i.1970: (**Verdi:** *Un ballo in maschera* – Teco io sto; **Meyerbeer:** *Les Hugueno* – Oh ciel! où courez-vous?; **Giordano:** *Andrea Chénier* – Vicino a te; **Puccini:** *Manon Lescaut* Tu, tu, amore? Tu?; **Donizetti:** *Poliuto* – Ah! Fuggi da morta) **EMI LP (ASD 2723)**

* The item from *Anna Bolena* is the only one so far transferred to CD (on *Montserrat Caballé sings Bellini & Donizetti* RCA/BMG 09026 61458 2 and *Eternal Caballé* RCA/BMG PL-75260 (2)5Z).

Metropolitan Opera Gala Honouring Sir Rudolf Bing

New York, live, 22.iv.72: (Puccini: *Manon Lescaut* – Tu, tu, amore? Tu? [with Plàcido Domingo] and other artists) **DG LP (DGG 2530 260); CD (431 103-2)**

Operatic Arias

Barcelona, studio, 12–28.vi.74: (Verdi: *Rigoletto* – Caro nome; **Il Trovatore** – Dell'amor sull'ali rosee; *I Vespri Siciliani* – (a) Arrigo!... Ah parli a un core, (b) Mercè, dilette amiche; *Un ballo in maschera* – Morrò, ma prima in grazia; **Cilea:** *Adriana Lecouvreur* – Io son l'umile ancella; **Bellini:** *La sonnambula* – Ah! se una volta sola... Ah, non credea mirati... Ah, non giunge; **Puccini:** *Suor Angelica* – Senza mamma) **Spanish Columbia, issued on Decca LP (SXLR 6690); Forlane CD (UCD 10905)***

Montserrat Caballé au Château du Thôlonet

Thôlonet/Aix en Provence, live, 25.vii.74: (Donizetti: *Roberto Devereux* – Vivi ingrato; **Bellini:** *Il pirata* – Col sorriso d'innocenza; **Rossini:** *La donna del lago* – Tanti affetti; **Verdi:** *Il corsaro* – Non so le tetre; *Aroldo* – O, dagli scanni eterei) **Rodolphe LP (RP 12455); CD (RPC 32455)**

Montserrat Caballé and Giuseppe di Stefano

Madrid, studio, 2–5.ix.74: (Massenet: *Manon* – Et je sais votre nom; **Bizet:** *Les pêcheurs de perles* – Ton coeur n'a pas compris; **Zandonai:** *Francesca di Rimini* – E così vada; **Massenet:** *Werther* – Il faut nous séparer; **Gomes:** *Il guarany* – Sento una forza indomita; **Donizetti:** *L'elisir d'amore* – Una parola, o Adina) **Spanish Columbia, issued on Dischi Ricordi LP (OCL 16250)**

Operatic Arias

Barcelona, studio, 12–16.vii.76: (Verdi: *Macbeth* – Nel dì della vittoria... Ambizioso spirto... Veni! t'affretta... Or tutti sorgette; *Il Trovatore* – Che più t'arresti... Tacea la notte... Di tale amor; **Mascagni:** *Cavalleria rusticana* – Voi lo sapete; **Puccini:** *Turandot* – In questa Reggia; **Catalani:** *La Wally* – Ebben, ne andrò solo e lontana; **Ponchielli:** *La Gioconda* – Suicidio!; **Giordano:** *Andrea Chénier* – La mamma morta) **Spanish Columbia, issued on Decca LP (SXLR 6825)†**

Bernstein Symphony No. 3 (Kaddish)

New York, studio, ix.1977: DG LP (DG 2709 077); CD (423 582-2)

Montserrat Caballé and José Carreras à Paris

Paris, live, 19.iii.79: (Rossini: *La donna del lago* – Tanti affetti; **Charpentier:** *Louise* – Depuis le jour; **Donizetti:** *Poliuto* – Questo pianto favelli‡; **Verdi:** *La forza del destino* – Pace, pace, mio Dio; **Giordano:** *Andrea Chénier* – (a) La mamma morta, (b) Vicino a te‡) (Items marked ‡ are with Carreras) **Rodolphe/INA CD (RPC 32501)**

Madrid Masterclasses (6 CDs)

Madrid, live, 23–27.x.88: (Lectures on singing technique and student masterclasses) Zafiro CDs (50812763-I to VI)

Eternal Caballé

Madrid/London, studio, ix and x.1991: (Cano – Hijo de la Luna; **Quiroga** – Ojos verdes; **Serrat** – Paraules d'amor; **Mostazo** – La dia que naci yo; **Rodrigo** – En Aranjuez con tu amor; **Donizetti:** *Lucrezia Borgia* – Tranquillo ei posa ... com'e bello; *Maria Stuarda* – Final

---

* Issued by Forlane under the title *L'Art de Montserrat Caballé: Les Maîtres Italiens de l'Art Lyrique Vol. 2*.

† An additional item recorded at these sessions – 'Un bel dì vedremo' – appeared on the Acanta release (DC29389) which was otherwise composed of selections drawn from this and the accompanying disc issued by Decca (SXLR 6690).

Scene; *Roberto Devereux* – Vivi ingrato; *Anna Bolena* – Al dolce guidami‡; **Massenet:** *Le Cid* – Pleurez, pleurez mes yeux; **Bizet:** *Carmen* – Habanera; **Saint-Saëns:** *Samson et Dalila* – Mon coeur; **Puccini:** *Gianni Schicchi* – O mio babbino caro; **Rossini:** *L'Assedio di Corinto* – L'ora fatal s'apressa... Giusto ciel!‡; **Bellini:** *Norma* – Casta diva‡; **Verdi:** *I vespri Siciliani* – Mercè, dillette amiche‡; **Rigoletto** – Caro nome‡; *La traviata* – E'strano ... sempre libera‡; *Il trovatore* – D'amor sull'ali rosee‡; **Cilea:** *Adriana Lecouvreur* – Io son l'umile ancella‡; **Luna:** *El niño judio* – De España Vengo; **Lloyd-Webber:** *The Phantom of the Opera* – Wishing you were somehow here again) (items marked ‡ are from previously released discs) **RCA/ BMG LP (PL-75260 (2)5Z) (in Spain only); CD (RD 61044)**

Opera for Africa

Verona, live, 18.viii.85: (Bellini: *Norma* – Casta diva; **Verdi:** *La traviata* – Brindisi‡) **Opera for Africa/Polygram LP (419 280-1)** (item marked ‡ with José Carreras)

Barcelona (with F. Mercury)

London, studio, 1987: (Barcelona; La Japonaise; The Fallen Priest; Ensueño; The Golden Boy; Guide me Home; How can I go on?; Overture piccante) **Mercury Songs Ltd LP (POLH 44 in UK, 837277-1 Internat.); CD (837277-2)**

Barcelona (with F. Mercury)

London, studio, 1987: (Barcelona (orig. version); Exercises in Free Love; Barcelona (extended version)) **Polydor 7-inch single (POSPX 887)**

Gala Lirica

Seville, live, iv.1992: (Massenet: *Le Cid* – Pleurez, pleurez mes yeux; **Verdi:** *La Traviata* – Brindisi‡) **RCA/BMG LP (RL 61191); CD (RD 61191); Video (791183)** (item marked ‡ with Carreras, Domingo, Kraus, Berganza et al.)

1992 Olympic Games Opening Ceremony

Barcelona, studio, 7–9.i.92: (Bellini: *Norma* – Casta diva; **Massenet:** *Hérodiade* – Il est doux, il est bon; Extracts from *Les contes d'Hoffmann, La bohème, Norma, Aïda**) **BMG/RCA CD (09026-61204-2)**

(ii)PIRATE

Montserrat Caballé and Gianfranco Cecchele

Philadelphia, pirate, 3.ii.67: (Donizetti: *Anna Bolena* – Al dolce guidami; *Roberto Devereux* – Vivi, ingrato; **Verdi:** *Aïda* – O terra, addio‡) (item marked ‡ with Cecchele) **Melodram CD (CDM 28051)**

Gala Operatic Concert (with Franco Corelli) and Bonaldo Giaiotti

New York, pirate, iii.1967: (Donizetti: *Lucrezia Borgia* – Com'è bello; **Rossini:** *La donna del lago* – Tanti affetti; **Verdi:** *Aroldo* – Ah! dagli scanni eteri; **Puccini:** *Manon Lescaut* – In quelle trine morbide; **Giordano:** *Andrea Chénier* – La nostra morta... Vicino a te‡) (item marked ‡ with Corelli) **Legato Classics CD (LCD-101-1); Melodram CD (CDM 28051)**

Houston Concert (acc. M. Zanetti)

Houston, pirate, 21.x.67: (Handel: *Giulio Cesare* – Piangeró la sorte mia; V'adoro pupille; **Schubert:** Du bist die Ruh; Ungeduld; **Strauss:** Allerseelen; Ständchen; **Rossini:** *Tancredi* – Di tanti palpiti; *La donna del lago* – Tanti affetti; **Debussy:** Beau soir; Mandoline; Air de Lia (from *L'enfant prodigue*); **Montsalvatge:** Punto de habañera; Canto negro; **Granados:** Llorad corazon; Gracia mia; **Rodrigo:** De donde venis amor; De los àlmos vengo; **Galvez:** Variantes de petenera; **Swiss Folk Song** – G'sätzli; **Verdi:** *La traviata* – Addio del passato) **Voce LP (VOCE-63)**

---

* Extracts performed as part of an operatic medley arranged by Tony Parera.

Un bel dì vedremo
Various, pirate, 1965–1970: (Items from *Il trovatore, Il pirata, Luisa Miller, Agnese di Hohenstaufen, Un ballo in maschera; La Donna del lago, Ernani, Don Carlos, Manon, Madama Butterfly*) **Foyer CD (1 CF 2039); Deja Vu CD (DVRECD 59)**

UPDATE TO THE PAPERBACK EDITION

Two and a half years is a long time in the record industry, and since this critical discography was first published there have been a number of changes, particularly in the volatile half-world of pirate releases. The Foyer, Melodram and Rodolphe marques are no longer with us, though the last's cache of releases, all emanating from the French National Sound Archives, are reappearing on the aptly named Phoenix label. Myto and G.O.P. (Great Opera Performances) – Italian labels both – have each produced a significant number of releases, some of performances never previously available. Happily, more of the known buried treasure has also finally made it on to CD, although much still remains in limbo. Since it is clear that Caballé's pirates sell, it is likely that the demand will prompt a continued supply.

The following are the new entrants to the Caballé CD discography.

COMPACT DISC

Norma, pirate, Milan, 1972: GOP CD (GOP 726)

Roberto Devereux, pirate, Venice, 1972: GOP CD (GOP 764)

Un ballo in maschera, pirate, Barcelona, 1972: Ornamenti CD (FE 103–4)

Un ballo in maschera, pirate, Milan, 1975: GOP CD (GOP 770); Myto CD (MCD 951.123)

Manon Lescaut, pirate, Buenos Aires, 10.vii.68: Eklipse CD Highlights (EKR P.11)

La Bohème, pirate, New York, 1974: GOP CD (GOP 753)

Zarzuela Arias and Duets, (with B. Martí), studio, 1967 & 1969: RCA/BMG CD (09026 68148 2)

Montserrat Caballé: Casta Diva, studio, 1964–76: RCA/BMG CD (74321 23675 2)

Montserrat Caballé at the Teatro Colón, pirate, Buenos Aires, 11.ix.65: Eklipse CD (EKR P2)

Montserrat Caballé in Concert, Verona, Milan & Zurich, pirate, 11.viii.69, 16-vi-70, 11-iii-73: (GOP 738-3)

Carreras & Caballé at the Bolshoi, live, Moscow, 5.ix.89: Belart CD (450 193-2)

Two voices, One Heart (with M. Martí), studio, 1995: RCA/BMG CD (74321 29646 2)

Madama Butterfly, pirate, Madrid, 1968, Legato CD (LCD 210-2)

VIDEO

Adriana Lecouvreur,
Tokyo, 1976: Legato Video (LCV 2)

Notes and References

CHAPTER THREE
(To Basel and Beyond)

1. *Le Chant Retrouvé: Sept divas – renaissance de l'Opéra* (Fayard, Paris, 1979).

CHAPTER FOUR
(Blood, Sweat and Tears)

1. *Bremen Tageblatt*, 4 September 1959.
2. *Opera*, vol. 12, no. 4, April 1961, p. 261.
3. *La Vanguardia*, 9 January 1962.

CHAPTER FIVE
(Finding Fulfilment)

1. Hugo von Hofmannsthal, *Arabella*, Act I. 'Aber der Richtige – wenns einen gibt für mich auf dieser Welt – der wird einmal dastehn, da vor mir, und wird mich anschaun, und ich ihn, und keine Zweifel werden sein und keine Fragen, und selig werd' ich sein and gehorsam wie ein Kind.'
2. John L. Walsh in *Opera*, vol. 12, no. 2, February 1965, p. 130.
3. Ibid., no. 3, March 1965, p. 209.

CHAPTER SIX
(A Trip to Stardom)

1. Bernard Jacobson in *Opera*, vol. 12, no. 5, May 1965, p. 495.
2. Harold Rosenthal in *Opera*, Autumn Festival Edition 1965, p. 26.
3. Raymond Ericson, *The New York Times*, 23 December 1965.

4. *Opera*, vol. 17, no. 3, March 1966, p. 204.
5. *Opera*, vol. 17, no. 6, June 1966, p. 455.

CHAPTER SEVEN
(Yankee Doodle Diva)

1. *Opera*, vol. 18, no. 5, April 1967, p. 295.
2. Ibid., vol. 19, no. 2, February 1968, p. 142.
3. Ibid., no. 3, March 1968, p. 210.
4. Ibid., no. 5, May 1968, p. 371.
5. The London Weekend Television *South Bank Show* documentary, broadcast 31 January 1993.
6. Frank Granville Barker, *Music and Musicians*, vol. 17, December 1968, p. 47.
7. Roger Alier i Aixalà and Francesc X. Mata, *El Gran Teatro del Liceo (Historia Artística)* (Edicions Francesc X. Mata S.L., Barcelona, 1991), p. 319.
8. *Opera*, vol. 20, no. 2, February 1969, pp. 115–16.
9. Allen Hughes, *The New York Times*, 11 April 1969.
10. *Opera*, vol. 20, no. 8, August 1969, p. 739.
11. *Music and Musicians*, vol. 17, August 1969, p. 44.

CHAPTER EIGHT
(Prima Donna Assoluta)

1. Frank Granville-Barker, *Music and Musicians*, vol. 18, March 1970, p. 23.

2. Alan Blyth in *Opera*, vol. 21, no. 5, May 1970, p. 472.

3. Roger Dettmer, ibid., no. 11, November 1970, p. 1115.

4. *Opera News*, 12 December 1970, p. 30.

5. Michael Scott, *Maria Meneghini Callas* (Simon & Schuster, London, 1991), p. 92.

6. Catherine Clément, *Opéra, ou la Défaite des Femmes*. Translated as *Opera, or the Undoing of Women* (Virago, London, 1989).

7. *Opera*, vol. 22, no. 5, May 1971, p. 447.

8. *Music and Musicians*, vol. 19, July 1971, p. 57.

9. John Greenhalgh, ibid., p. 58.

10. Gilbert Price, ibid., vol. 21, no. 4, April 1970, p. 359.

11. Mario Messinis, *Il Gazzettino*, 11 February 1972.

12. Max Wyman, *The Vancouver Sun*, 5 May 1972.

13. *Opera*, vol. 23, no. 9, September 1972, p. 862.

14. *Opera on Record* (vol. 1), ed. Alan Blyth (Hutchinson, London, 1979), p. 169.

15. Lorenzo Arruga, *La Scala* (Praeger Publishers Inc., New York, 1976), p. 232.

CHAPTER NINE
(Triumphs, Troubles and Transition)

1. Harold C. Schonberg, *The New York Times*, 14 February 1973.

2. Andrew Farkas, *Opera*, vol. 24, no. 7, July 1973, p. 600.

3. Roger Alier i Aixalà and Francesc X. Mata, *El Gran Teatro del Liceo (Historia Artística)* (Edicions Francesc X. Mata S.L., Barcelona, 1991), p. 363.

4. Luis Angel Catoni, *Opera News*, 2 March 1974, p. 24.

5. Private correspondence to Caballé, 27 April 1973.

6. *The New York Times*, 2 February 1974.

7. *Music and Musicians*, vol. 22, August 1974, pp. 33–4.

8. In May 1975 on Decca SXL-R 6690.

9. Harold Rosenthal, *Opera*, vol. 26, no. 6, June 1975, p. 566.

10. *Opera on Record*, 3 (Hutchinson, London, 1984), p. 107.

11. *The Gramophone*, vol. 52, no. 624, May 1975, p. 2019.

12. Ibid., vol. 64, no. 762, November 1986, p. 751.

13. Duilio Courir, *Corriere della Sera*, 29 January 1975.

14. William Ashbrook, *Donizetti and his Operas* (Cambridge University Press, Cambridge, 1982), p. 365.

CHAPTER TEN
(Heavyweight Contender)

1. Leighton Kerner, *Opera*, vol. 27, no. 8, August 1976, p. 716.

2. Joseph Wechsberg, ibid., no. 11, November 1976, p. 1034.

3. See Chapter 8, p. 159.

4. Luis Angel Catoni, *Opera News*, 2 April 1977, pp. 42–3.

5. Peter Taylor, *Musical Opinion*, vol. 100, April 1977, p. 370.

6. *Opera*, vol. 28, no. 6, June 1977, p. 560.

7. *Music and Musicians*, vol. 26, February 1978, p. 45.

8. Janos Gereben, *San Jose Mercury*, 16 October 1978.

9. *The Last Prima Donnas* (Limelight Editions, New York, 1990), p. 384.

10. Ibid., p. 247.

11. *Opera*, vol. 30, no. 7, July 1979, pp. 667–8.

12, Ibid., Autumn Festival Edition, 1979, p. 88.

CHAPTER ELEVEN
(Plain Sailing, Sudden Shipwreck)

1. *Nouvel Observateur*, July 1980.

2. *Opera*, Autumn Festival Edition, 1980, p. 69.

3. Tony Mayer, ibid., vol. 32, no. 5, May 1981, p. 506.

4. Gérard Mannoni, *Le Quotidien de Paris*, 26 April 1981.

5. Ibid., 18 May 1981.

6. *Opera*, vol. 32, no. 10, October 1981, p. 1050.

7. Ibid., no. 12, December 1981, p. 1234.

8. Ibid., vol. 33, no. 4, April 1982, p. 408.

9. *Monsalvat*, January 1987.

10. Robert Buning in private correspondence with the authors.

CHAPTER TWELVE
(The Undiscovered Country)

1. Charles Pitt, *Opera*, Autumn Festival Edition, 1983, pp. 91–2.

2. Ibid., p. 117.

3. André Tubeuf, *Opéra de Paris*, no. 9, 15 May 1983.

4. Oleg Kerensky, *Music and Musicians*, June 1984, p. 45.

5. Tim Page, *The New York Times*, 18 April 1984.

6. Luigi Bellingardi, *Opera*, vol. 36, no. 6, June 1985, p. 679.

CHAPTER THIRTEEN
(Mercury Rising)

1. *Opera*, Autumn Festival Edition, 1985, p. 63.

2. Marco Vallora, ibid., vol. 36, no. 12, December 1985, p. 1376.

3. Michael Redmond, *The Star-Ledger*, 25 September 1985.

4. Luigi Bellingardi, *Opera*, vol. 37, no. 2, February 1986, p. 201.

5. Ibid., no. 8, August 1986, p. 966.

6. *Le Monde de la Musique*, November 1986.

7. V. Molina-Foix, *Opera*, vol. 38, no. 11, November 1987, p. 1312.

8. Ibid., vol. 37, Autumn Festival Edition, 1987, pp. 112–14.

9. *The Times*, 26 August 1987.

CHAPTER FOURTEEN
(The Last of the Liceo)

1. *La Vanguardia*, 24 February 1989.

2. Bert Wechsler, *Daily News*, 3 April 1989.

3. Gerald Larner, *Guardian*, 19 August 1989.

4. *El País*, 6 December 1990.

5. *The Times*, 20 February 1992.

6. *ABC*, 14 February 1992.

7. *Le Monde de la Musique*, 1992, p. 75.

8. *El País*, 15 January 1992.

CHAPTER FIFTEEN
(Silver and Diamonds)

1. Hilary Finch, *The Times*, 25 May 1991.

2. Antonio Fernández-Cid, *ABC*, 9 February 1992.

3. *Mail on Sunday*, 12 July 1992.

4. Rodney Milnes, *Opera*, Autumn Festival Edition, 1992, p. 13.

CRITICAL DISCOGRAPHY

1. *Gramophone*, Vol 53, No. 630, November 1975, pp. 893–4.

2. Richard Fairman, *Opera on Record 2*, ed. Alan Blyth, Hutchinson, London, 1983, p. 124.

3. Alan Blyth, *Gramophone*, September 1977, p. 475.

4. Frank Granville Barker, *Records and Recording*, September 1977.

5. Alan Blyth, *Gramophone*, January 1991, p. 1409.

6. Sergio Segalini, *Opéra International*, November 1990, p. 70.

7. Vivian Liff, *American Record Guide*, Vol. 55, No. 6, November/December 1992, p. 258.

8. Andrew Porter, *Gramophone*, Vol. 46, No. 548, January 1969, p. 1055.

9. Sergio Segalini, *Opéra International*, September 1989, pp. 66–7.

10. *Gramophone*, September 1971, Vol. 59, No. 590 p. 496.

Bibliography

Alavedra, Joan, *Conxita Badía: Una Vida d'Artista* (Editorial Pòrtic, Barcelona, 1975)

Alier i Aixalà, Roger, and Francesc X. Mata, *El Gran Teatro Liceo (Historia Artística)* (Edicions Francesc X. Mata S. L., Barcelona, 1991)

Ashbrook, William, *Donizetti and his Operas* (Cambridge University Press, 1982)

Beeveor, Antony, *The Spanish Civil War* (Orbis, London, 1982)

Blyth, Alan (ed.), *Opera on Record* (3 vols) (Hutchinson, London, 1979, 1983, 1984)

Brenan, Gerald, *The Spanish Labyrinth: An Account of the Social and Political Background of the Spanish Civil War* (2nd ed.) (Cambridge University Press, 1974)

Budden, Julian, *The Operas of Verdi* (revised ed.). *Volume I: From Oberto to Rigoletto; Volume II: From Il Trovatore to La Forza del destino; Volume III: From Don Carlos to Falstaff* (Clarendon Press, Oxford, 1992).

Carner, Mosco, *Puccini: A Critical Biography* (2nd ed.) (Duckworth, London, 1974)

Carreras, José, *Singing from the Soul: An Autobiography* (Souvenir Press, London, 1991)

Celletti, Rodolfo, *A History of Bel Canto* (transl. Frederick Fuller) (Clarendon Press, Oxford, 1991)

Chadwick, Lee, *A Cuban Journey* (Dennis Dobson, London, 1975)

Chase, Gilbert, *The Music of Spain* (2nd ed.) (Dover Publications, New York, 1959)

Cockburn, Jacqueline, and Stokes, Richard, *The Spanish Song Companion* (Victor Gollancz, London, 1992)

Colomer, Claude, *Montserrat Caballé ou l'anti diva* (Société de Musicologie de Languedoc, Béziers, 1988)

Dent, Edward J., *The Rise of Romantic Opera* (ed. Winton Dean) (Cambridge University Press, 1976)

Domingo, Plácido, *Plácido Domingo: My First Forty Years* (Weidenfeld & Nicolson, London, 1983)

Drake, James A., *Richard Tucker: A Biography* (E. P. Duttton Inc., New York, 1984)

Duey, Philip A., *Bel Canto and Its Golden Age: A Study in its Teaching Concepts* (King's Crown Press, New York, 1951)

Fontbona, Francesc (ed.), *El Círculo del Liceo: Historia, Arte, Cultura* (Edicions Catalanes, Barcelona, 1991)

Giner, Salvador, *The Social Structure of Catalonia* (Anglo-Catalan Society, Sheffield)

Horne, Marilyn, and Scovell, Jane, *Marilyn Horne: My Life* (Atheneum, New York, 1984)

Hughes, Robert, *Barcelona* (Harvill, London, 1992)

James, Burnett, *Manuel de Falla and the Spanish Musical Renaissance* (Victor Gollancz, London, 1979)

Karnow, Stanley, *In Our Image: America's Empire in the Philippines* (Century, London, 1990)

Keates, Jonathan, *Handel: The Man and his Music* (Victor Gollancz, London, 1985)

Kesting, Jürgen, *Maria Callas* (transl. John Hunt) (Quartet Books, London, 1992)

Lang, Paul Henry, *George Frederick Handel* (Faber & Faber, London, 1966)

Major, Norma, *Joan Sutherland* (Queen Anne Press, London, 1987)

Marco, Tomás, *Spanish Music in the Twentieth Century* (Harvard University Press, Cambridge, Massachusetts, 1993)

Millington, Barry, *Wagner* (Dent, London, 1984)

Mordden, Ethan, *A Guide to Opera Recordings* (Oxford University Press, New York, 1987)

Orrey, Lesley, *Bellini* (Dent, London, 1969)

Osborne, Richard, *Rossini* (Dent, London, 1986)

Pérez Senz, Javier, *José Carreras: El Placer de Cantar – Un retrato autobiográfico* (Ediciones de Nuevo Arte Thor, Barcelona, 1988)

Rasponi, Lanfranco, *The Last Prima Donnas* (2nd ed.) (Limelight Editions, New York, 1990)

Reid, Cornelius L., *Bel Canto: Principles and Practices* (Joseph Patelson Musical House, New York, 1971)

Rust, Brian, *Brian Rust's Guide to Discography* (Greenwood Press, Connecticut, 1980)

Scott, Michael, *The Record of Singing to 1914* (Duckworth, London, 1977)

Scott, Michael, *The Record of Singing from 1914 to 1925* (Duckworth, London, 1979)

Scott, Michael, *Maria Menighini Callas* (Simon & Schuster, London, 1991)

Sills, Beverly, and Linderman, Lawrence, *Beverly: An Autobiography* (Bantam, New York, 1987)

Stassinopoulos, Arianna, *Maria Callas* (Weidenfeld & Nicolson, London, 1980)

Steane, John B., *The Grand Tradition: Seventy Years of Singing on Record* (2nd ed.) (Duckworth, London, 1993)

Stendhal, *The Life of Rossini* (2nd ed., transl. Richard N. Coe) (John Calder, London, 1985)

Thomas, Hugh, *The Spanish Civil War* (3rd ed.) (Penguin, London, 1986)

Tubeuf, André, *Le Chant Retrouvé: Sept divas – renaissance de l'Opéra* (Fayard, Paris, 1979)

Turnbull, Robert, *The Opera Gazetteer* (Trefoil Publications, London, 1988)

Weinstock, Herbert, *Vicenzo Bellini: His Life and His Opera* (Weidenfeld & Nicolson, London, 1971)

Weinstock, Herbert, *Donizetti and the World of Opera in Italy, Paris and Vienna in the First Half of the Nineteenth Century* (Methuen, London, 1963)

REFERENCE WORKS AND JOURNALS

American Record Guide, Vol. 47 (1984) to Vol. 57, No. 1 (January/February 1994)

Das Opern Glas, 1984 to 1993

Gramophone, Vol. 22 (1964)–Vol. 70 (May 1993) (General Gramophone Publications, London)

Kobbé's Complete Opera Book (10th ed.), ed. the Earl of Harewood (The Bodley Head, London, 1987)

Monsalvat, No. 1 (1974) to No. 212 (February 1993)

Music & Musicians, Vol. 15 (September 1966–August 1967) – Vol. 37 (September 1988–December 1988) (Orpheus Publications, London)

Opera, Vol. 1 (1950) to Vol. 44 (1993), London

Opéra International, No. 1 (1978) to No. 174 (December 1993)

Records and Recording, Vol. 10 (1967) – Vol. 23 (August 1980) (Hansom Books, London)

Scherzo, No. 1 (1984) to No. 71 (January/February 1993)

The New Grove Dictionary of Music and Musicians (20 vols), ed. S. Sadie (Macmillan Publishers Ltd, London, 1980)

The New Grove Dictionary of Opera (4 vols), ed. S. Sadie (Macmillan Press Ltd, London, 1992)

Index

'MC' in sub-entries refers to Montserrat Caballé.
Composers' works are organized alphabetically without the definite and
indefinite articles of the languages in which they are given.
Bold page numbers refer to entries in the discography.